DICTIONARY OF

Ancient & Medieval Warfare

DICTIONARY OF
Ancient & Medieval Warfare

STACKPOLE
BOOKS

First published in paperback in North America in 2001 by

STACKPOLE BOOKS
5067 Ritter Road
Mechanicsburg, PA 17055 USA
www.stackpolebooks.com

Originally published as *The Hutchinson Dictionary of Ancient and Medieval Warfare* in Great Britain in 1998 by Helicon Publishing Ltd

ISBN 0-8117-2610-X

Typeset by TechType, Abingdon, Oxon
Printed and bound in Slovenia by DELO tiskarna
by arrangement with Korotan Ljubljana

Papers used in this publication are natural recyclable products made from wood grown in sustainable forests. The manufacturing process of both raw materials and paper conform to the environmental regulations of the country of origin.

All photographs courtesy of AKG Photo, London.

Back and front image: Thracian helmet, from Sofia, Bulgaria
Front images, from left: armour of Count Johann von Brandenburg-Küstrin, 1513–1571; Shield and helmet; the French Pertuissance and Esponton lances, 16th century; Venetian halberd from the 17th century from the Palace of the Doges; the Assyrian King Assurbaipal in relief from his palace, Niniveh, Iraq

Editorial Team

Managing Editor
Katie Emblen

Project Editors
Simon Hall, Sarah Hudson

Editors
Lisa Isenman Sullivan,
Susan Mendelsohn,
Michelle Patient, Kathy Peltan, Edith
Summerhayes

Art and Design
Terence Caven

Production
Tony Ballsdon

Database Management
Nick Andrews, Graham Bennett, Lorraine
Cotterell, Louise Richmond

Contents

Introduction

Warfare is as old as humankind, and a universal experience. Its evidence is all around us, from Neolithic wall-paintings of spear and bow skirmishes to the Kalashnikovs and landmines of today. Yet when we examine the warfare of the past, we confront also its ephemeral nature: we struggle to interpret the evidence before us, because the military world that gave it such urgent meaning has now all but vanished. How do the stylized 3,000-year old friezes depicting the victories of the Egyptians relate to real military experience? Who were the Greek hoplites, and what does the term *othismos* (shoving) tell us about their type of fighting? What was Greek Fire, or a *gonfanon*, or a *chevauchée*? What happened at Dura Europus, at Dyrrachium, or at Constantinople in 1453? And the military histories of China, Japan, South Asia, Persia and Central Asia all demand our attention too – but consist of events even less familiar to most of us, and terminology even more obscure. It is this obscurity that the *Dictionary of Ancient & Medieval Warfare* is intended to dispel, in as concise and convenient a format as possible. We have brought together specialists in many different periods of military history and many different regions of the world, to ensure that the *Dictionary* offers unprecedented range and authority in its coverage.

Our coverage begins with the earliest recorded military events, and ends at AD 1500. We chose this end-date not because the so-called European Middle Ages conventionally end around this time, but because the first real impact of gunpowder weaponry, the emergence of new naval and siege technology, and the rise to world dominance of the countries of northwestern Europe began around 1500 and marked a shift in the balance of military power that is still with us today. The *Dictionary* is therefore a key to the whole military experience of pre-modern times.

Warfare is not only a matter of terminology. The *Dictionary* is full of battles and wars, and of heroes too: the great commanders, and also the ordinary soldiers – Egyptian charioteers, Roman legionaries, Mongol horse-archers, English bowmen, Chinese rocketeers, Burgundian artillerymen, Swiss halberdiers. The most important subjects are explored in longer articles, boxed off from the main A–Z sequence of entries; some of these cover the wars and campaigns that provide the context for shorter entries, while others outline the careers of the greatest commanders, or analyse key battles in depth. These articles provide a quick guide to the highpoints of ancient and medieval military history, but we hope the range of shorter entries, and the comprehensive cross-references, will encourage the reader to browse, too. There cannot be many experts in European history whose understanding of warfare in past times will not be broadened by an encounter within these pages with the Green Woodsmen, Princess Trung Trac, or Tahir the Ambidextrous.

Matthew Bennett
Hartley Wintney, July 1998

General Editor

Matthew Bennett, Royal Military Academy Sandhurst, joint author of the *Cambridge Atlas of Medieval Warfare* (1995), *Agincourt* (1991), and numerous articles.

Consultants

Peter Connolly, Honorary Research Fellow, Institute of Archaeology, University College, London. He is author of numerous illustrated books including *Pompeii, Jews in the Time of Jesus, The Legend of Odysseus and Greece,* and *Rome at War.*

John Gillingham, Professor of History at the London School of Economics. His books include *Richard the Lionheart, the Kingfisher Historical Atlas of Britain, Richard III,* and *The Cambridge Historical Atlas of Medieval Warfare.*

John Lazenby, Professor of Classics at the University of Newcastle. He is author of *First Punic War* and many other titles.

Contributors

Ancient Warfare

The Rev Ian Russell Lowell, contributor to *A World Atlas of Warfare* (1988) and specialist in warfare of the pre-classical period.

Classical Warfare

Peter Connolly, author of *Pompeii, Jews in the Time of Jesus, The Legend of Odysseus, Greece and Rome at War,* and many others.

Dr Catherine Gilliver, School of History and Archaeology, University of Wales, Cardiff.

Dr Adrian Goldsworthy, formerly of the School of History and Archaeology, University of Wales, Cardiff, author of *The Roman Army at War 100BC–AD200* and others.

Professor John Lazenby, Department of Classics, University of Newcastle, author of *First Punic War* (1996).

Andrew Pegler, research student in Roman Archaeology at the University of London.

Dr Louis Rawlings, School of History and Archaeology, University of Wales, Cardiff.

Late Romans

Simon MacDowell, specialist in the Dark Ages and late Roman period, author of a series of books on the late Roman army and the Germanic warriors of the migrations.

Medieval Warfare

Matthew Bennett: see above.

Jim Bradbury, medievalist and author of *The Medieval Archer, The Medieval Siege, The Civil War of 1139–53,* and *The Battle of Hastings.*

Julie Potter, medievalist and author of many articles.

Castles and Fortifications

Ian V Hogg, editor of *Jane's Infantry Weapons* (1982–95), author of over 120 books on military subjects, including *Coast Defences of England and Wales, Fortress, History of Fortification, Weapons that Changed the World, A History of Artillery,* and the *Guinness Encyclopedia of Weaponry.*

India, Eurasia, Persia

Dr Tony Heathcote, museum curator at the royal Military Academy Sandhurst and specialist in warfare in South Asia, author of *Military in British India: The Development of British Land Forces in South Asia 1600–1974.*

Oriental Warfare

Duncan Head, technical author and historian, and author of *The Achmaenid Army* (1994).

Dr Thom Richardson, Royal Armouries, Leeds.

Japan and Japanese Equipment

Greg Irvine, Assitant Curator, Far Eastern Collection, Victoria and Albert Museum, London.

Abd al-Rahman III (891–961) (byname *al-Nasir*, 'the Victorious') Umayyad caliph from 912 and ruler of al-Andalus (Spain). A successful proponent of ◊jihad against the Christian kingdoms until his defeat at Alhandega in 939, and expert at siege warfare, he brought the power of the Cordoban caliphate to its zenith. At the time of his death Umayyad military power was unchallenged.

Abd al-Rahman recaptured the Muslim cities in Spain by techniques ranging from the use of ◊mangonels at Beja in 929 to blockade and a permanent siege camp at Toledo in 930. During the course of his reign his personal force of slave troops grew from 3,750 to 13,750, enabling him to defeat the Christians in battle. He was victor over the Basques and Leonese near Pamplona in 920, and sacked the city in 924. In 929 he declared himself caliph with the regnal title 'al-Nasir'. After 939 he was less active in Spain, but aggressive in North Africa, taking Ceuta in 931 and Tangier in 951.

Abinger castle ◊motte-and-bailey castle built about 1100 in Surrey, England, excavated in 1949. The motte had a flattened summit, with postholes as evidence of a wooden palisade around it containing a 4 m/12 ft square rectangular wooden keep, probably on four corner posts like stilts. The keep was rebuilt in the 12th century. A bridge linked the bailey to the motte.

Abu Bakr (573–634) first Muslim caliph 632–34, the political successor to the prophet ◊Muhammad. He imposed Muslim authority over all the Arab tribes and began the expansion of Islam beyond Arabia.

Acre, Siege of (1189–91) siege in 1189–91 of the fortified port of Acre in the Holy Land (taken by the Muslims in 1187) by King ◊Guy de Lusignan of the Christian Kingdom of Jerusalem, reinforced by crusaders. The Ayubbid sultan ◊Saladin was unable to break the siege lines and the arrival of the English king ◊Richard (I) the Lionheart secured the capture of the city.

King Guy besieged Acre with a small number of troops and it seemed that Saladin would overwhelm him, but the determined attackers held on. Crusader reinforcements built up the besieging forces, and the arrival in May 1191 of the kings of France and England gave them a numerical advantage and established a naval blockade. Constant Muslim attacks failed to dislodge them, and the garrison was forced to surrender. Saladin refused to pay ransom for its members, resulting in their execution.

Acre, Siege of (1291) conflict of 1291 in which Acre, the last Christian crusading bastion in the Holy Land, was captured by the Muslims, bringing about the end of the Latin Kingdom. The Muslim leader Qalawun set out to reduce Acre after provocative attacks on Muslims in the city, but died en route; his son al-Ashraf completed the attack.

He captured the city with a force of 220,000 troops. The Grand Master of the Temple was killed in the fighting, and Acre was left to decay.

Actium, Battle of naval battle in which Octavian defeated the combined fleets of ◊Mark Antony and Cleopatra on 2 September 31 BC to become the undisputed ruler of the Roman world (as the emperor ◊Augustus). The site of the battle is at Akri, a promontory in western Greece.

Antony had encamped in Greece with a powerful force of infantry and cavalry, and was waiting for Octavian's smaller force to attack. However, engagements on land proved indecisive and in the meantime Octavian's naval commander Marcus Agrippa had managed to cut off Antony's supply route by sea, despite commanding a fleet of only 400 ships against Antony's 500. Antony and Cleopatra could have escaped over land to continue the fight but Cleopatra demanded to return to Egypt by sea and they were defeated in the ensuing sea battle.

Having unsuccessfully requested peace terms they fled to Egypt but Octavian pursued them there the following year. Alexandria surrendered without a fight and they committed suicide.

Adad-nerari I (lived 13th century BC)
Assyrian ruler 1295–1264 BC, the first to claim
the title 'Great King' after having conquered
the Hittite client kingdom of Hanigalbat
(northern Mesopotamia) and cowed the
Kassite kingdom of Karduniash (Babylonia).

After defeating the Hittite vassal Shattuara,
Adad-nerari reinstated him in Hanigalbat as an
Assyrian vassal, but his son and successor
Wasashatta rebelled. In response, Adad-nerari
crushed all resistance and occupied Hanigalbat
as an Assyrian province. He then defeated the
Kassite king Nazi-Muttarash at the Battle of
Kar-Ishtar and extended Assyrian control over
Karduniash.

adarga Spanish term for the heart-shaped or
double oval-shaped shield used in Spain and
Portugal throughout the medieval period,
adopted from the Muslim Berbers. It was principally used by the *jinetes*, the characteristic
medieval Iberian light cavalry.

Adda, Battle of battle on 11 August 490 near
the river Adda in northern Italy, between
◊Theodoric the Great's Ostrogoths and
◊Odoacer's Italian ◊*foederati*. Theodoric's victory secured control of Italy for the Ostrogoths.

Following his defeat at Faenza earlier in the
year (see ◊Faenza, Battle of), Theodoric's army
had fallen back on the town of Pavia in
Lombardy, northern Italy, where they were
besieged by Odoacer's forces. When some of
the Italians were drawn off to deal with a
Visigothic and Burgundian incursion into
Liguria, Theodoric seized the opportunity to
attack. Odoacer was defeated and forced to
retreat to Ravenna.

Ad Decimum, Battle of victory for the
Roman army, commanded by ◊Belisarius, in
the first engagement in the East Roman campaign to reconquer Africa from the Vandals.
The battle, which took place in 533, developed
into a series of fierce skirmishes around the
defile at the tenth milestone from Carthage
(hence *Ad Decimum*). The Vandal army disintegrated and the victory cleared the way to
Carthage for the Romans.

After landing on the coast of Africa and
establishing a base camp, Belisarius left his
infantry behind and led approximately 6,000
horsemen on to Carthage as the Vandals,
under ◊Gelimer, were marching out to meet
them. The two armies blundered into each
other. The Roman advance guard of 300 men
defeated a much larger Vandal force as they
were deploying, but failed to warn the main
Roman army. Both sides consisted entirely of
cavalry, resulting in very fluid combat, and initially the battle went well for the Vandals who

succeeded in routing 800 Roman ◊bucellarii.
However, they did not press their pursuit vig-
orously enough and Belisarius was able to rally
the Roman survivors against their disordered
pursuers.

Adherbal (lived 3rd century BC)
Carthaginian general. He was admiral of the
Punic fleet at Drepana in 249 BC (see ◊Drepana,
Battle of), and was probably commander in
chief in Sicily for that year. Despite his great
victory over the Roman fleet of Publius
Claudius Pulcher at Drepana, little else is
known of his career, and Hamilcar Barca
replaced him in Sicily from 248 BC.

admiral (or *amir*) Western term taken from
the Muslim term 'emir', originally just meaning a commander; it was first used in a naval
context in the West.

adoubment (French *adouber*) medieval
English term for being dubbed a knight; the
ceremony of knighting. The meaning of the
original French verb was to equip warriors,
usually in knightly harness; it did not necessarily imply the same rise in status.

Adrianople, Battle of (324) battle fought in
324 at Adrianople (present-day Edirne, Turkey)
between the Roman emperor ◊Constantine (I)
the Great and his eastern rival and co-ruler
Valerius Licinianus Licinius. Each army
allegedly fielded 130,000 men. Constantine
feinted against Licinius' flank, but then led his
centre in a decisive thrust, routing Licinius
with the loss of 40,000 men.

Adrianople, Battle of (718) battle fought in
718 at Adrianople (present-day Edirne, Turkey)
in which the Bulgars, led by King Terbelis,
were victorious over an Arab blocking force
deployed to prevent reinforcements reaching
the besieged city of Constantinople (see
◊Constantinople, Siege of 717–18). The Bulgar
intervention to help their Byzantine allies
forced the Arabs to abandon the siege.

Adrianople, Battle of (1205) battle for the
city of Adrianople (present-day Edirne,
Turkey) on 15 April 1205 between the Fourth
Crusaders led by the Latin emperor ◊Baldwin
of Flanders, aiming to extend his realm into
mainland Europe, and the forces of the
Bulgarian tsar Kalojan, assisting the Greek
occupiers of the city. Baldwin was captured
and his forces retreated.

The crusaders responded rashly to the
harassing attacks of Kalojan's Cuman horse
archers. They embarked on a disorderly pur-

ADRIANOPLE CAMPAIGN (376–78)

Campaign of 376–78 culminating in the great Gothic victory over the Romans at Adrianople in 378 that marks the beginning of the decline of Roman military power. It resulted in the permanent residence of the Goths inside imperial territory, and from this point onwards the Roman Empire was driven to an ever-increasing reliance on allied Germanic peoples to man its armies.

Gothic refugees, driven westward by the Huns, sought refuge across the Roman Danube frontier in 376. Initially permission was given, but as numbers began to grow the Romans tried to close the border. Those who had made it across became vulnerable to corrupt Roman officials who deliberately starved them of supplies to drive up prices. In 377, when the Romans treacherously killed some of the leading Goths, the remainder, under the leadership of ◊Fritigern, took up arms. The Goths easily defeated the local *limitanei* (border troops) near Marcianople (now Shumla, Bulgaria) and armed themselves with Roman equipment. They moved south, their numbers swelled by reinforcements from across the Danube and deserters from the Roman army. After failing to capture the city of Adrianople (now Edrine, Turkey) they broke up into smaller groups to forage throughout Thrace. A hastily gathered Roman field army managed to trap a large group of Goths in a mountainous defile and fought a bloody all-day struggle that came to be known as the Battle of *Ad Salices* (the Willows). The Goths managed to slip away to be joined by bands of Huns and Alans who had also crossed the Danube.

Several small engagements followed as the Romans tried to deal with the roving bands of Goths and their allies. By the summer of 378, worried that his separated bands would be defeated piecemeal by the Romans, Fritigern had gathered his forces together in a large wagon laager (encampment) near Adrianople. The Eastern emperor ◊Valens was urged to wait for reinforcements from the West before attacking the Goths, but after listening to faulty scouting reports that underestimated the Gothic numbers, he decided to seize the opportunity of destroying the marauders in one quick decisive stroke. On 9 August 378, on a blisteringly hot day, Valens led his forces against the Gothic wagon laager. Light troops, leading the advance, became engaged almost immediately, before the rest of the army was completely deployed. What the Romans did not know was that most of the Gothic cavalry and their Alan allies had been away foraging. They returned to hit the Romans in the flank as the latter were deploying from column of march. The Roman cavalry were routed, and the infantry were surrounded and destroyed. The emperor, his senior commanders, and 40,000 of the best imperial troops were slaughtered in what was the most significant Roman defeat since the Battle of Cannae almost 600 years earlier.

The Gothic victory at Adrianople can be attributed to the successful combination of infantry deployed defensively with cavalry delivering the punch, aided by faulty Roman reconnaissance and poor command and control.

---

suit of the Cumans, fell into an ambush, and Baldwin was seized. His forces had to conduct a three-day fighting march back to the security of Constantinople's walls, led by Enrico ◊Dandolo and Geoffrey de ◊Villehardouin.

adulterine castle castle built in England during the civil war of King Stephen's reign (c. 1097–1154) without the permission of a recognized authority. When ◊Henry II became king he destroyed most of these illicit castles.

The concept of a licence to build existed at this time but could not always be enforced. Chroniclers numbered the destroyed castles between 126 and 1,115; the lower figure is the more likely.

Aegates Islands, Battle of the sea battle fought in 241 BC between the Romans, under G Catulus Lutatius, and the Carthaginians, led by Hanno, near the coast of western Sicily, in which the Romans won a decisive victory. It was the final battle of the First Punic War (see ◊Punic War, First).

The Carthaginian fleet of 250 warships and transports, overloaded with reinforcements and supplies bound for ◊Hamilcar Barca's forces based around Mount Eryx on the island of Sicily, was intercepted by Lutatius and brought to battle. In heavy seas, 50 ships were sunk and 70 captured, along with approximately 10,000 men.

Aegospotami, Battle of naval battle fought in 405 BC off Aegospotami (now Gelibolu on the northern shore of the Dardanelles) between the Spartans and the Athenians; the final battle of the ◊Peloponnesian War. The virtual annihilation of the Athenian fleet meant that Sparta could cut off seaborne supplies from the Black Sea to Athens, and so led to the Athenian surrender the following year.

The historians ◊Xenophon and ◊Diodorus Siculus broadly agree that the Spartan commander Lysander surprised the Athenian fleet when most of its ships were moored, partly or wholly unmanned, and that only nine or ten escaped.

Aeneas the Tactician Greek author of possibly the earliest known works on tactics. Only one survives, *Poliorceta/On Siegecraft*, which deals with defence against siege and internal treachery and provides a fascinating glimpse into the life of the average Greek city state in times of stress. Aeneas may also be the Stymphalian general of the Arcadian League mentioned by ◊Xenophon.

AETIUS, FLAVIUS (390–454)

Roman patrician and warlord who became virtual ruler of Gaul (France) in the mid-5th century. He is renowned for defeating the Huns of ◊Attila at Châlons in 451 (see ◊Châlons, Battle of).

As a child, Aetius was a hostage to the Huns and he developed a friendship with the people and their king, Rua. In 423 he used his influence with the Huns to raise an army in support of Johannes, a bureaucrat favoured by western generals to succeed Honorius as emperor of the Western Roman Empire. His force of allegedly 60,000 men arrived in Italy three days too late. The infant Valentinian III was on the throne and Johannes had been deposed by an Eastern Roman army. Placidia, Valentinian's mother, bought Aetius off with a command in Gaul, depending on his support and that of another powerful general, ◊Boniface. In 429 Aetius had her ◊*magister militum* assassinated and supplanted him. In 430 Boniface challenged Aetius, and Aetius was forced to flee to the Huns. He returned in 433 with yet another Hun army, defeated Boniface and emerged as the most powerful man in the Western Roman Empire.

Preservation of Roman Gaul was the keystone of Aetius' policy, and by 440 Gaul was relatively peaceful. The situation was far less stable in the rest of the Empire. In 433 King Rua's successor, Attila, had forbidden Huns to serve in the Roman army. Attila launched a series of campaigns against the Eastern Empire in 441–42 and 447, then in 450 turned his attention to the West. He assembled a large army of Huns and Germans and crossed the Rhine in 451, where Aetius defeated him at the Battle of Châlons. This battle saved Roman Gaul, but the following year Attila invaded Italy and, unable to draw on any allies, Aetius could not stop his advance. Aquileia, Milan, and Pavia were sacked before the Huns were forced to withdraw. With the end of the Hun threat, political machinations began to threaten Aetius. He was murdered on the orders of the emperor Valentinian on 21 September 454.

African *limes* (or *Fossatum Africae*) Roman ◊*limes* (frontier) built by the emperor ◊Hadrian in the 2nd century AD to control the annual migrations of the nomadic desert peoples into the Roman province of Africa (roughly equivalent to present-day Tunisia), enabling them to levy taxes and duties more effectively.

It consisted of three detached sections, the Gemellae (approximately 60 km/37 mi long), the Mesarfelta (45 km/28 mi long), and the Hodna (a 120-km/75-mi ring around the Hodna Mountains in present-day Algeria), which served as barriers to funnel the nomads into the easily patrolled gaps between them. Each section consisted of a mud-brick wall with watchtowers and small gates at regular intervals and was fronted by a ditch.

Agathocles (c. 361–c. 289 BC) king of Syracuse from 305 BC, chiefly remembered for his invasion of Africa. He became commander of the Syracusan army in about 319 then overthrew the ruling oligarchy to seize power in 316. Eleven years later he assumed the royal title.

After a Carthaginian army defeated his forces in Sicily in 311, he boldly carried the war to Africa, where he marched on Carthage. Obligations took him back to Sicily and his army was almost annihilated in his absence. He did return but only to abandon the survivors and flee back to Sicily where, in 306, he made peace with Carthage. He went on to establish an empire in Sicily and southern Italy, and was preparing to renew war with Carthage when he was assassinated.

agema (Greek 'something leading') in ancient Greek warfare, the leading unit of a column. Later, an elite or guard unit.

Agesilaus II (c. 445–c. 359 BC) king of Sparta from 400 BC. Four years after taking the throne he campaigned in Asia Minor, ostensibly to free Greek cities from Persian rule. He returned to Greece in 394 to defend Sparta against a coalition of Athens, Thebes, and Corinth, winning at Coronea (see ◊Coronea, Battle of) on the way.

He later played a leading role in bringing Sparta's ally Phlius to heel, and in the warfare of the 370s twice invaded Boeotia. He campaigned in Arcadia in 370 and organized the defence of Sparta in both 370 and 362. He served as a mercenary general in Asia Minor in 364 and 361–359 in Egypt. He died in Cyrenaica, eastern Libya, journeying home from Egypt.

agger (from Latin *agger* 'a heap') siege mound, ramp, or terrace built out of earth, stone, timber, or debris from demolished buildings, used throughout ancient warfare and probably into the medieval period. It allowed attacking armies to bring heavy machinery such as siege towers closer to city walls and overtop them.

The 9th-century BC Assyrian reliefs from Nimrud illustrate such ramps. Julius Caesar's ramp at ◊Avaricum was some 90 m/300 ft wide and 23 m/75 ft high.

Agincourt, Battle of battle fought on 25 October 1415 in northern France, during the ◊Hundred Years' War, between ◊Henry V of England and a much larger force of French under a divided command. Henry decimated the French and enabled the English conquest of Normandy. Some 6,000 French died and hundreds, including the richest nobles, were taken prisoner.

Following his siege of Harfleur, Henry attempted a ◊*chevauchée* to Calais, but his small forces were diverted by the French and further weakened by disease and hunger. Forcing a crossing of the river Somme, Henry was brought to bay 48 km/30 mi south of Calais. He had barely 1,000 men-at-arms and 5,000 archers, which he deployed on the flanks. The French force numbered some 10,000 men-at-arms with 15–20,000 supporting infantry. Its leaders were so confident of victory that they did not dispose their forces properly: most dismounted, leaving wings of cavalry intended to charge and drive off the archers. Henry seized the initiative by advancing into a narrow gap between two woods, negating the French numbers. The English archers shot down the cavalry charges and disorganized the packed men-at-arms so that they were unable to fight properly.

Agis II (died 400 BC) king of Sparta from 427 BC, at the time of the ◊Peloponnesian War. He led Sparta's invasion of Attica in 425 and an abortive attack on the Argolid in 418 for which he was severely criticized. He recovered his reputation by winning at Mantinea (see ◊Mantinea, Battle of 418 BC) and went on to command Spartan forces occupying Decelea in Attica from 413 until the war ended in 404. He led the invasion of Elis in northwestern Greece, 402–400.

Agis III (died 330 BC) king of Sparta from 338 BC who attempted to revive Sparta's fortunes after ◊Philip (II) of Macedon stripped it of territory. He raised a revolt against Alexander the Great in 331, securing the services of some 8,000 Greek mercenaries who fought for Persia at Issus (see ◊Issus, Battle of

333 BC). He also attracted the support of some of the Peloponnesian states, but was defeated and killed near Megalopolis by Alexander's viceroy ◊Antipater.

Agis IV (died 240 BC) king of Sparta from 244 who tried to revive traditional Spartan ideals by implementing sweeping economic and social reforms. To force through his proposals, he exiled Leonidas II, fellow king of Sparta at the time, and deposed the ephors (senior magistrates). These high-handed methods antagonized many and before the reforms could be implemented Leonidas led a coup d'état. Agis, away on campaign during the coup, was executed when he returned.

agoge (Greek) training system used in ancient Sparta to toughen and discipline boys from the age of 7 to 20 in preparation for military service. Notoriously, boys were encouraged to steal extra food and beaten if caught, not as a punishment for stealing but for being caught.

Agra ancient fortified city in present-day Uttar Pradesh, northern India, on the river Jumna (or Yamuna). One of many Rajput strongholds sacked in the early 11th century during the raids of ◊Mahmud of Ghazni, Agra again became prominent in the reign of Nizam Shah Sikandar Lodi, Sultan of Delhi 1489–1517.

He established a residence there and used it as a base of operations in his campaigns against ◊Gwalior.

Agricola, Gnaeus Julius (AD 40–93) Roman general and politician. Born at Forum Julii (Fréjus) in Provence, he became consul in AD 77, and then governor of Britain about 78–84. He extended Roman rule to the Firth of Forth in Scotland and in 84 won the Battle of Mons Graupius. His fleet sailed round the north of Scotland and proved Britain an island.

Agricola served in Britain as tribune about 60/61 and legate about 70–73/74 before his unusually long appointment as governor. He campaigned in North Wales and Anglesey before carrying the conquest of Britain north to the Firth of Forth–Clyde line. After defeating the British tribes in 84 the Romans claimed that the whole island was under their control.

Agrigentum, Siege of siege conducted by the Romans under Lucius Postumius and Quintus Mamilius of the Carthaginian-held city of Agrigentum (now Agrigento), south-west Sicily, in 262 BC. After a seven-month siege the Carthaginians under Hannibal were defeated in a battle outside the walls.

Hannibal's garrison escaped but the city was sacked and its 50,000 inhabitants were enslaved.

Five months into the siege the Roman base at Herbesos fell to a Punic relief force. Both sides suffered deprivations for a further two months (the Romans being supplied by ◊Hiero II of Syracuse) until the Carthaginians were defeated.

Agrippa, Marcus Vipsanius (63–12 BC) Roman general and admiral. He was instrumental in the successful campaigns and rise to power of Octavian (later the emperor ◊Augustus). Agrippa commanded the victorious fleet at Actium (see ◊Actium, Battle of) in 31 BC. He continued to serve Octavian after the civil war in the west 20–18 BC, where he conquered the Cantabrian tribes in Spain and suppressed a rebellion in Gaul (France) provoked by the imposition of the census.

Ahenobarbus, Gnaeus Domitius (died 31 BC) Roman general. He participated in Caesar's assassination and allied himself with ◊Brutus and ◊Cassius. After Philippi (see ◊Philippi, battles of) he defected to ◊Mark Antony with the naval squadron under his command. He defected to Octavian (later the emperor ◊Augustus) just before the Battle of Actium in 31 BC, but died of fever before the battle.

Ahmadabad ('the city of Ahmad') city built by Ahmad Shah I of Gujarat (ruled 1411–41) on the raised bank of the river Sabarmati, western India, with easy access to the sea. It was constructed on the site of an earlier ◊Rajput stronghold as his new capital city.

The fortifications consisted of a curtain wall 4.5–6 m/15–20 ft high, pierced with 14 gates and a tower or bastion every 45 m/50 yds, the whole enclosing an area of about 5 sq km/2 sq mi.

Ahmad Shah (1373–1435) (known as *Ahmad the Saint*) king of the Bahmani Muslim dynasty of the Deccan 1422–35. He usurped the throne from his brother Firuz Shah Bahmani and waged numerous successful wars against neighbouring Hindu and Muslim kingdoms. His disastrous attack on Ahmad Shah I of Gujarat, a fellow Muslim, in 1430 diminished Bahmani prestige and power.

Before usurping the throne, he fought a victorious campaign under his brother Firuz against the Hindu kingdom of Vijayanagar (see ◊Goldsmith's Daughter, War of the). In 1423, with an army of 40,000 horsemen, he defeated a million-strong Hindu army on the river Tungabhadra.

He was given the title 'the Saint' in recognition of his zeal in waging war on the Hindus and destroying their temples.

Ahmose (lived 16th century BC) (or *Amosis*) Egyptian king 1539–1514 BC. He was the successor (possibly the son) of the Theban ruler Kamose and the founder of the 18th dynasty, the Egyptian New Kingdom. He reunited Upper and Lower Egypt (the Delta) and secured the southern Egyptian border.

He ended the war against the ◊Hyksos by forcing them out of their Delta capital of Avaris and pursuing their retreat to the eastern border fort of Sharuhen, which he sacked after a three-year campaign, thereby reuniting Upper and Lower Egypt. After restoring Theban control over the north, Ahmose then marched into Nubia to secure his southernmost border.

Ain Jalut, Battle of battle fought on 3 September 1260 in modern northern Israel in which the Mameluke sultan ◊Qutuz defeated the Mongols under ◊Hülegü's general Kitbuqa, saving Muslim Egypt from conquest.

Preparing for attack, Qutuz mustered 12,000 Mamelukes and took up a defensive position in a valley. When the Mongols attacked, Qutuz's general ◊Baibars conducted a feigned retreat, leading them into a trap. The hard fighting was decided by Qutuz's charge with the reserve. Despite Mongol invasions of Syria up to 1300 and beyond, the Mameluke victory ensured there would be no conquest.

Ajmer city in Rajasthan, India, strategically important for its command of the routes across the desert from Gujarat and Malwa to northern India. It was founded in AD 145 by Aja Raja, a chief of the ◊Rajput Chauhana clan. Its principal fort, the Taragarh, contains the tomb of the Muslim governor Sayyad Husayn.

Ajmer paid ransom to ◊Mahmud of Ghazni 1023–24. It was captured in 1193 by ◊Muhammad of Ghur, who installed Govinda Raja, illegitimate son of ◊Prithviraja Chauhana III, as his tributary. Govinda was later deposed in a Rajput uprising led by his uncle, Hari Raja (or Hemraj), who ruled as an independent prince until, twice defeated by ◊Qutb al-Din Aibak, he committed suicide. Ajmer continued to change hands between Muslims and Rajputs until 1470, when it became part of the sultanate of Malwa.

Ajnadayn, Battle of victory for the Arabs, commanded by ◊Khalid ibn al-Walid, over the Byzantines under Theodore, brother of Emperor ◊Heraclius, in the first clash between the new forces of Islam and the Eastern Roman Empire, which took place in Palestine in 634. The Arabs engaged the Byzantines in a fearsome head-on struggle in a battle that lasted two days, with high casualties on both sides. Although the Arabs managed to break the Byzantine army, they did not succeed in destroying it.

aketon quilted garment worn either as an independent protective covering or under ◊mail armour throughout medieval Europe. It is most probably the garment which evolved into the arming doublet in the 15th century.

akinakes straight, two-edged sword with a 20–25 cm/8–10 in blade, used from the 7th century BC by Scythians, Persians, and others. It was worn in a scabbard suspended from a waistbelt and held in place by a thong tied around the right thigh.

Both hilt and scabbard, particularly the large trefoil scabbard-chape typical of Persian examples, could be decorated with figured plates of bone, ivory, or gold.

akritos (plural *akritoi*) semi-independent Byzantine border warrior who defended the Byzantine Empire's remote frontiers, especially in the 9th century.

ala (plural *alae*) (Latin 'wing') cavalry unit in a Roman army. Traditionally flanking the deployed army, the *alae* were drawn from Rome's ◊socii and ◊auxilia. The design of the Roman saddle (see ◊saddle, Roman) allowed the *alae* to be highly effective.

Ala al-Din Husain (died 1161) (called *Jahansuz*, 'the World-Burner') prince of Ghur (near modern Charikar, Afghanistan) 1149–61 and founder of the Ghurid dynasty. He defeated ◊Bahram Shah of Ghazni (central Afghanistan) and challenged the Seljuk sultan ◊Sanjar, but was defeated by Sanjar at Herat in 1152. He took the title 'the World-Burner' from his destruction of Ghazni by fire in 1151.

His attack on Ghazni was in revenge for his brother Saif al-Din Suri's humiliation and murder there by Bahram Shah. Encouraged by his three victories over Bahram, 'the World-Burner' ceased to pay tribute to Sanjar and invaded Khurasan (northeastern Iran). After being defeated and captured by Sanjar he had to pay a large ransom to secure his release.

Ala al-Din Khilji (died 1316) sultan of Delhi 1296–1316. Noted for his oppression and cruelty, he conquered the Hindu kingdoms of Rajasthan and southern India and defended his northern boundaries against Mongol incursions.

His first major campaign was in the Deccan in 1294, after which he murdered his uncle and benefactor ◊Jalal al-Din Firuz Shah and usurped his throne. Between 1297 and 1303 he conquered the ◊Rajput kingdoms of Gujarat, Ranthambhor, and Chitral, and in 1310–11 sent his army, led by ◊Malik Kafur, into the previously unconquered Tamil lands of the far south, defeating them in battle and taking tribute from them.

In 1299 his troops defeated a Mongol horde which had reached the outskirts of Delhi. Between 1303 and 1307 various other Mongol forces penetrated as far as Delhi, but all were defeated and turned back.

Ala al-Din Khwarazm Shah (died 1221) sultan of Khwarazm, the area around the southern shores of the Aral Sea, 1200–21. He built up a rich and powerful kingdom covering the eastern half of the former ◊Seljuk Empire, but then provoked the Mongol invasion which led to the destruction of the greatest cities of central Asia and the massacre of their inhabitants.

His reign began with a decade of successful campaigns, during which he recovered Khurasan (northeastern Iran) from the Ghurid ◊Muhammad of Ghur and took Samarkand from the western Qara-Khans (1212).

Despising the Mongols as heathen savages, he authorized the execution of 450 Mongol merchants in 1218. When he subsequently put to death the ◊elchis sent by ◊Genghis Khan to seek redress by diplomatic means, war was the inevitable outcome. Within the space of two years his armies were defeated, his cities captured, and their populations massacred or enslaved. He died a refugee on an island in the Caspian Sea.

Alaca Höyük Bronze-Age Anatolian settlement 25 km/15.5 mi north of ◊Hattusas (modern Boğazkög, Turkey), the Hittite capital. It is possibly the Hittite city of Ankuwa, where Hittite kings overwintered.

The 4-hectare/10-acre site was encircled by a 700-m/766-yd cyclopean wall and two monumental gates. On the inner sides of the southern Sphinx Gate are the weathered forms of a Hittite Great King and Queen, each surmounting a double-headed eagle, an emblem of Hittite power. Excavated goods include gold objects and other items from royal tombs dating from about 2450 BC.

al-Afdal (died 1121) Armenian slave who rose to rule Fatimid Egypt 1094–1121. He reorganized its forces but was defeated by the First Crusaders at Ascalon (see ◊Ascalon, Battle of) in 1099. He was the victor at Ramlah in 1102 (see ◊Ramlah, Battle of), and preserved Egyptian independence. He was mur-

dered by a member of the Assassin sect in 1121 following defeat at Ibelin.

An able field commander with a flair for administration, he saw the revival of the Fatimid army and fleet and the capture of Jerusalem 1096. He was probably overconfident at Ascalon, when his larger forces were swept aside by campaign-hardened crusaders. After overcoming defeat at Ramlah, he returned to defeat ◊Baldwin I the next year, but he was unable to exploit this victory and remained largely on the defensive.

a la jineta medieval style of riding with a short stirrup, as practised by the Muslims of Spain, and by extension a skirmishing style of cavalry warfare.

'alam Arabic and Persian term for a standard or banner.

Alarcos, Battle of battle fought on 17 July 1195 in which the Christian king ◊Alfonso VIII of Castile attacked the Almohad (Berber Muslim) caliph al-Nasir, who had challenged his construction of a fortress town on the hill of Alarcos to the south of Toledo, Spain. Alfonso was defeated, Alarcos was abandoned, and several other important castles were subsequently taken by the Muslims.

Alfonso was challenged by the Almohad caliph in a position between two hills. Advancing overconfidently, the Castilians charged into the Muslim vanguard and drove them back. A left flank counterattack downhill from the Almohad reserve turned the tables, routing the Castilians.

Alaric (c. 370–410) Visigothic king 395–410 who campaigned against the Romans in the Balkans and Italy, finally capturing and sacking Rome in 410.

After successfully leading the Visigothic contingent in the Battle of Frigidius (see ◊Frigidius, Battle of) in 394, Alaric was angered by the Eastern Roman emperor Theodosius (I) the Great's refusal to give him a permanent command in the Roman army, and led the Visigoths, who were settled in the Balkans, against his former employer. In 400 he was given a Roman command position in the Balkans. He then made several attempted invasions of Italy but was defeated each time by the Roman general ◊Stilicho.

When Stilicho was executed in 408, Alaric marched unopposed on Rome, his army swelled by Roman troops who had been loyal to Stilicho. On 24 August 410 the gates were opened to him and he led the first foreign army in 800 years into the city. After three days he led the Goths south, intending to invade Sicily and then Africa, but died of a sudden illness.

Alashiya, battles of one of the earliest recorded series of sea battles, involving three Hittite naval victories off the coast of Cyprus against an enemy fleet and a subsequent battle on shore, led by Great King Suppiluliumas II (reigned 1275–1205 BC).

The Hittites had claimed Alashiya (Cyprus, or a part of it) as within their sphere of influence since the reign of Tudhaliyas II (1390–1370 BC), when it was attacked from the ◊Lukka lands. Lukkan raids, accompanied by Danuna (or Danaans, from Cilicia), were probably the provocation for the battles of Alashiya.

al-Babein, Battle of battle fought on 19 March 1167 between King ◊Almaric of the Christian Kingdom of Jerusalem allied with Shawar, Vizier of Egypt, and ◊Shirkuh, the commander of Sultan ◊Nur al-Din of Egypt and Syria's forces, some 320 km/200 mi south of Cairo. Almaric was outmanoeuvred and forced to retreat northwards, saving Egypt from Christian conquest.

Al-Babein means 'gate', referring to a position between two hills where Shirkuh had drawn up his army defensively. The Franks charged successfully, but the steep, sandy hillsides made it impossible for them to exploit their initial advantage, and their Egyptian allies seem to have played little part. The future Ayubbid sultan ◊Saladin took an important role in the battle, attacking Almaric's rear.

Albigensian Crusades series of wars fought in southern France 1209–18 and 1226, supposedly to suppress the Cathar heresy but effectively a conquest by the northern French for the French kings.

In 1208 Pope Innocent III preached a crusade against Raymond V, Count of Toulouse, for supporting heresy. Simon de ◊Montfort (the Elder) was given the task of subduing the south. This involved long sieges of inaccessible castles and, in 1211, a failed siege of Toulouse. The northerners proved better in the field, though, winning at Muret in 1213 despite Aragonese support for the southerners (see ◊Muret, Battle of). In 1215 the arrival of Prince Louis with a large army forced the surrender of Toulouse. In 1217 Raymond recovered the city and de Montfort was killed in a new siege in 1218. His son Amaury failed to prosecute the campaign and lost most of his father's conquests by 1224. Finally, ◊Louis VIII of France returned to overwhelm the war-weary southerners in 1226.

Albinus, Decimus Clodius (died AD 197) Roman governor of Britain from c. 192. He was one of the contenders for the imperial throne following the murder of the emperor Publius Helvius Pertinax in 193, and was granted the title of Caesar (imperial ruler) by ◊Septimus Severus. He was proclaimed Augustus (emperor) by his army, but was defeated at Lugdunum (see ◊Lugdunum, Battle of) and committed suicide.

Alcala de Guadaira fortress in Andalusia, Spain, built by the Moors to defend Seville from the southeast. It was conquered in 1246 by Ferdinand III of Castile and restored in the 15th century by the Marquis of Cadiz.

A typical Spanish-Moorish feature was the *enciente* (curtain wall) supported by eight towers. One tower, defending the gate, was set apart from the wall and connected to it by a bridge.

Alcazaba de Almeria powerful coastal fortress in Spain, about 100 km/62 mi east of Granada. Built by the Moors in the 10th century, it was subsequently strengthened and extended by the Christians and then later by Ferdinand and Isabella (late 15th century), thus becoming one of the most important medieval fortifications in Spain.

The early part was built of *tapis,* a form of concrete, and consisted of the usual Moorish features of a curtain wall with square towers. Later additions are in masonry, including a number of round towers.

Alcázar of Segovia walled and fortified area of Segovia, overlooking the junction of the Adaja and Eresma rivers. It was established by the Moors and after their expulsion extended and modified by the kings of Castile.

The perfectly proportioned John II's Tower (built by King John II in the first half of the 15th century) was rectangular, with 12 half-cylindrical turrets, and was designed to match the height of the cathedral which then existed.

Alcibiades (451/0–404/3 BC) Athenian admiral during the ◊Peloponnesian War.

In 415 BC Alcibiades was appointed one of the commanders of an Athenian expedition against Sicily, but was recalled to answer charges of sacrilege and fled to Sparta. Further scandal led to his flight to Persia, but he rehabilitated himself with the Athenians and played a leading part at Cyzicus (see ◊Cyzicus, Battle of 410 BC). He was given command of Athenian forces in Asia Minor but was replaced after his lieutenant's defeat off Notium in 407. He was murdered shortly after the war.

Alençon, Battle of frontier battle fought in France in 1118 between the Norman forces of ◊Henry I of England and the count of Anjou, Fulk V. Fulk had besieged Alençon which Henry came to relieve. Fulk's sorties from his siege camp failed, but he was rescued by the arrival of reinforcements under Lisiard de Sablé. Fulk then emerged from his camp and Henry was trapped; his army broke and fled.

Alençon, Siege of attack in 1053 on the Norman border stronghold of Alençon, northwest France, by ◊William (I) the Conqueror, then duke of Normandy, who recovered the town from Geoffrey Martel, count of Anjou. William appeared to be planning an attack on ◊Domfront castle but suddenly changed direction, and Alençon was taken by storm.

Alessandria, Battle of battle in 1391 in which the Milanese gained a victory over Florence in a war begun in 1390 for control in northern Italy.

Charles VI of France (1368–1422) had threatened to intervene but abandoned his expedition. A pro-Florentine force under the French Count of Armagnac and the English mercenary Sir John ◊Hawkwood was attacked and defeated by the Milanese outside Alessandria; Armagnac was killed.

Alexander Nevsky (1220–63) ruler of Novgorod in 1236 and Grand Prince of Russia in 1252. He survived Mongol attacks 1237–40, enabling him to defeat the Swedes in 1240 and the Germans in 1242.

Alexander pursued a policy of compromise with Russia's Mongol rulers following the conquest of 1237–40. This enabled him to beat off attacks by Sweden at the Battle of the Neva 1240 and, most famously, in the 'Battle on the Ice' against the Teutonic Knights (see ◊Military Order) and crusaders on Lake Peipus in 1242 (see ◊Lake Peipus, Battle of). Alexander lured the Germans into an ambush, and his allied Mongol horse archers played an important role in defeating their left flank.

Alexius (I) Comnenus (1048–1118) Byzantine emperor 1081–1118. With meagre resources, he dealt successfully with internal dissent and a series of external threats from the Turks and Normans. He managed the difficult passage of the First Crusade through

ALESIA, SIEGE OF

Siege of a hillfort of the Mandubii tribe at Alesia in Gaul (at modern Alise-Ste Reine in central France) by the Romans in 52 BC. Julius ◊Caesar gained a victory over the rebellious Gauls even though the town's situation on a steepsided plateau made it impregnable except by blockade, and a large Gallic army occupied the eastern slope of the hill.

In his war commentaries, Caesar describes the Alesia campaign in great detail. His siegeworks were very elaborate with camps and redoubts constructed at strategic points, and he made his soldiers dig a defensive trench before starting work on the main circumvallation some distance behind this. Two trenches, one filled with water, fronted a rampart and palisade 3.5 m/11.5 ft high. Towers were built every 23.5 m/ 77 ft, and antipersonnel traps were placed in front of the trenches. Once this 16 km/ 10 mi line was completed the Romans constructed another identical line of fortifications facing outwards, some 20 km/12 mi long, to counter the threat of a Gallic relieving army.

Concerted attacks on the Romans were made first by the besieged and then simultaneously by them and the relieving force which had finally arrived. The situation for the Romans became critical, but when Caesar arrived on the scene in his conspicuous red cloak they gained heart and repulsed the attacks. The next day the Gauls under ◊Vercingetorix surrendered and the Gallic revolt was virtually over.

The site of Alesia was excavated by Napoleon III in the 19th century. This showed that much of Caesar's record of his siegeworks was correct and that the Roman lines of defence were positioned to make optimum use of the terrain.

ALEXANDER (III) THE GREAT (356–323 BC)

King of Macedon 336–323 BC and conqueror of the Persian Empire. As commander of the powerful Macedonian army he conquered Greece in 336, defeated the Persian king Darius III in Asia Minor in 333, then moved on to Egypt where he founded Alexandria. He defeated the Persians again in Assyria in 331, then advanced further east, invading India in 327. He conquered the Punjab before mutinous troops forced his retreat.

He won his spurs in 338 BC, commanding the cavalry at the Battle of Chaeronea, and succeeded to the throne after the assassination of his father ◊Philip (II) of Macedon in 336. Though Thebes seized the opportunity to revolt while he was absent campaigning in the northwest, he rapidly reimposed his authority by destroying the city in 335.

Alexander inherited not only a magnificent army from his father but also plans to invade the Persian Empire, and in 334 he crossed the Hellespont (now the Dardanelles), never to return. Victory at the river Granicus that year (see ◊Granicus, Battle of the) gave him control of western Asia Minor, and then, ignoring Persian superiority at sea, he turned east, winning his second victory at Issus in the autumn of 333 (see ◊Issus, Battle of 333 BC), this time over the Persian king Darius himself. After taking Tyre and Gaza in epic sieges, he next invaded Egypt, where he spent the winter of 332/1.

This enabled Darius to assemble a new army, but Alexander's victory at Gaugamela on 1 October 331 (see ◊Gaugamela, Battle of) laid open the heartland of the Persian Empire and Babylon, Susa, and Persepolis were in turn occupied. Finally, the murder of Darius by his own entourage in the summer of 330 enabled Alexander to pose as his rightful successor. Widespread revolts in the northeast, however, took some three years of marching, sieges, and savage fighting to subdue, and this was followed by the invasion of India in 327, victory at the river Hydaspes (now Jhelum), and a further march eastwards until, at the river Hyphasis (now Beas), the army refused to go any further.

Turning back, Alexander descended the river Indus, subduing any tribe which refused to submit, and reached the delta in July 325. He then sent his fleet westwards, while he marched through the deserts of southern Baluchistan to rendezvous with it in southeast Iran in December, and to return to Susa early in 324. Further plans of conquest were cut short by his death in June 323.

Byzantine territory on its way to Jerusalem, and by the end of his reign he had, with the help of the Crusaders, restored much of Byzantine control over Anatolia.

Alfonso I (c. 1073–1134) ('the Battler') king of Aragón and Navarre, 1104–34. He spearheaded the Christian reconquest of Spain (see ◊Reconquista), recovering most of the Ebro Valley, Zaragoza, and Tudela. His expeditionary raid south to Valencia, Granada, and Málaga 1125–26 demonstrated the success of his efforts.

Alfonso VIII (1156–1214) king of Castile from 1158, aged two. He came to power in 1169, after a disputed regency. He led the Christian coalition that broke the power of the Moors, and was a leader in the victory at Las Navas de Tolosa (see ◊Las Navas de Tolosa, Battle of) in 1212, a turning point in the Christian ◊Reconquista of Spain. He also helped develop the Military Order of Santiago (see ◊Military Order).

Alfred the Great (c. 849–c. 901) Anglo-Saxon king 871–99. He succeeded his brother Aethelred to the throne of Wessex in 871 during the bitter struggle with the Danes for control of England. Through a combination of hard fighting and diplomacy Alfred managed to keep Wessex free of Danish control after the other Anglo-Saxon kingdoms had succumbed.

Alfred's skill as a military commander first came to light at the Battle of Ashdown (see ◊Ashdown, Battle of) in 871 when he led the Saxon army to victory against the Danes. Not all his campaigns were so successful; on a number of occasions he had to resort to buying off the Danes for a brief respite. His great victory at Edington (see ◊Edington, Battle of) in 878 secured the survival of Wessex and his peace treaty with the Danish king ◊Guthrum in 886 established a boundary between the Danelaw, east of Watling Street, and the Saxons to the west. The *Anglo-Saxon Chronicle* says that following his capture of London in 866 'all the English people submitted to him, except those who were in captivity to the Danes'. In some respects, therefore, Alfred could be considered the first king of England.

During periods of peace Alfred reformed and improved his military organization. He divided his levies into two parts with one half at home and the other on active service, giving him a relief system he could call on to continue a campaign. He also began to build fortified strongpoints (see ◊burh) throughout the kingdom to form the basis of an organized defensive system. Alfred is popularly credited as being the founder of the Royal Navy; he did build a fleet of improved ships manned by Frisians and on several occasions successfully challenged the Danes at sea.

Algidus, Battle of the battle fought about 431 BC between an allied force of the Aequi and Volsi and a Roman and Latin allied army led by the dictator Aulus Postumius. The Algidus was a strategic pass in the Alban hills, 20 km/ 12 mi southeast of Rome, controlled by the hill tribes of the Aequi. According to the Roman historian Livy, the Romans defeated the Aequi and Volsi encamped there.

Aljubarrota, Battle of battle fought on 14 August 1385 in west-central Portugal between a Portuguese force including English troops and the invading Castilians of King John I with their French allies; the invasion force was defeated.

The 6,500 Portuguese took up a defensive position, with the English archers on the left flank behind a field of pits to break up a cavalry charge. When the Castilians (said to have numbered 30,000) charged they were routed.

Allia, Battle of the battle fought about 390 or 386 BC between the Roman army and a Gallic warband led by the chieftain ◊Brennus. The Romans were routed on the banks of the river Allia, 18 km/12 mi north of Rome. The survivors withdrew to Veii and the Gauls advanced to sack Rome.

The defeat had such a traumatic effect on the Roman psyche that the anniversary (18 July) was regarded subsequently as a day of ill omen (*dies nefastus*).

Allington fortified manor house in England, northwest of Maidstone, Kent. Originally a residence, it was given licence to crenellate (build battlements) by Edward I in 1281, thus converting it into a defensive work.

The conversion included building a new outer wall with towers around the original walled house, and adding a wet ditch and a substantial gatehouse.

al-Mansur, Muhammad ibn Abu'Amir (lived 10th–11th centuries) ruler of al-Andalus (Spain) 981–1002 and the last great Umayyad general to oppose the Christians. Although lacking military training, he built up Umayyad forces by balancing indigenous Andalusian and Berber troops, using them in over 50 campaigns in the peninsula, including the sack of Barcelona in 985 and Santiago de Compostella in 997. He recovered well from defeat by the Castilians in 1000 and operated aggressively in North Africa, taking Fez in 998.

Almaric (lived 12th century) king of Jerusalem 1162–74. He recognized that the security of the Latin Kingdom depended upon control of Egypt, but, despite three campaigns, he failed to subdue it, eventually facing defeat by the young ◊Saladin.

In 1163 Almaric was invited into Egypt to support its caliph against ◊Nur al-Din's general ◊Shirkuh, leading to a stalemate. A renewed invasion in 1167 saw him defeated at al-Babein (see ◊al-Babein, Battle of). An alliance with the Byzantine emperor Manuel (I) Comnenus in 1168 encouraged Almaric to attack in 1169, but a joint siege of Damietta failed amidst acrimony, and the Christians did not return to Egypt for 50 years.

Almourol castle castle in Portugal, on an island in the river Tagus east of Entroncamento. It was built by the Knights Templar (see ◊Military Order) in the 12th century and maintained by them until 1312, when King Dinis handed it over to the Order of Christ. There was a central square keep and *enciente* (boundary wall) with ten towers.

almugavar lightly equipped warrior, originally from Iberia and inspired by Muslim warriors, who played an important role in the campaigns of the mercenary Catalan Company in the 13th century. *Almugavars* carried javelins for skirmishing but were also prepared to engage in hand-to-hand combat. They had a reputation for ferocity.

Alnwick castle border fortress 56 km / 35 mi north of Newcastle-upon-Tyne, England; stronghold of the Percy family and seat of the duke of Northumberland. It was built about 1096 by Yves de Vescy, 1st Baron of Alnwick, and passed to the Percys in 1309. Alnwick was the scene of much border fighting between the English and Scots, and was also prominent in the Wars of the Roses. Expansion and building continued into the 15th century.

Alnwick, Siege of siege ending on 13 July 1174 in which ◊William (I) the Lion of Scotland, invading England in support of the 1174 rebellion against ◊Henry II of England, was surprised outside Alnwick castle in Northumberland by the English and captured.

He was encamped outside the castle when an English force came out of the mist and attacked. William fought bravely but his horse was killed and he was trapped underneath it and seized by his opponents.

Alp-Arslan (c. 1029–72) sultan of the Seljuk Turks 1063–72, who expanded Turkish control over much of Anatolia and Syria. He destroyed the Byzantine army at Manzikert (see ◊Manzikert, Battle of) and captured Jerusalem in 1071. This was the event that set off the ◊Crusades from western Europe.

Alp-Tegin (died 963) (or *Alptigin*) Turkish ◊*ghulam* who rose to become chief *habib* (commander) of the Samanid empire of Iran and was appointed amir (governor) of Ghazni (central Afghanistan) 962–63. He continued to acknowledge Samanid suzerainty, but in practice ruled as a virtually independent prince, and founded the Ghaznavid dynasty.

Altrip fort (Roman *Alta Ripa*) 4th-century AD Roman fort near modern Ludwigshafen, Germany, built by the emperor ◊Valentinian I as part of the defences of the middle Rhine. It was trapezoidal in shape with projecting towers at each corner and one interval tower probably in the centre of the longer north wall. In common with many of the Rhine forts constructed by Valentinian, Altrip had a smaller bridgehead fort across the river on the right bank at Neckerau.

Alzey fort Roman fort to the southwest of present-day Frankfurt, Germany, built to bolster the defences of the Rhine. The date for its construction is not secure; it dates either to the building programme of the emperor Julian (ruled AD 360–63) or that of Valentinian I (ruled AD 364–75).

Ambhi (Greek *Omphis*) king of Takshashila (Greek 'Taxila') in the northwest Punjab, India, 327/326–320 BC. In accordance with the Hindu doctrine of ◊*mandala*, he welcomed Alexander the Great as a potential ally against his eastern neighbour, a king of the Parava dynasty, known to the Greeks as 'Poros', and fought on Alexander's side at the battle of the Hydaspes in 326 BC (see ◊Hydaspes, Battle of the).

Ambiorix (lived 1st century BC) Gallic chief of the Eburones. He was induced by ◊Indutiomarus of the Treveri to revolt against Julius ◊Caesar in the winter of 54/53 BC.

He tricked a legion and five cohorts led by Quintus Titurius Sabinus and Lucius Aurunculeius Cotta into abandoning their camp and ambushed them as they attempted to rejoin Caesar. During a parley he killed Sabinus and then destroyed the rest of the force. Caesar's subsequent campaigns in northern Gaul stripped him of allies but he managed to elude capture.

Amboise castle stronghold in the Loire valley, France, between Tours and Blois. The site was fortified from the Frankish period.

Amida fortified Roman town on the banks of the river Tigris (the present-day city of Diyarbakir in southeast Turkey), the capital of the Roman province of Mesopotamia. It was captured by the Persians three times and finally fell to the Arabs in 640. It was constructed by the emperor Constantius II (ruled 337–61) as a garrison town, and was enlarged and restored following the first Persian siege in 359.

Amida was retaken by the Byzantine emperor Julian in 363. In 502 it was captured by King Kavad of Persia, but it was recaptured by the Byzantine emperor Anastasius in 504. In 602 it was again taken by the Persians, to be recovered by the Byzantine emperor Heraclius in 628. It was captured by the Arabs in 640 and remained under Arab control.

Amida, Siege of assault on Amida (modern Diyarbakir, Turkey) on Rome's eastern frontier by the Persian king Shapur in 358. The town fell in a final attack led by Shapur himself, after a valiant defence by its Roman garrison.

During the siege the basalt walls and sheer cliffs on the east side were able to resist the Persians for 74 days. The town finally fell when an earthen mound raised to counter a Persian siege ramp collapsed and filled in the gap between the ramp and the wall, creating a direct route through the defences.

Ammianus Marcellinus (lived 4th century) Roman army officer who wrote a history of Rome. His later books covering the period 354–78 survive and provide invaluable detail about the Roman army in the 4th century.

Amphipolis, Battle of clash between Athens and Sparta in 422 BC that left both the Athenian commander, ◊Cleon, and his Spartan counterpart, ◊Brasidas, dead. The Spartan victory cleared the way for the Peace of Nicias, which brought the first ten years of the ◊Peloponnesian War to an end. Amphipolis was an Athenian colony controlling the valley of the river Strymon and the river's most important crossing.

This battle is of interest because of Cleon's mistake in exposing the right, unshielded side of his forces to attack. Amphipolis had gone over to the Spartans in 424, and Cleon was defeated while withdrawing from a reconnaissance of the area.

Amunhotep II (also known as *Amenophis II*) Egyptian pharaoh 1427–1396 BC, the son and successor of Tuthmosis III. He continued the war with Mitanni for control of the Levant, leading three northern expeditions to maintain Egyptian supremacy over the area won by his father. By the end of his reign Egyptian influence stretched as far north as Ugarit.

In a campaign in 1420 BC his army was almost ambushed as he crossed the river Orontes (modern 'Asi) in the vicinity of Kadesh; however, he beat off the attack to receive the allegiance of Kadesh and moved on to capture Ugarit, the most important Syrian port on the Mediterranean. In 1398 BC he campaigned in the area of Megiddo to defeat Mitannian countermeasures.

Amurru Akkadian ('Westerners') a tribal hill people, the biblical Amorites, who lived north of Mount Lebanon and whose land became the focus of the struggle between Mitanni, Egypt, and the Hittites in the 14th and 13th centuries BC.

Under the leadership of 'Abdi-Ashirta, the Amurru threw off Mitannian vassalage and began the conquest of the coastal city-states, gaining Sumur (or Simyra) for their capital, attacking Gubla (Byblos) to the south, and threatening Ugarit to the north. Aziru, 'Abdi-Ashirta's son and successor, offered fealty to the Hittites in about 1338 BC, but the land of Amurru was reconquered by Egypt under Seti I in about 1290 BC, then retaken by the Hittites under Muwatallis II some time after the Battle of Kadesh (see ◊Kadesh, Battle of) in 1275 BC. In the 12th century BC Amurru became the base for the operations of the ◊Peoples of the Sea.

anabasis (Greek 'going up') mounting a horse or, in ancient Greek warfare, a march from the coast into the interior. It is used as the title of ◊Xenophon's story of his adventures as a mercenary in 401–400 BC and also of ◊Arrian's account of Alexander the Great's campaigns.

Anagui (died 552) (also known as *A-na-kui, A-na-huai,* or *A-nu-kuei*) last *khagan* (emperor) of the Ruanruan nomads in Mongolia, who ruled 519–52. In 523 he led a massive attack on China, which helped precipitate the revolt of the Six Garrisons (see ◊Six Garrisons, rebellion of the). In 546 one of his subject tribes, the Turks of the Altai Mountains, rebelled against him and defeated the Ruanruan. Anagui committed suicide and the Turks took over his territory.

After his succession, Anagui was expelled by an uncle but regained power with help from the Toba of north China. When the strain of his attacks on China in 523 provoked the revolt of the Six Garrisons, the Toba court called in Anagui to subdue their mutinous soldiers.

In 546 the Turks of the Altai Mountains defeated another nomad confederacy on Anagui's behalf, and their ruler Bumin (or Tumen) asked for a Ruanruan princess as his reward. When this was refused, he rebelled and allied with ◊Yuwen Tai's Western Wei in China. After the Turkish victory over Anagui the Ruanruan remnants fled to China and a Turkish empire replaced theirs.

anastrophe in ancient Greek warfare, an about turn. In this manoeuvre, files (rows of men from front to back in marching formation) on the wings of a phalanx moved behind the phalanx to strengthen the formation's wings, or moved back into line after swinging forward. At sea, it is the turn a galley makes, particularly after breaking through a line of enemy ships.

An, Battle of battle in 589 BC in which the Chinese state of Qi was pitted against rivals Lu and Jin. Qi attacked Lu, and the Jin commander Ke Xi was sent with an army of 800 chariots to join up with Lu's army. Ke led the allied charge in person and was wounded, but broke the Qi army.

Qi commander Marquis Hui was almost captured in the pursuit, but was saved by his charioteer, who impersonated him. The commander was then allowed to escape by disaffected Di barbarian auxiliaries in the Jin army.

Anchialus, Battle of battle in 708 in which the Bulgars under Khan Tervel (r. 700–21) defeated the Byzantines in Thrace (modern Bulgaria). Faced with internal dissent and Muslim attacks, the Byzantines were unable to stop the Bulgars from overrunning Thrace. By 712 Tervel's men had reached the walls of Constantinople, but in 717 a peace was concluded under which the Bulgars allied themselves with the Byzantines to fend off a large-scale Muslim invasion.

Andernach, Battle of (876) battle in October 876 between the Germans under Louis III and the West Franks, at Andernach on the river Rhine. The German victory prevented Louis's uncle, Charles the Bald of France, from annexing the German territories of the Frankish Empire.

Andernach, Battle of (941) victory in 941 of the forces of the German emperor Otto I over the rebellious Eberhard of Franconia, Giselbert of Lorraine, and Otto's younger brother Henry, which brought Lorraine firmly under German control.

Angers castle citadel castle of Angers, Maine-et-Loire *département*, France, fortified in some form from the 9th century. The surviving castle dates mainly from the 13th century, with an irregular pentagon-shaped keep with 17 round towers, lowered to make gun platforms in the 16th century. It contains the 14th-century Apocalypse Tapestries.

angon heavy spear used primarily by western Germanic warriors of the migration period (250–600). The *angon* was probably a prestige weapon, similar in construction to the earlier Roman ◊*pilum*. Archaeological evidence shows that most were about as long as the warrior's body, with the barbed iron head accounting for at least half the length.

The 6th-century writer Agathius describes the weapon in detail: 'The greater part of the *angon* is covered with iron and very little wood is exposed. In battle the Frank throws the *angon* and if it hits an enemy ... the barbs hold inside the flesh. If the *angon* strikes a shield, it is fixed there, hanging down with butt on the ground. The *angon* cannot be pulled out because the barbs have penetrated the shield, nor can it be cut off with a sword because the wood of the shaft is covered with iron'.

Aniruddha (lived 11th century) (or *Anôratha, Anawrahta*) Burmese king of Pagan 1044–77 and the first unifier of Burma. He usurped the throne by killing King Sokkate in single combat. His conquests of several Mon states led to the creation of a unified Burmese-Mon kingdom and the triumph of Mon culture at Pagan's court. He permanently strengthened

Pagan by irrigating fertile land near the capital and settling it with captives from his conquests.

Wishing to convert his kingdom to Theravada Buddhism, Aniruddha requested scriptures from the Mon king of Thaton in Lower Burma. The king refused, and Aniruddha attacked Thaton in 1057, took the city after a three-month siege, and deported the population to Pagan. He then conquered and garrisoned other Mon states in the lower Irrawaddy and Salween valleys. Aniruddha also conquered part of the coastal kingdom of Arakan, campaigned in the southeast to secure his frontier against Khmer expansion, and fought an indecisive border war against the Nanzhao kingdom in Yunnan.

Ankara, Battle of battle fought on 28 July 1402 in central Anatolia between the Mongol ruler ◊Timur Leng (Tamerlane) and the Ottoman sultan Bayezid I, whose Anatolian troops deserted him, resulting in his capture by the Mongols.

Bayezid had proved himself the master of Asia Minor when he annexed the Karaman and other principalities in 1398. This, combined with the victory of Nicopolis (see ◊Nicopolis, Battle of) in 1396, gave him an empire stretching from the Danube to the Euphrates. Against Timur, however, he was ill matched. Timur besieged Ankara, then constructed field fortifications to defy the Turks. Bayezid's attacks were fruitless, and the defection of his recently conquered Anatolian troops produced a rout and led to his capture.

An Lushan (703–757) half-Turkish, half-Sogdian general in Tang Chinese service, who rebelled in 755 and proclaimed himself emperor of the Yan dynasty. He was killed and his rebellion ended, but the Tang regime never quite recovered.

An became governor (*jiedu shi*) on the northeastern frontier in 742, campaigning against the Khitan and Xi. As his power increased it was threatened by rivals at court, and in December 755 he rebelled with 150,000 Chinese and tribal troops. He overran the northeast but was held up at Tongguan (see ◊Tongguan, Battle of); eventually he defeated the loyalists there and took Changan, forcing the emperor ◊Tang Xuanzong to flee and proclaiming himself emperor.

Further advances were prevented by loyalist risings, and An was murdered and replaced by his son An Chingxu. A Tang counterattack then defeated the rebels at Changan (see ◊Changan, Battle of) and Xiandan, and the rebellion gradually died out.

Anshizheng, Battle of (or *An-shih-cheng, Ansisong*) siege and battle in the summer of 644 for the fortress of Anshizheng in the northern Korean kingdom of Koguryo, initiated by the Chinese emperor Tang Taizong during the Tang wars in Korea (see ◊Korea, Tang Chinese wars in). The Koreans suffered huge losses in the battle but resisted the siege for 63 days, after which Taizong withdrew.

A large Koguryo army under the Korean general Gao Yanshou, including many Manchurian tribal cavalry, came to Anshizheng's relief. When the Koreans deployed for battle, Taizong opposed them with part of his army, sent another force to work round into their rear, and placed his own reserve in ambush. Gao pushed back the main Chinese force, and then Taizong attacked his right flank. As the Koreans redeployed to meet this threat, the outflanking force arrived in their rear. With their retreat cut off, they lost large numbers of men.

Despite this setback, Anshizheng continued to resist. The Chinese built a siege ramp to assault the walls, but the Koreans defeated the attack and captured the mound. Knowing that he could not supply his forces into the winter, Taizong eventually withdrew.

Antigonus (I) Monophthalmus (c. 382–301 BC) (or *Antogonus Cyclops*, 'One-Eye') general and 'successor' of ◊Alexander (III) the Great (see ◊Diadochi), after whose death in 323 BC Antigonus made himself briefly master of Asia Minor and then 'king' of Macedon 306–301 BC. He was defeated and killed by ◊Seleucus (I) Nicator at Ipsus (see ◊Ipsus, Battle of).

Antigonus governed Phrygia for Alexander 334–323 BC, and became one of the contenders for supreme power after his death, particularly after the defeat of ◊Eumenes of Cardia and ◊Perdiccas in 319. After Eumenes' death in 316, he briefly held sway from the Hindu Kush to the Aegean, but wars with other successors led to loss of influence in the east.

From 310 his claims to promote autonomy and reactivation of the Corinthian League won him much support in Greece, and after being accorded extravagant honours by Athens in 307, he and his son, ◊Demetrius (I) Poliorcetes, proclaimed themselves 'kings'. But a war with ◊Ptolemy (I) Soter, the Greek ruler of Egypt, and Demetrius' attempt to coerce Rhodes were unsuccessful, and Antigonus was finally defeated at Ipsus.

Antigonus (II) Gonatas (319–239 BC) king of Macedonia c. 277/6–239 BC, who restored Macedonia's power. He defeated Athens and Sparta, and victories off Cos (255?) and Andros (245?) over Ptolemy II of Egypt's fleet extended his influence in the Aegean. However, his support of tyrants in Greece caused widespread disaffection which the Achaean League exploited to secure Corinth, one of the principal Macedonian bases in Greece, in 243, though Demetrias, Chalcis, and the Peiraeus were retained.

Antigonus (III) Doson (c. 263–c. 221 BC) regent and king of Macedonia from 229–221 BC. Antigonus achieved more by diplomacy than as a soldier, but when the Achaean League appealed to him in the face of Spartan aggression, he decisively defeated ◊Cleomenes III at Sellasia (see ◊Sellasia, Battle of). He died the following year after bursting a blood vessel during a battle against the Dardanians, in the modern Republic of Macedonia.

antilabe (Greek) cord or strap at the rim of a hoplite shield (*aspis*) which was gripped in the left hand.

Antioch, Battle of (272) first battle, fought in 272, between the army of the Roman emperor ◊Aurelian and Queen ◊Zenobia of Palmyra's forces commanded by her general Zabdas. The battle ended in a Roman success, despite the defeat of Aurelian's Illyrian and Moorish cavalry by the more heavily armoured Palmyrenes.

The Palmyrenes pursued too far and became exhausted, allowing the rest of their army to be defeated.

Antiochus (I) Soter (c. 324–c. 246 BC) ('the Saviour') king of Syria 281–261 BC, the son of ◊Seleucus (I) Nicator. He is famous as a founder of cities and for his victory over the Celts of Galatia in 275, for which he was given the title 'Soter'.

After acting as co-regent with his father in the east, he had to crush revolts in many areas at his accession, and Bithynia and Pontus became independent. He also fought Ptolemy II of Egypt over the Lebanon and Palestine.

Antiochus (III) the Great (c. 241–187 BC) king of Syria 223–187 BC. He earned his title 'the Great' by restoring the Seleucid empire in 25 years of continuous campaigning from western Asia Minor to Afghanistan. He also finally wrested the Lebanon and Palestine from Egypt, despite defeat at Raphia in 201 BC (see ◊Raphia, Battle of).

His western ambitions, which led him to seize Ptolemaic possessions in southwest Anatolia and to further Seleucid claims to Thrace, brought him into conflict with the Roman Republic. He invaded Greece, but was

ANTIOCH, BATTLE OF (1098)

Crucial siege by the forces of the First Crusade of the Muslim city of Antioch from 21 October 1097 to 3 June 1098, during which the crusaders were constantly attacked. When they had taken Antioch (now Antakya, Turkey), they were besieged themselves until decisively defeating the army of the caliph of Baghdad on 26 June 1098, freeing themselves to march south to Jerusalem in 1099.

After crossing the harsh Amanus mountains, during which many knights lost their horses, the crusaders attempted to besiege the city, originally fortified by the Byzantines. A near ten-mile circuit of 9 m/30 ft walls studded with 400 18 m/60 ft towers extended from the western frontage on the river Orontes up to a mountain in the east 300 m/1,000 ft high, with a strong citadel on the ridge. Yaghi-Siyan, the city's semi-independent governor, had a garrison of about 7,000 cavalry and twice as many foot, together with a large population. The crusaders could only try a blockade, as any kind of assault was impossible. Initially, they could only oppose the northwestern quarter of the city, although they launched strong attacks on the Bridge Gate, on the south-west side, since this dominated the route to St Simeon's port 19 km/12 mi away on the Mediterranean coast, from which crusader supplies came. In November 1097,

they built the castle Malregard to cover the road north to Harem, and the Bridge of Boats (a pontoon) to give them access to the right bank of the Orontes.

On 30 December 1097 ◊Bohemond led a foraging force into battle against a Muslim relief force from Homs, which he soundly defeated. However, food became so scarce that many crusaders deserted. On 8 February 1098, another Muslim army from Aleppo launched a surprise attack but was driven off in the Battle of Lake Antioch. In March 1098 the Provençals constructed La Mahommerie, a fort based around a mosque opposite the Bridge Gate. In April the southern approach was blocked by Tancred's Castle, opposite St George's Gate. It took treachery – Bohemond bribed a tower commander – finally to let the crusaders in on the night of 2–3 June. A couple of days later, Kerbogha of Mosul, representing the caliph of Baghdad, arrived outside the walls with a huge army. He had been delayed besieging Edessa, held by Baldwin of Le Bourg (see ◊Baldwin I), which saved the crusade. Kerbogha's forces were large but disunited. When the starving and desperate crusaders launched a surprise attack on his camp on 28 June, the Muslims scattered. The citadel of Antioch immediately surrendered to the crusaders, who had achieved the seemingly impossible.

---

defeated at Thermopylae (see ◊Thermopylae, Battle of 191 BC), and withdrew to Asia Minor, where he was again defeated at Magnesia (see ◊Magnesia, Battle of) late in 190 BC. By the Treaty of Apamea (188 BC), he surrendered all his possessions in Anatolia apart from Pamphylia and Cilicia. He finally died of wounds after plundering a temple in south-west Iran.

Antipater (c. 397–319 BC) Macedonian viceroy of ◊Alexander (III) the Great and regent of Macedonia 334–319 BC. With ◊Craterus he

defeated the Greeks, led by Athens and the Aetolians, in the ◊Lamian War in 322 BC. Again with Craterus, he invaded Asia Minor on hearing of ◊Perdiccas's intrigues, and presided over a peace conference in 320 BC.

Antipater was Alexander's viceroy in Europe during his campaigns in the east, and crushed revolts in Thrace and the Peloponnese, defeating Agis III of Sparta at Megalopolis in 330. After Alexander's death, he patched up relations with Craterus, who had been sent to replace him by Alexander.

After Perdiccas's death he presided over the peace conference at Triparadeisus, and returned to Europe as regent with Alexander's son and half-brother Alexander IV and Philip Arrhidaeus, but died shortly afterwards.

Antonine Wall short-lived fortified Roman frontier in Scotland built by the emperor Antoninus Pius (ruled AD 138–61) as a shorter and more practical (in resource terms) alternative to ◊Hadrian's Wall. Running for 60 km/37 mi across the Forth–Clyde isthmus, the Antonine Wall consisted of a turf rampart fronted by a wide ditch.

Rows of small pits which held sharp stakes (*lillia*) have been found in several places and may have been part of the defences. At least 16 forts garrisoned the wall and small fortlets and timber watchtowers were placed at intervals along it. The frontier was abandoned after the death of Antoninus Pius.

Aō early Chinese city, now Zhengzhou in Henan. It was the second capital of the Shang dynasty (about 1560–1530 BC). The city stood on a low mound in the broad Yellow River flood-plain. Its wall had a roughly square circuit of 7 km/4.5 mi.

The wall was made of earth, with a yellow loess typical of north China, pounded down in layers between wooden frames. It was 20 m/65 ft thick at the base, narrowing towards the top, and originally at least 10 m/32.5 ft high. It has been estimated that this wall would have taken 10,000 men 18 years to build, yet Aō was the capital for only 26 years. There may also have been an outer wall enclosing the suburbs.

Aosta Roman fortified town in northwest Italy, founded by the emperor Augustus in 24 BC. It was enclosed by a 2.5-km/1.5-mi-long rectangular circuit of defences. Each corner was protected by a tower, while each side was defended by two interval towers and a fortified gateway, each of the gates built to a different design. The well-preserved Praetorian (east) gate is notable.

The Praetorian gate consisted of an inner and outer set of vaulted entranceways that were bonded together at each side by large flanking towers. This turned the central space into a large open courtyard through which attackers would have to pass while being exposed on all sides. This design was followed later in many city fortifications, notably ◊Trier in Germany.

Apollodorus (lived AD 97–130) Greek architect and military engineer. He was a native of Damascus. He designed Trajan's Forum and Trajan's Column, the Basilica Ulpiana, Hadrian's Temple of Venus and Rome (all in Rome), and the triumphal arch in honour of Trajan at Ancona. His treatise *On Siege Machinery* has survived.

Heavily influenced by earlier Greek writers, the treatise includes details of obsolete Hellenistic military equipment and has practical advice on other tools, including ladders, ignored by most other theorists.

Appian Greek historian who wrote a multi-volume history of Rome. Only parts of this survive, but they provide detailed narratives of the republican civil wars and the Roman conquest of the eastern provinces and Spain, as well as accounts of the Punic Wars.

Appleby castle border stronghold in England of the de Vipont and later the Clifford families, located 19 km/12 mi southeast of Penrith, Westmoreland (now Cumbria).

Begun in the 12th century as a ◊motte-and-bailey castle, Appleby was rebuilt in stone towards the end of the century, with the curtain wall erected on the original Norman earthwork. The keep was built by Henry II, but the mansion now in the bailey dates from the time of James II.

Apros, Battle of battle fought in July 1305 between the mercenary Catalan Company and the forces of the Byzantine emperor Michael IX in Thrace. The Catalans challenged the emperor as a consequence of the murder of their leader, Roger de ◊Flor, at Adrianople in April. Michael was deserted by his mercenaries during the battle, leading to a rout of the imperial forces.

The Catalans had about 2,500 cavalry together with their ◊almugavar light troops to oppose about 14,000 Byzantine cavalry and many infantry. Michael's Alan cavalry withdrew first, then the ◊turcopoles, who joined the Catalans.

Aqraba, Battle of (or *Akraba*) victory in 633 for the Muslim Arabs led by ◊Khalid ibn al-Walid over the followers of the false prophet Musailama. After this victory the Arabs were united under the banner of Islam and poised to launch their devastating assaults on the Persian and Byzantine empires.

Aquae Sextiae, Battle of battle fought in 102 BC at Aquae Sextiae (Aix-en-Provence, France) in which the Roman consul Gaius ◊Marius won a decisive victory over the Germanic tribes of the Teutones and Ambrones, ending the threat of an invasion of Italy by these tribes.

On the first day of the battle Marius attacked

and destroyed the contingent of 30,000 Ambrones. On the following day the Teutones assaulted the uphill position of Marius, but were surprised in the rear by a force of 3,000 legionaries led by Marcus Claudius Marcellus. The Greek historian Plutarch, in his *Life of Marius*, gives the undoubtedly exaggerated figure of 100,000 Germans killed.

aquila (Latin 'eagle') image of an eagle, the principal symbol of the Roman ◊legion, attached to a wooden shaft; it was carried by a standard-bearer known as an *aquilifer*.

The eagle was one of several animal standards used by Roman legions in the republic, but in the late 2nd or early 1st century BC the Roman general Gaius ◊Marius abolished the others and made the eagle the principal standard of the legion. The loss of its *aquila* was a severe disgrace for a legion and in the imperial period often resulted in the disbanding of the entire unit. The *aquilifer* was assigned to the first ◊cohort of the legion and was expected to show courage and leadership in battle.

Aquilonia, Battle of battle fought in 293 BC in Samnium (central-southern Italy) in which the Roman consul Lucius Papirius Cursor's legions decisively defeated a major Samnite army to capture Aquilonia. The reduction of other Samnite strongholds soon followed, ending the third Samnite War (see ◊Samnite Wars) and leaving Rome undisputed master of central Italy.

Arar, Battle of the battle fought in 58 BC on the river Arar (modern Saône, France) between the Helvetii (a confederation of tribes moving from Switzerland into France) and a Roman force under Julius ◊Caesar, who intercepted their migration and defeated them in battle.

Caesar destroyed one of the cantons, the Tigurini, and rapidly crossed the river to face the other tribes. They refused to engage him and continued their march. However, after two weeks of pursuit they were engaged and defeated 27 km/17 mi from Bibracte (Mont Beuvray), the capital of the Aedui.

Arausio, Battle of battle fought in 105 BC at Arausio (modern Orange, France) in Gallia Narbonensis in which the Germanic tribe of the Cimbri heavily defeated a Roman army led by the consul Gnaeus Manlius and Qunitus Servilius Caepio.

The defeat so alarmed the Romans that Gauis ◊Marius, recently victorious in the ◊Jugurthine War, was made consul for the second time. The expected invasion of Italy did not, however, occur at this point, as the Cimbri turned west into Spain.

Araxes, Battle of Byzantine victory in 589 that halted an attempted Persian invasion, following which the unpopular Persian King Hormizd attempted to dismiss his defeated general, ◊Bahram Chobin. However, Hormizd was unable to secure the support of the army, and was deposed and imprisoned. Chobin later seized the throne for himself.

arbalest (from Latin *arcubalista*, Old French *arbaleste* 'hand bow') hand-held medieval European crossbow, a personal weapon distinguished from the ◊balista, which could be either a hand weapon or a siege engine. The crossbow was not known in England before the Norman Conquest.

Arbedo, Battle of battle fought on 30 June 1422 to the north of Bellinzona (in modern Switzerland), in which the *condottiere* (mercenary commander) Carmagnola led Milanese troops to defeat a Swiss invasion of northern Italy. The Swiss ◊halberds proved tactically ineffective and the lesson of the defeat was the need for the Swiss to adopt pikes.

Four thousand Swiss troops crossed the St Bernard Pass to seize the Milanese city of Bellinzona, but were attacked by Carmagnola with 5,000 cavalry and 3,000 foot soldiers. He dismounted his men-at-arms and surrounded the Swiss square. The Swiss eventually fought their way out but left 500 dead on the battlefield.

Arbon fort (Roman *Arbor Felix*) Roman fort defending the southern shore of Lake Constance (in present-day Switzerland), built by the emperor Diocletian in 294 to improve the security of the Raetian frontier.

The loss of the walls on the east and west sides makes it difficult to reconstruct the plan, and no gates survive. The walls were 2.6 m/8.5 ft thick with projecting semicircular towers placed at intervals of 15–18 m/49–59 ft along it. Large rectangular towers (10 × 11 m/33 × 36 ft) were also used in places. The reduced spaces between towers compared to earlier forts, for example Alzey, demonstrate the increased reliance on defensive artillery.

Archelaus Pontic admiral and general under ◊Mithridates (VI) Eupator.

In 88 BC Archelaus conquered Bithynia (now part of Turkey) and led an invasion of Greece, where he was defeated by Sulla at Orchomenus (see ◊Orchomenus, Battle of). He defected to Rome in 83 BC and assisted ◊Lucullus in his campaigns against Mithridates.

Archidamus II (476–427 BC) king of Sparta c. 469–427 BC, chiefly remembered for his leadership of the invasions of Attica early in the ◊Peloponnesian War, hence the term 'Archidamian War' for its first ten years.

In 432 he opposed war with Athens, but subsequently led the invasions of Attica in 431, 430, and 428, and in 429 began the siege of Plataea (see ◊Plataea, Siege of).

Archidamus III (died c. 338 BC) king of Sparta from 359, son of ◊Agesilaus II. In 368, as heir apparent, he won the so-called Tearless Battle in Arcadia, in the central Peloponnese, where, it is believed, not a single Spartan fell. In 365 he captured the city of Cromnus in Arcadia, and was later wounded in a failed attempt to relieve it from an Arcadian attack. Three years later he heroically defended Sparta against ◊Epaminondas.

As king, he played a minor role in the Third Sacred War by supporting the Phocians in their battle for control of Delphi. He was killed at Manduria in southern Italy fighting for the city of Tarentum against the Lucanians, a people who inhabited the district now called Basilicata.

arcubalista early crossbow mentioned by the Roman military writer ◊Vegetius as being used by 5th-century Roman infantry.

Ardashir I king of Persia from about 209–42, founder of the Sassanid dynasty and the Sassanian Empire. After succeeding as vassal king of Fars, he reduced the province to submission before defeating the last of the Parthian kings, Artabanus V, in 224. His attacks on former Parthian vassals in Armenia and Hatra in Mesopotamia led to war with the Roman emperor Alexander Severus in 231. The Romans recovered Hatra, but Ardashir recaptured it in 240. He was succeeded by his son ◊Shapur I.

Argentoratum, Battle of battle fought in 357 in which a 13,000-strong Roman force, commanded by Julian (later the emperor '◊Julian the Apostate', was victorious over a confederation of Alamannic (German) tribes, allegedly 35,000-strong, under ◊Chnodomar and his nephew Serapio. The Roman victory brought temporary stability to the upper Rhine frontier.

The Alamanni, who had recently crossed the Rhine, failed in an attempted ambush of the Roman left wing but succeeded in breaking the Roman ◊cataphracts on the opposite flank and in pushing back the first line of the Roman infantry centre. Julian intervened personally to rally his cavalry. The second line of infantry restored the situation in the centre, and after hard fighting succeeded in breaking the Alamanni. The Romans lost 243 men and 4 officers, while 6,000 Alamanni are said to have lost their lives, many of them in the pursuit that followed.

Arginusae Isles, Battle of the greatest sea battle of the ◊Peloponnesian War, fought by Athens and Sparta in 406 BC around the small Arginusae Islands (modern Garipadasi and Kalemadasi, between Lesbos and the west coast of Turkey).

Athens' 150 triremes commanded by eight *strategoi* (generals) won a decisive victory over Sparta's 120 triremes commanded by Callicratidas. They formed in two lines abeam on either side of the islands to prevent the Spartans from outflanking them or cutting through their line, and destroyed some 77 enemy ships for the loss of only 25.

The Athenian success in this battle was marred when six of the eight *strategoi* were executed for failing to pick up survivors or recover the bodies of the dead because of a storm.

Ariovistus (lived 1st century BC) king of the Suebi. He gained control of central and eastern Gaul (France) but was defeated by Julius ◊Caesar in 58 BC and fled back across the river Rhine.

The Gallic tribe of the Sequani invited the German Ariovistus across the Rhine to help in their war against the Aedui. He broke the power of the Aedui and their allies at the Battle of Magetobriga and then took over central and eastern Gaul at the expense of the Sequani. He was named a 'Friend of the Roman People' in 59 BC, but the following year Caesar provoked a conflict. Ariovistus' veteran army was brought to battle in the Alsace region and destroyed. Although Ariovistus escaped across the Rhine he may have expired soon after; he was certainly dead by the winter of 54/53 BC.

Arles, Battle of battle fought in 425 in which the Roman forces of ◊Aetius defeated the Visigoths, led by ◊Theodoric the Great, repulsing the Visigoths from Arles and preventing them from adding Narbonensis (a large area of modern southern France) to their kingdom.

armet modern term (from French) used to define a close helmet (designed to protect the whole head and face, with a movable visor) in which the ◊bevor is formed of two large, hinged cheek pieces meeting and fastening together at the chin. Armets first appeared in the early 15th century in Italy. They were the most important form of head armour for men-at-arms in southern Europe during that century.

armiger (from Latin 'armour-bearer') medieval European squire, or knight's shield bearer, not necessarily of noble status. In the 11th and 12th centuries an armiger could also be an ordinary soldier.

Arminius (Germanic *Hermann*) German chieftain of the Cherusci tribe who led the army that destroyed the Roman force commanded by Quintilius Varus in the Teutoberger Forest in AD 9 (see ◊Teutoberger Forest, Battle of the). Although he had served previously as an auxiliary commander in the Roman army, he waged continuous warfare against Rome until AD 16 when he suffered a reverse at Idistaviso (see ◊Idistaviso, Battle of) After this he fought a war against the Suebic confederation headed by ◊Maroboduus, defeating him in a hard-fought battle. He survived an assassination attempt by Tiberius in AD 19, but was murdered the same year by rivals within his own tribe.

arquebus (medieval High German *hakebusse* 'hook-gun') portable gun, originally for field use. It was sometimes supported on a trestle, carriage, or forked rest, and a hook was cast on the gun for fixing it to its carriage. The mechanism for this weapon was developed in the 15th century in Europe, though it did not become widely used until the 16th century.

In about 1500 the use of a slow match fixed to a lever was developed so that the match could be made to touch the powder automatically. The arquebus became a personal weapon, and it was improved by carrying each charge in a leather case, several together forming a 'bandolier'.

Arques-la-Bataille castle fortress in the *département* of Seine-Maritime, France, 10 km/6 mi south of Dieppe, on a natural rise in the landscape. It was built by ◊William (I) the Conqueror's uncle, the Count of Arques, soon after 1038.

The Count of Arques rebelled in 1052 and the castle was besieged and taken by William. ◊Henry I of England rebuilt it and added a rectangular keep. Arques was the last stronghold to resist the conquest of ◊Geoffrey V of Anjou in 1145, and one of the last to resist ◊Philip (II) Augustus in 1204.

Arrian (c. AD 86–160) Greek historian, theorist, and Roman governor of Cappadocia in the early 130s under the emperor Hadrian. His *Anabasis/Campaigns of Alexander* is the chief literary source of information on the campaigns of ◊Alexander (III) the Great, drawn with care from much earlier material. He also wrote several textbooks on Greek and Roman military drills.

His province of Cappadocia was threatened by the seminomadic Alans but he successfully opposed them, probably without the need for pitched battle. His proposed order of march and battle plan survive in *Ektasis/Order of March*, containing interesting variations on normal Roman battle tactics.

arrière ban (French 'last resort') medieval French troops made up of ordinary citizens, whose responsibility it was to serve the king in wartime. The troops of the *arrière ban* were not of high military quality and were despised by the French chivalry.

arrow ancient and medieval missile, normally with a wooden shaft, a flight of feathers, and a tip which was either hardened by burning or had a metal head. It was shot by a bow and could have considerable impact. Examples of medieval arrows are portrayed in the ◊Bayeux Tapestry.

An arrow was described in 1298 as having a barbed iron head, 7.5 cm/3 in long and 5 cm/2 in broad, a shaft of ash 85 cm/34 in long, and a flight of peacock feathers. Horn was often used to protect the nock or notch that was fitted to the bow string. The arrows found on the Tudor warship *Mary Rose* were made mainly of poplar and about 75 cm/30 in long. Use of massed bowmen meant mass production of arrows: during the Hundred Years' War, Edward III of England ordered 130,000 sheaves of arrows in 1341.

Arsuf, Battle of battle fought on 7 September 1191 between the crusaders of the Third Crusade under English king ◊Richard (I) the Lionheart and Muslim forces under the Ayubbid sultan ◊Saladin, near Arsuf in the south of modern Israel. The crusader victory enabled the Third Crusade to reach Jaffa, a bridgehead for attacks on Jerusalem. Although described as a battle, Arsuf was an example of a fighting march conducted by the crusaders.

After leaving the recently captured port of Acre on 22 August, Richard organized a tight defensive formation in which wings of infantry covered the cavalry from Muslim archery and charges. Saladin launched waves of attacks on the rearguard of Hospitallers (see ◊Military Order) and forced a countercharge from them, but Richard kept most of his knights under close control, delivering three charges that routed the Muslims. Saladin reorganized his troops, but was unable to prevent the crusader advance.

Artah, Battle of battle fought on 20 April 1105 between ◊Tancred, Prince of Antioch, and Ridwan of Aleppo (now Halab, Syria). Tancred was eager to recover lands lost to the Muslims during the imprisonment of Prince ◊Bohemond. Leading his forces onto a boulder-strewn plain that negated the Turkish skirmishing tactics, Tancred defeated the Muslim cavalry and infantry piecemeal.

Artaphernes the Elder Persian general, brother of ◊Darius (I) the Great, and satrap (provincial governor) of Sardis during the Ionian Revolt (499–493 BC). He held the citadel when the Greeks took Sardis in 499 BC. When the lower city caught fire, he led Persian and native Lydian troops in a counterattack that drove the Greeks out of Sardis and back to the coast.

Artaphernes the Younger Persian general who commanded ◊Darius (I) the Great's expedition against Athens that was defeated at Marathon in 490 BC (see ◊Marathon, Battle of). He was the son of Artaphernes the Elder.

Artaxata, Battle of battle fought in 68 BC between the Roman general ◊Lucullus and the combined forces of ◊Mithridates (VI) Eupator of Pontus and Tiridates of Armenia. Lucullus' Roman army defeated the forces of Mithridates and Tiridates using aggressive tactics. However, Lucullus' eastward advance was stopped by the mutiny of his own men.

Artaxerxes (II) Mnemon ('the Mindful') Achaemenid Persian king 404–359 BC, son and successor of Darius II and elder brother of ◊Cyrus the Younger, who rebelled early in his reign and was killed at Cunaxa (see ◊Cunaxa, Battle of). A war with Sparta 399–394 BC drove the Spartans from Asia; it was followed 387–380 by a conflict with Evagoras I, King of Salamis, which brought the Asian Greeks back under Persian rule. Artaxerxes' attempts to regain Egypt, though, were unsuccessful.

In the 360s BC a coalition of western satraps (provincial governors) including ◊Datames rebelled against Artaxerxes and captured the western half of Persia. This rebellion collapsed shortly before his death.

Artemisium, Battle of first encounter between Persian and Greek fleets during Xerxes I's invasion of Greece, fought at the same time as Thermopylae (see ◊Thermopylae, Battle of 480 BC). The inconclusive three-day battle takes its name from a shrine to Artemis on the northern coast of Euboea.

The Greeks' 320 triremes, possibly outnumbered over four times by the Persians, took the initiative during the first two days. On the third, action was initiated by the Persians around midday, perhaps to coincide with the final assault on Thermopylae. Though the Persians finally broke off the action, the Greeks suffered so heavily that they were contemplating withdrawal when news of the fall of Thermopylae arrived.

Artevelde, Philip van (1340–82) Flemish patriot who sided with England against France, leading a Ghent rebellion in 1382 against the French hierarchy under Count Louis II in Flanders. The rebels won the Battle of Beverhoutsveld, using infantry tactics and the fire power of ◊ribaudequins on carts, but were defeated at Westrozebeke, where Philip was killed.

Arthur (lived 6th century) semilegendary Romano-British warleader who led British resistance against the Saxons, Picts, and Scots in the first half of the 6th century. He was probably a warlord rather than a king. He operated throughout Britain, commanding a small force of mobile warriors, reminiscent of the late Roman ◊comitatenses. Arthur is credited with a great victory over the Saxons at Mount Badon, possibly in Dorset.

His life is too shrouded in legend to be certain about any of the details. His legendary base, 'Camelot', has been tentatively identified as a hillfort at South Cadbury in Somerset.

Arundel castle castle-palace in Sussex, England, 32 km/20 mi west of Brighton. It was built in around 1080 to guard the strategic Arun gap through the South Downs, to a motte and double bailey plan. The original motte still stands, surmounted by a shell keep built probably by Robert de Bellême in Henry II's time; curtain walls were erected around the baileys at the same time.

asabiya Arabic term referring to the companionship of warriors. By extension, it meant the kind of team spirit that an army required, and was much encouraged by the Ayubbid sultan ◊Saladin.

asavaran (or *asawira*) Sassanian Persian cavalry, the mainstay of the Sassanian army. The *asavaran* included ◊*clibanarii*, a type of fully armoured ◊cataphract cavalry riding armoured horses, and its members were recruited from the *dihqan* (minor gentry) and the retainers of great nobles.

The name was also used by Persian cavalry who joined Muslim armies after the Arab conquest of Persia in 633–51.

asawira Sassanian Persian cavalry: see ◊*asavaran*.

Ascalon, Battle of battle fought on 12 August 1099 in the Holy Land in which ◊al-Afdal's Fatimid Muslim force advancing from

Egypt, seeking to recover Jerusalem, was surprised and routed by the crusaders of the First Crusade.

After the fall of Jerusalem to the crusaders, they had to defend it against al-Afdal's Egyptian forces. The crusader forces apparently numbered 1,200 cavalry and 9,000 foot soldiers, perhaps outnumbered two to one. On 11 August they seized the Fatimid supply train, and early the next day attacked the Egyptians outside Ascalon. While ◊Godfrey de Bouillon covered an attempted outflanking by Bedouin cavalry, Robert of Normandy's knights crashed into the Egyptian centre, precipitating a rout.

Asclepiodotus Greek tactical writer. His surviving work is a theoretical and highly technical account of the ideal ◊phalanx, perhaps based on lost works by his teacher Posidonius and the historian ◊Polybius.

Asculum, Siege of siege by the Romans in 89 BC of the rebel city of Asculum (modern Ascoli Piceno) in central-eastern Italy. Asculum was the first city to revolt against the Romans at the beginning of the ◊Italian Social War.

Despite a number of reverses, the Romans were able to invest the town. Rebel reinforcements of eight legions (40,000 men) failed to save it, and Asculum was reduced after a year-long siege.

Ashby-de-la-Zouch castle castle in England, 25 km/16 mi northwest of Leicester. The Hastings family built a hall here in the 12th century, and Lord Hastings received a licence to crenellate (build battlements) in 1473, but construction halted when he was executed in 1483. Substantial later building included two baileys, the 12th-century hall, a 15th-century tower house (known as Hastings Tower), and a chapel.

Ashdown, Battle of inconclusive victory in 871 for the Anglo-Saxons, led by King Aethelred and his brother Alfred (later known as ◊Alfred the Great) over the Danes, under the kings Bagsecg and ◊Halfdan. English chroniclers say many thousands of Danes were killed, but since they were fit to fight (and win) a fortnight later at Basing (see ◊Basing, Battle of), this is unlikely.

Recovering from their recent defeat at Reading (see ◊Reading, Battle of), the Anglo-Saxons of Wessex met the Danes at Ashdown. The Danes were drawn up in two divisions, one under their kings, the other under the Danish ◊jarls. The English divided their army similarly with King Aethelred facing the Danish kings and his brother Alfred facing the jarls. The battle apparently opened while King Aethelred was still saying mass. Alfred took command of the whole English army, leading them in an uphill charge which, after hard fighting lasting until nightfall, succeeded in driving off the Danes and killing King Bagsecg and five *jarls*.

Ashikaga Yoshimitsu (1358–1408) Japan's third shogun of the Muromachi period. He consolidated the power of the Ashikaga shogunate, resolved the conflict between the ◊Northern and Southern Courts, and established profitable trade links with China. He relinquished his office in 1395 to his son Ashikaga Yoshimochi, but effectively held the reins of power until his death.

Yoshimitsu, who assumed the title of shogun when he was only ten years old, skilfully manipulated the regional military governors and refined the tax system. He resolved the conflict between the two courts by persuading the southern emperor to return to Kyoto on the (false) assumption that the two lines would alternately succeed to the imperial throne.

Ashingdon, Battle of (or *Assandun*) battle fought in 1016 at Ashingdon, Essex, England, between the Danes led by ◊Cnut the Great and the Saxons of ◊Edmund (II) Ironside. The decisive Danish victory was brought about by the desertion of Eadric of Mercia at a critical point in the battle. After the battle, Edmund and Cnut concluded a peace treaty in which Edmund was to rule over Wessex and Cnut over the rest of England. When Edmund died suddenly later that year, Cnut became king of all England.

Ashoka (died 232 BC) (or *Asoka*) emperor of India and eastern Afghanistan 269–232 BC. In his conquest of Kalinga (the present-day Indian state of Orissa and northern coastal strip of Andhra Pradesh) in about 261 BC, 150,000 people were captured, 100,000 killed, and many more died of privation. Their sufferings led Ashoka, who became a Buddhist, to renounce aggressive war and instead to seek moral conquest by adopting a policy of enlightened and humanitarian government.

He retained his army, which continued to garrison the conquered territories, and was frequently in action against the tribesmen of the frontier hills and jungles. The triple lion which headed the stone pillars marking his imperial edicts is one of the official symbols of the modern Indian republic.

Ashurbanipal (or *Aššur-ban-apli*) king of Assyria 668–c. 627 BC, the son and successor of ◊Esarhaddon. He conquered all of Egypt in 667

BC and created the largest empire then known in the west, but his reign was troubled by rebellions and Egypt was finally lost in about 639 BC.

Ashurbanipal defeated Pharaoh Taharqa at Memphis in 667 BC and then pursued him south to Thebes, where he was proclaimed pharaoh. The Egyptians regained their independence, after a decade of fighting, under Pharaoh Psammtik I in 656 BC. Civil war then broke out in Elam in about 660 BC and Babylonia rebelled in 651 BC. Ashurbanipal regained control at the cost of sacking Susa and razing Babylon.

Ashurnasirpal II (lived 9th century BC)

(or *Aššur-nasir-apli*) Neo-Assyrian great king 883–859 BC, the son of Tukulti-Ninurta II (890–884 BC). He founded a new capital, ◊Kalhu (the biblical Kaleh), for the empire he created, and developed the use of cavalry in warfare.

In 877 BC he crossed the river Euphrates with his army by floats to take the Neo-Hittite city of ◊Carchemish. He then crossed the river Arantu (classical Orontes, modern 'Asi) into ◊Amurru and exacted tribute from Kaiza (Kadesh) and the Phoenician city-states of Tyre, Sidon, and Gubla (Byblos), making Mount Lebanon his boundary. Crossing into Anatolia in 882 BC, he received tribute from the Mushku (Phrygians) and the Neo-Hittite states. He also suppressed the hill peoples to the north of Assyria. He was succeeded by his son Shalmaneser III.

Ashur-uballit I (lived 14th century BC)

Assyrian king 1353–1318 BC. He threw off Mitannian overlordship and founded the Middle Assyrian Kingdom, which was to challenge Hittite control over Syria and to defeat the Kassites (or *Kaššu*) of Babylonia.

He rebelled against Tushratta during the time the Hittites were attacking Mitanni under Suppiluliumas I (c. 1340 BC), and established Assyria's independence. He also placed the Kassite ◊Kurigalzu II on the throne of Karduniash (Babylonia), but on Ashur-uballit's death his son Enlil-nerari had to fight the first of a series of wars against Kurigalzu that would eventually lead to the conquest of Karduniash.

ashvamedha (Sanskrit, meaning 'horse-sacrifice') ceremonial sacrifice of a specially consecrated horse performed by Hindu kings to mark their achievements as great conquerors.

All those on whose territory the horse wandered, escorted by a select band of warriors, were required to acknowledge the overlordship of the king to whom the horse belonged, or to fight. If the horse was not captured by the end of a year, it was brought home for sacrifice at a ceremony which all the king's tributaries, old and new, were required to attend.

askar medieval Arabic word for the household troops of a leader; a kind of standing army.

Aspar (died 471)

East Roman general (◊*magister militum*) of Alan descent, the military power behind the throne at Constantinople for much of the 5th century. Hostility grew against him in the 460s, partly because he was an Arian heretic, and in 469 he was replaced by Zeno (an Isaurian and later emperor). He was killed by the Isaurians in 471.

In 431 Aspar led an Eastern army to assist the Western general ◊Boniface in his attempted defence of Africa against the Vandals. In the 440s he campaigned against the Persians, but suffered a major defeat when he tried to oppose ◊Attila's invasion of the Balkans in 441. When the Eastern emperor Theodosius II died in 450, Aspar raised Marcian to the throne. He played kingmaker again when Marcian died in 457, elevating the Roman commander Leo to the position of emperor.

Although Aspar remained the dominant influence in the East for several more years, Leo gradually reduced his dependency on him by recruiting Isaurians from the mountainous regions of Asia Minor to balance the influence of the Germans (especially Goths) in the army. From these men he formed a new bodyguard (the ◊*excubitores*).

aspis (Greek) shield, particularly a hoplite shield. The 'shield side' meant the left side, and the depth of a formation was often expressed by the number of shields. The term was also used for a body of hoplites.

Assandun, Battle of

Danish victory in 1016 over the Anglo-Saxons: see ◊Ashingdon, Battle of.

atabeg (Arabic) ruler of the Seljuk successor states, often meaning the military guardian of a Muslim ruler, and by extension a general, for example Imad al-Din ◊Zengi.

Athanaric

king of the Goths who led an expedition against the Romans in 367, securing the release of some Gothic prisoners and fixing the Danube as the frontier between Gothic and Roman territory. After he led the failed Gothic resistance against the Huns in 376, many of his people abandoned him and sought refuge inside the Roman Empire.

Athelstan (895–939)

king of England 924–39. The son of ◊Edward the Elder, Athelstan brought about English unity by ruling both Mercia and Wessex. He defeated an

ATTILA (C. 406–453)

King of the Huns 445–53. He welded this nomadic people into a cohesive entity which ruled over many Germanic, Slavic, and Sarmatian peoples and successfully challenged the Eastern and Western Roman empires.

The Huns waged an intermittent war with the Eastern Roman Empire through-out the 440s in which they succeeded in obtaining substantial tribute. In 450 Attila launched an invasion of the Western Empire which was checked by the Romans and Visigoths at Châlons in 451 (see ◊Châlons, Battle of). Attila died in mysterious circumstances, and his empire fell apart almost immediately afterwards.

---

invasion by Scots, Irish, and the men of Strathclyde at Brunanburh in 937 (see ◊Brunanburh, Battle of). He overcame the Scandinavian kingdom based in York and increased English power on the Welsh and Scottish borders.

Athens Greek city with its defence based on the Acropolis Hill, an ideal natural citadel. Athens also committed itself to defending its harbour at Piraeus, building a wall around the harbour and linking the city and port via a corridor formed by two 'Long Walls'.

The Acropolis Hill was fortified by a wall from the Mycenaean period. Following its destruction by the Persians in 480 BC, the wall was rebuilt, without bastions or towers. For its strategic security Athens also needed to protect its port and ensure that communications with it would not be cut off. The two 'Long Walls' connecting Piraeus with Athens formed a corridor 100 m/109 yds wide and 6,500 m/7,108 yds long, protected by two-storied interval towers.

Atlakh, Battle of (or *Talas*) battle 27–30 July 751 in which Abbasid Arabs defeated the Tang Chinese in Central Asia (in what is now Uzbekistan). For China this was a minor border defeat, but it paved the way for the spread of Islam in Central Asia.

◊Gao Xianzhi captured Tashkent in 750, but the king's son fled to the Arabs. Ziyad ibn Salih, governor of Samarkand, marched east with Arab and Tukharistani troops and met Gao's 30,000 Chinese, Ferghanan, and Qarluq Turkish troops at Atlakh, near the city of Talas. After two days of indecisive fighting, the Qarluqs changed sides on the third day and attacked the Chinese rear. Gao had to retreat through narrow passes, cutting a path through his baggage-animals and his fleeing Ferghanan allies.

Attalus I (lived 3rd century BC) king of Pergamum 241–197 BC. He decisively defeated the invading Galatians in the 230s, and in the early 220s briefly won control of Anatolia north of the Taurus Mountains from the Seleucids. He sided with Rome in the first and second ◊Macedonian Wars.

Lavish gifts to Delphi and Athens gained him the friendship of the Aetolian League, and with the latter he sided with Rome against Philip V of Macedon in the First Macedonian War of 211–205, winning Aegina and being included amongst Rome's allies in the peace. Philip's aggressive policies in the eastern Aegean led to the Battle of Chios (see ◊Chios, Battle of) in 201, and Attalus and his fleet were active again on Rome's side in the Second Macedonian War of 200–197.

Attic helmet type of Greek helmet used from the 5th to 2nd centuries BC. There is no agreement on the exact definition, but the term is most commonly used to describe a ◊Chalcidian helmet without a nasal guard.

The term Samnite Attic is often applied to a type of helmet with a straight brow and hinged cheek piece, used by the peoples of central and southern Italy.

Auberoche, Battle of battle fought on 21 October 1345, during the ◊Hundred Years' War, in which the Earl of Derby, with only 1,200 men, attacked and routed a French force besieging Auberoche, an important castle in the Périgord, southwestern France. The English attack under Derby ended the French campaign in the south.

The castle was defended by the Gascon allies of the English. Louis of Poitiers laid siege to it with some 7,000 troops, but Derby's surprise attack captured him and many other noblemen and knights.

Augsburg, Battle of battle in 910 at Augsburg, Bavaria, between the nomadic Magyars and the southern Germans under Ludwig III resulting in a victory for the nomads. The highly mobile Magyars first defeated the two supporting divisions of the German army then drew out the central division by feigning flight then turning around to hit the disorganized pursuers in the flanks and rear.

Aurelian (c. AD 215–75) (Lucius Domitius Aurelianus) Roman emperor 270–75. A successful soldier, he was proclaimed emperor by his troops on the death of Claudius II. He campaigned on the Danube and then defeated a large raid into Italy mounted by the Alamanni and Juthungi. He moved east and captured Queen ◊Zenobia of Palmyra (now Tadmur, Syria) by the end of 272, destroying Palmyra itself in 273.

Returning to Europe, he defeated the Gallic usurper Tetricus and then began construction of much stronger defences for Rome. He was planning a campaign against the Persians when he was murdered by a group of his own officers.

Ausculum, Battle of battle fought in 279 BC in which ◊Pyrrhus, King of Epirus, and his Macedonian-style army defeated the Roman legions opposing him in Samnium (central-southern Italy). After a hard-fought battle the Romans were forced to give way, partly due to the shock of Pyrrhus' 20 war elephants.

Casualty figures vary: Dionysius of Halicarnassus, writing in the 1st century AD, recorded that the dead on both sides came to 15,000, while Pyrrhus' own commentaries recorded his losses at 3,500.

Aussig, Siege of (or *Usti*) siege of the town of Aussig (Usti), North Bohemia, by the ◊Hussites during the Hussite Wars. Duke Frederick of Saxony attempted to raise the siege on 16 June 1426, but was defeated by Hussite ◊*Wagenburg* tactics.

The Hussite commander Holy Procop led a Hussite force combining wagons and the cavalry of Prince Korybutovic. Apparently outnumbered three to one by the Germans, the Hussites drew up in a defensive wagon fort on a hill, keeping their cavalry behind for the pursuit. The German attack was broken up by artillery fire, halted by the wagons, then routed by a counterattack. The Germans suffered heavy losses.

Auszug elite troops of the Swiss Confederation armies, usually unmarried men aged between 18 and 30.

Autaritus Gallic mercenary chief. He was one of the rebel leaders of the ◊Mercenary War fought between Carthage and its mercenaries, and was eventually seized by ◊Hamilcar Barca and crucified before the walls of rebel-held Tunis.

Autaritus had served in Sicily in the First Punic War (see ◊Punic War, First), where part of his force of Gauls deserted to the Romans. After the peace treaty between Rome and Carthage was signed, he and the remaining band of 2,000 Gauls were returned to Africa where they helped begin the mercenary uprising. He and ◊Spendius were seized by Hamilcar Barca during the negotiations for the surrender of their troops.

Autophradates Persian general, loyal to ◊Artaxerxes (II) Mnemon during the revolts of

AUGUSTUS (63 BC–AD 14)

(originally *Gaius Octavius* or *Gaius Julius Caesar Octavianus* – 'Octavian')

First Roman emperor from 31 BC, the great-nephew of Julius Caesar. He formed the Second Triumvirate with ◊Mark Antony and Lepidus, by which the three dominated Roman politics after Caesar's assassination. He defeated the forces of Antony and Cleopatra at Actium (see ◊Actium, Battle of) and established himself as Rome's first emperor. He took the name Augustus in 27 BC.

Octavian was only 19 when his great-uncle was murdered, but when Caesar's will named him his adopted son and principal heir he immediately began a political career. Initially Octavian allied himself with the consuls Hirtius and Pansa. They defeated Mark Antony at Mutina in 43 BC, but both consuls were killed. Octavian then obtained the consulship through force and joined Antony and Lepidus in the Second Triumvirate. He and Antony campaigned against ◊Brutus and ◊Cassius, Caesar's principal murderers, and defeated them in pitched battle at Philippi (see

◊Philippi, battles of) in 42 BC, effectively destroying the senatorial party's final attempt to curb powerful individuals in the process. While Antony concentrated on Rome's eastern provinces and formed a liaison with the Egyptian queen Cleopatra, Octavian established his reputation as a general in conquests on the Dalmatian coast of the Adriatic. Civil war, however, was a constant threat. Octavian removed one potential rival, Sextus ◊Pompeius, in a sea battle at Naulochus in 36 BC (see ◊Naulochus, Battle of), and then defeated Antony at Actium in 31 BC to become sole ruler of the Roman Empire. Both victories were engineered by Octavian's friend and contemporary Marcus Vipsanius ◊Agrippa.

Once he had established himself as emperor, Octavian, now renamed Augustus, carried through wide-ranging political, administrative and military reforms. He established a professional army, reorganizing the semipermanent force in existence at the end of the Republic to a permanent standing army of some 300,000 men in 28 legions and many auxiliary units. A permanent fleet was based initially on the Italian coast at Misenum near Naples and Ravenna on the Adriatic. Most of the legions were stationed in important frontier provinces which were governed by high-ranking senators that Augustus chose himself, thereby reducing the threat of further civil wars. To increase security in Rome and Italy, Augustus created a form of police force and night watch in Rome (the Urban Cohorts and Vigiles), and the Praetorian Guard (see ◊Praetorium) which ensured his own safety as well as helping to maintain public order.

Augustus spent considerable time in the provinces for much of the period between 27–13 BC. Through Agrippa and his provincial governors he consolidated and rationalized the rapid, often cursory conquests of the late Republic, creating a more secure situation for Rome in western Europe and the eastern Mediterranean. Spain was conquered in a brutal campaign by Agrippa, much of the Alps were incorporated into a Roman province by Augustus' stepsons Tiberius and Drusus, and the eastern Alps were secured through the creation of a client kingdom. On the Danube, the frontier was moved to the Rhine with the creation of the provinces of Pannonia, Noricum, and Moesia, while German presence on the Rhine was secured after the consolidation of Caesar's campaigns in Gaul. An attempt was also made to create a province to the east of the river.

In the East, diplomacy ensured relatively peaceful relations with the neighbouring Parthian empire. Although the return of the standards captured by the Parthians at Carrhae (see ◊Carrhae, Battle of) was portrayed as a military achievement, it was in fact achieved without any military intervention. Augustus sent his grandson Gaius to the eastern provinces in 1 BC and the friendly relations with the neighbouring empire continued. Elsewhere in the East, client kings loyal to Rome ensured both internal stability and military security. The African provinces, including Egypt, were protected from serious military threat by their desert frontiers.

Augustus' military and frontier policy suffered setbacks with a serious revolt in Pannonia in AD 6, put down by Tiberius, and the Varian disaster of AD 9. The latter spelled the end of the province of Germany after three legions with their governor Publius Quinctilius ◊Varus were ambushed by the German chieftain ◊Arminius and annihilated. However, Augustus' long reign enabled him to re-found the Roman state in a manner that allowed it to endure for several centuries.

the satraps (provincial governors). He led an army against ◊Datames' revolt in Cappadocia in 367 BC, but was forced to offer a truce so that he could attack another rebel, Ariobarzanes of Daskylion, on the Hellespontine coast. He besieged Ariobarzanes in Adramyttium but was forced to withdraw by ◊Agesilaus II. His final campaign was against rebels in Anatolia in 354.

auxilia (Latin 'support troops') auxiliary troops in the Roman imperial army who served in units of 500 or 1,000 infantry or cavalry (◊*ala*), sometimes mixed. They were recruited from noncitizens in the provinces outside Italy. From the mid-1st century AD the *auxilia* were granted Roman citizenship after 25 years of service.

They were often employed as provincial garrisons, but were as important and effective in battle as the legions.

Avarayr, Battle of battle fought in 451 between the Sassanian Persians and Christian Armenian rebels against Persian religious persecution at Avarayr, Armenia (modern Azerbaijan). The Sassanian Persian victory ended the rebellion; the leader of the Armenians, Vardan Mamikonian, was killed along with 1,036 Armenians and 3,544 Persians.

The Sassanian army led by Mihrnerseh met the Armenian rebels at Avarayr in the spring of 451. The two armies deployed in a plain, separated by a river. When the Armenians crossed the river their left wing was quickly beaten by the Persians. Vardan led his reserves to their defence and the Persians fell back to their elephants. However, Vardan's force was unsupported by the rest of the Armenian army and Persian reserves surrounded it and killed him.

Avar campaigns series of three successful campaigns by the Franks under ◊Charlemagne and his son ◊Pepin the Short against the Avars in 791–96. As a result, Avar power was destroyed and a large area of southeastern Europe was incorporated into the Carolingian Empire.

Avaricum hillfort of the Gauls, near modern Bourges, France; it was captured by the Roman general Julius Caesar in 52 BC during his crushing of the Gallic revolt under ◊Vercingetorix.

The Romans built a massive ramp of earth and timber over 23 m/75 ft high to reach the walls while the Gauls tried to undermine and set fire to it. During a heavy rainstorm the Romans were able to storm the walls and the population and defenders (nearly 40,000 people) were slaughtered.

Avars nomadic people from the Eurasian steppe who arrived in Eastern Europe in the mid-6th century AD. Employed by the Byzantines in 558, under Khan Baian they created their own empire in Pannonia and the Balkans, taking the strategic city of Sirmium (now Sremska Mitrovica, Serbia) in 582. In 626 they combined with the Persians to besiege Constantinople (see ◊Constantinople, Siege of 626). ◊Charlemagne conquered the Avar realm in a series of campaigns in the 790s.

The military impact of the Avars related to their equipment, which included iron stirrups, lances, and composite bows. This style was copied by the Byzantines, and may have led to the adoption of stirrups by the Franks.

aventail (French *camail*) the ◊mail defence attached to the lower edge of a ◊basinet (European knight's helmet) in the 14th and early 15th centuries, covering the neck and shoulders. It was attached to the helmet by a pierced leather band which fitted over a series of pierced lugs of brass or iron called vervelles, through which in turn a cord was passed, securing the aventail in place.

Avila walled city 93 km/55 mi northwest of Madrid, Spain. It is enclosed by a granite wall almost 3.2 km/2 mi long supported by 88 towers and pierced by 9 fortified gateways. Richard of Burgundy, son-in-law of Alfonso VI of Castile, strengthened the ramparts, which had existed from Roman times, but the masonry work was carried out about 1090–1100.

Unlike most walled cities, Avila has no castle, but the cathedral is incorporated into the wall, the apse forming a half tower.

Axine, Battle of the battle fought in 57 BC between the Roman army and the Belgae tribe on the river Axine (now the river Aisne, France) during the ◊Gallic Wars of Julius Caesar. It was the result of a Roman pre-emptive strike, invading Belgae territory to break up an army that the tribe had been massing.

Caesar led his army across the river into Belgae territory, but was unable to lure the tribe into giving battle. Instead, the Belgae sent part of their army across the river to try to cut the Romans off from their communications. The Romans intercepted them and inflicted crippling losses.

Aydon castle castle in Northumberland, England, 24 km/15 mi west of Newcastle. Located in a naturally strong position, it was built originally as a simple manor house, but obtained licence to crenellate (build battlements) around 1310, when a curtain wall, towers, and ditch were added to produce a textbook example of a fortified dwelling. It changed hands several times between English and Scots owners during the 14th century but eventually remained an English property.

Azitawataya (modern *Karatepe*) Neo-Hittite fortress dating from the 8th century BC on the river Ceyhan, Turkey, which controlled the northern routes into the plain of Adana. The founder, Azitawatas, left a unique bilingual inscription in hieroglyphic Luwian and Phoenician describing his wars in the service of his overlord.

Azuchi castle (Japanese *Azuchi-jō*) castle built 1576–79 on Mount Azuchi, near Lake Biwa-ko, Honshu Island, Japan, by the *Sengoku daimyo* ◊Oda Nobunaga as a major fortification to defend Kyoto and to consolidate his authority over Japan. It provided the model for later castles and was extensively copied by other *daimyo* (military regional landholders).

The fortifications stretched to the mountain's summit, incorporating natural features into its defensive system. Azuchi castle was more than a purely military structure; it was also a mansion to impress rivals with its strength and elegance. The inner rooms were decorated by Kano Eitoku, the leading painter of the age. Following Nobunaga's assassination in 1582, the castle was looted and destroyed by fire.

Babylon (Akkadian *Bab-Ili* 'Gate of God') capital of Babylonia, straddling the river Euphrates; situated in present-day Iraq, 90 km/56 mi south of Baghdad. It is the city of the Greek historian Herodotus' 'hanging gardens' and the biblical 'Tower of Babel'.

Babylon rose in prominence as the capital of the 18th-century BC Amorite kingdom of Hammurabi, controlling most of Mesopotamia, until it was sacked by the Hittite army under Mursilis I about 1595 BC. Then it was taken by the Kassites and eventually became the capital of their kingdom of Karduniash, one of the Great Powers of the 14th–13th centuries BC. Its conquest by the Assyrians under Tukulti-Ninurta I led to rebellion and eventually subjugation by the Elamites in 1154 BC.

Shalmaneser III reasserted Assyrian lordship in 851 BC, but the city was destroyed by ◊Sennacherib in 689 BC. It was rebuilt by Esarhaddon, but destroyed again in 648 BC after again rising against Assyrian rule.

The destruction of Assyria in 612 BC left Babylon under the control of the Chaldaeans, whose kings Nabopolassar and ◊Nebuchadnezzar created a new metropolis of grand buildings: the stepped ziqqurat, the 'hanging gardens', and the blue-tiled Gate of Ishtar. After the destruction of Jerusalem in 598 BC, the transhumance of the Jews led to the biblical Exile.

Babylon surrendered without a fight to the Persian ruler Cyrus the Great in 539 BC, and remained a wealthy city of the Persian Empire until the Macedonian conquest under Alexander the Great.

Babylon, Hittite raid on daring raid on the city of ◊Babylon about 1595 BC by the Hittite king ◊Mursilis I, which brought to an end the Amorite kingdom founded by ◊Hammurabi I. The attack led to the Kassite conquest of Babylonia and the establishment of the longest serving dynasty in Babylon (c. 1415–1225 BC).

It also led to the murder of Mursilis, after a palace coup, and the limitation of Hittite territorial conquests to Anatolia for the rest of the Old Kingdom period (16th–15th centuries BC).

Bach-dang River, Battle of battle in AD 938 in which the Vietnamese ◊Ngo Quyen defeated a Southern Han Chinese seaborne expedition under commander Liu Hongcao on a branch of the river Hong in China.

Liu sailed up the Bach-dang, part of the Hong river delta. Ngo planted large iron-tipped stakes in the river, reaching just below surface level at high tide. He sent out shallow-draft boats to attack Liu's fleet and feign flight upriver. The heavier Chinese vessels pursued, but were caught on the stakes as the tide fell. As they lay helpless, the Vietnamese attacked with fire-arrows. Liu and over half his men were killed or drowned.

bacheler medieval French term for a bachelor, meaning a young knight still dependent upon wages, or a member of a military household. In order to acquire fiefs and heiresses a *bacheler* would be expected to demonstrate prowess in battle (see ◊youth).

baculum (Latin 'baton' or 'stick') medieval baton of command, much like later marshals' batons. In the ◊Bayeux Tapestry both Duke William of Normandy and his brother Bishop Odo of Bayeux are shown waving three-foot sticks. These have been described as maces (heavy clubs), but much has been made of Odo, a cleric, not being allowed to shed blood.

Badr, Battle of battle fought in 624 at Badr, modern Saudi Arabia, between Muslims under the prophet Muhammad and the Quraish tribe. The Quraish were routed and the foundations of Muslim power were secured.

The Muslims, who were weak in number, took up a defensive position along the side of a valley. Muhammad directed the use of archery to prevent them from being outflanked by the superior Quraishi cavalry. Heavy rain the night before had made the ground unsuitable for their charge, and the Quraish were repulsed.

Baecula, Battle of battle fought in 208 BC at Baecula (modern Bailén, Spain) in which the Roman commander Publius Cornelius ◊Scipio (later Scipio 'Africanus') engaged and successfully checked Carthinagian forces in Spain under general ◊Hasdrubal Barca, brother of ◊Hannibal the Great.

Hasdrubal took up a strong defensive position on a steep ridge, the rear of which was defended by a river. Scipio was reluctant to attack but, after several days, fear that other Punic armies might arrive induced him into offering battle. His ◊*velites* engaged the Carthaginian skirmishers on the lower slopes, and while the main Punic force was still deploying Scipio attempted to envelop it by pushing his legions uphill on the wings. Hasdrubal, however, was able to see what was happening and disengaged before his forces were fully committed. He abandoned his skirmishers and took his elephants, war treasury, and the core of his army off along the river Tagus.

Baghras castle Templar castle 19 km/12 mi north of Antioch, commanding a pass across the Amanus mountains, southern Turkey. The surviving ruins date mostly from about 1200, including an early Gothic chapel.

Crowning a small round hill, the three-walled fortress is built in several storeys and displays significant Armenian influence, including a long gallery of archers' loops. The extensive undercrofts contain several water cisterns and held 12,000 measures of grain when ◊Saladin captured the castle in 1188. Recovered by German crusaders in 1190, the castle was returned to the ◊Knights Templar who held it until ◊Baibars conquered the principality of Antioch in 1268, after which it remained in ◊Mameluke hands.

Baginton fort Roman fort (also known as 'the Lunt') at Baginton, Warwickshire, England. It was constructed in about AD 61, in the aftermath of the ◊Boudiccan Revolt, and served both to watch over the region and to train cavalry horses.

Baginton provides a unique example of a cavalry horse training centre, with the training enclosure (*gyrus*) being a conspicuous feature of the fort. Internal buildings and gates were built in timber and the perimeter defences consisted of a ditch and turf rampart, part of which has been reconstructed. The defences bulged out on the east side to accommodate the circular *gyrus*. The fort was abandoned about AD 78–80.

Bagradas, Battle of the battle fought in 204 BC, during the latter part of the Second Punic War (see ◊Punic War, Second), in which the Roman leader Publius Cornelius ◊Scipio Africanus defeated the combined forces of the Carthaginians ◊Hasdrubal (son of Gisco) and

◊Syphax on the river Bagradas, in the interior of present-day Tunisia. The Roman victory forced the recall of ◊Hannibal the Great from Italy.

The Carthaginian army probably numbered 30,000, including 4,000 Celtiberian mercenaries. The size of Scipio's army is likely to have been around 20–25,000. Both armies engaged after several days of skirmishing. The Carthaginians on the right were routed by ◊Masinissa, King of the Massylii of north Africa; the Numidians commanded by Syphax on the left were broken by C Laelius. However, pursuit of these forces was delayed by the tenacity of the Celtiberians in the centre who, when surrounded, fought to the death. Masinissa and Laelius were sent after Syphax while Scipio marched to Tunis.

Bahram Chobin (died 591) (or *Varahran Chobin*) Sassanian Persian general and usurper. After defeating the Turks near Balkh in 588, he was transferred to Mesopotamia where Roman forces defeated his army at Nisibis in 589. Fearing for his life, he murdered King Hormizd IV and seized the throne. King Hormizd's son ◊Chosroes II fled to the Romans and, with troops supplied by the Roman emperor ◊Maurice, defeated Bahram and his Turkish allies on the river Zab in 590 and again at Sargana in 591. Bahram escaped but was killed soon after.

Bahram Shah (died 1152) sultan of Ghazni (central Afghanistan) 1118–52. He came to the throne with ◊Seljuk assistance and waged numerous campaigns in Afghanistan and northwest India, but was ultimately defeated by the rising power of Ghur, a small state in the mountains of northern Afghanistan.

After Bahram's brother Arslan Shah usurped the throne in 1115, the Seljuk sultan ◊Sanjar invaded Ghazni in 1117 to avenge his sister, who had been insulted by Arslan Shah. He defeated Arslan Shah and installed Bahram as sultan in return for an annual tribute of 250,000 dinars. Arslan Shah reoccupied Ghazni, but was again defeated and eventually put to death by Bahram, who then dealt successfully with revolts in the Punjab. Bahram himself rebelled against Sanjar in 1135, but was obliged to submit and accepted reinstatement on payment of further tribute.

In 1148 Bahram grew suspicious of his son-in-law Qutb al-Din Muhammad, a prince of the family ruling in Ghur, and had him poisoned. Muhammad's brother Saif al-Din then seized Ghazni, but was captured and put to death. A third brother, ◊Ala al-Din Husain, descended on Ghazni, defeated Bahram in three battles, and destroyed the city by fire. When Ala al-Din, 'the World-Burner', left, Bahram returned, but from then on the Ghaznavid dynasty declined until it was finally overthrown by ◊Muhammad of Ghur in 1187.

Baibars (lived 13th century) (or *al-Malik al-Zahir Rukn al-Din Baybars al-Bunduqdari*) Mameluke sultan of Egypt 1260–77. He played an important role in the victories of Mansurah (see ◊Mansurah, Battle of) in 1250 and Ain Jalut (see ◊Ain Jalut, Battle of) in 1260, conquered most of the eastern Christian states, and defeated the Mongols in 1277. On his last campaign he defeated the Mongols again at Albistan in 1277, before dying at Damascus, possibly of poisoning. His dynasty ruled until 1512.

A ◊Mameluke of the Bahri ('River') Regiment, Baibars led the counterattack that routed the crusaders at Mansurah. He also led the vanguard at Ain Jalut, where the Mongol invasion of Syria was defeated, and soon afterwards murdered Sultan ◊Qutuz and took his place.

An energetic soldier, he campaigned tirelessly to establish Mameluke rule over Muslims and Christians alike. Thoroughly professional, he established an efficient spy network and constructed a formidable siege train. In combination they defeated all who stood against him. His armies took the southern Christian fortresses of ◊Kerak-in-Moab castle in 1263, Caesarea in 1265, ◊Safed castle in 1266, and Jaffa in 1268. He also operated in northern Syria, finally conquering Antioch in 1268 and overrunning much of the Christian kingdom of Cilician Armenia (now southern Turkey).

bakufu Japanese term for ◊shogunate.

Balathista, Battle of decisive victory in 1014 for the Byzantines under Emperor ◊Basil II, and the culmination of their campaign against the Bulgars, led by Tsar ◊Samuel. Basil blinded his 15,000 prisoners, leaving one man in each hundred with a good eye so he could lead his companions home. Tsar Samuel is said to have died of shock and Bulgar resistance crumbled. By 1018 the Byzantines had conquered the country.

In 996 the Byzantine emperor had defeated Samuel at Spercheios, recapturing Greece and Macedonia. A few years later the Bulgars again invaded Byzantine territory, forcing Basil to resume the offensive. Samuel tried to block the Byzantine route through the mountains in Macedonia by fortifying a pass, but they sent a flanking force through another route to hit his army from the rear in conjunction with a frontal assault.

Balban, Baha al-Din Ghiyas al-Din (1205–85) sultan of Delhi 1266–85. A ◊*ghulam* and son-in-law of Sultan Iltutmish (or Altamsh), he made his name in the internecine wars following Iltutmish's death (1236), gained the throne at an advanced age, and restored central authority by a policy of vigorous campaigning and ruthless cruelty.

He insisted on strict observation of court protocol and the laws of Islam, but gave Delhi a period of stability and security.

Baldwin I (1058–1118) king of Jerusalem 1100–18. Younger brother of ◊Godfrey de Bouillon, his personal bravery was undisputed and celebrated. Victory at Ramlah in 1101 (see ◊Ramlah, Battle of) may have made him overconfident. When he reattacked the following year he carelessly led 500 knights against about 20,000 Egyptians. He escaped from this disaster virtually alone, and the Latin Kingdom had to be rescued by ◊Tancred and Baldwin of Edessa together with some 200 ships of crusaders. When Baldwin attacked again in 1104, he charged carrying his own ◊standard, and this victory secured his southern border.

He also extended Latin rule over the Syrian ports. Egyptian raids against Jerusalem in 1113 and Jaffa in 1115 provoked an attack on Egypt in 1118, where he died, probably of dysentery.

Baldwin II (died 1131) count of Edessa 1098–1118 and king of Jerusalem from 1118. Cousin to ◊Godfrey de Bouillon, Baldwin played a maverick role on the First Crusade, deserting the main body to have himself made ruler of Edessa in 1098. His stalwart defence of the city for two weeks saved the crusade from destruction. Despite periods of imprisonment he continued to hold the north for the Latins.

He defeated Il-Ghazi at Hab (see ◊Hab, Battle of) and ruled Antioch until 1126. His last campaigns against Aleppo in 1126 and Damascus in 1127 almost brought these strategic Muslim cities under Christian control.

Baldwin of Flanders (1171–1206) Frankish emperor of Constantinople 1204–06, the first emperor of the Latin (west European) Empire. He succeeded as Baldwin IX, Count of Flanders, in 1195. In 1200 he was forced to agree the Treaty of Péronne by which he became the vassal of King Philip (II) Augustus of France, and then left on the Fourth Crusade. After the Crusader capture of Constantinople in 1204 he was elected emperor of a Frankish regime based on the former Byzantine capital. He was captured by the Bulgars in 1205 and killed in 1206.

Balearic sling medieval European stone-throwing engine, noted for its rate of fire. It is thought that the Balearic sling might have been an early counterweight ◊trebuchet. It could also be related to the *arcus balearis* ('Balearic bow'), probably a ◊mangonel operated on the crossbow principle. It is unknown whether or not the engine actually originated in the Balearic Islands.

balinger medieval English oared vessel used during the ◊Hundred Years' War. Clinker-built and with about 12 oars per side, the balinger served as the galley of northwestern waters. With fighting crews of 40 to 60 men, it was especially useful for cross-Channel raiding and attacking becalmed sailing ships.

balista in medieval European warfare, either a siege engine or a crossbow, depending on the historical context. Both were tension weapons requiring a string to be drawn back and released. A variety of missiles could be used including large crossbow ◊bolts and combustibles.

The engine was similar to a large crossbow, operated by a winch to draw back the string. A variant of the balista used the torsion of twisted ropes to power the bow arms.

ballista original name for a stone-shooting machine as opposed to a ◊*catapulta*, an arrow- or bolt-shooting machine, in Roman warfare. The two words exchanged meanings during the Roman Empire, probably around the 1st century AD.

Rome was slow to adopt artillery, relying on Greek engineers to supply it when required. However, by the end of the republic (1st century AD), artillery had become part of the standard equipment of the legions and at some point, according to ◊Vegetius, the standard legionary artillery was set at 10 stone-throwing and 55 bolt-shooting machines.

Bamburgh castle castle in England, 23 km/14 mi north of Alnwick, Northumberland, situated on a rock outcrop which had been continuously fortified since AD 547, overlooking the sea. The castle changed hands frequently during the 12th and 13th centuries, and was added to and rebuilt from time to time. It fell into disuse in the late 15th century.

The present structure was begun in the 12th century, and the keep, which is some 6 sq m/70 sq ft, dates from this period. The area was surrounded by a curtain wall with towers and divided into three baileys (see ◊motte-and-bailey), with the main entrance through a barbican at the western end.

Ban Chao (died AD 102) (or *Pan Ch'ao*) Han Chinese general. He distinguished himself

as second in command of an expedition against the northern ◊Xiongnu in AD 73 and was then sent to the Western Regions, the kingdoms of the Tarim Basin silk-trade route in modern southern Xinjiang, where he served until just before his death, successfully restoring Han authority.

bandon late Roman/Byzantine tactical unit of approximately 300 men. The term derives from the German word for 'banner' and was also applied to the unit's standard. Such a unit was also called by its Greek name ◊*tagma*.

banner medieval standard. In medieval European warfare, a banner was a square flag carried by a ◊banneret. In a formal ceremony a knight's swallow-tailed ◊pennon was cropped to indicate his rise in status.

Banner standard carried by medieval Swiss troops bearing the coat-of-arms of the city or canton: for example, for Bern, a bear.

banneret (or *knight banneret*) knight of sufficient wealth and status to lead 20 other knights; he carried a ◊banner as a symbol and rallying point in battle.

Bannockburn, Battle of battle fought on 24 June 1314 at Bannockburn, Scotland, between ◊Robert (I) the Bruce, King of Scotland, and Edward II of England. The defeat of the English led to the independence of Scotland.

Edward II, attempting to relieve Stirling castle, led over 2,000 knights and 15,000 foot soldiers, including about 5,000 archers. Bruce had only 500 light cavalry and some 7,000 foot soldiers. He took up a defensive position behind a stream and dug pits to hamper the English cavalry. An English attack was repulsed, so Edward's forces made a night march to outflank the obstacles. This manoeuvre was badly executed, leaving Edward's knights in boggy ground and the archers out of position in the rear. Bruce blocked the English advance with ◊schiltrons of pikemen, then, as the archers tried to deploy, charged with his cavalry and routed them. The English knights' charges against the Scottish schiltrons suffered heavy casualties, with 500 noblemen being taken for ransom.

Banos de la Encina castle in Spain, 140 km/87 mi north of Granada. Built in the 10th century by the Moors to defend the line of the river Guadalquivir, it was captured by the Christians just before the Battle of Las Navas de Tolosa (see ◊Las Navas de Tolosa, Battle of) in 1212. It had the usual Moorish form of a curtain wall with square towers, and a large *torre del homenage* (castle keep) added by the

Christians to strengthen the defences and celebrate their victory over the Moors.

baojia and **baowu** (or *pao-chia* and *pao-wu*) Song Chinese militia organizations. ◊Wang Anshi introduced the *baojia* to supplement the ◊*yangbing* professional army. *Baowu* local defence forces already existed in some areas before Wang. They coexisted with and sometimes shared officers with the *baojia*, taking over in the 12th century the local defence function that the *baojia* abandoned.

The *baojia* had a set organizational structure in the community. Ten households formed a *xiaobao*, or 'small guard', in which all adult males except one per household were to serve. Five small guards formed a 'large guard', and ten of these formed a *dubao*, or 'superior guard'. They received military training during slack periods in the agricultural year and were responsible for keeping local order as well as being available for the army. After Wang's resignation in 1086 policing became their only responsibility, though some *baojia* units fought against Jurchen invaders 1127–36.

Barbastro, Siege of siege and capture in 1064 of the Muslim-held town of Barbastro, in the Spanish kingdom of Zaragoza, by the Duke of Aquitaine in alliance with the Catalans and the Aragonese. The Muslims recaptured the city, but the 1064 event retained significance as the first major success in the Christian ◊*Reconquista*.

Barbiano, Alberigo da (lived 14th–15th centuries) Italian ◊*condottiere*, Great Constable of Naples, Viceroy of Calabria in 1390, and joint commander of the army of Milan 1390–1402. Serving Gian Galleazo ◊Visconti in conjunction with Jacopo dal Verme, he defeated the Florentines at Casalecchio in 1402, delivering Bologna to Milan.

Barbiano was seen as the 'liberator of Italy' by Italian Renaissance humanists and Italian nationalist historians alike. In fact, his chequered career was no different from Transalpine *condottieri* and even his defeat of the Breton Company in 1380 did not end foreign mercenary involvement in Italy. He was a successful soldier, however, responsible for training other *condottieri* leaders.

barbote alternative name for the ◊bevor, the medieval European face defence worn with the sallet or kettle-hat.

barbute (Italian) helmet made in Italy in the 15th century, normally classified as a type of ◊sallet and often called a 'Venetian sallet', with a characteristic T-shaped opening at the front. These helmets are thought to have developed from the ◊basinet by extending the sides and rear downwards, obviating the need for an ◊aventail. Their similarity to ◊Corinthian helmets suggests that they might be copies of excavated examples from antiquity, or of ancient sculptures.

bard general term for horse armour. Bards were used extensively in the later Roman Empire, disappeared in the 5th century, and reappeared in Europe in the mid-12th century in the form of mail trappers. Plate bards appear in inventories from the mid-14th century.

Bari, Siege of (871–75) successful joint effort by the Byzantine Emperor ◊Basil (I) the Macedonian and the Holy Roman Emperor Ludwig II to drive the Muslims from southern Italy, carried out between 871 and 875. The Byzantine fleet blockaded the port of Bari, while Ludwig's Germans conducted operations on land.

Bari, Siege of (1068–71) siege of the last Byzantine stronghold in southern Italy by the Norman knight ◊Robert Guiscard during the gradual Norman conquest of Sicily. The siege lasted from 5 August 1068 to 16 April 1071. Guiscard used siege engines and a blockade to take the city.

Bari was set on a promontory with strong walls and a well-protected harbour, and was well defended. Early on in the siege the defenders launched a sally to burn the Norman siege engines. Guiscard then resorted to blockade. In the spring of 1071, supported by the ships of his brother Roger of Sicily, he established a naval blockade to complete the isolation of the city. When the Norman forces drove off a well-planned night attack by the previously invincible Byzantine fleet, the city surrendered.

Bar Kochba Rebellion Judean rebellion from AD 131 to 135 provoked by the Roman emperor ◊Hadrian's edict restricting Jewish religious practices, as well as his decision to build a temple to the Roman god Jupiter on the site of the Great Temple in Jerusalem. The charismatic leader Simeon Bar Kochba gave the rebellion a messianic element lacking in the earlier ◊Jewish War of AD 66–73. The Judeans were finally put down by the Romans.

The first Roman forces sent against the rebels suffered a series of defeats, but reinforcements were sent to the province from all over the empire. In 134 the experienced Roman governor of Britain Gaius Julius Severus was given charge of the Roman forces. In a long series of raids, skirmishes, and small-scale sieges, the Romans wore down the Judeans until all were destroyed or forced to surrender. Judea was renamed Syria Palestina and large communities of Gentiles were settled there.

Barnard castle castle in England in the town of Barnard Castle, 24 km/15 mi west of Darlington. It was named after Bernard de Balliol, who built the castle in 1112–32. Sited on a rock about 30 m/100 ft above the River Tees, the castle originally had four wards, a curtain wall, and a large round ◊donjon (keep), built in the late 13th century.

Barnet, Battle of battle fought on 14 April 1471, during the English Wars of the Roses (see ◊Roses, Wars of the), in which ◊Edward IV defeated and killed the Earl of Warwick in a confusing encounter in the fog at Barnet (now in northwest London).

Edward returned from exile in Burgundy with a few mercenaries and landed in Yorkshire in March. He marched south, gathering forces, and established himself in London. His forces now numbered 9–10,000 men. Taken off guard, Warwick had to approach from the north with a similar number and camped opposite Edward at Barnet. Overnight, on 13 April, he attempted an artillery bombardment, but his guns overshot. The next day was very foggy, and the armies did not line up against one another. As a result both right wings overlapped and defeated the enemy left. The Earl of Oxford, fighting for Warwick, showed great skill in getting his men back into the fray, but his badge, the Rising Sun, looked very like that of Edward's Sun with Streams, so archers of Warwick's centre shot at them. Oxford's men cried treason and fled. Edward chose this moment to drive forward, breaking through. Warwick was killed in the flight.

Barons' War (1215–17) civil war waged by the English barons against King John of England, provoked by his bad faith after signing the Magna Carta on 15 June 1215. The war involved Scottish and French invasions in support of the rebels. Royalist victories after John's death brought the conflict to an end.

John's bad faith caused widespread rebellion. His successful siege of Rochester castle from mid-October to 30 November 1216 freed him to turn against Alexander II, King of Scots, and drive him back from Norham and Berwick, after which he crushed northern English resistance in a winter campaign.

In May 1216 Prince Louis of France landed with substantial forces and besieged Dover and Windsor. John's determined strategy thwarted both attempts, but he died in October. Louis then brought reinforcements and conquered much of East Anglia and the

south between November 1216 and January 1217. Henry III's aged guardian William ◊Marshal led a recovery in royalist fortunes with victories at Lincoln on 20 May 1217 (see ◊Lincoln, Battle of) and at sea off Sandwich on 25 August, ending the war.

Barons' War (1264–67) civil war initiated by the English barons under Simon de ◊Montfort (the Younger), leader of a reform movement against King Henry III of England's government. Success at Lewes in 1264 (see ◊Lewes, Battle of) led to the king's capture, but at Evesham in 1265 (see ◊Evesham, Battle of) the rebellious barons were brutally massacred.

The Montfortians' power base was around Kenilworth castle, Warwickshire. Marching south, Simon challenged the royalists outside Lewes in Sussex on 14 May. Despite a successful charge by Prince Edward, the royalists were routed by Simon's tactics and Henry was captured.

Isolated by political defections in 1265, Simon was outmanoeuvred and drawn into a killing ground at Evesham, where he was killed, along with many other rebel barons. Montfortian castles continued to hold out until 1267. Kenilworth, surrounded by sophisticated water defences, withstood six months' intense siege until forced to surrender in December 1266.

barritus Latin term for the German war cry adopted by the Romans, described by the Roman historian Tacitus as 'a harsh, intermittent roar' which was amplified into a deep crescendo by the soldiers holding their shields in front of their mouths.

Basel fort (Roman *Basilia*) Roman fort at Basel, in present-day Switzerland, built to strengthen the Rhine frontier defences in Raetia and protect the bridge and bend in the river. Its most notable feature was a large granary within the fort, demonstrating one function of late Roman frontier forts as secure storage bases. Construction dates from the reigns of the emperors ◊Aurelian, ◊Probus, and ◊Diocletian are argued.

The fort occupied a good defensive position that had been exploited in Gallic times, situated on a hill with steep cliffs down to the Rhine on the east side. The walls have been located on the south (170 m/557 ft) and west (220 m/720 ft) sides. ◊Valentinian I constructed a small fort across the Rhine to protect the bridgehead, 13 m/43 ft square with walls 4 m/13 ft thick.

Basil (I) the Macedonian Byzantine emperor 867–86 who successfully campaigned against the Muslims and re-established

Byzantine naval control of the Eastern Mediterranean. He also expanded Byzantine-controlled territory in Italy and eastern Anatolia (part of modern Turkey).

Basil II (c. 958–1025) Byzantine emperor 976–1025. He completed the work of his predecessors ◊Nicephorus (II) Phocas and John ◊Zimisces and expanded the borders of the Byzantine Empire to their greatest extent since the 5th century. He eliminated political rivals, drove the Muslims from Syria, and destroyed the power of the Bulgars.

basinet (or *bacinet*) characteristic head armour worn by European knights in the second half of the 14th century and early 15th century. It appears to have developed from the plate reinforcement to the mail ◊coif, often called the *cervellière*, worn under the ◊great helm in the earlier part of the 14th century. By the 1340s it was worn without a great helm and with a visor, either pivoted at the temples or attached by a single pivot at the forehead (the latter type being known as a ◊*Klappvisier*).

The long point or snout of the former defences gave rise to the terms 'hounskull' and 'pig-faced' basinet.

Basing, Battle of battle in 871 at Basing in Wessex, England, in which the Danes, led by ◊Halfdan, defeated the Anglo-Saxons of Wessex, under Aethelred and his brother Alfred (see ◊Alfred the Great). The battle occurred just two weeks after the Anglo-Saxon victory at Ashdown (see ◊Ashdown, Battle of).

bastard sword sword with a long, straight blade, plain cross guard and rounded pommel, used in western Europe in the 15th and 16th centuries. It was also known as a *hand-and-a-half sword* because its long grip allowed the swordsman to use three fingers of his second hand for extra power if required.

bastide new town founded in Gascony, France, by Edward I of England in the late 13th century, sometimes in partnership with local lords. *Bastides* were surrounded by arcades and had a quadrilateral plan with a central market square. They served mainly as administrative and economic centres; only some of the original *bastides* were fortified.

battle (from Old French *bataile*) division of a medieval European host (army). A conventional deployment was of three 'battles'. The van (or vanguard), centre, and rear (rearguard) battles in a line of march became the right, centre, and left divisions respectively of a battle line. A 'battle' could also mean any grouping of knights or other troops on a more impromptu basis (rather like the modern 'battle group').

battle wagon Sumerian onager-drawn vehicle used in warfare by the cities of Sumer, Akkad, and Anatolia. As depicted on the 'Standard of Ur' and 'Stele of Vultures' (c. 2500 BC), it was a four-wheeled, two-person vehicle, armed with javelins in a quiver and drawn by four onagers. The solid wheels were made of two halves, and the front of the car was higher than the sides.

On the Standard, battle wagons are shown operating in conjunction with helmeted, cloaked, and spear-armed infantry, but as a separate military unit. On the Stele, King Eannatum of Lagash, mounted alone on his battle wagon, leads a detachment of helmeted and spear-armed infantry. The illustrations indicate a distinction between light troops accompanying the battle wagons and heavy troops operating en bloc.

Another contemporary relief shows a two-wheeled saddled vehicle for a single person, who probably sat astride the saddle. Clay models also depict single-crewed vehicles, with the crewman standing.

Baugé, Battle of battle fought in 1421 in northwest France during the ◊Hundred Years' War between a Franco-Scottish force and the English under the Duke of Clarence, Henry V of England's brother, who was killed.

Clarence launched a rash attack with 1,000 cavalry across the bridge at Baugé. At first he successfully drove back the defenders, but then advanced too far. He was surprised by the Earl of Buchan, commanding 5,000 Franco-Scots. Unable to keep good order and separated from their archer support, the English men-at-arms were overwhelmed.

Bayan khan of the ◊Avars, a nomadic Turkic people, who were driven westwards in the mid-5th century. Bayan campaigned successfully against the Eastern Roman Empire and various Germanic tribes to establish a powerful and influential empire in central Europe.

Bayeux Tapestry unique embroidered record of the Norman Conquest of England (1066), including a detailed portrayal of the Battle of Hastings (see ◊Hastings, Battle of). It was made in England about 1077 at the instigation of Bishop Odo of Bayeux, William the Conqueror's half-brother.

The Tapestry tells the story of the conquest from the Norman point of view. By showing the close relationship between Harold Godwinson (later Harold II of England) and Duke William of Normandy (later William I the Conqueror), including Harold's oath to

William, it justifies the Norman invasion when Harold took the throne on King Edward the Confessor's death.

The Tapestry provides unique details of the logistics, fleets, horses, weapons, and military equipment of 11th-century Europe. Its depiction of the battle is also full of incident, making clear how narrow was William's victory.

Bayezid II (1448–1512) Ottoman sultan 1481–1512. He was victorious against the late Christian crusade of Nicopolis, but was defeated at Ankara (see ◊Ankara, Battle of) in 1402 by the invading Mongol horde of ◊Timur Leng.

Bayezid attempted to take Constantinople from the Christians but was forced to abandon the attempt by the Nicopolis crusade. After his capture at Ankara he was exhibited as a prisoner in an iron cage, and died of poisoning by his own son.

beaked galley distinctive vessel of the ◊Peoples of the Sea depicted on the temple relief of Medinet Habu, Thebes, Egypt, illustrating the sea battle against the Egyptian king ◊Ramses III in 1175 BC. The Sea Peoples' vessels are depicted as having no distinctive stern, but rather a prow at either end, each with a beaked bird's head. They were equipped with oars and sails.

beaked galley, medieval medieval southern European warship. Unlike the galley of antiquity which had a sub-surface ram for holing and sinking, the medieval galley had a projecting, spiked beak for fixing onto enemy vessels and providing an avenue for boarding. Frescoes in the Palazzo Pubblico in Siena, Italy, portray this type of fighting.

Beaumaris castle castle in northwest Wales, on the Isle of Anglesey overlooking the Menai Strait. Beaumaris was the last Welsh castle to be built by ◊Edward I (1272–1307) and the finest example of a concentric fortification in Britain.

Intended to hold a garrison to control North Wales and protect the rich agricultural lands of the island, it was built by James of St George 1295–98 at a cost of over £7,000, but the original design was scaled down due to economic restraints.

Bedford, John, Duke of (1389–1435) first duke of Bedford from 1414, younger brother of ◊Henry V of England. When Henry was in France during the ◊Hundred Years' War in 1415, Bedford acted as regent. He was a distinguished commander in the later stages of the Hundred Years' War, winning at the Battle of Verneuil (see ◊Verneuil, Battle of) in 1424. Joan of Arc defeated his forces at Orléans (see ◊Orléans, Siege of)

and Patay (see ◊Patay, Battle of) in 1429; he later allowed her execution.

His first marriage to the sister of Philip the Good, Duke of Burgundy, cemented an alliance that strengthened England's position in the war. His second marriage to Jacquetta of Luxembourg, however, fostered division with Burgundy. He was designated protector for his nephew Henry VI.

Bedford castle castle in England about 80 km/50 mi north of London. It was built in around 1070, although no details of its construction are recorded, but it was the scene of a siege in 1224 when Fawkes de ◊Bréauté incurred King Henry III's wrath. When the castle was taken, Fawkes was allowed to go free on oath to take the Cross (go on a crusade), as were three Templars (see ◊Military Order), but most of the remainder of the garrison were hanged and the castle destroyed.

Bedriacum, Battle of decisive battle in AD 69 between the Roman emperor ◊Vespasian's Flavian forces led by the general Antoninus Primus and the rival emperor Aulus Vitellius' main Vitellian field army. The battle decided the outcome of the civil war known as the ◊Year of Four Emperors.

The Vitellian forces were stationed in the Po valley, but they lacked a clear commander, resulting in poor coordination. A large part of the army had endured a long march before they entered the battle. Approaching Bedriacum near the end of the day, the Flavian troops pressured their commander into attacking the Vitellians. The battle lasted through the night. At dawn the Flavian 3rd Legion (*Legio III Gallica*) saluted the sun in the manner prevalent in their Syrian station. The Vitellians misunderstood the gesture as a sign that more Flavians had advanced, and most of the Vitellian army panicked and routed. The Flavians pursued the Vitellians up to the walls of Bedriacum and stormed and sacked the city with great savagery.

Beeston castle castle in Cheshire, England, 16 km/10 mi southeast of Chester. The castle dates back to around 1220, though the naturally commanding site had been used before Roman times. The castle was isolated from the ridge upon which it stood by a man-made ditch 11 m/35 ft wide and 9 m/30 ft deep, cut into the rock.

Beizhou, Siege of (or *Pei-chou*) battle in 1048 in which Song Chinese forces defeated rebels under commander Wang Ze, besieged in Beizhou. The Song troops tunnelled under the walls, and 200 men entered the city and let their comrades in. In street-fighting Wang stampeded cattle at the Song troops, but they were turned back with missiles, and Song troops took the city.

Belatoba, Battle of alternative name for the Battle of Silistra of 1086: see ◊Silistra, Battle of.

belfry mobile siege tower, known to the ancient world and common in medieval sieges. Belfries served a dual purpose: covering activity by the besiegers against the lower part of the defensive wall, and providing a platform from which they could reach its top, usually by bridge. Belfries were usually higher than the walls themselves, so as to enable the besiegers to use missile weapons effectively against the defenders, and sometimes mounted throwing engines.

Belfries were usually built of wood, with the exterior protected against fire by skin coverings such as ox hides. Ladders were used for internal movement. James the Conqueror (1208–76) used belfries in Majorca, Spain, with two fighting platforms, one halfway up, the other at the top.

Bellême, Robert of (c. 1058–c. 1131) Norman commander and castle builder in England. He inherited lands in England, Normandy, and Maine, and the earldom of Shrewsbury, and acquired 34 castles.

Robert was his own architect for structures like ◊Bridgnorth castle and ◊Gisors castle, and

BELISARIUS (505–65)

East Roman general who led Rome's reconquest of the West. Though given inadequate resources by a jealous emperor, Belisarius achieved notable victories against the Persians, Huns, Vandals, and Goths.

Born in the Balkans, Belisarius served in the emperor's bodyguard, and at age 25 received command of the Roman army in the East. He defeated a superior force of Persians at Daras in 530 and although he was defeated at Callinicum (see ◊Callinicum, Battle of 531) his reputation remained high. His firm action during the Nika riots in Constantinople in 532 saved the emperor ◊Justinian from being overthrown. His greatest and most complete triumph was the rapid conquest of the Vandal North African kingdom in 533–34 with only 15,000 men. In the campaign against the Ostrogoths in Italy that followed, Belisarius secured Sicily with barely a struggle then, following a brief interlude to deal with a rebellion in Africa, took Naples and Rome. In 537 he showed great personal courage, inventiveness, and leadership to hold Rome against a Gothic siege. After throwing the Goths back from the walls of Rome, he took the offensive and forced the surrender of the Gothic king Witiges at Ravenna. The Goths offered to make Belisarius the western emperor, but he refused.

Despite Belisarius' loyalty, Justinian saw him as a potential rival and recalled him to deal with a Persian threat in the East. Over three years Belisarius recovered lost Roman territories in Syria and Mesopotamia in a war of manoeuvre with no major battles. Belisarius' absence from Italy led to a Gothic resurgence and he was sent back to deal with it, but Justinian remained suspicious and refused to give him enough troops to destroy the Gothic kingdom completely. After five years of fruitless campaigning, Belisarius was recalled and replaced by ◊Narses who brought the campaign to a successful conclusion.

Belisarius was recalled from retirement in 559 to defeat an army of Slavs and Bulgars who had invaded Moesia and Thrace and reached the walls of Constantinople. Despite saving the capital, Belisarius continued to arouse the emperor's jealousy and he was charged with treason and imprisoned in 562. Although later released, he was never again employed in Imperial service. He died 13 March 565.

designed and directed siege machines. He was 'commander of knights' for ◊William (II) Rufus, but became involved in rebellions against Rufus and King Henry I, eventually losing his English lands. He was imprisoned for life in 1112.

Belmont castle castle in Israel, 10 km/6 mi west of Jerusalem, that was built on a hill top by the Hospitallers (see ◊Military Order) in around 1150. The castle fell to ◊Saladin in 1187 and was razed in 1191. A village was subsequently built on the site.

The outer wall was roughly octagonal, and there are the remains of an inner wall. In the centre was the 'inner ward', a rectangular building of which three sides formed accommodation and the remainder a small courtyard.

Belmonte castle star-shaped castle-palace in Spain, about 80 km/50 mi southwest of Cuenca. There was a tower at each of the six points, and the structure was enclosed by ramparts which were originally part of the wall surrounding the village of Belmonte. Begun in 1456 by the Marquis of Villena, it was primarily a defended residence with a detached keep.

Belmonte was the prison of La Beltraneja, daughter of Henry IV, after her claim to the throne of Castile was rejected in favour of Isabella in the 15th century.

Belvoir castle castle in modern Israel, south of the Sea of Galilee. It was built by the Knights Hospitaller (see ◊Military Order) from 1168 onwards to a roughly rectangular concentric design. There was an inner court-yarded building, inner and outer walls, and a barbican. The central building and the outer wall had square towers at the corners, and a ditch surrounded the whole castle.

Benevento, Battle of battle fought on 26 February 1266 between Charles of Anjou and Manfred Hohenstauffen, King of Sicily, at Benevento in the Italian kingdom of Naples. Manfred was defeated and killed, assuring French rule in Italy.

Charles held a position behind the flooded river Calore. His crossbowmen were in front, followed by his cavalry: 900 Provençal, then 1,000 French, and finally 400 Italians. Manfred advanced across the river to attack, his Muslim archers in front, then 800 German cavalry, followed by his Italian cavalry, but his forces became separated in the advance. His archers were scattered by the Provençal charge, and although the Germans counter-charged effectively, they were surrounded

and the reserve was too far back to help. Manfred rushed into the skirmish and was killed.

Beneventum, Battle of (275 BC) battle fought in 275 BC between the Roman army of consul Manius Curius and ◊Pyrrhus, King of Epirus, at Beneventum (now Benevento) in southern Italy. The Roman victory forced Pyrrhus finally to abandon Italy and return to Epirus.

Pyrrhus' attempted night attack on the Roman camp fell foul of rough terrain and was delayed until after dawn. The Romans were able to create disorder among the king's war elephants, and this spread to the rest of the army.

Beneventum, Battle of (214 BC) battle fought in 214 BC at Beneventum (now Benevento) in southern Italy during the Second Punic War (see ◊Punic War, Second), between the Roman Titus Sempronius Gracchus, leading an army of slave volunteers (*volones*), and a Carthaginian force led by ◊Hannibal the Great's commander Hanno. The Carthaginian force comprised 1,200 Numidian and Moorish cavalry and 17,000 Lucanian and Bruttian infantry. The Carthaginians were defeated, but Hanno escaped the ensuing slaughter with 2,000 men, mostly cavalry.

Gracchus apparently offered freedom to any of his men who brought him an enemy head. During the battle it was noticed that they were decapitating the slain instead of fighting the living. A general promise of freedom on victory was made, and the Carthaginians were subsequently defeated.

Benkei (died 1189) renowned, semile-gendary Japanese warrior monk of the Kamakura period. He was a loyal retainer of ◊Minamoto Yoshitsune, whom he accompanied during the ◊Taira–Minamoto Wars.

Legend has it that Benkei had posted himself at the Gojo Bridge in Kyoto where he challenged all comers and relieved them of their swords. Having taken 999 swords, he challenged the young Yoshitsune, and was beaten by him. From then on Benkei followed Yoshitsune. When Yoshitsune was surrounded by enemies sent against him by his brother ◊Minamoto Yoritomo, Benkei fought on alone to his death, allowing Yoshitsune time to commit honourable suicide rather than be captured.

benming (or *pen-ming*) Han Chinese militia, recruited from conscripts who had served their regular tour of duty, but could be recalled for emergency service until they reached the age of 56.

Berkeley castle castle in England, 24 km/15 mi south of Gloucester, tracing its origin to the dwelling of Earl Godwin (father of King Harold II Godwinson), on this site around 1050. After the Norman Conquest William gave the estate to William FitzOsbern, Earl of Hereford, who erected a ◊motte-and-bailey wooden castle. The castle is famous for the imprisonment and murder of Edward II in 1327 and, architecturally, for its shell keep.

After FitzOsbern's wooden castle was destroyed in a local rebellion in 1088, his ◊castellan Roger de Berkeley began rebuilding in stone. The third generation of the de Berkeley family supported King Stephen and were evicted by Henry II, who gave the property to Robert FitzHarding in 1154, since which time the castle has remained in the same family.

Berkhamstead castle Norman ◊motte-and-bailey castle in England, 16 km/10 mi west of St Albans, Hertfordshire. Believed to have been built by Robert de Mortain around 1100, it now reveals few masonry remains, but probably the best-preserved Norman earthworks in existence.

Later modifications provided bastions flanking the ditch encircling motte and bailey. Prince Louis of France placed it under siege in 1226.

berserk Scandinavian term referring to a battle-madness that overcame warriors. Historians have speculated on how this 'shield-biting rage' came about, ranging from hallucinogenic mushrooms to mental instability theories.

Although there is no doubting Viking ferocity in battle, the term berserk, which is mainly found in skaldic poetry and saga literature written two centuries after the Viking age, may have no genuine historical basis.

Berwick, Siege of siege of the Scottish-held English castle of Berwick in Northumberland, England, by ◊Edward III of England from April to 20 July 1333.

An assault by land and sea on 27 June was held off, and Edward was unable to prevent the Scots reprovisioning the castle on 11 July. The garrison surrendered only after he defeated the Scots at Halidon Hill (see ◊Halidon Hill, Battle of) on 19 July.

Bessus (died 329 BC) Achaemenid Persian general. Under his kinsman ◊Darius III, he was satrap (provincial governor) of Bactria and commanded the left wing at Gaugamela (see ◊Gaugamela, Battle of) in 331 BC. During the Persian retreat he murdered Darius and claimed the throne as Artaxerxes IV. He was betrayed to Alexander the Great and executed.

Despite the help of his ally ◊Spitamenes, Bessus was unable to withstand an attack by Alexander the Great after claiming the Persian throne. He fled to Sogdia, where he was betrayed by Spitamenes to Alexander's general Ptolemy (I) Soter.

Beth-Horon, Battle of battle fought to the northwest of Jerusalem in AD 66 between a Roman force retreating from the city and Jewish rebels at the beginning of the ◊Jewish War. The Roman force suffered heavy losses and lost its siege equipment.

The governor of Syria, Cestius Gallus, marched with the 10th Legion (*Legio X Fretensis*), plus ◊vexillatios of several others and a large force of auxiliaries and allies, to confront the uprising in Jerusalem. He camped at Gabao and was attacked on the sabbath; his main line was routed, but disaster was avoided by the arrival of reserves. Unable to forage and subject to raids on his baggage train, Gallus decided to withdraw, but was hotly pursued through the Beth-Horon Pass – terrain where the superiority of his cavalry and his army's tactical organization were negated. The Romans lost 5,780 troops, while the Jewish rebels gained in confidence and captured military equipment.

bevor piece of plate armour to protect the lower front of the face. Bevors formed part of European medieval head defences such as the close helmet (see ◊armet), and the term is sometimes used of the wrapper or reinforcing bevor worn as an additional piece over the front of an armet. As an independent piece of armour, bevors were worn in the 15th century in northern and western Europe with helmets such as sallets and kettle-hats.

Bhadravarman I (lived 4th–5th centuries) first king of Champa (modern central Vietnam), 380–413. Known from inscriptions, he can be identified with the 'Fan Huda' (Fan Hu-ta) of Chinese sources.

Bhadravarman attacked China's Vietnamese provinces in 399, besieging the capital, Longbian, but was defeated by the guerrilla tactics of Do Vien, a Vietnamese official of the Chinese Eastern Jin dynasty. Bhadravarman attacked again in 405, and in response a Chinese fleet raided the Cham coast. He was defeated in another attack in 413, and disappeared.

Bi, Battle of (or *Pi*) battle in 595 BC in which King Zhuang's Chu army defeated a Jin army under commander Xun Linfu. This was another round in the contest between the two

Chinese states begun at Chengpu (see ◊Chengpu, Battle of).

Chu invaded Zheng, and a Jin army marched to its relief. At the Yellow River Xun Linfu learned that Zheng had surrendered and wished to withdraw, but his officers forced him to continue. When the armies met, King Zhuang of Chu was also reluctant to fight, but single combats broke out between the chariot-eers on both sides, and both sides sent in more troops to support these skirmishers. Because King Zhuang was with one of these units, the Chu officers feared for his safety and ordered a general advance, which swept the unprepared Jin forces away. The Chu reserve of 40 chariots completed the victory.

Bibracte, Battle of battle fought in July 58 BC in present-day central France between the Roman army of Julius ◊Caesar and the migrating tribe of the Helvetii, during the ◊Gallic Wars. The Roman victory removed the Helvetii as a military threat.

The Romans gave battle on a hill near Bibracte, the capital of the allied Aeduan tribe. A frontal assault by the Helvetii was routed and they were driven back to a hill about 1.6 km/1 mi away. As the Romans attacked this position the enemy rearguard appeared on their flank, opening the battle into two fronts. The Helvetii finally collapsed after nightfall, and subsequently retreated back to their homeland.

bidaut medieval French term for a light infantryman. Traditionally the *bidauts* came from mountainous southern France and carried javelins, ◊bucklers, and swords. In battle they could swarm around a stationary knight, slipping under his horse's belly to kill it and capture him.

Bindusara (died 274 BC) king of ◊Magadha c. 299–274 BC, the son and successor of ◊Chandragupta Maurya and father of ◊Ashoka. He maintained the existing territories of his empire, stretching from eastern Afghanistan to the Bay of Bengal, and added to them by conquests in the Deccan.

He also established diplomatic relations with distant rulers including 'Antiyoka' (◊Antiochus (I) Soter of Syria).

bireme galley with two banks of oars, anglicized from the Latin words for 'two-oared'. The corresponding Greek term, *dieres*, literally means 'two-fitted' and probably refers to two files of rowers from bow to stern on each side of the ship. In the bireme and ◊trireme, rowers sat at different levels so the galleys could be described as having, respectively, two and three banks.

Blore Heath, Battle of battle fought on 29 September 1459 during the English Wars of the Roses (see ◊Roses, Wars of the) in which the Yorkist Earl of Salisbury took up a defensive position and defeated rash Lancastrian charges. The Lancastrians lost about 2,000 troops, the Yorkists very few.

Salisbury was advancing westwards to join Richard, Duke of York, at Ludlow. Near Market Drayton (in present-day Staffordshire) he was challenged by the Lancastrians under Lord Audley. The 2,000–3,000 Yorkists took cover and Audley's much larger force (possibly 10,000 strong) launched cavalry charges, which suffered heavily from Yorkist archery. Audley was killed and Lord Dudley assumed command. He attacked with dismounted men-at-arms, but his remaining cavalry rode off and about 500 archers defected to the Yorkists.

Bodiam castle castle in Sussex, England, 19 km/12 mi north of Hastings. It was built 1386–90 in a rectangular design inside a moat, with a barbican and outworks, and a curtain wall with four round corner towers, square intermediate towers, and a powerful keep-gatehouse.

Sited as a defence against French incursions up the river Rother, it was located in a wide ditch entered by a causeway, which turned at right angles to enter the gates. The earliest known English cannon was unearthed here, although the castle probably never saw action.

Bodrum castle crusader castle on a peninsula of the west coast of Turkey, overlooking the Bay of Bodrum. The site was granted to the Hospitallers (see ◊Military Order) in 1415, and the castle was built by 1450, next to the ancient Mausoleum, using stone from it. The Knights withdrew to Malta in 1523.

The castle has a curtain wall and the great Towers of France and Italy. Heraldic arms are carved on the towers. The entrance is through a series of seven gates.

Bohemond (c. 1050–1111) (Bohemond I de Tankerville) prince of Antioch from 1098 and Italian-Norman leader of the First Crusade. He was an opportunist and great tactician, winning lands in the east, but he was a poor strategist and was outmanoeuvred by the Byzantine emperor ◊Alexius (I) Comnenus.

Son of the Norman knight ◊Robert Guiscard, Bohemond was named after a legendary giant. He supported his father's campaigns against Alexius (I) Comnenus at Durrazzo (now Dures, Albania) and northern Greece. Bohemond seized the opportunity of the First Crusade to win lands in the east, proving himself a commander of genius at

Dorylaeum (see ◊Dorylaeum, Battle of) and several battles around the siege of Antioch (see ◊Antioch, Battle of 1098). His final campaigns were under the banner of the crusade against the Byzantine Empire 1106–07. Again his siege of Durazzo failed 1109–11, and Alexius' navy destroyed his fleet.

bohort (from German, 'to push, shove') medieval European joust (see ◊tournament) in which no weapons were used, a kind of barging match on horseback. Punching with shields and wrestling was allowed. Later, in Old French, *bouhorder* meant to joust with blunted lances, safeguarding the rider and horse from serious injury.

bokuto imitation Japanese sword, usually wooden, carried by those, such as doctors, who were not of the ◊samurai class and therefore not permitted to carry a real sword.

They often gave the appearance of a real weapon and could occasionally be drawn like a real sword, but had a wooden blade and contained writing equipment in the hilt. Others were carved from solid pieces of wood into fanciful shapes such as dragons; these were in fact useful weapons as a form of cudgel.

Bolang, Battle of (or *Po-lang*) battle in September 207 at Mount Bolang in China in which ◊Cao Cao defeated two sons of ◊Yuan Shao. This battle confirmed Cao's control of north China won at Guandu (see ◊Guandu, Battle of).

Shao's sons had taken refuge with the Wuhuan nomads in northeast China. Cao led a lightly-equipped force to surprise them, marching through a narrow pass to attack the Wuhuan camping grounds from the west. The armies met as Cao climbed Mount Bolang. He was outnumbered but charged suddenly at the badly-deployed Wuhuan. They were broken and their chief killed. The Yuan brothers took refuge with another warlord, who beheaded them.

bolt (or *quarrel*) in medieval warfare, a ◊crossbow missile. The early medieval bolt was often made of ash or yew, about 3 m/1 ft long with a tapered and flattened butt. It was lightweight, perhaps less than 84 g/3 oz. The head, or pile, of the bolt was usually four-sided and pyramidal, and made of metal. It was similar to an arrow and had a flight, commonly made of goose wing feathers.

One type of bolt, known as a 'vireton', was made with a spiral flight so it would rotate in flight, improving its accuracy.

Bolton castle castle in Yorkshire, England, 18 km/11 mi southwest of Richmond. Richard le Scrope, Lord Chancellor of England, was granted a licence in 1379 to build it to defend Wensleydale. As befitted its austere surroundings, the castle was a simple rectangle with a large square tower at each corner.

bombard early medieval cannon that normally fired stone balls. It was short with a large bore and could be raised to a considerable elevation, but had a short range. Because bombards were heavy, difficult to move, and vulnerable to enemy fire, their use was generally restricted to sieges.

The Crécy bombard, found in the moat of Bodiam castle in Sussex, England, has a cast-iron interior with iron hoops shrunk upon the inner core. The chamber holds about 1.36 kg/3 lb of powder and it could fire a shot of 37.5 cm/15 in diameter.

Bonaguil castle stronghold on a rocky promontory west of Cahors, Lot-et-Garonne, France, built in the 13th century by the de la Tour family. It has strong, round corner towers and a wall up to 5 m/15 ft feet thick. The keep is pentagonal and makes a spur to the north. In the 15th century the Roquefeuil family modified it with outer works specifically designed for artillery.

These works include towers with cannon loops for firing from a low level, a purpose-built buttressed artillery terrace, and impressive ◊machicolation.

Boniface (died 432) (Bonifatius) Roman count of Africa, the main rival of ◊Aetius. He failed in his defence of Roman Africa against the Vandals 429–31 and was mortally wounded at Ravenna (see ◊Ravenna, Battle of 432) when he attempted to wrest power from Aetius.

Boniface of Montferrat (died 1207) king of Thessalonika, Greece. An Italian noble, Boniface was encouraged by his cousin Philip (II) Augustus of France to command the Fourth Crusade against the Byzantines. Although he successfully captured Constantinople, his fellow crusaders preferred ◊Baldwin of Flanders as Latin emperor. Boniface married Margaret, daughter of Béla II of Hungary, and became king of Thessalonika.

He was ambushed without armour by the Bulgars in the Rhodope mountains in Bulgaria in 1207; a wound in the arm proved fatal.

Borleng, Odo (lived 12th century) captain of ◊Henry I of England's household troops in the 1120s. He led the king's army that defeated the rebellion by Waleran of Meulan at Bourgthéroulde (see ◊Bourgthéroulde, Battle of) in 1124. Waleran was captured and imprisoned.

Before the battle (according to Norman historian Orderic Vitalis) Odo explained the tactic of dismounting knights to fight on foot against the rebels, which included placing crossbowmen at the front to wound the charging horses of the enemy.

Boromoraja I (died 1388) Thai king of Ayutthaya from 1370. He was the brother-in-law of ◊Rama Tibodi I, whose son Ramesuen he deposed in 1370 after a few months' reign. He defeated the Sukhothai kingdom and annexed its western districts, but intervened unsuccessfully in a succession dispute in the northern Thai kingdom of Chiengmai. He was succeeded by his 15-year-old son Tonglan, who after seven days was deposed by Ramesuen's return to the throne.

He defeated the older Sukhothai kingdom in the war of 1371–78, enslaving the prisoners taken in captured towns. In 1376 at Kamphaeng Phet an allied force from Sukhothai and Chiengmai attempted to ambush him, but was defeated. In 1378 Boromoraja began a second siege of Kamphaeng Phet, but this time King Tammaraja (Mahadharmaraja) II of Sukhothai agreed to peace terms. Boromoraja annexed western districts of Sukhothai, including Kamphaeng Phet, and Tammaraja became his vassal. He was defeated in 1387 at Sen Sanuk near Chiengmai in a battle noted for the exploits of the heavily pregnant Chiengmai princess Nang Muang, who fought on elephant-back dressed as a man. Chiengmai forces then attacked Kamphaeng Phet. Boromoraja drove them off but died on the way home.

Boromoraja II (died 1448) Thai king of Ayutthaya from 1424, the youngest of three sons of ◊Intharaja I. The two elder sons waged a war of succession; in a duel on elephant-back both were killed, so Boromoraja succeeded. During his reign he briefly conquered Cambodia, extinguished the Thai kingdom of Sukhothai, and invaded Chiengmai. He died in an attack against Chiengmai in 1448 and was succeeded by his son Ramesuen, who took the title ◊Boromo Trailokanat.

In 1431 Boromoraja attacked Cambodia, took the Khmer capital Angkor, and briefly imposed his son Intaburi as king. Intaburi soon died, however, and Boromoraja could not prevent the Khmers from reasserting their independence. In 1438 Boromoraja finally extinguished Sukhothai, a vassal of Ayutthaya since its defeat by ◊Boromoraja I. In 1442 he intervened in a succession dispute in the northern Thai kingdom of Chiengmai. He took much of the population captive, deporting them to Ayutthaya, but the candidate he was

backing had been killed before the Ayutthayan army arrived. Chiengmai spies infiltrated Boromoraja's army, stampeding his elephants to coincide with an ambush by the Chiengmai army. Boromoraja abandoned the expedition. In 1446 he sent an army over land right down the Malay peninsula to attack Malacca, but without success.

Boromo Trailokanat (lived 15th century) (or *Trailok*) Thai king of Ayutthaya, 1448–88. As Prince Ramesuen, he was a provincial governor under his father, ◊Boromoraja II. As king he created a centralized administration, with a separate military administration under the *kalahom*, divided into ministries. He spent much of his reign at war against the northern Thai kingdom of Chiengmai.

Trailokanat fought an indecisive war against Chiengmai 1452–56. In 1456 he sent a naval expedition against Malacca, but it was defeated by the Malaccan *bendahara* (chief minister), Tun Perak. In 1461 Chiengmai invaded Ayutthaya and was only forced to withdraw by a Ming Chinese invasion from Yunnan.

Trailokanat moved his capital north to P'itsanulok in 1463 to be closer to the front, and defeated another Chiengmai invasion. He counterattacked far into Chiengmai territory, but was driven into a swamp and defeated at Doi Ba, in a battle fought by moonlight. After ten years' peace Trailokanat invaded Chiengmai again in 1474, forcing Sri Sutham Tilok of Chiengmai to sue for peace. Trailokanat was succeeded by his son Boromoraja III, who restored Ayutthaya as the capital.

Boroughbridge, Battle of battle fought on 16 March 1322 between Sir Andrew de Harclay (for King Edward II of England) and the Earl of Lancaster, in present-day North Yorkshire, England. De Harclay defeated Lancaster's rebel forces as they attempted to cross the river Ure.

De Harclay's Border troops, a mixture of ◊schiltrons of Cumbrian pikemen and archers giving support, held the crossing of the river. Lancaster attacked with mounted and dismounted men-at-arms but was unable to force the position in the face of fierce archery.

Borthwick castle castle in Scotland, 16 km/10 mi southeast of Edinburgh. Built in around 1430, it was one of the most imposing tower-houses of Scotland. Rectangular, 30 m/100 ft high, and with two wings projecting from one of the longer sides, the great tower has a hall, kitchen, and solar (private chamber) on the ground floor and living accommodation above connected by spiral staircases. A curtain wall later enclosed it, with a large circular tower protecting the entrance gate.

Bosworth, Battle of battle fought on 22 August 1485, during the English Wars of the Roses (see ◊Roses, Wars of the), in which Henry Tudor (the future Henry VII) defeated and killed the Yorkist king ◊Richard III despite having fewer men, due to intelligent manoeuvre and the defection of Lord Stanley.

Henry Tudor inherited the Lancastrian claim and invaded England through Wales, landing at Milford Haven on 7 August. Richard had 11–12,000 men and a strong position on Ambion Hill. Henry had 5–7,000 troops, but the Stanley brothers commanded 5,000 and 3,000 men to the north and south of the royalists, respectively.

Accounts of the battle are unclear, but it is possible that the Lancastrian Earl of Oxford was able to swing around the right flank of the royal army. This enabled a better concentration of force, left Northumberland unengaged on the royalist left, and brought Henry closer to Lord Stanley. After some fierce fighting, Richard saw Henry's banner moving northwards. Richard charged with his cavalry and almost cut his way through to Henry before he was killed as the Stanley troops joined the fray.

Boucicault, Jean le Maingre (lived 14th–15th centuries) marshal of France 1361–1421. Although a model chivalric warrior and subject of the *Book of His Deeds*, he lost major battles at Nicopolis (see ◊Nicopolis, Battle of) and Agincourt (see ◊Agincourt, Battle of) and died in English captivity.

Boucicault is remembered for his chivalry, including the foundation of a knightly order of the 'White Lady with the Green Shield'. He was also a consummate athlete and a great warrior, capable of somersaults in full armour. He was captured on the Burgundian crusade at Nicopolis by Sultan Bayezid, having fought bravely but unwisely. He was ransomed and led the French vanguard on the Agincourt campaign. Boucicault advised a Fabian (cautious) strategy, avoiding battle, and devised tactics to counter the English bowmen by outflanking them. He was not allowed to put either plan into operation and fought in the front rank, where he was captured.

Boudiccan Revolt revolt in AD 61 by the Iceni and other native tribes against Roman rule in southern Britain. Led by Boudicca (Boadicea), queen of the Iceni of modern East Anglia, the rebels sacked Camulodunum (Colchester), Londinium (London), and Verulamium (St Albans) before meeting the Roman governor Suetonius ◊Paulinus in a pitched battle at a site now unknown. The Roman victory was swift and decisive.

The revolt was sparked off by the harsh treatment of the Iceni following the death of the client king Prasutagus and the incorporation of the kingdom into the Roman province. Underlying corruption and mistreatment by Roman administrators and veterans led other tribes, including the Trinovantes, to join in.

In the battle to suppress the revolt the Romans deployed in a narrow defile to prevent outflanking manoeuvres, with infantry in the centre and cavalry on the wings. British casualties were high because those fleeing the battlefield were trapped by the family wagons set up at the rear of their force to watch the battle.

boulevard (or *bulwark*) early medieval addition to town or castle defences, in the form of a projecting fortification, otherwise known as a barbican or bastion. Boulevards were low, usually semicircular defences, often built before the main gate and made of earth, stone, or wood. They were widened in the later medieval period to accommodate cannons.

Bourgthéroulde, Battle of battle fought in 1124 in Normandy, in which ◊Henry I, King of England and Duke of Normandy, gained a victory over Norman rebels led by Waleran, Count of Meulan. The victory helped to establish the king's authority firmly in the duchy.

Henry was not present in person at the battle, but a royal army led by Odo ◊Borleng, William de Tancarville, and Ralph de Bayeux fought the rebels. The royalist force dismounted some knights to fight as infantry and also used archers, who halted the rebel charge. Waleran was captured, though Henry later released him.

Bouvines, Battle of battle fought in 1214 near Bouvines, Flanders, between an imperialist coalition and ◊Philip (II) Augustus of France. The Holy Roman Emperor ◊Otto IV led the coalition forces in the north and King John of England (1167–1216) led those in the south. The French victory had repercussions throughout Europe: Otto lost his throne, the barons in England rebelled against John, and Flanders came under French control.

Philip was forced to fight the northern allied army near Bouvines when crossing the river Marq. He did not expect Otto to fight on Sunday but was proved wrong. Philip was unhorsed, but saved by his armour; Otto fled.

Bovet, Honoré (c. 1340–c. 1405) French priest and writer on morality and conduct of warfare. His book *Tree of Battles* helped to define chivalric loyalties and proper behaviour during the ◊Hundred Years' War.

bow hand weapon used for shooting arrows, known from prehistoric times and used in most parts of the world. In its simplest form it consisted of a wooden stave with a string attached to both ends. Pulling the string bent the stave; releasing the string then shot the arrow as the stave straightened. There were various types of bows, including ordinary wooden bows, shortbows, ◊crossbows, composite bows, springbows, and longbows.

The *shortbow* was a composite bow, with the stave in three pieces fixed together with glue, sinew, and horn. It was the common weapon for the nomadic horse warrior. The *crossbow* was mechanical with a release mechanism and a trigger. The *springbow* was probably a kind of crossbow. The *longbow* was a longer form of the ordinary wooden bow with a length somewhere between 1.5 m/5 ft and 1.8 m/6 ft. It was usually made of yew with hemp for string.

bow, classical Indian the standard infantry bow, used by Hindu armies from as early as the 10th century BC until the Muslim conquest at the end of the 12th century AD, was a powerful weapon up to 2 m/6.5 ft long, made of bamboo, and shooting iron-tipped cane arrows. The more convenient composite or horn bow, about 1.4 m/4.5 ft long, was preferred by those fighting on horseback or from elephants.

The prescribed method of use of the infantry bow was for the archer to rest one end of the bow on the ground and steady it between his toes, but early images show it also being used in the more conventional manner.

The bow was regarded as a weapon fit for the hands of princes, and there are many references to its use in battle by the heroes of ancient Indian mythology. The *Dhanur-veda* (Sanskrit 'archery-hymn'), a standard Hindu text on all aspects of warfare, derives its name from the perception of the bow as the most important weapon in war.

bow, composite type of bow, used by charioteers, that was the most important weapon of the late Bronze Age. It was designed with multiple parts made from different types of wood and bone glued together to provide extra tension, the bow being bent back on itself in use. This gave it an effective range of 200 m/220 yds, with an absolute range double that distance.

By comparison, the self bow, made from a single piece of shaped wood, was limited in range and penetrating power, having an effective distance of only 60 m/65 yds.

◊Amunhotep II, and other pharaohs, practised shooting with a composite bow from a moving chariot at copper 'oxhide' ingots.

bow-land Achaemenid Persian military tenure. The term usually refers to military colonists in Babylonia who held bow-land (Aramaic *bît qasti*) in return for infantry service, horse-land (*bît sisi*) for cavalry service, or chariot-land (*bît narkabti*) for chariot service. Many such fief holders would hire substitutes rather than fight.

In Persia the soldiers of the ◊*kara* served in exchange for bow-land.

boyar medieval Russian term referring to a nobleman. In military terms this meant a cavalryman with full equipment, armour, a lance, and bow, as opposed to the skirmishing horse-archers also employed by the tsars.

bracer in archery, a leather guard strapped onto the lower part of the archer's arm at the wrist. The bowstring, after shooting, snaps back with force; the bracer protects the inside wrist of the arm that holds the bow.

The term was also used in the medieval period to refer to a piece of metal armour that protected the lower part of the arm. It eventually became the term for the whole armour for the arm, including the shoulder. By the 14th century the individual parts were named separately as the vambrace, rerebrace, couter, spaudler, and pauldron.

Brasidas (died 422 BC) Spartan general at the time of the ◊Peloponnesian War, chiefly remembered for his campaign in Thrace between 424 and 422.

He saved Methone from the Athenians in 431, was twice adviser to Spartan admirals in 429 and 427, and was wounded commanding a trireme at Pylos in 425. While collecting troops for his Thracian campaign, he helped prevent the defection of Megara.

After marching to Thrace, he joined ◊Perdiccas of Macedon in an abortive campaign against Lyncestis, and then proceeded to win over many of Athens' allies in the area, including the strategically important Amphipolis. Following another abortive campaign with Perdiccas, he retreated when deserted by his ally. He was mortally wounded in a battle outside Amphipolis.

brattice (or *bretèche*) (from Old French *bretesque*) in medieval fortifications, a breastwork, parapet, or gallery made of wood. The term has been used to refer to the central wooden tower of a motte-and-bailey castle, or wooden fortifications at the gate. When a breach was made in the castle wall, a brattice could be built within to serve as a new temporary defence.

The term was also applied to the overhanging wooden hoardings that were built at the top of castle walls. They could be entered from the walls, and featured holes for dropping stones, hot oil, and missiles on the attackers. This was later the function of stone-built ◊machicolation.

Bréauté, Fawkes de (lived 13th century) mercenary for English kings in the early 13th century, the illegitimate son of a Norman knight.

He served King John against the barons, and then Henry III. He fought against the French at Lincoln (see ◊Lincoln, Battle of) in 1217. He gained many castles and the earldom of Devon, but when the earldom was claimed back, he rebelled. In 1224 Henry besieged Bedford castle, held by Fawkes's brother. Fawkes surrendered at Elstow, south of Bedford, and was exiled, forfeiting his lands.

Brémule, Battle of battle fought in 1119 on the plain of Brémule, Normandy, between ◊Henry I of England and Louis VI of France. The English victory halted a French invasion of Normandy.

Henry's nephew William Clito, son of Robert Curthose, the brother Henry had imprisoned since 1106, hoped to win Normandy and allied himself with Louis VI when the latter invaded Normandy. Some of the Anglo-Norman knights dismounted to fight on foot and stopped the French cavalry charge. Henry was wounded by a blow on the head, but was saved by his helmet. His sons led a cavalry charge that broke the French. Louis fled to safety at Les Andelys.

Brennus Gallic chieftain, probably of the Senones, who traditionally sacked Rome in 390 or 386 BC.

He failed to capture Clusium (modern Chiusi, Italy) and moved on to Rome, meeting the Roman army at the river Allia north of the city. His forces of about 70,000 overwhelmed the 40,000 that the Romans were able to muster and there was nothing to prevent him from then entering the city. By delaying his advance until late the next day he gave the Romans time to secure the Capitol, from which they held out for six months as his army had no experience with siege tactics. Tiring of the situation, he agreed to a Roman offer of a ransom of 1,000 pounds of gold and withdrew.

Brennus leader of the Galatian invasion of Greece in 279 BC. He penetrated as far as Delphi, but was unable to find anywhere for his tribe to settle and the migration ended in failure.

The Galatians (Gauls who were migrating eastwards) overran Macedonia in 279 BC and in the autumn Brennus led a column into Greece. A Greek coalition attempted to stop them at Thermopylae, but the secret route through the mountains was betrayed to Brennus and he led half his army to attack the Greeks from behind. The Greeks escaped by sea. Instead of reuniting his army, Brennus advanced into Greece and attacked Delphi. It was defended by only 4,000 men, but they thwarted the Galatian assault and Brennus was seriously wounded. He ordered a retreat north, but died en route.

Brian Boruma (c. 941–1014) king of Munster from 976 and high king of Ireland from 999. His campaigns represent the rise of Munster as a power in Ireland, symbolized by his victory over Leinster and the Dublin Norse at Glen Mama in 999. He was renowned as a builder of forts, and this may have been his most significant military legacy. He died in victory over the Vikings at Clontarf (see ◊Clontarf, Battle of).

Brian Boruma is an Irish national hero, celebrated as the conqueror of the Vikings, although Clontarf made very little difference to the Irish position in Ireland. *The War of the Irish against the Foreigners*, a piece of 12th-century dynastic propaganda, provides details of his campaigns 968–1014, which saw him emerge as high king.

Bride, the great ◊ballista in the siege-train led by Ja'wiyyah, commander of artillery in the Arab army with which Imad al-Din Muhammad bin Qasim conquered Sind in 711. It was worked by a detachment of 500 men, and at the siege of Debul succeeded in demolishing the city's tutelary shrine after only two ranging shots.

Bridgnorth castle castle in Shropshire, England, 19 km/12 mi southwest of Wolverhampton. Located on a ridge above the river Severn, it was built before 1102. The square tower keep dates from around 1170, after Henry II took the castle from supporters of King Stephen. There was also a bailey with a curtain wall.

brigandine plate armour made of small overlapping plates or bands of iron, steel, or leather riveted inside a tight-fitting coat of leather or heavy canvas, often covered in some finer material. It was used in western Europe from the 13th to 15th centuries and much longer in the east. Most commonly worn by soldiers on foot, it offered the advantages over heavier plate and mail of being both very flexible and relatively light.

broch in medieval Scotland, a type of tall, round, stone tower first employed by the Picts,

BRUTUS, MARCUS JUNIUS (C. 85–C. 42 BC)

Roman senator and general, chief conspirator with ◊Cassius in the assassination of Julius ◊Caesar.

Brutus supported Pompey in the civil war of 49–45 BC (see ◊Civil Wars, Roman Republican), but Caesar pardoned him after the Battle of Pharsalus and made him governor of Cisalpine Gaul in 46 BC. After Caesar's murder, he and Cassius raised an army to fight Mark Antony and Octavian, persuading most of the Macedonian forces to join them. Brutus suppressed a rebellion in Lycia, on the coast of southwest Asia Minor, using a mixture of force and moderation. Eventually Brutus and Cassius met Antony and Octavian at Philippi (see ◊Philippi, battles of). Brutus inflicted a sharp reverse on Octavian's soldiers in the first battle, but could not prevent the defeat and suicide of Cassius. He was defeated in the second battle and killed himself to avoid capture.

that continued to play a military role during the medieval period.

Brougham castle castle in England, just southeast of Penrith, Westmoreland (now Cumbria). Like its neighbour, ◊Brough castle, it was built on the remains of a Roman border fort. Begun in the mid-12th century, it had a wall with towers and a ditch and a large square keep built around 1275. It was used during the border wars of the 14th and 15th centuries.

Brough castle castle in England, 13 km/8 mi southeast of Appleby, Westmoreland (now Cumbria). Adapted by the Normans in the late 11th century from an earlier Roman fort by cutting off one corner with a ditch, this first castle was destroyed by the Scots in 1174. A new keep was built in 1180, after which the castle passed to the Clifford family, one of whom built the drum tower in 1300.

Broughton castle castle in England, 5 km/3 mi southwest of Banbury, Oxfordshire. It was originally an unfortified manor house, but its owner was given licence to crenellate (build battlements) in 1386, with a further licence in 1405. A moated bailey with an entrance via a barbican was built.

Bruce, Edward (died 1316) Scottish general and brother of ◊Robert (I) the Bruce, King of Scots.

Landing in Ireland in May 1315 as part of a Scottish diversionary operation, Edward was initially successful. In a series of devastating raids that undermined the authority of English rule, he also defeated Anglo-Irish forces at Connor in 1315 and Skerries in 1316. Supported by his brother in the autumn of 1316, Edward threatened Dublin, but Robert's withdrawal in December and the arrival of English reinforcements led to his defeat and death.

Brunanburh, Battle of engagement in 937 between the English and the Scots that confirmed ◊Athelstan's position as king of the English. The site of the battle has never been identified, although a location on the Scottish border, in Scotland, or in Yorkshire is possible, the last the most likely.

Athelstan's hold on Northumbria was uncertain and disputed by the Scots. In 937 the Scots, with allies from Ireland, Wales, Scandinavia, and Strathclyde, invaded England and defeated a force under the Earl of Northumbria. The English under Athelstan withstood attacks and then counterattacked, their troops pursuing the enemy on horseback. Five kings, seven earls, and a Scottish prince were killed on the allied side.

bucellarii late Roman/Germanic/Byzantine term for the private armies that followed many commanders in the 5th–6th centuries. They owed their allegiance to the commander personally rather than to any central authority. By the 7th century, after the reforms of the Eastern Roman emperor ◊Maurice, the *bucellarii* had become a regular unit in the Byzantine army.

Buch, the Captal de (died 1376) (Jean III de Grailly) Gascon mercenary captain. He played an important part for England in the ◊Hundred Years' War, fighting for ◊Edward the Black Prince at Poitiers in 1356 (see ◊Poitiers, Battle of 1356), where he led a vital surprise attack. He was rewarded with the Order of the Garter and made Constable of Aquitaine. He was captured at the Battle of Soubise in 1376, dying in captivity.

His other contributions to the war included the command of an army for Charles of

Navarre, but he was defeated by Bertrand du ◊Guesclin at the Battle of Cocherel in 1364. He commanded the right wing for the Black Prince's victory in Castile at the Battle of Navarette in 1367.

Büchsenmeister late medieval German term for a master artilleryman, the person responsible for the management of explosive devices, especially during a siege.

buckler small round shield used in Europe, Persia, and India from the 13th to 17th centuries. In the West it was most commonly used for fencing. Designed to be used with an outstretched arm, it was light and had a central grip.

Bueil, Jean de (c. 1410–70) marshal of France, field commander, and military theorist who analysed trends in 15th-century warfare. His use of artillery at Castillon (see ◊Castillon, Battle of) ended English rule in Gascony. His treatise *Le Jouvencel*, published in around 1466, was set out as a chivalric manual, but was also a valuable pragmatic guide to warfare as a tool of the ruler, anticipating Machiavelli by a generation.

His advice on strategy and the tactics of both battle and siege shows an awareness of changing warfare, as does his advice on creating units and uniforms for the French royal army.

Buhen large, rectangular, defensive fortification built on the west bank of the river Nile (in present-day Sudan), near the Second Cataract, during the Middle Kingdom of Egypt as the Egyptian garrison headquarters for controlling Nubia. It was surrounded by a dry moat and outer and inner turreted defensive walls, with a glacis (slope) in between, and enclosed an area of 14.5 ha/6 acres.

The outer wall, 700 m/766 yds long, was up to 4 m/13 ft thick. The inner wall was 5 m/16 ft thick and stood up to 11 m/26 ft in height. A fortified gateway, 47 × 30 m/51 × 33 yds, faced to the land in the middle of the northwestern wall, and two gateways led out of the southeastern wall onto the fortified quay.

In the New Kingdom, Buhen was the headquarters of all the forts to the south as far as Semna, 70 km/44 mi upriver.

buih sukri (Burmese 'headmen of the troops') commanders of the four arms of the Burmese army – cavalry, infantry, elephants, and the fleet – in the kingdom of Pagan (10th–13th centuries).

The *buih sukri* reported to the *mahasenapati* or commander in chief. Beneath each *buih sukri* were three grades of officer. In the cavalry, these were the *mran mhu, mran ciy,* and *mran kon*: roughly, colonels, captains, and sergeants.

Command structures in the other arms are not fully known but were similar.

buke the military houses of Japan; the warrior class, as opposed to the aristocracy (*kuge*).

bukehō term for the rules, regulations, and laws applied to the Japanese warrior class (*buke*) from the 12th century until the abolition of the ◊samurai class in the late 19th century. These laws were based on the feudalistic customs originating within the military family hierarchies, and were first codified by the ◊Kamakura shogunate in 1232.

buke seiji another name for the Japanese ◊Warrior Government, under the leadership of a shogun.

Bulgar-Byzantine War long, hard campaign fought 811–17 by the Byzantines against the Bulgars. It ended when the Byzantine emperor Leo V defeated the Bulgars at the Battle of Mesembria and forced them to agree to a 30-year peace.

In 811 the Byzantine emperor Nicephorus I personally led an army to capture and sack the Bulgar capital of Pliska, but in the pursuit of the survivors that followed he was ambushed in a mountain pass and killed. The Bulgars then gained the upper hand, defeating the new emperor Michael I at Versinikia, capturing Adrianople, and reaching the walls of Constantinople. Michael was overthrown and it was his successor, Leo V, who finally defeated the Bulgars.

Bureau, Jean (lived 15th century) medieval French artillery master. Jean and his brother Gaspard transformed the artillery of ◊Charles VII of France, and played an important part in the French successes of the later phases of the ◊Hundred Years' War.

He first served the English as master of artillery. His cannons were responsible for victory in 60 sieges 1449–50. He was successful in improving the range and strength of cannons. The first shot of his new cannon against the town of Harfleur, Normandy, in 1449 went through the rampart. In 1451 he became mayor of Bordeaux. His advice was instrumental in the French victory at Castillon in 1453 (see ◊Castillon, Battle of).

Burg fort late Roman fort at Stein am Rhein (Roman Tasgaetium), in present-day Switzerland, built to protect the southern bank of the river Hochrhein on the Raetian frontier. It was constructed by the emperor Diocletian (reigned 245–313).

The fort was built in the shape of a rhomboid 91× 88 m/298 ×288 ft. The walls enclosed an area of 0.8 ha / 1.98 acres and vary in width between 3.1 m / 10.2 ft thick on the southern landward side and 1.75 m / 5.75 ft on the northern river side. Round towers strengthened each corner and the west, south, and east sides each had two semicircular interval towers projecting 4 m / 13 ft beyond the wall. The fort gate was located on the south side, protected by twin flanking towers. The walls were later raised in height, perhaps by Valentinian I.

Burghal Hideage early 10th-century document which lists the ◊burhs of the English kingdom. It describes in great detail the locations, extent, and number of men required for the upkeep of these large, communal fortifications constructed by ◊Alfred the Great and his successors against the Vikings. It is not certain whether its instructions were still in force by 1066, at the time of the Norman Conquest.

Burgh Castle fort late 3rd-century Roman fort built to protect the coast of Norfolk, England, as part of the Saxon Shore defence system in Britain. It was constructed in the shape of a quadrilateral and also guarded the large estuary of the Yare and Wensum rivers.

The defences originally consisted of a 3-m- / 10-ft-thick free-standing wall, but the plan was soon altered to add massive solid external buttresses to the corners and the curtain wall. The walls survive on three sides to a height of 6 m / 20 ft.

burh Anglo-Saxon fortified stronghold combining urban and military functions. Burhs protected the local population and offered refuge, mainly against Viking or Danish attack. They were begun by ◊Alfred the Great, probably in imitation of Frankish examples, as a national defensive system against the Vikings, and were developed by his successors.

By the 890s there were over 30 burhs throughout Wessex, no more than 32 km / 20 mi apart. Several were double forts, guarding both sides of a river.

Burwell castle castle in Cambridgeshire, England, built by King Stephen against Geoffrey of Mandeville's 1143 rebellion. It had a rectangular stone curtain wall round an earth platform, a stone gatehouse, and possibly a keep. A wide ditch was dug for a moat but never filled. Geoffrey attacked Burwell in September 1144, was wounded by a crossbowman, and died a week later; the castle was abandoned.

bushi Japanese term meaning 'military gentry', applied to the ◊samurai.

bushidan term applied to the independent groupings of Japanese warriors with ties based on kinship that began to develop in Japan during the 10th century. The origins of the ◊samurai class are to be found in the *bushidan*.

These warrior groups tended to be maintained only for the duration of a particular military campaign, returning afterwards to their farming activities. They later developed into groupings with loyalties based less on kinship than on regional allegiances. This gave rise to the system of feudal *daimyo* with independent powers and effectively private armies which assembled during times of national political instability.

bushidō (Japanese 'the way of the warrior') term describing the ethos and spirit of the Japanese ◊samurai. The concept combines the Confucian principles of absolute loyalty to one's master, even above that to one's family, with the martial skills of weaponry and the willingness and ability to lay down one's life in battle or sacrifice as a matter of honour or principle in the name of one's lord or master.

Although the concept became codified in the late 16th century, it evolved naturally from the close family and kinship ties in the Japanese provinces and the warrior ethic which led to the founding of the first ◊Warrior Government of Japan towards the end of the 12th century.

buss medieval European fishing boat adapted as a horse transport (see also ◊tarida).

In 1190 ◊Richard (I) the Lionheart of England took 14 busses with him on crusade. Each carried 40 horses, 40 knights and squires, and 40 foot soldiers.

butsecarl (or *boatcarl*) rarely used Anglo-Scandinavian term describing the naval equivalent of the ◊housecarl, probably hired sailors with some standing and experience who owned boats, possibly soldiers used at sea. The term is only found in sources after 1066.

William the Conqueror used butsecarls to attack Ely in 1070–71 (see ◊Ely, Siege of), and in 1100 ◊Henry I of England 'ordered his butsecarls to guard the sea and watch in case any force from Normandy should reach the shores of England'.

Buyur Nor, Battle of battle in May 1388 in which the Ming Chinese defeated the Mongols at Buyur Nor in Mongolia.

After their defeat at Karakorum (see ◊Karakorum, Battle of), Ming armies raided Mongolia rather than attempting conquest. Lan Yu crossed the Gobi desert with 150,000 men to capture the Mongol khan Toghus

Temür. By forced marches he surprised the Mongols at Buyur Nor (Lake Buyur), trapped them against the lake and defeated them, capturing one of the khan's sons.

Toghus Temür himself was murdered soon after by one of his own followers. The Chinese captured 70,000 people and 150,000 head of livestock.

Byrhtnoth (died 991) English ◊ealdorman of Essex under Ethelred II who resisted the Danish invasion of eastern England.

He led the English at Maldon (see ◊Maldon, Battle of) in 991. The battle was recorded in a famous poem, in which Byrhtnoth, on horseback, encouraged brave conduct. He refused to pay the Danes tribute, and his overconfidence allowed the enemy to cross the narrow causeway from Northey Island to the mainland, where the battle was fought; he died in the battle, which the Danes won.

byrnie (or **brunia**) Anglo-Saxon term for the ◊hauberk or mail shirt.

Byrsa hill in the north African city of Carthage; it is the traditional site of the foundation of the city, which was later fortified as a citadel. The Carthaginians made their last stand against the Romans here in 147 BC (see ◊Punic War, Third).

The citadel included a temple precinct of Eshmun, and was large enough to serve as a refuge for 50,000 people during the final siege of Carthage. It was defended by 900 Roman deserters under the command of ◊Hasdrubal Barca. Though Hasdrubal surrendered, his family and all the defenders committed suicide in a fire they started in the temple.

caballaro villano medieval Spanish 'peasant knight' lightly equipped Spanish horseman, recruited from their lands and towns by Christian rulers in need of manpower for the ◊*Reconquista*. Caballaros villanos were widely employed in the raiding-style border warfare epitomized by ◊El Cid.

Caecus, Appius Claudius Roman politician, the most famous member of the Appii Caludii, one of the great patrician families of the Republic. Nicknamed Caecus ('the Blind') in old age, his loss of eyesight did not prevent him from winning undying fame by dissuading the Senate from negotiating with Pyrrhus after his victory at Heraclea (see ◊Heraclea, Battle of) in 280 BC.

Caen castle citadel castle on the river Orne, Calvados, Normandy, overlooking the town. It was built by ◊William (I) the Conqueror about 1047. Henry I of England built a keep which was destroyed during the French Revolution (1789–99). The remaining walls date from the 12th century, and the Exchequer Hall dates from about 1100. Philip (II) Augustus of France captured Caen while conquering Normandy in 1204; the castle finally fell to France in 1450.

Caen, Siege of (1346) attack on 26 July 1346 on the town of Caen in northern France by ◊Edward III of England at the beginning of the Crécy campaign and the start of the ◊Hundred Years' War. The French defenders were massacred.

Edward landed in the Cotentin peninsula in western Normandy. Caen was garrisoned by about 1,000 French troops, including Genoese crossbowmen. The city was strongly fortified, including a large castle, but the citizens of the undefended suburb of St Jean demanded protection. As a result the French were spread too thinly and the English soldiers, eager for booty, rushed the west gate.

Caen, Siege of (1450) one of the final conflicts of the ◊Hundred Years' War between the French and English. The recovery of the town of Caen in northern France was a vital stage in the French reconquest of Normandy from England.

The Duke of Somerset had retired to Caen after the loss of Rouen, as the French advanced through Normandy. The French besieged Caen in June 1450. The efficiency of the ◊Bureau brothers' cannons was apparent during three weeks of bombardment: one cannonball crashed into the room where Somerset's wife and children were sheltering. They were unharmed, but he surrendered on terms.

Caer Caradoc, Battle of popular name for the battle between ◊Caratacus and Ostorius ◊Scapula in AD 50, possibly fought in central Wales. After reconnaissance, Scapula allowed his soldiers to attack in a direct assault. His legionaries and auxiliaries faced no serious difficulties, but Caratacus escaped after being defeated.

Caerlaverock castle castle in Scotland, on the north shore of the Solway Firth, near the mouth of the river Nith. Built 1290–91, for 400 years it was the seat of the Maxwells, earls of Nithsdale. Triangular in plan, it is surrounded by an inner moat, earth ramparts, and an outer moat, with a powerful twin-towered gatehouse facing north.

It was captured by Edward I of England in 1300 and held until 1312, then much strengthened in the 15th century.

Caerleon fortress Roman legionary fortress on the bank of the river Usk at Caerleon (Roman Isca), southeast Wales, that guarded southern Wales from the late 1st to late 3rd centuries AD, providing the home for the 2nd Legion (*Legio II Augusta*). It was founded in AD 75 and was constructed in typical 'playing card' shape (rectangular with rounded corners).

Facilities for the soldiers included a large bathhouse built within the fortress and an amphitheatre outside. Though it was designed to house the 5,500 soldiers and officers of the legion, most were often serving on the distant frontier in northern England. By the late 3rd century the legion was finally moved from Caerleon and the site was abandoned.

Caernarvon castle (Welsh *Caernarfon*) castle in Wales, at the southwestern end of the Menai Strait.

Caernarvon was first fortified by Hugh Lupus, Earl of Chester, who built a wooden castle here at the end of the 11th century. By 1115 he had been driven out, when the country was recovered by the Welsh. The present castle was begun in 1283 by Edward I and was habitable by 1292. In 1294 a revolt led by Prince Madog burned the castle, and after settling the revolt Edward extended the defences 1295–1301.

More work was carried out 1304–05 and 1309–27, the principal constructor being James of St George. For many years it was a prison,

CAESAR, GAIUS JULIUS (100–44 BC)

Roman general and dictator, considered Rome's most successful military commander. He formed with ◊Pompey the Great and Marcus Licinius ◊Crassus (the Elder) the First Triumvirate in 60 BC. He conquered Gaul in 58–50 and invaded Britain in 55–54. By leading his army across the river Rubicon into Italy in 49, an act of treason, he provoked a civil war which ended in 45 with the defeat of Pompey and his supporters. He was voted dictator for life, but was assassinated by conspirators on 15 March 44 BC. Caesar was a skilled historian whose Commentarii, recounting his campaigns, has had a major impact on the way military history is written up to the present day.

Caesar's early career was conventional, in marked contrast with that of his later rival Pompey. He served as a military tribune in Asia, 80–78 BC where he received Rome's highest decoration, the *corona civica,* usually awarded for saving a fellow citizen's life. As governor of Further Spain (equivalent to modern Portugal and much of western, central, and southern Spain), he carried out some highly successful policing actions against the tribes of the area in 61–60 BC. His political alliance with Pompey and Crassus led to a consulship in 59, and in 58 he was given a five-year governorship, extended to ten years in 55, of the provinces of Illyria on the eastern shore of the Adriatic Sea and both Transalpine and Cisalpine Gaul (corresponding to present-day northern Italy, France, Belgium, part of Germany, and the southern Netherlands). During his tenure as governor, Caesar conquered Gallic territory up to the river Rhine, suffering only two reverses in this period: a detachment of 15 cohorts was annihilated in the winter of 54, and his attack on the Gallic fortress-town of Gergovia in 52 which ended in a costly failure. When his governorship ended in 49, Caesar was immensely wealthy and the leader of a highly efficient and fanatically loyal army. Pompey had become his rival after Crassus died at Carrhae in 53 (see ◊Carrhae, Battle of), and sided with factions in the Senate who wished to prosecute Caesar. Caesar led his army across the river Rubicon to meet Pompey's army in Italy, provoking a civil war that lasted until 45 BC. Caesar's brilliance as a general led to his great victories at Pharsalus (see ◊Pharsalus, Battle of) in 48, Thapsus (see ◊Thapsus, Battle of) in 46, and in 47 against King Pharnaces II (ruled 63–47 BC) in Asia Minor, a campaign he summarized succinctly as *veni, vidi, vici* (I came, I saw, I conquered'). His final victory, in 45, over the sons of Pompey at Munda in Spain, ended the war. However, Caesar failed to create a permanent peace and on 15 March 44 was stabbed to death at the foot of Pompey's statue in the Senate (see Marcus Junius ◊Brutus, ◊Cassius).

but in 1404 it was still strong enough to resist a siege by Owain ◊Glyndwr.

Caerphilly castle (Welsh *Caerffili*) castle in Wales, 16 km/10 mi north of Cardiff, built by Gilbert de Clare, Earl of Gloucester, in 1271. The second-largest castle in Europe, it had an immensely strong system of defence which, although besieged three times, was never overcome by an enemy.

Laid out to a concentric plan, it had a square inner ward with four towers and two combined keeps and gatehouses, surrounded by an outer ward with an eastern gatehouse leading over a bridge to a form of barbican. The outer ward was surrounded by a ditch that expanded to a flooded area to the north and south. This inundation was kept in place by the barrage or barbican structure that protected the entire eastern side of the castle and consisted of a double wall with towers. The western entrance led across a bridge to a hornwork, or advanced defensive position, that also acted as a barbican.

caetra buckler (small round shield) carried by Iberian warriors from about 300 BC to about 100 BC. This distinctive shield, about 30–45 cm/12–18 in across, was used by light troops, and provided the name – *caetrati* – for javelin troops who used it. Many representations exist in sculpture and painted vases.

Cahir castle castle in Ireland, 23 km/14 mi southeast of the town of Tipperary, Co. Tipperary. Building began in the 13th century on an island in the river Suir. The first construction was a roughly rectangular ward at the north end of the island, with three corner towers and a hall forming the fourth corner, and a two-towered gatehouse in the middle of the south wall.

In the 15th century this structure was converted into a great tower, and a curtain wall was placed around the southern half of the island to form a second ward or bailey. A barbican was also constructed to the west side of the northern ward. In the following century a wall was placed across the northern end of the southern ward so as to form a third ward between the north and south.

Caishi, Battle of (or *Ts'ai-shih*, 1161) battle in 1161 in which the Song Chinese defeated a Jurchen invasion led by ◊Wanyen Liang at Caishi on the river Yangtze.

Liang's army attempted to cross the lower Yangtze into southern China. The Song fleet under Yu Yunwen burned 300 of Liang's boats and seized a key island in the middle of the river. As Liang prepared for a further attack – ordering the execution of his naval officers if they could not cross within three days – his soldiers, hearing of rebellion at home, murdered him in his tent.

Caishi, Battle of (or *Ts'ai-shih*, 1356) battle in March 1356 during the Chinese civil wars in which ◊Zhu Yuanzhang defeated a Yuan river-fleet commanded by the Mongol admiral Manzi Khaya at Caishi on the river Yangtze.

Zhu was expanding from his base at Taiping on the south bank of the Yangtze. The victory enabled him to move on Nanjing.

Caister castle brick and limestone castle in England, 5 km/3 mi north of Great Yarmouth. It was built 1432–35 by Sir John Fastolf almost entirely of locally-made bricks. During the Wars of the Roses (1455–85) it was held by the Yorkist Paston family until it was besieged and taken by the Duke of Norfolk in 1429. The brickwork was considerably damaged by cannon fire.

It took the form of two quadrangles surrounded by water, with access between the inner and outer structures by drawbridge. The principal feature was the 27-m/90-ft-high circular brick tower keep of five stories. This castle is of particular interest because of the extensive records of its building which have survived.

Caizhou, Siege of (or *Ts'ai-chou*) fall of the last city held by Jin forces during the Mongol campaigns in China (see ◊China, Mongol campaigns in), to a combined force of Mongols under Tatsir and Song Chinese under Ming Tong, 1233–34.

After the fall of Kaifeng (see ◊Kaifeng, Siege of), the Jin emperor continued resistance in Caizhou, a small eastern provincial city. In autumn 1233 Mongol troops approached the city but were at first repulsed. Soon afterwards, 20,000 Song troops joined the siege, attacking across a lake which they drained in order to storm a key tower, while the Mongols attacked from land. When they breached the outer wall the Jin emperor tried to escape, but could not get out of the city. Early in 1234 the besiegers stormed the inner wall; the emperor hanged himself, and the city fell.

Calais, Siege of major siege during the conflict between ◊Edward III of England and Philip VI of France during the ◊Hundred Years' War. From 4 September 1346 to 3 September 1347, Edward besieged the strategically important French port of Calais and finally captured it. Calais remained in English hands for over two centuries as a bridgehead for the ambitions of the English kings in France.

Following his victory over the French at Crécy on 25 August, Edward moved directly to besiege Calais with a force of 10,000–12,000 troops. The English fleet blockaded the port but the first naval victory went to Philip's Genoese fleet, which captured all 25 of the first English supply ships on 17 September. Gradually the English gained the upper hand, with some 32,000 men serving during the course of the siege. Philip's relief attempts in October 1346 and May and July 1347 failed and the defenders were abandoned to their fate. They held on for 11 months, famously sending an embassy of six burghers to seek pity from Edward's queen.

Calatrava la Nueva castle in Spain, now called Calzada de Calatrava, 28 km/17 mi south of Cuidad Real.

Built 1213–16 after Las Navas de Tolosa (see ◊Las Navas de Tolosa, Battle of) in 1212, it became the fortress of the Order of Calatrava, an important ◊Military Order. It remained their headquarters until the suppression of the order in the 14th century. In the late 15th century the castle was then acquired by Ferdinand and Isabella, who commenced restoration. After their reign it fell into disuse.

Calatrava la Vieja castle in Spain, on the river Guadiana, 19 km/12 mi northeast of Cuidad Real. It was the original seat of the Order of Calatrava, an important ◊Military Order, and by the 10th century it had become a powerful stronghold on the route from Toledo to Cordoba.

The castle was taken by Alfonso VII in 1147 and given to the Knights Templar, who held it for ten years before being evicted by the Moors in 1158. King Sancho III then offered the castle to any warrior bold enough to take it. Two accepted the challenge, retook the castle and founded the Order of Calatrava. Early in the 13th century the castle was besieged for three years by the Moors and eventually surrendered. It was retaken in 1212, but it was so badly damaged that it was abandoned and the Order moved to ◊Calatrava la Nueva.

Calatrava, Order of order of Crusading knights: see ◊Military Order.

caliga tough military boot used by the Romans in the late republic and early empire (1st century BC–1st century AD). It was made of hide, with the upper cut into a series of V-shaped straps which were laced up the foot and ankle. The sole was made of several layers of hide studded with iron hod nails.

caliver European firearm, strictly a short musket used by cavalrymen, like the later 'car-bine'. The name dates from the latter part of the 16th century, but it is frequently encountered in translations of 15th-century texts to describe the handgun or ◊arquebus.

Callinicum, Battle of (296) battle fought in 296 between a Roman army under Galerius, the adopted son of the emperor ◊Diocletian, and a Persian army, at Callinicum (Sura) in western Persia. Galerius was defeated when he advanced against the far larger and more mobile Persian forces. He retreated to join Diocletian at Antioch, who treated him with contempt.

Callinicum, Battle of (531) inconclusive battle in 531 between the East Romans, under Belisarius, and the Persians commanded by Azarethes at Callinicum (Sura) in western Persia. Although the Persians gained the upper hand, they were unable to destroy their opponents, thanks to a firm stand by the Roman infantry, who held their position in the face of repeated cavalry charges.

caltrop metal object with spikes pointing upwards that was placed in a ditch to hamper attackers of a town or castle in medieval European warfare, or a globular metal object with projecting spikes that was used in battle. The latter type was fixed into the ground with one spike and projected upwards to halt the charging horses of enemy cavalry.

Calveley, Sir Hugh (c. 1320–94) English knight adventurer who fought in France and Spain. He became seneschal of Limousin in 1370, governor of Calais 1374–79, and governor of the Channel Islands in 1382. Still leading charges in his 60s, he typified the active military knights who served Edward III.

In 1347 Calveley served under Sir Thomas Dagworth in Brittany and fought in the famous mortal 'Combat of the Thirty' in 350, before engaging in guerrilla warfare. He accompanied ◊Edward the Black Prince to Spain, fighting at Najéra (see ◊Najéra, Battle of), then in the wars in Gascony. An active captain of Calais, he destroyed the French castles of Marke and Ardres. Returning to Brittany he saved the English siege of Nantes in 1380 with a sortie, and his experience rescued the 1383 Flanders expedition led by Thomas, Earl of Buckingham, from disaster.

Cambyses II (Persian *Kambujiya*) king of Persia 530–522 BC, the second Achaemenid king, son of ◊Cyrus (II) the Great. In 525 BC he led a campaign that resulted in the conquest of Egypt. An expedition against the Kushite kingdom of Nubia was a failure, and he died in Syria on the march home.

CANNAE, BATTLE OF

Battle fought in southern Italy in 216 BC between the Romans and Carthaginians, during the Second Punic War (see ◊Punic War, Second). The Carthaginian victory earned ◊Hannibal the Great immortality as a commander, while the Roman army suffered its heaviest defeat ever.

The Romans abandoned the cautious containment policy of Quintus ◊Fabius Maximus and decided to confront Hannibal in a decisive pitched battle. The Roman army of 80,000 men was under the command of the two consuls Gaius Terentius Varro and Aemilius ◊Paullus, and they gave battle on a narrow plain beside the river Orfanto, below the town of Cannae. The site was chosen because it had hills on the left and the river to the right, ensuring that the Carthaginian cavalry would be unable to outflank the Romans. The latter used their standard formation (see ◊velites, ◊hastati, ◊principes, and ◊triarii) with the allies on the flanks and the cavalry on the wings. Hannibal formed his light troops and pikemen into a front line and formed the Spanish and Celtic infantry behind them in an outward curve. His cavalry were also placed on the wings.

The light troops and cavalry opened the battle with a brief clash, after which both sides withdrew these troops. The Roman legion then charged and pushed back the Celts and Spaniards. However, the collapse of the Carthaginian curve was intended. As the Romans pushed forward they found that the pikemen had formed a phalanx on either side of the Carthaginian line and that they were penned in. Hannibal was then able to outflank them, and he sent his light troops around the pikemen to attack the Romans from behind. The Numidian cavalry returned and also attacked the Romans in the rear, completing the trap. Between 45,000 and 70,000 Romans were killed in the battle, including Paullus.

During his campaign of 525 BC the local Arabs helped him cross the desert beyond Gaza and he defeated Pharaoh Psammetichos III in battle, then captured Memphis. On his return journey to Persia an accidental leg wound became infected and killed him. ◊Darius (I) the Great won the ensuing succession struggle.

candidati (Latin 'the shining whites') soldiers who formed the inner bodyguard of the late Roman emperors. As their name suggests, it is probable that they wore white uniforms.

cannon (from the Greek *kanun*, Latin *canna* 'tube') large gun developed in the later medieval period, sometimes used in battle but most often in sieges. Cannons were known in western Europe by the 14th century. The earliest types were made with iron rods fitted around a core and bound with rings to form a tube. The later medieval period saw an increase in the efficiency, size, and impact of cannons. By the mid-15th century wrought iron was generally used.

Cannons were initially tied to a wooden board that could be tipped to provide elevation. Later they were attached to an adjustable wooden frame (trunnions were developed in the 15th century). The early weapons were loaded either by a mobile chamber with handles for lifting, or at the breech.

Canton Bay, Battle of the final action in the Mongol campaigns in China (see ◊China, Mongol campaigns in), ending on 19 March 1279. Song loyalists Zhang Shijie and Lu Xiufu, with the last Song child-emperor, fled by sea and were blockaded on Yaishan island in the bay of Canton (Guangzhou) by a superior Mongol fleet. They tried to break out but were defeated.

After the surrender of Linan, Song loyalists fled south to continue the struggle against ◊Khubilai Khan. The emperor's ship was sunk, and Lu took the child-emperor in his arms and leapt overboard rather than surrender. Zhang fled for southeast Asia with the 16 ships that did break out, but was killed in a hurricane.

Canukya alternative name of ◊Kautilya, chief minister of the Indian emperor ◊Chandragupta Maurya.

Canute see ◊Cnut the Great, king of England from 1016, Denmark from 1018, and Norway from 1028.

Cao Cao (AD 155–220) (or *Ts'ao Ts'ao*) Chinese general in the civil wars of the late Han dynasty. After defeating the Han warlord ◊Yuan Shao at Guandu in 200 (see ◊Guandu, Battle of) and his sons at Bolang in 207 (see ◊Bolang, Battle of), he gained control over all of northern China, but an attempt to conquer the south was defeated at the Red Cliff (see ◊Red Cliff, Battle of the), setting the boundaries for the ◊Three Kingdoms of China. In 216 he took the title 'King of Wei', and on his death his son deposed the last Han emperor.

cap à pied (French 'head to foot') term applied to a complete set of plate armour. The term is post-medieval, first appearing in English in the 16th century.

caparison covering for the horse of a medieval man-at-arms (heavily armed mounted soldier), usually made of padded cloth or leather and often decorated with the rider's coat of arms.

Cape Bon, Battle of naval battle in 468 between the Vandals and the East Romans at Cape Bon on the coast of modern Tunisia. The Vandals won a decisive victory, destroying more than half the Roman vessels by launching a surprise attack with fire ships while they were engaged in negotiations. The loss of their fleet forced the Romans to abandon a campaign to reconquer Africa.

Cape Ecnomus, Battle of see ◊Ecnomus, Battle of, sea battle fought in 256 BC between the Romans and Carthaginians.

capitano del populo medieval Italian term for the commander of a city militia. As the Italian cities freed themselves from higher authorities and became city-states, they required military commanders to conduct their campaigns. There was always a danger, however, that someone elected to the post might become a tyrant (see ◊*podestà*).

Capua, Siege of (212 BC) siege in 212 BC by the Roman army of the Carthaginian-allied city of Capua, central Italy, during the Second Punic War (see ◊Punic War, Second). The surprise arrival of ◊Hannibal the Great and a Carthaginian relief force compelled the Romans to withdraw before they had completed their siegeworks.

Capua had defected to Carthage in the aftermath of the Battle of Cannae in 216 BC (see ◊Cannae, Battle of). Capua was Italy's second city and dominated the Campania region, making Rome desperate to regain it. By a rapid march Hannibal led his army to the city and broke through the unprepared Roman lines. Battle was briefly joined, but the Romans chose to retreat in the successful ruse of convincing Hannibal that the threat to Capua had passed. After he had left to campaign in the south, they made a second, successful attempt to take the city (see ◊Capua, Siege of 212–211 BC).

Capua, Siege of (212–211 BC) second Roman siege, 212–211 BC, of the city of Capua (see also ◊Capua, Siege of 212 BC). When Hannibal came to relieve the city for the second time he had to engage in a pitched battle with the Romans. After this and a march on Rome had failed, Hannibal withdrew and the city surrendered.

Three Roman armies besieged the city, building a double circumvallation around it. Hannibal was campaigning in southern Italy at Tarentum at this time, and when he finally arrived at Capua almost half of Rome's legions in service in 211 BC, perhaps 50,000–60,000 men, were in the vicinity. After failing to dislodge the Romans, Hannibal withdrew to Bruttium. When Capua surrendered, much of its citizen population was sold into slavery and the city became the property of the Roman people.

Caractacus common spelling of ◊Caratatus, the British king.

Caradoc alternative, Celtic name of the British king ◊Caratacus.

Caratacus (died c. AD 54) (or *Caractacus*; Celtic *Caradoc*) British king who headed resistance to the Romans in southeast England and Wales AD 43–51, but was defeated on the Welsh border by Ostorius ◊Scapula. Shown in Claudius' triumphal procession in Rome, he was released in tribute to his courage and lived there in retirement.

After defeat by the Romans at the Medway (see ◊Medway, Battle of the), Caratacus organized resistance to the Romans amongst the tribes of south and central Wales. After his defeat in 51, he fled to the Brigantes but was handed over to the Romans by their pro-Roman queen Cartimandua.

Carausius, Marcus Aurelius Mausaeus Roman commander of the fleet based at Gesoriacum (present-day Boulogne, France) under ◊Maximian. Carausius cleared the English Channel of Saxon raiders, then declared himself an independent Augustus (emperor), controlling Britain and much of the coast of Gaul (France). In 293 he lost his territory in Gaul, including Gesoriacum, and was soon afterwards murdered by Allectus, one of his subordinates.

Carausius was involved in the construction or improvement of the line of forts around the coast of southern Britain, known as the Saxon Shore (see ◊Saxon Shore, forts of the).

caravel Iberian two- or three-masted lateen rigged ship dating from the 13th century but closely associated with the Spanish and Portuguese voyages of discovery of the 15th and 16th centuries. The galleon derived many of its characteristics from the caravel, but was square rigged.

Portuguese caravels were used to set up bases in north and west Africa in the late 15th century. In 1494 a squadron equipped by the Portuguese King John II mounted heavy guns to protect the Straits of Gibraltar. Large vessels carried some 30–40 pieces.

Carcassone walled town in France, on the river Aude 90 km / 56 mi southeast of Toulouse. The fortification consisted of two ramparts protected by 54 towers and pierced by two gates. A stronghold of the heretical Christian sect known as the Albigenses during the ◊Albigensian Crusades, it was sacked and burned by ◊Edward the Black Prince in 1355, during the ◊Hundred Years' War.

Carchemish (ancient *Kargamiš*) late Bronze Age–early Iron Age fortified city, situated on the west bank of the river Euphrates near Cerablus, Turkey. Its citadel stands on a 1,000-m-/1,094-yd-long ridge dominating a walled and banked inner town and a walled outer ward.

The last bastion of Mitannian resistance, it fell to the Hittite king Suppiluliumas I after an eight-day siege in 1327 BC. He installed his son Piyassilis (or Sharri-Kushuh) as appanage king to defend this border against Assyrian and Egyptian incursions. With the collapse of the Hittite Empire (about 1175 BC), the descendants of Piyassilis declared themselves great kings, gained control of Milid (or Malatya), and continued to resist Assyrian attacks, allying themselves with other Neo-Hittite states and Aramaean kingdoms until it was taken by ◊Ashurnasirpal II in 876 BC. Carchemish continued as a focus of resistance to Neo-Assyrian domination until its final subjugation under ◊Sargon II in 717 BC, after its king Pisiris had formed an alliance with ◊Mita of Muski. In 605 BC at Carchemish (see ◊Carchemish, Battle of) the Chaldeans under ◊Nebuchadnezzar took control of the Neo-Assyrian Empire.

Carchemish, Battle of final battle for the Neo-Assyrian Empire fought in 605 BC between the Egyptians and the Chaldeans of Babylonia and their allies the Medes. The Egyptians were finally defeated by the Babylonian leader ◊Nebuchadnezzar at Carchemish, allowing the Chaldeans to expand south into the Levant and the Medes west into Anatolia.

After ◊Cyaxares had successfully led the Medes against Ashur in 613 BC, Nabopolassar, the father of Nebuchadnezzar, led the Chaldeans into a pact with them and together they besieged and destroyed the Assyrian capital of Nineveh in 612, during which Sin-shar-ishkun, the last Neo-Assyrian ruler, died. After defeating a small remnant of Assyrians at Harran in 610, the Medes and Chaldeans retired. In 609 Pharaoh Necho II marched north to lay claim to the Assyrian western provinces, defeating and killing Josiah of Judah at Megiddo (see ◊Megiddo, Battle of), but the Egyptian forces were themselves defeated at Carchemish in 605.

Carew castle castle in Wales, 6 km / 4 mi east of Pembroke. It was begun in timber in around 1110, probably by Gerald of Windsor, Constable of Pembroke castle, to serve as an eastern outpost. Around 1200 the timber structure was replaced by stone, and the bulk of the castle dates from the 14th century. It was constructed as a tapering rectangle with corner towers and a barbican at the southeastern end.

Carisbrooke castle ◊motte-and-bailey castle on the Isle of Wight off the south coast of England, built in around 1070 by William FitzOsbern, a Norman leader at the Battle of Hastings. It reverted to the Crown in 1077 and was thereafter granted to a series of noblemen. Held by the Earl of Salisbury, it resisted a siege by the French in 1377.

Carlisle castle castle in Cumbria, England. Built in the 12th century on the site of a Norman stockade, it comprised a powerful stone keep within an inner bailey connected to an outer bailey.

Carmarthen castle (Welsh *Caerfyrddin*) castle in Dyfed, Wales. Probably begun in the latter years of the 11th century, this was a Norman ◊motte-and-bailey castle which saw considerable fighting during the 12th century and was captured by ◊Llewellyn the Great in 1215. Retaken by the English, it was rebuilt in stone and by 1275 had an inner bailey with five towers, a tower-keep, curtain wall, and other buildings.

As the administrative centre of South Wales it was continuously garrisoned, though it was lost to Owain ◊Glyndwr in the early 15th century and held by him for several years before being retaken.

carrack medieval ship, an early 14th-century Italian adaptation of the northern ◊cog but twice the size and having two masts; by the 1420s it had become a three-masted vessel. The four carracks built for ◊Henry V of England's royal fleet in 1413–20 were over 500 tons burden and carried several guns. Carracks transformed warfare at sea from land battles fought on water into true naval engagements.

Henry VIII's *Mary Rose* (700 tons, 1510) represents the full development of this ship type.

Carrhae, Battle of battle fought in 53 BC at the ancient town of Carrhae, near Haran in modern Turkey, between the Parthians led by Surena and a force led by Marcus Licinius ◊Crassus (the Elder), the first Roman army to invade Parthia. The Roman army, composed primarily of infantry, was unable to overpower the large and more mobile Parthian cavalry.

The Romans, who had seven ◊legions, 4,000 cavalry, and 4,000 light infantry, suffered steady losses from the arrows fired by the Parthians' composite bows. Crassus' son Publius was lured away from the main body and killed along with 5,000 men. The morale of the Roman army collapsed, and it began a disorganized retreat, but was harried and destroyed by the Parthians. Some 20,000 Romans died and 10,000 were captured. Crassus was killed while negotiating a surrender. A small Roman force led by ◊Cassius escaped to Syria and successfully defended the province.

Carrickfergus castle castle in what is now County Antrim, Ireland, 16 km/10 mi north of Belfast. Dating from the early 1190s, it was probably the first stone castle to be built in Ireland, and was built in three stages. Taken by King John in 1210, after the death of its founder, it remained Crown property thereafter, although besieged and damaged by Edward ◊Bruce in 1315–16.

The first stage of construction was the inner ward and commencement of the great tower. The second stage (around 1216–23) saw the completion of the tower and the addition of a middle ward by walling off an additional enclosure and adding towers. The third stage (around 1226–42) added a further curtain wall to make an outer ward, complete with towered gatehouse.

carroballista light field artillery that was easy to move, introduced in the Roman army in about AD 100. The *carroballista* was worked by torsion and had two arms that moved horizontally, like a crossbow; it was mounted on wheels.

carroccio medieval Italian wagon. The *carroccio* was the heart of an Italian city army, bearing the banners of its patron saints and serving as a command centre and a rallying point.

The *carroccio* of Milan was draped in red and white, bore the cross of St George, was drawn by white oxen, and had a guard of 300 men. ◊Frederick (I) Barbarossa was unhorsed trying to take it at Legnano in 1176.

English armies also used a *carroccio* at the Battle of Northallerton, or the Battle of the Standard, in 1138, as well as on ◊Richard (I) the Lionheart's crusade at Arsuf in 1191, bearing a dragon standard.

Carthage ancient Phoenician city in North Africa founded by colonists from Tyre in the late 9th century BC; it lay 16 km/10 mi north of Tunis, Tunisia. It was surrounded on three sides by the Gulf of Tunis and maintained an invincible navy to protect its shores. It was a leading trading centre and capital of the city-state of Carthage, and its defences were as much a display of wealth as a military necessity.

The defences were at first focused on the isthmus on the western side and on the ◊Byrsa hill citadel. The western wall consisted of three lines of fortifications. A ditch with rampart was followed by a substantial stone wall. Behind this was a third wall 14 m/45 ft high and 9 m/30 ft wide which contained within it accommodation for 300 elephants, 4,000 horses, and 24,000 men as well as stores. A single wall was constructed around the city to protect the sea front. All these fortifications were complete by the time of the Third Punic War and withstood a Roman siege from 149 to 147 BC, when the city finally fell to its attackers.

Carthage, Battle of battle fought in 238 at Carthage, North Africa, between Gordian I, the Roman governor of Africa, and Capellianus, governor of the neighbouring Roman province of Numidia. Gordian had proclaimed himself emperor, but was defeated by Capellianus' small army, which was supported by a large number of irregular troops.

Carthage, Siege of Roman siege of the Carthaginian capital on the coast of North Africa 147–146 BC, led by ◊Scipio Aemilianus, at the end of which the city was razed to the ground. This marked the end of the Punic Wars (see ◊Punic War, Third), and the Carthaginian possessions became the Roman province of Africa (roughly equivalent to present-day Tunisia).

CARTHAGINIAN ARMIES

The Carthaginian army was an enigmatic creation formed by a city-state whose chief priority was commercial enterprise and the preservation of civil power. For these reasons Carthage had only a small standing citizen army and fought its wars using foreign troops.

Military command was originally held by the two *suffets*, the chief Carthaginian magistrates. By the 5th century BC a separate military command was created, drawn from the aristocracy. The commanders, who had attained their status through wealth qualifications, were at first appointed directly as admirals or generals by the Council, and were later elected by the Citizen Assembly. The determination of the ruling class to protect its position ensured that the military commanders were kept under the supreme command of the civil authorities. The Council had the right to crucify or impale those commanders with whom it felt dissatisfied – a right which was frequently exercised. However, by the end of the First Punic War in 241 BC the Carthaginian commander ◊Hamilcar Barca had obtained a position of such popularity that he was effectively handed extraordinary command, and this was perpetuated through his family.

Up to the 5th century BC the Carthaginian citizens had formed a militia which was called up at times of national emergency or military necessity. After this had been disbanded only a force of 2,500 knights known as the Sacred Corps was maintained as a professional permanent force. The underlying reasons for this were that the ruling class of Carthage was fearful of armed citizens staging a military coup, and that employing citizens as soldiers would take them away from the trade and commercial activity that Carthage had made its chief enterprise.

To provide the bulk of their fighting force the Carthaginians therefore hired mercenaries or levied contingents from their allies and subjects. Celts from Gaul and the Po Valley, Celtiberians, Greeks, Ligurians, Balearic islanders, Numidians, and Libyans were all employed within the Carthaginian army. They fought with the weapons and tactics of their homeland and were placed under a Carthaginian commander. War elephants (see ◊elephant, in Carthaginian warfare), supplied by North African allies, replaced the chariot in the 3rd century BC.

Carthage had been blockaded (and even assaulted) since 149 BC, but Scipio's vigorous investment of the city weakened its inhabitants by hunger, particularly after his victory at Nepheris (see ◊Nepheris, battles of). Having taken the Megara (the suburban area outside the walls), Scipio forced his way into the harbours and seized the ◊Cothon (military harbour). Fierce and courageous resistance by the inhabitants during the final assault led to bloody street fighting around the Byrsa (the citadel of Carthage) lasting several days. Of an estimated population of 200,000, only 50,000 survived to be enslaved. Nine hundred Roman deserters, along with the wife and children of the Carthaginian commander ◊Hasdrubal Barca, burned themselves to death in the temple of Eschmoun rather than surrender.

Casilinum, Battle of last major battle of the Italian Wars (534–54), which took place in 553. A Roman army of 18,000 men, commanded by ◊Narses, defeated and annihilated a much larger force of Alamanni and Franks.

Narses deployed in a strong defensive position reminiscent of his dispositions at Taginae (see ◊Taginae, Battle of). His infantry centre was arranged with heavily armoured men in front supported by dismounted Germans, including Goths who had recently joined the Imperial cause. On the wings were the bow-armed cavalry. The Alamannic/

Frankish army, mainly fighting on foot, attacked in dense columns. They succeeded in driving back the Roman infantry centre but the cavalry closed in on the wings, weakened the Alamanni and Franks with archery, then charged home and broke them.

Cassander (died 287 BC) king of Macedonia c. 305–287 BC, son of ◊Antipater, and 'successor' of Alexander the Great (see ◊Diadochi). He played a leading part in the war against ◊Antigonus (I) Monophthalmus, and was recognized as general in Europe at the peace conference of 311. In about 305 he was proclaimed 'King of the Macedonians', after having had Alexander's son Alexander IV killed.

Cassel, Battle of battle fought in 1328 at Cassel in Flanders (now in northern France) between Philip VI of France and the Flemings, provoked by the revolt of Flanders against French rule. Philip VI marched against the rebels, and the Flemings made a fatal attack; half the communal forces of Flanders perished.

The French took this opportunity to avenge the slaughter of French knights at Courtrai in 1302 (see ◊Courtrai, Battle of). As a remembrance of the victory, Philip VI offered an equestrian statue of himself to Notre Dame in Paris.

Cassius (c. 85–42 BC) (*Gaius Cassius Longinus*) Roman general and one of Julius ◊Caesar's assassins. He fought with Marcus Licinius ◊Crassus (the Elder) against the Parthians and distinguished himself after Carrhae (see ◊Carrhae, Battle of) by defending the province of Syria. Cassius fought under Pompey in the civil war between Pompey and Julius Caesar. With Brutus he led the republican armies against Octavian and Mark Antony at Philippi (see ◊Philippi, battles of).

In 43 BC he returned to Syria to raise an army to oppose the forces of Caesar's supporters. At Philippi in 42 BC he commanded the left flank and was defeated by Mark Antony. Cassius, unaware that the right flank under Brutus had achieved success, despaired of the situation and committed suicide.

Cassius Longinus, Gaius Roman consul. In 171, having been denied command in the Third Macedonian War (see ◊Macedonian Wars) and sent instead to defend Italy's northern frontier, he attempted to march his troops over land to Macedonia. He was discovered by the Senate and ordered to return.

Castagnaro, Battle of battle fought on 11 March 1387 in which the *condottiere* (professional mercenary commander) Sir John ◊Hawkwood representing the Italian city of Padua used characteristically English archery

tactics to defeat the forces of the city of Verona. The Veronese suffered 1,500 casualties and had 4,500 men-at-arms captured, including all their leaders.

Hawkwood led 7,000 men-at-arms, 1,000 foot soldiers, and 600 mounted English archers. Giovanni dei Ordelaffi's Veronese forces numbered 9,000 men-at-arms, 2,600 pikemen and crossbowmen, and a large number of untrained militia. Hawkwood drew up his men in marshy land behind a stream. Dismounting his men-at-arms, he deployed his archers and crossbows on the flanks and kept a cavalry reserve. Successive waves of Veronese charges failed, and then Hawkwood delivered a cavalry charge into their left rear, capturing the Veronese ◊*carroccio*.

castellan governor of a castle. As the authority of the Carolingian dynasty waned in western Europe, power in the 10th–11th centuries fell increasingly into the hands of castellans. They controlled fortifications and as a result acted as quasi-rulers in their localities during periods of weak kingship.

Castel Sant'Angelo 6th-century fortress on the river Tiber east of the Vatican, Rome, Italy, on the site of Hadrian's tomb, known as the Mausoleum. Cencius Stephani built a tower here in the 11th century, which shortly afterwards became a papal stronghold.

Later additions include the round corner towers, the four polygonal towers, the outer bastions, and the loggia (open-sided gallery) crowned by an angel statue which gives the building its name, reflecting the angel which appeared to St Gregory I the Great. The fortress was also used as a prison.

Castillon, Battle of battle fought on 17 July 1453 at Castillon on the lower Dordogne, southwestern France, in which the French under Jean de ◊Bueil repelled the attacks of the English under Sir John ◊Talbot, who was killed, effect-ively ending the ◊Hundred Years' War. Although both Edward IV and Henry VIII led subsequent expeditions to France, English ambitions in France had been brought to an end.

Talbot led a small expeditionary force of 6,000 soldiers and recaptured Bordeaux in October 1452. In July 1453 the French, with almost 10,000 soldiers, advanced to Castillon, where Jean ◊Bureau, their master gunner, constructed a large artillery camp, some 640 m/700 yds long and 183 m/200 yds wide, equipped with 300 guns. Talbot hoped to rush the camp and drive off the French outposts, but the massed guns hurled back the attackers with heavy losses. A ball hit Talbot's horse; he was pinned underneath it and killed with a battleaxe.

castle-guard obligation of a medieval European knight to provide garrison service at a castle. It appeared in continental Europe earlier than in England, and was often separated from other military obligations; it was considered to be a lesser service than that in the host (army). It was often organized on a rota basis. In the later medieval period it was often commuted for a money payment.

Castle Hedingham castle in Essex, England, 6 km/4 mi northeast of Halstead. Probably the finest Norman keep in England, built in 1150, and home of the de Vere family for 550 years. Originally a ◊motte-and-bailey castle, all but the keep and part of the ditch have been destroyed in the course of various sieges.

Castle Rising castle in England, northeast of Kings Lynn, Norfolk. Built in around 1150, it consisted of a strong rectangular keep inside an oval mounded earthwork. A curtain wall probably crowned this earthwork, completely concealing the castle from view, and a masonry gatehouse let into the earthwork was the sole means of entry.

The curtain wall was surrounded by a ditch, with a drawbridge in front of the gateway leading to the bailey, surrounded on three sides by another mounded earthwork. This second element was surrounded by an extension of the ditch, the entire ditch bounding a rectangular area of some 9 ha/12 acres.

Castle Sween castle in Argyll, Scotland, on Loch Sween, 16 km/10 mi southwest of Lochgilphead. The earliest existing stone castle in Scotland, it was probably built in the late 11th or early 12th century. It now consists of four walls, with gates to land and sea, and traces of internal structures that were built against this wall. Two small towers were added at some time, and records indicate that additional construction took place as late as the 14th century.

Castracane, Catruccio (1282–1328) ◊Condottiere and ruler of Lucca from 1316. Exiled from Lucca at age 16, he spent 17 years fighting in France and as a mercenary in Italy. In 1314 he joined the forces of Uguccione della Faglione, lord of Pisa, and led them to victory over the Florentines at Montecatini, which resulted in the conquest of Lucca. In 1316 he deposed his master and took over as ruler. In 1325 he again defeated the Florentines at Altopascio. Political philosopher Niccolò Machiavelli later celebrated Castracane's achievements as a soldier-prince.

cat (or *Welsh cat*; also called *sow, mouse, tortoise, weasel*) mobile roofed platform or hut used in siege warfare to give cover to the attackers, who would creep it close to a defensive wall. It was sometimes attached to the wall with iron nails. Animal hide was often used on the roof as protection against fire. The cat was especially useful for covering mining activity at the foot of a wall.

The cat used by Simon de Montfort the Elder at Toulouse, France, in 1218 was made of wood, iron, and steel, had a platform and a door, and sheltered 400 knights and 150 archers.

Çatal Höyük Neolithic/Chalcolithic settlement in southern Anatolia, Turkey, occupied from 7000–5600 BC, covering a 13-ha/32-acre site with an estimated population of 10,000 people. The centre of an extensive trading complex, it exported obsidian tools and weapons, plentiful from the nearby volcanoes of Hasan Dag and Karaca Dag. There is no outer wall or defined citadel, but the houses are built together for defence with an entry from the roof.

In the earlier site of Asikli Höyük (c. 8000 BC), a settlement also based on obsidian trading, on the shore of Tuz Gölü, 250 km/155 mi to the northeast, there is a walled citadel area, showing a wide differentiation in social structure, though the houses are still entered from the roof.

cataphract technical term for the heavily armed Eastern cavalry that appeared in the West in the 3rd century BC. It was also sometimes applied to heavily armoured ships.

Cataphracts were used by ◊Antiochus (III) the Great against the Romans at Magnesia in 190 BC (see ◊Magnesia, Battle of), and also by the Parthians, Sassanians, Alans, and Sarmatians during the Roman imperial period (1st century BC–5th century AD).

catapulta original name for an arrow- or bolt-shooting machine, as opposed to a ◊ballista (stone-throwing machine), in Roman warfare. The two words exchanged meanings during the Roman Empire, probably in the 1st century AD.

Confusingly, the Greek-derived term 'catapult' also continued in use into the European Middle Ages as a general term for siege artillery. Roman stone-throwing machines with a single, vertical arm were usually referred to by the more precise term ◊onager.

Cato, Marcus Porcius (c. 234–149 BC) Roman politician, historian, and soldier. He served in the Second Punic War (see ◊Punic

War, Second). As consul in 195 BC he was sent to Spain where he won a battle outside the city of Emporion, and fought a series of campaigns against the tribes of the area. He then served as legate in Macedonia, playing a major role in the victory at Thermopylae (see ◊Thermopylae, Battle of 191 BC).

A prominent figure in the Senate, he dedicated the last years of his life to encouraging the Romans to destroy Carthage, dying a few months after the start of the Third Punic War.

Caudex, Appius Claudius Roman general and politician who advocated war with Carthage in 264 BC over the city of Messana, Sicily (see ◊Mamertine). The resulting conflict would become the First Punic War (see ◊Punic War, First).

When the members of the Senate were unsure how to react over the Messana incident, Caudex used his influence as consul to sway them into declaring war and supporting their new ally. Caudex commanded the Roman army sent to relieve the city in 264 BC. He fought no military engagements before returning to Rome in 263 BC.

Caudine Forks, Battle of the battle fought about 321 BC between the Roman army and the Samnites during the ◊Samnite Wars. The invading Roman army was captured and forced to submit to a crushing public humiliation.

Trapped at the Caudine Forks (described by Roman writers as a narrow defile, the location of which is unknown) while marching through Samnium, the Roman army was unable to break out and was forced to capitulate. The Samnites spared the Roman legionaries, but compelled them to surrender all their possessions and bow down to pass beneath a yoke before they could return to Rome.

CELTIC ARMIES

Celtic armies held a fearsome reputation for fanatical bravery and overwhelming ferocity. Developed through intertribal warfare, the Celtic way of fighting would take Italy, Spain, and the Baltic states by surprise. The drive of the Celtic warriors, the mobility of their chariot or horse-mounted troops, and the irresistible force of their mass infantry charge were at first shocking for the foreign states they encountered. However, once the initial shock had worn off, Celtic armies were shown to have fatal weaknesses.

Celtic warfare had evolved to suit the codes and morals of Celtic society. Emphasis was on the individual and battle was the means to obtain personal glory that would enhance status. Ritual display and acts of single combat between champions were an important preliminary to the battle, with the battle itself being simply a frontal charge by both sides until one side lost its nerve or was pushed from the field. There was no need for any organization other than the tribal hierarchy, as battle strategy might deny a warrior the chance to find his moment of glory. The army consisted mostly of infantry (see ◊soldurii) with the nobles and upper-class citizens fighting on horseback (see ◊trimarcisia) or from a chariot (see ◊essedarius). These all seem to have engaged the enemy together and not acted as separate forces until the enemy had been routed, at which point the cavalry would pursue them.

The only significant development in the Celtic army was the introduction of the four-pommel saddle. This allowed the horse to be used as a mobile fighting platform, making the less manoeuvrable chariot redundant. In general though, the Celts failed to adapt to the fighting methods of their non-Celtic opponents. Professionalism, sustained campaigns, battle manoeuvres, body armour, stabbing swords, and a central unified command were the antithesis of Celtic armies. Only in rare instances and under extreme pressure could leaders such as ◊Vercingetorix, chieftain of the Averni tribe, forge an effective Celtic multi-tribal army with a long-term tactical strategy.

Centumalus, Gnaeus Fulvius Roman general during the Second Punic War (see ◊Punic War, Second) who captured the Italian city of Capua in 211 BC, following the siege of 212–211 BC (see ◊Capua, Siege of), and commanded the Romans at Herdonia (now Ordana) in 210 BC (see ◊Herdonia, Battle of).

Centumalus was elected consul in 211 BC and assumed command of the army investing Capua. Dividing his forces between the inner and outer lines of the siege circumvallations, he repulsed the combined Carthaginian attempt to break in and the Capuan attempt to break out. Unable to escape the stranglehold, the city surrendered. Following this success he was sent to besiege the city of Herdonia (Ordana) in Apulia, southeast Italy, but was ambushed by Hannibal's army and died in the battle.

century basic unit of the Roman ◊legion from the time of the early republic. It was originally probably a unit of 100 men, but consisted of 60 to 80 men in the 3rd to 2nd centuries BC and was then fixed at 80. A century was commanded by a *centurion*, a long-serving officer who wore a transverse crest on his helmet and carried a *vitis* (vine-stick) as a badge of office.

Cerealis, Quintus Petilius Roman general. In AD 60, as legate of the 9th Legion (*Legio IX Hispana*), he attacked the Boudiccan rebels before the main ◊Boudiccan Revolt in Britain, but suffered a serious reverse with only himself and a few cavalry escaping. In 70 he successfully defeated the rebel Germanic Batavian auxiliaries of Julius Civilis in a series of hard-fought battles. He was governor of Britain 71–74, expanding the province to the north by conquering the Brigantes, a Celtic tribe.

Cerealis was an able but sometimes reckless commander. His career profited from the rise of the future emperor ◊Vespasian.

cervellière (French) skull cap, synonymous in the 13th century with the term 'basinet', worn in medieval Europe. It appeared as a small, hemispherical skull cap from about 1220, usually worn underneath the mail ◊coif, a practice which disappeared about 1330.

Chabrias (c. 420–357/6 BC) Athenian general and mercenary captain. He is first attested commanding on Aegina in 388, during the ◊Corinthian War, and then appears guarding a pass over Cithaeron against the Spartans, in 378, and in the fighting in Boeotia in 377. In 376 he won his greatest success when he defeated the Spartan fleet off Naxos.

He was instrumental in extending the second Athenian alliance. In 369 he was commanding mercenaries in the Peloponnese, and he subsequently served one of the Egyptian rebels against Persian rule, and in the Hellespont. He was killed at the Battle of Chios, in the Social War.

Chaeronea, Battle of (338 BC) battle fought in 338 BC at Chaeronea (modern Khaironia) in central Greece between ◊Philip (II) of Macedon and the Athenians allied with the Thebans, in which Philip broke the power of the southern Greek states and ensured Macedonian dominion over Greece.

It is uncertain what happened, but Philip possibly feinted withdrawal with his right, and when the Athenians pursued, a gap appeared in the right of the allied line. Into this swept the Macedonian cavalry, commanded by Philip's 18-year-old son Alexander (◊Alexander (III) the Great), and the battle was won.

Chaeronea, Battle of (86 BC) battle fought in 86 BC at Chaeronea (modern Khaironia) in central Greece between an army under the Roman general ◊Sulla and a far larger Pontic army commanded by ◊Mithridates (VI) Eupator's general Taxiles, during the First Mithridatic War. The Roman forces defeated the inefficient Pontic army.

Sulla dug trenches to protect the flanks of his army of 15,000 infantry and 1,500 cavalry from envelopment by the huge Pontic force that supposedly consisted of 100,000 infantry, 10,000 cavalry, and 94 scythed chariots. Although large, the Pontic army contained relatively few effective units. The Pontic chariot charge floundered on a line of concealed pits dug by the Romans. The clash between the infantry lines resulted in a fierce struggle, but Sulla was able to gain the victory by judicious use of his reserves. In his memoirs he claimed to have lost only a dozen men, and only 10,000 of the Pontic troops escaped.

chahar 'aineh (Persian 'four mirrors') form of Asian armour comprising four circular, octagonal, or rectangular plates of steel strapped around the chest over a mail shirt. It appeared in central Asia from the 16th century in the circular form, and in India and Persia in the 17th century in the other two forms.

Chalcidian helmet Greek helmet in use from the 6th to the 4th centuries BC. It was an evolved form of the ◊Corinthian helmet, cut away between the cheek and neck to leave the ear uncovered and allowing the wearer to hear. The cheek pieces were often hinged.

Chalcis, Battle of minor sea battle fought in 429 BC, during the ◊Peloponnesian War, which provides one of the best illustrations in

CHÂLONS, BATTLE OF

Battle fought in 451 near Châlons-sur-Marne in Gaul (France) between the Romans and their allies commanded by ◊Aetius and the Huns led by ◊Attila; the victory was won by the Romans. The battle is considered by many to have been one of the decisive battles of the Western world since it stopped the Huns from overrunning what is now France and prevented the potential destruction of much of what remained of classical civilization in the West. The decisiveness of the battle is debatable, but if the Huns had defeated the Romans the history of western Europe would certainly have followed a very different course.

Throughout the 440s the Huns waged a series of campaigns against the Eastern Roman Empire. They devastated the Balkans and exacted a heavy tribute. In 450 they turned their attention to the West. Several factors brought this about: the Eastern emperor Marcian adopted a stronger policy towards the Huns; the Franks were fighting amongst themselves and one prince sought the support of the Huns, another the support of the West Romans; the Vandals were urging the Huns to move against their enemies the Visigoths; and finally Honoria, the sister of the Western emperor Valentinian III, became involved in a scandal at court and appealed to Attila for help.

Attila marshalled all the forces of the Hunnic empire for the war. Marching alongside the Huns were many allied and subject peoples: Gepids commanded by Ardaric; Ostrogoths under their three leaders Valamir, Theodemir, and Videmir; Thuringians; Rugians; Sciri; Heruls; Burgundians from the east of the Rhine; and the Ripuarian Franks. After crossing the Rhine in 451 Attila captured and sacked Metz and then moved on to Orléans where he hoped that kindred Alans would join him.

Aetius, the Roman commander in the West, had previously relied on the Huns to man his armies. He now needed to find troops to oppose them. With some difficulty he persuaded his old enemies the Visigoths under King Theodoric to join him in an alliance. Other peoples of Gaul followed suit: the Salian Franks under Merovech; the federate Burgundians of Savoy; Armorican Britons, Saxons, and Breones; Aetius' army presumably also included some Roman troops, though their details are not recorded.

Sangiban, King of the Alans of Orléans, had apparently promised to betray his city to Attila but instead he joined the Roman cause and Attila was thrown back from Orléans. The Huns withdrew towards the plains of Champagne where their mobile mounted forces might hope to meet the Romans at an advantage. They were hard pressed by Aetius' army and forced to fight a constant rearguard action. On one occasion a major battle resulted from a clash between Aetius' Franks and Attila's Gepids in which 15,000 men are said to have died.

The two armies finally closed with each other on the Catalaunian Plains in Champagne in a vast battle. The battlefield was a flat, open plain with a hill on the outer edge. Aetius drew up his forces with the Visigoths on the right, Alans in the centre, and the Romans and other nations on the left. Opposing them, the Huns arrayed themselves in the centre with their main German allies on each wing: Ostrogoths on the left and Gepids on the right. The deployment of the other German allies is not known.

The battle opened with Aetius sending a force of Visigoths under Thorismund (King Theodoric's son) to seize the height dominating the battlefield on the Roman right. Possession of the hill was disputed by the Huns but Thorismund succeeded in driving them off. The struggle for the hill was preliminary to the battle proper which opened with the Huns breaking through the Alans (whose enthusiasm was doubtful) and swinging around to join the Ostrogoths in an assault on the main Visigoth position. The Visigoths held firm despite wavering initially at the rout of the Alans and despite the loss of King Theodoric. Meanwhile, on the other flank, the Gepids made no headway against the Romans and Franks. The battle raged all day with high casualties on both sides (figures as high as an unlikely 300,000 being recorded). The decisive stroke came when Thorismund charged down the hill he had captured earlier, into the flank of the Ostrogoths and Huns, and succeeded in driving them back to their wagon laager. Darkness had fallen by this time and a confused fight developed amongst the wagons until Thorismund was thrown from his horse, rescued by his companions, and urged to withdraw.

At this point Aetius was unaware of the Visigothic victory. Anxious to learn their fate, he rode over to the right wing, dodging the various scattered groups that filled the battlefield. Once he learned of victory Aetius did not order a pursuit. The reason for this has been variously explained. The Goths claimed that Aetius did not want to destroy the Huns as he needed them to counterbalance growing Visigothic power. The Franks claimed that Aetius wanted all the booty for himself. Whatever the reason, Attila was allowed to withdraw in good order and remained strong enough to invade Italy the following year.

classical warfare of the advantages of fast, manoeuvrable galleys.

Putting out with 20 triremes from Chalcis (modern Krioneri), a town on the north shore of the Gulf of Corinth, the Athenian Phormio intercepted a Peloponnesian fleet of 47 ships on its way to Leucas in the Ionian Sea. The Peloponnesians formed a defensive circle, prows outwards, with lighter craft and five of their fastest ships in the centre. When the Athenians rowed around them in line ahead formation, they backed water until they began to fall foul of one another. With the morning wind adding to the confusion, Phormio seized the opportunity to ram several enemy ships. The rest fled, but 12 were captured in pursuit.

Châlus-Chabrol, Siege of siege of a rebel castle in Limoges, central France, in 1199 during which ◊Richard (I) the Lionheart of England was killed. Although chroniclers mention a disputed hoard of treasure, Richard besieged Châlus to quell a rebellion (encouraged by ◊Philip (II) Augustus of France) against his authority in the region.

Richard, surveying the castle of Châlus while not wearing full armour, was hit by a crossbow bolt shot from the walls. The efforts of a surgeon to save him seem to have hastened his death.

Champa, Mongol invasion of invasion by sea of Champa (modern central Vietnam) 1282–87 by the Mongol commander Sodu under ◊Khubilai Khan, with 5,000 men and 100 ships. After Vietnam refused passage to their reinforcements, the Mongols took Hanoi, but they were forced to withdraw. The rulers of both Vietnam and Champa offered tribute, and Khubilai – effectively accepting defeat – settled for that.

Sodu took the port of Vijaya and advanced into the interior against King Jaya Indravarman VI, but was defeated by Cham guerillas in the mountains. Despite reinforcements he made little progress. Khubilai therefore sent an army under Toghon in 1284 to march through Vietnam to support Sodu. After Vietnamese emperor Tran Thanh-Ton refused to allow passage to the Mongols, Toghon and Sodu cooperated in a joint attack on Vietnam. They took Hanoi and defeated several Vietnamese detachments, but suffered from the climate, disease, and guerilla attacks. Toghon therefore withdrew in the summer of 1285, leaving Sodu isolated in the south. He was defeated by Vietnamese forces under Prince Tran Nhat-Canh, and was surrounded and killed trying to retreat. Further Mongol-Chinese forces invaded Vietnam 1286–87 and took Hanoi again. Their fleet was defeated and they could not engage the main Vietnamese army, so they were again forced to withdraw.

Champaner city in western India, first recorded in historical accounts in about 1300, when it was seized from a rival clan by the Chauhana ◊Rajputs. Its main defensive feature was the Pavagarh or 'fire-hill', a hillfort 760 m/2,500 ft above the surrounding plain protected by a series of massive stone walls and with its innermost gateway approachable only through a winding passage cut through solid rock.

Champaner was besieged by ◊Mahmud Shah Bigarha of Gujarat for 21 months 1482–84. The Rajput garrison finally slew their wives and children in the rite of ◊*jauhar* before sallying out to a final attack.

Chanderi town and fort in central India, probably founded by the ◊Rajput Chandela dynasty in the 9th or 10th centuries. The citadel stands 70 m/230 ft above the town, and is entered through the *Kirat Sagar* ('gate of blood'). The southwest gateway (1490) is approached via a passageway cut through solid rock.

The town was raided by Muslims in 1030, captured by Ghiyas al-Din ◊Balban in 1251, and captured again in 1438 by Mahmud I, the Khilji sultan of Malwa.

Chandragupta I (lived 4th century) king of ◊Magadha 320–30, and founder of the Gupta dynasty which established an Indian empire comparable in size with that of ◊Chandragupta Maurya.

Chandragupta I was an adventurer who came to power through marriage to Kumaradevi, a princess of the ancient Lichchavi dynasty of northern India, which re-emerged on the decline of the ◊Kusana dynasty. He adopted the title Maharajadhiraja, 'Great King of Kings', despite his humble origins.

Chandragupta II (lived 4th–5th centuries) king of ◊Magadha 380–415. He defeated the Shakas (Scythians) of Rajasthan shortly after 388 and took the title Vikramaditya, 'Sun of Valour'. He is remembered in Indian folklore as the beneficent Raja Bikram, the 'Sun King', of Ujjain (a Shaka satrapy captured by Chandragupta II early in his reign).

He was the son and successor of ◊Samudragupta.

Chandragupta Maurya (died c. 297 BC) ruler of northern India and first Indian emperor c. 325–296 BC, founder of the Mauryan dynasty.

He overthrew the Nanda dynasty of ◊Magadha in 325 BC and then conquered the Punjab in 322 BC after the death of ◊Alexander (III) the Great, expanding his empire west to Iran. He is credited with having united most of India.

As army commander under Danananda, the last king of the Nanda dynasty of Magadha, he made an unsuccessful attempt on the throne and fled with his wily Brahman adviser Kautilya to join the invading army of Alexander, where he was recorded as 'Sandracottos'. Having urged Alexander to press on against Danananda ('Xandrames'), without success, he gathered his own army against Danananda, eventually becoming king in his place.

With Kautilya's aid he established a centralized empire on the model of the Achaemenids of Iran, and defeated ◊Seleucus (I) Nicator, who had attempted to restore Macedonian rule in the east in 305 BC. Seleucus ceded India (present-day Pakistan and part of the Punjab) and eastern Afghanistan in exchange for 500 war elephants for use in his western campaigns.

chanfron piece of armour that protected a horse's head, widely used in the ancient world. Many examples dating from the 5th to the 3rd centuries BC have been found in southern Italy and ◊Alexander (III) the Great's horse is wearing one on the Issus mosaic from Pompeii, depicting the battle of 333 BC against the Persian King Darius III.

The *chanfron* also appears on several triumphal monuments, such as the 2nd-century BC Pergamum reliefs. The Romans used versions made of decorated hide or metal for cavalry displays (*hippica gymnasia*).

Changan capital of several Chinese dynasties, near what is now Xian. Under the Sui (581–617) and Tang (618–906) dynasties, its walls enclosed the classic rectangle on a huge scale – 9.4 by 8.4 km/5.9 by 5.3 mi – although a rectangle (the Daming Palace) was added to the north wall. Inside the north wall, the imperial city and the imperial palace were separately walled. The streets within the city followed a rigid grid pattern. There were three gates in each wall, massive structures incorporating outworks and wooden towers.

Changan, Battle of battle near the Tang capital of Changan on 13 November 757 in which the Tang Chinese defeated rebels under An Chingxu, who had murdered his father ◊An Lushan and taken over his regime.

A counterattack was led by imperial commander Guo Ziyi and the new emperor Suzong's son Li Shu. The rebels marched out of

Changan to face the imperial army south of the city. The Tang army included numerous foreign contingents, notably 4,000 Uighur nomad cavalry under Yehu, the son of the Uighur *khaghan* ('Great Khan'). Its advance guard, consisting of swordsmen under Li Siye, was driven back but held out. A rebel cavalry force tried an outflanking movement, but was defeated by the Uighurs, who then rode round and attacked the rebel rear. Caught between Yehu and Li Siye, the rebels were defeated. The imperialists reoccupied Changan the next day.

Changan, capture of Tibetan occupation of Changan, the capital of Tang China, in 763. The Tibetans had steadily taken over the northern provence of Gansu when it was stripped of troops to fight ◊An Lushan. The court, dealing with the remains of An's rebellion, did not take the Tibetans seriously until they were close to Changan. Then both the emperor and the local troops fled the city, allowing the Tibetans to take it unopposed. They burned and looted Changan and set up a puppet emperor, but withdrew after two weeks.

changcong suwei (or *ch'ang-ts'ung su'wei*) Tang Chinese guards force raised in 723. The ◊*wei* guards units manned by ◊*fubing* militiamen had declined in numbers and efficiency, so a new force was recruited from picked veteran soldiers. It rose to 120,000 men. The force was renamed ◊*kuoqi* ('mounted archers') in 725 and amalgamated with the ◊Palace Army.

Changping, Battle of (or *Ch'ang-p'ing*) battle in 260 BC in which the Chinese state of Qin defeated its rival Zhao in the Changping gorge, near Gaoping in central China. The Qin general Bo Qi (victor at Ying: see ◊Ying, fall of 278 BC) invaded Zhao, outmanoeuvred the Zhao general Zhao Kuo and his army of 450,000 men with a feigned retreat, cut off his supplies, and penned him up in Changping gorge. Zhao Kuo held out for 40 days awaiting relief, then sortied with a picked force but was shot and killed. The 400,000 remaining Zhao troops surrendered, but the Qin massacred them all.

changsheng jun (or *ch'ang-sheng chün*) (Chinese 'Ever-Victorious Army') Chinese force commanded by Guo Yaoshi, which remained ever-victorious by consistently defecting to the winners. Originally serving the Khitan Liao dynasty, they deserted to the Song Chinese in around 1120 when the Liao collapsed under the attacks of the Song and the Jurchen under ◊Wanyen Aguda. When the Jurchen invaded Song territory in 1125, the *changsheng jun* surrendered to the Jurchen

without a fight and assisted their conquest of Hebei province.

chanson de geste (medieval French 'song of (great) deeds') one of a genre of epic poems of medieval Europe, based on a legendary Carolingian past and dealing with matters of importance to the military classes – loyalty, lineage, courage, fighting skills, and battle tactics – often against an imaginary 'Saracen' foe.

Chansons de geste, an invaluable source for the ethos of warrior knights, were translated into German and Scandinavian languages as the concept of ◊chivalry appeared in those regions.

chapel de fer French term synonymous with ◊kettle-hat, a type of helmet used in medieval Europe.

chariot, Chinese war chariots comprising large wheels with 18–34 spokes, rectangular cab floors, and openwork railed bodies. They appeared in late Shang period burials in around 1300 BC, but the peak of chariot use was the Spring and Autumn period (770–476 BC). They remained in use, though less important, until the 2nd century BC. Similarities to examples from the Caucasus and Siberia suggest introduction from the northwest.

At first drawn by two horses, teams of four were common by 1000 BC and standard by 700 BC. Horses were originally yoked to a single pole, but by the 4th century BC a sophisticated breast-strap harness was used. Most chariots had a crew of three: driver, archer, and spearman or halberdier (though some Shang examples have cabs only large enough for two). Early chariot-tactics involved close cooperation with infantry in formations such as the ◊fish-scale formation. The larger Spring and Autumn chariot forces were the decisive arm by themselves, fighting other charioteers according to an elaborate chivalrous code but sometimes vulnerable to a sudden rush by barbarian infantry. In the ◊Warring States chariots were gradually supplanted by increasing numbers of infantry and the cavalry introduced by ◊Wuling.

chariot, scythed four-horse chariot with large, scythelike blades attached to its axles, yoke ends, and poles, used by Persian and Hellenistic armies from about 401 to 47 BC. Unlike standard chariots which carried fighting crew, scythed chariots carried only a driver who hurtled them at speed into the enemy formation.

Scythed chariots were rarely successful as weapons of war for several reasons: they required flat and open terrain; the drivers and horses were reluctant to crash suicidally into

CHARIOT, NEAR EASTERN

The light two-horse war chariot dominated Near Eastern armies of the late Bronze Age, used in companies for missile fire, harassing enemy lines, and the pursuit of routing foes. It was crewed by two people, the driver-archer and the shieldbearer, both of whom wore a helmet, gorget (neck guard), and scale corselet. The chariot car held one or more quivers for arrows. Charioteers became an elite group in society, the Hurrian ◊*mariyanna*, and Egyptian pharaohs of the New Kingdom portrayed themselves as powerful charioteers overcoming their enemies.

Evidence of the importance of the chariot has come from burials as far apart as the Caucasus and Mycenaean Greece, as well as from horse training manuals from the Hittite capital ◊Hattusas (modern Boğazköy, Turkey) and the important Syrian seaport of Ugarit (modern Ras Shamra). Temple and palace reliefs from Egypt and Assyria depict the chariot in action.

Horse teams were trained in the style of modern-day interval training, with a mixed combination of walks, trots, gallops, and circuit training. Feeds were deliberately irregular and varied. The crew were trained to shoot arrows, using a composite bow (see ◊bow, composite), from a rocking stool. The horses were stallions, no larger than 14 hands. A chariot exercise ground has been found at Western Thebes, Egypt, near the palace of Pharaoh Amunhotep II.

With the development of cavalry under the Neo-Assyrian king ◊Ashurnasirpal II, the chariot of the Iron Age became a heavy vehicle of secondary importance, often with a span of four horses and up to four crew.

solid bodies of enemy troops; and they were easily swamped by light infantry before they got up speed.

They are first reliably mentioned at Cunaxa in 401 BC (see ◊Cunaxa, Battle of) where they were fielded both by Artaxerxes and his opponent Cyrus the Younger. Darius III used 200 scythed chariots at Gaugamela in 331 BC (see ◊Gaugamela, Battle of) and Persian armies continued to use them until the fall of their empire. Thereafter ◊Seleucus (I) Nicator, his descendants, and Mithradates VI of Pontus fielded scythed chariots. Their last known appearance was in Pharnaces' army at Zela in 47 BC (see ◊Zela, Battle of).

chariot, Vedic light chariot used by the horse-taming Aryans who entered northern India from the northwest during the 2nd millennium BC. It was carried on a single pair of spoked wheels and drawn by a team of two horses yoked abreast. The crew of two (driver and warrior) were armed with bows, spears, and swords.

There are many references to this vehicle in early Vedic poems.

Charlemagne (Charles I the Great) (742–814) king of the Franks from 768 and Holy Roman emperor from 800. By inheritance (his father was ◊Pepin the Short) and extensive campaigns of conquest, he united most of western Europe by 804, when after 30 years of war the Saxons came under his control.

Pepin had been mayor of the palace in Merovingian Neustria until he was crowned king by Pope Stephen II (died 757) in 754, and his sons Carl (Charlemagne) and Carloman were crowned as joint heirs. When Pepin died in 768, Charlemagne inherited the northern Frankish kingdom, and when Carloman died 771, he also took possession of his domains.

He was engaged in his first Saxon campaign when the Pope's call for help against the Lombards reached him; he crossed the Alps, captured Pavia, and took the title of king of the Lombards. The pacification and Christianizing of the Saxon peoples occupied the greater part of Charlemagne's reign. From 792 north Saxony was subdued, and in 804 the whole region came under his rule.

In 777 the emir of Zaragoza asked for Charlemagne's help against the emir of Córdoba. Charlemagne crossed the Pyrenees 778 and reached the Ebro but had to turn back from Zaragoza. The rearguard action of Roncesvalles, in which ◊Roland, warden of the

Breton March, and other Frankish nobles were ambushed and killed by Basques, was later glorified in the *Chanson de Roland*. In 801 the district between the Pyrenees and the Llobregat was organized as the Spanish March. The independent duchy of Bavaria was incorporated in the kingdom 788, and the ◊Avar people were subdued 791–96. Charlemagne's last campaign was against a Danish attack on his northern frontier 810.

The supremacy of the Frankish king in Europe found outward expression in the bestowal of the imperial title: in Rome, during Mass on Christmas Day 800, Pope Leo III crowned Charlemagne emperor.

He died 28 Jan 814 in Aachen, where he was buried. Soon a cycle of heroic legends and romances developed around him, including epics by Ariosto, Boiardo, and Tasso.

Charles (V) the Wise (1337–80) king of France 1364–80. He was regent during the captivity of his father ◊John II in England, 1356–60, and became king upon John's death. He reconquered nearly all of France from England 1369–80, and diminished the power of mercenary companies (see ◊mercenaries, medieval) in France.

Charles commanded at a distance rather than in the field, a method that had rarely succeeded in the past. He chose an excellent commander in Bertrand du ◊Guesclin, who defeated the rebel Charles of Navarre at Cocherel in 1364.

Charles VII (1403–61) king of France from 1422, final victor over England in the ◊Hundred Years' War, and the organizer of France's first standing army.

The son of Charles VI (1368–1422), Charles was excluded from the succession by the Treaty of Troyes agreed between his father and the English in 1420, but was recognized in the south of France. In 1429 ◊Joan of Arc raised the siege of Orléans and had him crowned at Reims.

In 1435, by the Treaty of Arras, he detached Burgundy from its English alliance. He recovered Paris from the English in 1436, and by 1453 had expelled the English from all of France except Calais.

Charles Martel (c. 688–741) ('the Hammer') illegitimate son of Pepin II, from 719 the ◊Mayor of the Palace of Austrasia (northeastern Frankish territories in what is now France, Belgium, and Germany).

Charles brought the other Frankish territories under his control and expanded Merovingian control over the Alamanni and Thuringians. His decisive victory over the invading Umayyad Arabs at Tours in 732 (see ◊Tours, Battle of) earned him the name Martel ('the Hammer'). He ruled over the Merovingian kingdom as a de facto king and from 737 governed without a king on the throne.

Charles (II) the Bald (823–77) Holy Roman emperor from 875 and (as Charles II) king of West Francia from 843. The younger son of Louis (I) 'the Pious' (778–840), he warred against his brother the emperor Lothair I (c. 795–855). The Treaty of Verdun (843) made him king of the West Frankish Kingdom (now France and the Spanish Marches). He entered Italy in 875 and was crowned emperor.

Charles improved Frankish defences against the Vikings, including river fortifications. His *Capitula* included military reforms on fortification, raising armies, and armaments.

Charles the Bold (1433–77) duke of Burgundy from 1463 who fought in the French civil war at Montlhéry in 1465 (see ◊Montlhéry, Battle of), then crushed Liège in 1464–68. He reformed his army before engaging on an ambitious campaign for conquest, unsuccessfully besieging the imperial town of Neuss in 1474–75 before being defeated in his attack on the Swiss Federation in 1476–77 and dying in battle near Nancy, in Lorraine.

Charles's experiences in the civil 'War of the Public Weal' and against Liège, including his victory in the Battle of Brustem in 1467, taught him the value of well-coordinated forces. His annual military Ordinances of 1471–73 were intended to create a flexible all-arms force of cavalry, artillery, and foot soldiers combining pikemen and archers, divided into uniformed units under ◊banners. He gathered 12,000 men and an extensive artillery train to besiege Neuss. However, his largely mercenary forces proved fragile in the face of determined opposition and were defeated three times by the Swiss: at Grandson (see ◊Grandson, Battle of) and Mürten (see ◊Mürten, Battle of) in 1476, and at Nancy in 1477.

charnel hasp used from around the mid-15th century in Europe to secure a ◊great helm to the back and breastplate for jousting. It took the form of a hinged flap with rectangular holes corresponding with a series of pierced rectangular lugs, and replaced the leather straps and buckles found on earlier jousting helmets.

Charny, Geoffrey de (1305–56) French knight, warrior, and paragon of chivalry. He fought at Gascony in 1337, at the siege of Tournai in 1340, at Morlaix in 1342 (see

◊Morlaix, Battle of), on the Smyrna Crusade in 1346, at Ardres in 1351, and at Poiters in 1356, where he was killed. A counsellor and diplomat for Philip VI, he wrote a book of chivalry and created a chivalric order for John (II) the Good.

De Charny's career won him fame, despite his lack of success in the field. His book analysed and celebrated military virtues, stressing, 'he who does more is worth more'. French defeats in the 1340s led him to advocate a revival of chivalry, including the formation of the Company of the Star, who vowed never to retreat. The order was decimated at Morlaix in a head-on charge. De Charny bore the ◊oriflamme royal banner at Poiters, where he was killed fighting to the end.

Chastel Pelerin (or *'Atlit*) (from medieval French 'Pilgrim's Castle') Templar castle built in 1218 on a promontory overlooking the coast road 24 km/15 mi south of Haifa in the Holy Land (modern Israel), strategically vital for the defence of the Syrian coast. It withstood the attack of ◊Baibars in 1268 and was the last surviving crusader outpost after the fall of Acre in 1291 (see ◊Acre, Siege of 1291).

The castle features a triple wall of massive masonry, the outer wall standing 9 m/30 ft high above a deep moat, and two huge 34 m/110 ft towers protecting a typically circular Templar church and living quarters. It is named after the pilgrims who worked on its rapid construction.

Chastel Rouge (or *Qalaat Yahmur*) small, square ◊donjon castle with a rectangular curtain wall situated 24 km/15 mi north of Tortosa (Tartus) in Syria, built about 1112.

Chastel rouge is typical of the blockhouse-style castles of the early crusades. It was held by the Knights Hospitaller (see ◊Military Order) in about 1200, but was lost to the ◊Mamelukes in 1289.

Chateau Gaillard castle in France, overlooking a bend in the river Seine near Les Andelys, 80 km/50 mi northwest of Paris, guarding the route to Rouen. Built 1196–98 by ◊Richard (I) the Lionheart, it lies on a spur protected by a wide ditch, an outer bailey, a second ditch, a middle bailey, a third ditch commanded by a curtain wall, a third bailey, and finally the powerful, circular keep.

Built as a deliberate challenge to the kings of France (its name means 'Saucy Castle'), Chateau Gaillard represents a system of concentric defences carried to the highest level of sophistication and integration over a century before such designs became common in European castles. In 1204 ◊Philip (II) Augustus

of France took it from King John of England after a siege lasting six months.

Château Gaillard, Siege of key siege in 1203–04 during ◊Philip (II) Augustus of France's conquest of Normandy from King John of England. Philip's previous invasions had led ◊Richard (I) the Lionheart to build Château Gaillard at Les Andelys on the river Seine on the Norman-French border. The castle surrendered on 6 March 1204 and was followed by the collapse of the Angevin Empire in western Europe.

Philip began the siege in August 1203; Roger de Lacy held the castle for John, who was ruler of the Angevin lands as well as king of England. John attempted a relief by land and water, but coordination of these efforts failed and Philip destroyed each force separately. The outer bailey (wall) was mined, and the inner bailey was mined under cover of a permanent rock bridge, while the besiegers entered by a chute.

chausses close-fitting mail armour for the legs, either laced up the back of the leg or designed as a hose. It was used in western Europe from the early Middle Ages.

Che Bong Nga (died 1390) king of Champa (modern central Vietnam) from 1360 and leader of a striking but short-lived military revival. From 1361 he led a series of campaigns against Vietnam, recovering provinces ceded in 1306. He was succeeded by a general who ceded the north back to Vietnam in return for peace. Che Bong Nga's victories therefore had no permanent consequences, but delayed the Vietnamese conquest of Champa, which was achieved by ◊Lê Thanh Ton in 1471.

In 1371 he invaded the heart of Vietnam and took Hanoi (see ◊Hanoi, sack of). In 1377 a Vietnamese counterattack was defeated at the old Cham capital, Vijaya, and the Vietnamese King Trân Duê-tông was killed. When Ming China pressured him to stop these campaigns he launched naval expeditions against pirates, sending the booty to China. Under cover of this he resumed attacks on Vietnam in 1380, 1384, and 1389–90. In a naval battle during this final campaign his ship was surrounded and he was killed.

chelandion (plural *chelandia*) Byzantine vessel for transporting horses across water, able to carry 12 mounts (see also ◊tarida). *Chelandia* played a large part in the recovery of the Mediterranean islands by the Byzantines from the Arabs in the mid-10th century. At Crete in 960 they carried armies of several thousand men, apparently landing cavalrymen, armed and mounted, on the beach.

chemise outer wall surrounding the keep of a medieval castle with a raised platform at the back that could be reached from the keep by a postern or drawbridge.

Chencang, Siege of (or *Ch'en-ts'ang*) siege of the Wei city of Chencang in February 229 by ◊Zhuge Liang of Shu Han, whose 10,000 troops fought against only 1,000 defenders. The defenders put up a strong fight, however. Running short of supplies after 20 days, Zhuge gave up the siege. Wei cavalry pursued his retreating army, but he ambushed and defeated them.

The Shu Han army assaulted with towers and scaling-ladders, but the defenders dropped millstones on the towers and set fire to the ladders. Zhuge then had the moat filled in and attacked again. He destroyed the outer wall, but the defenders had built an inner wall to stop him. Attempts at mining were defeated by countermines.

Chengdu campaign (or *Ch'eng-tu*) surrender in AD 36 of the Chinese city of Chengdu to ◊Han Guangwudi and the end of the regime of Sichuan leader Gonsun Shu. This battle was the last stage of the civil war which made Han Guangwudi master of China.

The regime of Gongsun Shu held out in Sichuan, and a Han army marched up the Yangtze against him. He blocked the gorges with a floating bridge between fortifications on both banks. In spring the Han fleet attacked and, helped by an east wind, burned the bridge. In December they finally reached Chengdu but were very short of supplies. They might have given up but on 24 December Gongsun Shu led a sally and was wounded in a Han counterattack. He died during the night, and the city surrendered.

Chengpu, Battle of (or *Ch'eng-p'u*) battle in 632 BC in which a northern Chinese coalition under Duke Wen of Jin defeated a southern coalition under general Ziyu of Chu.

The Jin army numbered 700 chariots and some 50,000 men, and the Chu force was probably similar in size. First, the Jin left fiercely attacked and broke the unreliable allied forces on the Chu right. Next, the Jin right feigned a retreat, luring the Chu left-wing chariots after them, then turned to charge their pursuers while troops from the Jin centre hit them from the other side. The Chu left was scattered. Ziyu, rallying his centre, withdrew, and the Jin army captured his camp.

Chen She (died 208 BC) (or *Chen Sheng*) leader of the first rebellion against the Chinese Qin dynasty after the death of the emperor ◊Qin Shi Huangdi. His example was more important than his military achievement, and rebellion continued after his death under ◊Xiang Yu and Liu Bang (later the emperor ◊Han Gaozu).

Chen She rebelled in 209 BC with a group of conscripts he was leading to garrison service. With widespread popular support against Qin oppression, he revived the Yangtze valley kingdom of Chu. However, an army he sent to attack the capital Xian was defeated by the Qin general Zhang Han, who armed the labourers working on Huangdi's tomb, and after more Qin victories Chen She was murdered by his own charioteer.

Chepstow castle (Welsh *Casgwent*) Welsh border castle overlooking the mouth of the river Wye. Originally a Norman castle of the late11th century, it was the principal base from which the Normans conquered west Wales. Built by William FitzOsbern, Earl of Hereford, in the usual ◊motte-and-bailey form, it was rebuilt in stone from about 1120 onwards by Walter de Clare, and was extended by various successors.

Chester, Battle of victory in 605 for the Angles, under King Aethelfrith of Northumbria, over the Britons, led by Scrocmagil, which resulted in the capture of Chester and the separation of the Britons in Wales from those in the north. 'Countless numbers' of Britons were reportedly slain, including an unlikely 200 priests who were said to have accompanied the British force to pray for their victory. Scrocmagil was one of only 50 Britons to survive.

Chester castle castle in England, 48 km/30 mi southwest of Manchester. The first castle here was built by William the Conqueror around 1069–70 and was occupied by the earls of Chester, who made additions during the 12th century. In 1237 the castle was taken over by the Crown, leading to considerable extension and improvement.

Henry III (1207–72) added a curtain wall and tower and rebuilt the great hall, while Edward I (1239–1307) rebuilt the gatehouse. The castle was integral with the city walls, some 3.2 km/2 mi of which are still in existence.

Chester fortress (Roman *Deva*) Roman legionary fortress at Chester, northwest England, that controlled western England and northern Wales and served as the home of the 20th Legion (*Legio XX Valeria Victrix*) from about AD 100 to 250. It was occupied until the late 3rd century.

The first fortress was constructed in about AD 79 for the 2nd Legion (*Legio II Adiutrix*), but the legion was withdrawn from Britain within a decade, leaving the base vacant. Following the arrival of the 20th Legion the timber internal buildings and earth and timber defences were systematically replaced in stone. Though soon far behind the northern frontier, the position of the fortress on the navigable river Dee provided an important military harbour to supply western Britain.

Chesters fort (Roman *Cilurnum*) Roman fort that protected the frontier of ◊Hadrian's Wall in northern England. It guarded the bridge carrying the wall and military road over the river Tyne and was constructed in the 'playing card' shape (rectangular with rounded corners) used by the Romans from the late 1st to early 3rd centuries. It sat astride the wall with three of its four main gates giving access to the enemy side of the wall, to allow quicker response to meet an enemy attack.

Chesters was usually occupied by an auxiliary cavalry unit as cavalry were more effective in the flat ground of the area. The fort bathhouse, built beside the river, remains well preserved.

chevalier medieval French term for a knight, sometimes given qualifying words such as *engagé* (paid) or *d'un écu* (with heraldic arms). The French word makes it clear that an essential part of a knight's equipment was his horse (*cheval*). The English word 'cavalier' is derived from it.

chevauchée (medieval French 'ride') in the medieval period, a raid through enemy territory. The aim was to damage crops, buildings, and property and drive the peasantry into hiding, so reducing the productivity of a region. This undermined the revenues of its ruler and proved that he was unable to protect his subjects. Pillagers were sent out from an army's line of march, up to 20 km/12 mi each side.

For examples of the *chevauchée* see ◊Edward III, ◊Edward the Black Prince, and ◊Hundred

Years' War. English armies were notably successful with this strategy until the French learned not to try to engage them in battle, but to hang on their flanks and prevent them foraging, so reducing the English soldiers and horses to starvation.

Chevy Chase, Battle of another name for the Battle of Otterburn in 1388, between the Scots and the English: see ◊Otterburn, Battle of.

Chichi (lived 1st century BC) (or *Chih-chih*) ◊Xiongnu prince of Maodun's imperial dynasty. He seized the throne in a war of succession between several candidates, but his brother Huhanye won over his followers and Chichi fled west to Kangju (southern Kazakhstan; see ◊Kangju campaign) where he settled by agreement with the local king and began to subdue neighbouring tribes. The Chinese, fearing that he would build up a new hostile confederation, sent an expedition that defeated and killed him in 36 BC.

chiliarch (Greek 'commander of a thousand') generally, a commander or Persian court official; specifically, an official at the court of Alexander the Great and the ◊*Diadochi.* In the works of ancient tactical writers the term refers to the commander of a unit of 1024 men.

Chingiz Khan The more correct transliteration of the name of the Mongol conqueror generally referred to as ◊Genghis Khan.

Chinhung (died 576) king of Silla 540–76 in the ◊Three Kingdoms of Korea period. By an alliance with the southwestern kingdom of Paekche and a series of territorial conquests, he made Silla the dominant state in the peninsula.

Chinghung allied himself with Paekche in 551 to take the important Han River Valley from the northern kingdom of Koguryo, dividing it between the allies. He then turned on Paekche in 553, taking the lower Han Valley which had been Paekche's share; this separated Paekche from Koguryo, hindering any future cooperation against Silla. A Paekche counterattack was defeated in 554, and King Song of

CHINA, MONGOL CAMPAIGNS IN

Mongol occupation of China 1205–79, the greatest of Mongol military achievements. Although other tribes had conquered the north, no nomad army had ever occupied all of China. The north was conquered by the mobility, discipline, and fighting power of the Mongol cavalry, assisted by disunity on the Chinese side. The conquest of the south, where climate and terrain were less suited to Mongol cavalry tactics, was achieved largely by northern Chinese manpower under Mongol leadership.

When ◊Genghis Khan came to power, China was divided between the Jurchen Jin dynasty in the north, the Tanguts of Xixia in the northwest, and the native Chinese Song dynasty in the south. He attacked the Tanguts from 1205, making them tributary in the 1209–10 campaign, after which they provided auxiliaries against the Jin. In his last campaign he defeated them at Lingzhou (see ◊Lingzhou, Siege of 1226) and destroyed their state.

In 1211 Genghis invaded the Jin empire, with perhaps 75,000 troops against 600,000. He defeated a Jin army at Huanerzui (see ◊Huanerzui, Battle of), and his general Jebe raided the outskirts of their capital Zhongdu (modern Beijing). Unable to take the strong Chinese fortified towns (see ◊fortified towns, Chinese), however, the Mongols merely raided and withdrew. In 1212 the Khitan leader ◊Yelü Liuge revolted against the Jin in southern Manchuria, submitting to Genghis, who attacked again in 1213. ◊Mukhali besieged several towns while Genghis attacked Zhongdu, but withdrew in exchange for tribute. Expecting more attacks, the Jin moved their capital south to Kaifeng. Seeing this as preparation for new hostilities, Genghis besieged Zhongdu again and took it. He sent Mukhali to conquer the northeast, where he defeated resistance at Yongde (see ◊Yongde, Battle of).

Mukhali then commanded the Mongol war-effort in China while Genghis fought in the west against Khwarazm. He had 50,000–70,000 troops, only 15,000 of whom were Mongols, the rest other tribal cavalry and Chinese. This small force made only slow progress, but with Chinese artillery Mukhali was able to take towns. Until his death in 1223 he conquered everywhere north of the Yellow River, as well as some districts to the south. But in the next few years the Jin regained territory, defeating the Mongols at Dachangyuan (see ◊Dachangyuan, Battle of). The Song also attacked, losing at Zanhuang (see ◊Zanhuang, Battle of).

When ◊Ogedei succeeded Genghis he resumed the offensive. A great western sweep in 1232 outflanked Jin defences by passing through Song territory, and the Mongols took the Jin capital, Kaifeng (see ◊Kaifeng, Siege of). The Jin emperor continued resistance in the provinces but was defeated by Mongol and Song forces at Caizhou in 1234 (see ◊Caizhou, Siege of). The Song were granted some ex-Jin territories as a reward, but were dissatisfied and attacked Kaifeng and Loyang. They were driven out, but Ogedei resolved to conquer the Song empire. This war lasted 45 years, interrupted by the deaths of successive khans and by the civil war that established ◊Khubilai Khan on the Mongol throne. He commanded forces in China under Mangu, conquering Yunnan after Jinsha (see ◊Jinsha River, Battle of). The war with the Song intensified with Tiaoyushan (see ◊Tiaoyushan, Battle of). The turning point was the successful sieges of Xiangyang and Fancheng (see ◊Xiangyang and Fancheng, sieges of). After this the offensive under Bayan met little real opposition. He forced a crossing of the Yangtze in January 1275, defeated the main Song army in March, and took the capital Linan in 1276 (see ◊Linan, Siege of). Thereafter he only had to mop up local resistance, defeating the last Song fleet in Canton Bay in 1279 (see ◊Canton Bay, Battle of). China was reunified under the rule of Khubilai's Yuan dynasty.

Paekche died in battle at Kwansan fortress just inside Silla. In 562 Chinhung conquered Kaya, the last independent area between Silla and Paekche. He then conquered the east coast of modern North Korea from Koguryo.

Chinon castle castle in France, 50 km/31 mi southwest of Tours. It was originally a Roman entrenched camp overlooking the river Vienne,

in which three separate structures: Fort St Georges, Château de Milieu, and Château de Coudray have been erected, separated by ditches.

Built by Henry II of England, who died here in 1188, it fell to ◊Philip (II) Augustus of France in 1205 after an eight-month siege. He strengthened the work, and it was later used as a prison for the Templars (see ◊Military

CHIVALRY

Warrior code of Christian Europe, which originated in the 12th century as a means of controlling knightly violence but took on a range of ideological, literary, and social values that defined the medieval knight.

The French word *chevalerie* is derived from *chevalier* (knight) and stood for the whole social code associated with being a noble warrior. The idea first appeared in the 1130s, notably in the work of Geoffrey of Monmouth's legendary *History of the Kings of Britain*, which featured the court of King Arthur. Its tenets required the warrior to adhere to Christian values of protecting the weak and fighting the wicked. By about 1150 the ideals of courtly love, developed in southern France, became part of chivalry. Each knight was supposed to love a lady made unattainable by reason of distance or different station, and to be inspired to deeds of valour in her honour. Chrétien de Troyes was just one of many poets who celebrated the court of King Arthur and explored the darker side of passion, for example in the tragic tale of Lancelot and Guinevere (Arthur's queen).

At the same time (in the 1170s) great princes like 'Young King Henry', the son of Henry II of England, sponsored tournaments where knights could display their military skills in wartime. Elaborate rituals developed for knighting ceremonies also, as arranged by the Holy Roman Emperor Frederick (I) Barbarossa in Germany in 1180. Since knighthood

was seen as an order (in the same way as the priesthood) a new entrant was bathed and endured a night-long vigil of prayer before being given armour, sword, and lance in a ceremony loaded with Christian symbolism. By 1200 chivalry was a full-blown ideology. Military orders of warrior monks grew up to defend Christendom and extend its borders (see ◊Military Order). In the 14th century kings began to create orders of chivalry to celebrate their power and the status of their military aristocracy, for example the ◊Order of the Garter.

It used to be thought that the chivalric code hampered the ability of its proponents to pursue warfare in a pragmatic style. While it is true that a sense of knightly class superiority could lead to some rash actions, most chivalric generals practised war as harshly as the code allowed. Both ◊Richard (I) the Lionheart and ◊Henry V massacred prisoners, and ◊Edward the Black Prince sacked Limoges; these actions were justified by the failure of their opponents to conduct warfare according to a convention which in some ways anticipated the Genevan code.

The influence of chivalry upon Western culture has been profound. Tied in with visions of crusading, it became the driving force behind the great period of exploration and discovery of the 'New World' of 15th- and 16th-century Europe. Without King Arthur there would have been no Columbus.

Order) and as a residence by ◊Joan of Arc in 1429.

Chios, Battle of indecisive sea battle in 201 BC between Philip V of Macedon and ◊Attalus I of Pergamum and his Rhodian allies. Philip claimed the victory although he suffered the heavier losses.

The battle developed into two separate actions in the channel between the Aegean island still called Chios and the west coast of modern Turkey. To the east, Attalus had some success before he was isolated and forced to run ashore. Although he escaped, the sight of the royal ship in enemy hands caused the rest of his fleet to withdraw. To the west, the Rhodians demonstrated their naval expertise, shearing off oars as they rowed through the line then swinging to ram the enemy's stern or side. The Macedonians eventually managed to disengage and the Rhodians withdrew to Chios.

Chippenham, Battle of victory of a Danish army under ◊Guthrum over the Anglo-Saxons of Wessex at Chippenham (in modern Wiltshire) after a surprise attack in January 878, during the mid-winter festival. The Saxons were scattered and King ◊Alfred the Great was driven into hiding with a small band of companions. Alfred built a fortification at Athelney (probably in Somerset) and resorted to guerrilla attacks against the Danes while he rebuilt his force.

Chitor the greatest fortress in Rajasthan, India, traditionally built by the legendary Pandava King Raja Bhima, but named after a king of the ◊Rajput Mori clan who flourished in the 7th century. It stands 150 m/500 ft above the surrounding plain, defended by walls enclosing an area of some 280 ha/690 acres within a perimeter 5.25 km/3.25 mi long and 0.8 km/0.5 mi wide.

The fortress was taken from the Moris by the Rajput rulers of Mewar in 734, and thereafter remained a tributary of that kingdom. It was captured by the sultan of Delhi ◊Ala al-Din Khilji in 1303, but was retaken by the Rajputs in 1340.

Chnodomar king of the Alamanni (a German tribe) who led a large army against Roman territory in Gaul and was defeated by the future emperor Julian the Apostate at Argentoratum in 357 (see ◊Argentoratum, Battle of). He was captured after the battle and died in captivity in Rome.

chokutō straight, single-edged Japanese sword principally used during the Nara period (645–794). Both imported Chinese and native Japanese blades of this period have survived in the collections of temples and shrines.

The blades are relatively light and of well-forged steel with a straight tempered edge (*hamon*), a longitudinal ridge (*shinogi*) on one side near the cutting edge, and a small, sharply angled point (*kissaki*). Some blades also have a slight curvature.

chong elite cavalry originally stationed in the capital of the kingdom of Silla during the ◊Three Kingdoms of Korea period. As Silla expanded, *chong* units were sent to conquered territory; there were six *chong* in the late Three Kingdoms period, commanded by tribal aristocrats.

After unification in the 7th century there were ten *chong*, now provincial garrison units contrasting with the ◊*sodang* of the capital.

chongbyong Korean conscript troops under the Yi dynasty, in the 15th century. They were part-time soldiers levied from peasants between the ages of 16 and 60. Some served in the ◊*owi* garrisons in the capital, others were assigned to serve by rotation in a *chinsugun* provincial garrison. The system was not thoroughly enforced and many evaded service.

Chosroes (I) Anushirvan (Persian *Khusrau*) Sassanian Persian king 531–79. He signed a 30-year peace with Rome in 561. About 558 (or 568) he allied himself with the new Gök Turk empire of the steppes to destroy and partition the Hephthalite *White Hun* empire, taking the lands south of the river Oxus (present-day Amu Darya). He also conquered Yemen in southern Arabia.

Chosroes made peace with the Roman emperor ◊Justinian soon after his accession, but renewed war in 540 by sacking Antioch. In 542 he was defeated in Palestine by Justinian's general ◊Belisarius. Prolonged fighting in the Caucasus against the Romans and their allies had mixed results, and peace was finally agreed.

At home, Chosroes reformed the administration and attempted to turn the ◊Sassanian armies into one centralized, professional force.

Chosroes II, Parviz (died 628) (or *Aparvez Chosroes;* Persian *Khusrau*) Sassanian Persian king from 590. He attacked the Eastern Roman Empire in 602, and in 626 planned an attack on Constantinople. The Roman emperor ◊Heraclius counterattacked in 627 and captured the Persian capital Ctesiphon in 628. Chosroes refused to surrender and was killed by his own nobles.

After Bahram Chobin murdered his father Hormizd IV in 590, Chosroes fled to the Roman emperor ◊Maurice, who supplied him with troops that defeated Bahram and restored

Chosroes to the throne. When Maurice was killed by Phokas in 602, Chosroes seized the excuse to attack the Eastern Empire, claiming he was avenging the crime. In 626, at the height of its success, his army along with Avar allies planned to attack Constantinople, but the city was saved when Chosroes's forces could not be transported across the straits. The following year, the new Roman emperor Heraclius attacked from the Black Sea coast, marching south through Armenia. He defeated the Persians in Azerbaijan and went on to capture their capital.

Chrysopolis, Battle of final battle, fought in 324, between the Roman emperor ◊Constantine (I) the Great and his eastern rival and co-ruler Valerius Licinianus Licinius, following the Battle of Adrianople (see ◊Adrianople, Battle of 324). Licinius was captured and executed, leaving Constantine as sole emperor.

Churyu, Battle of battle fought in 663 in the Korean kingdom of Paekche, during the Tang wars (see ◊Korea, Tang Chinese wars in), in which the Chinese defeated a Japanese force that had come to help Paekche.

Japanese-Paekche forces held the fortress of Churyu at the mouth of the river Kum. Chinese and Silla Korean armies besieged the city while a Chinese fleet of 170 ships attacked and defeated a Japanese fleet of 400, forcing it to withdraw. In a second encounter ten days later, the Chinese surrounded the Japanese fleet and inflicted heavy losses. The city surrendered soon afterwards.

Cibalae, Battle of battle fought in 315 between the Roman emperor ◊Constantine (I) the Great and his eastern rival and co-ruler Valerius Licinianus Licinius. It was Constantine's first battlefield success against Licinius. His 20,000 soldiers defeated the latter's 35,000 in a hard-fought action, finally decided by a breakthrough on the right led by Constantine himself.

Licinius managed to keep his army in order during the retreat, but lost 20,000 soldiers.

Cilgerran castle castle in Wales, 5 km/3 mi southeast of Cardigan. An Anglo-Norman castle sited on a rocky promontory above the river Teifi, south Wales, it occupied the site of a stronghold built by Gerald of Windsor, Lord of Pembroke, in the reign of ◊Henry I of England (1100–35) and was strongly fortified by 1109.

It was taken by the Lord Rhys of Deheubarth in 1165 and recaptured by William Marshall in 1204. In 1215 Cilgerran fell to Prince ◊Llewellyn the Great. Its surviving structure dates largely from 1223, when it was recaptured and extensively rebuilt by William Marshall the Younger. It later passed into the Hastings family, who became earls of

CICERO, QUINTUS TULLIUS (102–43 BC)

Roman senator, younger brother of the famous orator and statesmen Marcus Tullius Cicero. Although he seems to have been a capable soldier, his successful career was largely due to the fame of his brother.

As legate to Julius Caesar in Gaul, 54–52 BC, the younger Cicero participated in Caesar's second British expedition. He distinguished himself in the winter of 54–53 when the inexperienced legion under his command successfully defended its winter quarters from attacks by the rebellious tribes of the Eburones and Nervii. This provided Caesar with a much-needed success after the humiliating annihilation of 15 ◊cohorts at Atuatuca (possibly near modern Liège in Belgium). In 53 Quintus remained at Atuatuca to guard the army's baggage while Caesar led a punitive expedition against the Gauls, but three of his cohorts were badly cut up when they were surprised by German raiders while foraging. Cicero went to Cilicia (the region around modern Adana) as his brother's legate in 51 BC. He played a major part in preparations against the expected Parthian invasion, and was prominent in a short campaign to punish the tribes of Mount Amanus, on the border between Syria and Cilicia, for banditry. He sided with Pompey in the civil war against Caesar, but was pardoned, only to be executed in the proscriptions of ◊Mark Antony and Octavian.

Pembroke, but was in ruins by 1326. Some rebuilding was done around 1389 in apprehension of a French invasion.

Cimon (c. 510–450 BC) leading Athenian admiral of the 470s and 460s BC, son of ◊Miltiades. His greatest triumph was the victory over the Persians at Eurymedon (see ◊Eurymedon, Battle of) in 466, which possibly led them to sue for peace.

His first exploits were the capture of Eïon and Skyros in 476/5, and after the Battle of Eurymedon he commanded Athenian forces against Thasos in 465–62.

Acquitted of taking bribes from the King of Macedon on his return home, he persuaded the assembly to send him to help Sparta against the rebel ◊helots (?462), but was ostracized, probably in 461, when sent home by the Spartans. He was recalled in 451 to help negotiate a truce with Sparta, and was sent to Cyprus in command of a fleet, dying at the siege of Citium in 450.

CIVIL WARS, ROMAN REPUBLICAN

Series of civil wars during a period of great instability in Roman history, 91–31 BC.

The first of these conflicts, the ◊Italian Social War, 91–88 BC, resulted when many of Rome's Italian allies rebelled after being refused Roman citizenship. Successful campaigns by ◊Marius, ◊Sulla, and Pompeius Strabo, along with generous concessions for the allies who remained loyal, helped turn the tide in Rome's favour.

A second civil war occurred in 88–82 BC, when Sulla marched his legions on Rome after Marius had attempted to usurp his command to fight ◊Mithridates (VI) Eupator in Asia. Marius fled to Africa, but returned to retake the city in 87 BC, dying soon after. In 83 BC Sulla returned to Italy and inflicted several defeats on the senators opposed to him, sometimes called the Marians, before gaining final victory in 82 BC at the Colline Gate, one of the gates of the city of Rome. Pockets of resistance held out briefly in Sicily and Africa and more successfully in Spain under the leadership of Sertorius.

In 49–45 BC civil war broke out again when ◊Pompey the Great sided with Caesar's enemies in the Senate. When Caesar's consulship in Gaul ended, the Senate wished to prosecute him for his behaviour as a consul. He refused to submit and in 49 BC quickly captured Italy, forced the Pompeians in Spain to surrender, and crossed the Adriatic Sea. Caesar came close to disaster at Dyrrachium (see ◊Dyrrachium, Battle of 49–48 BC), but crushed Pompey at Pharsalus (see ◊Pharsalus, Battle of). Pompey was murdered in Egypt and Caesar, who had pursued him there, placed Cleopatra on the throne before defeating Pharnaces at Zela (see ◊Zela, Battle of) in 48–47 BC. He defeated strong Pompeian forces at Thapsus in Africa in 46 BC and at Munda in Spain in 45 BC.

The final civil war of the republic, 44–31 BC, was precipitated by Caesar's murder and only ended when Octavian established the principate. After the Ides of March, ◊Mark Antony raised an army to fight the two conspirators responsible for Caesar's death, Marcus Junius ◊Brutus and ◊Cassius. Octavian at first supported the conspiracy, but when the Senate seemed ready to discard him after Forum Gallorum in 43 BC (see ◊Forum Gallorum, Battle of), he changed sides and formed the Second Triumvirate with Antony and Lepidus. After defeating Brutus and Cassius at Philippi in 42 BC (see ◊Philippi, battles of), Octavian and Antony divided the empire between themselves. But the alliance broke down, provoked in part by Antony's association with Cleopatra, and Octavian defeated him at Actium (see ◊Actium, Battle of) to become the sole master of the Roman world.

cingulum Roman military belt consisting of rectangular metal plates riveted to a leather belt. Although use of such belts was widespread, the earliest indisputably Roman examples come from the Roman siege camps at Numantia and date from 133 BC. This type of *cingulum*, to which both sword and dagger were usually attached, remained in use until the 2nd century AD.

cingulum militiae (Latin 'soldier's belt') sword belt of a medieval knight. The sword and belt were strapped to a new knight during the dubbing ceremony and symbolized his entry into the order of knighthood. Both the term and associated meaning were derived from the ◊*cingulum* of the later Roman Empire.

Cinque Ports group of ports in southern England, originally five – Sandwich, Dover, Hythe, Romney, and Hastings – but later including Rye, Winchelsea, and others. They were probably founded in Roman times, but from the reign of the Danish king ◊Cnut the Great were obliged to supply ships and men for the royal fleet against invasion, in return for trade privileges. Their defence of England's southern coast was mostly successful, save for periods in the ◊Hundred Years' War.

The surrounding area, the Liberty of the Cinque Ports, included about 40 settlements. King John (1167–1216) issued charters in favour of the individual ports in 1206. The Liberty received its Great Charter in 1278.

Civitate, Battle of battle waged on 17 June 1053 between the Norman knight ◊Robert Guiscard and other Normans, and Pope Leo IX and his forces near modern San Severo, Italy. Leo was attempting to establish authority over the Norman barons of southern Italy, but he was taken prisoner and realized that he needed Norman military support.

The papal army included a detachment of Swabian infantry who fought with double-handed swords. The Norman forces, about 1,000 cavalry in three divisions, were successful on both flanks but were checked by the hard-fighting Swabian foot soldiers. Eventually the Norman right swung in behind them and they were slaughtered.

Clari, Robert de (died 13th century) knight and chronicler of the Fourth Crusade 1200–04 (see ◊Crusades). De Clari's account is valuable because it parallels that of ◊Villehardouin but is seen from the ordinary crusader's point of view, spiced with clear military detail.

He is critical of the diversion of the crusade to ◊Constantinople, but accepts the rigours of the siege uncomplainingly. He celebrates the involvement of his brother Alelme for being a member of the first group to break into the city; but he is unhappy about the distribution of the booty.

Clastidium, Battle of battle fought in 222 BC between the Roman army and Gaulish tribes at the Roman town of Clastidium (now Casteggio) in the Po Valley, Italy. The battle is notable for the winning of *spolia opima* (armour and weapons of the Gallic chieftain Viridomarus killed in single combat) by the Roman general Claudius ◊Marcellus and strengthened Rome's domination over the Italian Celts.

By attacking the Roman supply base at Clastidium, the Gauls hoped to draw the Roman army away from besieging their chief town of Acerrae. Marcellus sent his light infantry and cavalry to Clastidium's defence and succeeded in driving off the tribes.

Clearchus (lived late 5th century BC) Spartan general. He was twice governor of the former Athenian colony of Byzantium after the city's defection to Sparta, then joined the Persian prince ◊Cyrus the Younger as a mercenary and commanded the Greek right wing at Cunaxa in 401 BC (see ◊Cunaxa, Battle of).

Cleomenes I (lived 6th–5th centuries BC) king of Sparta c. 520–c. 490 BC, noted for his interventions in Athenian affairs in the late 6th century (seeking to bring Athens under Spartan influence), and his victory over Argos at Sepeia in 494 BC (see ◊Sepeia, Battle of).

He rejected an Ionian appeal for help in a revolt against Persia, and, allegedly, a grandiose Scythian proposal for an invasion of the Persian Empire. He secured the deposition of his fellow king Damaratus by bribing the Delphic oracle to declare him illegitimate. Forced to flee when the story leaked, he gathered support in Arcadia and frightened Sparta into restoring him. He committed suicide.

Cleomenes III (died c. 220 BC) king of Sparta from about 235 BC who tried to re-establish Spartan power in the Peloponnese. After defeating the Achaean League at Mount Lycaeum and Ladoceia in 227, he seized absolute power in Sparta and reformed the army on Macedonian lines. His attacks on Argos and Corinth in 225 and 224 caused the alarmed Achaean League to appeal to the Macedonian king ◊Antigonus (III) Doson for help.

At Sellasia in 222 (see ◊Sellasia, Battle of), he soundly defeated Cleomenes, who fled to Egypt and committed suicide.

Cleon (died 422 BC) Athenian politician and general in the early years of the ◊Peloponnesian War. He advocated tough measures against rebel allies, and in 425 BC was instrumental in having Spartan peace proposals rejected. In 422 he recaptured Torone and Galepsus in Thrace, but failed at Stagirus, and was killed by the Spartans outside Amphipolis.

clibanarius (Latin 'oven man') late Roman heavily armoured cavalry soldier. ◊Cataphracts were given this nickname in the 3rd to 5th centuries AD because they became extremely hot when wearing their armour.

Clontarf, Battle of battle fought in 1014 at Clontarf, Dublin, Ireland, between the forces of the Irish High King ◊Brian Boruma and the Dublin Vikings and their Leinster allies, who challenged Brian's authority but were defeated. Although the Irish victory eliminated the Norse threat to Ireland, Brian and his son were both killed in the battle.

The Dublin Vikings had been reinforced from Orkney and Man together with contingents from all over the Viking world including, possibly, some Normans. They drew up with the Leinstermen in the centre and Viking contingents on the flanks. Initially the Leinstermen drove back the Irish centre, while the High King's men pushed back the flanks. However, the Leinstermen advanced too far, became isolated, and were driven back in disorder. The left wing then also collapsed and although the Vikings on the right attempted to withdraw to Dublin in good order, most of their men were killed.

Losses are recorded at over 6,000 Vikings and 4,000 Irish, including Brian, his son Murchadh, and his grandson Tordelbach. Jarls Sigurd of Orkney and Brodir of Man were also killed.

CLOVIS (465–511)

(or *Chlodovech*)

King of the Salian Franks 481–511, who extended his realm from a small area around Tournai to encompass most of modern France and parts of modern Germany.

At the age of 15 he succeeded his father Childereic, inheriting the leadership of the Salian Franks who were settled in what is now Flanders. In 486 he moved against the Gallo-Roman warlord Syagrius, defeating him near Soissons and incorporating the area north of the river Loire into his kingdom. He then moved east to intervene in a Burgundian dynastic dispute, but failed to bring the Burgundians under his rule. He waged a long war against the Alamanni, eventually extending the boundaries of his kingdom east of the Rhine, and he succeeded in conquering most of the Visigothic possessions in France. He maintained his power through strength of personality and playing rivals off against each other. When necessary he would not hesitate to use treachery or brutality.

In 493 Clovis married Clotilda, daughter of the Burgundian Chilperic II. Clotilda was a Catholic and exerted a great influence over him. She is said to have inspired him to convert to Christianity at a critical moment in the Battle of Tolbiac in 496. Whatever the truth, he and 3,000 of his followers were baptized as Catholics at Rheims at Christmas 496.

Clovis seized the banner of Catholicism to rally support and undermine the other Germanic kingdoms. In 507 he moved against the Visigoths. His victory at Vouillé (see ◊Vouillé, Battle of) was decisive and Clovis became ruler of most of what is now France. By now he ruled over a vast area and several peoples. The Eastern emperor Anastasius granted him an honorary title of 'consul' , no doubt seeing him as a counterweight to Theodoric the Great in Italy. Clovis moved his capital to Paris and laid the foundations for what was eventually to become the French nation. He died unexpectedly in 511 and his kingdom was divided up amongst his four sons.

Clos des Galées medieval French royal naval arsenal based at Rouen, on the river Seine, France. It was copied from Italian models and was designed to provide the French king with a fleet to dominate the English Channel. The Clos des Galées was constructed by Philip IV in 1294–98. By 1338 it had 17 covered bays and could support probably twice that number of vessels.

After an inauspicious start to the ◊Hundred Years' War, suffering defeat at Sluys (see ◊Sluys, Battle of), the French galley fleet steadily proved its worth in raids on the English coast. In 1372 a combined force of Franco-Genoese galleys destroyed a becalmed Anglo-Castilian sailing fleet.

Clypea (modern *Kelibia*) Carthaginian fortress on the southeastern horn of modern Cap Bon, Tunisia. It was one of a series of fortifications that commanded the coastline of Cap Bon (including Ras-el-Fortass, Ras-el-Drek, and Kerkouane), and was occupied between the 5th and 2nd centuries BC.

Its strategic value is clear from the landings on Cap Bon by ◊Agathocles in 310 BC, Marcus Atilius ◊Regulus (who captured the position in 256 BC), and ◊Scipio Aemilianus in 147 BC.

Cnidus, Battle of sea battle in the ◊Corinthian War which ended the brief period of Spartan's dominance at sea that began with Aegospotami (see ◊Aegospotami, Battle of). It was fought near Cnidus, which lay at the end of the peninsula now called Resadiye on the southwest tip of Turkey, in 394 BC.

Forces involved were 85 Spartan triremes commanded by Peisander and over 90 Persian-built triremes jointly commanded by the Persian ◊Pharnabazus and the Athenian ◊Conon. What happened is uncertain, but Peisander's allies fled, he was killed and his fleet was driven ashore, losing 50 ships.

Cnut the Great (c. 995–1035) (or *Canute*) king of England from 1016, Denmark from 1018, and Norway from 1028. Having invaded England in 1013 with his father Sweyn, King of Denmark, he was acclaimed king on Sweyn's death in 1014 by his Viking army. Cnut defeated ◊Edmund (II) Ironside at the Battle of Ashingdon (or Assandun), Essex, in 1016 and became king of all England on Edmund's death.

He succeeded his brother Harold as king of Denmark in 1018, compelled King Malcolm II to pay homage by invading Scotland about 1027, and conquered Norway in 1028. His empire was crumbling at his death, after defeat by Swedes in 1025 and the loss of Norway. He was succeeded by his illegitimate son Harold I 'Harefoot' (died 1040).

coat armour (French *cote à armer*) contemporary historical term for the ◊surcoat, a long fabric garment, usually sleeveless, worn over armour in medieval Europe.

The surcoat, thought to have been adopted from the Muslims during the Crusades as a method of keeping ◊mail armour cool, first appeared about 1150 and was worn in approximately the same form until the 1320s. In the 13th century some surcoats are illustrated with elbow-length sleeves. By about 1340 the surcoat had become a tight-fitting garment with long sleeves and skirts extending to the knee, and by about 1350 it was shortened to the hips, a form in which it survived until the early 15th century. Although the term coat armour was still used, the term 'jupon' or 'gipoun' was also used from about 1350.

coat of plates (or *pair of plates*) protective body covering made of iron plates riveted inside a fabric coat. It was widely worn by the European knightly classes from the second half of the 13th century until the introduction of the one-piece breastplate at the end of the 14th century.

Coca castle (or *Castillo de Fonseca*) castle-palace in Spain, about 60 km/37 mi south-southeast of Valladolid. Built by Alfonso de Fonseca, Archbishop of Seville, in the 15th century, it is considered to be one of the finest examples of the Moorish-influenced Spanish style known as *mudejar*.

Built of brick in rectangular concentric form, it is surrounded by a dry ditch into which the walls fall in a sharply-inclined plinth. These outer walls enclose an inner walled rectangle, with the powerful keep at one corner. Construction was never completed as the archbishop had intended, the work being overtaken by the wars of the 15th century against the Moors, during which the interior was severely damaged.

Cockermouth castle castle in Cumbria, England, 39 km/24 mi southwest of Carlisle. Built at the confluence of the Cocker and Derwent rivers, this was a keep-and-two-bailey design which cleverly used the rivers to provide an efficient water barrier. It was begun some time in the 13th century, and a curtain wall, outer bailey, and barbican were added some time in the 14th century.

cog northern European ship common from about 1200 to 1400, often over 200 tons in burden, used for both transport and war. A cog was clinker-built, single-masted, and had a high, boxlike hull and steep stem and stern posts, with castles fore and aft. It represented a significant advance over the ◊longship in carrying capacity.

Vessels of this type played a role in the 13th-century crusader conquest of the southern Baltic shores, being practically invulnerable to the skiffs (light rowing boats) used by their heathen opponents. They were also the main ship type in 14th-century English navies, the castles providing shooting platforms for the archers, as at Sluys and Winchelsea (see ◊Sluys, Battle of and ◊Winchelsea, Battle of).

cognizance medieval European heraldic term for a coat of arms or a representation of part of it carried by retainers or subjects.

cohort principal subunit of the Roman ◊legion usually consisting of 6 ◊centuries or 480 men from at least the 1st century BC onwards. It was the commonest unit of the ◊auxilia. The first cohort of imperial legions and many auxiliary units consisted of 800 men.

coif medieval European protective head covering made of ◊mail. Coifs were worn continuously by men-at-arms until the mid-14th century when the ◊basinet and ◊aventail become the commonest form of head defence.

Colchester castle castle in Essex, England, 103 km/64 mi northeast of London. It had the greatest Norman keep in England, with foundations 9 m/30 ft deep. Built in around 1078, at the same time as the ◊Tower of London, it had improvements such as corner towers, which give flank protection to the wall, and a solid plinth beneath the ground floor, which was impervious to rams and mining.

In 1091 it was given to the High Steward of Colchester, from whom it passed to the Clare family. They built a wall around the bailey and made some improvements in the accommodation.

Co-Loa capital of the Au Lac kingdom in northern Vietnam, in the Red River flood plain, 15 km/9 mi northwest of what is now Hanoi. Fortified in the late 3rd century BC by An Duong, founder of Au Lac, it fell in around 180 BC to ◊Zhao Tuo, but remained in use under Chinese rule.

It was called 'snail city' from its concentric fortifications – an inner rectangular rampart surrounded by two outer moated oval ramparts, covering 600 ha/1,500 acres. The outer wall covered an 8 km/5 mi circuit and was 12 m/39 ft thick.

comes Latin title for European continental magnates usually translated as 'count', but used in England for 'earl'. An early British use was for the Roman commander of the Saxon Shore forts. It was also commonly used to refer to someone in a high position at court or a provincial commander. A dependent area commanded by a *comes* became a county. The title often retained a military sense though its prime use came to signify rank.

comitatenses line units of the mobile field army of the late Roman Empire (4th–6th centuries). Created in the early 4th century, they originally formed the Emperor's ◊comitatus (central reserve). They soon evolved into regional field armies based in key locations throughout the Empire.

comitatus group of personal companions of a late Roman or Germanic leader. The first *comitatus* belonged to the Roman emperor Diocletian in the late 3rd to early 4th centuries. From the end of the 4th century most Roman and Germanic military commanders were accompanied by a *comitatus:* troops who owed direct allegiance to the individual commander, rather than to the army as a whole.

Scholars are divided as to whether the first *comitatus* of Diocletian was simply his inner circle of friends and advisors, or the embryo of the mobile field army (◊comitatenses).

commission of array system developed by ◊Edward I of England to improve the numbers and quality of foot soldiers recruited. In 1277 county sheriffs were used for the task, and by 1282 household knights were involved. The small number of commissioners could not interview all the potential recruits and had to employ local people, which led to corruption. The system produced soldiers in quantity rather than quality.

Commius king of the Atrebates (or Trebates) tribe in Gallia Belgica (now northern France and Belgium) 57–50 BC. Commius was an ally of Rome before supporting the Gallic revolt of about 51 BC (see ◊Gallic Wars). As a result his tribal lands were seized and he was sent into exile in 50 BC, establishing a new kingdom in southern England.

Commius was awarded his kingdom by the Roman general and proconsul Julius ◊Caesar in 57 BC, and was sent on a mission to England in 55 BC to try and persuade the Belgae peoples there to submit to Rome peacefully. Returning to Gaul he pledged support to the Gallic revolt, but a serious injury resulting from a Roman assassination attempt left him and his tribe out of the fighting.

compagnon d'armes (medieval French) companion or brother-in-arms. The most famous pair were Roland and Oliver, the legendary heroes of the ◊chansons de geste, especially the 11th-century ◊Chanson de Roland. Their friendship epitomized military loyalty. This type of companionship was not restricted to literary figures, however, and could have genuine military value.

The English knight and jouster William ◊Marshal had a companion on the tournament circuit about 1170, and in the 14th century Bertrand du ◊Guesclin and Sir Hugh ◊Calveley were brothers-in-arms despite fighting on opposite sides in the Hundred Years' War.

condottiere (plural   **condottieri**) Italian term for a leader, used from the 13th to 16th centuries to describe a mercenary soldier, originally a captain who commanded his own company and sold its services to any state or prince ready to pay. The contract signed to employ such a company was called a 'condotta'.

The concept originated in Italy and spread throughout Europe. Many *condottieri* were foreigners, for example from Spain, France, Germany, and England. Notable companies were the White Company, the Great Company (mainly French and German), and the Catalan Company.

Conisbrough castle castle in England, 8 km/5 mi southwest of Doncaster, built around 1180 by Hamelin Plantagenet, half-brother of Henry II, on a natural mound improved by ditching. Among the earliest curtain walls built in Britain, the wall surrounding the top of the mound was 11 m/35 ft high and 2 m/7 ft thick and had solid towers projecting at intervals. A long and narrow walled barbican protected the entrance gate.

At the opposite end of the bailey was the great circular keep, 29 m/95 ft high, with six buttresses. The keep was almost 'blind', having few windows other than the arrow-slits, but the ingenious design concealed a chapel, pigeon-loft, water cistern, guardrooms, and other domestic offices within the buttresses.

Conon (c. 450–389 BC) Athenian admiral. In 407 BC he superseded ◊Alcibiades in the eastern Aegean. After the Athenian defeat by the Spartans at Aegospotami (see ◊Aegospotami, Battle of) in 405, he fled to Cyprus. In 394, as joint commander of a Persian fleet, he won a decisive victory over the Spartans at Cnidus (see ◊Cnidus, Battle of).

After recovering control of much of the Aegean, he returned to Athens in 393, but was denounced to the Persians by the Spartans in 392 and arrested. Though he escaped to Cyprus, he died soon afterwards.

conquest, Hindu doctrine of in Hindu doctrine from the 4th century BC onwards, conquests were categorized into three types: *dharma-vijaya* ('righteous victory'), after which the defeated king was reinstated as a vassal or tributary; *lobha-vijaya* ('greedy victory'), after which the defeated side surrendered treasure and territory; and *asura-vijaya* ('demoniac victory'), the complete destruction of the defeated state and its annexation by the victor.

Most texts approved only the first category, which allowed kings to make war to achieve glory and status but permitted the defeated side to survive. The realistic Brahman minister ◊Kautilya advised a defeated king to submit in the hope that one day he might turn the tables on his new overlord, but recommended 'demoniac conquest' as the best policy for a victorious king.

conroi medieval French term for a unit of knights, some 20 to 60 in number, usually the following of a particular lord. Dating to the 12th century, usage of the word proves that knightly cavalry was capable of battlefield manoeuvre, including feigned flights. Sometimes the word *conroi* could mean the whole battle array.

constable (Latin *comes stabuli* 'count of the stable') in medieval Europe, an officer of the king, originally responsible for army stores and stabling, and later responsible for the army in the king's absence. In England the constable subsequently became an official at a sheriff's court of law. In France the constable became the commander-in-chief under the king, a post held by such men as Bertrand du ◊Guesclin.

constabulary medieval term meaning a group (or troop) of ten knights, the smallest unit of knightly cavalry.

Constantine (I) the Great (285–337) first Christian emperor of Rome 306–37 and founder of Constantinople (modern Istanbul, Turkey). He defeated Maxentius, joint emperor of Rome, in 312, and in 313 formally recognized Christianity. As sole emperor of the west of the empire, he defeated Licinius, emperor of the east, to become ruler of the Roman world in 324. Constantine moved his capital to Byzantium on the Bosporus in 330, renaming it Constantinople.

Constantine was born at Naissus (modern Niš, Serbia), the son of Constantius. He was already well known as a soldier when his father died in York, England, in 306 and he was acclaimed by the troops there as joint emperor in his father's place. A few years later Maxentius, the joint emperor in Rome (whose sister had married Constantine), challenged his authority and mobilized his armies to invade Gaul (France). Constantine won a crushing victory at the Milvian Bridge near Rome in 312 (see ◊Milvian Bridge, Battle of the).

During this campaign he was said to have seen a vision of the cross of Jesus superimposed upon the sun, accompanied by the words: 'In this sign, conquer'. By the Edict of Milan of 313 he formally recognized Christianity as one of the religions legally permitted within the Roman Empire. In 337 he set out to defend the Euphrates frontier against the Persians, but died at Nicomedia in Asia Minor before reaching it.

Constantinople ancient city founded by the Greeks as Byzantium about 660 BC and refounded by the Roman emperor ◊Constantine (I) the Great in AD 330 as the capital of the Eastern Roman Empire. Constantinople (modern Istanbul, Turkey) was the impregnable bastion of the Eastern Roman Empire and the Byzantine Empire, its successor, until it fell to the Turks in 1453.

For over a thousand years the walls established by the emperors of Rome and of the Eastern Empire defended the city against all assailants. Nothing is known of the early defences before Constantine began construction of fortifications to protect his new capital; these ran in an exterior arc from the present-day Atatürk Bridge to the Istanbul Hospital, but have not survived.

The emperor Theodosius II (reigned 408–50) began construction of a new land wall 6 km/3.7 mi long, 1.3 km/0.8 mi west of Constantine's fortifications. These new walls, improved and enlarged during Theodosius' reign, became the basis of Constantinople's defence. Consisting of an inner and outer wall with a deep moat in front, the two walls were of descending height, allowing artillery fire to be directed from both. The inner wall was fortified by 96 towers and had 8 main gates as well as several posterns. Walls were also constructed along the seashore, completely enclosing the city. In about 510 the Long Wall was constructed 65 km/40 mi to the west, but at over 45 km/28 mi in length it was impractical to defend and it was abandoned in the 7th century.

Constantinople, capture of recapture of the city of Constantinople from the Latin Empire by the Byzantine emperor ◊Michael (VIII) Palaeologus' general Alexios Strategopoulos on 25 July 1261, when it was undefended. The Latins (western crusaders), who had held the city since 1204, left it unprotected when their fleet was away. Alexios

moved 500 troops in through the Pege Gate, killing the guards and recovering the city without fighting.

Constantinople, Siege of (626) unsuccessful siege of the Byzantine capital in 626 by a large force of ◊Avars and Slavs (allegedly 100,000 strong), supported by two Persian armies. The defence of Constantinople was conducted by the Byzantine emperor ◊Heraclius' son Constantine. The siege began on 29 July; after suffering terrible losses, the Avars burned their siege engines on 10 August and withdrew.

An earlier attempt by the Avars to take Constantinople in 619 had been bought off by the Byzantines. Encouraged by the absence of Heraclius, who was campaigning in eastern Anatolia against the Persians, the Avars and their allies began a siege of the city, while the two Persian armies moved to support them.

While Constantine defended Constantinople, the emperor's brother Theodore attacked and defeated one of the Persian armies, killing its commander Shahin. Meanwhile Avar assaults on the walls were repulsed and the Slav fleet in the Bosporus was completely destroyed by the Byzantine navy, effectively preventing any linkup between the Avar and Persian armies on opposite sides of the waterway.

Constantinople, Siege of (669–77) intermittent and unsuccessful siege of the Byzantine capital by the Muslim Arabs, who attacked the city from both land and the sea. They were repeatedly repulsed, and finally forced to agree a truce with the Byzantines.

An attempted assault on the walls in 669 was driven back and the Arab army was then defeated at the Battle of Armorium. A naval attack in 672 was repulsed, and the Arab fleet was destroyed at Cyzicus (see ◊Cyzicus, Battle of 672). For the next five years skirmishes at land and sea continued around Constantinople until the Byzantines again destroyed the Arab fleet, forcing Caliph Mu'awiya to give up Cyprus, pay an annual tribute, and agree to a 30-year truce.

Constantinople, Siege of (717–18) unsuccessful siege of the Byzantine capital by the Arabs under the general Maslama. The failure of the Arabs to take Constantinople saved eastern Europe from possible Muslim conquest.

Taking advantage of anarchy in the Byzantine Empire, Maslama led 80,000 troops across the Hellespont. He dispatched part of his force into Thrace to block any attempt by the Byzantines' Bulgar allies to break the siege, and prepared the rest for an assault, which was

CONSTANTINOPLE, SEIGE OF (1203–04)

Siege in 1203 and capture and sack in 1204 of Constantinople by crusaders of the Fourth Crusade, largely as a result of Venetian political and economic machinations. They ended the city's reputation as an impregnable Byzantine fortress and established a short-lived Latin Empire, which lasted until 1261.

The crusaders, numbering some 2,000 knights and 10,000 foot, were transported by the Venetian fleet to try to install a pretender on the Byzantine throne. The fleet arrived on 24 June 1203, and established camp at Scutari on the Asian side of the Bosporus. On 6 July the Venetians broke the chain across the Golden Horn while knights stormed the Galata Tower on its eastern bank. This enabled the besiegers to shift their camp to opposite the Blachernae Palace in the northeastern corner of the city walls, accessible by combined assault from land and sea. Their first attempt on 17 July employed flying bridges from the masts of Venetian ships. These were lowered onto the tops of the walls, while rams were swung at their base and shipboard artillery gave supporting fire. Enrico ◊Dandolo, the Venetian doge, led the attack which seized 25–30 towers in the Petrion sector. The next day the crusaders faced attack by the Byzantine emperor Alexius' superior forces and nearly charged impetuously into their midst, but ◊Baldwin of Flanders's control prevented disaster. As a result the city surrendered and Isaac Angleus was declared emperor.

In 1204 the crusaders found themselves having to attack the city again to oust the Byzantine usurper Alexius V. They defeated his cavalry outside the walls, then resumed preparations to attack the walls. Rams and siege engines were constructed on land to attack the Blachernae Palace, while the Venetian ships also mounted stone-throwers and leather-covered siege towers, together with flying bridges. An attack on 8 April was driven back by contrary winds, which prevented the ships from lying alongside the walls. Then, on 12 April, with a favourable wind, they attacked again. Some broke in through a postern gate, while others seized the towers. This time the city was sacked, losing half of its houses to a great fire.

beaten back with heavy losses. When a fleet of Arab reinforcements was destroyed by the Byzantine navy the attackers settled down for a long siege.

After the winter, the Byzantine emperor Leo III launched a counterattack. His fleet destroyed the Arab blockade in the Bosporus and his army broke the enemy surrounding Chalcedon. In the summer the Bulgars attacked and defeated the Muslim blocking force at Adrianople (see ◊Adrianople, Battle of 718). The surviving Arabs lifted the siege and retreated back across Anatolia.

Constantinople, Siege of (1394–1402) siege lasting from 1394 to 1402 in which the Ottoman sultan Bayezid I blockaded Constantinople despite Christian relief attempts, until his defeat at Ankara (see ◊Ankara, Battle of) in 1402 by ◊Timur Leng (Tamerlane).

Bayezid was determined to take the city and besieged it from the spring of 1394 with 10,000 troops. While the siege continued, he defeated Mircea of Wallachia in 1395 and the crusade of Nicopolis in 1396. Jean le Maingre ◊Boucicault, who was captured in the battle, returned with over 2,000 men in 1399 and skirmished aggressively for six months. But while help from the West failed, Bayezid's utter defeat by Timur Leng (Tamerlane) at Ankara spared the city until 1453.

Constantinople, Siege of (1453) final siege of the Byzantine capital, from 5 April to 29 May 1453, by Ottoman Turkish forces under ◊Mehmet (II) the Conqueror. Mehmet conquered Constantinople using a combination of naval blockade, battery by gunpowder artillery, and mass assaults. This siege brought an end to the Byzantine Empire.

Mehmet mustered 100,000 men, including 12,000 elite Janissaries (members of the standing Ottoman army) against 7,000 defenders under the Genoese ◊*condottiere* Giovanni Giustiniani. Mehmet sealed off the city by land and sea and commenced bombardment with huge cannon. A naval attack on 12 June was held off, and the Venetian fleet inflicted another defeat on 20 April, but the brilliant ploy of transporting Turkish ships over land on rollers into the Golden Horn (the narrow inlet that was the city's main harbour) negated the Venetian naval superiority. Assaults on the walls on 12 and 17 May were repulsed, but eventually the Janissaries stormed in through a breach and the city fell.

contubernium mess unit in a Roman army. Each ◊century in a Roman legion or auxiliary unit was divided into *contubernia* of about eight men who messed together. Although these were not tactical units, the system encouraged morale in battle.

Conway castle (Welsh *Conwy*) castle in Conway, Wales, at the northeastern end of the Menai Strait. It was one of several castles built by Edward I in order to subjugate the Welsh. Begun in 1283, it was built to the design of James of St George. Its principal purpose was to protect the trade route through the Vale of Conway, and the design included walling the town.

Completed by 1290, it withstood a siege by the Welsh in 1294, but within 30 years it was showing signs of decay and was rebuilt in 1346.

Conwy, Siege of Welsh action against ◊Edward I of England at Conwy castle, Wales, in 1294–95, part of a revolt led by Madoc ap Llewellyn against English overlordship. Edward spent Christmas at Conwy, where the Welsh besieged him. They were driven off and in January 1295 Edward advanced to Bangor, but he was forced back to Conwy.

The revolt had begun in 1294. Edward's new Welsh castles were weakly garrisoned and Caernarfon had been razed, causing Edward to turn back to Wales from a planned expedition to France.

Coolus helmet (or *Mannheim helmet*) helmet of Celtic origin found mainly in France and the Rhineland, which appears to have been adopted by the Roman legions operating in Gaul in the 1st century BC. It was very similar to the ◊Montefortino helmet, but had a spherical skull cap without a topknot and apparently no cheek pieces.

In the early 1st century AD the neck guard was enlarged and a brow guard and large cheek pieces fitted. The Coolus helmet was superseded by the ◊Imperial Gallic helmet in the second half of the 1st century AD.

Corbridge fort (Roman *Coriosopitum*) Roman auxiliary fort at Corbridge, England, on the early northern frontier in Britain. It was soon refounded as a military supply base and civil town that catered for ◊Hadrian's Wall.

The original fort guarded the crossing of the main route north over the river Tyne from the AD 80s. A few decades later it served as a garrison post on the Stanegate frontier, an east–west patrol road constructed across the north of England. The construction of Hadrian's Wall left Corbridge fort 4 km/2.5 mi to the south and no longer of use, but the strategic location of the site on an important road junction and river crossing made it ideal for supplying the new frontier. A civilian town and military supply depot was soon developed with the military presence consisting of two walled compounds, later united, which contained workshops and accommodation.

Corbulo, Gnaeus Domitius (died c. AD 67) Roman general under the emperors Claudius and Nero, governor of Germany (in 47) and later Syria. He campaigned against the Chauci in Germany, and won outstanding victories in a series of campaigns against the Parthians 58–63. He was executed by Nero, who may have suspected his loyalty.

Renowned as a disciplinarian, Corbulo was appointed by Nero to command the eastern frontier against a Parthian threat in 54. He surprised the Parthians by a forced march through Armenia, capturing several key cities by storm, and ultimately brokered a peace between Rome and Parthia that lasted nearly 50 years.

Corfe castle castle in England 16 km/10 mi southwest of Bournemouth, Dorset. It was founded by William the Conqueror and built on a hilltop scarped to form a mound and ditch. A keep was added in the reign of Henry I (1068–1135).

Reputedly one of the strongest castles in England, in the 12th century it featured prominently in the wars between Stephen and Matilda. Later used by King John as a prison, it was considerably strengthened by Henry III who added the curtain walls.

Corfu, Battle of battle fought off the Greek island of Corfu in the autumn of 1084 between the Norman knight and ruler of southern Italy ◊Robert Guiscard, making another attempt to conquer Byzantium after the loss of Durazzo in 1083, and the Venetian fleet of the Byzantine emperor Alexius (I) Comnenus. The Venetian fleet was defeated by Guiscard's superior naval tactics.

Alexius had a fleet of nine great Venetian ◊triremes and three large Greek galleys. The Venetian vessels took up a close formation known as the 'sea harbour'. Guiscard attacked on all sides with three groups of five lighter, more manoeuvrable galleys, supported by smaller craft. He drove off the Greek vessels, sank seven of the Venetian ships, and captured the other two.

Corinthian helmet commonest form of Greek hoplite helmet in use from the 8th century to the beginning of the 5th century BC. It was ideal for fighting in a ◊phalanx formation, where the head was the most vulnerable part of the body. The helmet completely encased the head, but had a T-shaped split down the front leaving the eyes, mouth, and nose uncovered, although the nose was still protected by a ◊nasal.

The late form is arguably the most elegant helmet ever designed. The only flaw in the design was that the wearer could not hear through the helmet. Attempts, such as making holes in the sides, were made to try to solve the problem, but the type was finally abandoned in favour of the ◊Chalcidian helmet, ◊Attic helmet, and ◊Thracian helmet.

Corinthian War war fought 395–386 BC between the Greek city-state of Sparta and an alliance of other Greek city-states that feared Sparta, primarily Boeotia, Corinth, Athens, and Argos. Persia became involved to remove Spartan forces from Asia Minor, and negotiated a peace settlement.

The war was sparked off by a border incident between Locris and Phocis, which drew in Boeotia on the Locrian side and Sparta on the Phocian side. Sparta failed to crush Boeotia and the Spartan commander ◊Lysander was killed at Haliartus in 395, but it defeated the allies at the Nemea in 394 (see ◊Nemea, Battle of the) before they could invade Laconia. Meanwhile, King Agesilaus of Sparta, summoned home from Asia Minor, also defeated an allied army which attempted to block his path at Coronea in 394 (see ◊Coronea, Battle of), just after a Persian-financed fleet under the Athenian commander ◊Conon had crushed the Spartans off Cnidus (see ◊Cnidus, Battle of).

The war on land now became a series of skirmishes around Corinth, but at sea Conon's successes alarmed Persia into thinking they heralded a revival of the Athenian empire in the Aegean. Eventually, in 387, Persia negotiated a treaty with Sparta which led to the cutting of Athens' supply line through the Hellespont and to the 'King's Peace', dictated by the King of Persia with Spartan backing.

Cornwall, Sir John (lived 15th century) English commander who fought under Henry V at Agincourt in 1415 (see ◊Agincourt, Battle of), commanding the advance guard during the march and covering the Somme crossing. He also fought in the subsequent English conquest of Normandy. After his son was killed at Meaux, northeastern France, in 1422 he decided to abandon warfare. He declared that Henry's war was unjust and vowed never again to take arms against Christians.

Coronea, Battle of battle fought in 394 BC during the ◊Corinthian War in which King ◊Agesilaus II of Sparta, returning from Asia Minor, defeated an army of Thebans and other Boeotians, Athenians, Argives, Corinthians and others at Coronea, about 4 km/2.5 mi south of the modern village of Koroneia.

Xenophon described the battle as 'like none of the others in our time', probably because when both sides won on their right, as often happened in hoplite encounters, Agesilaus countermarched his phalanx and met the victorious Thebans head-on as they tried to rejoin their defeated allies on the slopes of a nearby hill. Though they suffered heavy losses, the Thebans broke through, probably by massing their hoplites deeper than usual.

corsalet general term for armour covering the chest and back; see also ◊cuirass.

Cortenuova, Battle of battle fought in Italy in 1237 between the Holy Roman emperor ◊Frederick II of Hohenstaufen and the Lombard League, an association of northern Italian towns asserting their independence from imperial rule. The Lombards were defeated and Frederick held a Roman-style triumph march, but German power in Italy was to be short-lived.

Frederick had planned to winter in Cremona and he followed the Lombard army northwards. They met by the river crossing at Cortenuova, where the imperial advance engaged the enemy. The Lombard army formed around the Milanese ◊carroccio. The battle continued all day. During the night the Lombards withdrew, abandoning the carroccio, which was stuck in the mud.

corvus (Latin 'raven') Roman naval device used for boarding enemy vessels.

The corvus was a drawbridge with a spike (resembling the beak of a raven) at the end, which was dropped onto an enemy vessel, allowing the ship to be held while Roman marines crossed to take possession. The *corvus* was designed to counter Carthaginian naval superiority and to gain maximum advantage from legionary fighting power. It was tactically successful, but made the ship to which it was fitted unstable and difficult to manoeuvre.

Cosa city (modern Ansedonia, Italy) founded as a colony by Rome in 273 BC in order to control the western coast road through Etrusca. Situated on a rocky hill that commanded the coastal plain, the defences enclosed an area 900 × 950 × 600 × 870 m/984 × 1,040 × 655 × 950 yds.

A citadel was constructed on the hill in the southwest corner, the highest point of the area enclosed by the defences. This refuge had a small postern gate giving access through the west wall. The city had gates on only three sides, as the steep terrain on the west side made it impracticable. The west and south sides had square towers placed along their length at regular intervals of roughly 50 m/165 ft. Only one is known on the east side.

Cothon military harbour of the North African city of Carthage. The Cothon was a circular harbour with a central island shielded from external view by a double wall. Access was through the rectangular 'merchant's harbour', although during the Roman siege of Carthage 147–146 BC part of the sea wall was demolished to allow a surprise Punic sortie.

Excavations have revealed ship sheds dating from the 2nd century BC. These berths probably housed 160 to 170 ships. This figure is close to the number of 220 triremes given by the Greek historian ◊Appian as the capacity of the harbour.

Cotrone, Battle of decisive defeat in 982 for the German army under Emperor Otto II in southern Italy in 982 by the Byzantine Empire's Muslim allies led by Abul Kasim.

The Germans managed to drive off the Muslim advance guard, then charged and broke the centre of the Muslim main line, killing Abul Kasim in the process. The Muslim reserve intervened to hit the Germans in the flank, and succeeded in breaking them. Meanwhile the German fleet was destroyed by the Byzantine navy at Stilo. The emperor Otto is said to have escaped on a Byzantine ship whose crew did not recognize him.

cottereau term applied to mercenaries in medieval France and neighbouring regions, first recorded in 1127 and taken to mean 'disturbers' or 'destroyers'. They came mainly from Provence, the Pyrenees, and the Low Countries.

They were denounced at a papal council in 1179 and attacked by local populations in 1183.

Cotyaeum, Battle of defeat of Isuarian rebels in 493 at the hands of an East Roman army consisting mostly of Goths. The Isuarians were semi-independent, warlike mountain people who formed a vital part of the East Roman armies of the 5th and 6th centuries.

couched lance medieval technique of holding the ◊lance firmly under the right armpit and resting it on the saddle bow in order to unite the impetus of rider and charging horse to deliver a blow.

Coucy castle castle in northern France, 20 km/12 mi north of Soissons on the river Aisne. Roughly triangular, the castle's most impressive feature was the ◊donjon (keep) on the southern wall, consisting of a circular tower 18 m/59 ft wide and 32 m/105 ft high, which acted as a residence as well as a stronghold.

The castle passed to the French crown in 1498 but was then neglected.

Courtrai, Battle of battle fought on 11 July 1302 in Flanders (present-day Belgium) in which Flemish townsmen, seeking independence from King Philip IV of France, defeated a force of French knights. Their victory surprised contemporaries. The Flemish called it the 'Battle of the Golden Spurs', from the 700 pairs of gilded spurs that were taken from the defeated knights.

The Flemings were besieged at Courtrai on 26 June. Their 10,000 troops, mostly infantry equipped with crossbows and ◊goedendags, were opposed by 2,000–3,000 French knights and about 5,000 foot soldiers. The Flemish defended water-filled ditches, which Count Robert of Artois rashly assaulted with cavalry. He was killed in the ensuing debacle, along with half his knights.

Courtrai castle stronghold at the heart of a Flemish castellany, split from Tournai. It was built between 1394 and 1396 for Philip the Bold, Duke of Burgundy. The plans were worked on by master masons from St Omer, France, and on the spot by Henry Heubens. The works were under the supervision of a local canon and an official known as the *bailli*.

couter piece of plate armour for the elbow, used by European men-at-arms (and occasionally ordinary soldiers) by the early 14th century. Towards the end of the 14th century the couter became part of the fully articulated ◊vambrace (arm defence).

cranequin device for drawing a ◊crossbow in later medieval Europe. It was developed in the 15th century, during the later period of crossbow use. It consisted of a metal ratchet bar with a winder that had cogs. The archer would wind the handle to draw back the crossbow string. It was light and easy to use, although slow, and became popular for use in hunting on horseback.

crannog medieval Irish term for an artificial island created in a lake for use as a refuge and fortification.

Crannon, Battle of battle in 322 BC, during the ◊Lamian War, that ended attempts by the Greek city-states to break away from Macedonian control after the death of Alexander the Great.

Under ◊Antipater, a Macedonian army of 40,000 heavy infantry, 3,000 archers and slingers, and 5,000 cavalry met a Greek army of 3,500 cavalry, mainly from Thessaly, and 25,000 hoplites at Crannon, about 9 km/15 mi southwest of Larisa in Thessaly. The Macedonians drove the Greek infantry to higher ground and the Thessalian cavalry, which was having the better of things, fell back to join them. Antipater opened negotiations to end hostilities, but insisted on negotiating with each state's troops separately. Although the Greeks refused to accept this, he decided to break off the engagement because the Greek hoplites were in such a strong position.

Crassus, Marcus Licinius (115–53 BC) (the Elder) Roman general who crushed the ◊Spartacus Revolt in 71 BC and became consul in 70 BC. In 60 BC he joined with Julius Caesar and Pompey the Great in the First Triumvirate and obtained a command in the east in 55 BC. Eager to gain his own reputation for military glory, he invaded Parthia (Mesopotamia and Persia), but was defeated by the Parthians at Carrhae (see ◊Carrhae, Battle of), captured, and put to death.

Crassus, Marcus Licinius (the Younger) Roman general, grandson of the triumvir Marcus Licinius Crassus the Elder. He fought first with Sextus ◊Pompeius and Mark Antony before defecting to Octavian (later the emperor Augustus). In 29 BC he defeated the Bastarnae of modern Romania and Bulgaria, killing their king, Deldo, in single combat.

Crassus, Publius Licinius (85–53 BC) Roman commander, the younger son of the triumvir Marcus Licinius Crassus the Elder. He served with Julius Caesar in Gaul (France), distinguished himself as a cavalry commander against the German tribal chief Ariovistus, led the 7th Legion against the Veneti (a seafaring Celtic tribe), and led the conquest of Aquitania

(southwestern France). In 54 BC he led a contingent of Gallic cavalry to join his father's Parthian campaign, and was killed at Carrhae (see ◊Carrhae, Battle of).

Crasus, Battle of battle between Arabs and Byzantines in Cyprus in 805, the most significant in a series of victories of the Abbasid Caliphate of Harun al-Rashid over the Byzantine emperor Nicephorus. Although the victory led to Muslim Arab conquest of Cyprus and much of Anatolia, the Byzantines recovered most of their lost territory when Harun left to deal with a rebellion.

Craterus (died 321 BC) Macedonian general. When Alexander the Great died in 323 BC, Craterus became joint regent of Macedonia and Greece with ◊Antipater. He helped Antipater to win the ◊Lamian War and joined him in the invasion of Asia Minor. He died in battle against ◊Eumenes of Cardia.

Cravant, Battle of battle fought on 31 July 1423 between the English Earl of Salisbury and his Burgundian allies and a Franco-Scottish force under ◊Charles VII, who had mustered a large army to invade Burgundy. Salisbury surprised and defeated Charles's force, besieging the town of Cravant, France, and capturing its commanders.

Salisbury's force of 4,000 English and about 2,000 Burgundians was outnumbered by three to one. Despite this, Salisbury attacked across the river Yonne and uphill, covered by the supporting fire of his archers. After a difficult fight he broke the opposing French, while Lord Willoughby opposed the Scots. The French count of Ventadour and the Scottish constable Sir John Stewart were captured.

Crécy, Battle of successful defence by ◊Edward III of English territory in France against an attack by Philip VI of France on 25 August 1346. The English archers played a crucial role in Edward's victory, which allowed him to besiege and take Calais, (see ◊Calais, Siege of).

Following a failed attack on Paris in early August, Edward was chased northward by superior French forces. His army had to fight across the ford of Blanchtaque on the river Somme before turning to fight some 8 km/5 mi north, in Ponthieu. He led some 10,000 men, including 2,000 men-at-arms, 5,000 archers and 3,000 infantry. Philip was said to have had 12,000 mounted men-at-arms, 6,000 Genoese crossbowmen, and perhaps 10,000 other infantry. He could not bring his larger forces to bear because he was unable to deploy from line of march. First, the crossbowmen were outshot by the English, then a series of uncoordinated cavalry charges were flung against the defenders. Edward had disposed his archers and men-at-arms in mutually supportive ◊battles that hurled back these attacks. Some 1,500 French knights were killed and Philip withdrew, humiliated.

Crema, Siege of key siege in the conflict between the northern Italian cities of Crema and Cremona in 1160. The Holy Roman emperor ◊Frederick (I) Barbarossa intervened, allying with the latter and besieging the former. The siege was noted for atrocities on both sides. Crema surrendered on terms, but Frederick was soon to be defeated at Legnano in 1176 (see ◊Legnano, Battle of).

crenellation in medieval military architecture, a toothed effect along the top of battlements (defensive walls), with gaps between each vertical 'tooth'. The stone teeth were called 'merlons', the openings 'crenels'. Crenellation often fronted a wall walk, providing protection and openings for the use of weapons.

Crenellation became the criterion to determine the level of fortification; as recorded from the 12th century, a licence was required to crenellate. In the later medieval period crenellation became fashionable decoration rather than genuine defensive architecture.

Criccieth castle castle in Wales, 11 km / 7 mi northwest of Harlech, Gwynned. This castle was originally built by the Welsh around 1200 as a triangular stone enclosure on a peninsula overlooking the sea. Cliffs protected one side and the other sides were ditched. Two large rectangular towers were incorporated into the walls.

After the conquest of Wales by Edward I towards the end of the 13th century, the English improved the castle by building an inner enclosure with a tower-keep and a powerful gatehouse, oriented so that the body of the inner ward was between the inner and outer gatehouses. It was taken by Owain ◊Glyndwr in 1404 and appears to have fallen into disuse shortly afterwards.

Crimisus, Battle of climactic battle, in 341 BC, of the Corinthian general Timoleon's crusade to free Sicily from the Carthaginians.

Timoleon's army caught the Carthaginians as they crossed the river Crimisus (probably the modern Belice Sinistro). At the height of battle a thunderstorm broke, driving rain into the Carthaginians' faces and turning the ground into a quagmire. Over 10,000 Carthaginians were reportedly killed, many drowned in the swollen river and others were hunted down by Greek light troops.

crinet protective neck covering forming part of a set of horse armour (see ◊bard). The separate mail or plate defence for the horse's neck appeared in Europe in the late 14th century and continued in use through the later medieval period.

Crocus Field, Battle of the ◊Philip (II) of Macedon's first significant victory over the Greeks, in 353 BC, which established Macedonian control over Thessaly.

The battle probably took place in the Crocian plain on the western side of the Gulf of Pagasae. Philip had been asked to support the Thessalians against Lycophron, tyrant of Pherae. The Phocian general ◊Onomarchus met Philip and a large contingent of Thessalians. In a hard-fought battle, Philip's superiority in cavalry proved decisive and the Phocians fled towards the sea. Many of them, including Onomarchus, drowned in an attempt to swim out to the ships of their Athenian allies.

Croesus (died 547 BC) last king of Lydia (in western Asia Minor) 560–547 BC. He expanded Lydian power to its greatest extent, conquering all Anatolia west of the river Halys and entering alliances with Media, Egypt, and Sparta. He invaded Persia but was defeated by ◊Cyrus (II) the Great; Lydia was subsequently absorbed into the Persian Empire.

When contemplating war with Persia, Croesus consulted the Delphic Oracle and received the famous response that he would 'destroy a great empire'. He invaded but was beaten at Pteria. Retreating to Lydia, he dismissed many troops as he expected hostilities to pause for the winter, but Cyrus pursued immediately, won another battle outside the Lydian capital Sardis, and besieged it. When the city fell Croesus immolated himself on a funeral pyre.

crossbow bow with a mechanism to draw back the string and a trigger to release it, used in medieval European warfare. The bow was fixed to a stock fitted with a catch to hold the string in place. There was usually a projecting nut on the stock over which the string was drawn, the nut being retracted to release the string by a trigger.

Bending the bow was initially done by the hands and feet. Improvements included the use of a stirrup fitted to the stock into which the archer's foot could be placed while drawing the bow. To draw the string a claw could be fixed to the archer's belt. Other devices for drawing included the pulley, the ◊goat's-foot lever, the windlass, and the ◊cranequin. Steel bows were developed in the 15th century. The crossbow missile was known as a ◊bolt or quarrel.

Croton, Battle of battle fought in 204 BC between a Roman army and the Carthaginian forces of ◊Hannibal the Great during the Second Punic War (see ◊Punic War, Second). Croton was to be Hannibal's last battle in Italy. Though winning an initial engagement, he was defeated in a second bout of fighting.

The battle was fought near the southern Italian town of Croton (modern Crotona), one of the towns in the Bruttium region still loyal to Hannibal. A Roman army was sent into the region to put pressure on Hannibal, but it was intercepted near Croton and defeated. The arrival of a second Roman army soon afterwards forced Hannibal to take refuge in the city.

Crusades (from French *croisade*) European wars against non-Christians and heretics, sanctioned by the pope; in particular, the series of wars 1096–1291 undertaken by European rulers to recover Palestine from the Muslims. Motivated by religious zeal, the desire for land, and the trading ambitions of the major Italian cities, the Crusades were varied in their aims and effects.

The Crusades ostensibly began to ensure the safety of pilgrims visiting the Holy Sepulchre and to establish Christian rule in Palestine and they continued for over two centuries, with hardly a decade passing without one or more expeditions. Later they were extended to include most of the Middle East, and attacks were directed against Egypt and even Constantinople.

In Palestine the tolerant rule of the first Muslim conquerors had for centuries allowed a Christian protectorate (first established under ◊Charlemagne) to exist in Jerusalem, and Christian pilgrims were allowed to come and go quite freely. However, peaceful coexistence was shattered in 1010 when the caliph Hakim destroyed the sanctuary. After 1071 the Saracens were driven out by the Seljuk Turks and Christian pilgrimage became difficult and dangerous. In 1095 Pope Urban II appealed for protection for the pilgrims, giving the turbulent feudal knights of Europe a new outlet for their energies, and the first Crusades were launched.

In 1095 several undisciplined hosts, such as those of Walter the Penniless and Peter the Hermit, set out for the East, but perished on the way. A more serious expedition, the *First Crusade* was mounted 1096–97: a great army under Godfrey de Bouillon, Bohemund de Tankerville, and other leaders, fought its way through Asia Minor, taking Antioch in 1098, and Jerusalem in 1099. A Christian kingdom was established, with Godfrey as its first king, his brother Baldwin as Count of Edessa (Upper Mesopotamia), and Bohemund ruling at Antioch. Godfrey died in 1100 and was succeeded by Baldwin.

During the next half-century, in spite of reinforcements, including fleets from Genoa, Norway, and Venice, the Christians in Syria were hard-pressed and the orders of Knights Hospitaller and Knights Templar (see ◊Military Order) were formed to assist in the defence of Jerusalem. Edessa was lost in 1144, and the *Second Crusade*, under Louis VII of France and Conrad III of Germany (1146–48), ended disastrously. Its failure for a time discouraged any similar ventures, while Muslim pressure increased on all sides.

The crusading spirit was revived toward the end of the 12th century in response to the conquests of ◊Saladin, Sultan of Egypt. Having captured Damascus in 1174 and Aleppo in 1183, he swept down through Galilee with an immense force, defeated a Christian army at the Horns of Hattin, (see ◊Hattin, Battle of) and took Jerusalem in October 1187. The news was received in Europe with consternation and rage. Several fresh expeditions were mounted, of which the most important was the *Third Crusade* led by ◊Philip (II) Augustus of France, ◊Frederick (I) Barbarossa of Germany, and ◊Richard (I) the Lionheart of England in 1189. The Germans went through Asia Minor, losing their emperor on the way; the French and English went by sea to Muslim-held Acre, which had already been besieged for nearly two years by the crusader Guy de Lusignan. Richard distinguished himself in the capture of the city, but quarrelled with his allies, who left him to carry on the war alone. After a year of brilliant but strategically insignificant exploits, he made a truce with Saladin, and returned to Europe.

The *Fourth Crusade,* starting from Venice in 1202, became involved in Venetian and Byzantine intrigues, and instead of reaching Jerusalem, assisted the deposed Isaac Angelus to regain the Byzantine throne; in 1204 Constantinople was stormed and sacked by the crusaders, and a Latin empire was established there under Baldwin of Flanders.

The *Seventh Crusade,* led by Louis IX of France in 1249 was, like an earlier expedition in 1217, directed against Egypt, and proved even more disastrous. Louis was captured with the greater part of his army, and had to pay 800,000 pieces of gold as a ransom. Even after this, he headed another crusade in 1270, but died at Carthage.

Ctesiphon, Battle of conflict at the Persian capital, Ctesiphon, on the river Tigris about 100 km / 60 mi above Babylon, which was attacked by the Romans in 363. Under Julian the Apostate, the Romans successfully crossed the Tigris at night, then drove the Persians back after a daylong battle. The Persians suffered 2,500 casualties to the Romans' 70.

cuirass (or *cuirie*) protective plate covering for the trunk of the body, used throughout Europe from the 13th century. By the 15th century cuirasses of iron or steel plate, formed of a breastplate and backplate, and often made of a number of separate pieces, were a standard part of a complete set of armour.

cuir boulli (French 'boiled leather') term for leather hardened by heating. Inventories show that a large portion of 13th- and 14th-century plate armour was made of hardened leather rather than iron, and that whalebone (baleen) was also extensively used.

cuirie medieval armour: see ◊cuirass.

culet rear part of a skirt made of plate in European armour. The synonymous terms 'culet' and 'garderein' appear in the 17th century for this defence, which was probably regarded as half of the ◊fauld in the 15th century.

culverin (French *coulevrine* 'snakelike') term originally used for a small cannon but later applied to a handgun with a small bore for its length. Generally the smallest of the gunpowder weapons of the medieval period, it was relatively light and portable and was commonly used in 15th-century battles, particularly by Burgundian troops.

The culverin was made of forged iron and fixed to a wooden stock, and usually placed on a rest for firing. It used lead shot, which was less expensive than other available materials.

Cuman nomadic horse-archer from the Eurasian steppe; the Cumans were both a threat to the Byzantine Empire and mercenaries in its service in the 11th to 13th centuries. The King of Hungary recruited them to fight the Mongol invasion in about 1240.

Cunaxa, Battle of battle fought in 401 BC on the river Euphrates near Baghdad (in present-day Iraq) between ◊Artaxerxes (II) Mnemon of Persia and his rebel brother ◊Cyrus the Younger, who was killed. The battle is memorable for the part played in it by

◊Xenophon and his fellow Greek mercenaries, hired by Cyrus.

The Greeks routed Artaxerxes' left in a charge vividly described by Xenophon, and even after Cyrus' death and the defeat of the rest of his army, managed to fend off a second attack. Some time after the battle, many of the Greek commanders were treacherously killed, and it was then that Xenophon, among others, emerged to lead his comrades home by way of the Black Sea coast, in the epic march described in his *Anabasis*.

cuneus battle formation used by the Germans and late imperial Romans. Although the word is usually translated as 'wedge', it was in reality more like a deep attack column. The *cuneus* was described by the 1st-century Roman historian Tacitus as 'closely compressed on all sides and secure in front, rear and flank', and in the 6th-century Byzantine military manual *Strategikon* as 'even and dense'.

Cyaxares (lived 7th–6th centuries BC)

(Babylonian **Umakištar**) king of the Medes c. 625–585 BC. He conquered the Persians in about 625 BC and then led his army against the waning Neo-Assyrian Empire, taking Ashur in 614 BC and, jointly with the Babylonians under Nabopolassar, taking the capital Nineveh in 612 BC. The alliance with Babylon was sealed with the marriage of Cyaxares' daughter to Nebuchadnezzar, Nabopolassar's successor. Cyaxares pushed further west into Anatolia and defeated the Lydians (or *Ludu*) under Alyattes in 590 BC. The limit of Median expansion was set at the river Halys (modern Kizilirmak).

Cynoscephalae, Battle of decisive battle of the second of the ◊Macedonian Wars of 197 BC, in which a Roman army under Titus Quinctius ◊Flamininus defeated the Macedonians under Philip V, leading the latter to seek peace. The battle demonstrated that the Hellenistic pike ◊phalanx lacked the flexibility of the Roman ◊legion.

The Macedonians had 21,500 infantry (16,000 of whom formed the phalanx) and 2,000 cavalry. The Roman army was roughly similar in size, but had a slight advantage in cavalry. The armies had been marching on a parallel course on either side of a line of hills, each unaware of the other's presence. When their scouts collided at the pass on the hills of Cynoscephalae, fighting between the advance guards escalated into a battle. On each side the right wing quickly formed into battle order and drove back the enemy left. An unknown Roman ◊tribune, exploiting the flexibility of the ◊*triplex acies* formation, led 20 maniples (legion subdivisions) from the rear lines of the Roman right and outflanked Philip's successful troops. The Macedonian deployment in a single deep phalanx made it difficult to face this threat. Some 8,000 Macedonians were killed and 5,000 captured, against a Roman loss of 700.

Cynossema, Battle of Athenian naval victory in 411 BC, during the latter part of the ◊Peloponnesian War, important because it was Athens' first success after the expeditionary force it sent to Sicily was annihilated in 413.

The Athenians' 76 triremes met 86 triremes from the Peloponnese and Syracuse off the cape east of the modern Turkish town of Kilibakir on the Gallipoli peninsula. At first the Peloponnesians had the better of it, but the Athenian right defeated their left then rounded on their centre. The Peloponnesians fled up the channel, carrying away the Syracusans in the panic.

Cyprus, Battle of Byzantine naval victory in 745 over an Arab fleet, after which the Arabs were forced from Cyprus – which they had controlled jointly with the Byzantines since their victory at Sebastopolis in 692 (see ◊Sebastopolis, Battle of).

Cyrus (II) the Great (died 530 BC) king of Persia 559–530 BC and founder of the Achaemenid Persian Empire.

The son of the vassal king of Persia and of a daughter of his Median overlord Astyages, Cyrus rebelled in about 550 BC with the help of mutiny in the Median army and replaced the Median Empire with a Persian one. In 547 he defeated ◊Croesus of Lydia at Pteria and Sardis, conquering Asia Minor. In 539 he captured Babylon from Nabu-naid (Nabonidus) the Chaldaean, formerly his ally against the Medes, and extended his frontiers to the borders of Egypt. He was killed while campaigning in Central Asia, and was succeeded by his son ◊Cambyses II.

Cyrus probably founded the ◊Immortals and ◊spear-bearers, and may have been the first to organize an effective force of Persian cavalry.

Cyrus the Younger (c. 423–c. 401 BC) Achaemenid Persian pretender and younger son of King Darius II of Persia. He attempted to seize the throne from his brother ◊Artaxerxes (II) Mnemon in 401 BC and was killed in battle at Cunaxa (see ◊Cunaxa, Battle of).

About 408 Cyrus was sent to Anatolia to coordinate the activities of local satraps (provincial governors) such as Tissaphernes and Pharnabazus. He cooperated with ◊Lysander to gain an ally in Greece. When his elder brother succeeded to the throne, Cyrus, with Spartan support, raised a large army of Greek mercenaries, including ◊Xenophon. He marched east, surprising Artaxerxes before his army was fully assembled, but was killed in battle at the head of his cavalry.

Cyzicus, Battle of (410 BC) important Athenian victory over Sparta in 410 BC, in the latter part of the ◊Peloponnesian War, at Cyzicus, a Greek colony on the southern shore of the Sea of Marmara (modern Balikhisar, Turkey). The victory led to Athens' temporary recovery of dominance in the Hellespontine region.

Led by ◊Alcibiades, Theramenes, and ◊Thrasybulus, the Athenians managed to catch the Spartan commander Mindarus out at sea and cut him off from his base at Cyzicus. Mindarus fled to shore where, in a confused fight, he was killed.

A Spartan dispatch, quoted by Xenophon, describes the extent of the disaster: 'The ships are gone. Mindarus has disappeared. The men are hungry. We don't know what to do.'

Cyzicus, Battle of (74–73 BC) battle fought in 74–73 BC between the Roman general Lucius Licinius ◊Lucullus and King ◊Mithridates (VI) Eupator of Pontus.

Lucullus' small Roman army relieved the city of Cyzicus (present-day Balikhisar, Turkey), under siege by a large Pontic army, by cutting Mithridates's supply lines. The Romans effectively destroyed the Pontic army when it tried to withdraw.

Cyzicus, Battle of (193) battle fought at Cyzicus (modern Balikhisar, Turkey) in AD 193 between the Roman emperor Lucius ◊Septimus Severus and Asellius Aemilianus, a supporter of the Roman governor of Syria, Percennius Niger. The battle was a victory for Septimus Severus, which followed his successful crossing of the Bosporus. Asellius died in the conflict.

Cyzicus, Battle of (672) battle in 672 in which the Byzantines gained a naval victory over an Arab fleet, under Caliph Mu'awiya, blockading Constantinople (see ◊Constantinople, Siege of 669–77).

The use of ◊Greek fire by the Byzantine forces (possibly for the first time) played a significant part in their victory.

Dabhoi (Sanskrit *Darbhavati*) town in central India, dating from the 11th century and fortified in the mid-13th century by the ◊Rajput King Visaladevi Vagheli of Dhalka. The 15-m-/50-ft-high walls formed a quadrilateral with sides approximately 915 m/1,000 yds long, a round tower at each corner, and defended gateways in the centre of each wall.

Dabhoi was occupied by ◊Muhammad ibn Tughluq, Sultan of Delhi, in 1345.

Dachangyuan, Battle of (or *Ta-ch'ang-yuan*) battle in 1228 during the Mongol campaigns in China (see ◊China, Mongol campaigns in). The Jurchen commander Wanyen Chengheshan with 400 tribal cavalry and a force of Chinese infantry defeated 8,000 Mongols attacking Dachangyuan.

Dacian War (AD 89) campaign fought by the Roman Emperor Domitian in AD 89 against the Dacians, who threatened the Roman frontier on the central Danube.

Under their King Decebalus, the Dacians defeated Roman armies on two occasions, in one of which they may have completely destroyed the 5th Legion (*Legio V Alaudae*). The imperial campaign led to a Roman victory, but Decebalus was recognized as the legitimate king of Dacia.

Daegsanstan, Battle of invasion of Northumbria by King Aidan's Dalriadan Scots (Irish who had settled on the west coast of Scotland) which was decisively defeated in 603 by the Angles under King Aethelfrith. Aethelfrith's brother Theobald was killed in the battle.

Dafei, Battle of (or *Ta-fei*) battle in August 670 in which Tang Chinese commander Xie Rengui was sent with 50,000 men to recover the ◊Four Garrisons, taken by the Tibetans. This battle was the key victory in the rise of the Tibetan Empire.

Leaving his baggage-train behind, Xie Rengui marched swiftly to surprise a Tibetan detachment, but meanwhile the Tibetans captured his baggage. As Xie returned, he was in turn defeated by the Tibetan minister mGar Khri-brin.

Dagworth, Sir Thomas (died 1350) English captain in the early phase of the ◊Hundred Years' War.

Dagworth served in Brittany from 1345, where he led a ◊*chevauchée*. In 1346 he won a notable victory at St-Pol-de-Léon, possibly the first triumph in the war for the English longbow. In 1347 Dagworth was wounded and captured during the relief of La Roche-Derrien. He was rescued and the fight ended in English victory. He was ambushed at Auray in 1350 and put to death.

daimyo (Japanese 'great landholding name') Japanese term for a major regional military landholder. The term was first used in both a military and civil context from the 11th century, but soon became used exclusively for the military appointee.

With the establishment of the ◊Kamakura shogunate, the provincial military families were given landholding appointments by the reigning ◊shogun and were termed ◊*shugo* (military governor). The instability following the fall of the Kamakura shogunate enabled local leaders to gain real power through the acquisition of land and subsequent military and political might as they attracted more followers. They became the de facto rulers of the provinces, being termed ◊*shugo daimyo*.

With the advent of the Onin Wars (1467–77), most of the existing *shugo daimyo* were obliterated, eventually being replaced by the ◊*Sengoku daimyo* who established their own military domains centred on the castle towns (jōka-machi) of the 16th century.

daishō (Japanese, literally 'large and small') matched pair of long (◊*katana*) and short (◊*wakizashi*) swords worn by the Japanese ◊samurai.

In the Muromachi period (1333–1568), with the adoption of the *uchigatana* (the early name for the *katana*) as the principal fighting weapon and the greater use of infantry, the *daishō* became standard wear for the samurai both in times of battle and in daily life.

DACIAN WARS (101–06)

Two campaigns fought in AD 101–02 and 105–06 by the Roman emperor ◊Trajan against Decebalus, the king of Dacia, which resulted in Decebalus' defeat and death and the annexation of his kingdom into the Roman Empire as the province of Dacia (modern Romania).

The literary sources for the campaigns, provided by the 3rd-century historian Dio, are very poor so it is hard to establish a detailed narrative of events. The carved reliefs on Trajan's Column in Rome, which may actually have been added to the Column by Trajan's successor ◊Hadrian, illustrate scenes from the campaign but do not constitute a narrative account of them.

The Dacian Wars followed a period of peace on the central Danube, partly due to Roman pay-offs to the Dacians which were agreed as part of a settlement between Decebalus and the Roman emperor Domitian. The first campaign began ostensibly because Decebalus was building up military strength and Trajan was reluctant to pay him any longer. Trajan may also have been eager to establish his reputation as a military emperor just three years after succeeding Nerva. In AD 101 Trajan crossed the Danube and advanced into Dacia. A pitched battle at Tapae, near the Dacian capital of Sarmizegethusa, resulted in a Roman victory. Decebalus agreed terms but was permitted to retain his crown; the Romans recovered the military equipment and legionary standard that had been captured during Domitian's campaigns, and Trajan set up a memorial to the Roman soldiers who had died in the campaign. This may be one of the large monuments at Adamklissi in eastern Romania that, like a modern cenotaph, listed the names of those who lost their lives.

Peace did not last, and Decebalus seems to have begun attacks on Roman garrisons along the Danube. Trajan prepared for a second campaign in AD 104 by constructing a stone bridge, designed by Apollodorus, over the Danube. He invaded Dacia the following year, leading to a period of hard campaigning with the stubborn Dacians. Eventually the Romans besieged and captured Sarmizegethusa, probably taking it by storm. With most of his kingdom now occupied by the Romans, Decebalus attempted to flee but was almost captured by Roman cavalrymen. To avoid capture he committed suicide. One of the cavalrymen, Tiberius Claudius Maximus, presented Decebalus' head to Trajan, and later had a scene of himself nearly capturing Decebalus engraved on his tombstone. Dacia became a Roman province with a legion stationed in Sarmizegethusa.

Damascus, Siege of unsuccessful siege attempted on 24 –28 July 1148 by the crusaders of the Second Crusade (under King Louis VII of France and the Holy Roman Emperor Conrad III, allied with Baldwin III of Jerusalem) against the strategically important city of Damascus, Syria. It was mishandled and ended in failure.

Arriving in the east after a difficult journey across Asia Minor, Louis and Conrad persuaded a reluctant Baldwin to attack Damascus, with whose citizens he had a treaty. The impatient crusaders attacked first through the orchards to the west of the city, but then switched to the waterless lands to the east where they were exposed to harassment by Muslim mounted archers. They were driven off in confusion and lost many men in the retreat.

Damietta, Siege of siege of the well-fortified city of Damietta at the mouth of the river Nile, Egypt, undertaken by the crusaders of the Fifth Crusade in spring 1218. They took the city on 5 November 1219, but were later cut off and captured, and handed it back as ransom.

The success of the siege depended upon maintaining crusader numbers over almost two years. Leopold of Austria played an important role in leading the assaults and fighting against the Egyptian Sultan al-Kamil's attacks, but the final surrender was produced by the invention of a floating siege tower on two ships, which dropped flying bridges onto the chain tower, the key to the defences.

The crusaders' attempt to march on Cairo after their success at Damietta left them cut off from supplies and led to their capture at Baramun on 29 August 1221.

Damme, Battle of battle fought in Flanders in 1213 by King John of England's Flemish allies against King ◊Philip (II) Augustus of France. The outcome was a victory for Flemings, and Philip's invasion of Flanders was halted.

In 1213 the French invasion of England was called off and the fleet raided inland against Flanders. The Flemings attacked Philip's fleet at Damme, formerly the port for Bruges, in alliance with the Earl of Salisbury and the Count of Boulogne. Some 400 of the 1,500 ships were captured, and Philip's mercenary captain Cadoc was probably killed. Philip ordered the rest of the fleet burned, and abandoned his land campaign.

Dandanqan, Battle of battle fought in Khurasan (northeastern Iran) in 1040 in which the ◊Seljuk Turkomen, led by Toghril Beg, won a decisive victory over a numerically superior and better-trained regular army under Sultan Mas'ud of Ghazni. Control of Khurasan subsequently passed from the Ghaznavids to the Seljuk Empire.

Exasperated by the continued failure of his generals to suppress the nomadic Turkomen whose depredations were ruining the economy of ◊Nishapur and other great cities of Khurasan, Mas'ud (son of Mahmud of Ghazni) took the field in person. He was drawn by the elusive Turkomen into the waterless desert between Merv and Sarakh. He finally reached the fort of Dandanqan, where Toghril attacked and routed the exhausted Ghaznavids.

Dandolo, Enrico (c. 1108–1205) doge of Venice 1193–1205 and architect of the conquest of ◊Constantinople in 1204. Allegedly aged 85 at his election and almost blind, Dandolo might seem an unlikely candidate for military glory, but it was his wisdom and energy which made Venice's capture of the Byzantine Levant trade possible.

He negotiated the 1201 treaty with Geoffrey de ◊Villehardouin to transport the French crusaders. He engineered the crusade's detour to Zara, Dalmatia, in 1203 and its arrival at Constantinople in support of an imperial pretender. Venetian ships made the storming of the city's walls possible, and Dandolo was the first man to top them. He rescued the Franks after their defeat at Adrianople in 1205 (see ◊Adrianople, Battle of 1205), organizing the retreat, but these exertions killed him.

Danevirke linear fortification consisting of a rampart and ditch built about the year 800 across the base of the Jutland Peninsula, Denmark.

The Danevirke was about 19 km / 12 mi long, with its eastern end at the fortified port of Hedeby. It was attributed to King Gotfred (died 810). The Danevirke could only slow an invading force and was not defended against one. The Danish kings kept it in use to about 1200.

Dan no Ura, Battle of decisive naval victory of the Minamoto forces in 1185 in the ◊Taira–Minamoto Wars of Japan. ◊Minamoto Yoshitsune defeated the Taira forces so thoroughly that the clan was all but annihilated.

Following their defeat at the Battle of Yashima (see ◊Yashima, Battle of), the Taira forces had been reduced to a small force of some 4,000–5,000 warriors. They were surrounded by armies under Minamoto Yoshitsune at Dan no Ura, the western exit from the inland sea just north of the island of Shikoku. Allied with local forces well versed in sea warfare, Yoshitsune defeated the Taira forces in a resounding victory.

Dantidurga first king of the Rashtrakuta dynasty of the Deccan (southern India), which lasted from the mid-8th century to 973. He overthrew his overlord Kirtivarman II, last of the kings of the Chalukya dynasty, whose resources had been drained by continual warfare against neighbouring rulers.

dao Chinese term for the single-edged sword introduced during the Han dynasty, made of iron and steel. From the 1st to the 10th centuries it was straight-bladed, and thereafter curved.

Daphnai (or *Defenneh*) Egyptian fortress near Pelusium in the eastern Nile Delta, commanding the land approach from Palestine. Saïtic Pharaohs used it to garrison Greek mercenary troops in the 6th century BC and it remained a major garrison during the subsequent Persian period, about 525–332 BC.

Dapur, battles of two battles between the Egyptian pharaoh ◊Ramses II and the Hittites, which took place after the Battle of Kadesh (see ◊Kadesh, Battle of) in 1275 BC and before the peace treaty between Egypt and the Hittites in 1258 BC.

Both battles were sieges, portrayed in Ramses' temple reliefs. The first, in 1271 BC, as depicted at the Ramesseum Temple, shows Hittite chariots with two-member crews, armed with bows, engaging in a chariot battle. Also shown are Egyptians using a scaling ladder against the fortifications and sappers at work under protective coverings undermining the glacis (slope in front of the fortifications). Dapur is one of 18 listed fortified towns attacked by Ramses. The relief of the second battle, as shown at Luxor Temple, depicts it as a siege only.

Daras, Battle of decisive victory in 530 for the Romans, led by Belisarius, over the Persians under their *Mirranes* (commander) Perozes, which marked the start of the Roman leader's career and the resurgence of the East Roman Empire.

Faced with 40,000 Persians, Belisarius entrenched his 25,000 men in front of the city of Daras and waited for their attack. After several days of stand-off and inconclusive skirmishing, Perozes formed his men in two lines and attacked in successive waves, hitting the Romans with a constant rotation of fresh troops, but holding his elite cavalry unit of Immortals in reserve. ('Immortals' usually refers to a set number of troops, constantly replaced as they fall.) Aided by a wind from behind them, the Romans had the best of the missile exchange, but at close quarters the Persians succeeded in routing the Roman left. The situation was saved by a unit of 300 Heruls who hit the pursuers in the rear. More Roman cavalry closed in on the flank of the Persians and forced them back. Perozes then switched his attack to the other flank, throwing in the Immortals to support the regular cavalry. The results were similar with initial Persian success countered by Belisarius' cavalry reserve which hit and routed the pursuers. With the best cavalry warriors beaten, the infantry levies fled. Belisarius did not pursue, fearing the still numerous Persians would rally and turn on his men while they were in disorderly pursuit.

dardier medieval European term for a lightly armed javelin-carrying soldier who served on land and at sea, named after the short 'dart' he carried.

Darius III (died 330 BC) last king of Achaemenid Persia, reigning from 336 BC. He outmanoeuvred the invasion force of ◊Alexander (III) the Great in northern Syria in

334 BC, but a year later was defeated by Alexander at Issus (see ◊Issus, Battle of 333 BC). He was again defeated by Alexander at Gaugamela (see ◊Gaugamela, Battle of) in 331 BC. During the Persian retreat he was murdered by his general ◊Bessus.

As a prince Darius distinguished himself by killing an enemy champion in single combat during a campaign against the Cadusians south of the Caspian Sea. After his Anatolian satraps (provincial governors) failed to stop Alexander's invasion at the river Granicus in 334 BC (see ◊Granicus, Battle of the), he assumed command of the resistance. When Alexander went on to subdue Syria and Egypt after his victory at Issus, Darius assembled half a million men for his final battle at Gaugamela.

Dartmouth castle castle in England 43 km/27 mi south of Exeter, Devon. The earliest remaining English castle specifically designed to accommodate artillery, Dartmouth was built around 1485–90. Of simple design, it consisted of two large towers with small holes for cannons and with crenellated gun platforms alongside them.

Dasymon, Battle of victory in 838 for the Arabs, under Caliph al Mu'tasim, over the Byzantines, led by the Emperor Theophilus, in which Byzantine power was severely weakened for the remainder of Theophilus' reign. After a siege lasting 55 days, the caliph captured and sacked Amorium, the original object of his campaign.

The caliph led a large Muslim Arab force over the Tarus mountains with the aim of destroying Amorium, the birthplace of the Byzantine emperor. Theophilus launched an attack on the Arab infantry while their cavalry were away foraging and was at the point of victory when the Arab cavalry returned and drove the Byzantines off in disarray.

Datames (died 362 BC) Achaemenid Persian general. He fought in ◊Artaxerxes (II) Mnemon's Cadusian campaign and became satrap (provincial governor) of Cappadocia. Threatened by enemies at court, he rebelled against Artaxerxes; the Persian general ◊Autophradates failed to squash this rebellion in 367 BC. Datames eventually turned his attentions to Mesopotamia, but his invasion failed and he was murdered by a presumed ally.

After capturing the rebellious prince of Paphlagonia about 378 BC, Datames was appointed to command an attack on Egypt, but he was diverted by another rebel, Aspis, whom he captured before returning to Cappadocia to deal with his enemies at court.

DARIUS (I) THE GREAT (C. 558–486 BC)

King of Persia 522–486 BC, the last to expand the Empire significantly. A member of a younger branch of the Achaemenid dynasty and spear-bearer to ◊Cambyses II, a distant relative, he won the throne from the usurper Gaumata after Cambyses' death. In 512 BC he marched against the Scythians, a people north of the Black Sea, and subjugated Thrace and Macedon. An expedition in 492 against the Greek supporters of the Ionian revolt under his general ◊Mardonius failed, and the army sent into Attica in 490 BC was defeated at Marathon (see ◊Marathon, Battle of). Darius founded the city of ◊Persepolis, and completed the organization of the Persian Empire into some 20 satrapies.

Several provinces immediately rebelled when Darius claimed the throne; in the first year of his reign he claimed to have won 19 battles and defeated 9 rebel kings. With the Empire in disarray Skunkha, chief of a Saka tribe in Central Asia, attacked; Darius defeated him, imposing a friendly king in his place. While in the east he conquered an Indian province in modern Pakistan. In the west he was less successful against Skunkha's Scythian relatives, chasing them for months without bringing them to battle.

In 499 BC Histiaos of Miletos led a revolt of the Ionian Greeks which liberated Ionia, Karia, and Cyprus. The Ionians were reconquered, and Darius vowed revenge against Athens and Eretreia and sent an expedition into Thrace in 492 BC under Mardonius, who further expanded the empire towards Greece by land. His defeat off Mount Athos led to a change of plan, an attack directly across the Aegean. Led by Artaphernes the Younger and Datis, this was defeated at the Battle of Marathon. Darius was prevented from further operations against Greece by an Egyptian revolt. He was succeeded by his son ◊Xerxes I.

Date family family of provincial Japanese warriors, later ◊*daimyo*, from the Kamakura period (1185–1333) through to the end of the Edo period (1868).

Isa Tomomune, the founder of the Date clan, was given the fiefdom of the Date district (from where the family took its name) of Mutsu province (modern Miyagi and Iwate prefectures) in the north of Japan in about 1189 as a reward for assisting ◊Minamoto Yoritomo to destroy his younger brother ◊Minamoto Yoshitsune. During the late 14th century they sided with the Muromachi shogunate and greatly increased their territories, and in the early 15th century created an exemplary legal system for their domains.

Date Masamune (1567–1636) (nicknamed 'the one-eyed dragon') renowned warrior of the ◊Date family, head of the family 1584–1636. He fought with ◊Toyotomi Hideyoshi in the ill-fated invasions of Korea in 1592 and 1597 (see ◊Korea, Japanese invasions of). Following Sekigahara (see ◊Sekigahara, Battle of) he was given the domain of Sendai in the north of Japan.

Dateng xia campaign (or *Ta-t'eng hsia*) campaign in 1465–66 in which the Ming Chinese, led by imperial commander Han Yong, defeated tribal rebels in what is now Guangxi. The frequently rebellious Yao rose in 1464 under Hou Dagou, and were joined by the Zhuang and other tribes. Imperial commander Han Yong was sent against them with 30,000 northern troops, including 1,000 Mongol cavalry and 160,000 local soldiers. Yao forces outside their heartland were defeated; 7,000 were killed and others joined the Ming army.

Against local advice, Han Yong pushed on to the Yao bases, stockades in the precipitous gorge where the river Xun runs through steep jungle-covered mountains. In several battles, two columns fought their way through the gorges, setting fire to the stockades. Rebel commander Hou Dagou and 800 men were captured, and over 3,000 Yao were killed. Captive Zhuang tribal archers were then based in the gorges to keep the Yao subdued.

Daulatabad (originally *Deogiri*) fortress in the Deccan, India, built about 1187 by the ◊Rajput chieftain Bhillama I, founder of the

Yadava dynasty. Three lines of walls, the outer one some 4.4 km/2.75 mi in circumference, enclosed a hill rising 183 m/600 ft above the plain, each defended by moats and turrets. The innermost enclosure was approached through a tunnel, closed at each end with iron doors, in which fires could be lit to make the tunnel unusable.

It was captured in 1294 by ◊Ala al-Din Khilji, Sultan of Delhi. He restored it to its Hindu ruler, Ramchandra Raja, for an immense ransom and the promise of annual tribute, but when this was not paid his armies reoccupied Deogiri in 1307 and 1310. Sultan ◊Muhammad ibn Tughluq renamed it Daulatabad, 'the city of wealth', in 1339 and made it his capital. In 1347 it became the capital of the newly established Bahmani sultanate.

David (lived 11th–10th centuries BC) king of the Hebrews 1004–965 BC. He became king of Judah on the death of King Saul at Mount Gilboa in 1004 BC (see ◊Mount Gilboa, Battle of), then king of Israel in 997 BC. He united the tribes against the Philistines, conquering their cities (such as ◊Ekron), and extending his kingdom over Moab and other surrounding lands. He captured Jerusalem to make it the City of David, capital of the united tribes of Israel and Judah. He was succeeded by his son Solomon.

David initially served under Saul but later became a renegade and then a mercenary leader for the Philistines under Achish of Gath, who refused to let him fight with the Philistines against Saul.

After the death of Solomon in 928 BC, the kingdom was split in two again. The Davidic line kept ruling in Jerusalem until its destruction by ◊Nebuchadnezzar in 586 BC.

De-an, Siege of (or *Te-an*) siege of the southern Chinese city of De-an from December 1206 to March 1207 by the Jurchen of northern China in retaliation for an invasion by the Song Empire of the south.

The Jurchen besieged Xiangyang (see ◊Xiangyang, Siege of) as well as De-an, both in modern Hubei. The Song commander Wang Yunchu had 6,000 troops, mostly militia, to resist about 100,000 attackers. The Jurchen bombarded the city with ◊trebuchets, built a siege-tower which the defenders managed to burn, and undermined part of the wall, but failed to take the city.

decurion junior officer of an ◊ala in the Roman army. A decurion was the commander of a ◊turma (cavalry unit), for which he received double pay and preferential accommodation in forts.

Defence of Pylos set of eight clay tablets found at ◊Pylos, written in Linear B (an early form of Greek writing), describing the preparations for the defence of the Late Bronze-Age kingdom of Pylos in about 1180 BC. Two tablets list rowers and their stations or places of origin and six tablets list ten commands (*o-ka*, or *orkha*) of land-based watchers. These tablets provide the only surviving contemporary written information about the structure and command of Mycenaean forces.

Each command is led by a named member of the nobility, assisted by one or more named officers, with a detachment of 50 or more men. Some of these are described as infantry while others are called by their tribe name. Some of the watchers and the rowers originate from the island of Zakynthos.

degel Aramaic term for an Achaemenid Persian garrison unit, or regiment, in 6th–5th-century BC Egypt. Garrisons at ◊Elephantine and ◊Syene were divided into *degels*, possibly numbering 1,000 soldiers, and subdivided into ◊*mata*. The term is also used for units of the native Egyptian ◊*machimoi*.

dekarch section commander in the Byzantine army, who commanded approximately ten men.

Delhi, Battle of battle fought in 1398 in northern India in which the invading army of ◊Timur Leng (Tamerlane), Amir of Samarkand, was victorious over the forces of Mahmud Shah, Sultan of Delhi, and his chief minister Mallu Khan.

Faced by a numerically superior army, including large numbers of elephants, Timur protected his front and flanks by ◊caltrops, ditches, barricades of thatch, and lines of carts and tethered buffaloes. These halted the Indian charge in the centre, while he launched decisive counterattacks with his cavalry on both flanks and in the Indian rear. Delhi was occupied after the battle; a rising of its citizens prompted a massacre that silenced the city.

Delium, Battle of battle fought in 424 BC on the coast of Boeotia, Greece, one of the bloodiest battles of the ◊Peloponnesian War, in which the Boeotians defeated an Athenian army returning from garrisoning an outpost in Boeotia. The battle is remarkable for the 25-deep Theban phalanx on the Boeotian right and the heavy Athenian losses, at 14% possibly the worst ever suffered by a ◊hoplite army in a pitched battle.

Each side had about 7,000 hoplites and some cavalry, and although the Boeotians allegedly had many more light troops, they played no part. On the Boeotian right, the Thebans pushed the 8-deep Athenians back, and although the Athenian right was at first victorious, it fled at the appearance of two squadrons of Boeotian cavalry sent to support their left, thinking that another army was approaching. The Athenian left then also fled.

Dellius, Quintus Roman lieutenant and historian who served ◊Mark Antony in a variety of military and diplomatic roles. He had changed sides several times in the Roman civil wars and defected to Octavian (later the emperor Augustus) just before the Battle of Actium of 31 BC.

He wrote an account of Antony's Parthian expedition, now lost, which may have been the main source for the Greek biographer Plutarch's account in his biography of Mark Antony.

Demetrius (I) Poliorcetes (336–283 BC) ('the Besieger') Macedonian general and king 294–288 BC, the son of ◊Antigonus (I) Monophthalmus and 'successor' of ◊Alexander (III) the Great (see ◊Diadochi), who fought with his father against the other 'successors'. He destroyed Egypt's naval power by his victory over Ptolemy (I) Soter off Salamis, Cyprus, in 306, but lost both Macedonia and Greece. He finally surrendered to ◊Seleucus (I) Nicator in 285 and died in captivity.

He restored Athenian democracy in 307, but failed in his attempt to capture Rhodes (though he was given the title 'Poliorcetes' for his efforts there) and concluded a treaty in 304. His impetuous cavalry charge at Ipsus (see ◊Ipsus, Battle of) was largely responsible for his father's death in 301 BC.

Demosthenes (died 413 BC) Athenian general in the ◊Peloponnesian War.

In 426 BC, after a disastrous invasion of Aetolia, he retrieved his reputation by winning minor victories at Olpae (see ◊Olpae, Battle of) and Idomene nearby, before achieving his greatest success at Pylos in 425 (see ◊Pylos, Battle of). In 413 he was sent to Sicily with reinforcements (see ◊Syracuse, Siege of), and after failing to take the Epipolae heights, advocated abandoning the siege. He was captured in the Athenian retreat and executed.

Denbigh castle castle in Wales. The site was originally occupied by Dafydd ap Gruffydd's wooden castle, which was captured by Edward I in 1282 and given to the Earl of Lincoln. He began construction of a stone castle but died in 1311 before the building was finished.

The castle passed through various hands before being owned by Henry Percy (Hotspur)

in 1399. During the Wars of the Roses (1455–85) it was held by both sides in turn, then besieged and burned by Jasper Tudor.

Dendra Panoply suit of 14th-century BC (Late Bronze Age) armour found in a Mycenaean chamber tomb near Dendra in the Peloponnese, Greece. It consisted of 15 shaped plates of beaten bronze forming a cuirass of two halves, with skirts stretching down to the knees, plus a one-piece gorget (neck guard) and shoulder and upper-arm guards.

This suit is distinct from contemporary Hittite and Egyptian scale corselets, but has similarities with the Linear B *to-ra-ka* (thorax) tablets from ◊Knossos, which show banded corselets. By the 13th century BC lighter armour is depicted on the Pylos tablets (see ◊Defence of Pylos) and in pottery illustration and reliefs.

Deng Ai (lived 3rd century) (or *Teng Ai*) Chinese general of the ◊Three Kingdoms of China period who led the northern Chinese Wei Empire's conquest of Shu Han (modern Sichuan) in 263.

The Wei attacked in overwhelming strength, and while their main army was held in mountain passes Deng Ai marched through terrain believed to be impassable, building roads and bridges as he went. He defeated the Shu Han reserve army and captured the capital Chengdu, leading to the surrender of the kingdom.

Dentatus, Marius Curius (died 270 BC) Roman general during the ◊Samnite Wars. He became known as a model example of a patriotic and honourable Roman commander.

As consul in 290–289 BC he commanded an army during the last campaign of the ◊Samnite Wars, conquering the mountain area of the tribe. Known less for these military achievements and more for his personal behaviour, Dentatus' frugality and incorruptibility were much praised in Roman literature.

Dependent States (*shuguo* or *shu-kuo*) tribal groups on the northern border of Han dynasty China, including surrendered ◊Xiongnu or proto-Tibetan Qiang groups, retaining local independence in return for supplying troops. They were a source of good cavalry.

Derinkuyu one of 30 underground cities near Nevsehir, Turkey (in classical Cappadocia). It was built into the soft tufa thrown out by the nearby extinct volcano of Erçiyes Dag (classical Mount Argaeos) and was occupied from 2000–1000 BC and from the 6th to 17th centuries AD. The excavated city covers an area of 4 sq km/1.5 sq mi with at least 18–20 levels descending down to 55 m/180 ft underground, and had an estimated population of 20,000.

Derinkuyu was a Hittite city from the Old Kingdom period until the fall of the Neo-Hittite states. It was occupied again as Byzantium retreated from the Turkish advance and became a refuge for Christians, with many churches being built underground.

destrier medieval European name for a knight's warhorse or charger, always a stallion. The name could have meant either that the horse led with its right leg or was led on the right by its groom.

Dhar (Sanskrit *Dhara*) fortified city in central India. It was the capital of the Rajput kingdom of Malwa from the 11th to the early 15th centuries. The fortifications were composed mostly of a brick curtain wall and a citadel of red sandstone.

It became the capital of Malwa during the reign of Bhoja Raja of the ◊Rajput Paramara clan. It was sacked by rival Rajput clans in 1020 and 1040, and captured by ◊Ala al-Din Khilji, Sultan of Delhi, in 1305. In 1531 it was annexed by Muzaffar Shah I of Gujarat, then fell to the Mogul Emperor Akbar in 1560.

Dharmapala (lived 8th–9th century) second king 790–815 of the Pala Buddhist dynasty, ruling over the eastern Gangetic plains of India. He defeated his western rivals, the Gurjara-Pratihara dynasty, in about 800 and seized their capital Kanyakubja (modern Kannauj), but they recovered most of their territories by the time of his death.

Dharmaraja Chandrabhanu (lived 13th century) king of the Malay state of Tambralinga, active in the period 1230–70. He spent more than 30 years in the conquest of Sri Lanka, but was finally decisively defeated in 1270 by Pandya princes from south India.

In 1247 he sent an expedition to Sri Lanka with the ostensible aim of obtaining a Buddhist relic, and occupied part of the island. His troops used poisoned arrows in this campaign. In 1258 a Pandya prince, Jatavarman Sundara Pandya, invaded Sri Lanka, and in 1263 his brother, Jatavarman Vira Pandya, defeated an alliance of Tambralinga forces commanded by Chandrabhanu's son and two Sinhalese princes. In 1270 Chandrabhanu attacked Sri Lanka again and was defeated by the Pandyas, badly enough that Tambralinga had not recovered when attacked by the Thais twenty years later.

Diadochi (Greek 'successors') Macedonian generals who fought one another for the empire of ◊Alexander (III) the Great after his death in a series of conflicts known as the Wars of the *Diadochi*. They were ◊Antigonus (I) Monophthalmus and his son ◊Demetrius (I) Poliorcetes, ◊Cassander, ◊Seleucus (I) Nicator, ◊Ptolemy (I) Soter, ◊Eumenes of Cardia, and ◊Lysimachus.

diekplous (Greek 'sailing through and out') classical Greek naval manoeuvre in which galleys attempt to row through the enemy line then turn to ram the side or stern of individual enemy ships.

Dienebrüdern (German 'serving brothers') German term describing the knights of the military orders who fought in Prussia and Livonia, later known as the Teutonic Knights (see ◊Military Order).

Dingxian, Battle of (or *Ting-hsien*) battle in 946 in which the Chinese defeated the Khitan. The Khitan invaded northern China but were defeated by commander Fu Yanqing of the Later Jin dynasty, who attacked them frontally with infantry and in one flank with 10,000 cavalry. The Khitan were driven out and their emperor fled on a camel.

Dingxi, Battle of (or *Ting-hsi*) battle 3–4 May 1370 in which the Ming Chinese under commander Xu Da defeated the Mongols, led by general Kökö Temür, who lost 86,000 men. This battle finally lost northern China for the Mongols, but Kökö Temür remained powerful in Mongolia, meeting Xu Da again at Karakorum (see ◊Karakorum, Battle of).

After ◊Zhu Yuanzhang's Ming forces ejected the Mongols from northeast China, an army under Xu Da pursued the Mongol general Kökö Temür into the northwest. At Dingxi in Gansu, Xu found the Mongol encampment. The Chinese deployed with part of their front covered by a stream and the rest by field fortifications. The Mongol attack turned one flank, and Xu Da had to intervene personally to prevent rout. The next day an unexpected Chinese attack broke Kökö Temür's force and took his camp.

Dinh Bo Linh (923–79) first independent Vietnamese emperor. Son of an official of ◊Ngo Quyen, he became a local leader in the anarchic 'Twelve Warlords' period following Ngo's death. He proclaimed himself first king and in 966 emperor of Dai Co Viet, a decisive assertion of Vietnamese independence from China.

He was based on the southern frontier, gained control of the coast through alliances, and then pushed inland, defeating the weakened remnants of the Ngo dynasty at Do-dong River in 963. His personal followers became the ◊Sons of Heaven, supported by the ◊Ten Circuit Army he founded in 974. He was assassinated in 979.

Diocletian (AD **245–313**) (*Gaius Aurelius Valerius Diocletianus*) Roman emperor 284–305. The commander of the *protectores domestici* (see ◊*domestici*) under the emperor Numerian, he was proclaimed emperor by his troops following Numerian's death, and defeated his rival Carinus in 285. In 293 he appointed ◊Maximian as co-ruler and reorganized and subdivided the empire, with two joint and two subordinate emperors. This was known as the Tetrarchic system. In 305 he abdicated in favour of Galerius, living in retirement until his death.

During his reign Diocletian fought a successful war against the Persians, defeated Achilleus in Egypt, and subdued ◊Carausius and Allectus in Britain. Diocletian also reformed the army, creating or reorganizing many of the units that would form the core of the later, much larger *comitatenses*, or field armies.

Diodorus Siculus Greek historian, born in Sicily, who wrote a 40-volume history covering events from mythological times to 60 BC. Fifteen of the volumes have survived intact. The remainder are fragmentary.

Although Diodorus' work is marred by a confused use of earlier sources and a rhetorical and moralizing tone, it is useful for providing evidence where few or no other source survives. It is particularly important for the history of classical Sicily and for Greek history from 359 to 301 BC.

Dionysias fort Roman fort at Dionysias (modern Qasr Qarum) in the Egyptian Fayum. It is a good example of the defensive forts built by the emperor ◊Diocletian on the Roman frontiers.

Built in brick, it was rectangular in shape with an area 94.4 × 80 m/310 × 262 ft. It had only one gate, and was protected by a wall almost 4 m/13 ft thick and at least 7 m/23 ft high. External projecting towers were placed at the corners and at intervals along the curtain wall.

Dionysius I (c. 430–367 BC) tyrant of the Greek city of Syracuse in Sicily, who came to power in 405 BC. He fought four wars with the Carthaginians and confined them to western Sicily, but was unable to drive them completely from the island.

In the 380s BC he extended his sway into Italy and the Adriatic, and in Greece he helped Sparta to impose the King's Peace of 387 and assisted Sparta in the struggle with Boeotia in 369/8.

He is credited with introducing catapults and the quinquereme to classical warfare.

dismounted knight medieval European battle tactic in which knights, normally used as heavy shock cavalry, dismounted to fight on foot. This was done in many historical periods, but it was used consistently as a tactic in battles involving the Anglo-Norman realm in the 12th century. It made for a stable defence against charging cavalry before the development of more highly trained specialist infantry.

Dismounted knights fought at Tinchebrai in 1106, Brémule in 1119, Bourgthéroulde in 1124, Lincoln in 1141, and probably Alençon in 1118 (see separate entries for these battles).

Diviciacus (lived 1st century BC) chieftain of the Aedui tribe and leader of its pro-Roman faction, in opposition to his brother ◊Dumnorix. He became such a trusted and respected ally of the Roman general and proconsul Julius Caesar during the ◊Gallic Wars that he was able to successfully plead for his brother's life.

Diviciacus had fled to Rome in 61 BC following the conquest of his tribe by the neighbouring Sequani. His pleas for help to the Senate were rejected, but answered in Caesar's early Gallic campaigns, winning his devoted loyalty. Caesar frequently consulted him on matters of intelligence and reconnaissance and he was often appointed as the spokesman for Gallic deputations.

Di Xin (lived 12th century BC) (or *Ti Hsin*) last king of the Shang dynasty in China, who reigned about 1154–1122 BC (traditional dates; an alternative chronology gives his death in 1027 BC). He was nicknamed Zhou, 'tyrant'.

Di led campaigns in the east, against the state or tribe of Yufang, and twice against the more important Renfang. These eastern preoccupations enabled his western vassals, the Zhou, under kings Wen and ◊Wu, to build up support and defeat him at Mu in 1122 BC (see ◊Mu, Battle of).

dō Japanese term for the main part of a suit of armour which serves to protect the torso. The term covers all types of body covering, including plate and scale armour.

dolabra pickaxe used by Roman ◊legions for constructing field fortifications, siege ramps, and camps. Although it was not a weapon, it enabled the Roman legionaries to win many campaigns.

Dolforwyn castle castle in Powys, Wales, 6 km/4 mi northeast of Newtown; a rare example of a Norman-style castle actually built by a Welsh prince to keep the Normans out.

Consisting of a rectangular curtain wall with a large round tower and a range of apartments inside the wall, Dolforwyn was built by ◊Llewellyn the Last around 1272–76. It was besieged and captured by Roger de Mortimer in 1277. The castle was forfeit to the king in 1321 due to the treasonable actions of the Mortimer family, and by 1398 is recorded as being in ruins

dōmaru (Japanese 'trunk wrapping') form of Japanese armour developed during the Muromachi period (1333–1568) from the earlier ◊ō-yoroi, and in use until the 19th century. The dōmaru incorporated modifications demanded by the changes in warfare during this period from predominantly one-to-one combat by cavalry to the use of larger units of foot soldiers.

It retained many of the characteristics of the ō-yoroi, but dispensed with the additional side covering plate (waidate) and simply fastened on the right. As the bow was no longer the primary weapon, the leather covering (tsurubashiri) over the cuirass (dō) was also abandoned. Likewise the protective pieces covering the shoulder strap fixings (sendan and kyubi no ita) were replaced with smaller pieces (gyōyō) which simply served to cover and protect the suspension cords. The large hanging shoulder pieces (ō-sode) became smaller and served little protective function.

The hanging skirtlike tassets (◊kusazuri) were divided into smaller sections to facilitate easier movement when fighting on foot. Additional leg and thigh protection was introduced by means of a split armoured apron (haidate) formed of iron or leather lacquered plates (◊kozane) which hung below the tassets and in some instances fastened onto the upper thigh.

The helmets associated with the dōmaru tended to be of the ◊suji kabuto type, and the turned-back side plates (◊fukigaeshi) had become smaller, serving as decorative devices frequently bearing the family crest, or mon. A flexible gorget (nodowa) was also introduced together with various types of metal face masks.

domestici (in full **protectores domestici**) title given to late Roman staff officers forming the emperor's inner circle to distinguish them from ordinary ◊protectores.

Domfront castle major border fortress east of Avranches in the modern département of Orne, France, between Normandy and Maine.

Domfront towers above a small town on a 60 m/200 ft rocky height over the river Varenne, with a ditch cutting off the only easy approach. It was built by William de Bellême in 1011. The rectangular keep was constructed by Henry I of France. Domfront was captured by ◊William (I) the Conqueror in 1052. ◊Henry II of England received the papal nuncio sent to reconcile him to Archbishop Thomas à Becket at the castle.

Dong Zhuo (died AD 192) (or *Tung Cho*) Chinese warlord who seized power at the Han court in 189, marking the effective end of Han imperial power and beginning a period of civil war leading to the ◊Three Kingdoms of China.

He was campaigning in the east against the Yellow Turbans (see ◊Yellow Turbans, rebellion of the) and other rebels when the unpopular Emperor Han Lingdi died in May 189. Dong marched on the capital Loyang, seizing it in September after the Han warlord ◊Yuan Shao's massacre of the court eunuchs who were trying to seize power. Yuan Shao, ◊Yuan Shu, and ◊Cao Cao fled east, built up a coalition against Dong, and killed him in 192.

donjon castle keep or separate central tower. Donjon is an Old French term preferred to 'keep' by some historians. It derived via dominionem from Latin dominus ('lord'), the tower being a sign of lordship.

Donnington castle castle in England, 3 km/2 mi north of Newbury, Berkshire. It was built under licence to crenellate (build battlements) in 1386 and was subsequently extended into an irregular oblong with round towers at the corners and square towers in the longer sides. The shorter end had a strong two-towered gatehouse which survives, while the fourth side was extended into an irregular hexagon.

Dorchester, raid on first recorded Viking raid on England, which took place in 789.

Dorostalon campaign decisive defeat by the Byzantines, under the Emperor John ◊Zimisces, of a Russian attempt, led by Prince Sviatoslav, to establish an empire on the river Danube (in modern Bulgaria) between 969 and 972. The Russians were allowed to withdraw after agreeing to abandon any attempts to occupy Bulgaria.

After defeating a Russian invasion at Arcadiopolis near Adrianople, the Byzantines pursued Sviatoslav back to the Danube, where he took a stand in front of a fortified position at Dorostalon (modern Silistria). The Russian light cavalry auxiliaries were induced to desert, leaving the Russian infantry to face the Byzantines alone. The Russians stood firm in face of a combination of cavalry charges and archery, but eventually they were forced back on their fortifications. They withstood a siege that lasted 65 days before surrendering. On the way home to Kiev they were ambushed by the Pechenegs and Sviatoslav's skull apparently ended up as a Pecheneg drinking cup.

Dorylaeum, Battle of battle fought on 1 July 1097 between the crusaders of the First Crusade and the Seljuk Turks in central Asia Minor. The crusaders routed the Seljuks and were able to go on to attack Syria.

Following their successful siege of Nicaea in 1097 (see ◊Nicaea, Battle of), the crusaders split into two columns to aid foraging. The vanguard under ◊Bohemond was attacked at Bozüyük. Sultan Kilij Arslan led 7,000–8,000 Seljuk mounted archers in an ambush, throwing the crusaders into confusion. Bohemond took up an improvised position, defended by the foot soldiers, while the knights made countercharges to keep the Turks at bay. Rescue came at the end of the day with the second column, led by the papal legate Adhémar of Le Puy. Its cavalry fell on the Seljuk rear, routing them with heavy casualties.

Doué-la-Fontaine castle (also known as *La Motte*) the earliest known castle in Europe, southeast of Angers in the Loire Valley, France. The stone keep was built by Theobald, Count of Blois, in about 950 and a motte was built around the tower about 1000. Although the building did not survive into the modern era, when excavation was undertaken in 1967–70 it was recognized as a model for early keeps.

The keep was a conversion from a rectangular stone hall dating from about 900, carried out after a fire. The ground floor entrance was blocked, and an upper storey and a forebuilding added. Fulk Nerra, Count of Anjou, captured Doué-la-Fontaine in about 1025.

Dover castle castle in Kent, on the south coast of England and 'the key of England' upon which no expense was spared by successive monarchs from the 9th to the 14th centuries. Originally a keep with outbuildings, it was modified to a concentric plan in the 12th cen-tury. The Constable's Gate, built in the 13th century, is among the most impressive in the country.

draco standard used by the nomadic Indo-European Sarmatians, which consisted of a dragon's head made of metal, attached to a pole. On Trajan's Column in Rome it is shown with a long tail probably made of cloth. The Romans adopted it some time after Trajan's Dacian Wars at the beginning of the 2nd century AD.

Drepana, Battle of sea battle fought in 249 BC, during the First Punic War, outside the western Sicilian harbour of Drepana (modern Trapani) between the Carthaginian fleet commanded by ◊Adherbal and a large Roman force commanded by Publius Claudius ◊Pulcher. The Romans were significantly defeated.

They had attempted to surprise the Punic fleet in its base at Drepana. However, Adherbal avoided the threat of blockade, leading his fleet rapidly into open sea and pinning the Romans close inshore. The battle was dominated by the superior construction of the Punic ships and the skills of their crews. The Romans managed to escape with 30 ships but 93 were captured.

Drobeta fort Roman fort at present-day Turnu Severin, on the southern border of Romania, that protected the bridgehead of the Danube bridge from the early 2nd century AD until perhaps as late as the 5th century. It was built by the Emperor Trajan (reigned AD 98–117) to guard the northern approach to the bridge of Apollodorus, and is the first auxiliary fort known to have had stone walls. Though retaining its original 'playing card' shape (rectangular with rounded corners), its defences were systematically upgraded and improved over the centuries.

It measured 140×130 m / 153×142 yds with gates in all four sides and small internally projecting towers. A rebuilding by Aurelian or Valentinian I blocked off three of the gates and turned them into large projecting bastions. The surviving gate was enhanced with new round towers that projected over 6 m / 19.7 ft, compared to the original 1 m / 3.3 ft. New large projecting towers were also added to each corner of the fort, taking a 'splayed fan' shape to create a straight 90-degree angle with each of the side walls.

dromon medieval Byzantine war galley. The standard warship from the 10th century, and the mainstay of the Byzantine navies, the dromon usually had 200 rowers in total, consisting of two banks of oars with 50 benches per side, each seating 2 rowers. The oarsmen might be expected to fight, but each vessel also had a complement of 70 marines.

It is possible that many carried the ◊siphon in the bow to spray ◊Greek fire over enemy vessels, together with torsion artillery pieces.

Drusus, Nero Claudius (c. 38 BC–AD 9) (called *'Drusus Germanicus'*) Roman general, the younger brother of the future emperor Tiberius and father of ◊Germanicus Caesar. He was a skilful commander who, after a successful war against the Rhaetians, advanced the Roman frontier in Germany to the Elbe region in 9 BC. He died as a result of injuries incurred in a riding accident.

duel, medieval (from the archaic Latin *duellum* 'war') single one-to-one combat, used to settle disputes in medieval Europe. The duel was a generally accepted legal recourse for most of the early medieval period. Culturally, the duel was the right of a noble in defence of his honour. A knight could throw down his gage (a token of defiance, usually a glove or hat) and demand combat with an accuser. The church gradually moved to condemn the practice.

The joust (see ◊tournament) was a duel without the judicial aspect, but the term duel survived for any one-to-one combat. Duels and jousts were a popular topic in *chanson* (French 'song') literature.

Duffus castle castle in Grampian, Scotland, 8 km/5 mi northwest of Elgin. Built by a Norman baron in the early 12th century, the structure began as a simple ◊motte-and-bailey work with a wooden hall. Held by a supporter of King Edward I of England in the latter years of the 13th century, it was burned down and was then rebuilt around 1300 in stone, with a great tower and curtain wall.

It was to become the great object-lesson in not building stonework onto artificial mounds, since at some time, probably in the 14th century, the mound subsided and the corner of the great tower collapsed. Even so, further construction was done during the 15th century, though the castle fell into disuse shortly afterwards.

Duilius, Gaius Roman commander during the First Punic War (see ◊Punic War, First). He served as both admiral and general and achieved Rome's first naval victory, at Mylae in 260 BC (see ◊Mylae, Battle of).

As consul in 260 BC he commanded the Roman forces in Sicily and received command of the navy, following the loss of the admiral. He led the fleet, the first Rome had ever commissioned, into battle off Mylae (modern Milazzo) and there defeated the Carthaginians. As a general he raised the Carthaginian siege of Segesta (modern Egesta, Sicily). In 259 BC he returned to Rome to celebrate its first naval triumph.

Dumnorix (lived 1st century BC) chieftain of the Aedui tribe, who pursued an anti-Roman stance during the ◊Gallic Wars.

Dumnorix supported the migration of the Helvetii and hindered Roman efforts to crush it in 58 BC. This contravened his pledge of allegiance and he was betrayed by pro-Roman factions and arrested. His life was spared through the pleas of his brother ◊Diviciacus.

He continued to spread dissent and refused to obey the Roman general and proconsul Julius Caesar's order to accompany him on the second expedition to Britain in 54 BC. He was killed resisting Roman arrest.

Dunbar, Battle of battle fought at Dunbar in Scotland in 1296 between the English under John de Warenne, Earl of Surrey, on behalf of Edward I of England and the Scots under King John Balliol (c. 1250–1314). Surrey's victory led to the English occupation of Scotland, and the Stone of Destiny was removed from Scone to Westminster.

Balliol had been made king with Edward's support, but had afterwards rebelled against him, so Edward sought to take direct control of Scotland. Surrey's cavalry was victorious, and many prisoners were taken, though Balliol escaped.

Dunnichen Moss, Battle of battle fought in 685 between a Pictish army and the forces of King Ecgfrith of the Anglo-Saxon kingdom of Northumbria. Ecgfrith had advanced north to Forfar when he was ambushed from Dunnichen Hill. His army was caught with its back to Nechtan's Mire, a marsh, and destroyed. The Northumbrian dominance of what became southern Scotland was thus brought to an end.

Dunstanburgh castle castle in England, on the Northumberland coast near Alnwick. Built by the Earl of Lancaster 1313–16, it played a significant role in the Wars of the Roses (1455–85). Twice besieged, it was taken by Yorkist troops for Edward IV in the second half of the 15th century.

Dupplin Moor, Battle of battle fought by a largely English army under Edward Balliol, claimant to the Scottish throne, against a Scottish army south of Perth, Scotland, in 1332 in order to gain the throne. He defeated his opponents and was crowned king of Scotland at Scone the same year. The English tactics were adopted for use during the ◊Hundred Years' War.

Balliol invaded Scotland with 500 men-at-arms and 1,000 archers. He was confronted by the Earl of Mar, the regent of Scotland, with several thousand men. Balliol took up a defensive position at the head of a valley, with his men-at-arms flanked by the archers. The Scots advanced into this trap and suffered heavy casualties; Mar and other nobles were killed in the confusion.

Dura Europus fortified city on a broad promontory above the river Euphrates in Syria (Roman Mesopotamia), founded about 300 BC as a colony by the Seleucid Empire. It was taken by Parthia about 100 BC, by Rome in AD 165, and by the Sassanids in about 252.

Its commanding position was naturally provided with defences in the form of steep slopes and wadis on the north and south sides and the river on the east. A citadel was built on the east side to command the river; though now mostly eroded, it was 300 m/985 ft long. The main walls were on the landward western side, 2 m/6.5 ft thick and strengthened by 11 square interval towers.

In around AD 210, some 9 ha/22 acres of the northern city were walled off to form a military compound. This accommodated the legionary force garrisoned in the city and three more towers were added to the west wall in this corner. The city was the headquarters of the regional Roman commander of the frontier, the *Dux Ripae*, but the city was too isolated from reinforcements and despite fierce resistance it fell to the Sassanian King Shapur I in about 252. The city was destroyed and never reoccupied.

Durazzo, Battle of battle in 1081 between the Normans under ◊Robert Guiscard and the Byzantines under ◊Alexius (I) Comnenus; see ◊Dyrrachium, Battle of 1081.

Durbe, Battle of battle fought in 1260 between the Teutonic Knights (see ◊Military Order) and the Lithuanians, resulting in a revival of pagan fortunes in the eastern Baltic. Master von Hornhausen of Livonia was ambushed by the Lithuanians and killed along with 150 knight brothers. As a result, the subjected pagans of Prussia, Livonia, and Lithuania rebelled, overthrowing their Christian rulers.

durga (Sanskrit) fortified city in Indian military architecture, standard from about the 4th century BC to the 14th century AD. The ideal *durga* was surrounded by a mud rampart covered in spiny shrubs and carrying a wall 6 m/20 ft high, with many square towers and roofed embrasures for archers, the whole protected by three concentric wide moats.

The cities of Pataliputra in ancient ◊Magadha and ◊Vijayanagar in the Deccan both conformed to this design.

Durham castle Norman castle in northeast England, founded by William the Conqueror and dating from around 1070.

It was originally a wooden ◊motte-and-bailey castle that was later considerably extended in stone. The castle became the residence of the prince-bishops of Durham, who held absolute power over their lands (the County Palatine of Durham) on the condition

that they raise and maintain when necessary an army to oppose Scottish invasions of northern England.

Dur-Sharrukin (modern *Khorsabad*) short-lived capital (c. 710–705 BC) of the Neo-Assyrian Empire under ◊Sargon II, after whom it was named ('Fort Sargon'). It replaced ◊Kalhu (Nimrud) and was superseded by Nineveh. The city was square in shape and enclosed by a wall 7 km/4.3 mi long which had seven gates. The citadel with its royal palace straddled the line of the wall to the northeast, while the imperial arsenal, containing a secondary royal palace, was similarly constructed to the southeast.

Impressive scenes of Sargon's conquests were discovered in the halls of the palace, such as his siege of ◊Ekron in 712 BC.

duwei fu (or *tu-wei fu*) garrison headquarters in Han dynasty China, particularly on the ◊Great Wall of China. The headquarters were known by the name of their location, and commanded by an officer known as a *duwei*. The *duwei fu* were divided into two to five ◊houguan (companies).

dux (Latin 'general', 'governor', or 'commander') person of high rank, translated variously as ealdorman, doge, or duke among the successor states to the Roman Empire. In Europe there were early medieval dukes of Francia, Paris, Brittany, and Aquitaine, for example. The Scandinavian rulers of Normandy from 911 were not initially known as dukes but assumed the title before 1066.

Dyle, Battle of battle fought in 891 between Arnulf, King of the East Franks, and the Viking raiders of Francia, who had killed the Archbishop of Mainz during their raid. Arnulf attacked their camp at Louvain (in present-day Belgium) near the river Dyle, taking them by surprise. The battle was brief but fierce, and two Viking kings, Siegfrid and Godafrid, died in the conflict.

The Battle of Dyle was an early example of cavalry dismounting to fight on foot, Arnulf declaring: 'I first will dismount from my horse'.

Dyrrachium, Battle of (49–48 BC) drawn-out encounter in 49–48 BC near Dyrrachium (modern Durrês, Albania) between Julius ◊Caesar and ◊Pompey the Great shortly before the decisive battle at Pharsalus (see ◊Pharsalus, Battle of). Caesar attempted to besiege Pompey's camp and numerous minor skirmishes occurred before he was forced to raise his blockade.

Dyrrachium, Battle of (1081) failed attempt in 1081 by a large Byzantine army of 70,000 men under the Byzantine Emperor ◊Alexius (I) Comnenus to relieve the city of Dyrrachium (Italian Durazzo, modern Durrês, Albania), which was being besieged by a Norman army of 15,000–18,000 men under the Norman knight ◊Robert Guiscard, who had ambitions in the Byzantine Empire, and his son ◊Bohemond.

Guiscard's large fleet had been beaten by Alexius' Venetian allies in June 1081, isolating the Normans on a hostile shore, before they began the siege of the city. Soon they were starving and suffering from dysentery. Alexius brought up his mercenary army, which included Serbs, Macedonian Slavs, ◊Varangians, and Turks, to finish them off, but in the ensuing battle the Norman cavalry won an unlikely victory. Alexius withdrew and after resistance over the winter, the city surrendered in February 1082.

Eadred (c. 925–55) king of England 946–55. Youngest son of ◊Edward the Elder, he followed his two brothers on the throne. He was accused of murdering his predecessor and brother, Edmund I, in 946, but may not have been responsible. Eadred increased the power of the Wessex kings in northern England. On returning from his first expedition north in 948 he was attacked crossing the Aire and defeated at Castleford, Yorkshire. Eadred later expelled ◊Erik Bloodaxe from York and took over Northumbria.

eagle standard of the Roman legion. It is described as being made of silver with gold feet in the first half of the 1st century BC and completely of gold thereafter. To lose the eagle was the greatest disgrace a legion could suffer. There are numerous examples of the eagle-bearer (*aquilifer*) losing his life defending the precious standard. Caesar recounts two such incidents and Augustus went to great lengths to recover the eagles lost by Crassus in Syria 55 BC and by Varus in Germany AD 9.

ealdorman Anglo-Saxon nobleman and royal governor of a shire. He would command the ◊fyrd of the shire in battle.

Earlier Nine Years' War military campaigns carried out 1051–62 by the Japanese imperial court against the Abe family of Mutsu province (modern Miyagi and Iwate prefectures) who were taking land by force and refusing to send taxes to court. The ◊Minamoto family fought on behalf of the court, finally destroying the Abe family with assistance from the Kiyoharu clan.

The war was only fought for a period of 9 of the 11 years. Its name distinguishes it from the ◊Later Three Years' War, which broke out in the same area in 1083.

echielle (medieval French) term for a squadron of knightly cavalry, of no fixed size but made up of several ◊conrois.

Ecnomus, Battle of sea battle fought off the coast of Sicily in 256 BC between the Romans, under Marcus Atilius ◊Regulus, and the Carthaginians, during the First Punic War. It was the largest sea battle of antiquity. The Roman victory enabled the Romans to land in Africa at ◊Clypea and continue the war in Carthage's own territory.

The Greek historian Polybius reports the numbers in the Roman fleet as 330 quinqueremes (each with a crew of 300 rowers and 120 marines) and transports for 4 legions (20,000 men) and cavalry, giving a grand total of little under 160,000 men. The Carthaginians manned 350 warships (over 150,000 men).

Regulus divided his force into four squadrons. Two formed the left and right sides of a wedge, and a third formed the base of the triangle towing the transports. The fourth formed a reserve line. The Punic fleet deployed mostly in line attempting not only to outflank the Romans, but to detach the wedge from its base by backing water. Although the Carthaginians had the advantage of manoeuvrablilty, the Roman use of the ◊corvus to grapple enemy ships proved decisive. The Carthaginians lost 94 ships (30 sunk, 64 captured); the Romans lost 24 (sunk).

écorcheur (medieval French 'flayer') brutally evocative term used to describe the mercenary companies which ravaged France during the ◊Hundred Years' War.

Edessa rectangular citadel in eastern Turkey isolated from its town (modern Turkish **Urfa**) by a rock-cut ditch. An acropolis site in ancient times, Edessa was developed by its Byzantine and Armenian rulers.

When Baldwin le Bourg seized Edessa in 1097, he initiated the excavation of a 12-m-/40-ft-deep rock-cut ditch, faced with large polygonal bastions and a large square ◊donjon. His defence of Edessa in 1098 saved the First Crusade and the city remained important to the crusaders until it fell to Imad al-Din ◊Zengi in 1144, after which it remained in Muslim hands.

Edessa, Battle of battle fought in 260 between the Persian ruler Sharpur I and the Roman emperor ◊Valerian. Sharpur I was victorious over Valerian's weak Roman army, which he first defeated in battle, then blockaded in its camp and eventually forced to surrender.

Edgecote Moor, Battle of battle fought on 26 July 1469 during the English Wars of the Roses (see ◊Roses, Wars of the) in which the Earl of Warwick and Duke of Clarence, in rebellion against ◊Edward IV, defeated his smaller forces and captured him.

Edward did not respond quickly to the rebellion and may have underestimated its danger. He relied upon the efforts of the Earl of Pembroke with his Welsh troops and the Earl of Devon, whose archers arrived late at the encounter. As a result, the royalists were easily overcome in a confused encounter, with 2,000 Welsh dying.

Edinburgh castle castle in southeast Scotland. First recorded in 1093 as the 'castle of the maidens', it was probably a Bronze-Age defensive site. The early work was destroyed in 1314 by the Earl of Moray to deny it to the English. Taken by Edward III in 1335, it was recovered by the Scots in 1341 and besieged by Henry IV in 1400 without success.

Edington, Battle of battle fought in May 878 between the Saxons and Danes in Wessex. After a two-week siege ◊Guthrum, leader of the Danes, sued for peace. He agreed to provide hostages, to leave Wessex, and to be baptized as a Christian. The resulting six-year truce enabled King ◊Alfred the Great of Wessex to consolidate his position and build up his forces, including a fleet.

Guthrum's Danes had overrun Wessex after their surprise winter attack at Chippenham (see ◊Chippenham, Battle of). King Alfred had gone into hiding and conducted a campaign of harassment against the invaders over the winter and early spring. With the coming of spring, Alfred's small band of companions was reinforced by the levies of Somerset, Wiltshire, and Hampshire and in May he marched against the Danes. The Saxons routed the Danes at Edington, Wiltshire, driving them back to their fortifications at Chippenham.

Edmund (II) Ironside (c. 981–1016) king of England in 1016, the son of Ethelred II 'the Unready' (c. 968–1016). He led the resistance to ◊Cnut the Great's invasion in 1015, and on Ethelred's death in 1016 was chosen king by the citizens of London, whereas the Witan (the king's council) elected Cnut. In the struggle for the throne, Cnut defeated Edmund at Ashingdon (or Assandun; see ◊Ashingdon, Battle of), and they divided the kingdom between them; when Edmund died the same year, Cnut ruled the whole kingdom.

Edward I (1239–1307) king of England from 1272, son of Henry III (1207–72). He led the royal forces against Simon de ◊Montfort (the Younger) in the ◊Barons' War of 1264–67, and was on a crusade when he succeeded to the throne. He established English rule over all of Wales 1282–84, and secured recognition of his overlordship from the Scottish king, although the Scots under Sir William Wallace and ◊Robert (I) the Bruce fiercely resisted actual conquest. He was succeeded by his son Edward II (1284–1327).

Edward was a noted castle builder, including the northern Welsh ◊Conway castle, ◊Caernarvon castle, ◊Beaumaris castle, and ◊Harlech castle. He was also responsible for building ◊*bastides* to defend the English position in France.

Edward III (1310–77) king of England from 1327, son of Edward II. He assumed the government in 1330 from his mother, through whom in 1337 he laid claim to the French throne and thus began the ◊Hundred Years' War. Edward was the victor of Halidon Hill in 1333, Sluys in 1340, Crécy in 1346, and at the siege of Calais 1346–47 (see separate entries for these actions), and created the ◊Order of the Garter.

Edward's early experience was against the Scots, including the disastrous Weardale campaign in 1327. Forcing them to battle outside Berwick at Halidon Hill he used a combination of dismounted men-at-arms and archers to crush the Scots. Apart from the naval victory of Sluys his initial campaigns against France were expensive and inconclusive. Resorting to ◊*chevauchée*, he scored a stunning victory at Crécy, which delivered the crucial bridgehead of Calais into English hands. Due to the brilliant success of his son Edward of Woodstock (see ◊Edward the Black Prince) at Poitiers in 1356 (see ◊Poitiers, Battle of 1356), and later campaigns, Edward achieved the favourable Treaty of Brétigny in 1360. He gave up personal command in the latter part of his reign. An inspiring leader, his Order of the Garter was a chivalric club designed to bind his military nobility to him, and was widely imitated.

Edward IV (1442–83) king of England 1461–70 and from 1471. He was the son of Richard, Duke of York, and succeeded Henry VI in the Wars of the Roses (see ◊Roses, Wars of the), temporarily losing his throne to Henry when Edward fell out with his adviser Richard Neville, Earl of Warwick (◊Warwick the Kingmaker). Edward was a fine warrior and intelligent strategist, with victories at Mortimer's Cross and Towton in 1461, Empingham in 1470, and Barnet and Tewkesbury in 1471.

Edward was physically imposing and had a quick intelligence. He made his mark, aged 19, in a simple victory at Mortimer's Cross (see ◊Mortimer's Cross, Battle of). In contrast, Towton was a hard-fought, long encounter in which his physical strength played a part in assuring victory (see ◊Towton, Battle of). Once crowned, the rebellions were dealt with by Warwick and his family. When Warwick himself rebelled in 1469, Edward responded by defeating the northern rebels, then travelling abroad to gather more forces. The campaign of 1470–71 showed him at his best. Landing with a small army recruited in Burgundy, he soon gathered enough troops to challenge Warwick at Barnet (see ◊Barnet, Battle of). A rapid march to oppose Henry's VI's queen, Margaret, at Tewkesbury caught the Lancastrians off balance (see ◊Tewkesbury, Battle of). Edward's victory snuffed out any possibility of further opposition.

Edward the Black Prince (1330–76)

(Edward of Woodstock) prince of Wales, eldest son of Edward III of England. A fine soldier but a harsh ruler, he was victor at Poitiers in 1356 (see ◊Poitiers, Battle of 1356) and Nájera in 1370 (see ◊Nájera, Battle of), sacker of Limoges in 1370 (see ◊Limoges, Siege of), and prince of Aquitaine from 1362. His nickname relates to his magnificent effigy in full armour in Canterbury Cathedral, now restored to gilded splendour.

Famously, Edward proved himself an effective leader of men at Crécy (see ◊Crécy, Battle of) in 1346. His 500-mile ◊chevauchée of 1355 from Bordeaux to Narbonne brought much booty and probably provoked King John II to battle at Poitiers the following year. Edward fought on the defensive and captured the French king, bringing a huge ransom and freezing the French war effort. Invited to support a claimant to the Castilian throne, he invaded Spain in 1366 and achieved victory over a Franco-Castilian force at Nájera. The murder of his ally, King Pedro, negated this victory. Returning to Aquitaine, his rule was unpopular due to the cost of the Spanish expedition, and his recapture of Limoges was seen as unnecessarily cruel. He died of dropsy (oedema).

Edward the Elder (c. 870–924)

king of the West Saxons. He succeeded his father ◊Alfred the Great in 899. He reconquered southeast England and the Midlands from the Danes, uniting Wessex and Mercia with the help of his sister Aethelflaed. By the time of his death his kingdom was the most powerful in the British Isles. He was succeeded by his son ◊Athelstan.

Edward extended the system of burghal defence begun by Alfred, building new ◊burhs, for example at Hertford and Buckingham, and twin burhs at Bedford and Stamford.

Eigenotze medieval Swiss term denoting the sworn brotherhood of the cantons which made them such a formidable force in battle.

Eight Princes, rebellions of the

disturbances 291–306 that undermined the Western Jin dynasty (266–316), which had briefly re-unified China. Princes of the Imperial house controlled a dangerously high proportion of the army, and after the death of the dynasty's founder they fought among themselves for the succession, particularly around the capital. Some contenders hired barbarian auxiliary troops, including the ◊Xiongnu, who in 304 rebelled on their own account, and eventually under ◊Liu Cong overthrew the Jin.

Ekron Philistine city (modern Tel Miqne, Israel), closely linked with Ashdod, Ashkelon, Gath, and Gaza, together forming the biblical Pentapolis (five cities). Dating back to the 4th millennium BC, it came under the control of the ◊Peoples of the Sea about 1200 BC, and was destroyed about 1000 BC. It was rebuilt and in 712 BC was besieged by the Assyrians. It was recovered, only to be destroyed by the Babylonians under ◊Nebuchadnezzar in 604 BC. The 20-ha/50-acre site was enclosed by a thick wall 1.6 km/1 mi in length, and centred upon the palace.

The people of Ekron refused to house the Ark of the Covenant after the Philistine army defeated the Hebrews at the Battle of Aphek about 1040 BC, and its subsequent destruction about 1000 BC could be linked with David's conquest of the Philistia.

elchi (Turkish) diplomatic representative or envoy; a term that came into use in the 11th to 12th centuries throughout central Asia and neighbouring areas under Turko-Mongolian linguistic and cultural influence.

El Cid, Rodrigo Diaz de Vivar (1043–1099)

Spanish hero of the ◊*Reconquista,* mercenary and adventurer, conqueror of Valencia in 1094, and twice victor over the Almoravids (Berber dynasty). His Arabic title means 'the lord'. Although seen as a Christian hero, after being exiled from Castile in 1082, he operated as a military opportunist. He served the Muslim ruler of Lerida 1083–88 before leaving to found his own realm. His military activities produced a royal income and funded his conquest of Valencia.

He defeated the Count of Barcelona in the contest for Valencia, and also outmanoeuvred Alfonso of Castile. He routed the previously invincible Almoravids at Cuarte in 1094 and Bairén in 1096, before seizing Almenara in 1097 and the supposedly impregnable rock of Murviedro in 1098 to secure his realm. This did not long survive his death, being surrendered to the Muslims by his widow Jimena in 1102.

elephant, in Carthaginian warfare elephants were used by the Carthaginians in the First and Second Punic Wars with initially devastating effects (see ◊Punic War, First and ◊Punic War, Second). However, the Romans learned to exploit their preference for flat ground and their tendency to become uncontrollable when panicked, and were able to render them obsolete.

The elephants were mostly of the small North African forest type (now extinct), with some African bush elephants also being used. They were too small to carry fighting towers and were instead ridden like a horse. They were first used against Rome at the siege of Agrigentum in 262 BC, but by the Battle of Panoramus in 251 BC, 130 out of the 140 Carthaginian elephants were killed and the remainder captured. They enjoyed shock value with Hannibal in Italy, but they were too few in number, and at the Battle of Zama in 202 BC they were a liability.

elephant, in Chinese warfare Asiatic elephants were used in warfare in southern China. Common throughout China in the Bronze Age, when Shang dynasty armies may possibly have employed them, they survived thereafter only in the south, where local armies occasionally used a few in battle.

The Southern Han state (917–71) had the only standing elephant-corps, local animals carrying ten men each, commanded by the 'Legate Dirigent and Agitant of the Gigantic Elephants'. They were deployed in the front line, and were successful in battle against neighbouring Chu in 948, but were defeated by Song dynasty crossbowmen in 971. In general, Chinese archery was an effective anti-elephant tactic, as ◊Liu Fang found.

Elephantine (or *Yeb*) island fortress in Upper Egypt, in the river Nile before the first cataract near Syene (now Aswan). Under the Persians in the 5th century BC it had a Jewish garrison, the 'Aramaeans of Yeb the fortress', inherited from the Saïtic pharaohs (26th dynasty, 668–525 BC).

The garrison was commanded by a *rab haila* and organized into ◊degel and ◊mata. It left a quantity of interesting records, written in Aramaic on papyrus.

elephant, in Indian warfare elephants were a major part of Indian armies throughout the classical and medieval periods. The largest and fiercest bulls were used for shock action on the battlefield and for assaults on palisades and gateways, while smaller bulls and cows served as transport animals, and could also be used for clearing obstacles.

Fighting elephants might have their tusks fitted with spikes or blades and be armoured with metal plates, mail, leather, quilting, or bamboo. In addition to a driver, fighting elephants could carry two or three people, armed with bows, darts, quoits, or combustible missiles, and with a long lance (*tomara*) for close combat. They might also have a dedicated infantry squad for their local protection and support.

Ely, Siege of siege undertaken in 1071 by ◊William (I) the Conqueror to crush the last resistance to his rule in England under the Anglo-Saxon rebel ◊Hereward the Wake, who had seized the abbey of Ely on an island in the Cambridgeshire Fens. A combined operation using ships and land forces caused the English to surrender.

Hereward had taken the abbey in 1070 with assistance from other Englishmen and some Danes. William mustered a fleet and landed forces in 1071. His ships sailed down the river Ouse to blockade the abbey, while the army constructed causeways, protected by wooden castles, to cross onto the island.

Emesa, Battle of battle fought in 272 between the forces of the Roman emperor ◊Aurelian and Queen ◊Zenobia of Palmyra. Aurelian's decisive victory in the war against Palmyra was in part owed to the defeat of the Palmyrene armoured cavalry, or *clibanarii*, by a unit raised in Palestine and armed with heavy clubs, with which they were able to injure the cavalry without penetrating their armour.

enarmes straps for the forearm and hand on the inside of a shield. They are comparatively rare in shields, most of which are held by a handgrip (even Islamic shields which have two fabric straps and a square pad attached by four bosses are held in this way).

Enarmes appeared on European kite-shaped cavalry shields in the 11th century, and are clearly shown in artistic representations such as the Bayeux Tapestry. They continued to be the standard method of holding European heater- or flat-iron-shaped shields during the remainder of the medieval period, and were also used on some later round shields (◊targets).

Englefield, Battle of first engagement, in 870, in the Danish invasion of Wessex which resulted in an inconclusive Saxon victory. Few details of the battle are known other than Sidroc, one of the Danish *jarls* was killed. Although a Saxon victory, the battle seemed to have little adverse affect on Danish operations and was probably little more than a skirmish.

Having overrun Northumbria, Mercia, and East Anglia, the Danes in England turned their attention to Wessex. The Danish army moved south in 870 and established a base at Reading. Two ◊*jarls* raided up-country and were defeated at Englefield by a Saxon force commanded by the ◊ealdorman Aethelwulf.

enomotia (plural *enomotiai*) (Greek) the smallest unit in an army, particularly the Spartan army. It consisted of 40 men ranging from 20 to 60 years of age, probably five from each of the eight groups of age classes (20–24, 25–29, 30–34 and so on). Literally, it may have meant 'sworn band'.

entaxis in Greek warfare, the deployment of units of lightly armed troops between the units of heavily armed foot soldiers.

Epaminondas (died 362 BC) Theban general and politician. He was credited with the revolutionary tactics that won at Leuctra (see ◊Leuctra, Battle of) in 371 BC. He invaded the Peloponnese twice, penetrating as far as Sparta and freeing Messenia. His third invasion, in 367, caused the break-up of Sparta's alliance. But as fear of Sparta began to be replaced by fear of Thebes, Epaminondas found himself fighting old friends, now in alliance with Sparta, and was killed at Mantinea (see ◊Mantinea, Battle of 362 BC).

equites (singular *eques*) (Latin 'horsemen') Roman cavalry. They were usually deployed on the wings of the battle line so that they could wheel round behind the enemy lines and attack them from the rear, thus often playing a decisive role in Roman battles.

The *equites* were originally recruited from among the wealthiest citizens as only they could afford to provide a mount and their equipment. By the 6th century BC the horses were provided by the state and the property requirement was lowered, giving rise to the *equites* becoming a distinct social class below that of the senator. By the 3rd century BC the cavalry began to be largely provided by the allies (see ◊*socii*) and the wealth element was entirely removed.

equites singulares cavalry who acted as personal bodyguards for Roman generals, providing them with an elite force at their immediate disposal. They were temporary formations specially selected from the cavalry units of an army. The *Equites Singulares Augusti* were a permanent unit that provided the Praetorian Guard with a cavalry arm.

Erik Bloodaxe (died 954) king of Norway 942–47. He succeeded to the throne on the abdication of his father ◊Harald Fairhair, but was deposed by his brother Haakon and driven from Norway in the 930s. He fled to England, where he became ruler of the Norse kingdom of Northumbria in 948. He was expelled in 954 and killed in battle at Stainmore, Yorkshire (now in Cumbria).

Eryx, battles of two battles, in 249 BC and about 244 BC, fought between the Romans and Carthaginians for the Sicilian town of Eryx during the First Punic War (see ◊Punic War, First).

Despite defeat at Drepana in 249 BC (see ◊Drepana, Battle of), the Romans were able to seize the town of Eryx and the mountain (Monte San Guiliano), with its shrine of Astarte (Venus) the same year. The town was recaptured a few years later by ◊Hamilcar Barca who used it as his base for operations, despite it being situated between two Roman armies.

Erzhu Rong (died 530) (or *Erh-chu Jung*) Erzhu tribal general in China who took the Wei capital of Loyang in northern China in 528 and set his own imperial candidate on the throne. A year later he lost the capital to a southern Chinese force under Chen Chingzhi, sent by the Liang emperor ◊Liang Wudi. Rong eventually overwhelmed Chen, regained Loyang, and defeated all other opposition in northern China, but was assassinated by his puppet emperor.

When the emperor Wei Suzong died in suspicious circumstances in 528, Rong marched on Loyang with 10,000 tribal cavalry. Imperial troops defending the Yellow River bridge defected to him, so he took the capital unopposed, massacring thousands. In 529, however, he lost it to a mere 7,000 southern Chinese.

Esarhaddon (died 669 BC) (Akkadian *Aššur-aha-iddin*) Assyrian Great King 680–669 BC. He seized the throne after the murder of his father ◊Sennacherib, conquered Egypt, and used the plunder to rebuild the city of ◊Babylon.

Esarhaddon defeated Cimmerian (biblical Gomer) incursions in Anatolia in 679 BC and an Elamite invasion of Babylonia in 675, and installed a pro-Assyrian, Urtaki, on the throne of Susa. In 672 he attacked Egypt but was repulsed on the border, only to return in 671 and defeat Pharaoh Taharqa at Memphis. In 670 Esarhaddon put down a plot to overthrow him, while Taharqa returned from Nubia to threaten Assyrian control of Egypt. Esarhaddon died on the way to Egypt and was succeeded by his son ◊Ashurbanipal.

Escalona castle exceptionally large defended enclosure above the river Alberche in Spain, 50 km/31 mi northwest of Toledo. Originally fortified by the Moors, it was of major importance in the defences of Toledo.

After being captured by the Christians in the 13th century, a curtain wall with eight towers and a ditch was constructed. The area was later divided into two wards by a wall and ditch. In the 15th century a large keep was built and the castle became a residence.

espionage and secret service, Indian in classical Hindu kingdoms (c. 500 BC–AD 500), the secret service was a system of collecting information and disseminating official propaganda; it employed spies and secret service agents. Muslim rulers in medieval India (AD 500–1500) appointed official informers or newswriters in most of the important cities under their control as a means of keeping themselves informed.

The Hindu spies, drawn from any walk of life, kept a ruler in touch with public opinion and maintained his popularity by spreading favourable stories. The secret service agents were used for acts of special daring and violence, including assassinations in domestic or enemy territory.

espringal (or *springald*) (French 'spring') medieval European siege engine, probably with a wooden arm drawn backwards against torsion and released to strike a bolt placed in the frame. The arm would have been drawn back by a windlass. The term may have also been used to describe a hurling machine. It is also possible that it was used for an ◊onager, which used a spring device for hurling stones.

essedarius chariot or charioteer employed by the Celts to attack cavalry. The chariot, also known as the esseda, provided a mobile fighting base for a warrior who used the chariot box as a platform for throwing javelins before dismounting to fight on foot. It was pulled by two horses and controlled by a driver.

Celtic chariots were of similar design and use in both mainland Europe and Britain. They are last recorded in continental Europe at the Battle of Telamon in 225 BC and in Britain

during Claudius' invasion of AD 43.

Estrithson, Swein (Danish *Svend Estridsen*) king of Denmark from 1046, who won Danish independence from Norway.

When King Magnus of Norway took control of Denmark around 1040, Swein led a failed attempt to overthrow him. He then ruled as the ◊jarl (chieftain or noble) of Jutland under Magnus' authority. When Magnus died in 1047, Swein was proclaimed king of Denmark, and he fought for 17 years to protect his claim against the Norwegian ◊Harald Hardrada. In 1064 he made peace with Harald, who was then preparing to attack England, and was able to rule an independent Denmark from that time until his death.

Eumenes (II) Soter (died 160 or 159 BC) king of Pergamum 197–158 BC, son and successor of ◊Attalus I. He maintained his father's alliance with Rome, and was rewarded with large additions of territory, but was kept in check by Rome.

As Rome's ally in the war against Antiochus (III) the Great of Syria, he fought at Magnesia (see ◊Magnesia, Battle of) in 190, and by the Peace of Apamea (188) received a considerable slice of Antiochus' territory in Anatolia. Rome interfered in his wars with Bithynia in 187–183 and Pontus in 183–179, though a victory over Bithynia's allies, the Galatians, in 184 brought him the title 'Soter' (Saviour) from the Greeks.

His attempts to ingratiate himself afresh with Rome by playing upon its suspicions of Macedonia backfired when the latter's defeat in the Third Macedonian War (170–167) made his own power an object of suspicion, and Rome looked to Bithynia and even the Galatians to keep him in check.

Eumenes of Cardia (c. 361–316 BC) Macedonian general and secretary to ◊Philip (II) of Macedon and ◊Alexander (III) the Great, after whose death Cappadocia, Paphlagonia, and Pontus were assigned to him as a 'successor' of Alexander (see ◊Diadochi). He defeated the Macedonian general ◊Craterus in 321 BC, but was himself defeated and slain by ◊Antigonus (I) Monophthalmus in 316.

Eurymedon, Battle of decisive battle fought between Greeks and Persians around 467 BC, following the defeat of Xerxes' invasion of Greece and possibly leading to a peace between the Athenian alliance and Persia.

At the approach of the Athenian fleet, commanded by ◊Cimon, the Persian fleet took refuge with land forces on the river Eurymedon (modern Köprü Çayi) which flows into the Mediterranean on the south coast of

Turkey. Cimon boldly sailed up the river and won a dramatic land and sea battle, capturing the entire enemy fleet and its camp.

Eustace the Monk (died 1217) naval mercenary employed at various times by King John of England and ◊Philip (II) Augustus of France. It was claimed that he revolutionized warship design by increasing the size of the wooden fore- and after-castles that formed the principal fighting platforms of medieval ships. He also made use of throwing engines from ships. He commanded the fleet for Philip's son Louis (later ◊Louis VIII) in the invasion of England against John and Henry III. Eustace's fleet was defeated near Sandwich, Kent, in 1217, when he was captured and executed on board ship.

Evesham, Battle of battle fought on 4 August 1265 in Worcestershire, England, during the ◊Barons' War of 1264–67, in which Edward, Prince of Wales (later ◊Edward I) defeated Simon de ◊Montfort (the Younger), Earl of Leicester, who was killed. Henry III (1207–72) was held prisoner by the rebels who were trapped in a loop of the river Avon, but he was escued and restored as king.

excubitores members of a Roman bodyguard unit of 300 men, consisting of soldiers recruited from Isauria, a mountainous region of Asia Minor. The unit was created by the Emperor Leo I (r. 457–74) as part of a successful effort by the Eastern Roman Empire to reduce its military dependence on the Germanic tribes, especially the Goths.

exeligmos (Greek) countermarch, practised in three different ways by ancient armies. Macedonian file leaders performed an about turn then stood fast while their file moved to their rear. Spartans preferred to give the impression that they were advancing, so their file closers performed an about turn and stood fast while the file leaders led their files to their front. In Cretan or Persian armies, the file leaders took the position of the file closers and vice versa, and intervening ranks swapped positions in such a way that the phalanx remained in the same place.

Exeter (Roman *Isca*) site of a Roman legionary fortress that guarded the southwest of England in the mid-1st century AD and was then refounded as a city and local tribal capital (Roman *Isca Dumnoniorum*).

The fortress was established on the river Exe about AD 55–60. It marked the end of the march of conquest of the 2nd Legion (*Legio II Augusta*) through southern England, as it established its base in a position to dominate the newly conquered tribes of the region and isolate the Devon and Cornwall peninsula. The timber fortress was laid out in 'playing card' shape (rectangular with rounded corners) and a substantial stone bathhouse was begun before the legion was moved to Caerleon about AD 75.

extraordinarii cohortes special unit consisting of one-third of the cavalry and one-fifth of the infantry of the allied units attached to a Roman republican army. They were at the immediate disposal of the consul, camping near his tent, and were used as shock troops.

FABIUS MAXIMUS, QUINTUS (C. 280–204 BC)

(Quintus Fabius Maximus Verrucosus)

Roman general and politician during the Second Punic War (see ◊Punic War, Second). Fabius was called upon to protect Rome at its most critical moments. His cautious leadership gave the Roman army time to rebuild itself by avoiding pitched battles with the Carthaginian general ◊Hannibal the Great and concentrating on keeping the loyalty of the allied Italian cities. This policy came to be known as 'containment', for it sought to restrict Hannibal as much as possible and limit the damage caused to Rome. Though unpopular for its lack of tangible results (Fabius was given the nickname Cunctator, 'the Delayer'), his policy was instrumental in guiding Rome through its immediate crisis.

Fabius was an experienced politician (consul in 233 and 228 BC, censor in 230 BC) and general (having won at least one triumph, or victory procession) by the time he was appointed dictator of Rome

for six months in 217 BC, following the Battle of Lake Trasimene. He recognized that the only way to beat Hannibal was to wear him down, overstretch his resources, and deny him supplies. Within the first few months of the war he trapped Hannibal's army in the Volturno Valley, but it managed to escape. In 216 BC his deputy Minucius ◊Rufus was elevated to equal status, but at the Battle of Gerunium in 217 BC only Fabius managed to save the situation. In respect Minucius resigned and voted Fabius the civic crown, the award for saving the lives of Roman citizens.

Retiring to the Senate, Fabius was given command of the defence of the city of Rome following the Battle of Cannae in 216 BC and elected consul again in 214 BC and 209 BC, regaining several important cities. Within the Senate he provided a strong voice on the conduct of the war until his death.

fabricae state-run arms factories of the late Roman Empire.

Faenza, Battle of victory in 490 for the Italian army of Germanic ◊*foederati* led by ◊Odoacer, over the Ostrogoths, led by ◊Theodoric the Great. After receiving reinforcements, Odoacer broke out from Ravenna, where he had been besieged following his defeat at Verona (see ◊Verona, Battle of 489). He succeeded in driving the Ostrogoths to Pavia where they took refuge and were in turn besieged.

Faestulae, Battle of battle fought in AD 405 at Faestulae (modern Fiesole, outside Florence, Italy) in which a Roman force of 20,000 troops under ◊Stilicho defeated a much larger army of various Germanic peoples under the leadership of ◊Radagaisus and saved Florence from falling to Radagaisus.

Florence was on the verge of surrender when Stilicho's army arrived. The Romans succeeded in reprovisioning the city and drove the Germans from the walls, trapping them in the rough country outside the city where they were surrounded and destroyed after being weakened by thirst and hunger.

Fähnlein medieval Swiss term denoting the small triangular or swallow-tailed banner carried by their troops of missile-men and hand-gunners, and by extension the name of such units. Such flags had been used earlier in 14th-century Italy, implying a similar organization.

Falaise castle early 11th-century ducal castle south of Caen, France, on a cliff overlooking the Ante Valley. The rectangular keep was added by ◊Henry I of England and the Talbot Tower by ◊Philip (II) Augustus of France after capturing Falaise. The castle was restored in the 19th century, but suffered damage in World War II.

It was from here that Robert I, Duke of Normandy, saw the tanner's daughter Herlève at the Fontaine d'Arlette. Their illegitimate offspring was ◊William (I) the Conqueror, who was born at Falaise.

falcata short, single-edged, cut-and-thrust sword, the Spanish version of the Greek ◊*kopis*, used from the 6th century BC to the 3rd century AD.

falchion (from the Latin *falx* 'sickle') curved short sword or dagger favoured by medieval European archers. It had a wide blade towards the point, with a convex edge and a concave back.

falcon (or *falconet*) medium-sized late medieval gun. Falcons were lighter than the large cannons and ◊bombards and easier to move and therefore often more useful in battles and sieges.

Falkirk, Battle of battle fought on 22 July 1298 at Falkirk, 37 km/23 mi west of Edinburgh, Scotland, at which ◊Edward I of England defeated the Scots.

William ◊Wallace faced the English in open battle, but his cavalry fled and his spearmen were outmatched by the English archers. Wallace's previous victory at Stirling had depended on the use of pikemen in ◊schiltrons. Edward's combination of archers and cavalry overcame this formation. The battle led to Wallace's fall from power.

falx (Latin 'scythe' or 'sickle') forward-curved, single-edged, two-handed slashing sword used by the Dacians around the 1st century AD. As depicted on a monument at Adamklissi, Romania, commemorating the Roman emperor Trajan's victory over the Dacians, however, it was a scythelike blade attached to a long handle.

familia alternative (Latin) name for a medieval military household; see ◊household, military.

fanhan mixed tribal *fan* and Chinese *Han* armies of the Shatuo Turks in northern China under ◊Li Keyong and his successors, containing Shatuo, Tatar, and other cavalry, Chinese regulars, and ◊*tuanlian* militiamen. They were originally undisciplined, but ruler Li Cunxu (908–26) introduced regulations that improved their discipline on the march and in battle.

Fan Ruoshui (lived 10th century) (or *Fan Jo-shui*) Chinese military engineer who in 975 bridged the river Yangze for ◊Song Taizu's conquest of the southern state of Jiangnan.

Having failed the official examinations, Fan spent months rowing a small boat on the Yangtze, trailing a silken thread to chart the currents. He used several thousand boats tied together with bamboo ropes and topped with a floating walkway, and built his bridge within three days.

Fan Yangmai II (died 447) king of Champa (modern central Vietnam) from 421. He raided China's Vietnamese provinces throughout his reign, but was eventually defeated by a Chinese invasion in 446.

Yangmai raided the coast of Vietnam in 431 with over 100 ships. A Chinese fleet counterattacked, and in an indecisive nighttime naval battle Yangmai's helmsman was wounded and forced to flee in a small boat. Yangmai raided Vietnam several times in the 430s, demanding that China cede it to him.

In 446 the Chinese governor Tan Hezhi (T'an Ho-chih) invaded Champa. He besieged the border city of Qusu, defeated a relief army, and captured and sacked the city, beheading all adult inhabitants. The Chinese then marched south. Yangmai met them outside the capital, Linyi, with a huge army spearheaded by elephants. To counter them the Chinese manufactured lions of bamboo and paper, perhaps something like modern lion-dancers. These frightened the elephants, who fled and trampled through their own army. The Chinese massacred Yangmai's army and sacked the capital, looting 48,000 kg/105,600 lb of gold. Yangmai fled into the mountains and died, supposedly of grief, on his return after the Chinese had left.

faris medieval Arabic horseman, often compared to the Western knight. His basic military skills were described in the ◊*furusiya* (cavalry training manuals), stressing obedience, individual skills, tactical awareness, bravery, and the possession of good armour and weapons, including a bow and lance. A professional ◊*faris* was also trained to fight on foot.

Fastolf, Sir John (1380–1459) English captain in the latter part of the ◊Hundred Years' War. He fought for Henry V at Agincourt in 1415 (see ◊Agincourt, Battle of), at Verneuil in 1424 (see ◊Verneuil, Battle of), and at 'Battle of the Herrings', near Orléans, in 1429.

Son of an esquire to Edward III, he built Caister castle in Norfolk using his war profits. He escaped from the English defeat at Patay in 1429 (see ◊Patay, Battle of). He was captain of Le Mans and governor of Maine, Anjou, and the Channel Islands. Fastolf may have been an inspiration for William Shakespeare's character of Sir John Falstaff.

Fauconberg, Thomas (died 1471) English sea commander, active for the Lancastrians in the Wars of the Roses (see ◊Roses, Wars of the). The illegitimate son of Lord Fauconberg, he led an attack on London from Kent, one of the few sieges of the war, attempting to cross London Bridge but failing. He was given a charter of pardon for his war activities in return for surrendering his fleet. He ignored the agreement and was beheaded in 1471.

fauld hooped plate skirt attached to the lower edge of a plate ◊cuirass. Faulds first appeared in Europe in the early 15th century with the earliest homogeneous sets of plate armour, which retained the relatively deep skirts of the earlier ◊coats of plates. They continued as essential elements of plate cuirasses to the end of the 16th century.

Faventia, Battle of decisive victory for a small army of Goths, commanded by their new king, ◊Totila, over a much larger East Roman force, led by eleven commanders, which took place in northern Italy in 542. The Roman army disintegrated leaving Totila in control of northern Italy.

After the surrender of ◊Witiges at Ravenna (see ◊Ravenna, Siege of 538–39), the Goths went through a rapid succession of kings, with the able Totila gaining the crown in 541. With ◊Belisarius away in the east, the Roman command in Italy was divided amongst eleven commanders. Totila seized the opportunity to break out of his area of control around Verona and led a small army of 5,300 men against a much larger Roman force of 12,300. The battle opened with the Gothic hero Valaris issuing a challenge to single combat which was taken up by an Armenian in the Roman army. Both men died in the exchange, which might have been a deliberate delaying tactic on Totila's part to give time for a flanking force of 300 men to ride around the Roman position. Once the main forces were engaged, the Gothic flanking force hit and routed the Romans.

Fei River, Battle of the battle in November 383 in which ◊Fu Jian's invasion of south China was quashed.

After the defeat of a detachment at Luojian (see ◊Luojian, Battle of), the main body of Fu's huge army tried to cross the river Fei further west, and were met by 70,000 southern troops under Xie Xuan. Fu's advance guard crossed the Fei and defeated one southern detachment, but withdrew from the main enemy army to hold the river line. Fu's general Fu Rong then pulled the advance guard back further to allow the southerners across the river, hoping to attack as they were part way across; but the poorly coordinated northern army began to panic, and the southerners attacked, killed Rong, and put them to flight. As the panic spread, Fu's whole army collapsed. The retreat was covered by Murong Chui's Xianbei cavalry, the one unit that remained intact.

Fengzhou, relief of (or *Feng-chou*) river battle in 928 between two states in divided southern China. A large fleet from Chu attacked the Southern Han city of Fengzhou on the West River. A Han relieving force strung two huge iron chains across the river, with winches to haul them up. They then attacked with light boats, luring the Chu fleet into pursuit. When the Chu ships pursued past the chains these were hauled up, cutting off their retreat. Crossfire from Han ◊ballistae on the riverbanks then slaughtered the trapped fleet.

fetiales college of Roman priests with responsibility for upholding the procedures and laws concerning formal declarations of peace and war. The role of the *fetiales* was to ensure that all wars fought by Rome were just (*bellum iustum*) and not liable to divine retribution. The priesthood consisted of 20 members, with the chief priest known as the *pater patriatus*.

The *fetiales* originated in archaic Rome and the Latin states. Opposing sides would send two *fetiales* as ambassadors to demand redress; if they were not satisfied after 33 days, war was declared. The *pater patriatus* would return to the enemy border and symbolically throw a spear into it. Treaties would also be formally concluded by the *fetiales*, enacting a curse to ensure the sanctity of the arrangement. Following Roman expansion the *fetiales* enacted their rites within Rome.

Field of Blood, Battle of the battle fought on 28 June 1119 near Artah, Syria, in which Ilghazi of Aleppo overwhelmed Roger of Antioch, capturing his entire force.

Roger had been gradually capturing the forts around Aleppo, so the citizens turned to

Ilghazi for protection. Expecting reinforcements from ◊Baldwin II, King of the Christian Kingdom of Jerusalem, Roger led 700 knights and 4,000 foot soldiers to a defensive position in the foothills 24 km/15 mi west of Aleppo. Ilghazi moved swiftly to surround them with about 40,000 troops. Roger was captured and held to ransom and his soldiers were killed.

Fiesole, Battle of battle fought at Fiesole, or Faestulae, in Italy in AD 405 between Roman and Germanic forces; see ◊Faestulae, Battle of.

fighting top (or *top-castle*) naval term referring to a basket or platform attached to the top of a ship's mast to provide a vantage point against an opponent in close contact.

The Venetians fighting for the Byzantines against the Norman fleet at Dyrrachium used this device, dropping metal-studded logs through the bottoms of the Norman vessels to make a hole in the hull and sink them.

fish-scale formation (*yuli*) Chinese mixed formation of chariots and infantry, recorded in descriptions of Xuge in 707 BC (see ◊Xuge, Battle of). Each squadron of 25 chariots was followed by five files of five infantry to cover the gaps between the vehicles.

At Kangju in 36 BC (see ◊Kangju campaign) enemy infantry were described in fish-scale formation, but the meaning here is unclear. It could mean a ◊testudo-like formation of overlapping shields, a wedge, or a chequerboard of subunits.

flail medieval Bohemian weapon based on the agricultural flail used for winnowing grain. The ◊Hussites used it as an infantry weapon and also as a symbol to represent their non-aristocratic origins as a popular religious and military movement. Ball-and-chain attachments usually replaced the original wooden end to the weapon.

Flamininus, Titus Quinctius (228–174 BC) Roman general who ended the Second Macedonian War by defeating King Philip V of Macedon in 197 BC at Cynoscephalae, Thessaly (see ◊Cynoscephalae, Battle of). He helped to make the peace a lasting one by his sympathetic treatment of the communities in Greece. He also served in the later stages of the Second Punic War (see ◊Punic War, Second).

Flaminius, Gaius (died 23 June 217 BC) Roman general who commanded the Roman army at Lake Trasimene in 217 BC (see ◊Lake Trasimene, Battle of) during the Second Punic War (see ◊Punic War, Second). Flaminius was unprepared for the Carthaginian general ◊Hannibal the Great's unconventional tactics and perished in the ambush.

A successful general in campaigns against the tribes of Cisalpine Gaul, Flaminius was elected to a second consulship in 217 BC, commanding an army stationed to block Hannibal's passage through Etruria. Carrying out orders not to lose contact with Hannibal's army, he had to follow it wherever it went, a situation perfectly set for an ambush. Flaminius is credited with fighting to the death and not attempting to escape.

flanchard side part of a set of European horse armour (see ◊bard). The first reference to a solid plate flanchard is in the de Nesle inventory of 1302, and from the late 14th century pairs of flanchards were standard elements of a plate bard.

Flarcheim, Battle of indecisive battle fought in Thuringia in 1080 between the Holy Roman emperor ◊Henry IV and Rudolf, Duke of Swabia, supported by the papacy. Accounts of the battle are confusing, both sides claiming victory, but it was Henry who withdrew and Rudolf claimed at least a technical victory.

The battle led to additional criticism of the German emperor by the papacy during the ongoing conflict between the church and the state, and Henry was excommunicated for a second time.

Flint castle castle in Wales 32 km/20 mi southwest of Liverpool. One of the first of Edward I's Welsh castles, it was built 1277–85 by Master James of St George. It consisted of a rectangular curtain wall with three towers. The flanks were protected by a marsh, and the unusual detached tower is said to have been inspired by Aigues Mortes in France (a walled town with a detatched keep).

Flor, Roger de (died 1305) captain of the Spanish-Italian Catalan Company. Actually a German (named von Blumen), Roger was expelled from the Templars (see ◊Military Order) and took to mercenary adventure, leading the Catalan Company to Constantinople in 1303.

His unruly troops were responsible for the death of the son of the leader of the Byzantine's Alan mercenaries. After bickering over inadequate pay, and occupying the Gallipoli peninsula, Roger agreed to visit Emperor Michael IX's camp. Here he was murdered by vengeful Alans, an action which prompted his leaderless troops into a campaign of devastation, eventually leading to their establishment of a state at Athens.

flyssa national sword of the Islamic Kaybeles of North Africa. The *flyssa* has a straight, single-edged blade with a long point and a pommel in the form of a stylized horse's head.

foederati in the late Roman Empire, trusted native tribes which defended coasts or frontiers from further incursions as Imperial authority receded. *Foederati* were established in Britain in the 4th century AD, for example the Damnonii of southern Scotland who seem to have entered into an alliance with the Romans in the reign of Theodosius. Gildas and Bede record that in the mid-5th century AD Vortigern invited the Anglo-Saxons to settle in Kent to defend the coastline.

Fogliano, Guidoricco da (lived 14th century) ◊*condottiere* and mercenary captain of Siena 1327–34 who later served Verona. Not a particularly distinguished general, he is chiefly famous for featuring in a magnificent painting by Italian painter Simone Martini (c. 1280–1344), which depicts him riding through the Tuscan countryside clad in cloth of gold, with a military siege in the background. This powerful image is often used to represent the power of the *condottieri*.

Fontenay, Battle of battle in 841 near Sens (in northern France) between the grandsons of Charlemagne, in which Charles the Bold and Louis the German combined forces to defeat their elder brother, Emperor Lothair. Lothair sued for peace and, in the Treaty of Verdun (signed in 863), Lothair was recognized as Emperor of Lorraine, Burgundy, and Italy; Louis was given the German territories east of the Rhine; and Charles got the remaining territory to the west.

Lothair's Aquitainian allies held their ground against Louis' Saxons and Bavarians. Lothair's own troops, however, were driven back by Charles' Neustrians and Burgundians. The army then routed. Losses were high on all sides, particularly amongst the nobility who bore the brunt of the fighting.

Formigny, Battle of battle fought on 15 April 1450 near the coast of Normandy, France, during the ◊Hundred Years' War, in which Clermont's French forces defeated the English forces of Thomas ◊Kyriell. The latter was making an attempt to recover Normandy. The battle was decided with the arrival of Richemont.

Kyriell led 800 men-at-arms and 3,000 archers against Clermont's force of 5,000. The English took up a defensive position covering a bridge and were initially successful in throwing back French attacks and then following up to capture their artillery. However, the arrival of Richemont's 2,000 soldiers in the English left rear decided the encounter. Kyriell was captured and his men dispersed; there would be no reconquest.

Fornham, Battle of battle of 1173 between ◊Henry II of England and Flemish mercenaries led by the rebel Robert, Earl of Leicester, who was defeated and captured. The battle was fought at Fornham, near Bury St Edmund, England, during the great rebellion against Henry which spread throughout the Angevin (Anjou dynasty) Empire in 1173–74.

When the Earl of Leicester arrived in England with his mercenary army he was met by a royal force under Richard de Lucy and Humphrey de Bohun, joined by the earls of Gloucester, Arundel, and Cornwall, who blocked his way at Fornham near Bury St Edmund and defeated the rebel forces.

Fornovo, Battle of battle of 1495 in which Charles VIII of France, retiring from Italy, was ambushed by Venetian forces near Parma and fought his way out. There were heavy casualties on both sides.

Charles led 4,500 men-at-arms, 3,000 Swiss infantry, 600 archers, and 1,000 artillerymen against 25,000 Venetians and their allies, including 2,500 five-man ◊lances, 2,000 ◊*stradiots*, and 8,000 professional infantry. The Venetians' captain Francesco Gonzaga planned to attack the marching column's right flank with the bulk of his forces, while the stradiots harried the left flank. The Milanese infantry, who tackled the vanguard, were driven back by the Swiss, the *stradiots* turned to plundering, and the main cavalry charge was delivered too late. Gonzaga was mortally wounded at the height of the battle, allowing the French to escape.

fortified towns, Chinese towns in China since the Neolithic period (about 2,000 BC), fortified typically on a rectangular plan oriented towards the cardinal compass points. The wall was usually of pounded earth, though stone was used where available, and from the Han dynasty (202 BC–AD 20) onwards, walls were often faced in brick.

Pounded-earth walls were massive structures well suited for absorbing the shock of rams or missiles, but immensely labour-intensive to build. ◊Ao is an early example, and ◊Lu a typical city of later antiquity. Some towns had an outer wall enclosing suburbs from an early date. From the ◊Warring States period, a succession of defences became common, starting with a water-filled moat. Small secondary walls were often erected between the moat and the main wall; one was the 'sheep-horse wall' which provided a refuge for country dwellers and their livestock.

Towers were used from Warring States times, either wooden constructions atop the wall or projecting 'horse-face' bastions. From the Tang period (618–907), outworks included 'crossbow-platforms' built some distance in front of the gates as an advance protection. Later these were linked by covered walkways to the main wall.

Forum Gallorum, Battle of battle of 43 BC during the Roman civil war following Julius ◊Caesar's death, in which a senatorial army inflicted a sharp reverse on ◊Mark Antony. The battle marked an important stage in the rise of Octavian (later the emperor Augustus).

On 14 April Mark Antony led two ◊legions with auxiliary troops and attacked the army of the consul Pansa, driving it back despite the resistance of the veteran *Legio Martia*. In their success Mark Antony's troops became disordered and were routed by the sudden arrival of the other consul, Hirtius, with two legions.

Forum Trebonii, Battle of battle fought between Roman and Gothic forces in 251. The Gothic victory followed their success at Philippopolis (see ◊Philippopolis, Siege of) and resulted in the death of the Roman emperor Decius and his son along with a large part of their army.

The Goths had deployed in three lines, the rearmost behind a marsh. Although the Romans managed after a struggle to defeat the forward lines, their assault on the third line failed.

Fougères castle castle in France, 50 km/31 mi northwest of Rennes. Dating from the 11th century, it was razed by Henry II in 1166. It was rebuilt by 1173, after which it was gradually strengthened and extended. Situated on a hill overlooking the town, the castle has been partially restored, and 11 towers remain.

One of the strong places of Brittany, and captured several times by the English, it was a pioneer in the use of water defences, with sluices allowing ditches to be filled or drained at will. In around 1480 two towers were built, which were among the earliest French attempts to provide artillery-proof works.

Four Garrisons the main Tang Chinese fortresses in the Tarim basin in Central Asia from the 640s to the 790s. The four were Kashgar, Khotan, Kucha, and Karashahr. These cities retained their own kings and internal autonomy but had Chinese garrisons and governors.

framea simple spear used by the early Germans.

Framlingham castle castle in England, 14 km/9 mi northeast of Ipswich, Suffolk. It was

the stronghold of the Bigods and later the Howards, both families holding the Earldom of Norfolk. Built as a wooden ◊motte-and-bailey work by Hugh Bigod, it was demolished by the King's order, but then rebuilt in stone by his son Roger in about 1190–1200.

On a mound surrounded by a ditch, the structure had a curtain wall 13 m/44 ft high and 2.5 m/8 ft thick with 13 projecting towers. The entrance was built into the central tower on the southwest side and had a drawbridge across the ditch to the bailey, which was also surrounded by its own ditch.

franc-archer (or *free-archer*) medieval French 'free bowman' member of the forces raised by ◊Charles VII of France in 1448 in return for tax exemptions, following the success of English longbowmen in the ◊Hundred Years' War. There were 8,000 franc-archers under captains. Parishes provided equipment; every unit of 'hearths' (50–120) provided a franc-archer.

In practice franc-archers included pikemen and gunners as well as archers. They fought in the War of the Public Weal and their numbers were doubled by Louis XI. Their limitations were exposed in the war against Burgundy and they were replaced with a standing army including mercenaries.

francisca hatchet used as a weapon by the Germans of the migration period (250–600), especially along the Rhine frontier, which could be thrown at an opponent or retained for use as a side arm.

Frederick (I) Barbarossa (c 1123–90) Holy Roman emperor 1152–90, conqueror of Italy despite his defeat at Legnano in 1176 (see ◊Legnano, Battle of), and crusader 1146–48 and 1189–90. Like all kings of Germany who wished to become emperor, Barbarossa needed to control the wealthy Italian parts of his domains, and to be crowned by the pope in Rome. He faced the new assertiveness of the north Italian cities, however, which required two decades of warfare to subdue.

His coronation campaign of 1154–55 was successful. When he returned in 1158, Frederick met sterner opposition. He took Crema (see ◊Crema, Seige of) in 1160 and Milan in 1162 after long and bitter sieges. His expedition of 1167 was devastated by disease and led to the formation of the Lombard League of northern Italian cities against him. In 1176 the League proved strong enough to defeat the emperor at Legnano. He was unhorsed and believed dead for several days. In the end, it was diplomacy, rather than military force, which led to the Peace of Constance in 1183. Inspired to return to the

Holy Land by the fall of Jerusalem to ◊Saladin in 1187, Barbarossa drowned in a river in southern Asia Minor.

Frederick II (1194–1250) Holy Roman emperor 1212–50, called 'the Wonder of the World'. He was the son of ◊Henry VI. He led a crusade 1228–29 that recovered Jerusalem by treaty, without fighting. Frederick quarrelled with the pope, who excommunicated him three times, and a feud began that lasted with intervals until the end of his reign. His later years were marred by rebellions of his chief minister and his son.

Frederick fought for his inheritance, taking the imperial crown from Otto IV in 1212 but not being formally crowned as emperor until 1220, after an early life as king of Sicily.

Free Companies groups of mercenaries under captains who sold or contracted their services. They first appeared in the 12th century and plagued Europe in the 14th century, especially France, living off the land, plundering and ransoming. As France recovered the Free Companies were suppressed.

Other similar groups were the ◊*écorcheurs* after 1435 and the Great Companies.

Fréteval, Battle of skirmish of 1194 in the Vendômois, France, during the war between ◊Richard (I) the Lionheart of England and ◊Philip (II) Augustus of France. It was a setback for Philip, though not a major defeat.

Philip sought to avoid battle, but his rear was attacked and the baggage train taken. This, rather than the fighting, was the disaster, since Richard captured the royal seal, financial accounts and archives, plus documents which revealed treachery by some of Richard's magnates. Philip eluded Richard by chance rather than design, Richard missing him when he stopped in a church to pray.

Frigidius, Battle of scene of a decisive victory in northern Italy on 5 September 394 for the East Romans, led by the emperor ◊Theodosius, over a West Roman army commanded by the Frankish general Arbogast and his puppet emperor Eugenius. After this victory Theodosius ruled as sole emperor until his death four months later.

Arbogast deployed in a strong defensive position blocking the route from the Alps towards Aquileia in northern Italy. Theodosius, aided by up to 20,000 Goths, launched a frontal assault with disastrous results when half his Gothic allies became casualties. The following day Theodosius attacked again, catching his opponents off guard. The battle swayed back and forth until a violent mountain wind storm

(the *Bora*) suddenly blew up in the faces of the Western troops and tipped the balance in Theodosius' favour. Eugenius was captured and executed and Arbogast committed suicide.

Fritigern Gothic warleader of the Tervingi clan who led the Goths in a war against Rome in 376. He outmanoeuvred several Roman armies and inflicted a crushing defeat at Adrianople in 378 (see ◊Adrianople campaign). He died in 382 while still campaigning against the Romans in the Balkans.

Froissart, Jean de (c. 1338–c. 1410) French priest and author. His *Chronicles* describe the ◊Hundred Years' War to 1400, and provide important insights into the ethos and conduct of medieval warfare. Long known as the 'chronicler of chivalry', Froissart blended narrative, anecdote, and documentary sources to describe the wars of his era.

His account of Crécy in 1346 (see ◊Crécy, Battle of) is the most detailed, as is his moving description of the siege of Calais in 1347 (see ◊Calais, Siege of), which followed. Much of his information came from talking to serving soldiers, and he conveys well their mixture of chivalric impulse and lust for booty that motivated them.

Frontinus, Sextus Julius (c. AD 40–102/3) Roman governor of Britain AD 73/74–c. 77 and military theorist. He campaigned in Wales and the north of Britain, paving the way for the early conquests of ◊Agricola. He wrote a general treatise on the art of war, of which the appendix *Strategemata/Stratagems* survives, and *De aquis urbis Romae/On the Water Supply of Rome*.

Frontinus was a leading senator in Rome in the late 1st century AD and held the consulship three times before his appointment as governor of Britain.

His *Strategemata* appendix takes the form of four books of 'stratagems'. These are examples from history of tactics, actions, and tricks to gain the upper hand in war.

fubing (or *fu-ping*) Chinese selective militia, the mainstay of Sui and early Tang armies. The system goes back to the Western Wei territorial ◊*xiangbing*. Under the Tang, 630 *fu* units existed, mostly in the northern provinces. Units could be of 800, 1,000, or 1,200 men, and were divided into ◊*tuan* of 200. A typical *fu* contained 100 cavalry and 900 infantry.

Soldiers supplied their own clothing, swords, and bows, but armour and other weapons were issued. Cavalrymen bought horses with government money. Between the ages of 21 and 60 they did short tours of duty in the ◊*wei* guards at the capital, longer tours in frontier garrisons, and served on campaign in a ◊*xingjun*. The *fubing's* limited service period became less useful as the Tang Empire expanded. The *fubing* frontier service was abolished in 737, their guard service in 749.

Fuchai (died 473 BC) (or *Fu-ch'ai*) last king of the Chinese kingdom of Wu 496–473 BC, the son of ◊Holu. He avenged his father's death by defeating ◊Goujian of Yue at Fujiao in 494, but allowed Goujian to keep his throne as a tributary. In the 480s he campaigned in the north against Qi (present-day Shandong), and his capital was attacked by Goujian in his absence. Fuchai surrendered to Goujian in 473 and committed suicide when his state was annexed.

Fu Hao (lived 14th–13th centuries BC) one of the queens of the Shang Chinese king ◊Wu Ding, entrusted by him with the leadership of repeated military campaigns against neighbouring tribes. For one campaign against the Qiang she commanded 10,000 ◊*lu* troops and 3,000 from her own ◊*zu*.

Her tomb at Yin (present-day Anyang, Henan province, China) yielded one of the major collections of Shang weapons, both practical and ceremonial.

Fu Jian (died 385) (or *Fu Chien*) tribal ruler 357–85 of the Former Qin state founded in 352 after the collapse of ◊Shi Le's Later Zhao dynasty, during the ◊Sixteen Kingdoms period. Jian was of the 'proto-Tibetan' Di (Ti) tribe. He conquered northern China and attempted an invasion of southern China. He was killed during a revolt by a rival clan.

Jian and his Chinese chief minister Wang Meng ran the state as an autocratic military bureaucracy, alienating the Di tribesmen but enabling Jian to raise huge conscript armies. In 365 he was attacked by the Murong ◊Xianbei of Yan, and then had to put down revolts by the ◊Xiongnu and his own imperial clan. He defeated all these, and in 370 conquered Yan. Soon he controlled all north China, and in 383 even sent an expedition against the city-kingdoms of the Tarim Basin silk-trade route. In the same year he invaded south China, but his massive army (allegedly 600,000 infantry and 270,000 cavalry) was defeated at Luojian (see ◊Luojian, Battle of) and the Fei River (see ◊Fei River, Battle of The). The Xianbei revolted, defeating his forces at Zheng in 384 (see ◊Zheng, Battle of), and amid other revolts Fu Jian was strangled by a member of a rival Di clan.

Fujigawa, Battle of the battle (or non-battle) of 1180 in the ◊Taira–Minamoto Wars of 12th-century Japan, important as the first major victory for the emergent forces of ◊Minamoto Yoritomo.

Yoritomo led his troops against the Taira army who were encamped on the banks of the river Fujigawa. Legend has it that as Yoritomo and a small exploratory force undertook a night crossing of the river, they disturbed a flock of wild geese. The noise startled the Taira forces, who thought that they were being attacked by a huge force, and they panicked and fled.

Fujiwara Michinaga (966–1028) major court official of the Heian period who, by skilful political alliances and shrewd control of the imperial throne, effectively ruled Japan from about 988 to 1019. He was the father of four empresses and grandfather of three emperors.

Aware of the rising power of the military families in the provinces, themselves often related to the imperial household, he allied the Fujiwara family with the ◊Minamoto family, thereby extending his political, military, and economic power.

Fujiwara Sumitomo (died 941) Japanese court official of the Fujiwara family. He led a major rebellion against the emperor Suzaku in 939, invading several provinces and expelling their governors, but was eventually captured and killed by an army under another Fujiwara general loyal to the court.

fukigaeshi upper turned-back plates, or lames, on both sides of the Japanese helmet which are a continuation of the neck guard (◊*shikoro*).

In the helmets of the Kamakura period (1185–1333) the *fukigaeshi* were extremely large and lay almost flat over the rest of the *shikoro*. Later developments saw them transformed into simple decorative devices which were often adorned with the family crest.

fulcum formation used by late Roman and Byzantine infantry in which 'the men in the front ranks close in until their shields are touching, completely covering their midsections almost to their ankles. The men standing behind them hold their shields above their heads, interlocking them with those of the men in front of them, covering their chests and faces, and in this way move to attack' (*Strategikon*). In earlier periods the formation was called a ◊*testudo*.

Fulk (III) Nerra (987–1040) count of Anjou, of the Angevin dynasty in northwestern France, who transformed Anjou into a major power in western Europe. An effective military leader, he defeated Conan I of Brittany at the battle of Nantes in 992, and Odo II of Blois at the Battle of Pontlevoy in 1016. Also an innovator in fortification, his works included ◊Doué-la-Fontaine castle and ◊Langeais castle, among the oldest in Europe.

furusiya medieval Arabic ◊Mameluke cavalry training manual of the 13th and 14th centuries. These manuals are well illustrated and show how the individual warrior learned to fight with the ◊lance and ◊bow, including many manoeuvres on horseback.

futuwa medieval Arabic code of ethics, usually compared to Western chivalry, developed in Iran about 1200. Its origins were in ancient traditions of the region associated with tribal solidarity, and it had an important impact on military loyalty.

Caliph al-Nasir moved to ensure that the *futuwa* movement was faithful to the Abbasids, and after the fall of Baghdad to the Mongols, the ◊Mamelukes inherited this tradition.

fyrd Anglo-Saxon local militia. All freemen were obliged to serve in the defence of their shire but, by the 11th century, a distinction was drawn between the **great fyrd**, for local defence, and the **select fyrd**, drawn from better-equipped and experienced warriors who could serve farther afield.

Gaesati transalpine Gallic warriors probably armed with the *gaesum*, a long, heavy Gallic throwing-spear. According to the Greek historian Polybius, in 225 BC they were hired by the north Italian Gallic tribes called the Insubres and Boii for a campaign into central Italy that ended at Telamon (see ◊Telamon, Battle of). In the imperial period *numeri* (see ◊*numerus*) of Raeti Gaesati appear from inscriptions to have been stationed throughout the Roman Empire, although little is known about them.

Stationed in front of the main army at Telamon, the Gaesati displayed their naked physiques and gold torcs in an intimidating fashion (they may have fought naked for ritual reasons). However, they were ill-equipped to deal with the skirmishing tactics of the Roman ◊velites and broke under a prolonged hail of missiles.

A further 30,000 Gaesati were hired by the Insubres in 223 BC and were probably present at the Celtic defeats of Clastidium and Mediolanum (see ◊Clastidium, Battle of and ◊Mediolanum, Battle of).

Gaiseric (428–77) Vandal king, who was brother and successor of ◊Gunderic. Although lame and with a reputation for ruthlessness and cruelty, Gaiseric proved to be one of the ablest of the Germanic leaders of the migration period. He led the Vandals and Alans from Spain to conquer Roman Africa, and established the Vandal Kingdom as the dominant power in the western Mediterranean. Although on several occasions the Western and Eastern halves of the Roman Empire sent combined forces against him, he always emerged triumphant. Sometimes he achieved victory through diplomacy (allying himself with ◊Attila, for example) and on other occasions by defeating the Romans in battle both on land and at sea. Gaiseric's kingdom, however, was built on shaky foundations and held together primarily by the force of his personality. The Arian Vandals were few in number and hated by their primarily Catholic subjects whom they persecuted. On Gaiseric's death in 477 Vandal power quickly faded.

In May 429 he took advantage of civil war in Roman Africa to lead 80,000 people (about 10,000–15,000 warriors) across from Spain. He twice defeated the Roman forces sent against him and captured the city of Hippo in 431. Bowing to the inevitable, the West Roman government recognized Gaiseric's control of Mauritania and Numidia in 435. Gaiseric used the peace to build up his strength, particularly that of his fleet, and on 19 October 439 seized Carthage, gaining the best harbour in the western Mediterranean and access to rich agricultural land. In the years that followed Gaiseric combined skilful diplomacy with sea power to strengthen his hold on Africa and expand the Vandal kingdom. All of the Mediterranean littoral suffered from Vandal raids, including Rome, which was sacked in 455. Gaiseric also captured Tripoli, Sardinia, and Sicily.

Gaixia, Battle of (or *Kai-hsia*) battle in 202 BC marking ◊Han Gaozu's final defeat of ◊Xiang Yu in China. Several Han armies converged on Xiang, surrounding him at Gaixia, in modern Anhui. Worn down by successive attacks by fresh Han units, outnumbered and out of supplies, he broke out with 800 cavalry and was pursued by 5,000 Han cavalry. When the Han caught him he had only 28 followers left. Surrounded, he fought desperately but eventually cut his own throat.

Gaja Mada (lived 14th century) chief minister of the Majapahit Empire of Java, in government service 1319–64. He served as a palace guards officer under King Jayanagara and as chief minister under his successors, princess regent Tribhuvana and her son, Hyam Wuruk. Gaja Mada expanded Java's power throughout Indonesia.

In 1319 he escorted King Jayanagara, son of Majapahit's founder ◊Vijaya, when a revolt forced him to flee the capital. Gaja Mada returned and organized a counter-revolt, restoring the king. In 1328 Jayanagara died – allegedly assassinated on Gaja Mada's behalf after taking his wife. The princess Tribhuvana succeeded as regent, and from 1330 Gaja Mada was her chief minister; when her son Hyam Wuruk became king in 1350, Gaja Mada remained in charge until his death in 1364.

Bali was conquered under Gaga Mada 1331–43. The king of Sunda in west Java was lured into a trap and killed in 1351, and Sunda was forced to acknowledge Majapahit's suzerainty. Majapahit sources also claim rule over Sumatra, parts of the Malay peninsula, parts of Borneo, Celebes, and the Moluccas, though these claims may be exaggerated.

Galba, Servius Sulpicius (lived 2nd century) Roman politician and military commander who massacred a tribe of Lusitanians in 150 after he had disarmed them on promise of fair treatment. He was prosecuted on his return to Rome but escaped justice by bringing his children into court and appealing to the jury's pity.

galley, beaked see ◊beaked galley.

Gamala, Siege of siege and assault on the Galilean town of Gamala by the Roman army under the emperor ◊Vespasian in AD 67. The site, modern Gamla in the Golan Heights, has been excavated and traces of the siege have been discovered.

The town was built on the steeply angled slope of a narrow spur, making approach difficult. The first Roman assault broke through the outer defences, but lost momentum in the narrow streets. The Romans climbed onto the flat roofs of the houses, but when some of the houses collapsed the attack ended in a costly disaster. Vespasian was cut off in the city, and barely escaped. The second storming was led in person by the Roman general ◊Titus, who quickly secured the town.

GALLIC WARS

Series of campaigns conducted in Gaul (roughly equivalent to present-day France, Belgium, and some of western Germany) by the Roman general Julius ◊Caesar between 58 and 51 BC, which brought a huge expanse of new territory under Rome's control and established Caesar as one of the most popular military and political figures of the age. The campaigns, well documented by Caesar himself in *The Gallic War*, were to become famous for exploits such as the first bridging of the river Rhine and the first Roman expedition to Britain. The conquered territory was subsequently organized into provinces by the emperor Augustus.

Needing to gain a military reputation to enhance his political career, Caesar obtained the proconsulship of Roman Gaul in 59 BC with the intention of using its large provincial armies against the unconquered tribes of Celtic Gaul. His first campaign in 58 BC was designed to clear Gaul of external invaders, routing the migrating Helvetii at Bibracte (see ◊Bibracte, Battle of) and then forcing back the Germans who had conquered the Aedui tribe (see ◊Diviciacus and

◊unnamed battle). These actions had the advantage of securing the support of those tribes who regained their lands and freedom, but also of ensuring that the annexation of Gaul was not prolonged by outside intervention. The Germans had to be pushed back again in 55 BC; Caesar defeated them at the river Meuse (see ◊Meuse, Battle of the) and bridged the Rhine to ravage their territory. His expeditions to Britain in 55 and 54 BC were also intended to isolate Gaul from any outside assistance.

Within Gaul itself, the powerful Belgae tribal confederacy was the subject of the campaign of 57 BC (see ◊Axine, Battle of the), and year after year Caesar's operations continued to subdue the other tribes. A mass revolt broke out in 53 BC, led at first by ◊Indutiomarus and then by ◊Vercingetorix. The rebellion was gradually broken down to a final stand at the hilltop fortress of Alesia, where the Roman siege resisted desperate Gaulish assaults until Vercingetorix and his army were starved into surrender. The remaining tribes submitted and Caesar entered Rome in triumph.

gambeson quilted coat used as armour in European warfare from the 12th century. It was worn under chain or plate armour in order to reduce chafing and the shock of blows. Some were made of fine material such as silk and worn over armour for display and added protection.

Gannascus member of the Canninefates tribe who deserted from the Roman ◊*auxilia* and led a band which raided the coast of northern Gaul using small ships. In AD 47 he led a major raid by the Chauci, a Germanic tribe, against Germania Inferior. Gnaeus Domitius Corbulo defeated him and then arranged for Gannascus to be murdered by the eastern branch of the Chauci.

gantaolu (or *kan-t'ao-lu*) (Chinese 'seekers after loot') unpaid Chinese irregular troops employed by the Mongols in China before the establishment of the regular ◊*Han jun*. The *gantaolu* were officially disbanded in 1273, although on later occasions similar unregistered 'volunteers' following the army for loot were rounded up and enlisted as regulars.

Gaolianghe, Battle of (or *Kao-liang-ho*) battle in 979 in which the Khitan defeated Song China. The Song defeated a Khitan attempt to rescue the last independent Chinese state, Northern Han, so were encouraged to attack the areas of northeast China already held by the Khitan. The second Song emperor, Taizong, (◊Song Taizu's brother) personally besieged the Khitan 'southern capital', modern Beijing, but was heavily defeated at the Gaoliang River. The Song were thereafter on the defensive.

Gao Xianzhi (died 755) (or *Kao Hsien-chih* (Korean *Ko Sonji*) Korean general in Tang Chinese service. He defeated the Tibetans at Wakhan and Balur in 747 and was appointed military governor of the ◊Four Garrisons in Central Asia in 748. In 750 he supported China's client state Ferghana in a war against Tashkent and captured the city, but was defeated by the Arabs at Atlakh in 751 (see ◊Atlakh, Battle of) and relieved of command. In 755 he prepared the defences of Tongguan (see ◊Tongguan, Battle of) against ◊An Lushan, but Emperor Tang Xuanzong had him executed for failing to defeat An.

Gaoyu, Battle of (or *Kao-yu*) battle in 685 in what is now Jiangu in which a Tang Chinese army under commander Li Xiaoyi defeated rebels led by Li Jingye. The rebels defended a river line, and their best troops defeated imperial attempts to cross by boat. Xiaoyi then had the reeds set alight and crossed under cover of the smoke. His troops broke the rebel front line, and the rebel elite, waiting in reserve, were swept away in the rout.

Gasgan one of a group of tribal enemies of the Hittites who occupied the coastlands along the Black Sea from the time of the Old Kingdom (1500 BC onwards). They were a constant threat to the capital Hattusas (modern Boğazköy, Turkey) and overran most of the Hittite heartland – the bend of the river Marassanda (classical Halys, modern Kizilirmak) – in the time before Suppiluliumas I, and again when Muwatallis fought against Ramses II at Kadesh (see ◊Kadesh, Battle of) in 1275 BC.

The Gasgans may have contributed to the collapse of the Hittite empire: Tiglath-Pileser I in his first campaign (1114 BC) mentioned renegade Gasgans, and ◊Sargon II defeated Gasgans as far south as Hilakku (classical Cilicia) in the 8th century BC.

Gate Fulford, Battle of battle of 1066, preceding the Battle of Hastings, when ◊Harold (II) Godwinson, King of England, was defeated to the south of York in an invasion by King Harald III Hardrada of Norway.

Harold's brother Tostig was in alliance with Hardrada. Edwin and Morcar, earls of Mercia and Northumbria, came from York to oppose Hardrada. The battle was fought south of York, in what is now a suburb of the city. The earls survived and made peace with Hardrada.

Gaugamela, Battle of battle fought in 331 BC on the east bank of the river Tigris in Upper Mesopotamia, in the Persian satrapy (province) of Adiabene, between ◊Alexander (III) the Great and ◊Darius III of Persia. It was the scene of Alexander's final and decisive victory over Darius, by which he effectively gained control over the whole of Asia Minor.

Alexander seems to have deployed a second line of allied infantry behind his main phalanx. An attempt to outflank the Macedonian right was beaten off, as was the charge of the Persian chariots, and this apparently left a gap in the left centre of the Persian line which Alexander exploited with his Companion cavalry and the right and centre of his phalanx, whereupon Darius fled with Alexander in pursuit. As news of Darius' flight spread, the rest of the Persian army disintegrated.

Gaul, Frankish invasions of widespread series of raids or invasions in AD 256 into the Western Roman Empire by the tribal confederation of the Franks. Although they may have suffered some defeats at the hands of the Romans led by Posthumus, they nevertheless reached Spain.

gauntlet protective covering for the hand, wrist, and later the lower forearm, usually made of plate. Plate gauntlets were an essential part of European armour from the 13th to the 17th centuries.

Gaza, Battle of battle of 17 October 1244 in which Christian forces under Walter of Jaffa, allied with Syrian Muslim rulers, fought the Egyptians and their Khwarasmian Turkish allies. It was the most important battle since Hattin in 1187 (see ◊Hattin, Battle of) and, following the loss of Jerusalem in July (see ◊Jerusalem, sack of), sounded the death knell for Christian rule in the Holy Land. The defeat provoked Louis IX of France's crusade of 1248–50.

The alliance between the Christians and Muslim Syrian rulers had been formed in response to the Mongol invasions. After taking Jerusalem in July, about 10,000 Khwarismian Turks moved south to join Baibars' Ayyubid Egyptian army of 5,000 outside Gaza. Walter of Jaffa mustered almost 1,000 knights and many infantry, together with his allies, totalling possibly 20,000 men, and attacked. The Frankish charge on the right flank was succeeding against the Egyptians, but the Khwarasmians drove off the Muslim centre and left flank. The Turks then surrounded the Christians, who suffered about 5,000 casualties and lost 800 as prisoners.

gekokujō Japanese term applied to the overthrow of the ruling military or political classes by those of inferior social standing. Examples can be found throughout Japanese history, notably the destruction of the ◊Kamakura shogunate in 1185 and the civil unrest of the ◊Ōnin Wars (1467–77).

Gelimer last king of the Vandals (530–34), who was defeated by ◊Belisarius, and his kingdom taken over by the Romans.

Gelimer deposed his pro-Roman cousin Hilderic in 530, after the latter had lost much of the Vandal hinterland to the Moors. This gave the East Roman Emperor ◊Justinian the excuse to attempt the reconquest of Africa. Gelimer's leadership in the field was weak, and even cowardly. His armies collapsed and he surrendered in 534. He ended his life in exile in the Eastern Empire.

Gelon (c. 540–478 BC) tyrant of Syracuse. Gelon took power in Gela, then capital of Sicily 491, and then transferred the capital to Syracuse. He refused to help the mainland Greeks against Xerxes 480 BC, but later the same year defeated the Carthaginians under Hamilcar Barca at Himera, on the north coast of Sicily, leaving Syracuse as the leading city in the western Greek world.

Geluofeng (died 778) (or *Ko-lo-feng*) king of the tribal kingdom of Nanzhao (in present-day Yunnan, southwest China) 748–78. Nanzhao had been allied with Tang China, but its growing wealth led to Chinese aggression. Geluofeng defeated the Chinese attacks and turned Nanzhao into a formidable local power.

The first Chinese attack on Nanzhao came in 751. Geluofeng defeated the Chinese on the upper river Yangtze, and turned to an alliance with the powerful Tibetan Empire. When the Chinese attacked again in 754, he fell back deep into his own territory and, with Tibetan help, defeated them at Dengchuan. The rebellion by ◊An Lushan prevented further Chinese expeditions and Geluofeng was able to invade Chinese frontier territory. He also conquered neighbouring tribes in southern Yunnan and attacked the Pyu kingdom in present-day Myanmar (formerly Burma).

Gempei Wars another name for the ◊Taira–Minamoto Wars of 1180–85, a major conflict between the Taira and Minamoto families of Japan.

gen d'armes (medieval French 'man-at-arms') fully equipped warrior in 14th- and 15th-century Europe, when many people did not take up knighthood. The French and Burgundian rulers had elite squadrons of *gens d'armes*, equipped with barded (breastplated) horses, and the term survived into the 16th century and later.

Genghis Khan (c. 1155–1227) (more correctly, *Chingiz Khan*) Mongol conqueror, ruler of all Mongol peoples from 1206. He conquered the empires of northern China 1211–15 and Khwarazm 1219–21, and invaded northern India in 1221, while his lieutenants advanced as far as the Crimea. When he died his empire ranged from the Yellow Sea to the Black Sea; it continued to expand after his death to extend from Hungary to Korea. Genghis Khan controlled probably a larger area than any other individual in history. He was not only a great military leader, but the creator of a stable political system.

Temujin, as he was originally called, was the son of a Mongol chieftain, whom he succeeded at the age of 13. He spent the first 25 years of his rule in the unification of the nomadic tribes south of Lake Baikal into a great kingdom of the steppes, taking the title Chingiz Khan ('World Conqueror') in 1206. The rapidity, discipline, manoeuvrability, and ruthlessness of the Mongol army he created made him one of the greatest military leaders of history. To his Muslim enemies he was 'the Wrath of God'.

Geoffrey (II) de Mandeville (died 1144)

English noble who became sheriff of Essex, Hampshire, London, and Middlesex, and earl of Essex under King Stephen of Blois. In 1141, with Stephen in prison, he briefly deserted the royal cause but soon returned to his allegiance. He was arrested by the king in 1143 and after his release, rebelled from his base in Ely. Geoffrey was wounded attacking ◊Burwell castle in 1144 and died a week later.

Geoffrey V (died 1151) count of Anjou

from 1129 and duke of Normandy from 1144. He conquered Normandy 1135–45 in the name of his wife Matilda, daughter of Henry I of England. Their son, as Henry II, was the first of the Plantagenet line of English rulers.

Geoffrey used ◊Greek fire at the siege of ◊Montreuil-Bellay castle 1149–51, where he was also described as reading the Roman work on warfare by Flavius ◊Vegetius.

Georg von Frundsberg (1473–1528)

'Father of the Landsknechts', mercenary who fought in the Italian Wars, and victor of Bicocca in 1522 and Pavia in 1525. Von Frundsberg is connected from 1499 with the development of the Landsknechts, imperial troops who challenged the Swiss supremacy that had developed in the late 15th century. Although his career was mainly post-1500, he represents the continuity between medieval and Renaissance warfare.

Gergovia Gallic hillfort in the territory of the Arverni, attacked by the Romans in 52 BC.

Julius ◊Caesar's troops assaulted the well-defended hillfort following their successful action at ◊Avaricum. The Romans carried out the attack too enthusiastically, ignoring Caesar's orders to halt, and were repulsed by the Gauls with heavy losses.

Germanicopolis, Battle of (or *Gangra*) victory in 778 for the Byzantines over the Arabs, which halted an attempted Arab invasion of Anatolia.

GERMANIC ARMIES

Organized military forces of the Germanic peoples from 1st century BC to 4th century AD. Their structure and military practices changed little during this period, although there was considerable diversification afterwards. War leaders were usually elected for the duration of a campaign and some tribes appointed a pair of commanders. An army was composed of all freemen able to equip themselves and was organized on a family, clan, and tribal basis. The only distinct groups were the *comites* (permanent retainers) of particular noblemen. These were full-time warriors who lived at the expense of their leader under an obligation to fight and die for him, and were usually better equipped than most warriors. Cavalry were very effective, although they were poorly mounted and not very numerous. The number of archers in Germanic armies also appears to have been low.

Most men were armed with a shield and one or several *frameae* (light spears). Swords were uncommon and armour and helmets very rare. Men skirmishing with javelins are described, but it is unclear whether these formed distinct units or were simply ordinary warriors running forward from the main line as the mood took them. Several sources describe a formation used by the Germans known as the *cuneus* (wedge). It is unclear precisely what this was and suggestions have varied from a deep, densely-packed column to some sort of triangular formation. Since Germanic noblemen needed glory and booty to maintain their position in society, warfare was an integral part of Germanic culture during this period, especially raiding, which was commonly used against Rome. Large armies took a long time to muster, were clumsy in their movements, and could be easily surprised. They were dangerous because of the bravery of individual warriors and the large numbers that a charismatic tribal leader might command.

Germanicus Caesar (15 BC–AD 19) Roman general. He was the son of ◊Drusus Germanicus and adopted son of Tiberius, and married Agrippina, the granddaughter of the emperor ◊Augustus. He campaigned in Pannonia and Dalmatia in AD 7–10, and then in Germany 11–12. In 14 he quelled a mutiny of the legions on the Rhine provoked by the death of Augustus.

He then embarked on two more years of operations against the German tribes, winning a series of victories. Sent to the Middle East to negotiate with the Parthians, he died near Antioch, possibly murdered at the instigation of Tiberius.

He was the father of Caligula and Agrippina, mother of ◊Nero.

gerrhon Greek term for a shield made of reeds, canes, or wickerwork. The ancient Greeks used the word to describe the Persian ◊*spara* and other types of shields. In modern usage it refers to large Assyrian reed siege-shields.

Gewalthut medieval Swiss term for 'main body': see ◊*Vorhut*.

ghazi (Arabic 'soldier of the faith') religious warrior fighting in the cause of Islam against infidels (Hindus, polytheists, and idolators). *Ghazis* first appeared as members of dedicated and organized bodies in Anatolia in the early 14th century. Their Christian counterparts were the Byzantine *akritos* or the Frankish crusaders.

The term *ghazi* was later applied to any individual ready to sacrifice himself in battle and became a synonym for 'hero'.

ghulam (Arabic 'slave') member of a force of military slaves kept throughout history by most Islamic rulers and their senior officers as household troops. They were often prisoners of war, or their descendants, drawn from a wide spread of ethnic groups.

As regular troops, they were generally better trained and more dependable than contingents produced by landholders under quasi-feudal systems, but they were more expensive to keep up and liable to participate in palace coups.

gisarme medieval European infantry polearm. The name dates from the 12th century and probably represents a range of weapon types, including the single-edged bill or ◊halberd, fork, and pike.

Gisors castle 11th-century stronghold occupying a key position in Eure *département*, Normandy, France. The motte was built by Rufus in 1096. The walls and octagonal shell keep were added under ◊Henry I of England. ◊Philip (II) Augustus of France added the round 'Prisoners' Tower' after his conquest of Normandy in 1204, an early example of the *en bec* structure (strengthening stone spur).

Givald's Foss, Battle of Viking victory in 852 over the Carolingian Franks under Charles the Bald at the height of Viking power in France.

gladius general term for the legionary sword used during the Roman republic and early empire (around 300 BC–AD 200). It was replaced by the ◊*spatha*.

gladius hispaniensis legionary sword of the late Roman republic (around 200 BC–AD 25), originating in Spain. It had a metal-framed scabbard and was suspended from a belt on the right side of the body.

This long-pointed and slightly waisted cut-and-thrust weapon was gradually replaced by the short-pointed, straight-edged Pompeian sword (essentially a hacking weapon) in the middle of the 1st century AD, which in turn was superseded by the ◊*spatha* in the 2nd century AD.

glaive medieval polearm, usually consisting of a large, single-edged, leaf-shaped blade used by foot soldiers.

Glendower, Owen alternative, Anglicized spelling of Owain ◊Glyndwr, Welsh nationalist leader.

gleve (medieval German) a knight and his 'team'. In 1373 a gleve was defined as three horsemen – one knight, another with missiles, and a page – but the term could also refer to common missile-men in combination.

Gloucester, Robert, Earl of (died 1147) eldest illegitimate son of Henry I of England, ennobled by him. His defiance of King Stephen (who had seized the throne after Henry's death) in 1138 made the civil war possible for his half-sister Matilda, whom he served as chief commander, winning at Lincoln in 1141 (see ◊Lincoln, Battle of) – in which action Stephen was captured.

Robert's own capture at Winchester (see ◊Winchester, Battle of) in 1141 was followed by the mutual release of both. Robert's death was a blow to Matilda's hopes of being crowned.

Glyndwr, Owain (born 1354) (or *Owen Glendower*) Welsh nationalist leader. He led a rebellion against Henry IV of England, taking the title 'Prince of Wales' in 1400, and successfully led the Welsh defence against English invasions 1400–02, although Wales was reconquered 1405–13.

He allied himself with English rebels, including the Percies, and also the French, but his allies were defeated. He went into hiding and disappeared from history.

goat's-foot lever device for operating a ◊crossbow, introduced in the mid-14th century, which looked like a goat's cloven foot. It worked with a purpose-made crossbow that had pins projecting from each side of the stock. The lever had dividing claws at one end that could be fitted under the string. The lever was rested over the stock, pivoting on the pins. By pressing the handle the lever pivoted and the string could be drawn back with ease.

Go-Daigo (1288–1339) Japanese emperor. He was responsible for the brief restoration to power of the imperial throne in the ◊Kemmu Restoration of 1333–36 when the ◊Kamakura shogunate was overthrown. Assisted by Ashikaga Takauji, the emperor's reforms were deemed too radical, and he in turn was deposed by Takauji.

Godfrey de Bouillon (c. 1060–1100) duke of Lower Lorraine, advocate of the Holy Sepulchre in 1099, and leader of the German contingent on the First Crusade. An experienced warrior in the service of Emperor Henry IV, he was only one of several leaders on the crusade, but he was wealthy and his followers played an important part in the successful sieges of Nicaea in 1097 (see ◊Nicaea, Battle of) and Jerusalem in 1099 (see ◊Jerusalem, Siege of), as well as at the battle of Ascalon (see ◊Ascalon, Battle of) in 1099. This may also be why he was elected as Jerusalem's protector, although he refused a crown in Christ's city.

goedendag (Flemish 'good day') ironically named weapon of medieval Flanders. It was a 1.3-m-/4-ft-long polearm in the form of a heavy wooden club, tipped with an iron band and spike, and was used by the Flemish militias against the French about 1300.

It is depicted on a contemporary chest kept in New College, Oxford University, England, commemorating the battle of Courtrai (see ◊Courtrai, Battle of).

gokenin (Japanese 'housemen') Japanese term applied to those vassals directly subject to the ◊shogun.

With the foundation of the ◊Kamakura shogunate many ◊samurai became the personal vassals of ◊Minamoto Yoritomo and received direct appointments as military governors in the name of the shogun. They formed the basis for the military control of the country.

Goldsmith's Daughter, War of the war fought in 1406 between Deva Raya I, ruler of the Hindu empire of ◊Vijayanagar 1406–22, and the Muslim Firuz Shah Bahmani of the Deccan, provoked by Deva Raya's attempted abduction of the daughter of a goldsmith living in territory ruled by Firuz Shah. The Muslims retaliated by attacking Vijayanagar.

When Deva Raya was told of the beautiful and talented girl, Parchal, he sent a force to abduct her. She and her parents fled, and the Hindu force plundered the countryside. Firuz Shah, ably supported by his brother ◊Ahmad Shah, then led an army to Vijayanagar. The Muslims were unable to take the city, but were victorious in the field. A marriage was arranged between one of Deva Raya's daughters and Firuz, but a breach of protocol by Deva Raya was taken as an insult, leading to further hostilities.

Goltho castle small castle in Lincolnshire, England, dating from about 1180, but more interestingly an Anglo-Saxon fortification called a 'pre-Conquest castle'. This is debatable since it was smaller in scale than Norman castles and is perhaps best seen as a transitional structure in the development of castles.

gonfanon (or *gonfalon* or *confanon*) (medieval French) medieval lance-head banner, larger than a knight's ◊pennon, and often fringed with tongues of cloth, but not as large as a ◊banner. The ◊Bayeux Tapestry portrays some fine early examples. The gonfanon was used to direct the movement of troops in battle.

As used by the order of Knights Templar (see ◊Military Order), an officer called the 'gonfanonier' directed the squires and handed the order's standard to the marshal to initiate a charge.

Gonzaga, Francesco (lived 15th–16th centuries) marquis of Mantua and Venetian captain-general. He fought against the French at Fornovo in 1495 (see ◊Fornovo, Battle of) and for them at Cerignola in 1503, where he was outclassed by the Spanish commander Gonsalvo de Cordoba. His battle-seeking strategy at Fornovo contradicts the stereotype of the ◊condottieri as seeking bloodless battles and no certain conclusion in order to prolong their employment. At Cerignola he encountered a new generation of commanders with superior tactical ability.

Goodrich castle castle in east Wales, between Monmouth and Ross, founded before the Conquest to defend against the Welsh. The keep of the later castle was built in the late 12th century, in the time of Henry II. Other architectural features include a barbican, spurs on the turrets to counter mining, and a ditch cut from solid rock. The castle was given to the earls of Pembroke by Henry III and then passed to the Talbots, earls of Shrewsbury.

Gopala Indian Buddhist founder of the Pala dynasty which restored order in the eastern Gangetic region of India after a period of anarchy; the dynasty lasted until about 1050. Under his successors ◊Dharmapala and Devapala (reigned 815–854) the Palas became one of the foremost powers in northern India.

gorget plate armour in the form of a collar designed to protect the neck, chest, and shoulders, in use in western Europe from the 15th century. It was generally made in two pieces joined by a hinge or pivoting rivet and locked together around the neck by use of a keyhole and stud.

Gormaz castle castle in Spain, 22 km/14 mi east of Aranda de Duero. Built by the Moors in the 10th century and one of their most important fortresses in Castile, it enabled them to keep control of the Duero River boundary. The castle was surrendered to the Christians in 975 after the defeat of its commander in battle, and was later associated with the celebrated ◊El Cid.

The castle consists of two main wards surrounded by about 915 m/3,000 ft of curtain wall, 9 m/30 ft high with numerous square towers. One ward was the residence of the ◊castellan and his garrison, and the other housed the livestock and servants. There were doubtless buildings in both wards but nothing remains of these today.

gorytos combined bow-case and quiver used by Scythian archers from about the 7th century BC. It was supported by a waistbelt and worn over the left hip. It held both the short, heavily recurved Scythian composite bow (see ◊bow, composite) and up to 75 arrows.

The *gorytos* was widely copied by neighbouring peoples, and a larger version was carried by the Medes and Persians. In the early centuries AD it was replaced by separate bow-cases and quivers.

Goujian (died 464 BC) (or *Kou-chien*) king of Yue (or Yüeh, present-day Zhejiang, China) 496–464 BC. In 496 Goujian attacked ◊Holu of the coastal kingdom of Wu at Zuili, killed him, and overran his country. He was defeated in 494 by Holu's son ◊Fuchai and submitted to him, but attacked Wu again and permanently annexed the kingdom in 473.

When Fuchai was engaged elsewhere, Goujian attacked Wu in 482 with 48,000 men,

capturing the capital and killing the crown prince. In 475 he attacked again, defeated the Wu army at the Lei marshes, and besieged the capital. Fuchai surrendered in 473.

Govinda III fifth king of the Rashtrakuta dynasty of the Deccan c. 783–815. An active and militarily successful ruler, he extended his dominions southwards into the Tamil lands ruled by the Pallavas and northwards into Rajasthan.

Gowran Pass, Battle of battle fought in 1169 in southeast Ireland in which Dermot McMurrough, King of Leinster, defeated MacGillpatric of Ossory's superior forces. Dermot and his mercenary Norman commanders Hervey de Montmorency and Robert FitzStephen were returning from a raid on Ossory. They were pursued, and turned to engage MacGillpatrick's forces in battle.

Archers opened the battle with an attempted ambush, but it was the Norman knights' charge that scattered their lightly armed opponents. The victory was exploited by Dermot's light Irish foot soldiers, who pursued the routed Ossorians.

Gracchus, Tiberius Sempronius (c. 210–154 BC) Roman general and politician whose campaigns as governor of Nearer Spain in 180–179 BC pacified the frontier for a generation. In 177 he gained the consulship and subdued Sardinia in a harsh two-year campaign.

Granada, Siege of conflict of 1491–92 in Granada, Spain, in which the Moorish-held city was taken by the Catholic monarchs Ferdinand V (1452–1516) and Isabella I (1451–1504) and incorporated into the new Spanish kingdom.

When Muley Hasan, Sultan of Granada, refused to pay tribute in 1491 the city and its citadel, the Alhambra, were besieged by Catholic forces. Terms were agreed for surrender, and the Alhambra became a Christian palace. With the capture of Granada, the Moorish power in Spain was finally extinguished; the last Moorish king, Boabdil (c. 1459–1528), went into exile.

Grandson, Battle of encounter between ◊Charles the Bold, Duke of Burgundy, and the Swiss on the shores of Lake Geneva, Switzerland, on 2 March 1476. Charles's force was advancing on Neuchâtel, as part of his plan to take the country, when the Swiss came across them. Although casualties were fairly even, the Burgundians fled and lost some 400 pieces of artillery.

GREAT WALL OF CHINA

General term given to a number of defensive lines of various periods on the northern Chinese frontier.

Several ◊Warring States rulers (5th–3rd centuries BC), including King Wuling of Zhao, built walls for defence against the new threat of mounted nomads. Following his ◊Ordos campaign, the emperor ◊Qin Shi Huangdi's general Meng Tian began work in 214 BC to link these existing defences into a single system against the ◊Xiongnu. Meng Tian's system was not a continuous wall; mountain barriers were deemed sufficient at some places, a series of fortified cities at others. This system did not last long; after the emperor ◊Han Gaozu's defeat at Pingcheng in 200 BC he ceded the Ordos back to the Xiongnu, and the frontier apparently followed an older Warring States wall. As the Han expanded, however, they developed a new wall system, and the emperor ◊Han Wudi extended it westwards to protect the newly acquired territories in Xinjiang. It was also under the Han that the Wall acquired psychological importance as the boundary between Chinese and barbarian, settlement and nomadism, and became a barrier to unregulated trade. The Han wall was an earthwork linking square watchtowers of plastered and whitewashed brick. It was manned by conscript soldiers well supplied with armour, crossbows, and ◊ballistae, with a sophisticated system of flags and torches for signalling. They regularly patrolled for traces of enemy activity; areas of sand beyond the Wall were raked smooth to reveal traces of passing nomads. The soldiers' other tasks included farming to supply themselves and brickmaking for repairs. When central authority collapsed from the late 2nd century AD, few regimes had the resources to maintain continuous frontier defences. In the 5th century the ◊Toba campaigns against the Ruanruan demonstrated an aggressive alternative to walls. But the Sinicization of the Toba aristocracy led to a reversion to Chinese methods, and up to ◊Sui Wendi several dynasties walled parts of the frontier – the Northern Qi built 3,000 *li* (about 1,600 km/995 mi) of wall in the mid-6th century. The aggressive expansion of ◊Tang Taizong again made frontier walls redundant, and after the fall of the Tang dynasty northern China was mostly ruled by foreign dynasties whose cavalry armies had little use for walls. Nonetheless, the Jurchen Jin dynasty of Wanyen Aguda built long frontier walls during the 12th century, in Inner Mongolia well north of any Chinese walls. The Jin structures were double walls with two moats, beacon towers, and 'horse-face' bastions, but they failed to keep out the Mongols.

The present Great Wall was built by the Ming dynasty. After ◊Zhu Yuanzhang expelled the Mongols, frontier strategy was based on mobile cavalry armies and advanced garrisons on the edge of the steppe. In the early 15th century the Ming found the advance policy difficult to maintain and started to build walls at certain strategic points. The ◊Tumu Incident of 1449 revealed the weakness of the frontier; Mongol raids from the Ordos continued until the victory at Hongyanchi in 1473 (see ◊Hongyanchi, Battle of) cleared them out and allowed the building of the ◊Ordos Loop Walls. The continuous wall along the rest of the frontier dates only from the 16th century.

It was a Swiss foraging column that bumped into the vanguard of Charles's 11,000-strong force of Burgundians. The remainder soon advanced and formed a 10,000-strong massed square. Charles intended to break up the square with artillery and exploit the gaps with his ◊gen d'armes cavalry. This tactic appeared to be successful, but Swiss reserves suddenly appeared on the Burgundian flank and created a rout.

Granicus, Battle of the Alexander's first victory over the Persians, fought on the banks of the river Granicus in northwest Asia Minor (probably now the Kocabas) in 334 BC.

The sources differ about what happened. According to ◊Arrian, Alexander fought his way across the Granicus against Persian cavalry late in the day, then annihilated the Greek mercenary infantry on the Persian side. He seems to have drawn the Persians out of position and into the river bed by sending a single squadron of Companions (Macedonian cavalry) into attack, then launching the rest obliquely into the left of the confused enemy mass. ◊Diodorus Siculus says that Alexander crossed the river unopposed at dawn and won a conventional battle on the far bank.

great helm large, cylindrical protective head covering made of plate. Properly called the 'helm' or 'heaume', the first great helms appeared in Europe in the early 13th century. They extended the current flat-topped helmet by the addition of a face defence, pierced at the front with sights and breaths, and then a neck defence, with all parts being solidly riveted together.

These early helms were worn over arming caps and mail ◊coifs. By the late 13th century the top had become a truncated cone, though some round-topped helms were also designed. The development of the visored ◊basinet relegated the great helm from the battlefield by the early 15th century, though helms continued to be used as jousting armour into the 16th century.

Great Raids, Hussite invasions of southern Germany in 1428–31 by the ◊Hussites under ◊Procopius to levy tribute and challenge Catholic religious observance.

Procopius attacked Moravia and Silesia in 1428, the Hussites' reputation cowing any opposition. In 1429 they penetrated as far north as Dresden and then swung back south to Leipzig in Saxony. In 1430 Procopius advanced to Nuremberg and had the Hussites' Four Articles of faith read in the town square. Papal crusades failed to recover Bohemia; it was only when the Hussites fell out amongst themselves that they were defeated.

greave (or *shin guard*) ancient piece of armour protecting the lower leg. Examples are known from the Mycenaean period (pre-1200 BC), but the full greave, covering the leg from the knee to just above the ankle, developed in Greece as part of the ◊hoplite armour.

Greaves may have been used by the front ranks of the Macedonian phalanx (mid-4th century–150 BC). Apart from their use as part of the traditional uniform of centurions, there is little evidence for their use by Roman legionaries.

greave, medieval piece of plate armour covering the lower leg. Greaves first appeared in medieval European inventories in the 1260s and become common in representations of early plate armour from the early 14th century, at first as demi-greaves, protecting only the outside and front of the shin, then as *grèves closes*, formed of two hinged plates completely enclosing the lower leg.

Greek fire combustible material used in medieval warfare, especially by the Byzantine Empire, against wooden ships or fortifications. Like a flame-thrower, it could be aimed, usually through a tube, and would explode on impact. The main ingredient was almost certainly naphtha or crude oil.

Greek fire was possibly invented in the 7th century by the Egyptian architect Callinicus who fled from Syria to Greece. The Byzantine Empire used it until its fall in 1453, and kept its recipe a closely guarded secret.

Green Woodsmen, rebellion of the one of the peasant revolts AD 17–26 provoked by natural disasters following the usurpation of ◊Wang Mang in China. A group in modern Hubei who based themselves in the Lülin or 'green-wooded' hills cooperated with local gentry, including Liu Xuan of the Han imperial family, whom they set up as emperor, and his cousin Liu Xiu.

They defeated Wang Mang's army at Kunyang (see ◊Kunyang, Battle of), enabling them to take Loyang and in October 23 the capital Changan. Disputes within the regime, however, prevented it from extending its control over much of China, and in AD 25 the Red Eyebrows took Changan (see ◊Red Eyebrows, rebellion of the). Liu Xuan fled but was caught and murdered by former supporters. The Green Woodsmen remnants were defeated by their former ally Liu Xiu, who became Emperor ◊Han Guangwudi.

grivpan piece of Sassanian Persian armour. Literally meaning 'neck-protector', it may have been the ◊mail or scale neck guard attached to

Parthian and Sassanian helmets. A less literal meaning may have been 'life preserver', denoting the lamellar cuirass worn over mail shirts by Sassanian cavalry.

Grosmont castle castle in east Wales, 16 km/ 10 mi north of Monmouth. One of the 'three castles of Gwent', it guards a crossing of the river Monnow. Built as a ◊motte-and-bailey castle in the late 11th century by one of William the Conqueror's followers, it eventually came into the house of Lancaster, and ◊John of Gaunt was born here. It was besieged during Owain ◊Glyndwr's insurrection in 1404, but thereafter fell into ruin.

Gruffydd ap Llewellyn (died 1063) king of Welsh Wales, and of all Wales from 1056. He defeated the English at Hereford in 1055 (see ◊Hereford, Battle of), but was defeated by ◊Harold (II) Godwinson. Like many Welsh princes, Gruffydd lived by raiding rich English lands, gaining victories in 1039, 1049, and 1052. This won him prestige against his rivals, the greatest of whom was Gruffydd ap Rhydderch of South Wales.

In alliance with exiled Earl Aelfgar of Mercia, Gruffydd disposed of his namesake in 1051. They then went on to raid England, defeating Earl Ralph the Timid at Hereford in pitched battle and sacking the town. Even Harold was forced to retreat and accede the All Wales title to Gruffydd. When Harold led a combined operation with his brother Tostig against Wales in 1063, Gruffydd was forced to retreat into the mountains where he was betrayed and murdered.

Grumentum, Battle of battle fought in 207 BC in southern Italy between the Roman army of Claudius ◊Nero and the Carthaginian army of ◊Hannibal the Great during the Second Punic War (see ◊Punic War, Second). Hannibal withdrew before he could be defeated.

Hannibal had moved his army into Lucania to try and regain some of the towns that had defected from him. He gave battle to Nero at Grumentum (present-day Grumento Nova) and when the battle began to turn in Rome's favour he broke off the engagement and waited for nightfall to withdraw.

Guadalete, Battle of decisive victory on 19 July 711 for a combined Muslim force, led by Tarik ibn Ziyad, over the much larger Visigoth army under their King, Roderic, which led to the Muslim conquest of Spain.

Aided by the Byzantines and the recently deposed Visigothic King Achila, Tarik ibn Ziyad led a small force of 7,000 Berbers and 300 Arab cavalry across the straits of Gibraltar (which is named after him: Gerbel el Tarik). He was met by Roderic with a much larger army (allegedly 90,000), probably on the banks of the river Guadalete near Medina Sidonia. Before joining battle Tarik was reinforced by an additional 5,000 Berbers.

The wings of the Visigoth army were commanded by the disaffected relatives of the recently deposed King Achila and they deserted at a critical moment. The unsupported Visigoth centre, under Roderic's command, held only briefly before breaking. Roderic disappeared, some legends say he drowned in a marsh while trying to escape, others claim he lived to fight on. Whatever the case, the Visigothic kingdom collapsed. The Muslims won another battle at Ecija and then the Visigoth capital of Toledo surrendered without a fight. Persecuted Jews and other malcontents welcomed the invaders as liberators.

guaizi ma (or *kuai-tzu ma*) ('horse team'), the tactical system of the Jurchen cavalry raised by the ◊mengan mouke organization. Two cavalrymen in every file of five were heavily-armoured lancers, the other three lightly-armoured archers. The archers, deployed behind the lancers, would advance through the ranks to shoot at and try to envelop the enemy, but pull back to the rear to escape enemy pursuit or allow the lancers to charge. Using these tactics, 17 Jurchen cavalry once defeated 2,000 Song Chinese infantry.

Guandu, Battle of (or *Kuan-tu*) decisive battle in the struggle between ◊Cao Cao and ◊Yuan Shao for control of north China, fought in 200 just south of the Yellow River. Shao's army eventually surrendered and never regained the initiative, allowing Cao to take over the whole north, setting the pattern for the ◊Three Kingdoms of China.

Losing initial skirmishes to Yuan Shao's larger army, Cao fell back to a fortified camp which Shao besieged. When both sides ran low on supplies, Cao marched to ambush one of Shao's convoys. In his absence Shao assaulted the camp with his main force, but was defeated, while Cao succeeded in capturing the convoy. These defeats undermined morale in Shao's army. One officer burned his siege-engines and deserted. Shao then panicked and fled across the Yellow River.

guerre couverte medieval French term for a war, commonly employed in medieval baronial feuds, in which the participants could wound and kill but not burn, take booty, or prisoners, the latter being restricted to the wars of princes.

Guesclin, Bertrand du (c. 1320–80) constable of France from 1369 who became celebrated as a paragon of chivalry, and was later a French national hero.

Du Guesclin rose from an undistinguished Breton family and made his name in defence of Rennes 1356–57, but then was captured by the English. Upon his release, he defeated the Navarrese royal army at Cocherel in Normandy in 1364 for the newly crowned Charles V of France. Later that year he was defeated by the English at Auray, and again captured. His second captor, Sir Hugh ◊Calveley, became his companion-in-arms, and they later raised troops together for the Spanish expedition of 1366. Du Guesclin's involvement in Spain was similarly unsuccessful, however, with Calveley joining Edward of Woodstock to defeat him at Nájera in 1367, where he was yet again captured (see ◊Nájére, Battle of). Ransomed once more, du Guesclin returned to France, where he served successfully against ◊John of Gaunt's *chevauchée* of 1373–74. In 1374–78 he served in Brittany, and died at a siege in 1380.

guige strap fitted to the inside of a shield for suspension over the shoulder, used on European shields from the 11th to 15th centuries.

Guildford castle castle in Surrey, England. Begun by the Normans, and with a large, square Norman keep, it was the only royal castle in Surrey. It was virtually abandoned in the 13th century, and as a result, it is a rare example of a Norman castle which has never been modified or extended.

Guiling, Battle of (or *Kuei-ling*) battle in 354 BC in which Qi commander ◊Sun Bin first defeated the state of Wei, in the Chinese ◊Warring States period. The state of Zhao appealed for Qi's help against a Wei attack. The ensuing stratagem, 'besieging Wei to rescue Zhao', became a classic of the 'indirect approach'.

Sun Bin and fellow commander Tian Jin marched against the Wei capital, Daliang, and Wei recalled its troops from Zhao, under commander Pang Juan, to meet the threat. Sun sent a small force to attack Daliang and then retreat. When Pang took the bait and pursued, Sun ambushed and defeated the Wei army at Guiling.

Guinegatte, Battle of battle fought in 1479 by ◊Maximilian I, before he became Holy Roman emperor, to defend the Netherlands against French attack under Louis XI. The battle was indecisive, though Maximilian remained on the field, making it technically his victory.

It was one of several occasions when Louis' ◊franc-archers failed, and soon afterwards France hired Swiss mercenaries and local French infantry instead.

gulai gorod medieval Russian moving fortress, comprised of wagons and mobile defensive screens, designed to protect its defenders from horse-archer enemies such as the Tatars. In the 15th century it included gunpowder weapons, like the Hussite *Wagenburg*.

Gulbarga ancient city in the Indian peninsula, taking its name from Raja Gul Chand of the Hindu kingdom of Warangal. It was the Bahmani capital in the 14th and 15th centuries and was fortified by strong walls with defended gateways and 15 towers.

Gulbarga was captured by ◊Muhammad ibn Tughluq, Sultan of Delhi, in 1313, then seized in 1347 by Ala al-Din Hasan Gangu Bahman, founder of the Bahmani sultanate of the Deccan.

Gunderic Vandal king from 406 who presided over the recovery of Vandal power in Spain following defeats by the Visigoths. Under his leadership, the Vandals and their Alan allies defeated the Suevi in Galicia (northern Spain), then attacked the Roman forces in the south. The Romans were crushed in 422 after their Visigothic allies deserted, leaving Gunderic in virtual control of Spain. The Vandals seized the Spanish ports and began to make use of sea power, capturing the Balearic Islands and raiding North Africa.

Gunki monogatari (Japanese 'war tales') romanticized collection of Japanese war tales, mostly dealing with events of the late Heian, Kamakura, and early Muromachi periods, written down from the 14th century. They exemplify deeds of heroism and present the acts of self-sacrifice of the ◊samurai as shining examples.

Many of the characters of these tales, particularly those who met poignant or tragic deaths, have become national legends, and the facts are often inseparable from the myths. Of particular note are the *Hōgen monogatari* (dealing with the ◊Hōgen Disturbance of 1156), the ◊*Heiji monogatari* (dealing with the Heiji Disturbance of 1160), and the ◊*Heike monogatari* (tales of the Heike, or Taira, family).

gunpowder powder which explodes on ignition. It was probably first invented in China, where it was chiefly used for fireworks. It is possible that knowledge of it was transmitted from the Middle East to Europe.

The writings of the English monk Roger Bacon show that he was experimenting with gunpowder in 1249. His mixture contained saltpetre, charcoal, and sulphur. The development of effective gunpowder was essential for the growing significance of cannons and handguns in the late medieval period.

Guo Ziyi (697–781) (or *Kuo Tzu-i*) Tang Chinese general. He defeated ◊An Lushan's rebels at Jiashan in 756 and masterminded Emperor Suzong's counterattack against Lushan's son, commanding the Tang army at Changan and Xindian in 757 (see ◊Changan, Battle of and ◊Xindian, Battle of). When the Tibetans attacked Changan in 763 (see ◊Changan, capture of), Guo was recalled from retirement to organize local troops for its defence.

For several years he struggled to fend off Tibetan attacks with an outnumbered, outclassed rabble. He is remembered for dealing with a joint Tibetan–Uighur attack in 764 by riding up to the Uighurs unarmed, reminding them of their old alliance with China, and persuading them to attack the Tibetans instead.

Gurgan, Battle of battle between the Hephthalite ◊White Huns and the Sassanian Persian king Peroz in 484. The Hephthalites captured most of the Persians by luring them across a covered ditch, and the rest were cut down by the main Hephthalite army.

The deep ditch had one crossing place wide enough for ten horses. After covering it over, a small detachment of Hephthalites lured the Persians into pursuit by feigning flight. The Hephthalites crossed the ditch at the safe point but most of the Persians fell in. Many, including Peroz, died from the fall.

gurz Persian term for a mace. Maces were used in Asia from prehistory onwards, and became particularly important from the 7th century with the establishment of armies largely composed of armoured cavalry, where a concussive weapon such as the mace was a more effective side arm than the sword.

gusset (or *voider*) panel of ◊mail used to protect a joint in plate armour. It became common in the 15th century, principally as a section of mail protecting the underarm and sewn to arming doublets (quilted jerkins worn beneath armour). The term 'gusset' is also used of the articulating plates fitted at the arm openings of breastplates of the second half of the 16th century.

Guthrum Danish king of East Anglia 880–90. He almost conquered Wessex after a surprise attack against the Saxons at Chippenham (see ◊Chippenham, Battle of) in 878, but was decisively defeated by King ◊Alfred the Great a few months later at Edington (see ◊Edington, Battle of) and as a result of the peace terms agreed to evacuate Wessex and convert to Christianity.

Guthrum kept the peace in his East Anglian base until 884 when he joined forces with Vikings who had come over from France to raid Kent. The Saxons counterattacked and succeeded in seizing London, once again causing Guthrum to sue for peace. The treaty established the frontier between Danes and Saxons along the Roman road known as Watling Street.

Guy de Lusignan (lived 12th century) king of Jerusalem 1186–90 and lord of Cyprus 1192–94. He was a brave knight but an undistinguished general who led the Latins to defeat at Hattin in 1187 (see ◊Hattin, Battle of). Guy became king of Jerusalem in the face of vehement baronial opposition by virtue of his marriage to the heiress Sibylla. He had proved himself a competent commander in the previous reign, notably when conducting a disciplined fighting march against ◊Saladin in 1183.

Seeking to relieve Saladin's siege of Tiberias in 1187, he allowed his army to march into waterless terrain, allegedly on the advice of Gerard de ◊Ridefort. Guy was captured at the Horns of Hattin, though later ransomed. He redeemed his reputation by initiating the siege of Acre (see ◊Acre, Siege of 1189–91), but was replaced as king 1192 and accepted retirement to Cyprus.

Gwalior (derived from *Gopadri* or *Gopegir*, 'cowboys' hill') fortress on an isolated sandstone crag 90 m/300 ft above the neighbouring town of Gwalior in present-day Madhya Pradesh, India, defended by a wall 9 m/30 ft high, with battlements, tall towers, and palace domes stretching for over 3 km/2 mi. It was probably founded in the 4th or 5th century by a member of the Gupta dynasty.

It was held by the Huna kings Toramana and ◊Mihirakula in the 6th century and by the ◊Rajput rulers of Jaipur from the mid-10th century to 1128, when they were ousted by the rival Parihar clan. ◊Mahmud of Ghazni and ◊Qutb al-Din Aibak laid siege to Gwalior in 1021 and 1196 respectively, but the Parihars reestablished their independence 1210–32. The Rajput Tonwar clan took Gwalior in 1398, surrendering it to Ibraham Lodi, Sultan of Delhi, in 1518.

Hab, Battle of battle fought on 14 August 1119 between ◊Baldwin II, King of the Christian Kingdom of Jerusalem, and Ilghazi of Aleppo. The battle took place to the southwest of Aleppo, Syria. Baldwin rescued Antioch (now Antakya, Turkey) by holding Ilghazi in a drawn encounter.

Following the disastrous defeat of Roger of Antioch at the Field of Blood in June (see ◊Field of Blood, Battle of the), Baldwin led 700 knights and several thousand foot soldiers north to save Antioch. He met the forces of Ilghazi at Hab, 48 km/30 mi southwest of Aleppo. The Christian right wing gave way, but the left and centre held, enabling Baldwin to launch a charge with the reserve that broke the Turkoman light cavalry. Ilghazi's ◊*ghulams* retired in good order.

habergeon (or *haubergeon*) term used in medieval Europe for the mail shirt. A diminutive of ◊hauberk, the term first appeared in the 14th century with the shortening of the mail shirt, and by the 15th century the two words were used interchangeably.

hachimanza decorative surround, often in the form of a stylized lotus, of the ◊*tehen no ana*, the opening in the top of a Japanese helmet. It was a feature of helmets from the Heian period (794–1185).

hachiwara solid iron or steel bar carried in Japan in a similar fashion to a sword. It has a small curved, hooked projection near the handle. Sometimes referred to as a 'helmet breaker', it is a device to parry blows or even break a sword.

Hadrian, (Publius Aelius Hadrianus) (AD 76–138) Roman emperor 117–138. He was adopted by the emperor Trajan, whom he succeeded. He pursued a policy of non-expansion and consolidation after the vast conquests of Trajan's reign. His defensive policy aimed at fixing the boundaries of the empire, which included the building of ◊Hadrian's Wall in Britain. He travelled more widely than any other emperor, and consolidated both the army and Roman administration.

Hadrian introduced administrative, financial, and legal reforms. To maintain discipline and ensure good relations with his soldiers he toured the provinces extensively, reviewing the army as he went. His review speech to the army of Africa survives on an inscription and is revealing about the skills expected of different units in the army.

Hadrian's Wall line of fortifications built by the Roman emperor ◊Hadrian (reigned AD 117–38) across northern Britain from the Cumbrian coast on the west to the North Sea on the east. The Wall itself ran from Bowness on the Solway Firth to Wallsend on the river Tyne, a distance of 110 km/68 mi.

Numerous modifications were made to the original plan, usually due to the need to conserve labour and resources for such an enormous project. In its most complete state, Hadrian's Wall consisted of a continuous linear stone wall 1.8 m/5.9 ft thick with a wide ditch in front. At distances of 1 Roman mile (1,480 m/1,618 yds) a gateway was placed in the wall protected by a fortlet, known as a milecastle. These gateways allowed local people to pass through the frontier and aided the deployment of troops. Two watchtowers were placed between each milecastle to ensure that any movement could be observed. Fifteen auxiliary forts were placed on or beside the wall (see ◊Housesteads fort and ◊Chesters fort) to provide the garrisons for patrolling the Wall and regulating the movement of traffic. Earth and timber fortlets continued down the Cumbrian coast to prevent outflanking by sea, and a fort at South Shields at the Tyne mouth fulfilled a similar function. Strong naval patrols would also have ensured that no one bypassed the Wall. Beyond the Wall itself were outpost forts. These acted as early-warning systems and probably also provided security for the local population who were allied to Rome and predated the boundary created by the Wall. Between 138 and 161 the Wall was shut down in favour of the ◊Antonine Wall, before being recommissioned after the death of the emperor Antoninus Pius. The manpower needed to patrol the Wall and maintain its fortifications could not be met by the depleted army in Britain and the Wall was breached at least twice before it was finally abandoned in the late 4th century.

Hafrsfjord, Battle of sea battle in the Hafrsfjord, Stavanger, Norway, in about 872 between ◊Harald Fairhair and an alliance of several minor kings and ◊*jarls* from northwestern Norway who opposed Harald's attempt to impose his rule over the whole country. Harald won the battle, and many of his opponents subsequently emigrated to Iceland.

Hakata Bay defence system huge stone wall constructed around Hakata Bay on the island of Kyushu, Japan, following the first Mongol invasion of 1274 (see ◊Japan, Mongol invasions of).

The Japanese had barely managed to contain the first Mongol invasion and were only saved by a huge typhoon which decimated the enemy fleet. In 1276 the Kamakura shogunate, ever fearful of further invasions, ordered the construction of a huge defence which stretched some 40 km/25 mi around Hakata Bay, scene of the first invasion. The wall was some 5 m/16 ft high and vertical on the seaward side, sloping back inland so that the Japanese cavalry could reach the summit.

In June 1281 the Mongol forces again attacked Kyushu, but the Hakata Bay defences held them back for over seven weeks until, once again, they were decimated by a typhoon.

halberd infantry weapon widely used from the 14th century, when infantry armies became dominant. It consisted of a wooden staff with a distinctive blade, one side of which was an axe, the other a pick. The shaft head was also extended as a spike, making it a three-in-one weapon. It was about 1.8 m/6 ft in length.

Halberds made for ceremonial use were longer and elaborately decorated.

Halfdan (died 877) one of the Danish kings who led the Danish Great Army, which invaded England in 865, conquering Northumbria, Mercia, and East Anglia. He rose to be the principal leader of the Danes and led the host south against Wessex, where a combination of hard fighting and payment of tribute induced Halfdan to turn his attention back to the north. By 876 he was in full control of Northumbria where he settled his followers. The following year he was killed by a Norwegian Viking during an expedition to Ireland.

Halidon Hill, Battle of battle fought on 19 July 1333 near Berwick, Scotland, between ◊Edward III of England and a Scots army under Archibald Douglas. Douglas and five earls were killed amongst thousands of Scottish casualties.

The Scots needed to defeat Edward to raise the siege of Berwick (see ◊Berwick, Siege of). Edward took a defensive position, with each of his three formations of men-at-arms supported by two wings of archers, in the same formation as had proved successful at Dupplin Moor in 1332. The Scots also dismounted their men-at-arms to stiffen their foot soldiers, and advanced uphill across boggy ground into an arrow storm. Exhausted and disorganized by the ground and the arrows, they were easily repelled.

halqa medieval Arabic bodyguard of a medieval Arabic ruler. The Ayubbid sultan ◊Saladin's *halqa* was remarked upon by Western observers at Arsuf in 1191 (see ◊Arsuf, Battle of), being dressed in yellow and fighting most determinedly.

Halys, Battle of climatic battle fought on 28 May 585 BC between ◊Cyaxares of Media and Alyattes of Lydia during the war of 590–585 BC. Their armies met near the river Halys (modern Kizil Irmak) in northern Anatolia, where fighting continued until an eclipse of the sun darkened the sky. They parted, and a treaty fixed the Halys as the border between the two empires.

This border was kept for 40 years until Cyrus the Great of Media was defeated by Croesus, the last king of Lydia.

Halys River, Battle of decisive Byzantine victory in 623, in which the Emperor ◊Heraclius uncovered and destroyed a Persian ambush set by Shahrbaraz. This victory cleared the Persians from Anatolia and opened the way for the Byzantines into Armenia. Heraclius' forces captured Dwin, the Persian capital of Armenia, drove King Chosroes II from Azerbaijan and destroyed important Persian religious shrines marking the birthplace of Zoroaster. In the following year (624) Heraclius, successfully operating against three Persian armies, penetrated deep into the Persian heartland advancing further than any previous Roman commander.

hamhippoi (Greek 'alongside horsemen') Greek infantry trained to charge into battle alongside the cavalry, possibly holding the horses' tails or manes.

Hamilcar (lived 5th century BC) Carthaginian general. He was appointed to lead an army to the aid of the Sicilian city of Himera, probably because he was the formal guest-friend (*xenos*) of Terillus, tyrant of that city. He was defeated in battle (see ◊Himera, Battle of) by ◊Gelon, tyrant of Syracuse.

Hamilcar (died 309 BC) Carthaginian general, son of the Carthaginian general Gisco (lived 339–338 BC). He commanded the Carthaginian army on the island of Sicily during the war between Carthage and Syracuse. He defeated the Syracusans at Himera, but was killed during the siege of the city of Syracuse.

In 309 BC he commanded the army sent to depose Agathocles, tyrant of Syracuse, and defeated him at the Battle of the River Himera. Some 7,000 Greeks perished for the loss of only 500 Carthaginians. Hamilcar began the siege of Syracuse but was unable to progress far. When Agathocles launched a surprise invasion of Africa, Hamilcar was caught unawares and failed to prevent the invasion fleet leaving. He was captured while leading a night attack on the city, and was executed by the Syracusans.

Hamilcar Barca (died 229 BC) Carthaginian general, the father of ◊Hannibal the Great. Hamilcar rose to prominence in 249 BC at the first Battle of Eryx, during the later stages of the First Punic War (see ◊Punic War, First). He negotiated the peace treaty with the Carthaginians at the end of the war in 241 BC, and suppressed the revolt of Carthage's foreign troops, the ◊Mercenary War (241–237 BC). He then campaigned in Spain until his death, substantially enlarging and enriching the Carthaginian Empire.

Despite a long-running feud with his political rival ◊Hanno the Great, Hamilcar masterminded the Barcid domination of Carthaginian foreign policy through a marriage alliance with ◊Hasdrubal and successes in Africa and Spain. Using both military genius and diplomatic skill, he conquered the Iberian tribes of southern Spain but was killed in battle against the Oretani. His three sons, Hannibal, ◊Hasdrubal Barca, and ◊Mago Barca, inherited his hatred of Rome.

Hammurabi I Amorite king of Babylon 1792–1750 BC. He created a great although short-lived kingdom, and left the lasting legacy of Babylon as the city of law, order, and culture. During his reign he consolidated his kingdom by encoding a set of common laws, the Code of Hammurabi.

In 1784 BC Hammurabi captured Isin and Uruk, key city-states to the south, and in 1782 he crossed the river Tigris to take Malgium. He contested Assyrian control over the middle Euphrates after the death of Shamshi-Adad in 1781, supporting Zimri-Lim in his rebellion at Mari (modern Tell Hariri) in 1779. In 1764 and 1762 Hammurabi twice defeated coalitions made up of Assyrians, Guti, the peoples of Eshnunna, and Elamites, from lands to the north and east, which led to the destruction of Eshnunna and the Tigris becoming the eastern boundary of Hammurabi's kingdom. In 1763 he conquered Larsa, the last of the rival southern Mesopotamian city-states. In 1757 he conquered Mari, the city of Zimri-Lim, whom he made his vassal. Hammurabi suffered from illness towards the end of his reign and for the last few years shared power with his son Samsu-ilin, who conquered and razed Ur.

hanburi (or *happuri*) most basic form of Japanese helmet consisting often of little more than a few steel or leather plates worn as a skullcap or simply covering the crown, forehead, or temples. It was usually constructed so as to fold up for ease of transport and was worn by the lowest rank of foot soldier conscripted for warfare, probably from the 16th century.

Han Guangwudi (died AD 57) (or *Han Kuang-wu-ti*) emperor of China AD 25–57, restorer of the Han dynasty after ◊Wang Mang's usurpation. Some of his opponents were supported by the ◊Xiongnu, so Guangwudi took sides in a civil war to weaken them, successfully splitting them into northern and southern hordes.

Born Liu Xiu, he joined the Green Woodsmen's rebellion (see ◊Green Woodsmen, rebellion of the), distinguishing himself at Kunyang when he escaped the city by night and raised troops to relieve it. The Green Woodsmen made his cousin Liu Xuan emperor in 24; Xiu broke with him and raised troops of his own. Next year, Xuan was defeated by the Red Eyebrows and killed (see ◊Red Eyebrows, rebellion of the).

Liu Xiu then claimed the throne, defeated the Green Woodsmen remnants and in 27 the Red Eyebrows, and mopped up resistance in the rest of China, defeating regionalist contenders and finally conquering the southwestern province of Sichuan in the ◊Chengdu campaign of AD 36.

Hangu Pass, Battle of (or *Han-ku*) battle in 318 BC in which the rising kingdom of Qin defeated a coalition of Chinese states. The allies advanced eastwards up the Yellow River, but were defeated by a Qin army defending prepared positions in the pass. Other attacks in 296 and 207 BC also failed to force the pass. The invulnerability of Qin's frontiers was one of the strengths that led it to unify China under ◊Qin Shi Huangdi.

HAN GAOZU (248–195 BC)

(or *Kao-tsu* or *Liu Bang*)

Emperor of China from 202 BC. He founded the Han dynasty after overthrowing the Qin dynasty in 206 BC. Although his success was hard-fought, he eventually defeated ◊Xiang Yu and all other rivals, partly due to his talent for recruiting able generals and administrators. After reunifying China, he took the title of Emperor Gaozu of the Han dynasty. This dynasty reigned over 400 years, until 220 AD.

As a petty official, Liu rebelled against the Qin, following the example of ◊Chen She and Xiang Yu. They agreed that the first rebel leader to take the Qin heartland, (roughly modern Sichuan and southern Shanxi) would become its king, and in 207 BC Liu Bang succeeded. But Xiang Yu cheated him of the prize, making him merely King of Han, a small area to the far south of Qin, and dividing the rest of Qin territory among three of its surrendering generals. In defiance, Liu conquered the three generals in 206 BC and attacked Xiang's base at Pengcheng (see ◊Pengcheng, Battle of), beginning a civil war that would continue until 202 BC. Although Liu was defeated at Pengcheng, his position was saved by the exertions of his subordinates Xiao He, who recruited a new army, and Han Xin, who seized a new base near the important Ao Granary at Xingyang on the Yellow River. In 204,Xiang Yu besieged the base, cutting Liu's army off from the granary. As supplies grew short, Liu escaped by a ruse with only a handful of followers. Meanwhile, Han Xin conquered most of eastern China on his behalf, winning battles at Jingxing Pass (see ◊Jingxing Pass, Battle of) and the Wei (see ◊Wei River, Battle of). In 203 Liu Bang and Xiang Yu made a truce based on mutual exhaustion and agreed to divide China between them, Liu taking the west and Xiang the east. But both sides immediately began preparations for a fresh struggle. In 202 Liu broke the agreement, believing his position to be the stronger, and destroyed Xiang Yu at Gaixia (see ◊Gaixia, Battle of). As Emperor, Han Gaozu granted over half the country to his generals and relatives as semi-independent kingdoms; but when the ◊Xiongnu, a hostile nomad confederacy on China's northern border, attacked the borders in 201 the local king defected to them and Han Gaozu had to deal with the problem himself. In 200 he was defeated at Pingcheng (near modern Datong in Shanxi) by the Xiongnu leader Maodun (see ◊Pingcheng, Battle of) and had to pay annual 'presents' to the nomads. Gaozu eliminated most of the kingdoms not ruled by his relatives, but even the surviving kingdoms later caused problems, such as the ◊Wu rebellion.

Han jun (or **Han chün**) 'Han army', the north Chinese part of the army of the Mongolian Yuan dynasty in China (1260–1368). They were recruited from Khitan and Jurchen as well as northern Chinese, and were of lower status than the ◊Menggu jun, but higher than the south Chinese ◊xinfu jun. Early Mongol armies in China employed ◊gantaolu irregulars and troops of semi-independent warlords like Li Tan. The *Han jun* organization was effectively formalized under ◊Khubilai Khan.

Hannibal (died 406 BC) Carthaginian general, the son of Gisco and grandson of ◊Hamilcar. He was one of the leading magistrates of Carthage who waged war on the Sicilian city of Selinus in 409 BC to avenge Hamilcar's death at Himera in 480 (see ◊Himera, Battle of).

Hannibal invaded Sicily with an army of 50,000 and quickly sacked Selinus, killing 16,000 inhabitants and enslaving the rest. He subjected Himera to a similar fate in 408, but died during his siege of Acragas (modern

HANNIBAL (247–188 BC) ('THE GREAT')

Carthaginian general, supreme commander of the Carthaginian forces during the Second Punic War (see ◊Punic War, Second). Hannibal's invasion of Italy, his seemingly endless string of devastating victories over the Romans, and his inspiring personality earned him immortality as a military genius and iconic hero. Fulfilling an oath sworn at the age of 9 to always hate the Romans, Hannibal ravaged Italy for 16 years. Though defeating the Roman army in almost a dozen battles, relentless Roman resistance and the problems of supplying his invasion army prevented him from achieving a decisive victory. When the Romans finally fielded a general willing to experiment and innovate in battle as much as he had done, Publius Cornelius ◊Scipio, Hannibal had to come to the defence of his own homeland.

As the son of the Carthaginian general ◊Hamilcar Barca, Hannibal was brought up in a strongly military family. His father had instilled in him a deep hatred of the Romans, fuelled by a belief that the peace imposed by Rome after the First Punic War had been unjust and that Carthaginian politicians had ended the war when it could still have been won. Hamilcar had brought his family to settle in Spain in 237 BC and died in action there in 229 BC. The prestige of his family and his own personal popularity and military ability lead to Hannibal's election as commander of the Carthaginian army in Spain in 221 BC at the age of 26.

He resolved almost immediately to undertake an invasion of Italy. Knowing that Rome controlled the seas, Hannibal decided to invade by the one route the Romans thought impossible – by land. When he provoked war in 219 BC the plans for invasion were in place, and in 218 he led his army across the Alps into the Po Valley of Italy. He would not leave again until 202 BC.

Needing a quick victory to restore his troops' morale and impress the Gallic tribes, he defeated the first Roman army sent against him by ambushing it. The Roman generals were slow to learn that Hannibal, though commanding an organized conventional field army, was not always interested in fighting battles conventionally. He varied his deployments, used feints, and kept reserves hidden for surprise attacks. He also had an exceptional interest in military intelligence and reconnaissance, acquiring as much knowledge as possible about his enemy. His abilities as a tactician were shown to the full at Cannae in 216 BC (see ◊Cannae, Battle of), his greatest achievement.

Hannibal's victories persuaded large numbers of Rome's Italian allies to defect. These were crucial as the Carthaginian supply lines from Carthage were long and unreliable, and the more troops and supplies he could obtain locally the stronger his position. However, despite his series of victories, Rome refused to capitulate, and breaching the walls of the capital were beyond the capability of the Carthaginian army. Hannibal slowly lost the initiative and in 202 BC he was recalled to Carthage to defend his own capital. There he was defeated at Zama by Publius Cornelius Scipio (later Scipio 'Africanus'). He tried a political career, but was forced out of Carthage by opponents in 195 BC and spent the remainder of his life as a curiosity and mercenary among foreign courts, finally committing suicide.

Agrigento). His brother ◊Himilco continued the campaign.

Hannibal Gisco (died 258 BC) (or *Gisgo*)

Carthaginian admiral and general in the First Punic War (see ◊Punic War, First). He demonstrated a remarkable ability for survival, suffering numerous heavy defeats but escaping punishment and regaining his commands. He was finally killed at the Battle of Sulci in 258 BC, by his own crew.

As admiral of the fleet in Sicily in 262 BC, he persuaded the city of Messana to become a Carthaginian protectorate, but it was soon to spark the outbreak of the First Punic War. As general he attempted to secure the Sicilian city and port of Agrigentum (now Agrigento) but was besieged there and only narrowly escaped. He was relieved of his army command, but was soon reinstated as an admiral and suffered heavy defeats at Mylae in 260 BC and Sulci in 258 BC.

Hanno the Great (lived 3rd century BC)

Carthaginian politician and general. He appears to have mismanaged the early stages of the ◊Mercenary War, and was defeated at Utica in 241. He quarrelled with ◊Hamilcar Barca and was relieved of command but was later reinstalled in time for the final victories of the war.

His opposition to the Barca family continued, and it is reported by the Roman historian Livy that he opposed the policies of ◊Hannibal the Great, advising the Carthaginians in 219 BC not to become embroiled with Rome in the Second Punic War.

Hanno the Navigator (lived 5th century BC)

Carthaginian navigator, the son of ◊Hamilcar. He is remembered primarily for the surviving account of his voyage down the Moroccan coast of Africa. He may be the Hanno who seems to have conquered much of the Carthaginian hinterland, subduing the Libyan tribes and creating the basis for the Carthaginian Empire in Africa.

Hanoi, sack of

capture and sack in 1371 of the capital of Dai Viet (modern Vietnam) under the Trân dynasty by King ◊Che Bong Nga of Champa during his campaign in the Tongking Delta.

Han Plain, Battle of

battle in 645 BC, in which the Chinese state of Qin defeated its neighbour Jin in a struggle for the Yellow River valley. Duke ◊Mu of Qin was at one point wounded and in danger of capture, but was rescued by his barbarian bodyguard. Marquis Huai of Jin's headstrong chariot-horses bolted into marshy ground and was bogged down and captured.

Hansi

city in the Punjab, India, fortified with high brick walls with loopholes and bastions, and a canal serving as a moat. It was probably a ◊Kusana dynasty stronghold, but local tradition attributes it to Anang Pala, Tomara Rajput king of the Delhi region in the 10th century.

In 1037, under the rule of Mahipala, King of Delhi, it was attacked by Mas'ud, son of ◊Mahmud of Ghazni. Mahipala recaptured Hansi in 1043, but it again fell to the Muslims, under ◊Muhammad of Ghur, in 1192. It was thereafter held by Rajput tributaries of the sultans of Delhi.

Han Wudi (died 187 BC) (or *Han Wu-ti*)

emperor of China 141–187 BC. He used the growing prosperity of China since ◊Han Gaozu's unification to launch wide-ranging expansionist campaigns. He ordered the ◊Korea, Han Chinese conquest of and the conquest of ◊Zhao Tuo's Nan Yue in Vietnam, but his main efforts were against the ◊Xiongnu in Mongolia and Central Asia.

The subsidies China paid the Xiongnu did not prevent raids, and in 133 BC Wudi tried to defeat them by treacherously ambushing the Xiongnu ruler. When this failed, Wudi engaged in open warfare. He occupied and fortified border areas, conquered the nearer kingdoms of modern Xinjiang to deny them to the Xiongnu, and extended the ◊Great Wall of China to protect the newly subdued areas. In 104–101 his general ◊Li Guangli defeated distant Dayuan, extending Chinese overlordship west of the Pamirs. His generals Wei Qing and ◊Huo Qubing led successful attacks on the Xiongnu, though the general ◊Li Guang was less fortunate. In 99 the general ◊Li Ling was defeated, and in 90 Li Guangli was defeated and captured.

Hao

capital of the Western Zhou empire of northern China from the 11th century BC, in the Wei river valley near what is now Xian. It was founded by King ◊Wu originally as a military stronghold and had double walls and a system of beacons to warn of attack. The sack of Hao by an alliance of barbarians and rebel Chinese nobles in 771 BC marked the end of effective royal Zhou power.

Hapiri

rootless or seminomadic peoples of the Late Bronze–Early Iron Ages (2nd–1st millennia BC), known to the Egyptians as *'Apiru*. They came to prominence during the reigns of the pharaohs Amunhotep III and

Akhenaten (14th centruy BC) when they attacked and conquered the Levantine city-states such as Gubla (Byblos) and Megiddo.

They were used by 'Abdi-Ashirta of ◊Amurru and Lab'ayu of Shechem, south of the Lebanon, to create their own kingdoms during the break-up of the empire of Mitanni and the weakness of the Egyptian late 18th dynasty. They have been linked to Hebrew tribes whose arrival in the Levant may be placed at this time.

happuri alternative form of ◊*hanburi*, a Japanese helmet.

hara-ate simple form of Japanese armour consisting of a breastplate which covered the front of the body, worn by the *ashigaru* from the Muromachi period (1333–1568) until the 16th/17th century. It could be worn under ceremonial dress.

hara-kiri (Japanese *hara* 'belly', *kiri*, 'cut') popular and more vulgar term for ◊*seppuku*, Japanese ritual suicide by disembowelment.

Harald Fairhair (c. 860–c. 940) (Norwegian *Harald Hårfagre*) king of Norway from around 870. As a minor king of Vestfold (a region around Oslo), he brought the various Norwegian kings and ◊*jarls* (chieftains or nobles) under his rule to become the first king of all Norway. He also extended his rule over the Shetland and Orkney islands in the late 800s.

Harald Hardrada (1015–66) ('Hard Ruler') king of Norway 1045–66, sharing power with Magnus I 1045–47, who also ruled over Denmark. When Magnus died in 1047 Swein ◊Estrithson was proclaimed king of Denmark. Harald fought against Swein for 17 years but was unable to bring Denmark back under his control. In 1066 Harald led an invasion of England where he was defeated and killed at the Battle of Stamford Bridge (see ◊Stamford Bridge, Battle of).

Harold (II) Godwinson (c. 1020–66) last Anglo-Saxon king of England, January to October 1066. He was defeated and killed by William of Normandy (◊William (I) the Conqueror) at the Battle of Hastings (see ◊Hastings, Battle of).

He succeeded his father Earl Godwin in 1053 as Earl of Wessex. In 1063 William of Normandy tricked him into swearing to support his claim to the English throne, and when the Witan (a council of high-ranking religious and secular men) elected Harold to succeed Edward the Confessor, William prepared to invade. Meanwhile, Harold's treacherous

brother Tostig (died 1066) joined ◊Harald Hardrada of Norway in invading Northumbria. Harold routed and killed them at Stamford Bridge on 25 September. Three days later William landed at Pevensey, Sussex, and Harold was killed at the Battle of Hastings on 14 October.

haramaki Japanese form of armour developed in the Muromachi period (1333–1568) from the earlier ◊*ō-yoroi* and similar in most aspects to the ◊*dōmaru*.

The *haramaki* was a simple form of armour, the term strictly referring only to the *dō* or ◊cuirass which laced up at the back. Early versions were extremely light and only provided basic protection. In the later Muromachi period the join at the back was given extra protection by a separate hanging plate of ◊*kozane* called the ◊*seita*.

Harfleur, Battle of conflict of 18 August–4 October 1415 between ◊Henry V of England and the French, during the ◊Hundred Years' War. Henry besieged and took the stategically important French town of Harfleur, at the mouth of the river Seine, but only after heavy losses to fighting and disease.

Henry's invasion fleet carried 2,500 men-at-arms and 8,000 archers. He was also well equipped with siege artillery. Harfleur was defended by only 400 men-at-arms, but it had strong walls and 26 towers and was surrounded by water. Mines and assaults proved equally ineffective, although the English cannon made headway against the bulwark by the west gate. The town surrendered because there was no sign of relief, but Henry lost 2,000 men to dysentery and 2,000 went home sick.

Harivarman IV (lived 11th century) king of Champa (modern central Vietnam) 1074–80, formerly Prince Thang. He defeated a Vietnamese attack in 1074, and in around 1074–76 defeated a Khmer invasion at the battle of Somesvara, capturing the Khmer prince in command. In 1076 both Harivarman and the Khmers were persuaded to cooperate with a Song Chinese attack on Vietnam. When the Chinese were defeated their allies withdrew, and Harivarman thereafter paid tribute to Dai Viet.

Harlech castle castle in Wales, built by Edward I 1285–90 at a cost of just under £8000. Besieged by the Welsh 1294–95 without success, it was taken by Owain ◊Glyndwr in 1404 and retaken by Talbot in 1408. It was captured by Yorkists in 1468, giving rise to the famous song 'Men of Harlech'.

harness medieval English term for a complete set of plate armour, used ubiquitously in contemporary sources.

Harshavardhana (**590–647**) last great Buddhist emperor of most of northern India, c. 605/6–46/47, before the invasion of the Muslims. Through a succession of military victories he established a large pan-regional empire across northern and central India, extending from the Bay of Bengal to the Arabian Sea and to Kashmir in the northwest. It was connected by loose quasi-feudal ties.

His father Prabhakaravardhana was king of Sthanvisvara (modern Thanesar). Harsha's sister Rajyasri was married to Grahavarman, a king of the Maukhari dynasty ruling Kanyakubja (modern Kannauj). Grahavarman was assassinated, and Rajyasri imprisoned, by Devagupta, King of Malwa. Harsha's elder brother Rajyavardhana, who succeeded Prabhakara as king of Sthanvisvara, was slain marching to avenge them, and Harsha succeeded to the two thrones left vacant by his brother and brother-in-law. He then embarked on a six-year campaign to extend his empire, checked only in the south by the Chalukya king ◊Pulakeshin II.

Hasdrubal (**lived 3rd century** BC) Carthaginian commander of mercenaries, son of Hanno, who was made a general in order to face the invasion of Africa in 256 BC by the Roman consul Marcus Atilius ◊Regulus. He was later (254 or 251 BC) sent to Sicily as commander in chief with 140 elephants. He spent some time training his troops before attacking the Romans at Panoramus in 251 BC (see ◊Panoramus, Battle of), but on his defeat there was condemned to death by the Carthaginians.

Hasdrubal (**died 221** BC) Carthaginian politician and general who was elected successor to ◊Hamilcar Barca in Spain. He extended Carthage's possessions there and founded its capital city of Carthago Nova (New Carthage, present-day Cartagena).

He was the leader of the popular party following the end of the First Punic War, and an influential ally and protector of Hamilcar Barca, becoming his son-in-law. His friendship was rewarded in 229 BC when he was elected as Hamilcar's heir and successor. In the nine years of his command he extended Carthage's territorial possessions in Spain by military and diplomatic prowess until his assassination in 221 BC by a Spanish slave.

Hasdrubal (**lived 3rd century** BC) Carthaginian general, son of Gisco, who fought in Spain during the Second Punic War (see ◊Punic War, Second). His army operated closely with the other Carthaginian forces in the war.

In 211 BC he combined with ◊Hasdrubal Barca and ◊Mago Barca to defeat the Roman armies led by the brothers Publius and Gnaeus Cornelius Scipio. He was defeated at Ilipa in 206 BC (see ◊Ilipa, Battle of) by the son of Publius, Publius Cornelius ◊Scipio (later called Scipio 'Africanus'), and forced to withdraw to Africa. Here he was instrumental in gaining the allegiance of ◊Syphax for Carthage. Their combined army was defeated by Scipio 'Africanus' at the Battle of the Bagradas in 204 BC (see ◊Bagradas, Battle of the).

Hasdrubal Barca (**died 207 BC**) Carthaginian general during the Second Punic War (see ◊Punic War, Second), brother of ◊Hannibal the Great. He commanded the army defending Spain.

He was defeated at Ibera by Gnaeus Cornelius ◊Scipio in 215 BC before defeating him in turn at Ilorci (present-day Lorqui) in 211. He made a stand against Publius Cornelius ◊Scipio (later Scipio 'Africanus') at Baecula in 208 and was defeated (see ◊Baecula, Battle of). In 207 he led the remainder of his army into Italy to reinforce his brother Hannibal, but it was intercepted by Gaius Claudius ◊Nero and Marcus Livius ◊Salinator at the river Metaurus (see ◊Metaurus, Battle of the) and Hasdrubal died in the battle.

Hasdrubal Barca (**lived 2nd century** BC) Carthaginian commander defeated in the war with the Numidian king ◊Masinissa in 152 BC. When the Romans sided with Masinissa, he was condemned to death by the Carthaginians as responsible for the war. He gathered his own army, and was later given command of the Carthaginian forces during the Third Punic War (see ◊Punic War, Third). He took personal command of the city of Carthage during the siege by Scipio Aemilianus (see ◊Carthage, Siege of).

Hasdrubal based his forces at Nepheris (see ◊Nepheris, battles of), from where he harried the Romans and sent supplies into Carthage. During the siege of Carthage he tortured and executed Roman prisoners on the walls of the city and instituted a strict regime that the Roman historian Appian compares to a tyranny. He surrendered himself when the city fell, although his wife and children perished rather than be captured.

hasta Roman word for a spear. The Roman ◊legion probably evolved from a spear-armed ◊phalanx, but by the mid-2nd century BC only one-seventh of the infantry still used the spear and by 100 BC it had disappeared altogether from the legionary's weapons. It returned to service in the 3rd century AD, and was widely used by auxiliary infantry and at all periods by most of the cavalry.

hastati (singular *hastatus*) type of infantry of the Roman republican army from the 4th century BC until the reforms of the general and politician Gaius ◊Marius between 107 and 104 BC. The *hastati* were young men who occupied the front line in battle. They were equipped with two heavy javelins and a sword, using the javelins to break up the enemy lines and then charging with their swords. (See also ◊*principes* and ◊*triarii*.)

The *hastati* were formed into maniples of 2 centuries of 30 men, with 15 maniples per legion. By the 2nd century BC the maniples had been reduced to 10, but the centuries had been doubled in size to 60 men.

hastiludes (Latin 'spear games') alternative name for jousting and a frequent 11th- and 12th-century description of what became known as the ◊tournament.

Hastings castle castle in England, on West Hill, Sussex. William the Conqueror actually built a wooden ◊motte-and-bailey castle here in 1066 before the battle of Hastings (see

HASTINGS, BATTLE OF

Decisive battle between ◊William (I) the Conqueror, Duke of Normandy, and ◊Harold (II) Godwinson, King of England, on 14 October 1066. Harold was killed in the engagement and William was crowned king of England two months later on Christmas Day.

After his victory at Stamford Bridge (see ◊Stamford Bridge, Battle of), Harold had driven his army on forced marches south. William, who had laid claim to the English throne, landed at Pevensey Bay in Kent with an army of Normans, Bretons, Flemings, and other Frenchmen. When the duke heard of Harold's advance, he advanced from Hastings towards London, and sighted Harold's army around 8 a.m. at the top of the ridge of Caldbec Hill, 10 km/6 mi inland from Hastings, at Senlac, Sussex. Harold spread his forces across the crest of the hill in a shield wall formation to block William's advance, placing himself and his ◊housecarls in the centre. William deployed in the valley below with his Normans in the centre, Bretons on the left and French and Flemish forces on the right. Harold's army consisted entirely of foot soldiers, though many of the English housecarls had ridden to the battlefield. William's army included contingents of mounted cavalry, foot soldiers, and archers.

The battle began with William's archers loosing a rain of arrows uphill at Harold's position. William then advanced his heavy infantry, and later his cavalry against the English line, all with little success. The Breton contingent began to retreat and panic spread through the Norman army, fuelled by false news that the duke had fallen. But the English failed to press home their advantage and William rallied his troops by riding the lines bareheaded to show he was still alive. As the Norman troops turned, the cavalry attacked the English who had left the shield wall in pursuit. Both armies regrouped, with neither having achieved a clear advantage.

In the afternoon William launched various infantry and cavalry attacks, with further periods of rest and regrouping. The shield wall remained unbroken. With nightfall approaching, William again sent his archers forward. This time they disrupted the English position enough for the infantry and cavalry to break through. Harold may have been wounded by an arrow in the eye during the archery assault, and in this final attack he was killed. The defeated English were pursued until nightfall and William was left in possession of the battlefield.

◊Hastings, Battle of), a fact attested to by the ◊Bayeux Tapestry. A stone castle with tower and gatehouse later replaced the original, but sea erosion was already making inroads into the site by the end of the 14th century and led to the abandonment of the castle, most of which has now disappeared.

hatomune dō Japanese solid plate armour of European style, or even of European manufacture, having a medial ridge, and often referred to as 'pigeon breast'. It was developed after 1543, as a result of contact with the West.

With the introduction of firearms to the Japanese battlefields, plate armour, being bulletproof, became necessary as well as fashionable, and the European style was copied or adapted to include Japanese features such as the ◊*kusazuri*.

Hatra, Siege of siege of the city of Hatra in Mesopotamia by the Roman emperor Septimius Severus in about AD 200. The semi-desert conditions and defensive capabilities of the Hatrenes (including the use of burning naphtha and rapid firing artillery) forced him to abandon the attempt after some months.

Hattin, Battle of battle fought on 3–4 July 1187 in which King ◊Guy de Lusignan of Jerusalem advanced into waterless terrain and was surrounded and captured by the Ayyubid sultan ◊Saladin, who then destroyed the military power of the Kingdom of Jerusalem.

Saladin had mustered 12,000 cavalry and almost 20,000 foot soldiers to besiege the town of Tiberias on Lake Galilee. King Guy led 1,200 knights and 15,000 foot soldiers. He attempted to rescue the town, leaving the Springs of Saforie and crossing waterless terrain. Saladin exploited this strategic error, using his superior cavalry to harass the march and setting fire to the grass. Thirsty and blinded, the crusaders stumbled into a defensive position at the ancient hillfort on the twin peaks known as the Horns of Hattin. Attacked on all sides, the infantry broke and the knights lost their horses to arrows. King Guy fought to the last but was captured.

Hattusas capital city of the Hittites 1650–1175 BC (present-day Boğazköy, or Boğazkale, in central Turkey). Founded by ◊Hattusilis I in 1650 BC, it expanded from the Büyükkale (citadel) to what is known as the Lower City with its huge Temple I complex. It was twice sacked by the ◊Gasgans – during the time of Tudhaliyas III (1355–1344 BC), and during the reign of Muwatallis II at the time of the battle of Kadesh (see ◊Kadesh, Battle of) around 1275 BC. It was rebuilt and refortified

during the reigns of Hattusilis III and Tudhaliyas IV (1264–1209 BC) when the city was expanded to the south, adding an Upper City to the Lower City and Büyükkale. It was finally sacked and deserted around 1175 BC, probably by the Gasgans.

Hattusilis I Hittite Great King 1650–1620 BC. He founded ◊Hattusas (Boğazköy, Turkey) as the Hittite capital and expanded the Hittite kingdom by conquests into western Anatolia and the northern Levant.

During six campaigns he gained control over the Black Sea coastland (later lost to the ◊Gasgans) immediately north of Hattusas, defeated Arzawa in southwestern Anatolia, and, crossing the Taurus Mountains, conquered Alalah and Halba (Aleppo) in northern Syria. The two-horse light chariot (see ◊chariot, Near Eastern) and siege warfare were used effectively to bring about his victories. He likened himself to Sargon I in that he crossed the river Mala (Euphrates). The end of his reign was riven by dynastic rivalry and he settled the kingship on his nephew ◊Mursilis I.

hauberk ◊mail shirt, synonymous in the early Middle Ages with *byrnie*. The term 'hauberk' was used throughout the medieval period in Europe, but in the 14th century the diminutive term 'habergeon' became increasingly common in inventories, at the same time as the shorter mail shirt was being depicted in contemporary art.

hautepiece upright flange formed by an extension of the ◊pauldron, guarding the neck. Hautepieces appeared in Italian plate armour from about 1425, and were used throughout Europe, especially Italy, France, England, and the Low Countries, until the 16th century.

Hawkwood, Sir John (lived 14th century) English captain employed as a mercenary in Italy. He fought for Edward III of England in France; the White Company then employed him in Italy. When employed by the papacy, he was ordered to act without mercy, but he disobeyed, apparently sparing the lives of 1,000 women.

The son of an Essex tanner, his abilities impressed the Florentines who provided him with a wealthy Visconti wife.

hayago Japanese gunpowder flask, or primer, in use following the introduction of the matchlock to Japan in 1543. It was generally made of leather or lacquered wood with an ivory or bone tube for pouring the powder. In design it was often similar to the *inrō*, a container for personal medicines.

hazarapatiš Achaemenid Persian military leader. Persian troops were organized into regiments of 1,000, and the term literally means 'commander of 1,000'. It also came to mean the chief minister or grand vizier of the empire because that official commanded the 1,000-strong ◊spear-bearer guards.

The same title was later used in Armenia, Sassanian Persia, and, translated as *chiliarchos*, the Hellenistic courts.

heater shield shield with a straight or slightly curved top and two curved sides meeting in a point at the bottom, in use in western Europe during the 11th and 12th centuries. It was strapped to the forearm or over the shoulder and covered from shoulder to mid-thigh.

Hedgeley Moor, Battle of battle of 1464 during the English Wars of the Roses (see ◊Roses, Wars of the) in which the Lancastrians under the Duke of Somerset and Ralph Percy were defeated by a Yorkist force under Lord Montagu in Northumberland.

Somerset had reneged on his agreement with ◊Edward IV of England and rejoined the Lancastrians. Percy was another deserter from the Yorkist cause. They attacked the Yorkist force at a site between Morpeth and Wooler. When their defeat became apparent, Somerset escaped but Percy fought to the last, his charging horse achieving a spectacular jump at what became known as 'Percy's Leap'.

Heidelberg castle castle situated on a spur northeast of the city of Heidelberg in modern Baden-Württemberg, Germany, built on a rectangular plan with round corner towers for the Count Palatine of the Rhine from 1225. Much of the surviving building dates from the 15th century. It was severely damaged by French troops during the Thirty Years' War in the 17th century.

Heiji Disturbance confrontation in 1160 between ◊Minamoto Yoshitomo and ◊Taira Kiyomori during which Minamoto influence at the Japanese imperial court was crushed and the Taira family gained complete control.

Both Yoshitomo and Kiyomori had shared in the victories of the ◊Hōgen Disturbance, but Kiyomori had received the greater rewards and was able to exert considerable influence over the retired emperor Go-Shirakawa. On an occasion when Kiyomori was absent from court in Kyoto, Yoshitomo seized power with the aid of other discontents. He imprisoned Go-Shirakawa and the reigning emperor Niō and appointed his own vassals to positions of influence. In the ensuing battle at the Rokuhara mansions in Kyoto, Taira Kiyomori led his troops to crushing victory over Yoshitomo, who was killed in a snowstorm while attempting to raise more troops.

Heiji monogatari (Japanese 'tales of the Heiji') one of the Japanese war tales (◊*Gunki monogatari*) which relate the story of the imperial power struggles in the middle of the 12th century and the rise and fall of the Taira clan (see also ◊*Heike monogatari*). It may have been written down in the early 13th century.

Heike monogatari (Japanese 'tales of the Heike') one of the Japanese war tales (◊*Gunki monogatari*) which deal with the height of power of the Taira family ◊(also known as the Heike) from their victories in the ◊Hōgen Disturbance to their crushing defeat in the ◊Taira–Minamoto Wars.

The tales have extremely vivid descriptions of battles, including details of the equipment worn and the conduct displayed during combat. They describe the commendable conduct and courageous deeds of the Taira warriors who willingly gave their lives in battle for the family.

helepolis (Greek 'city taker') multistorey siege tower on wheels, fitted with catapults and drawbridges.

Helge River, Battle of naval battle in 1026 at the mouth of the river Helge in eastern Skane, Sweden, during which the Danes under ◊Cnut the Great (Canute) defeated a combined force of Norwegians and Swedes. As a result of this victory, Cnut added Norway and parts of Sweden to his empire and established Danish control of the Baltic.

Heliopolis, Battle of battle fought in 640 at Heliopolis, Egypt, in which the Muslims under Amr ibn al-As gained a decisive victory, opening the way to the Muslim conquest of Egypt. Following their victory the Muslims went on to besiege and capture the nearby fortresses of Babylon (641) and Alexandria (642).

Hellespont, Battle of the two-day naval battle in 324 between the fleets of the Roman emperor ◊Constantine (I) the Great, commanded by his son Crispus, and his eastern rival and co-ruler Valerius Licinianus Licinius, led by Amandus. Constantine won the battle on the second day, when the wind favoured Crispus' ships.

Helmsley castle castle in northeast England, 40 km/25 mi west of Scarborough. Begun in around 1190, the castle had a curtain wall with towers and a large D-shaped keep projecting through the wall. A ditch, an embankment, and a second ditch surrounded all this.

The embankment was surmounted by a wooden palisade, or fence, except for a section in front of the castle gatehouse, which was built in masonry as a strong barbican, linked to the main curtain by walls crossing the inner ditch. A similar, but much smaller, barbican existed at the opposite end of the work, though this appears not to have had the linking walls.

helot state-owned serf used by the Spartans as an agricultural labour force and as soldier-servants. In the latter role they were armed, and from the 420s BC onwards they were increasingly used as ◊hoplites, being freed either before or after such service.

Henry (II) of Trastamara (c. 1333–79) king of Castile and Léon 1366–79. The illegitimate son of Alfonso XI of Castile, he was a claimant to the throne in the Castilian War of Succession. He allied himself with Charles V of France during the ◊Hundred Years' War, while England favoured his brother Pedro the Cruel. He invaded Castile in 1366, but was defeated by Edward the Black Prince at the battle of Najéra in 1367 (see ◊Najéra, Battle of). Henry gained his revenge at the battle of Montiel in 1369; in personal combat he stabbed Pedro to death.

Henry I (1068–1135) king of England from 1100. Youngest son of ◊William (I) the Conqueror, he succeeded his brother William II. He won the support of the Saxons by granting them a charter and marrying a Saxon princess, Matilda, daughter of Malcolm III of Scotland.

He defeated his brother Robert Curthose at Tinchebrai (see ◊Tinchebrai, Battle of) in 1106 and imprisoned him, reuniting England and Normandy. He defeated Louis VI of France at Brémule in 1119 (see ◊Brémule, Battle of), and Norman rebels at Bourgthéroulde in 1124 (see ◊Bourgthéroulde, Battle of). His only legitimate son, William, was drowned in 1120, and Henry settled the succession on his daughter Matilda.

Henry II (1133–89) king of England 1154–89. The son of Matilda and ◊Geoffrey V, Count of Anjou, he succeeded King Stephen (c. 1097–1154). He curbed the power of the barons, but his attempt to bring the church courts under control was abandoned after the murder of Thomas à Becket, Archbishop of Canterbury, in 1170. The English conquest of Ireland began during Henry's reign. On several occasions his sons rebelled, notably 1173–74. Henry was succeeded by his son ◊Richard (I) the Lionheart.

Henry was lord of Scotland, Ireland, and Wales, and Count of Anjou, Brittany, Poitou, Normandy, Maine, Gascony, and claimed Aquitaine through marriage to the heiress Eleanor in 1152. Henry's many French possessions caused him to live for more than half his reign outside England.

Henry IV (1367–1413) king of England from 1399, the son of ◊John of Gaunt. As a young man he fought with the Teutonic Knights and went to Jerusalem. In 1398 he was banished by Richard II (1367–1400) for political activity but returned in 1399 to head a revolt, and was accepted as king by Parliament. He was succeeded by his son ◊Henry V.

Henry had difficulty in keeping the support of Parliament and the clergy, and had to deal with baronial unrest and Owen ◊Glyndwr's uprising in Wales. The Percy family was defeated at Shrewsbury in 1403, and the Earl of Northumberland was beaten at Bramham Moor in 1408.

Henry V (1387–1422) king of England 1413–22, a cold and ruthless soldier respected by contemporaries as a chivalric warrior. He fought at Shrewsbury in 1403, was victor of Agincourt in 1415, conquered Normandy 1417–20, and died at Meaux in 1422.

Determined to revive the war in France, Henry's invasion of 1415 was impressively organized, but his siege of Harfleur took too long, reducing his intended grand ◊chevauchée to a reckless dash to Calais. Although his tiny, bedraggled army was cut off by a superior French force, it achieved a surprising victory at Agincourt (see ◊Agincourt, Battle of). When Henry returned it was with serious intent to reduce Normandy, which he did, including a long, bitter siege of Rouen (see ◊Rouen, Siege of 1418–19). Military pressure on Paris ensured the favourable Treaty of Troyes in 1420, making him heir to the French throne, but he contracted dysentery conducting the siege of Meaux.

Henry (I) the Fowler (c. 876–936) king of Germany from 919 and duke of Saxony from 912. He secured the frontiers of Saxony, ruled in harmony with its nobles, and extended German influence over the Danes, the Hungarians, and the Slavonic tribes. He overcame Wenceslas of Bohemia and defeated the Wends at Lenzen in 929. The ◊Magyars were beaten at Riade in 933 (see ◊Riade, Battle of). He was about to claim the imperial crown when he died.

Henry built a system of forts against the Magyars, and reorganized the army in East Francia. He imposed burdens on the landed to support defence. His forces underwent training.

Henry IV (1050–1106) Holy Roman emperor 1056–1106. He came into conflict with the nobles of Germany in an attempt to increase imperial power, making an agreement with the German princes at Tribur in 1076. He also clashed with the papacy in the Investiture Controversy. He made his peace at Canossa, Italy, in 1077.

Late in his reign his sons Conrad and Henry (the future emperor Henry V) rebelled. Henry was forced to abdicate and took refuge in Liège, where he died.

Henry VI (1165–97) Holy Roman emperor 1191–97. He conquered the Norman Kingdom of Sicily in his wife's name (Constance, aunt and heiress of William II of Sicily), and was crowned at Palermo, Sicily, on Christmas Day in 1194. This union of imperial lands north and south of Rome threatened papal independence.

King ◊Richard (I) the Lionheart of England was handed into Henry's power after falling into the hands of Duke Leopold of Austria when returning from crusade. Richard was only released for a large ransom, after agreeing that England should become a fief of the Holy Roman Empire.

Henry the Lion (1129–95) duke of Bavaria 1156–80, duke of Saxony 1142–80, and duke of Lünenburg 1180–85. He was granted the duchy of Bavaria by the emperor Frederick I Barbarossa. He founded Lübeck and Munich. In 1162 he married Matilda, daughter of Henry II of England. His refusal in 1176 to accompany Frederick to Italy led in 1180 to his being deprived of the duchies of Bavaria and Saxony. Henry led several military expeditions to conquer territory in the East. His son became the Holy Roman emperor ◊Otto IV.

Heraclea, Battle of battle fought in 280 BC in which ◊Pyrrhus, King of Epirus, led his army of 25,000 infantry, 3,000 cavalry, and 20 elephants to victory over the Roman legions led by the consul Laevinius.

In a long and hard-fought battle both sides suffered heavy casualties (15,000 Romans and 13,000 Epirotes according to Dionysius of Halicarnassus, writing in the 1st century AD). The Romans, despite the defections of some southern Italian allies, rejected Pyrrhus' overture for peace.

Heraclius (c. 575–641) Byzantine (East Roman) emperor 610–41. He restored order to the empire, decisively defeated the Persians, and carried out reforms to the Byzantine army and military organization.

He was proclaimed emperor by the people of Constantinople (present-day Istanbul, Turkey) after defeating and capturing the unpopular usurper Phocas. Having inherited a shell of an empire, with an empty treasury, broken armies, and its territories occupied by Persians, Avars, and Slavs, he set about restoring order, aided by the Orthodox church.

In a series of brilliant campaigns 622–28, culminating at Nineveh (see ◊Nineveh, Battle of), Heraclius completely outmanoevred his many opponents and recovered all lost territories from the Persians. However, he was beset by difficulties: the empire was worn out from years of war and split with religious controversy, and he was forced to raise taxes to an oppressive level to repay the loan provided by the church for the war with Persia and the Avars. Meanwhile, the new force of Islam was on the march and before his death on 11 February 641, Heraclius saw his armies routed and Syria and Egypt lost to the Arabs.

herald (Old French *heraut*, Old High German *hariwalt*) 'manager' of a medieval army. The word first appears in the 13th century, though its origins are older. Heralds played a role in military ceremonial as announcers for commanders – they would announce messages relating to war such as declarations of war, challenges, declarations of time of attack, the naming of battlefields, and so on. They received privileges as neutrals in war.

They later became announcers at tournaments and experts on the rules of blazon and rights of heraldic arms.

herce term used by the French chronicler Jean de ◊Froissart to describe a formation of English archers at Crécy (see ◊Crécy, Battle of) 'which wisely was open' and in 'two hedges'. Historians have taken this to mean triangular wedges between men-at-arms, from the meaning of *herce* as harrow. *Herce* derives from *ericius* (hedgehog), and a more likely meaning is hedged in with stakes or pikemen.

Froissart also describes a *herce* at the Battle of Nicopolis in 1396 with the Turkish army in wings in the manner of a '*herce...* the two wings were at the front in advance and closed at the rear... the two wings, fully opened when the Christians had entered within them, were closed up'. This describes a wing formation, forward and fanning out, which could close when the enemy attacked the centre.

Herdonia, Battle of battle fought in 210 BC, during the Second Punic War, in which a Roman army under Gnaeus Fulvius Centumalus attempted to recapture the town of Herdonia (in Apulia, southeast Italy) from the Carthaginians. The Carthaginian general ◊Hannibal the Great made a sudden attack on the Roman army and destroyed it.

Hannibal punished traitors within the city

itself, razed it to the ground, and transferred the population to Metapontum and Thurii. Such drastic action was an admission that he could no longer maintain a defence of all allied cities against Roman forces.

here Old English word for a force or army in a more general sense than ◊fyrd, associated with 'hergian' (harry). It was generally used of an enemy force, often Viking raiders, and sometimes very small forces.

In the West Saxon King Ine's law code it was a force of over 35, but the *Anglo-Saxon Chronicle* described a *here* as 'great' (893) and 'large' (921), and even refers to a naval *here* of 934.

Hereford, Battle of battle of 1055 between Aelfgar, Earl of Mercia, and Ralph the Timid, Earl of Hereford, fighting on behalf of the English King Edward the Confessor. Edward had exiled Aelfgar, who raised forces in Ireland and Wales and invaded England. The town of Hereford was pillaged, and terms were agreed with Aelfgar and he was restored.

One source says the English were forced 'to fight on horseback against their custom'. This suggests Ralph attempted continental cavalry methods, which failed through lack of experience in England.

Hereward the Wake (lived 11th century) legendary Saxon hero of the English resistance to the Normans, who defended Ely in 1070–71 (see ◊Ely, Siege of). Outlawed by Edward the Confessor 1062, Hereward returned home after 1066 to find his father dead, his brother murdered, and the Norman lord Peter de Bourne in possession. Hereward killed him in revenge and led 40 men to the last English strongpoint at the abbey of Ely. When William the Conqueror took the island 1071, Hereward retreated into the forest.

heriot (Old English *heregeatu* 'war equipment') in medieval England, the death duty owed to one's lord. Initially this was the restoration of what the lord had provided for a soldier in war: arms, armour, and a horse. A thegn (soldier) paid the heriot when his predecessor died. In ◊Cnut the Great's laws the heriot was a thegn's horse and equipment, while an earl owed eight horses. The death duty was cancelled for a soldier who was killed while fighting for his lord.

Anglo-Saxon wills record heriot payments as occasionally being made in money instead of equipment.

Herodotus (lived 5th century BC) Greek historian, described as the 'Father of History'. He wrote a nine-book account of the Greek-Persian struggle that culminated in the defeat of the Persian invasion attempts in 490 and 480 BC. The work contains lengthy digressions on peoples, places, and earlier history. Herodotus was the first historian to apply critical evaluation to his material, while also recording divergent opinions.

He was born in Halicarnassus in Asia Minor and appears to have spent most of his life travelling, eventually settling in Thouria, in southern Italy.

Herstmonceaux castle castle 6 km / 4 mi east of Hailsham in East Sussex, England. Originally a manor house, the owner received a licence to crenellate (build battlements) in 1440 and converted it into a fortified dwelling. One of the oldest English brick buildings, the bricks and bricklayers were imported from Flanders.

The castle is rectangular, with hexagonal towers at each corner, pentagonal towers on three faces, twin pentagonal towers forming a gatehouse on the fourth face, and pentagonal buttress towers between the main towers on all faces. A wide moat was crossed by a drawbridge.

Hertford castle castle in southeast England. Begun immediately after the Conquest as a wooden ◊motte-and-bailey castle, it was rebuilt in stone during the reign of Henry II (1154–89). Besieged and captured by the French in 1216, it was the prison of the kings of France and Scotland, and was frequently visited by the monarchs due to its proximity to London. The present 'castle' is actually the gatehouse built by Edward IV in around 1464.

hetairoi (Greek 'companions') comrades of a hero or aristocratic leader, especially members of Alexander the Great's Macedonian cavalry.

Hever castle castle in Kent, England, 13 km / 8 mi west of Tonbridge. A residence existed here in the 13th century, and in 1272 Sir Stephen de Penchester received a licence to crenellate (build battlements), but the present structure is due to Sir William de Hevre who built it in the time of Edward III (1327–77). Most of the building is now a residence but there are still elements of the fortifications, such as the gatehouse and wall towers.

In the 15th century it came into the hands of Sir Geoffrey Boleyn, who did much reconstruction, and his descendant Anne lived here prior to her discovery by Henry VIII.

Hexham, Battle of battle fought in 1464 in the north of England during the Wars of the Roses (see ◊Roses, Wars of the) in which the Lancastrians under the Duke of Somerset were defeated by the Yorkists under Lord Montagu.

The Yorkists blocked the smaller force of their opponents at Hexham, catching them by surprise. The Lancastrians were overcome and several of their leaders were captured and executed, including Somerset. Henry VI escaped, abandoning his helmet and crown.

Hiero II (c. 306–215 BC) tyrant of the Sicilian city-state of Syracuse 270–215 BC. He served as an ally to Carthage before joining Rome and becoming one of its most loyal allies in the First and Second Punic Wars.

Taking power through a military coup in 270 BC, Hiero pursued expansionist ambitions against the neighbouring ◊Mamertines. Despite defeating them at Mylae in 265 BC, he was unable to take their capital, Messana, and when the Mamertines allied themselves with Rome he formed an alliance with Carthage to try again in 262. On the outbreak of war with Rome, his army was defeated and Syracuse was besieged by the Romans. With no help arriving from Carthage, Hiero sued for peace and signed a treaty with Rome that confirmed Syracusan independence and his own sovereignty. In return he provided Rome with ships, troops, and the use of his ports.

Himeji castle (Japanese *Himeji-jō*) castle in Himeji, Hyōgo prefecture, Japan. It was constructed in the 14th century by the Akamatsu family as the *daimyo*'s residence and centre of administration, and became known as *Shirasagi-jō* ('Castle of the White Heron'). It was expanded during the Sengoku period (1467–1568) and by ◊Toyotomi Hideyoshi in the late 16th century.

The castle is located on a small hill with an intricate system of defensive moats, gates, and enclosures and a series of minor donjons connected to the main five-storey donjon. It was surrendered to Toyotomi Hideyoshi in 1580 and he greatly enlarged the original structure with the addition of many turrets to the original walls and donjon.

Himera, Battle of battle between the Sicilian Greeks and Carthage at the city of Himera, on the northern coast of Sicily, allegedly on the same day as Salamis (see ◊Salamis, Battle of 480 BC).

HINDU ARMIES

The Indian army of the classical period (c. 500 BC–AD 500) consisted of six different categories of troops, divided into four combat arms and four supporting services. The six categories comprised (1) hereditary troops, the kshatriyas or ◊Rajputs, who formed the military class of Hindu society and normally undertook military service on a quasi-feudal basis; (2) mercenaries, full-time professional soldiers serving for pay on a contract system; (3) troops provided by corporations, the private forces maintained by merchants for the protection of caravans and warehouses; (4) contingents provided by vassals and auxiliaries; (5) troops that had defected from the enemy; and (6) tribal war parties, especially suited for operations in difficult terrain. The four combat arms were elephants (see ◊elephant, in Indian warfare), cavalry, chariots (see ◊chariot, Vedic), and infantry, and the four supporting services were the navy, pioneers, intelligence, and the commissariat.

Elephants were the most prestigious, though often the least effective, of the combat arms. Horses bred in India were generally inferior to those from Central Asia, so that the Indian cavalry was both lighter and slower than its contemporaries in other armies. The light Vedic chariot of the early Aryans and their chestnut horses had, by classical times, given way to a larger vehicle drawn by four horses with a crew of four. This was a personnel carrier rather than a combat vehicle, and had mostly gone out of use by the early centuries AD. The infantry were made up of spearmen, swordsmen, and archers. Most logistic support came from private contractors and camp followers, but the best-organized armies included medical staff and veterinarians for elephants and horses.

◊Herodotus recorded that 300,000 Carthaginians were led into battle by ◊Hamilcar Barca who spent the day sacrificing and leapt into the fire when he realized all was lost. But ◊Diodorus Siculus claims that Hamilcar was killed by cavalry commanded by Gelon of Syracuse who had come to the aide of his father-in-law Theron of Akragas to defend Himera. After Hamilcar's death the main forces engaged in battle and the Greeks prevailed.

Himilco (lived 5th–4th centuries BC) Carthaginian general, son of Gisco, who succeeded his brother ◊Hannibal at Acragas (modern Agrigento), Sicily, in 406 BC. He captured the town that winter and in 405 seized Gela and Camarina and concluded an advantageous peace with ◊Dionysius I of Syracuse.

In 397 BC his attempt to relieve the Punic base at Motya failed (see ◊Motya, Siege of) and the city fell to Dionysius. In 396 he recaptured the town, reduced Messana, and won a naval victory that enabled him to besiege Syracuse. When this siege was made untenable by epidemic he withdrew in disgrace and starved himself to death.

hipparchos (or *hipparch*) (Greek) cavalry commander. Two were elected annually in Athens. From about 300 to 100 BC, the Achaean League used the term to mean 'vice president'.

hippeis (Greek 'horsemen') aristocracy of Greek city-states, so called because they were able to afford horses and chariots and later provided the cavalry. Homer uses the term to mean 'charioteers'. In Sparta *hippeis* was an elite force of 300 infantry who formed the royal guard.

hiza yoroi early Japanese knee armour originating in the Kofun period (c. 300 BC–AD 300) and used in conjunction with the ◊ō-yoroi until the Kamakura period (1185–1333).

hoarding wooden defence structure used in medieval siege warfare. When siege was imminent, many medieval fortifications had their roofs removed and hoardings were added to towers. Also, when attackers brought siege towers (see ◊belfry) up against fortifications, it was frequently necessary to raise the height of the walls and towers by constructing hoardings above them.

hoate Japanese iron face mask dating from the Muromachi period (1333–1568). It covered the lower part of the face, below the eyes, and was worn with a helmet. It usually had stylized facial features, together with a bristle moustache and side fittings to cover part of the ears.

The nose was frequently detachable. The *hoate* could also be fitted with a mail or lamellar neck guard.

hobelar horsed English infantryman used in Wales and Scotland in the 14th century. Originally they were brought from Ireland with small, speedy horses called 'hobinos' or 'ubinos'. These were used for transport rather than fighting, though historians have described them as 'light cavalry'. Some hobelars were archers, some spearmen. They were the precursors of mounted archers.

Hōgen Disturbance military confrontations of 1156 in the struggles of the Japanese imperial succession between the followers of the reigning emperor Go-Shirakawa and the cloistered emperor Sutoku. The court divided into factions with members of the Fujiwara family on both sides of the dispute and the ◊Taira family and ◊Minamoto family supporting Go-Shirakawa, who eventually emerged victorious.

Real power was, however, in the hands of the warrior families of the Taira and Minamoto and further struggles followed for political and military supremacy.

Hōjō family Japanese warrior family, descended from a branch of the Taira clan, who took their name from the region of Japan where they were appointed military governors in the late 11th century. They became the hereditary regents (*shikken*) of the Kamakura shogunate and effectively ruled Japan for over 100 years.

hoko (or *katakama yari*) short-bladed Japanese spear, originating in the Muromachi period (1333–1568), with either a single curved transverse blade or with two transverse blades, one being shorter than the other.

Holu (died 496 BC) king of Wu 510–496 BC, a 'barbarian' state at the mouth of the Yangtze River, China. He invaded Wu's traditional enemy Chu in 506, but in his absence Wu was invaded by King Yunchang of Yue (or Yüeh, in present-day Zhejiang, south of Wu). Holu returned to rescue his country, then attacked Chu again in 504. He was finally defeated by ◊Goujian of Yue at Zuili (or Tsui-li) and died of wounds.

After invading Chu in 506, Holu captured the capital Ying but 500 Qin chariots sent to help Chu defeated the Wu army. Holu remained fighting in Chu while his country was ravaged by Yue forces, provoking his brother to seize the throne until Holu returned to defeat him.

Homildon Hill, Battle of battle fought in northern England in 1402 between Henry

'Hotspur' ◊Percy and Scottish raiders under Archibald, Earl of Douglas. Douglas had crossed the Anglo-Scottish border for a second time that year and was confronted and captured on his return north.

Douglas received six wounds and fell from his horse. Henry IV of England refused to let Percy ransom his captives, notably Douglas, which caused the captives to rebel.

Hong River, Battle of (or *Hung*) battle in 638 BC in which the rising southern kingdom of Chu defeated the traditionalist Chinese state of Song. Duke Xiang of Song let the enemy cross the river, then refused to attack them until they were ready, thus facilitating their victory.

A Chu army invaded Song to relieve Song pressure on the state of Zheng. Duke Xiang of Song held the Hong river line against them, but when requested he drew back to allow the Chu to cross. His minister of war urged him to attack while the enemy were split by the river, but Xiang refused, saying it was improper to attack the enemy before they were ready. When the Chu forces were fully deployed he attacked them but was wounded and completely defeated.

Hongyanchi, Battle of (or *Hung-yen-ch'ih*) battle in 1473 in which the Ming Chinese under frontier commander Wang Yue defeated the Mongols at the northern Chinese border. First Wang attacked a Mongol camp, killing or capturing 350 people, then surprised the Mongol troop returning from their raid. The Mongols withdrew from the Ordos, enabling Wang to construct the ◊Ordos Loop Walls.

Hearing that Mongols were raiding Ningxia, Wang led 4,600 cavalry to surprise the Mongols' families left at Lake Hongyanchi. He split his forces into detachments and surprised the Mongol camp by attacking from several directions under cover of a dust-storm, trapping the Mongols against the lake. As Wang marched home he met the Mongols returning from their raid, and defeated them too.

Honnōji Incident the events of 1582 at the Honnōji, a temple in Kyoto, Japan, when the military warlord ◊Oda Nobunaga was assassinated by his vassal Akechi Mitsuhide.

Nobunaga was resting with a few attendants when Mitsuhide, who was supposed to be leading his troops (on behalf of Nobunaga) to western Japan to suppress a rival *daimyo*, took the opportunity to attack Nobunaga. Nobunaga was shot by musket and arrows and died in the burning buildings of Honnōji.

hoplite (Greek 'man-at-arms') term used to describe the heavy infantry who formed the core of Greek city-state armies from the 7th to the 4th centuries BC. The defensive armour of the hoplites included a bronze helmet, breastplate, greaves, and a round shield; their offensive weapons were an iron sword and a long spear.

hoplite sword (or *ksiphos*) commonest form of sword used from the 9th to the 3rd centuries BC, during the Greek classical period. It is arguably the most successful sword of the ancient world, dominating the central Mediterranean area from the 7th to the 3rd centuries BC.

The blade was normally waisted with its maximum width just before it tapered to a point. It was basically a slashing weapon weighted towards the point, but many examples are long cut-and-thrust weapons. A few are short and designed solely for thrusting. Blade lengths vary from 32–70 cm / 12.5–27.5 in.

hoplon (plural *hopla*) Greek word sometimes interpreted as 'shield', from which the term ◊hoplite derives. However, the usual term for a hoplite shield was *aspis*, and *hoplon* was very rarely used in the singular. Its plural, *hopla*, means 'arms' and hoplite probably means 'man-at-arms'.

Horatius (lived 6th century BC) Roman soldier who gained legendary status for his defence of Rome's Tiber Bridge against the Etruscans in about 508 BC. It is uncertain how much of the heroic tale of Horatius Cocles is true and how much was romanticized by Roman historians, but his shining example of courage, intelligence, and military skill served as a model for Roman aspirations.

Horatius was sentry on the Tiber Bridge when the Etruscan army of Tarquinus captured the Janiculan Hill. With nothing to stop them crossing into Rome, Horatius took command of the situation and ordered his companions to destroy the bridge while he fought the Etruscans off long enough for the task to be completed.

Hörice, Battle of battle fought in Bohemia on 20 April 1423 in which the radical Horebite Hussite leader Jan ◊Zizka of Trocnov opposed Cenek of Wartenburg, leading troops from the moderate Utraquist faction, in the first conflict between ◊Hussites. Zizka's victory epitomized his tactical method.

Cenek, who had supported the Hussites, returned to Rome and King ◊Sigismund, and raised troops to attack the radical Horebites around Hradec Králové. Zizka took two columns of wagons to confront Cenek in a defensive position at Hörice. Using a church tower as his command post, he deployed his wagons on a slope. His men were ordered to hold their fire until the enemy reached the top of the hill, then to deliver a volley, swiftly followed by a counterattack. After several assaults the Utraquists broke and fled.

horn armour horn was used in Europe and Asia for the manufacture of armour of several different types. Helmets of horn are attested in Anglo-Saxon England, and defences of baleen (whalebone), particularly popular for gauntlet manufacture, are found in medieval Europe. Scale coats made of horn are found occasionally in medieval Asia.

horo Japanese protective clothing, originating in the late 15th century and used until the 16th century. It consisted of strips of cloth sewn together and strengthened with braid, and was worn loosely with armour. When the mounted warrior rode into battle it would distend with the wind and effectively protected the rider's back from stray arrows.

It would sometimes be artificially distended by the use of a wicker, whalebone, or bamboo framework called an *oikago*.

hoshi kabuto style of Japanese iron helmet which originated in the Heian period (794–1185) and had large decorative rivets (*hoshi*, 'stars') to hold the vertical plates of the helmet together. Later helmets which used vertical ridges to join the plates (◊*suji kabuto*) would sometimes include the ◊*hoshi* as a purely decorative feature.

The helmet was used until the Muromachi period (1333–1568) and was revived several times subsequently.

Hosokawa family family of Japanese warlords and military governors under the ◊Muromachi shogunate, which they helped to found. They were a branch of the Ashikaga family and traditionally held the important post of kanrei (deputy) to the shogun, to whose fate their own fortunes were inextricably linked.

Hosokawa Katsumoto (1430–73) Japanese military governor of Settsu province, Japan, who held the position of kanrei (deputy to the shogun) for three terms, 1445–49, 1452–64, and 1468–73. He and ◊Yamana Sōzen, the real holders of power behind the Ashikaga shogunate at that time, disagreed over the succession in 1465 and sparked off the ◊Onin Wars.

They came into confrontation during one of the endless disputes of succession under the Ashikaga shogunate when they found themselves supporting opposing factions. During the ensuing Ōnin Wars the forces of Katsumoto

and Sōzen ravaged the capital Kyoto. Katsumoto died of an illness before he could see his forces gain eventual victory.

hostage political or military prisoner detained as a safeguard against rebellion or opposition – an important feature of medieval warfare. A hostage might be a representative of a noble family serving at a foreign court who was expected to fight in the lord of the court's war. Another type of hostage was taken on campaign, with a real threat of death or mutilation if the subjected group rebelled.

The future English king Harold II was a hostage when detained by William of Normandy (the future ◊William (I) the Conqueror) in 1064, and hostages were taken on campaign during the Viking conquest of England (1011–13).

houguan (or *hou-kuan*) (Chinese 'company') unit of Han Chinese frontier troops, especially on the ◊Great Wall of China, and a subunit of the ◊*duwei fu*. Its strength varied: a typical *houguan* consisted of five *hou* platoons, but could have up to 18. The *hou* was in turn divided into two to eight *sui* sections. Each of these comprised an officer and two to four, or sometimes up to ten men, depending on what was required to man a particular outpost or signal-tower.

hounskull another term for the visored ◊basinet (knight's helmet) of the 14th and early 15th centuries. The term, like 'pig-faced' basinet, does not appear to have been in contemporary use.

housecarl (or *huscarl*) member of the hired household troops used by the Danish kings of England in the 11th century as a form of bodyguard and standing army. The housecarls were introduced by King ◊Cnut the Great in 1016.

They were initially paid for by the heregeld (army tax), although they also received grants of land, in return for which they would fight when summoned.

household, military medieval European fighting unit. Also called the *familia* (Latin) or *maisnie* (French), the military household of a ruler formed the core of his fighting men. They were usually retained knights, receiving pay in return for providing military service utilizing the most up-to-date equipment.

The English kings Henry I and Edward I made extensive use of their households on their campaigns. All great lords, including some ecclesiastics such as Rhineland bishops, kept military households for instant active service.

Housesteads fort Roman auxiliary infantry fort on ◊Hadrian's Wall, northern England, notable for the good state of preservation of its defences and internal buildings. It was built in stone in the 'playing card' shape (rectangular with rounded corners) typical of Roman forts in the late 1st to early 3rd centuries.

Housesteads was added to the Wall after a change in the original plan, as can be seen in the remains of a wall turret within the fort, and accommodated a garrison of 1,000 infantry. The steep-sided plateau dictated that the fort should be built with its long access against the wall, with only the north gate providing passage through it. A large civilian village grew up on the slopes south of Housesteads fort.

Huaixi campaign (or ◊*Huai-hsi*) government campaign 815–17 against the rebellious province of Huaixi in Tang China. Huaixi, part of modern Henan, was one of several provinces left semi-independent, despite the restoration of Tang control after ◊An Lushan's rebellion. Government forces finally defeated the province in 817.

When Wu Yuanji succeeded his father as governor of Huaixi, the court demanded his submission. After his refusal, they assembled 90,000 troops from several provinces. Huiaxi had about 30,000 regulars, plus militia, to face this. The government forces were organized in five commands to converge on Huaixi. Throughout 815–16 they had limited success, thanks to poor coordination and an effective mobile defence by Huaixi troops, including mule-mounted infantry. In 817 Li Su became overall government commander. He raised new elite units, including 2,000 northern frontier cavalry. He wore Huaixi down by cutting off supplies, and then launched a surprise attack through a snowstorm on the rebel capital, finishing the war at a stroke.

Huan (died 643 BC) (Duke of Qi) First *ba* (hegemon) of the Chinese states 685–643 BC, which had been divided since the fall of ◊Hao. By invoking the prestige of the weakened Zhou monarchy instead of openly seeking power, Huan persuaded the states to cooperate against the northern tribes and the half-barbarian southern state of Chu, and to sign a common peace.

In 679 he prevented Zheng from invading Song. He also assisted the states of Yan and Wei against the Northern Rong and Di barbarians, and in 656 he led an alliance that forced Chu to pay tribute to the Zhou king. After his death the alliance collapsed, but his example was followed by later leaders including ◊Wen, Marquis of Jin.

Huan and his minister Guan Zhong reformed Qi's army on a standard territorial basis, organized into three ◊*jun* armies totalling 30,000 men and 800 chariots (see ◊chariot, Chinese).

Huanerzui, Battle of (or *Huan-erh-tsui*) battle in June 1211 in which the Jin were defeated during the Mongol campaigns in China (see ◊China, Mongol campaigns in). Jin commander Geishilie Jizhong, with an army of 300,000 Jurchen and Khitan cavalry and Chinese infantry, marched to meet ◊Genghis Khan in what is now Inner Mongolia. After faltering under Mongol archery, the Jin cavalry trampled over their infantry during their retreat, and the Mongols pursued almost to modern Beijing.

Advised to attack quickly with cavalry to catch the Mongols scattered, grazing their horses after crossing the desert, the Jin commander instead waited for his infantry to come up. He then advanced with cavalry in front and infantry behind. The Mongols engaged him where constricted ground would not allow him to use his numerical superiority. ◊Mukhali led a charge which broke them, and Genghis followed up leading his guards.

Huang Chao (died 884) Chinese rebel leader. He led a coalition of peasant rebels and bandit gangs on a great and devastating march to capture the Tang capital Changan, where he proclaimed himself emperor. He was defeated by Tang forces and killed himself.

Huang joined the rebel coalition in Shandong in 875 and became its leader after his colleague Wang Xianzhi was killed in battle in 878. He led the coalition south as far as Guangzhou (Canton), which he sacked in 879. In 880 he marched north to Loyang and west through the Tongguan Pass to capture Changan. However, he did not control the territory his hordes had marched through, and had no real base.

Tang forces, strengthened by new ◊*tuanlian* militias, surrounded Changan and cut off supplies. One of his generals, Zhu Wen, deserted to the Tang. In 883 ◊Li Keyong's Turkish cavalry defeated Huang at Liangtianshan, forcing Huang and his remaining followers to flee eastwards. Surrounded by Li's men near Mount Tai in Shandong, he took his own life.

Huanglong, Battle of two-day battle in 1115 in which 10,000 Jurchen troops under ◊Wanyen Aguda defeated the Khitan Liao Emperor Tianzudi with allegedly 700,000 troops, near Huanglong in what is now Kirin. On the first day the Jurchen attacked nine times, with limited success, but during the second day of fighting Khitan morale began to crumble, and a final Jurchen attack swept them away. Aguda took their camp and soon after captured the town of Huanglong.

huissier medieval ship for transporting horses. It had a door in its side that was caulked with tar while at sea and then broken open in order to disembark the knights' horses. The French historian Jean de Joinville describes huissiers on crusade in 1148. (See also ◊*tarida*.)

Hülegü (born 1217) Western Mongol khan 1253–65. He established the Il-khanid dynasty and conquered Baghdad in 1258. His army was defeated, however, in the conquest of Egypt at Ain Jalut (see ◊Ain Jalut, Battle of) in 1260.

Entrusted by his brother Great Khan ◊Möngke with the conquest of Muslim southwest Asia, Hülegü was initially very successful. His first task was the destruction of the ◊Ismailis sect which had attempted to assassinate Möngke in 1256. He then turned against the Abbasid caliphate, taking Baghdad, massacring 200,000 (he claimed) of its inhabitants and executing the caliph. The Ayyubid caliph was also captured and the city of Aleppo conquered in 1260.

The Christian rulers of Antioch and Cilician Armenia hastened to ally themselves with Hülegü and joined in the conquest of Damascus in 1260. Möngke's death, however, forced Hülegü to return east, leaving his general Kit-buqa to confront the Mamelukes at Ain

HUNDRED YEARS' WAR

Lengthy conflict between England and France from 1337 to 1453 that finally ended any significant involvement of the kings of England in Continental Europe. In effect it was several separate conflicts, or perhaps part of a greater struggle between the two nations that began with ◊William (I) the Conqueror's conquest of England, continuing with the struggle between the Plantagenet Angevin Empire and Capetian France, and ending with the French capture of Calais in 1558.

The war proper began with the English King Edward III's attempt to regain the French territories held by his Angevin ancestors, in part by claiming the French throne. English triumphs in this phase of the war included the naval victory at Sluys in 1340 (see ◊Sluys, Battle of) and Crécy in 1346 (see ◊Crécy, Battle of) under Edward, and Poitiers in 1356 (see ◊Poitiers, Battle of 1356) under ◊Edward the Black Prince, and the English capture of Calais in 1347. English success owed much to the impact of the longbow. This phase of the war concluded with the Treaty of Brétigny (1360) recognizing English gains.

From 1369 the English concentrated on a series of ◊*chevauchées*, adding to the destruction suffered in France as a result of the Black Death. Under Charles V (1364–80) France regained ground, particularly thanks to the efforts of the commander Bretrand du Guesclin.

England regained the initiative with the succession of the aggressive ◊Henry V. His greatest success was at Agincourt in 1415 (see ◊Agincourt, Battle of), again won by longbow tactics. Henry reconquered Normandy, and formed a powerful alliance with Burgundy; by the treaty of Troyes (1420) it seemed that the crown of France would pass to the English kings. Henry VI was crowned king of France in Paris in 1431.

But despite further English victories, the war went the way of France. England's Burgundian alliance collapsed in 1435. ◊Joan of Arc helped save Orléans (see ◊Orléans, Siege of) and Charles VII (1422–61) established his authority. France regained military superiority, partly through their improvement of cannon under the brothers ◊Bureau. They won significant battles, including Formigny in 1450 (see ◊Formigny, Battle of) and Castillon in 1453 (see ◊Castillon, Battle of). The latter is seen as marking the end of the war, though there was no final treaty.

Jalut. Hülegü was then involved until his death in fighting his Muslim brother Berke.

Hunyadi, János Corvinus (c. 1387–1456) Hungarian general and politician. He led late crusades against the Turks and was regent of Hungary 1446–52. His successful defence of Belgrade in 1456 saved Hungary from Turkish invasion.

Hunyadi expelled the Turks from Transylvania in 1442 and gained notable victories south of the Danube in 1443. He was defeated by the Ottoman sultan Murad II at Varna (in present-day Bulgaria) in 1444 and defeated again at Kosovo (Serbia) in 1448, leaving Wallachia in Turkish hands.

huoqiang (or *huo-ch'iang*) (Chinese 'fire-lance') Chinese incendiary weapon perhaps invented in the 10th century, though not common until the 13th. Originally a short bamboo tube filled with gunpowder on the end of a pole, it spurted flame at close range when a fuse was lit, and was often fitted with a spear-head for close defence. Bronze tubes replaced the bamboo, and the tube could be stuffed with stones or iron balls or used to fire an arrow – transforming the firelance into a primitive handgun.

Huo Qubing (died 117 BC) (or *Ho Ch'ü-ping*) Chinese 'Swift Cavalry General' of the emperor ◊Han Wudi, commander against the ◊Xiongnu, and nephew of the general Wei Qing.

Serving under his uncle from the age of 18, he distinguished himself leading lightly equipped cavalry forces in daring penetrations deep into enemy territory. In the spring of 121 BC he led a successful raid of 10,000 cavalry which captured 8,000 Xiongnu and a great golden idol; in the summer another raid killed or captured 30,000, including 10 chieftains. In 119 he led a force which killed 70,000, while a simultaneous attack by Wei Qing narrowly failed to capture the Xiongnu ruler, leading to the disgrace of Han Wudi's general ◊Li Guang.

Huoyi, Battle of (or *Huo-i*) battle on September 8, 617, in which Tang rebels under ◊Tang Gaozu defeated a large Sui army under commander Song Laosheng, in China.

As the rebels advanced on the capital, Changan, they were held up by a large Sui army blocking a narrow defile in the Fen river valley. Two days after the summer rains stopped, the Tang army lured Song out of his position by a feint attack, and Li Shimin (the future ◊Tang Taizong) charged into the Sui flank with cavalry concealed in ambush. The Sui broke and fled.

Hussite medieval term for a Bohemian warrior, derived from the followers of the proto-Protestant cleric Jan Hus, who was burned as a heretic in 1419. His largely Czech followers, fired by religious fervour, became some of the most feared fighters in Europe. Under the leadership of Jan ◊Zizka, who used gunpowder weapons and the ◊*Wagenburg* in an innovative way, they defeated several crusades against them (1417–35).

Hussite Great Raids Hussite invasions of southern Germany in 1428–31; see ◊Great Raids, Hussite.

hwarang (Korean 'flower of youth') 'knight-ly' order of young noblemen of the kingdom of Silla in the ◊Three Kingdoms of Korea period. *Hwarang* members received education in literature, music, and Buddhism as well as military training. They were dedicated to the king of Silla, and forbidden to retreat on the battlefield.

Hydaspes, Battle of the battle fought on the banks of the river Hydaspes (modern Jhelum, Pakistan) in 326 BC between ◊Alexander (III) the Great and the Indian king Porus. It was Alexander's last victory in pitched battle; a subsequent mutiny forced him to abandon hopes of conquering India.

By marching and countermarching he apparently so confused the enemy that he was able to cross the Hydaspes unopposed. In the battle itself, his cavalry massed on his right and drove their opposite numbers into their own infantry, despite Porus transferring cavalry from right to left, while the Macedonian infantry received some of Porus's elephants with opened ranks and drove others back into their own infantry. The result was a massacre, and Porus himself was captured.

Hyginus Roman military theorist, attributed author of *De metatione castrorum/On the Laying Out of Camps*, a treatise on how to encamp a Roman army. The work provides key information on the theoretical strengths of Roman units, how they were arranged in overnight or marching camps, and how such camps were fortified.

Hyksos from Egyptian *hekau hastiu* 'rulers of the desert people' Amorite princes who controlled the Levant during the 17th and 16th centuries BC and eventually invaded and controlled the Egyptian Delta. The Hyksos are credited with bringing new weapons of war into Egypt, notably the light two-horse chariot.

As the Hyksos moved southwards, Egypt fragmented into rival dynasties, based at Avaris in the Delta, Memphis, and Thebes. Nubia also broke away from Egyptian control, bringing an end to the Middle Kingdom. After the Hittite raid on Babylon (see ◊Babylon, Hittite raid on) in 1595 BC, the Hyksos invaded the Delta and Thebes became the centre of a reduced Egypt under local rulers (17th dynasty), while in the Delta numerous rulers vied for power (15th–16th dynasties).

The Hyksos quickly became 'Egyptianized' but, situated in the Delta, kept a firm economic and political hold over their southern neighbours along the river Nile. This led to war, and the pharaoh Kamose of Thebes (c. 1541–1539 BC) died breaking Hyksos control. The pharaohs of the 18th dynasty regained control over all of Egypt and Nubia, pushing the Hyksos ever further north. Tuthmosis III defeated the last Hyksos coalition at Megiddo in 1458 BC (see ◊Megiddo, Battle of).

hypaspist (Greek 'shield bearer') man who carried a hoplite's shield before he went into battle, usually a slave. The term was also used for an elite infantry unit in the Macedonian army, possibly originally derived from the king's shield-bearers.

hyperesia deck crew of a (Greek) galley, excluding the rowers. The *hyperesia* of a classical Athenian trireme would probably include 10 hoplites and 4 archers serving as marines and 16 sailors, including the bosun.

Hyrcanian Rock, Battle of ambush and destruction of a Turkish army by a small Persian force, under the able general Varahran Chobin, which took place south of the Caspian Sea in 588. The Persians regained control of much of the region, which had recently been overrun by the Turks.

Ichi no Tani, Battle of decisive battle fought in front of the cliffs of Ichi no Tani in 1184 during the ◊Taira–Minamoto Wars of Japan, where the forces under ◊Minamoto Yoshitsune attacked the Taira troops under the command of Tadanori and inflicted a crushing defeat on them.

A small company of troops under Yoshitsune scaled the steep cliffs at the rear of the Taira forces while the main part of his army attacked from the front. The unexpected surprise of this action turned the stalemate of the battle to Yoshitsune's advantage, and although many Taira escaped by sea, he gained a major victory over them.

Ichi no Tani castle (Japanese *Ichi no Tani-jō*) fortress at Fukuhara, near present-day Kobe, Japan, more of an extensive stockade than a castle. It was built facing the sea with cliffs as a natural defensive northern wall. It was the site of the Battle of Ichi no Tani (see ◊Ichi no Tani, Battle of) in the wars between the Taira and Minamoto.

Idistaviso, Battle of battle fought in AD 16 between the Roman general ◊Germanicus Caesar and the German cheiftain ◊Arminius near modern-day Minden, Germany. Although Germanicus' victory restored Roman prestige it did not break Arminius' power.

Arminius had gathered a large army, adding contingents from many Germanic tribes to his own Cherusci, and waited to meet the advancing Romans on a level plain bordered by the river Weser. Germanicus' eight legions and their auxiliary infantry and cavalry advanced in a hollow square ready to deploy into battle order. Arminius had hoped to keep the Cherusci in reserve, but they attacked prematurely. Germanicus counterattacked with his Roman infantry and used his cavalry to outflank the German infantry. The Germans were routed with heavy losses, but Arminius himself escaped.

Ido castle (Japanese *Ido-jō*) Japanese hill fortification near Dazaifu, north Kyushu island, Japan, believed to have been constructed around 756 in response to rebellions against the Tang court in China. The castle consisted of a series of breastworks which followed the three main ridges of Mount Takasu along with a number of observation towers and a series of stone walls which continued down the mountainside.

The site was abandoned at some time in the 8th century but was rebuilt in the Sengoku period (1467–1568) as a castle for the Harada family.

ikki Japanese term used in the early 14th century for the temporary assembly of military forces for a particular purpose, notably the alliances of local warrior bands against their military governors' attempts to impose control. The term later came to mean any group of peasantry or smaller bands of warriors who assembled for the purpose of insurrection.

ikkō-ikki Japanese term for the armed uprisings in the late 15th century by the forces of the Jōdo Shin militant Buddhist sect. They killed the military governor of Kaga province about 1488 and took control of the area for almost a hundred years.

Ilan castle Armenian castle situated on a sinuous ridge 6 km / 4 mi west of Ceyhan, southern Turkey. Armenian rulers constructed three progressively higher walls along the summit of the ridge in the 11th and 12th centuries. The Hospitallers (see ◊Military Order) held Ilan in 1233, probably until its conquest by the ◊Mamelukes.

Each of the three wards (areas between the walls) of the castle has a defended gateway, one bearing two lions rampant, the arms of the Armenian royal house, built after Leon's coronation in 1198.

ile (Greek) band of men, particularly a troop of cavalry.

Ilerda, Battle of first major confrontation between rival Roman field armies in the civil war between Julius ◊Caesar and ◊Pompey the

Great, near the hilltop town of Ilerda (modern Lèrida, Spain), in 49 BC. It was a decisive victory for Caesar and the Pompeian armies in Spain, commanded by Lucius Afranius and Marcus Petreius, were forced to surrender.

Caesar's army consisted of 6 ◊legions from his Gallic army, along with 7,000 cavalry and 5,000 light infantry, perhaps a total of 35,000–40,000. The Pompeian army of 7 legions, 5,000 cavalry, and a force of Spanish auxiliaries was roughly the same strength. The campaign consisted of much manoeuvring and several small actions fought near Ilerda as each side attempted to deprive the other of supplies. Caesar succeeded and the Pompeian army began to starve. Although Pompey offered battle, Caesar refused to commit himself, and within days Pompey was forced to surrender, with most of his legions being absorbed into Caesar's army.

Ilipa, Battle of battle fought in Spain in 206 BC, during the Second Punic War, in which Publius Cornelius ◊Scipio (later Scipio 'Africanus') led a Roman army of 45,000 to victory over a Carthaginian army of 4,500 cavalry and 50,000 infantry under ◊Hasdrubal and ◊Mago Barca. This battle marked the end of the war in Spain and demonstrated that the tactical skills of Scipio had reached maturity.

For several days prior to the battle both sides had deployed with their best troops, Roman legionaries opposite Africans, in the centre. Scipio's masterstroke was to suddenly attack the Punic camp one morning with an advance force of light infantry and cavalry. He then changed his line of battle so that the legionaries were on the wings and his weaker Spanish allies in the centre. The Carthaginians were rushed into their usual deployment, without time to breakfast. The Roman wings quickly defeated pro-Carthaginian Spanish forces stationed against them and enveloped the African centre before it had got to grips with its opposition. Despite being weakened by hunger, the Carthaginians were able to hold out until they were saved by a sudden storm. A night retreat by Hasdrubal misfired when, after vigorous pursuit by the Romans, the Punic forces became dispersed.

Illyriciani (or *equites Illyriciani*) troopers of the late Roman cavalry reserve. Formed by the emperor Gallienus in the 3rd century and based at strategic locations in northern Italy, Greece, and the Balkans, they provided a fast-moving reserve that could deploy quickly to trouble spots. The name is derived from the province of Illyricum (former modern Yugoslavia) from where a significant portion of the soldiers were recruited.

These units were instrumental in the restoration of order and stability by the Illyrian emperors (Claudius, Aurelian, Probus, Carus, and Diocletian). However, in the relative calm of Diocletian's reign (284–305) the bulk of the *Illyriciani* were distributed along the eastern frontiers and never regained their former status.

imago Roman standard, bearing an image of the emperor, or a member of his family.

Immortals Achaemenid Persian elite infantry, so named because they were continually kept at their full strength of 10,000 men. They were divided into regiments of 1,000 with the ◊spear-bearers perhaps serving as the senior regiment.

From 480 BC to 479 BC they fought at Thermopylae (see ◊Thermopylae, Battle of 480 BC) and Plataea (see ◊Plataea, Battle of) equipped as *sparabara*, but they had probably been disbanded by the time of ◊Darius III in the 4th century BC. If they did exist at that time it is likely that they were re-equipped as *takabara* instead of the older *sparabara*.

The Sassanian kings also had a unit of 1,000 cavalry termed Immortals who fought at Daras in 530.

imperator Roman military title, approximately equivalent to 'general'. Successful Roman commanders were hailed *'imperator'* after a victory in battle. The emperors from ◊Augustus onwards were granted this as a permanent title.

Imperial Gallic helmet very common type of Roman helmet in use at the beginning of the Empire (1st century AD). It evolved from the late Celtic Porte bei Nidau type iron helmet, probably brought into the Roman army by Gallic auxiliaries early in the reign of the first emperor Augustus. It disappeared in the 2nd century AD.

incastellamento medieval Italian fracturing of political authority down to the level of a castle. This was a feature of most of medieval western Europe outside England and Scandinavia and it had a profound impact on how rulers waged war. Castle warfare was slow and attritional, depending upon the loyalty of castellans (castle governors) to defend a lord's territory.

incendiary weapons, Indian in the classical period (c. 500 BC–AD 500), Indian warfare featured fireballs, flaming arrows, and similar missiles shot from siege engines. Incendiarism was condemned by most Hindu texts as a breach of the laws of war, but was strongly advocated by the Brahman chief minister ◊Kautilya.

The *Arthashashtra*, attributed to him, includes a formula for the composition of fire-raising material and suggests the use of birds and monkeys as delivery systems when attacking an enemy city.

incendiary weapons, medieval European weapons designed to start fires. In the medieval period barrels of burning pitch were dropped from castle battlements, often through specially designed ◊brattices or machicolation. Incendiary missiles were often hurled by throwing engines, and fire arrows were commonly employed. The most famous incendiary weapon of the period was ◊Greek fire.

indenture medieval English military contract between a ruler and a baron, knight, or even an esquire, specifying the numbers and types of troops to be provided for war service, usually overseas, during the ◊Hundred Years' War. Obligation varied from one campaign to life, in return for an annual fee. Many indentures survive, providing an invaluable record of the men-at-arms and archers involved in the war.

Indiculus loricatorum list of 2,080 armoured knights summoned for the Holy Roman emperor Otto II's invasion of Italy in 981. Extrapolation from this document shows that obligations of the great religious houses and bishops totalled some 3,000 knights, and the lay vassals provided twice as many, giving Otto a potential armoured cavalry of almost 10,000 men, a very large number for the period.

Indus, Battle of the battle fought on the river Indus in 1221 in which the Mongols, led by ◊Genghis Khan in person, were victorious over Sultan Jalal al-Din, the last of the Khwarazm Shahs. This was the last major engagement of Genghis Khan's western campaign (1219–21) and marked the southernmost limit of his advance into India.

INDIAN ARMIES, TACTICS AND DEPLOYMENTS

Early Hindu theorists of the classical period (c. 500 BC–AD 500) recommended the formation of all-arms sections, made up of one elephant, one chariot, three cavalrymen, and five foot soldiers. Three of these sections (*patti*) formed a combat team (*senamukha*), three *senamukhas* formed a battle group (*gulma*), and so on, in groups of three, up to the level of a complete army (*aksauhini*) of 21,870 *pattis*. In practice, armies were drawn up with each arm massed separately. Heavy infantry and elephants were concentrated in the centre, with archers placed behind the spearmen. Light infantry, cavalry, and chariots took the conventional position of mobile troops, on the flanks.

During the classical period much emphasis was placed on single combat between individual champions, and only elite household troops could be relied on to fight to the last. Hindu and Muslim generals in medieval times (AD 500–1500) relied heavily upon mass, and armies commonly included hundreds of elephants and tens of thousands of horsemen. Battles were usually decided by a charge of elephants and heavy cavalry, which had become the predominant component of Indian armies. Defensive tactics included the use of caltraps, entrenchments, and improvised barricades. Armies were commanded by a general (*senapati*), though the king himself was expected to lead in battle (the cautious theorist ◊Kautilya recommended him doing so from the rear). Captains (*nayaka*) were appointed to act as subordinate commanders, usually men of noble birth at the head of their own contingents.

In the medieval period, army units often had a continuing corporate life, with a welfare system, subscriptions, memorials, and so on, comparable to those of Roman legions or modern regiments and divisions. A well organized army was expected to be able to march two leagues (*yojanas*) in a day. Kings were advised to spend half their annual revenue on defence, and to place one-sixth of the remainder in their treasuries as a contingency fund.

After the defeat and death of ◊Ala al-Din Khwarazm Shah, his son and successor Jalal al-Din retreated into northwest India, where he was overtaken by Genghis Khan on the west bank of the Indus. Jalal al-Din's army attacked, making initial headway, but the Mongols rallied and successfully counterattacked on both flanks. Jalal al-Din finally jumped his horse down a 10-m/33-ft cliff to swim across the river. Marvelling at this feat, Genghis Khan stopped his archers from shooting at Jalal al-Din, who emerged safely on the far side.

Indutiomarus (died 53 BC) chieftain of the Treveri tribe during the ◊Gallic Wars, who supported the revolt against the Romans of 54 BC. Though vocal in encouraging hostility, his military action was a disaster and he was killed in 53 BC.

Indutiomarus committed his tribe to the revolt of 54 BC and encouraged several neighbouring tribes to join in. He led his own forces into battle against one of the Roman winter camps in an ill-conceived operation and his forces were routed in a surprise counterattack. A large bounty was placed on his head by the camp commander and he was pursued to his death by the entire Roman garrison.

infanzón lesser military aristocrat of medieval Spain, often engaged in border warfare. The legendary ◊El Cid came from the ranks of the *infanzónes*.

Intercisa fort Roman fort at present-day Dunaújváros in central Hungary that formed part of the Danube defences of Pannonia Inferior (Hungary). Measuring 180 × 200 m/197 × 219 yds, it was most likely constructed in the mid-2nd century, but near the end of the reign of Marcus Aurelius (161–80) improvements were already being made to strengthen the defences.

New towers were added to the gates which projected 2 m/6.5 ft beyond the existing stone wall, allowing artillery weapons to cover the base of the wall on either side and the gate portal itself. Under ◊Constantine (I) the Great or Valentinian I projecting towers were added at the fort corners. To create a straight 90-degree angle with the fort wall these new towers took a shape known as 'axe-head' or 'splayed fan' (also seen at ◊Drobeta fort). At the same time the west gate was closed off and converted into a single, large, projecting tower.

Intharaja I (died 1424) (or *Int'araja*) Thai king of Ayutthaya from 1408, nephew of King ◊Boromoraja I. As Prince Nakonin he was a provincial governor for King Ramraja, whom he deposed. He intervened in wars of succession in his vassal-state of Sukhotahi and in the northern Thai kingdom of Chiengmai. He was succeeded by his son ◊Boromoraja II.

In 1410 Intharaja supported Tammaraja (Mahadharmaraja) III in the Sukhothai war of succession. The following year Intharaja sent Tammaraja with an Ayutthayan army to support Prince Yi Kumkam against Prince Sam Fang Ken in a succession dispute in Chiengmai. Tammaraja besieged the town of Phayao on the northwestern border of Chiengmai territory. Both sides used cannon, an innovation in Thailand. Tammaraja built an earthwork fort which the defenders destroyed in a sally. After this stubborn resistance Tammaraja withdrew from Phayao and besieged Chiengmai itself but again failed to take it. The succession dispute was settled by single combat; when the defending champion wounded the Ayutthayan champion in the toe, he was declared the winner. The Ayutthayans recognized Sam Fang Ken as king and withdrew, capturing the town of Chiengrai on the way and carrying off the population as slaves to pay for the cost of the war.

Iphicrates (lived 4th century BC) Athenian general. He achieved fame as a commander of peltasts (mercenary light infantry) in the ◊Corinthian War, when he heavily defeated a Spartan force near Corinth in 390 BC, and is credited with a number of reforms to infantry equipment.

He served with the Persians in their unsuccessful attempt to recover Egypt in 373, then returned to Athens and commanded both on Corcyra (modern Corfu) and in the Peloponnese before returning to the north, where he intervened in Macedonian court intrigues on behalf of the future Philip II and his brothers. His part in Athens' defeat by its allies at Embata in 356 ended his career.

Ipsus, Battle of battle fought in Phrygia, Asia Minor, in 301 BC in which ◊Antigonus (I) Monophthalmus was defeated and killed by his fellow Macedonian generals Lysimachus and Seleucus I of Syria, thus effectively ending any chance that Alexander the Great's empire would remain intact.

Antigonus' defeat seems to have been due to a cavalry charge getting out of hand, led by his son ◊Demetrius (I) Poliorcetes, who went in overzealous pursuit of the defeated enemy cavalry, exposing his father's flank to Seleucus' Indian elephants. Antigonus waited too long for his son's return.

iqta medieval Arabic non-hereditary revenue-providing estate used by Muslim states to support a mounted warrior.

Ismaili member of a medieval Muslim sect, originally based in northern Iran. Under their legendary 'Old Man of the Mountains' leader the Ismailis played a role in the politics of the Holy Land in the 12th and 13th centuries, holding several important castles in northern Syria and providing dedicated fanatics for assassination of both Christian and Muslim rulers.

Issoudun castle early 12th-century citadel castle with a motte, situated between Châteauroux and Bourges in Bas-Berry, France. The area was disputed by the Angevins and the Capetians. ◊Philip (II) Augustus of France added a round tower, La Tour Blanche, about 1202 with the *en bec* (strengthening stone spur) defending its most vulnerable side.

Issus, Battle of (333 BC) battle fought in 333 BC in Cilicia, Asia Minor (in modern Turkey), between ◊Alexander (III) the Great and ◊Darius III of Persia. It was the scene of Alexander's second victory over the Persians.

It seems that after countering a cavalry attack on his left, Alexander was able to break through on the right with his Companion cavalry, and wheel to threaten the Persian centre. The right of his phalanx then crossed the river, whereupon Darius fled, with Alexander in pursuit. The left of the phalanx found it more difficult to fight its way across, and much of the Persian army was able to retreat when the Macedonians turned to plundering their camp.

Issus, Battle of (194) decisive battle fought in 194 at Issus, Cilicia (in present-day Turkey), in which the Roman emperor Lucius ◊Septimus Severus defeated Percennius Niger, the Roman governor of Syria, in the civil war following the death of the Roman emperor Publius Helvius Pertinax.

After Severus' success at Nicaea in 194 (see ◊Nicaea, Battle of), the main armies of each side clashed in open field. At first Niger's superiority in numbers appeared to be advantageous, but a sudden violent thunderstorm caused his troops to panic and flee, with the loss of 20,000 soldiers.

Issus, campaign of first stage, in 622, in the successful Byzantine counterattack, led by ◊Heraclius, against the Persians in Syria and Egypt (see ◊Syria and Egypt, Persian conquest of).

After buying off an Avar invasion and securing funds from the church, the Byzantine Emperor Heraclius broke with tradition by personally leading an army against the Persians. He sailed with his army from Constantinople in April 622 to land just north of Antioch, near the ancient town of Issus.

After several skirmishes he outmanoeuvred the Persian army under Shahrbaraz to break out towards the north, cutting across the Persian lines of communication and forcing them to pull back from Syria and western Anatolia.

Italian Social War revolt 91–89 BC of Rome's Italian allies, provoked by the denial of their Roman citizenship. The situation was resolved by agreeing to their demands: the citizens of peninsular Italy ceased to be allies and became Romans by the peace treaty concluded in 87 BC.

The issue of enfranchisement was causing increasing unrest amongst the Italians, who were frustrated that Rome relied on them for its army but gave them little in return. In 91 BC the Roman politician Livius Drusus raised a motion in the Senate to extend Roman citizenship to all those in Italy. It was rejected, and most of Italy rose in revolt, with fighting continuing until 89 BC. Realizing that they had pushed the allies too far and that Rome depended on them, the Senate recanted.

Italy, Lombard invasion of invasion and conquest of northern Italy by the Germanic Lombards (*Langobardi*) in 568, led by the Lombard king Alboin. The imperial army was defeated in 569, and most of the major cities of northern Italy fell. Alboin was murdered in 572 and the Lombards then ranged over Italy under the leadership of 35 independent dukes.

Before invading Italy, the Lombards had slowly migrated from the lower Elbe to the Danube valley. They had defeated the Heruls in 508, assisted the Romans in Italy against the Goths and Franks 551–54, and, with the aid of the Avars, destroyed the Gepids in 567. Fearing the growing power of the Avars, Alboin abandoned Pannonia to his allies and on 1 April 568 invaded Italy with his entire people, reinforced by some Saxons and others. Italy, having been devastated by the long wars of Roman reconquest 535–54, was ill equipped to resist invasion.

Italy, Merovingian invasion of intervention in northern Italy by the Merovingian Franks in 553, ostensibly to aid the Goths in their conflict with the Romans but in reality an attempt to seize what they could for themselves.

The Franks were led by two Alamanni brothers, Lothar and Butilin. Their army is claimed to have been 80,000 strong, comprising forces from several Germanic tribes, including the remnants of the defeated Gothic army. While these numbers are probably inflated, the army was clearly very large because the Romans were unable to mount any effective defence against it. After amassing enough plunder to satisfy his warriors, Lothar headed for home, but his forces were then defeated by the Romans. Meanwhile, Butilin set out to conquer Italy, and Narses defeated his reduced forces at Casilinum (see ◊Casilinum, Battle of).

ito maki no tachi style of Japanese ◊*tachi* (sword) mounting which developed in the late Momoyama period (1568–1600). The area of the scabbard between and either side of the suspension straps was wrapped with braid to prevent the lacquer on the scabbard from scraping against armour.

Iwafune no ki fortified Japanese ◊*saku,* or ◊*ki,* on Honshu island, Japan, believed to have been established around 648 during the military campaigns of Japan's Yamato court to suppress the tribes in the northeast of the island. The supposed remains of the stockade were discovered near Murakami in Niigata prefecture in 1957.

Izawa castle (Japanese *Izawa-jō*) fortress built around the year 802 in the northern Japanese province of Mutsu (now Iwate prefecture) as part of the Heian court's attempts to subdue the Ezo people. The fortress was strategically placed near the confluence of two rivers and was of such importance that the leader of the court forces transferred his regional headquarters to the site.

jack type of soft armour in the form of a quilted fabric doublet used in western Europe, principally England, from about 1390 to about 1540. It was the main protective body covering used by the majority of English archers during the Hundred Years' War and the Wars of the Roses. It was largely replaced by the plate jack after 1500.

Jacquerie French peasant uprising of 1358, caused partly by the ravages of the English army and French nobility during the ◊Hundred Years' War, which reduced the rural population to destitution. The word derives from the nickname for a French peasant, 'Jacques Bonhomme'.

The uprising began in the Beauvaisis and risings followed in various places, including Paris, where the rebel leader Etienne Marcel was killed with an axe. The nobility united to crush the rebellion.

Jaffa, Battle of battle fought on 1 August 1192 between ◊Richard (I) the Lionheart of England and the Ayubbid sultan of Egypt ◊Saladin over the fortified port of Jaffa (now Tel Aviv, Israel). Richard succeeded in driving off the far superior forces of Saladin's cavalry.

Saladin launched a surprise attack on Jaffa on 27 July. Richard was at Acre and when he learned that the garrison had agreed to surrender by 1 August if not relieved, he sailed south. After landing on the beach at Jaffa, he quickly formed a defensive line of alternating crossbow archers and spearmen. This held off the attack of hundreds of Muslim cavalry throughout a long day, at the end of which Richard charged with only ten knights to scatter them.

Jaichand Gaharwar (or *Jayachchandra Gahadavala*) Rajput king of the central Ganges plain, India. He was the father-in-law and rival of ◊Prithviraja Chauhana III. When ◊Muhammad of Ghur invaded India in 1191–92, Jaichand welcomed him as an ally against Prithviraja, but was defeated and killed by Muhammad's Muslim forces.

Jaichand was one of the last of the Hindu kings to perform the ◊*ashvamedha* or conqueror's horse-sacrifice. Prithviraja refused his summons to attend this ceremony, whereupon Jaichand erected a statue of Prithviraja to stand in place of a doorkeeper. When Jaichand's daughter Padmavati came to select a husband at the ceremony of ◊*swayamvara* she threw her garland over this statue, and Prithviraja carried her off.

Jaichand regretted his initial welcome of Muhammad of Ghur when he realized that Muhammad intended to establish a permanent rule in India, and met him at Chandwar in 1193. The Hindu forces were on the point of victory when Jaichand was struck in the eye by a Muslim arrow and fell from his elephant. At this, his army lost heart and fled.

Jaipal I (died 1001) (or *Jayapala I*) Rajput king of Und (or Waihind), the Punjab, and eastern Afghanistan. He was the first Hindu ruler to cross swords with the Muslim rulers of Ghazni (central Afghanistan), and lost eastern Afghanistan to them. After being captured by ◊Mahmud of Ghazni, he was ransomed by his son but committed suicide.

Jaipal made unsuccessful attacks against Alp-Tegin in 973 and his successor ◊Sebuk-Tegin in 979. Sebuk-Tegin took the offensive in 986 and 988, and Jaipal was forced to cede eastern Afghanistan to the growing power of Ghazni. Sebuk-Tegin's successor Mahmud of Ghazni invaded the Punjab in 1001, defeating and capturing Jaipal at the Battle of Peshawar.

Jaipur (or *Jainagar*) largest city in Rajasthan, India, founded by Maharaja Sawai Jai Singh in 1728 on the site of an earlier settlement. The main citadel, on the Nahagarh or 'Tiger Hill', consists of a crenellated masonry wall, 2.75 m/9 ft thick and 6 m/20 ft high, on a rock cliff 150 m/500 ft above the surrounding area.

Jaipur served as the capital of Amber state, founded in 1128 by Dulhai Rai (Tej Karan).

Jaisalmer city in Rajasthan, India, founded in 1156 by Rowal Jaisal, chief of the Jadon ◊Rajput clan, and fortified with a stone wall 5 km/3 mi in circumference and 1.5 m/5 ft thick, with numerous bastions and towers. The citadel is on a hill 76 m/250 ft high, defended by a wall of similar construction, with battlements and turrets, reaching a height of 9 m/30 ft.

It was captured and sacked about 1300 by the Muslims under ◊Ala al-Din Khilji, Sultan of Delhi.

Jalal al-Din Firuz Shah (1220–96) sultan of Delhi 1290–96, and founder of the Khilji dynasty of Delhi. He proved a beneficent ruler, but his failure to punish his enemies or reward his friends was counted against him and he was treacherously murdered by his nephew and successor ◊Ala al-Din Khilji.

Firuz Shah was descended from a Turkish family previously domiciled in Afghanistan, and came to the throne through the murder of Sultan Balban's grandson and successor Kaiqubad.

James (I) the Conqueror (1208–76) king of Aragón from 1213. He conquered the Balearic Islands and took Valencia from the Moors, dividing it with Alfonso X of Castile (1221–84) by a treaty of 1244. Both these exploits are recorded in his autobiography, *Libre dels feyts/ The Book of Feats*. He largely established Aragón as the dominant power in the Mediterranean.

His autobiography contains military information on strategy, tactics, and provisions plus accounts of his own warfare and diplomatic negotiations.

Japan, Mongol invasions of invasions of 1274 and 1281 by the forces of Khubilai Khan, Mongol emperor of China, sent against Japan when the ◊Kamakura shogunate refused to recognize his paramount authority and send tribute to his court.

On both occasions the Mongols landed in western Japan in huge numbers. In 1274 more than 900 vessels carrying 40,000 troops were dispatched. In 1281 over 4,000 vessels with more than 140,000 troops were sent out. They created great devastation, particularly around the town of Hakata on the island of Kyushu, before their fleets were destroyed by typhoons which the Japanese regarded as a divine wind (kamikaze) sent to defend the 'land of the gods'.

Khubilai Khan never totally gave up his plans to dominate Japan, and although preparations were made on several occasions for subsequent invasions, instability within his own empire prevented these schemes from coming to fruition.

jarid Persian term for a set of short javelins, usually carried in a quiver by cavalry.

jarl Scandinavian nobleman who, in the Viking period, controlled an area of land either independently or under the king. The term is closely relate to the Anglo-Saxon 'earl'.

jauhar (Sanskrit, meaning 'holocaust', 'mass suicide') medieval Hindu rite of self-sacrifice when the fall of a fortress was inevitable. The men of the garrison sallied out to die fighting to the last, while the bodies of their women and children burned in the inner chambers of the fortress.

It was intended to avoid the dishonour of captivity and enslavement, and was practised by the proud ◊Rajput kingdoms of northern India as they fell to the Muslim invaders.

jawshan Arabic term for the lamellar coat worn over ◊mail armour by early medieval Islamic cavalry. After the replacement of this armour style in about the 14th century by the *zereh baghtar*, or mail and plate coat, the term was generally used for any form of body armour.

Jaya Indravarman IV (lived 12th century) king of Champa (modern central Vietnam), active during the period 1163–92. An official under Jaya Harivarman I, he usurped the throne from Harivarman's son in 1167 and from 1170 fought against Cambodia. Despite innovations from China, he failed in his land attacks but was more successful at sea. He was eventually defeated and captured by a Cham army. He was released to fight Cham rebels, but was defeated and killed by ◊Sri Vidyanandana.

In 1172 a shipwrecked Chinese officer, Ji Yangjun, instructed the Chams in mounted archery. Jaya Indravarman commissioned him to import horses from Hainan, but China banned their export, so the Cham cavalry could not be increased as planned. Ji also introduced the Chinese ballista, which the Chams mounted on elephants. Despite these innovations Jaya Indravarman's land attacks against Cambodia failed. In 1177 he attacked unexpectedly with a fleet which sailed up the Mekong to the Tonle Sap (Great Lake), burned the wooden defences of the Khmer capital Angkor, sacked it, and killed the king. Under ◊Jayavarman VII the Khmers rallied and expelled the Chams. In 1190 Jaya Indravarman resumed the offensive, but a Khmer army under the exiled Cham Sri Vidyanandana defeated him and conquered Champa.

Jaya Paramesvaravarman II (lived 13th century) king of Champa (modern central Vietnam) 1226–52. Champa was under Khmer occupation 1203–20 after the defeat of ◊Sri

Vidyanandana. Prince Angsaraja became Cambodia's governor there, and led the occupying Khmer army, with Burmese and Thai troops, against Vietnam in 1207. The Khmers withdrew from Champa for reasons unknown in 1220, and in 1226 Angsaraja was crowned king as Jaya Paramesvaravarman II. Cham ships continued to raid the Vietnamese coast, and in 1252 the Vietnamese emperor Trân Than-tôn invaded Champa in reprisal. He carried off many prisoners, and Jaya Paramesvaravarman was apparently deposed or killed.

Jayavarman VII (c. 1125–1218) king of Cambodia from 1181, second cousin of ◊Suryavarman II. He conquered Champa (modern central Vietnam) and extended his rule into the Malay peninsula and part of Burma. He refortified Angkor with stone walls and moats and was also a great builder of monuments at Angkor and elsewhere, commemorating his victories over the Chams in battle-reliefs.

Under Yasovarman II (about 1160–65) Jayavarman led an army into Champa. He returned on hearing of Yasovarman's murder, but was unable to overthrow the usurper Tribhuvanaditya until ◊Jaya Indravarman IV of Champa captured Angkor and killed Tribhuvanaditya. Jayavarman led Khmer resistance, defeated the Chams in both land and naval battles, and after expelling them was crowned. He employed a refugee Cham prince, ◊Sri Vidyanandana, first against local rebels and then to conquer Champa. Vidyanandana turned against him and Champa had to be conquered again, but from 1203 until after Jayavarman's death it was a Khmer province. The future Cham king ◊Jaya Paramesvaravarman II was one of Jayavarman's governors.

jazerant rare type of armour in the form of a ◊mail shirt sewn inside a fabric doublet, used across Persia to western Europe from about 1200 to 1500. It was probably copied in Europe from Muslim originals.

The word is almost certainly a transliteration of the Persian (and later Arabic) term for this kind of armour, *kazhagand*, which first appeared in the 11th century as *qazhagand*.

Jericho Neolithic site (modern Tell es-Sultan, Jordan) dated to the 8th millennium BC, extending over 3–4 ha/7–10 acres. It is significant because of its defences, having the earliest known stone tower and stone defensive wall.

Jericho survived into the late 2nd millennium BC: by the Middle Bronze Age it had expanded and was surrounded by a mudbrick wall nearly 500 m/550 yds long. This development may have been in response to the use of the battering ram, a device which lay behind the biblical story of Joshua collapsing the walls of Jericho.

The D-shaped tower is 8.5 m/28 ft in diameter and its remains are over 8 m/26 ft in height. It abutted the defensive wall which had an outer ditch 8 m/26 ft wide and 2 m/6.5 ft deep. The tower is solid but has an entrance and internal flight of 22 steps.

Jerusalem, Roman in Roman times the city of Jerusalem consisted of five regions – the Old

JERUSALEM, SIEGE OF (70)

Culminating siege of the ◊Jewish War in which Roman forces recaptured Jerusalem and destroyed its Temple.

Although Jerusalem was heavily fortified with three great circuit walls, its defenders were fatally weakened by the bitter hostility between their three main factions. ◊Titus's army of four legions, plus auxiliaries and allied contingents, approached the conflict with confidence but nearly suffered a reverse when the 10th Legion (*Legio X Fretensis*), camping alone on the Mount of Olives, was attacked in a strong sally from the city.

After this, the Romans were more methodical, systematically battering their way through each circuit wall in turn, taking Jerusalem piece by piece, and constructing a wall of circumvallation around the city to prevent defenders from escaping. Even so, the three-month siege remained very hard-fought and several Roman assaults failed with heavy losses. Fighting was especially bitter around the Temple, which burned to the ground when the Romans finally captured it. After the fall of the Temple, the resistance of the Jewish defenders collapsed.

JEWISH WAR

Jewish revolt against Rome, 66–74, caused by a long period of provincial maladministration coupled with growing social and economic problems. Sometimes called the Great Rebellion, the war ended with the complete destruction of Jerusalem by the Roman governor ◊Titus. The narrative of Josephus and the rich archaeological record make this one of the best recorded conflicts of the Roman Empire.

The rebellion in the Roman province of Judaea broke out in AD 66, and the small Roman garrison in Jerusalem was quickly annihilated. When the governor of Syria, Cestius Gallus, led a hastily gathered army against the city, he was defeated and pursued with heavy losses through the Beth-Horon Pass (see ◊Beth-Horon, Battle of).The Jewish rebels, divided into a disparate collection of groups led by charismatic leaders, were often in open and violent dispute with each other. Popular support fluctuated and some whole communities defected to Rome at the earliest opportunity. In these circumstances, the rebels were unable to create an effective field army and the war became dominated by sieges as the Romans systematically captured one Jewish city after another. ◊Vespasian conquered Galilee, Samaria, Idumaea, and much of Judaea in 67–69 before leaving the war to his son, Titus. In 70 Titus stormed Jerusalem after a fierce siege (see ◊Jerusalem, Siege of 70), leaving subsequent governors of Judaea to mop up the last rebel strongholds at Herodium, Machaerus, and Masada (see ◊Masada, Siege of) in 71–74. Although some fighting occurred in Egypt, the uprising failed to spread among the Jews of the Diaspora.

Town, Upper Town, Temple, Middle Town, and New Town – each protected by its own wall. A fortress, known as the Antonia, was constructed at the corner of the Temple where the wall of the Middle Town joined it. During the Jewish Revolt of AD 66–73 the city was invested by the Romans for five months in AD 70.

Jerusalem, sack of fall on 11 July 1244 of the city of Jerusalem in the Holy Land to Khwarismian Muslim troops and finally out of Christian hands.

After its fall in 1187, Jerusalem had been recovered by the diplomacy of the Holy Roman emperor ◊Frederick II in 1228. The Kwarismian Turks were military exiles following the overthrow of their shah by the Mongols in 1231. Allegedly 10,000 strong, they overwhelmed the city's defences while the main Christain force was mustering at Acre, leading to a battle at Gaza (see ◊Gaza, Battle of). The garrison held out in the citadel, but finally agreed to surrender.

Jerusalem, Siege of (1099) siege of the Muslim-held city of Jerusalem in the Holy Land by Christians of the First Crusade from Europe, lasting from 13 June to 15 July 1099.

The crusaders used ships' timbers to construct siege engines and stormed the city after only four weeks.

Cut off from supplies, and short of water and timber for siege engines, the crusaders launched an ill-prepared assault on 13 June. The Fatimid governor had a small but veteran garrison, and the city's walls were in good repair. The crusaders initially concentrated on the northwest corner of the city. The arrival of the crusader fleet at Jaffa on 17 June provided a supply of timber to build a siege tower and ram. On 9–10 July the tower was moved 915 m / 1,000 yds east, near Herod's Gate, to launch a surprise assault. It was in position on 15 July; protected by damp hides, it resisted attempts to set it on fire, and a brutal sack followed.

Jewish Rebellion rebellion of the Jewish population in Egypt against the Romans, 115–17. The Romans suffered several early defeats but eventually suppressed the rebellion after a long campaign.

jian Chinese term for a straight, double-edged sword. It was first produced in bronze during the Zhou dynasty; though largely replaced by the iron ◊*dao* during the Han dynasty, the *jian* is still made today.

jianer (or *chien-erh*) (Chinese 'strong men') Chinese professional soldiers of the Tang period (618–906) used particularly in frontier garrisons to supplement the ◊*fubing* militia.

Many of the *jianer* were *fubing* who re-enlisted after their tour of frontier duty. Other frontier troops were foreign mercenaries. The proportion of professionals increased, and after the abolition of *fubing* frontier service in 737 the Tang armies were entirely professionals except for emergency local militias, the ◊*tuanlian*.

jiangjun (or *chiang-chün*) Chinese general's rank. Under the Han dynasty (206 BC–AD 220) this was the senior rank in the army, though the commander of a force including several generals was sometimes called *da jiangjun*, 'senior general' or 'generalissimo'. Under the Tang dynasty, the ◊*wei* guards units were commanded by a *da jiangjun* and two *jiangjun*.

Han Generals would be given a title corresponding to their task; ◊Li Guangli was *Ershi jiangjun*, since Ershi was the target of his expedition. Later in the dynasty the *jiangjun* was often commander of a ◊*ying*.

jibbah Sudanese term for a quilted coat, sometimes worn with ◊mail armour over the top or underneath. It is derived from an old Arabic word which may originally have referred to quilted armour but later came to mean armour in general.

jie (or *chieh*) one of the two standards carried on campaign by the commander in chief of a Tang Chinese ◊*xingjun* field army, the other being the ◊*jing*. It consisted of three painted wooden discs surrounded by feathers, mounted one above the other on a pole topped with a copper dragon's head.

jiedu shi (or *chieh-tu shih*) Chinese provincial military governors of the middle and late Tang period (618–907). The first were appointed in 710 to command the permanent armies that were developing on the frontiers. By 725 there were nine, covering the whole northern frontier. They controlled the majority of the empire's troops, mostly ◊*jianer* professionals more loyal to their commanders than to the central government and developing into ◊*yabing* private armies.

The rebellion of the over-mighty *jiedu shi* ◊An Lushan was almost inevitable. After the rebellion, the number of *jiedu shi* multiplied as the government sought to reward loyal generals and, by dividing the commands, prevent any from growing too strong. Some governorships, such as that in Huaixi, became hereditary. One *jiedu shi*, Chu Wen, eventually overthrew the Tang.

jihad Muslim term for 'holy war'. The original Islamic conquests initiated by Muhammad, the founder of Islam, justified the use of war as a means to bring his revelation to unbelievers. The concept was later used by secular rulers, especially on the frontiers of the medieval Christian world, to motivate frontier warriors' raids and help raise troops for more significant campaigns, such as those by which ◊Saladin reduced the Latin Kingdom of Jerusalem.

jimbaori surcoat worn over Japanese armour. It was popular from the late Muromachi period (1333–1568), and reached heights of decorative fancy during the Momoyama period (1568–1600).

Often made from elegant imported silks, brocades, and wool, the jimbaori could be adorned with almost any motif, including Western designs, or even decorated with rare and exotic feathers.

Jimo, Siege of (or *Chi-mo*) defeat in 279 BC of besieging Yan forces by ◊Tian Dan of Qi. After lulling the besiegers into believing that Jimo would surrender, Tian Dan sallied out at night. He sent out 1,000 oxen, swathed in red silk to look like dragons and with flaming straw on their tails. These were followed by 5,000 soldiers, while the citizens drummed and shouted behind them. Totally surprised, the besiegers panicked, and when their general was killed, they fled.

jing (or *ching*) Chinese all-round defence formation named from its resemblance to the Chinese character *jing*, a well. It could be made up of nine units of any size in a three by three square, or of five units arranged in a chequerboard. The *jing* formation is mentioned in Tang dynasty sources but is probably much older.

jing (or *ching*) one of the two standards carried on campaign by the commander in chief of a Tang Chinese ◊*xingjun* field army, the other being the ◊*jie*. It was a red silk flag painted with a tiger, with a red silk streamer and a copper dragon's head atop the pole.

jingasa Japanese shallow conical hat, usually made of iron in single or multiple plates but sometimes of lacquered wood, worn in battle by the *ashigaru* from the Muromachi period (1333–1568) onwards. In later periods it was worn during parades.

The *jingasa* has a padded interior and two padded loops which hang down past the ears and are tied under the chin with a cord.

Jingū (Empress) legendary Japanese empress. As described in the chronicle *Nihon Shoki* of

720, she completed the defeat of the people of Kyushu island after the death of her husband in the campaign and then went on, while pregnant, to defeat the armies of Korea. On her return she gave birth to the emperor Ojin, who was later deified as the war god Hachiman.

Jingxing Pass, Battle of (or *Ching-hsing*) battle in 204 BC in which ◊Han Gaozu's general Han Xin and his army outsmarted and defeated the kingdom of Zhao, an ally of ◊Xiang Yu.

Zhao commander Chen Yu held the fortified Jingxing Pass with 200,000 men against Han's 'few tens of thousands'. Han sent 2,000 light cavalry, each one with a flag, to outflank the Zhao position by night. At dawn he advanced with 10,000 men, and the defenders left their defences to attack. Han feigned flight, falling back to the rest of his forces and luring the Zhao troops further from their position. Meanwhile his outflanking cavalry seized the Zhao fortifications from behind, displaying their red Han flags on the battlements. Believing the force behind them was much larger than it was, the Zhao troops broke and fled. Chen Yu was beheaded.

Jinsha River, Battle of (or *Chin-sha chiang*) battle in November 1253 in which ◊Khubilai Khan defeated the Dali kingdom (the later name of ◊Geluofeng's Nanzhao kingdom) during the Mongol campaigns in China (see ◊China, Mongol campaigns in). Khubilai led a campaign into modern Yunnan province to outflank the Song Chinese Empire from the west. As he advanced south from Sichuan the Dali armies under the minister Gao Taixiang met him on the river Jinsha. The Mongols made rafts from inflated sheepskin bags and crossed the river by night, surprising and routing the defenders.

jinwei jun (or *chin-wei chün*) central army of the Western Wei state in China, organized in around 534 by ◊Yuwen Tai. It was stationed at the capital and probably mainly comprised ◊Xianbei cavalry. Its inadequate size forced the recruitment of Chinese ◊xiangbing troops as reinforcements.

Jinyang, Siege of (or *Chin-yang*) climax, 455–453 BC, of the wars between noble families that destroyed Jin, formerly the strongest state in China. After this siege, Jin was divided into the three states of Zhao, Han, and Wei, marking the start of the ◊Warring States period.

Clan leader Zhi Yao had expelled the Jin ruler and besieged Zhao Wuxu, his only remaining opponent, in Jinyang. The siege dragged on because of the reluctance of Yao's allies, the Han and Wei clans. Diverting the river Jin to flood the city, Yao let slip that he could use the same tactic against his allies' cities. This prompted them to conspire with Wuxu. They murdered Yao, and all central authority in Jin collapsed.

jitte steel baton with a projecting square hook near the handle carried by Japanese non-samurai officials from the 16th century. It could be used to catch the sword of an opponent and break his blade or disarm him. It was a useful instrument for an official when arresting a person of potentially higher rank or social status.

jiu jun (or *chiu chün*) frontier armies of the Khitan Liao dynasty (907–1125) recruited from Khitan tribesmen. After the conquest of the Liao by ◊Wanyen Aguda, they served his Jurchen Jin dynasty, but deserted to ◊Genghis Khan and assisted in his capture of Zhongdu.

jizamurai Japanese term for those warriors, *bushi*, or ◊samurai, who remained in their local villages rather than directly serving the shogunate and developed their own power base by seizing land as the influence of the shogun waned in the late Kamakura period (1185–1333). Many consolidated their power and later became ◊Sengoku daimyo.

Joan of Arc (1412–31) (the *Maid of Orlèans*) military leader who inspired the French at Orléans in 1428–29 (see ◊Orléans, Siege of) and at Patay, north of Orléans, in 1429 (see ◊Patay, Battle of). As a young peasant girl, she was the wrong age, class, and gender to engage in warfare, yet her 'heavenly voices' instructed her to expel the occupying English from northern France (see ◊Hundred Years' War) and secure the coronation of ◊Charles VII of France. Because of her strength of character, she achieved both aims. The experienced soldiers believed that she spoke the truth, and her enthusiasm was believed to have delivered Orléans to them. Her subsequent attempt to take Paris was overambitious, however, and she was captured May 1430 at Compiègne by the Burgundians, who sold her to the English. She was found guilty of witchcraft and heresy by a tribunal of French ecclesiastics who supported the English, and burned to death at the stake in Rouen 30 May 1431.

Charles made no attempt to save her, but after the recapture of Normandy he instituted a retrial, held 1450–56, that exonerated her. After the French defeat in the Franco-Prussian War in 1870–71, Joan experienced a revival as a military figurehead. She was canonized in 1928.

Jodhpur capital city of Marwar or Jodhpur state in Rajasthan, India, founded by the

◊Rajput Rao Jodha in 1459. It was defended by a massive wall, with gates studded with spikes to protect them from being pushed down by war elephants.

John (II) Comnenus (1087–1143)

Byzantine emperor 1118–43. Inheriting a revived empire from his father, Alexius, John's reign was dedicated to trying to regain old territories lost since Manzikert in 1071 (see ◊Manzikert, Battle of) and the First Crusade in 1096–99 (see ◊Crusades). All his campaigns ended in treaties which improved the Byzantine position without actually gaining much territory, but when John died in a hunting accident, his son ◊Manuel (I) Comnenus was able to build in his father's achievement.

John's campaigns included wars with the Venitians 1122–28 and with Danishmend Turks 1130–35. He crushed the Pechenegs in 1122 and attacked Antioch 1137–38 and 1142–43.

John (II) the Good (1319–64)

king of France 1350–64. During the ◊Hundred Years' War, he was defeated by ◊Edward the Black Prince and captured at the Battle of Poitiers in 1356 (see ◊Poitiers, Battle of 1356). He had to cede territory to England in the Treaty of London (1359). France rejected this but agreed the Treaty of Brétigny (1360).

John was held prisoner in the Tower of London until released on part payment of a large ransom. His son, the Duke of Anjou, hostage for the balance of the ransom, escaped and John kept his word, returning to captivity. He died a prisoner.

John of Gaunt (1340–99)

English noble and politician, fourth son of ◊Edward III of England, Duke of Lancaster from 1362. He distinguished himself during the ◊Hundred Years' War. During Edward's last years, and the years before Richard II attained the age of majority, he acted as head of government, and Parliament protested against his corrupt rule.

John was born in Ghent, Flanders. In 1359 he married Blanche, daughter of the Duke of Lancaster, and their son became ◊Henry IV of England. Blanche died in 1369 and three years later he married Constance, daughter of Pedro III of Castile. John assumed the title of king of Castile in 1372, but his efforts proved unsuccessful, and in 1387 he renounced all claims in favour of his daughter Catherine, who married Henry III of Castile (1379–1406) in 1393.

jōka-machi (Japanese 'castle town') Japanese fort-based settlement of a type that began to develop in the turbulent years of the late Muromachi period (1333–1568). Local lords built strategically placed wooden structures as centres of refuge and administration and to secure their domains against rival warlords, and their subjects and vassals congregated around them.

As conditions began to stabilize in the 16th century, and in spite of – or because of – the introduction of firearms from the West, they became huge regional commercial and administrative centres built around imposing stone castles.

Jomsviking one of the pirates who form a sworn brotherhood in the *Jomsviking Saga*, once believed historically accurate, but now treated cautiously and likely to be fictional. Cnut the Great's ◊housecarls were thought to be organized in the same manner. The saga dates from the late 12th century, over a century after Cnut.

Josephus, Flavius (c. AD 37–101)

Jewish historian and Roman collaborator during the Jewish rebellion (66–70). He was involved in the revolt against Rome in 66 and was sent to Galilee to prepare for the Roman invasion. In 67 he commanded the garrison at Jotopata, surrendering to the emperor ◊Vespasian when the town fell. He became a favoured member of ◊Titus entourage, being wounded during the siege of Jerusalem in 70 while encouraging the defenders to surrender.

Josephus produced a detailed account of the rebellion in *The Jewish War*, and also dealt with some aspects of his command in Galilee in *Life*, an autobiography.

Jotopata, Siege of siege of the Galilean hilltop town of Jotopata in AD 67 by a Roman army commanded by the emperor ◊Vespasian. The defence was led by ◊Josephus. Although Jewish defence was aggressive and several assaults were repulsed, the final attack was overwhelming and the Romans captured the town after 48 days with just one casualty.

Juba I (died 46 BC)

king of Numidia (roughly equivalent to present-day Algeria) 60–46 BC and opponent of Julius ◊Caesar in the Civil Wars (see ◊Civil Wars, Roman Republican). He supported ◊Pompey the Great in an attempt to stave off the annexation of his kingdom, but on Caesar's victory he lost both his life and his kingdom.

At the time of his coronation the supporters of Caesar were making open plans to annex Numidia. When the Civil Wars broke out Juba staked his crown on the Pompey faction and attacked Caesar's general Curio, killing him and defeating his army. Caesar invaded Africa in 47 BC and crushed Juba and the Pompeians at Thapsus in 46 BC (see ◊Thapsus, Battle of).

Juba committed suicide and his kingdom was annexed.

Jugurtha (died 104 BC) pretender to the throne of Numidia (roughly equivalent to present-day Algeria). He seized power from the royal family and became king in 118 BC but incurred the wrath of Rome and was finally ousted as a result of the ◊Jugurthine War.

The illegitimate nephew of King Micipsa, Jugurtha seized the Numidian throne and killed the two princes named with him as joint heirs. In the resulting war with Rome he exploited the knowledge of the Roman army that he had acquired while serving with it in the Second Punic War. His actions during that war had won him enough respect in Rome to carry out the murder of the first prince without Roman criticism. He was betrayed by his father-in-law Bocchus I, King of Mauretania, and delivered to Rome where he was executed at Gaius Marius' triumph (victory procession) in 104 BC.

Jugurthine War war fought 111–104 BC between Rome and the army of ◊Jugurtha, King of Numidia. The Romans invaded Numidia (in North Africa) in an attempt to oust Jugurtha from the throne he had seized. He was finally betrayed to them in 105 BC.

The war was sparked when Jugurtha's coup in 118 BC ignored Roman guarantees on the succession and involved the deaths of Roman citizens. War was declared in 111, but failed to defeat Jugurtha despite numerous strategic gains. In 107 the legate Gaius ◊Marius was given command, but was still unable to achieve a decisive victory. In 105 he induced Bocchus I, the king of neighbouring Mauretania, to betray Jugurtha in exchange for increased territory.

Julian (332–63) (*Flavius Claudius Julianus*) Roman emperor 361–63, known as 'Julian the Apostate' for his failed attempt to revive paganism. He proved to be an able military commander when appointed to defend Gaul against incursions by the Franks and Alamanni 356–59. In 363 he led a massive invasion of Persia but, although he won all his battles, he was unable to draw the Persians into a decisive engagement. He was killed in a night attack on his camp by a javelin, possibly thrown by one of his disaffected Christian soldiers.

Julius Civilis member of the Batavian royal family who led a large-scale rebellion against Rome in AD 70. Although he proclaimed a Gallic empire, his supporters were mainly German. He won several victories, notably when he forced two Roman legions to surren-der at Vetera, but was defeated in a series of battles against a Roman army commanded by Q Petilius ◊Cerealis.

jūmonji-yari Japanese spear, originating in the Muromachi period (1333–1568), that consisted of a long central blade with two equal-sized transverse blades forming a cross shape, or the Japanese character for the number ten (*jū*).

jun (or *chün*) Chinese military unit conventionally translated as 'army', though 'division' is often more appropriate. Under the Western Zhou (about 1027–770 BC), the feudal lords each had armies of one to three *jun*, while the kings had at least 14, the ◊Six Armies and the Eight Yin Armies. The strength of a *jun* is not certain, but a later commentator put it at 12,500 men.

In later periods the *jun* was not always part of the regular hierarchy of units but was often used in the names of particular forces. (See ◊shence jun, ◊Menggu jun, ◊Han jun, and ◊xinfu jun.)

jund Arabic term for an army.

junshi Japanese custom by which some of the chief retainers would commit ritual suicide to follow their lord after his death. The usual form of suicide was by disembowelment, ◊seppuku.

There were no fixed rules for this custom, and the manner of the suicide depended on the lord's importance, how highly he was regarded, and the circumstances of his death.

jupon (or *gipoun*) hip-length fabric garment, usually long-sleeved, worn over armour throughout Europe and synonymous in the late 14th century with the terms 'coat armour' and 'surcoat'. By about 1350 the surcoat was shortened to the hips, a form in which it survived until the early 15th century. Although the garment was still described as coat armour, it was also called a 'jupon' from about 1350.

Justinian (c. 483–565) (*Flavius Anicianus Justinianus*) East Roman emperor 527–65, renowned for overseeing the reconquest of Africa, Italy, and parts of Spain, and for codifying Roman law. His achievements, however, were short-lived. His reconquests and ambitious building projects overstretched the empire's resources and within a few years of his death much of his newly conquered territory had been lost.

Justinian did not take to the field himself but employed the most able generals to command his armies: ◊Belisarius, ◊Narses, and Germanius. He was, however, jealous and suspicious of successful generals and deprived them, especially Belisarius, of the resources they needed to complete their missions. Only Narses, who as a eunuch could not take the throne, was given full support.

Just War theory of how war should be conducted, developed by the Catholic Church during the 12th century and reaching some agreed definition by the late 13th century. Major contributions came from the Neapolitan philosopher and theologian Thomas Aquinas and Pope Innocent IV.

It restricted the occasions for war, and where war was permitted it was only to be conducted in approved circumstances. Generally war between Christians was condemned, and penalties were imposed for engagement in unjust war. Christians were expected to be the defenders, not the aggressors, and have just cause for action. Only a legitimate authority could undertake war.

kabuto general term for the Japanese helmet in use from the Heian period (794–1185). The main bowl of the helmet generally consisted of a number of iron plates riveted strongly together. If the rivets were prominent then the style was referred to as ◊*hoshi kabuto*, and if the plates had strong vertical ridges then the style was known as ◊*suji kabuto*.

The top of the helmet had a hole (◊*tehen no ana*) which afforded some ventilation (there has been speculation that the hair could be pulled through the opening). The bowl of the helmet had a small riveted peak (◊*maezashi*) to which a crest (◊*maedate*), as well as the decorative horn-like projections (◊*kuwagata*), could be affixed. The neck guard (*shikoro*) was made of between three and seven strips of lacquered leather or iron laced vertically together so as to be flexible around the neck. The top strip was riveted to the helmet bowl and the front portion was turned back (◊*fukigaeshi*). This was often, in later helmets, a separate, purely decorative addition.

Kadesh (or *Qadesh*; Hittite *Kinza*) Late Bronze Age fortress (present-day Tell Nebi Mend) on the river Aranta (classical Orontes, modern 'Asi), guarding the Beqa'a Valley, the route through the Lebanon and Anti-Lebanon Mountains.

It was the capital of the leader of the coalition defeated by Tuthmosis III at Megiddo in 1458 BC (see ◊Megiddo, Battle of) and it was subsequently attacked by Tuthmosis III in 1452 BC. In 1420 BC it was brought into the Egyptian sphere of influence by his son and successor ◊Amunhotep II. After being taken by the Hittite Great King Suppiluliumas I in about 1340 BC, it became the southernmost outpost of the Hittite Empire and the site of the Battle of Kadesh in 1275 BC (see ◊Kadesh, Battle of).

Kadesh-Barnea (possibly Ein el-Qudeirat) situated in the central Negev wilderness (in present-day Israel), where the Hebrew tribes encamped before entering Canaan; also the site of one of the 'Forts of Wilderness' probably set up during the reign of King Uzziah (767–740 BC) of Judah to protect his southern border.

Kadesh, Battle of (or *Qadesh*) battle fought in 1275 BC at ◊Kadesh, Syria, between the Hittites and Egyptians, the outcome of which determined the zones of Hittite and Egyptian control over the Levant. Though depicted as a resounding victory by the Egyptian pharaoh Ramses II in his temples, Hittite sources challenge this and place it in the perspective of a longer campaign to control ◊Amurru and the Beqa'a Valley.

Pharaoh Seti I, Ramses' father, had reconquered Amurru and taken Kadesh in about 1301 BC. The Hittites under Muwatallis had retaken Kadesh but not Amurru. In 1276 BC Ramses used Amurru for an inland raid against Kadesh, and in 1275 BC led a larger expedition against the Hittites. Leading the advanced guard, the Army of Amun, he had three other armies in the field: Sutekh (or Seth) in Amurru, Pre' moving up the Beqa'a Valley, between the Lebanon and Anti-Lebanon Mountains, and Ptah in Taminta, the region surrounding Kadesh. On reaching the foothills of Kadesh, Ramses was fooled by Hittite 'deserters' into believing that Muwatallis and the Hittite army was far to the north at Halba (classical Aleppo). The pharaoh and Army of Amun then encamped to the northwest of Kadesh, awaiting the other three armies.

As Army Pre' crossed the ford of the river Arantu (classical Orontes, modern 'Asi), a concealed Hittite force of 2,500 chariots attacked. As the routers were being pursued north towards the Egyptian camp, Ramses discovered through capturing two more Hittite scouts that Muwatallis and an army of 37,000 Hittites and allies were just to the northeast of his position. Then Ramses, according his temple records, sallied forth and defeated the Hittites single-handed, while sending a messenger to Army Ptah to rush to his aid. The advanced guard of Ptah, the Necrin, arrived and attacked the advancing Hittite chariots. Muwatallis sent in another 1,000 chariots, but the Egyptians regained the initiative. By the end of the second day, the scattered forces of the Egyptians regrouped around the camp of Army Amun, while the Hittites reformed around the city of Kadesh.

On the third day of the battle Ramses lined his

forces up in battle order, harangued them for letting him down, and then publicly executed numbers of them to the astonishment of the Hittites on the east side of the river. He then marched south. The Hittites pursued the Egyptians as far south as Upi, the region of Damascus, where Muwatallis left his brother Hattusilis to reorder the region as Hittite territory. Amurru, however, remained in Egyptian hands and Ramses used this as his base for two more attacks against the Hittites, besieging Dapur (see ◊Dapur, battles of) and Tunip in 1271 and 1269 BC, after which the Hittites regained Amurru.

The outcome of the Battle of Kadesh was a victory for Muwatallis. He had assembled an army from across the Hittite Empire, from Dardaniya ('Trojans') and ◊Lukka in the west to Ugarit, Halpa, and Kargamis (see ◊Carchemish) in the southeast. He had retained Kadesh and eventually regained Amurru.

In 1259 BC the conflicts between Egypt and the Hittites came to an end with a treaty between ◊Ramses II and Hattusilis III, the Hittite king. Two versions of this treaty exist: the Hittite and the Egyptian. Later on Hattusilis married two of his daughters to Ramses and the monarchs kept up a regular correspondence. Kadesh remained firmly in the Hittite sphere of influence.

Kagenoma Japanese fortification in present-day Fukuoka prefecture, Japan, constructed in the 6th to 8th centuries. The site consists of rows of stones which follow the natural contours of the hillside and is approximately 600 m/1,970 ft by 300 m/985 ft in area.

Kagenoma is of the type referred to as *kōgoishi* ('god-enclosing stones'), originally believed to be a sacred site. It was conceivably both a military and administrative centre during the period which saw a centralized form of government begin to emerge as the native Ezo people were subjugated.

Kaifeng, Siege of fall of the Jin capital 1232–33 during the Mongol campaigns in China (see ◊China, Mongol campaigns in). A Mongol army besieged the city of Kaifeng in 1232. Although the defenders held them off, famine and plague eventually set in. In May of the following year, amid popular unrest, the Jin commander in chief seized power from the royal clan and surrendered to Subudei.

After the first siege of Zhongdu (see ◊Zhongdu, sieges of), the Jin moved their capital south to Kaifeng. When it was besieged the defenders resisted fiercely, using trebuchets and gunpowder weapons including ◊huoqiang and ◊zhen tian lei, and frequently sallying out. The Mongols could make little impression on the

walls, but the Jin were eventually forced to surrender. In spring 1233 the Jin emperor fled the city.

kaiken small Japanese dagger traditionally carried by ◊samurai women from the Kamakura period (1185–1333) onwards. It was used both as a defensive weapon and as a means of committing suicide by cutting the main vein in the neck.

Kalhu capital of Assyria 884–710 BC (modern Nimrud, biblical Kaleh), situated on the east bank of the river Tigris, 31 km/19 mi south of Mosul in present-day Iraq. It was founded by Shalmaneser I in about 1250 BC, and rebuilt (completed in 879 BC) by ◊Ashurnasirpal II as the capital of Assyria, which it remained until superseded by Nineveh in about 710 BC.

Rectangular in design, the site covers 2 sq km/1.25 sq mi, with Ashurnasirpal's palace and the temple and ziggurat of Ninurta dominating the southwest citadel. It was also a vast treasure house for booty captured by the Assyrian army. The arsenal in the southeast was built by Shalmaneser III.

The palace was decorated with scenes of Ashurnasirpal's wars, portraying in great detail battering rams and siege towers, chariotry, and the early use of paired cavalry, one rider directing both horses while the other rider shoots. Transportation of equipment (including chariots) by boat is clearly depicted, as are Assyrian soldiers floating across moats on inflated bladders to besiege fortified cities.

Kalka River, Battle of the encounter between the Mongol forces of ◊Genghis Khan and an alliance of Russian princes in May 1222, in which the Russians were defeated. The battle was a mere skirmish to the Mongols, who were on a great raid from Persia and around the Caspian Sea. They continued on their way and did not return to conquer Russia for 15 years.

Following the destruction of the Khwarasm Empire (modern Iran, Iraq, and part of western Turkestan), Genghis Khan sent his generals Jebe and Sübedei to attack northward. The Russians probably underestimated the threat, but mustered a force led by the princes of Galicia, Kiev, and Chernigov to oppose it.

Kamakura shogunate first ◊Warrior Government of Japan 1185–1333, established by ◊Minamoto Yoritomo at Kamakura in the Kantō region of eastern Japan. It was controlled almost excusively by Yorimoto until his death in 1199; his sons were little more than figurehead shoguns and real power passed to the ◊Hōjō family through Yoritomo's widow in 1219.

The strengths of Yoritomo's government lay in the lord/vassal relationship with his vassals (*gokenin*) and military governors (◊*shugo*). He also established an efficient administrative office (the ◊*samurai-dokoro*). The major weakness of the shogunate was that it was run by Yoritomo himself and neither of his two sons who succeeded him had his leadership qualities. Through his widow, Hōjō Masako, control therefore passed to the Hōjō family after the assassination of the second son Minamoto Sanetomo, and its leaders became hereditary shogunal regents (◊*shikken*).

The end of the Kamakura shogunate was brought about in 1333 by Ashikaga Takauji and ◊Nitta Yoshisada, both vassals of the government, who turned against their leaders and forced the ruling Hōjō *shikken* and his family to commit suicide, thereby plunging the country into years of fighting and political turmoil.

kama yari Japanese pick, or sickle, with a cutting edge of about 20 cm / 8 in, used as a weapon in close combat by non-samurai and by the trained assassins, the ninja. It was sometimes combined with a flail, the ◊*kusari gama*, to become a particularly lethal close combat weapon.

The aggressor would pull the opponent towards himself by the chains of the *kusari gama* and then use the *kama yari* to cut the victim's throat.

kamikaze (Japanese 'divine winds') typhoons, which on both occasions of the Mongol invasions of Japan (see ◊Japan, Mongol invasions of) destroyed the invading fleets. The Japanese belief that their land was protected by the gods was greatly strengthened by these natural catastrophes.

kampaku Japanese title for an imperial regent acting for an adult emperor. It was first used in the Heian period (794–1185), and was last used by ◊Toyotomi Hideyoshi (1537–1598) and his son Hidetsugu.

kandys Achaemenid Persian military cloak of Median origin. Worn by officers and elite cavalry, the *kandys* was a sign of status, often coloured with expensive dyes such as purple, lined with fur, and trimmed with leopard skin. Although it had sleeves, the *kandys* was usually worn as a cloak.

According to the Greek historian Xenophon, cavalrymen only put their arms through the sleeves for royal inspections.

Kangju campaign (*K'ang-chü* or *Sogdiana*) battle in 36 BC, in which the ◊Xiongnu leader ◊Chichi was finally defeated. Han Chinese commander Chen Tang, with 40,000 troops, attacked Chichi in Kangju (often translated as 'Sogdiana', though the region is really the Chu and Talas valleys in southern Kazakhstan, north of Sogdia

proper), killed Chichi and destroyed the city.

Kangju was fortified with an inner earth wall and an outer palisade with archers' towers and a moat. While infantry in ◊fish-scale formation defended the gates, Xiongnu cavalry attacked the Chinese but were driven off by crossbowmen. The Chinese then surrounded the city and drained the moat under cover of great shields. Their crossbowmen outshot the defending archers, and Chichi himself was wounded. At night the Chinese burned the palisade and forced the remaining defenders inside the inner wall. Kangju cavalry attempted to relieve the city but were driven off by a Chinese counterattack at dawn. The Chinese then stormed the city and set fire to it. Chichi was among the 1,518 killed and beheaded.

Kangra mountainous district in the north of the Punjab, India. Prior to the Muslim invasions it was ruled by ◊Rajputs of the Katoch clan, who had their capital in the town of Nagarkot, defended by the neighbouring fort of Kot Kangra.

The fort was seized by ◊Mahmud of Ghazni in 1009, who carried away immense quantities of booty. In 1044 the local hillmen, supported by a Rajput army led by Mahipala, King of Delhi, recovered the fort. In 1360, under attack from Firuz Tughluq, Sultan of Delhi, the raja of Kangra surrendered the fort. He was allowed to remain in possession of it, in return for payment of tribute.

Kanishka greatest of the ◊Kusana dynasty kings, who ruled from Bactria to the central Gangetic plains of India c. 120–60. He founded the city of Purushapura (modern Peshawar), promoted Buddhism, and planned to marry a Chinese Han princess but was defeated in battle near the Caspian Sea by the Chinese general Pan Ch'ao.

After becoming a convert to Buddhism he promoted this faith with great zeal, though paying little regard to its pacifist teachings. Eventually his own officers grew weary of his continual campaigns and smothered him with a quilt.

Kannō Disturbance series of military conflicts 1350–52 in Japan's Nambokuchō period when rivalries between Ashikaga Takauji and his younger brother Tadayoshi split the Muromachi shogunate.

kanrei deputy of the Japanese shogun, particularly in the Muromachi period (1333–1568) when the holder of the post played an important role in negotiating with the increasingly influential provincial military lords (◊*shugo daimyo*).

Kantara site of a mountain fortress with triple defensive walls in northern Cyprus. Originally a watchtower, Kantara was increasingly fortified, especially in the 14th century when a strong tower and gatehouse were added. When the Venetians held Cyprus they concentrated on defending the ports, dismantling the site in 1525.

kantō tachi early form of straight, single-edged Japanese ◊*tachi* (sword) blade with an annular pommel beaten from the same piece of steel as the blade, originating in the Kofun period (c. 300–645) and used by warriors until the beginning of the Heian period (794–1185). Many of these blades were imported from China.

kara Achaemenid Persian national army comprised of Persians who owed military service in exchange for ◊bow-land. It was not a standing force but would be called out for major battles.

The term is used in inscriptions by the Persian king Darius (I) the Great, contrasting the 'small Persian army which was in the palace', meaning permanent units such as the ◊Kinsmen, ◊spearbearers, and ◊Immortals, with the *kara* or 'people-army'.

Karakorum, Battle of battle near the Mongol capital, Karakorum, on 7 June 1372. A Mongol army of 100,000 men under Kökö Temür defeated a Ming Chinese army claimed to be 400,000 men, including 150,000 cavalry, under general Xu Da. The result was that the Chinese evacuated Mongolia, and ◊Zhu Yuanzhang gave up plans to conquer it.

After expelling the Mongols from China, Zhu Yuanzhang's Ming dynasty continued the offensive into Mongolia. In spring 1372 Xu Da and his army crossed the Gobi Desert into Mongolia in search of Kökö Temür's 100,000 men. In April the vanguard, under Lan Yu, defeated one Mongol division at the river Tula, but Kökö Temür avoided contact until inflicting a decisive defeat on Xu Da near Karakorum.

Karatepe modern name of ◊Azitawataya, Neo-Hittite fortress in Turkey.

kardakes (or *cardaces* or *kardaka*) Achaemenid Persian infantry in the 4th century BC. According to the Greek historian Strabo, *kardakes* were Persian noble youths undergoing military training who took part in the royal hunt and carried out police work. The term also refers to bodies of infantry.

In 367 BC the Persian general Autophradates fielded a large force of *kardakes*, and they were probably at Issus in 333 BC (see ◊Issus, Battle of 333 BC), although the Greek historian Arrian called the infantry there ◊hoplites.

Kastenbrust box-shaped breastplate fashionable in Germany from about 1420 to 1450. It preceded the fluted, 'Gothic' type of breastplate.

katakama yari alternative name for a ◊*hoko*, a Japanese spear.

katana Japanese long sword worn thrust through the belt with the cutting edge uppermost, attached to the sash with a ◊*sageo*. The blade and its appropriate fittings developed in the Muromachi period (1333–1568) when fighting moved more from cavalry to infantry and the ◊samurai adopted the ◊*daishō* (*katana* and *wakizashi*) as standard wear.

In the early days of its use the *katana* was known as the *uchigatana*.

katana kake Japanese sword stand or rack, in use from the Muromachi period (1333–1568) onwards. Etiquette demanded that the long sword be placed in a position of honour when entering a house. Some stands would accommodate both *katana* (long swords) and *wakizashi* (short swords).

katana zutsu large, ornate Japanese sword case, usually of lacquered wood, into which the blade, already housed in a plain wooden scabbard (*shirasaya*), was placed. It was popular in the Momoyama period (1568–1600), and was frequently decorated with the owner's family crest, or *mon*.

Katō Kiyomasa (1562–1611) Japanese ◊*daimyo* (regional military landholder) of the Momoyama period. He was one of two leading generals under Toyotomi Hideyoshi in the invasions of Korea 1592–97 (see ◊Korea, Japanese invasions of), and helped both Hideyoshi and ◊Tokugawa Ieyasu in their efforts to unify Japan.

He became *daimyo* of Kumamoto prefecture following his suppression of a major rebellion of discontented samurai in 1588. After Hideyoshi's death in 1598, he sided with Ieyasu, but remained loyal to the memory of his former master and attempted to protect the interests of Hideyoshi's son.

Kätzi, Ulrich (lived 15th century) Schwytzer captain in the Burgundian Wars, 1476–77. He was commander of the Schwyz contingent at Grandson (see ◊Grandson, Battle of) and Mürten (see ◊Mürten, Battle of) in 1476, and at Nancy (see ◊Nancy, Battle of) in 1477. His presence alongside the banner in the massed pikes at Grandson helped to maintain Swiss morale.

Kauthal, Battle of the first great battle, 1367, in the 200-year-long war between the Hindu kingdom of ◊Vijayanagar and the Bahmani Muslim sultanate. The Bahmani sultan Muhammad I was victorious over the Hindu king Bukka I. It was also the first battle in southern India in which both sides used guns.

The Muslim force consisted of 10,000 cavalry

and 30,000 foot soldiers under the sultan's cousin Khan Muhammad, while the Hindus mustered 40,000 cavalry and 500,000 foot soldiers under Bukka's general Mallinath. Both Muslim wings were routed and their commanders were killed, but Muslim superiority in artillery and cavalry carried the day and the Hindus fled when Mallinath was killed.

Kautilya (or *Canukya, Chanakya,* or *Visnugupta*) able and unscrupulous Brahman chief minister of the Indian emperor ◊Chandragupta Maurya. He is the attributed author of the *Arthashashtra/Treatise on Statecraft* (though the work is probably of a later date), which gives detailed advice on every aspect of administration, including the organization of armies and the conduct of war.

Unlike many Hindu texts which praise the concept of death in battle even in a lost cause, the *Arthashashtra* is severely practical, recommending that victorious kings conciliate the defeated as the most efficient way of securing their continued subjection, and teaching the defeated that a live dog is better than a dead lion.

Kaviani banner (*drafs-i-kavian*) Sassanian Persian national army standard. Traditionally the great leather apron of the legendary blacksmith Kavi, this was a leather sheet measuring 7 m/23 ft by 5 m/16 ft. It was decorated with coloured embroidery, jewels, and streamers and was carried by priests.

Kawanakajima, battles of territorial disputes of 1553–64 between the Japanese *daimyo* ◊Takeda Shingen and his neighbour Uesugi Kenshi during the final years of Japan's Sengoku period. There were at least five battles on the same site, the plain of Kawanakajima, in present-day Nagano prefecture.

The battles were instigated by Shingen's advances into strategic territories, but few were significant and they offered the two factions an opportunity to test their military strength.

keikō Japanese armour of the Kofun to Nara periods (c. 300–794) which consisted of linked iron or leather plates laced horizontally with cotton or leather and with an opening at the front. This style of flexible lamellar armour was imported into Japan from mainland Asia at around the same time as the horse.

As a successor to the earlier ◊*tanko* it was far more suitable to cavalry use and led to the eventual evolution of all later types of distinctively Japanese armours.

Kemmu Restoration brief restoration of direct imperial control of Japan 1333–36 by the Japanese emperor ◊Go-Daigo through the overthrow of the ◊Kamakura shogunate. He was assisted by two of the shogunate's generals, Ashikaga Takauji and Nitta Yoshisada, who sought their own ends.

Go-Daigo was ill-prepared for the realities of controlling what was effectively a warrior-based society which had held power for over 150 years. Takauji had long coveted the position of shogun and under various pretexts the emperor dispatched an army under Yoshisada to deal with him. The end result was the period of civil war under the ◊Northern and Southern Courts.

ken Japanese straight, double-edged blade that widens slightly towards the point. Although a weapon in its own right, it is primarily used in esoteric Buddhist ritual and is the blade held by the protective Buddhist deity Fudo Myō-ō, who was regarded in high esteem by the ◊samurai.

Kenilworth castle castle in England, 10 km/6 mi southwest of Coventry. Founded by Geoffrey de Clinton in 1115; he or his son built Caesar's Tower, the great keep. They also built the barbican and other defences and dammed the stream to form a lake and ditch.

Henry II, John, and Henry III later added to the castle, and in 1254 it was leased to Simon de Montford. It figured prominently in the ◊Barons' War of 1264–67 and was captured by Henry III in 1266 after a six-month siege. John of Gaunt built Mervyn's Tower (the Strong Tower), the banqueting hall, and the White Hall.

Kephissos, Battle of battle fought on 15 March 1311 in which the Catalan Company defeated and killed Walter, Duke of Athens, taking his territories. Following the murder of their leader, Roger de ◊Flor, the Catalan mercenaries had ravaged European Byzantium 1307–09 before taking service with Walter. When he tried to dismiss all but 500, the rest turned on him.

Walter had 700 knights and several thousand foot soldiers against the Catalans' 2,000 cavalry and 4,000 ◊*almugavar* infantry. Taking a defensive position in a marsh, and aided by the defection of their old comrades, the Catalans annihilated the Frankish cavalry charge.

Kerak-in-Moab castle castle in what is now Al-Karak, Jordan. The largest of the Transjordan Crusader castles, building began in 1142. It had its own port on the Dead Sea and was able to communicate by fire signal with Jerusalem, 80 km/50 mi away. Besieged many times, it was finally starved out.

kern medieval Irish lower-class warrior, unarmoured and carrying only a sword and javelins, used in the raiding and burning warfare of Ireland and also by the English kings in France.

kettle-hat plate helmet with a broad brim, synonymous with the French term *chapel de fer*. Kettle-hats appeared in medieval Europe about the end of the 12th century and continued in use throughout the medieval period. They were the characteristic helmets of ordinary soldiers, but were also used extensively by the knightly classes.

Khalid ibn al-Walid meaning 'Sword of God' Islamic general responsible for many of Islam's early victories 629–36. His many victories included the defeat of the followers of the rival prophet Musailima at Aqraba in 633 (see ◊Aqraba, Battle of) and the defeat of the Byzantines at Yarmuk in 636 (see ◊Yarmuk, Battle of), which led to the seizure of Syria.

Although initially one of the prophet ◊Muhammad's military opponents, Khalid converted to Islam in 629 and became its greatest general. He led raids into Persian Mesopotamia and Byzantine Syria and between 634 and 636 defeated several Byzantine armies, culminating in the decisive victory at Yarmuk. He had a reputation as a brilliant but ruthless warrior, somewhat unscrupulous and not particularly religious.

Khizr Khan, Nasir al-Mulk Muslim governor of Multan, in the Punjab, under the sultanate of Delhi, until ousted by a rival in 1396. During the invasion of India by Amir ◊Timur Leng (Tamerlane) of Samarkand in 1399, Khizr Khan joined Timur's camp and was appointed viceroy of the Delhi sultanate by Timur when he returned to Samarkand; Khizr Khan subsequently became the founder of the Sayyad dynasty of Delhi.

By a series of successful campaigns he reunited the Punjab with Delhi and re-established Muslim authority over the neighbouring ◊Rajput kingdoms. He assumed no royal title for himself, and continued to recognize the overlordship of Timur's son and successor Shah Rukh.

Khrisong Detsen (died 797) (or *Khri-song-lde-brtsan*) *bTsan-po* ('emperor') of Tibet 755–97. He exploited Chinese weakness in the aftermath of ◊An Lushan's rebellion to recover from the Chinese offensives of ◊Tang Xuanzong's reign and conquer wide areas of western China, and brought Tibetan power to its peak.

In 763 he briefly occupied Changan (see ◊Changan, capture of), despite ◊Guo Ziyi's efforts. In 786 Tibetan armies occupied the Ordos loop of the Yellow River and in 787 took Dunhuang, cutting China off from the ◊Four

Garrisons of the Tarim Basin silk-trade route, which they proceeded to occupy. Khrisong Detsen then fought a war against China's Uighur allies for possession of this region; an Uighur army defeated the Tibetans at Kucha in 792.

Khubilai Khan (1215–94) (or *Qubilai Khan*) Mongol Great Khan from 1260, grandson of ◊Genghis Khan, and first emperor of the Yuan dynasty of China from 1271. Although he expanded Mongol power in China and southeast Asia, his rule became increasingly Chinese-based and the other Mongol khanates drifted towards independence.

As a prince he held territory in north China and fought in the Mongol campaigns in China (see ◊China, Mongol campaigns in), winning the Battle of the Jinsha River in 1253 (see ◊Jinsha River, Battle of) and campaigning against the Song dynasty. On the death of his brother Mangu, Khubilai was proclaimed Great Khan but was opposed by another brother, Arigh-böke, based in the Mongolian steppes. Khubilai's troops defeated him at Shimultai in 1261, occupying Mongolia. Arigh-böke was gradually worn down and surrendered in 1264. Other steppe-based Mongol rivals could not seriously challenge Khubilai's power.

Khubilai put down ◊Li Tan's rebellion of 1262 and completed the conquest of China. He brought the heterogeneous Mongol-Chinese armies under central control, organizing the Menggu ◊*jun*, Han *jun*, and ◊*xinfu jun*, and eventually dispensing with ◊*gantaolu* irregulars. As Chinese emperor he aimed to extend Chinese control throughout eastern Asia; hence the Mongol invasions of Champa (see ◊Champa, Mongol invasion of), Japan (see ◊Japan, Mongol invasions of), and ◊Yikomusu's expedition to Java – none of which were successful, though Vietnam, Champa, and Java paid tribute.

khud Persian term for a helmet, often expanded to *kolah khud*.

ki another name for ◊*saku*, a form of early Japanese palisade or stockade.

Kidwelly castle castle in Wales, 29 km/18 mi northwest of Swansea. The structure began as a wooden ◊motte-and-bailey castle in the late 11th century built by a local baron, but was rebuilt in masonry 1280–1300.

Concentric in form, though of an unusual semicircular shape, it had a square inner ward with four towers, a chapel, and residence. One wall of the structure was then extended in both directions to form the upright of the D, with a gatehouse at each end to which the semicircular curtain wall with its three towers was anchored. The straight side was bounded by a steep drop to the river Gwendraeth, and a ditch cut from the river surrounds the remainder of the work.

Kildrummy castle castle in Grampian, Scotland, 48 km/30 mi west of Aberdeen. Built around 1215 on the site of an earlier timber ◊motte-and-bailey work, this castle is D-shaped, with round towers at each end of the upright part, a double-towered gateway at the centre of the curve, and half-round towers midway along the curtain walls. The usual domestic buildings were built against the straight wall and the entrance was later improved by the addition of a barbican.

Kim Yusin (595–673) (or *Kim Yushin*) Korean general of the ◊Three Kingdoms of Korea state of Silla. In 629 he distinguished himself leading ◊*sodang* troops in the capture of a fortress in the northern Korean kingdom of Koguryo. In the Tang campaigns in Korea (see ◊Korea, Tang Chinese wars in) he and the Chinese general ◊Su Dingfang took Sabi, the capital of Paekche, in 660 (see ◊Sabi, Siege of). He defended Silla during the war against Koguryo in 668 and then served against China.

Kinsmen Achaemenid Persian household cavalry regiment of 1,000 men. They were the mounted equivalent of the ◊spear-bearers and held the honorary rank of royal kinsman.

Two such regiments appear in records of the Persian king Xerxes' invasion of Greece in 480 BC, one regiment at Gaugamela, and they also accompanied the king on other campaigns. Their Persian name may have been *xvaka* or *huvaka*, and it is likely that the *euakai* cavalry incorporated by Alexander the Great into the Macedonian army were probably Kinsmen.

Kirby Muxloe castle castle in England, 6 km/4 mi west of Leicester. This brick-built castle was begun in 1480 by Lord Hastings, who was already building ◊Ashby-de-la-Zouch castle, also in Leicester. All that now remains is the gatehouse, one tower and the water defences.

It was planned as a rectangle, with square towers at each corner, half-towers on three of the walls, and a turreted gatehouse on the fourth side. An artificial lake fed from a nearby stream surrounded it, and the design was unusual for its period in being liberally provided with gunports. However, Lord Hastings fell foul of his king and was executed in 1483 before the castle was completed, and his widow stopped the work.

Kirta possibly the founder of the Mitannian Empire, which challenged the powers of New Kingdom Egypt and the Hittites in the Late Bronze Age. Kirta is known only from a Mitannian 'dynastic seal' and an epic story from

the Syrian seaport of Ugarit (modern Ras Shamra).

The dynastic seal of 'Shuttarna, son of Kirta, king of Maitani' has been dated as early as 1525 BC, an age when the Hittites had lost the northern Syria gained by ◊Hattusilis I and ◊Mursilis I and when Egypt was fighting to regain control over the Delta from the ◊Hyksos. The 'Kirta Epic' – a legendary story discovered at Ugarit – is about Kirta obtaining an heir to the throne of his (unnamed) city and his journey to find one. The mention of horses and the cities of Tyre and Sidon fits in with the Mitannian expansion into the Levant which was challenged by Pharaoh Tuthmosis III at Megiddo in 1458 BC (see ◊Megiddo, Battle of).

kite shield slightly convex shield with a rounded top and elongated bottom to protect the legs of foot soldiers or mounted knights, used in western Europe during the 11th–12th centuries. The kite shield had a handgrip and a neck strap so that it could be slung over the shoulder or across the back.

Klappvisier visor for a ◊basinet (European knight's helmet) attached by a hinged bar to two studs at the centre of the forehead. It appeared in Germany about 1360–70 and continued in use until about 1410, principally in Germany but also in other parts of Europe.

Knaresborough castle castle in England, northeast of Harrogate, Yorkshire, built by Serlo de Bergh shortly after the Conquest. The murderers of St Thomas á Becket found shelter here for a year and Richard II was imprisoned here also. It was the residence of Piers Galveston, Henry III (1216–72), and John of Gaunt (1340–99).

Knecht medieval German 'lad' originally a squire or military servant, later extended to mean a knight (see ◊Landsknecht).

Knights Hospitaller (or *Hospitallers*) order of Crusading knights: see ◊Military Order.

Knights Templar (or *Templars*) order of Crusading knights: see ◊Military Order.

Knollys, Sir Robert (lived 14th century) English knight who fought in the ◊Hundred Years' War and became master of Edward the Black Prince's household. He was granted estates in Brittany, Wiltshire, Kent, and Norfolk, and made captain of ◊Fougères castle. He fought at the battles of Mauron in 1352 (see ◊Mauron, Battle of) and Poitiers (see ◊Tours, Battle of) in 1356, and went on several ◊*chevauchées*. He took employment with the Free Companies; his Grand Company held 40 castles in the Loire Valley.

Knossos Middle and Late Bronze Age settlement, 8 km/5 mi south of present-day Iraklion, Crete. Knossos is one of the main cities of what is known as the Minoan civilization (a modern name derived from the legend of King Minos), but its people were known as *Keftiu* by the Egyptians, and recognized as great traders in their sea-going *Keftiu* ships. It was later conquered by the Mycenaeans from the Greek mainland and became the dominant city of the island.

Knossos rose to prominence between 2000 and 1700 BC – the Old Palace Period – with the construction of a huge palace, similar to the Cretan palaces at Phaistos and Mallia and the Arzawan palace at modern Beycesultan in southwest Turkey, indicative of the growth of a powerful nobility. At all these sites the megaron (hall) with a central hearth and four supporting pillars is a distinctive feature.

During the Late Bronze Age, 1600 to 1180 BC – the New Palace Period – the palace was rebuilt and enlarged, constructed around a large court and covering an area of 2 ha/5 acres. Its complex layout gave rise to the Greek myth of the Minotaur and the labyrinth. It was surrounded by an inner city and a much larger outer city with a parameter of 4 km/2.5 mi. It was occupied by Mycenaeans from the Greek mainland around 1400 BC, who have left written evidence in the Linear B tablets of a much more warlike and centrally controlled society, listing chariots, corselets, arrows, and slingshot.

kōgai type of Japanese bodkin or skewer generally found in a pocket of the scabbard of a ◊*wakizashi* (short sword). It often bears the crest of the owner, and one suggested use is that of marking the severed head of an enemy on the battlefield by sticking it in his ear.

Other uses include arranging the hair and, when in the split form known as *wari-kōgai,* they could be used as chopsticks.

kogatana small Japanese knife kept in a side pocket of the scabbard of a sword, in use from the Muromachi period (1333–1568). See also ◊*kozuka.*

Koko Nor, Battle of (678) battle in 678 in which Tibet defeated Tang China at the Koko Nor, a large saltwater lake in north China. The Tang Chinese bureaucrat-general Li Jingxuan was outmanoeuvred and trapped against a canal, with the Tibetan army on a ridge above him. His advance guard was surrounded and wiped out. Only a night attack on the Tibetan camp by 500 men covered Li's withdrawal.

Koko Nor, Battle of (726–27) battle 726–27 in which Tang China defeated Tibet. Tibetans raid-

ing into Gansu in winter were pursued by the Tang Chinese governor Wang Junchuo. He led his troops across the frozen lake Koko Nor and caught the Tibetans as they crossed the river Dafei, capturing their baggage and many men.

Köln-Deutz fort (Roman *Divitia*) late Roman fort built to protect the Rhine bridge at Cologne in modern Germany and serve as a bulwark for the important city on the opposite bank. It was constructed by the emperor ◊Constantine (I) the Great.

The fort was square in shape (140 × 140 m/460 × 460 ft) and protected by 14 round corner and interval towers. It was provided with gates only on the east and west sides, the west giving access to the bridge.

Komaki Nagakute campaign series of battles and military campaigns of the succession struggles in Japan in 1584 following the assassination of the military warlord ◊Oda Nobunaga. On one side were the forces of the warlord ◊Toyotomi Hideyoshi, on the other those of Nobunaga's son Nobukatsu and of the warrior leader Tokugawa Ieyasu. Peace was agreed by the end of the year.

Following Hideyoshi's rapid rise in power, Nobukatsu and Ieyasu formed a alliance against him. After minor victories on both sides, and a major one by Ieyasu at Nagakute, the war became little more than a series of irritating skirmishes and it was seen by all parties that peace was the best measure, at least in the short term.

kondei (Japanese 'able-bodied young men' or 'stalwart youth') Japanese militia formed during the Nara period (710–94), made up of the young sons of noble families with skills in archery and horsemanship who were sent to serve in the provinces as an exemption against taxes. The system was abandoned in the 10th century.

kontos term generally thought to mean a pike or heavy spear, used by Greek writers in the Roman period. The word was used so widely that it is often impossible translate: the Greek historian Arrian, writing in the 2nd century AD clearly uses it for the ◊*pilum.*

kopis (or *machaira*) single-edged sword with an elongated S-shaped cutting edge, found in southern Europe from the 7th century BC. The non-cutting edge was normally in the form of a long regular curve and the blade was normally about 3 cm/1.2 in wide just below the hilt, increasing to as much as 7 cm/2.75 in wide before curving back to form the point. The handle was normally in the form of a bird.

The earliest examples (7th–8th century BC) come from Italy and are huge weapons, with a blade length of 55–60 cm/21.5–23.5 in, heavily weighted towards the point. The sword first appeared on Greek vase paintings in the 5th century BC. By the 3rd century BC the *kopis* as used in Greece and Italy had evolved into a much slimmer, sabrelike weapon. In Spain it developed into a much smaller cut-and-thrust sword (◊*falcata*), with a blade length of 40–50 cm/15.75–19.7 in.

Korea, Han Chinese conquest of

conquest by the Chinese emperor ◊Han Wudi in 109–108 BC of Choson, an ancient kingdom in northern Korea ruled since 195 BC by descendants of a Chinese adventurer. The conquest was part of his general expansionist policy and to forestall Choson's alliance with the Xiongnu.

In 109 an army of 60,000 under Xun Zhi and a fleet carrying 5,000 troops under Yang Pu converged on Choson. Xun's army was held by a firm Korean defence, so when Yang's men disembarked they were unsupported and were crushed. The following year Xun defeated the Korean army, linked up with Yang's survivors, and besieged the capital for several months, eventually forcing it to surrender.

China only ever controlled northwestern Korea, but kept that foothold until the ◊Three Kingdoms of Korea period.

Korea, Japanese invasions of

invasions of Korea 1592–97 led by the Japanese military leader ◊Toyotomi Hideyoshi, who planned to conquer Korea, move into China, and install the Japanese emperor in Beijing. Hideyoshi himself would then rule all of Japan, Korea, and China and be able to reward his followers with even greater domains.

Initially he negotiated with the Koreans for passage for his troops into China and it is believed that their refusal was the impetus to launch the first invasion of 1592. The Japanese armies made rapid advances but were overextended and had severe supply problems as their fleet was harassed by the Korean navy. By 1593 a stalemate had been reached and peace negotiations began, but without satisfactory conclusion. In 1597 Hideyoshi relaunched his attacks on Korea. After many initial victories against both the Chinese and Korean forces an impasse was again reached.

Hideyoshi died in September 1598, leaving instructions that all troops be withdrawn from Korea. Local truces ensued while the Japanese forces withdrew, but during the withdrawal a huge combined Chinese and Korean army and fleet decimated the returning Japanese forces.

Korea, Sui Chinese wars in

series of wars fought 598–614 between the Sui Chinese and Koguryo, northernmost of the ◊Three Kingdoms of Korea, which felt threatened by the emperor ◊Sui Wendi's unification of China and started the wars. The Chinese defeat contributed to the fall of the Sui and their replacement by ◊Tang Gaozu.

Koguryo first attacked Chinese Liaoxi in 598; the Chinese counterattacked across the river Liao but were defeated. Wendi's son, Sui Yangdi, was urged by the general and minister ◊Pei Ju to conquer Koguryo. After massive conscription, Wendi and Pei Ju invaded with an army of allegedly 1,130,000 men. The engineer ◊Yuwen Kai bridged the Liao, and the Sui army besieged Liaodong fortress. As the siege dragged on, Wendi sent a detachment to march directly on the Koguryo capital, but they were defeated by the Koguryo general Ulchi Mundok at the river Salsu in 612 (see ◊Salsu River, Battle of the). Wendi evacuated Koguryo as the late summer rains threatened to bog his army down. Attacks in 613 and 614 were also defeated.

Korea, Tang Chinese wars in

series of wars fought 644–96 between China and the Korean kingdoms, in which China was unsuccessful until it formed an alliance with Silla, the southeastern kingdom of the ◊Three Kingdoms of Korea. The allies destroyed the two other kingdoms of Koguryo and Paekche; China and Silla then fought and Silla won, uniting Korea.

In 644 the emperor ◊Tang Taizong invaded Koguryo. He captured Liaodong fortress and besieged Anshizheng, defeating relief forces, but could not take the city and withdrew (see ◊Anshizheng, Battle of). In 660 Tang and Silla attacked the southwestern kingdom, Paekche. The Chinese general Su Dingfang and Silla general Kim Yusin captured the capital Sabi (see ◊Sabi, Siege of). Resistance continued; in 663 a Japanese expedition was defeated at Churyu (see ◊Churyu, Battle of), and Paekche was pacified by 664.

Meanwhile, China and Silla attacked Koguryo in 662. Su Dingfang attacked by sea and besieged the capital without success. In 667 the Chinese general Li Shiji overran Koguryo's northern territory, then marched south to besiege Pyongyang with other Chinese and Silla forces, capturing the city in 668.

China organized these conquests as provinces, treating Silla also as conquered. Silla encouraged revolts in Koguryo, and in 671 attacked and conquered former Paekche. By 676 the Chinese were expelled from Korea south of the river Taedong. They held former northern Koguryo until 696, when Koreans and Manchurian tribes rebelled and set up the new kingdom of Parhae (Bohai).

Koryo frontier fortifications organized system of defences for northern frontier of the territories of the Koryo dynasty, in Korea, threatened by the Khitan and Jurchen of Manchuria. The frontier area was heavily fortified in the 11th and 12th centuries with two major systems of forts and the 'Long Wall', walling off the Korean peninsula from sea to sea.

The founder of the Koryo dynasty ◊Wang Kon occupied territory on the Khitan border, and after a Khitan invasion in 993, the kingdom of Koryo occupied territory further northwest, between the river Ch'ongch'on and the east bank of the Yalu, and built the 'Six Garrison Settlements East of the River' to hold it, confronting Khitan forts on the far bank. The Kuju campaign of 1018 (see ◊Kuju, Battle of) showed that the Khitan could bypass these forts, so between 1033 and 1044 the stone 'Long Wall' was built, defending the Korean peninsula against both the Khitan and the rising Jurchen power.

Shortly before ◊Wanyen Aguda united the Jurchen, the Korean general Yun Kwan led the new ◊pyolmuban forces in 1107 to seize territory in the northeast, beyond the Long Wall, from the Jurchen, and established the 'Nine Forts' to hold it.

koshigatana Japanese term for a small dagger or short sword of the Heian period (794–1185), usually lacking a sword guard (◊*tsuba*).

Kossovo, Battle of battle fought 17–19 October 1448 in Serbia between the Ottoman sultan Murad II (1404–51) and the Hungarian regent János ◊Hunyadi, resulting in the loss of Constantinople (modern Istanbul, Turkey) to the Turks in 1453.

Hunyadi led 24,000 men including 10,000 Wallachians, but should have waited to join up with the Albanian chief Scanderbeg's troops before confronting Murad's force of 40,000. His German handgunners fought well in the centre, but when their ammunition ran out and the Wallachians deserted, the Christians were overwhelmed by the combination of Janissary (standing Ottoman Turkish army) foot soldiers and timariot cavalry on the wings.

kote Japanese armoured sleeve with integral gauntlets, in use from the Nara period (710–94) onwards. The *kote* generally comprised mail attached to a textile backing with small solid plates of varying shapes attached to provide additional protection for the upper arm, elbows, forearms, and back of the hand.

kozane Japanese term for small plates of leather or iron, usually lacquered to provide effective weather proofing, which were laced or bound together to form flexible armour. They were used from the Nara period (710–94) onwards.

kozuka strictly, the Japanese term for the flat rectangular handle of the small knife kept in the scabbard of a sword (◊*kogatana*) from the Muromachi period (1333–1568) onwards, but commonly used to refer to both the handle and blade.

Krak des Chevaliers castle crusader castle in northern Syria protecting the inland route from the Tripoli coast. Built from around 1115 onwards, it became the principal garrison of the Knights Hospitaller (see ◊Military Order) in the 12th and 13th centuries and was frequently besieged by the Saracens. Constantly improved, it represents the best fortress technology of its day. It was finally overcome in 1271, by subterfuge rather than strength, and has remained in an excellent state of preservation.

Krishna III (939–968) eleventh king (939/940–968/970) of the Rashtrakuta dynasty of the Deccan. Whereas his predecessors had expanded their territories to the northwest, Krishna marched southwards into the Tamil lands, defeating and killing the Chola king ◊Parantaka I in 953.

Kucha, capture of capture in 648 of Kucha, a powerful trading city in the Tarim basin in modern southern Xinjiang, by a Tang Chinese army under the Turkish general Ashina She-er, with 100,000 mostly Turkish troops. Kucha subsequently became one of the Tang ◊Four Garrisons.

Attacking unexpectedly from the north, Ashina sent a decoy force of 1,000 cavalry to engage the 50,000 Kuchean troops. The decoy force retreated in a typical nomad feigned flight, and when the Kucheans pursued they were ambushed by the rest of the Tang army and defeated. The king fled and the city fell. He returned soon after with Turkish troops of his own and retook the town, killing the governor Ashina had left behind. The Chinese, however, soon recovered it.

Kuju, Battle of battle fought in 1018 in which the Koryo state in Korea defeated the invading Khitan. The invasion army was wiped out, and this was the last Khitan attack on Korea.

Bypassing the Korean frontier fortifications, the Khitan bridged the river Yalu and Xiao Paiya led 100,000 ◊*ordo* troops, conscript levies, and others into Korea. Kang Kamch'an, with 200,000 men, defeated them at Anju, breaking a dyke to flood the Khitan army and then launching a cavalry ambush. Xiao's retreat was cut off, so he resolved to advance south and attack the capital, Kaesong. He was unable to breach the city's strong defences and withdrew. On the way back, Kang Kamch'an defeated Xiao at Kuju, surrounding and destroying the Khitan army.

Kumaragupta I (died 453) fourth king of the Gupta dynasty, ruler of ◊Magadha 415–53. In the latter part of his reign his empire was invaded by the *Hunas* or ◊White Huns.

Kumbhalghar fortress in Rajasthan, India, built on a steep rocky crag and defended by a series of concentric walls with bastions, battlements, and heavily protected gates approached through winding passageways. The earliest fortifications are attributed to Samprati, a Jain prince of the 2nd century BC.

Kumbhalghar takes its name from Khumba Raja, one of the greatest ◊Rajput rulers of Chitor. He constructed or improved a total of 84 fortresses during his reign (1433–68), of which Kumbhalghar was the finest after Chitor.

Kunyang, Battle of (or *K'un-yang*) battle on 7 July 23, in which the Chinese rebel Green Woodsmen defeated imperial commander Wang Mang's army in Kunyang (in modern Henan) (see ◊Green Woodsmen, rebellion of the). The battle decisively weakened Wang Mang, and the prestige that rebel leader Liu Xiu gained would contribute to his eventually winning the throne as ◊Han Guangwudi.

Wang Mang mobilized an alleged 420,000 men (his propaganda claimed 1 million) under military leaders Wang Yi and Wang Xun, who besieged 90,000 rebels in Kunyang. Liu Xiu escaped and recruited troops outside. On 7 July he staged a surprise attack on the siege lines with 3,000 troops, killing Wang Xun and routing part of his army. The defenders of Kunyang sallied out to join him and the besieging army broke and fled. Many were killed trying to cross a river swollen by rainstorms.

kura Japanese saddle, generally made from four pieces of wood laced together and frequently decorated with lacquer and mother-of-pearl inlay. The style has remained basically unchanged from the Heian period (794–1185).

Kurigalzu II Kassite great king of Babylonia 1332–1308 BC. He conquered Elam and Susa, and his reign inaugurated a renaissance of Kassite culture that lasted until the reign of Kashtiliash IV (1232–1225 BC).

Kurigalzu was the son (or possibly the grandson) of Burna-Buriash II (1359–1333 BC), whose daughter married the Hittite king Suppiluliumas I and whose son married the daughter of the Assyrian king ◊Ashur-uballit I. When Burna-Buriash died in 1333 BC his son and heir was killed by an usurper, but Ashur-uballit intervened to place Kurigalzu on the throne. Kurigalzu defeated Hurbatila, the Elamite king, in about 1330 BC and went on to conquer the eastern lands of Susiana and Elam, sacking the capital city of Susa.

kuriltai assembly of Mongol chieftains at which military campaigning decisions were made. *Kuriltais* were also used for the election of a new khan.

The death of Khan Ogedei in 1241 led to the recall of Mongol forces engaged in conquering Eastern Europe for a *kuriltai* to find a successor. This withdrawal probably saved Western Christendom from invasion.

Kusana dynasty family of Turkic conquerors of the Shaka (Scyth) and Indo-Hellenic kingdoms of Bactria and northwestern India, who established a kingdom which lasted from about AD 50–250 and which at its peak, under ◊Kanishka, extended from central Asia to the lower Ganges in India. In decline by AD 176, the dynasty was finally overthrown by the Sassanians.

The Kusanas, an Indo-European-speaking nomadic people of central Asian descent, were forced from China when the Great Wall was extended west by the Han dynasty. A branch of the Kusanas, the Yueh-chi or Tokharians, displaced the Shakas from the area between the rivers Oxus (modern Amu Darya) and Jaxartes (Syr-Darya) and later moved into Bactra 130–126 BC, destroying the Shaka and Indo-Hellenic kingdoms there. Under Chief Kujula Kadphises (reigned AD 15–55) the Yueh-chi Kusanas moved into northwest India and conquered the last surviving Shaka, Pahlavi (Parthian), and Indo-Hellenic kingdoms there, establishing a capital city at Purushapura (modern Peshawar).

kusari gama Japanese flail consisting of two small, heavy weights connected by a length of chain, used by non-samurai from the Muromachi period (1333–1568) onwards. It was sometimes used in combination with the ◊*kama yari*.

kusazuri Japanese term for the tassels which hung from the main part of a suit of armour (the *dō*) to protect the upper thighs, used from the Heian period (794–1185) onwards. The ◊*kusazuri* comprised linked iron or leather plates (◊*kozane*) which were formed into between four and nine overlapping vertical strips.

Kusunoki Masashige (died 1336) Japanese warrior and military tactician who assisted the emperor ◊Go-Daigo in the ◊Kemmu Restoration. In the early stages of the emperor's power struggles, Masashige kept the forces of the Kamakura shogunate at bay through guerrilla tactics.

Kutna Hora, Battle of battle for the town of Kutna Hora fought on 21–22 January 1422 during the Hussite Wars between the ◊Hussites under Jan ◊Zizka of Tracnor and King ◊Sigismund of Bohemia's troops. The Hussites were outnumbered and surrounded, but fought their way out.

Kutna Hora, a Bohemian Catholic mining town, had been recently taken over by the Hussites. Because of its strategic importance Sigismund marched to its relief. Zizka opposed him with his usual wagon fort formation outside the town, and fended off the first attacks, but the miners, aided by royalist troops, broke into the town by the far gate, rendering Zizka's position untenable. Under cover of darkness he moved his forces onto the top of Kasik Hill. Sigismund did not risk an attack, and, opening with his artillery at midnight on 22 January, Zizka broke through the lines and escaped to Kolin.

kuwagata horn or hoe-like crest found on the front of Japanese helmets from the Heian period (794–1185). These crests became particularly large and ornate from the Nambokuchō period (1336–92) until the Momoyama period (1578–1600).

Kwanggaeto (lived 4th–5th centuries) king of Koguryo 391–413, in the ◊Three Kingdoms of Korea period, whose victorious campaigns dominated the Korean peninsula. He repeatedly drove off Japanese attacks, and also conquered forest tribes in Manchuria and took Liaodong on the Chinese border from the Murong ◊Xianbei.

In 396 he marched against the southwestern kingdom of Paekche, which had allied with the Japanese against Kwanggaeto's ally Silla. He took 18 Paekche fortified towns and captured the capital, withdrawing with hostages. The Japanese attacked Silla again, so in 400 Kwanggaeto sent 50,000 troops to Silla's assistance, chasing the Japanese out and recovering the Silla capital. In 404 and again in 407 the Japanese attacked Koguryo itself, but were beaten off.

kwanggun (Korean 'resplendent army') Korean provincial regular forces under the Koryo dynasty (981–1392), distinct from ◊Two Guards and Six Divisions.

The *kwanggun* were originally private forces under local gentry who had supported the founder of the Koryo dynasty ◊Wang Kon, but their organization was regularized under central government control in 947. They became provincial garrison forces, those in frontier provinces being assault and support units on a permanent combat footing while interior provincial troops were police and *chongyonggun* militia.

Kyanzittha (lived 11th–12th centuries) (or *Kalancacsa*) Burmese king of Pagan 1084–1111. He was ◊Aniruddha's general or, according to later sources, his son, but fell out with him and was banished. Aniruddha's son Sawlu (Co Lu) became king in 1044, and Kyanzittha assisted him against the rebellion of Ngayaman Kan, governor of the Mons of Pegu. Kyanzittha became king after the rebels killed his brother, and had a largely peaceful reign reconciling the Mons to Burmese rule.

In one battle during Ngayaman Kan's rebellion, Sawlu and Kyanzittha were lured into a marsh to attack a decoy army of stick-figures; the royal elephants got bogged down and the army fled. After Ngayaman Kan captured and killed Sawlu, Kyanzittha assembled an army and defeated and killed Ngayaman Kan with little difficulty in a battle near Pagan in 1084.

Kyrenia castle crusader promontory castle rebuilt as an artillery fort on the side facing land in Girne, northern Cyprus. The original castle was developed under the Lusignan kings following the establishment of the dynasty by King Guy in 1191. It was taken by the Genoese following a long siege in 1374. Its present appearance reflects 16th-century Venetian modernization.

Kyriell, Sir Thomas (died 1461) English commander in the ◊Hundred Years' War who became captain of Gisors and lieutenant of Calais. He was responsible for assembling a force and unsuccessfully attempting to save Normandy in 1449. He sailed for Cherbourg with 2,500 men in 1450, and attacked and took Valognes. At Formigny the English were beaten and Kyriell was captured.

He was released and in 1457 fought off a French attack on Sandwich. A Yorkist supporter in the Wars of the Roses (see ◊Roses, Wars of the), he was executed as a traitor after the defeat of the Yorkists under the Earl of Warwick at the battle of St Albans (see ◊St Albans, Battle of 1461).

kyūdō Japanese 'the way of the bow' Japanese term for the study and practice of archery. The bow was the traditional weapon of the mounted ◊samurai who would be trained in the formal aspects of its use from an early age.

Labienus, Titus Atius (100–45 BC) Roman soldier who was Julius Caesar's ablest subordinate in Gaul but fought against him in the civil war (see ◊Civil Wars, Roman Republican). In Gaul he was trusted with the largest and most responsible independent commands. He may, however, have been associated with Pompey the Great from the beginning of his career. He supported Pompey at Pharsalus (see ◊Pharsalus, Battle of), Ruspina (see ◊Ruspina, Battle of), and Thapsus (see ◊Thapsus, Battle of) before being killed in the aftermath of Munda (see ◊Munda, Battle of).

Lachish fortified city (modern Tell ed Duweir) of Judah that was besieged by the Assyrian king ◊Sennacherib in 701 BC and later destroyed by ◊Nebuchadnezzar of Babylonia in 589 BC.

First fortified about 1750 BC, Lachish became a seat of government about 1000 BC during the reign of King ◊David of Judah. It was refortified by his grandson Rehoboam with a 6-m-/20-ft-wide wall enclosing a 20-ha/50-acre site. During the reign of Hezekiah the city fell to the Assyrians, and the site was razed after being besieged by the Babylonians under Nebuchadnezzar.

lac tuong ancient Vietnamese military aristocracy of the Van Lang (about 700–220 BC) and Au Lac (about 220–180 BC) kingdoms. They and their *lac hau* civil equivalents retained local authority even after the conquest of ◊Zhao Tuo until the defeat of ◊Trung Trac's rebellion.

Lade, Battle of decisive sea battle between the Persians and the rebel Greeks of Asia Minor, about 494 BC, effectively ending the Ionian Revolt. It was fought off what was then a small island called Lade, now a small hill in the alluvial plain of the Turkish river Maeander, northwest of the ancient city of Miletus.

The Greeks, commanded by Dionysius of Phocaea, mustered only 353 triremes against the Persian 600. Dionysius drilled them in a manoeuvre known as the ◊*diekplous* until they refused to train any more. Worse still, when the

battle began 49 of the 60 Samian ships fled, along with all 70 ships from Lesbos and most of the others. The 100 ships from Chios fought gallantly, allegedly using the *diekplous*, but were overwhelmed.

laeti Barbarian military settlers (or prisoners) who were allocated land in Roman territory and were required to provide recruits for the Roman army.

Lahore fortified city on the river Ravi, Punjab, in present-day Pakistan, first recorded in 630. It was taken by the Muslim invader ◊Mahmud of Ghazni in 1020, fell to the Mongols in 1241, was sacked by ◊Timur Leng (Tamerlane) in 1398, and was rebuilt by Mubarak Shah, Sultan of Delhi, in 1422.

In 1432 Bahlol Khan Lodi, governor of Lahore, marched to Delhi and founded the line of Lodi sultans who ruled until the rise of the Mogul Empire early in the 16th century.

Lake Peipus, Battle of battle fought on 5 April 1242 on a frozen Russian lake in which the Russian leader ◊Alexander Nevsky defeated Danish and German crusaders, including Teutonic Knights (see ◊Military Order), who were operating along the southern Baltic and had attacked Novgorod.

Alexander met the crusaders at Raven's Rock, the narrowest crossing point between the two frozen lakes of Peipus and Pskov. The ice was banked and uneven, providing good cover. The crusaders deployed Danish knights on the left, Teutonic knights in the centre, and Livonians on the right, supported by Estonian foot soldiers. The Russians were fewer and more lightly armed, but their right flank horse-archers forced back the Danes, causing the Estonian foot soldiers to flee. The German knights were left isolated and suffered heavily.

Lake Regillius, Battle of battle fought in Tusculan territory in 496 BC between the Romans and the Latini tribes of Italy. The Roman victory restored Roman supremacy over the region and re-established the Latin League (an alliance of the Latini tribes and

Rome) as a defensive military alliance, the core of Rome's military policy in the early republic.

The precise reasons why war broke out between Rome and the Latins are unknown, but in 496 BC Rome was tense enough to appoint a dictator for the first time. In the same year the two armies met at Lake Regillius. Both sides repeatedly gained and lost the upper hand until the Romans ordered their cavalry to dismount and join the infantry in a final desperate assault that broke the Latin lines.

Lake Trasimene, Battle of battle fought in 217 BC between the Roman army of Gaius ◊Flaminius and the Carthaginian army of ◊Hannibal the Great during the Second Punic War (see ◊Punic War, Second). Hannibal lured the Romans into an ambush beside Lake Trasimene in central Italy and inflicted a resounding defeat.

Hannibal bypassed Flaminius' army, which was blocking his route, and forced it to follow him to keep him under observation. The Romans kept to a safe distance, affording Hannibal time to choose an ambush site and deploy his troops. As Flaminius led his army along the narrow shore of the lake, tricked into believing that Hannibal was still in front, the Carthaginians fell on the Roman army from the sides and trapped it against the lake. Some 15,000 Romans were killed and an equal number were captured; only 1,500 Carthaginians were lost.

Lake Vadimon, Battle of battle fought in 283 BC in the Tiber Valley, 80 km/50 mi north of Rome, between the Romans and an alliance of Etruscans and Boii, the outcome of which would suppress the Etruscan revolt. Their defeat at Lake Vadimon and a further defeat the following year induced the Boii to sign a peace treaty that would last 50 years. The Etruscans, who did not sign the treaty, lost their allies and were no longer able to oppose the Romans.

lambrequin piece of fabric worn over a helm in medieval Europe as a covering. The term is a 19th-century heraldic one.

lamellar armour type of armour made of scales, usually of leather or iron, pierced with pairs of holes and laced together into strips with leather laces which were then laced together with leather or silk laces to form complete body coverings. Lamellar armour was in use in eastern Asia from about AD 400 and throughout Asia and the Muslim world by about 1000. It spread into Scandinavia, and was still in use in parts of China and central Asia in 1500.

Lamellar armour seems to have developed on the central Asian steppes as an excellent defence against horse archery. It may be related in origin to the Chinese laced-plate style of armour. It is distinguished from scale armour by the upward overlapping of the rows of lamellae and by the lacing of the scales flexibly to each other rather than to a fabric lining, or inflexibly to each other by wiring. In the Muslim west, lamellar coats were called *jawshan* while in the east they appeared as ◊*keikō*, and subsequently were developed into ◊*ō-yoroi* and other forms of Japanese armour.

Lamian War war fought 323–322 BC after the death of ◊Alexander (III) the Great, King of Macedon, when many of the Greek city-states combined against Macedon in an attempt to recover their independence. They were defeated at Crannon, in Thessaly, in 322 BC by the Macedonian generals Antipater and Craterus. The war took its name from the Greek city of Lamia, around which it initially centred.

Before his death Alexander had released his Greek mercenaries, and 8,000 of these were recruited by the Athenian Leosthenes to form the core of the Greek army. After Alexander's death, Leosthenes and the Athenian orator Hyperides persuaded Athens to declare war on Macedonia, and negotiated an alliance with other Greek city-states, including Aetolia.

When Antipater marched south to suppress the rebellion, the allies succeeded in bottling him up in Lamia, but Leosthenes' death in a sortie left the alliance without a general of equal skill, and in early 322 Antipater's fellow Macedonian general Leonnatus relieved the siege and Antipater withdrew to Macedonia.

After the defeat of the Athenian fleet off Amorgos, Craterus crossed from Asia Minor to join Antipater in Macedonia, and their combined forces defeated the allies at Crannon in Thessaly. This led to the dispersal of the allied forces, and Antipater was then able to subdue the rebels piecemeal, occupying Athens in September 322.

Lancaster castle castle in Lancashire, England. It was founded late in the 11th century by Robert de Poitou, who forfeited through treason shortly afterwards. The keep was added in the time of King John, around 1192, together with walling and a circular tower. The 13th-century gateway is generally credited to John of Gaunt (1340–99), and further construction and additions continued as late as Henry VI (1422–71).

lance medieval cavalry weapon with a wooden shaft and, usually, a metal head. It was originally thrown or thrust overarm. Later, when the development of the stirrup allowed the rider to brace against impact, it was couched, tucked under the arm, and used for piercing in a charge. The lance diverged from its spearlike shape, tending towards a longer, thicker shape with a specially formed grip.

In jousting tournaments lances were sometimes blunted or given special non-lethal heads. A shorter lance was useful when cavalry tactics included dismounting to fight on foot. In the later medieval period lance-rests were fixed to the breastplate which could bear the weight of the lance when required.

lancea light spear that could either be thrown or retained for hand-to-hand fighting. It was the preferred weapon of many 4th- and 5th-century Roman soldiers.

lanciarii imperial Roman legionaries armed with light spears called ◊*lancea*. Initially these men formed the rear ranks of a ◊legion, later they were brigaded together and may have been used as light troops.

The senior legion of the late imperial field army was the *legio lanciarii*, which, although possibly armed with *lancea*, was probably a heavy infantry unit.

Landsknecht (medieval German 'servant of the country') term first used for troops raised by ◊Charles the Bold, Duke of Burgundy, in 1470 in imitation of the Swiss pikemen. Landsknechts were also used extensively in the campaigns of the Holy Roman emperor ◊Maximilian I, who took an oath of loyalty from his troops in 1490.

Landsturm in medieval Switzerland, the troops of the mass levy, only called upon in times of emergency.

Landwehr in medieval Switzerland, reserve forces raised from older men, often married, who were prepared to serve at some distance from their homes.

Langeais castle fortress overlooking the Loire Valley, in present-day Indre-et-Loire *département*, France, on the border between Blois and Anjou. It was built by Fulk Nerra, Count of Anjou, in the 10th century. The remains of the original castle can be seen in the gardens of the Renaissance château (by Jean Bourré under Louis XI of France).

Langeais was thought to be the oldest castle in Europe until the discovery of ◊Doué-la-Fontaine castle. Charles VIII of France married Anne of Brittany here.

Lanze medieval German term for an armoured horseman or knight.

La Roche-Guyon castle fortress overlooking the river Seine, near its confluence with the river Epte, in present-day Val d'Oise *département*, France. It was built about 1190 on an isthmus, across which a ditch was cut to isolate it, and had transitional architectural features. The keep was round with an *en bec* (strengthening stone spur).

It preceded the planning of Château Gaillard.

La Rochelle, Battle of sea battle of 1372 in which France's ally Henry II of Castile attacked the English fleet under the Earl of Pembroke as he approached La Rochelle, France. The English lost the city to the French and Pembroke was captured and taken to Spain.

After the English defeat at sea, the mayor of La Rochelle aided the French siege force under Bernard du ◊Guesclin by tricking the English garrison commander Philip Mansel into surrender. Mansel could not read and was persuaded by a false letter of instructions from Edward III of England that was presented by the mayor. He followed 'orders', parading his men in a spot outside the gates where they were attacked. La Rochelle then surrendered.

Las Navas de Tolosa, Battle of battle fought in Spain on 16 July 1212 in which an alliance of Iberian kings defeated the Almohad (Berber Muslim) caliph al-Nasir, surprising him by crossing mountains through a secret pass. This proved to be the pivotal battle of the ◊Reconquista; Muslim fortunes were never recovered.

Following his defeat at Alarcos in 1195 (see ◊Alarcos, Battle of), Alfonso VIII of Castile built an alliance with the kings of Aragon and Navarre, initially supported by large numbers of French crusaders. Al-Nasir waited behind the defence of the Sierra Morena, confident that the Christians would starve trying to cross this mountain range. The French deserted, but a shepherd showed the Spanish the way through a side valley, allowing them to appear in the left rear of the Almohad force. Taken by surprise and unwilling to fight, al-Nasir's unpaid army mostly took flight. Al-Nasir returned to North Africa, where he was assassinated.

Later Three Years' War series of military campaigns 1083–87 fought in northeastern Japan between Yoshiie, the Minamoto governor of Mutsu province from 1083, and the Kiyohara family, the military commanders of Dewa province.

Conflict within the Kiyohara family was creating chaos in the region. Yoshiie's intervention resolved the conflict and established a strong independent political and military power base for the Minamoto family in the northeast.

latten alloy of copper, tin, and zinc used in medieval Europe for decorative borders on armour, and occasionally for whole pieces (such as the gauntlets of Edward the Black Prince preserved at Canterbury Cathedral, Canterbury, England).

Launceston castle castle in England, 35 km/21 mi northwest of Plymouth, Cornwall. It is generally believed that this was the site of a pre-Conquest castle of the earls of Cornwall, but it was usurped by William de Mortain, (William the Conqueror's half-brother), who raised a ◊motte-and-bailey castle there shortly after the Conquest.

A shell keep was built around the motte in the 13th century, and shortly afterwards a tower was built inside the shell. The motte sides were later revetted (faced with stones), probably as a form of insurance against possible collapse, and a large hall was built in the bailey.

Laupen, Battle of battle fought on 21 June 1339 in which Swiss troops under Rudolph van Erbach defended the Swiss city of Laupen against Burgundian besiegers under Count Gerard de Vallangin.

The Count de Vallangin led 12,000 men from Fribourg and Burgundy, while Rudolph van Erbach led the contingents of Berne and the Forest Cantons in the attack, some 6,500 men. The Bernese on the right drove back the Friburgers, but the Swiss left struggled against the Burgundian knights. It was remarkable for infantry to attack cavalry, and when the Bernese joined the Swiss left the knights were surrounded and defeated.

Laws of War medieval term describing the constraints on the conduct of warfare. Before the 14th century these were mostly customary, but in the later Middle Ages many treatises sought to codify them (see Honoré ◊Bovet). They considered such issues as who or what was legitimate target warfare, whether burning to devastate territory was allowed, the treatment of conquered fortresses and cities, and the management of ransoms.

Lechfeld, Battle of decisive victory in 955 for the Germans, led by Emperor Otto I, over the Magyars under Karchas Bulcsu, which finally ended the Magyar incursions into Germany.

Karchas Bulcsu's large Magyar army of between 50,000 and 100,000 men had swept through Bavaria, France, Burgundy, and Italy and had laid siege to Augsburg. Otto led an army of 10,000 Bavarians, Franconians, Saxons, Thuringians, Swabians, Bohemians, and some Slavs against them. The Magyars launched a frontal assault, while sending a small force around the German flanks. The flanking force succeeded in getting around behind the German position and seized their baggage train, but was eventually defeated by the Franconians. The frontal assault failed to break the German line and when the Germans adopted the offensive the Magyars were driven off. Many were killed in the vigorous pursuit that ensued.

Leeds castle castle in England, 8 km/5 mi southeast of Maidstone, Kent. A castle was built here shortly after the Conquest and held by the Crèvecoeur family until it fought on the wrong side in Henry III's reign (1227–72), after which the castle passed into Crown hands. The castle was rebuilt in its present form around 1280.

It straddles three islands on a branch of the river Medway which, with the help of a dam, forms the moat. The smallest island is walled and approached by three causeways, each with a gate and drawbridge. A fortified mill further protected one of the causeways and connected to an outer wall, a design intended to protect the dam upon which the water defences depended. A stone bridge led to the second island and a powerful gatehouse in a high wall enclosing the island. Inside this ran the wall of the inner ward surrounding the modern mansion. An arched building connects this area with the third island, upon which the remains of the original castle stood. This was a powerful circular keep with central court, and various buildings from the 14th and 15th centuries.

legate Roman officer whose power was derived from the legal authority of his general. Legates were originally the senior subordinates of a Roman commander. By the time of the early empire the title was given to the commanders of ◊legions (*legatus legionis*) and the governors of most of the provinces in the empire which contained legionary garrisons (*legatus Augusti*).

Legnano, Battle of battle fought between the Holy Roman Emperor ◊Frederick (I) Barbarossa and members of the Lombard League (an association of northern Italian towns fighting to retain independence from imperial rule) in 1176 at Legnano, northwest of Milan, Italy. Frederick was defeated. He escaped to Pavia, but made peace with the papacy and recognized the freedom of the Italian communes.

LEGION

Latin *legio*

Main unit of the Roman army for most of its history.

Originally 'legion' meant only 'levy', and represented the entire military manpower of the Roman state. Tradition credits King Servius Tullius of dividing the levy into five classes in the 6th century BC. Membership was based on property qualifications, and each class was equipped differently. The levy probably fought as a ◊hoplite phalanx. At some stage it was divided into two so that each of the year's consuls commanded one legion. Gradually, the legion's organization and tactics became more sophisticated and by the end of the 4th century, the manipular legion (see ◊maniple) had developed. It normally deployed for battle in the ◊*triplex acies* formation, but remained a citizen militia. At the time of the Second Punic War (218–201 BC), the legion included 300 cavalry, 1,200 light infantry, and 4,200 heavy infantry arranged in three lines: 1,200 *hastati* recruited from the younger men; 1,200 *principes* drawn from men in the prime of life; and 600 *triarii*, the veteran soldiers. All were equipped with a helmet, body armour, oval shield, and ◊*gladius*. The *hastati* and *principes* carried two *pila* (see ◊*pilum*) per man, while the *triarii* were armed with long spears. The light infantry, armed with a round shield, *gladius*, and a bundle of light javelins, fought in support of either the infantry or cavalry. In a crisis the size of the legion could be increased, but the

numbers of *triarii* and cavalry always remained the same. Each line was divided into ten maniples, each led by two centurions. The legion was commanded by six military tribunes. The Roman army became a professional force in the late 2nd–early 1st centuries BC. Credit usually goes to ◊Marius for this reform, but it was probably part of a gradual transition completed under ◊Augustus. The property qualification was abandoned and all legionaries were armed alike with long-shield, helmet, cuirass, *gladius,* and *pilum*. They were organized into ten ◊cohorts of 480 men, each divided into six centuries of 80, each century commanded by a centurion. Legions were commanded by a legate supported by one Senatorial tribune, a Camp Prefect who was usually an experienced officer, and five equestrian tribunes. Soldiers served for 25 years and received a bounty or plot of land on discharge. In the later 1st century the first cohort, commanded by the ◊*primus pilus,* was enlarged to five centuries of 160 men apiece with an additional 120 cavalry acting as scouts and messengers. There were many specialists within the ranks of the legion, such as engineers, artillerymen, architects, and artisans. Facts about the legion in the late imperial period are uncertain. During the 3rd century most were reduced in size, probably to about 1,000 strong. The majority of legionaries were heavy infantry equipped with a variety of spears and javelins instead of the *pilum* and used the longer ◊*spatha* instead of the *gladius*.

The outcome of the battle was a major setback to the emperor's plans for imperial domination over Italy, and showed the power of infantry against feudal cavalry.

Lê Hoan (lived 10th century) Vietnamese emperor 980–1005. Commander in chief under Dinh Bo Linh, he won a brief civil war after Dinh's murder and defeated a Song Chinese

invasion. In 982 he invaded Champa (modern central Vietnam), killing King Paramesvaravarman I and gaining great booty from sacking the capital Indrapura. He invaded northern Champa again in 983 and 990, and beat off Cham counterattacks in 995 and 997, forcing the Cham to move their capital south to Vijaya.

leidang the levying of ships, warriors, and equipment in Viking Denmark.

Lê Lo'i (c. 1385–1433) Vietnamese general, founder of the Later Lê dynasty. Vietnam was occupied by Ming China in 1408, and repeated revolts failed. Lê Lo'i, an officer of the previous Trân dynasty, led a revolt in 1418, and after defeats in the following years he finally besieged Chinese forces in Hanoi in 1427, forcing them to withdraw from Vietnam. The Chinese recognized Lê Lo'i as King of Annam in return for theoretical Chinese overlordship.

Lê Lo'i was defeated in battle in 1419 and 1420, but began a guerilla struggle with the support of the rural population. In winter 1425 he began a major offensive which penned Chinese forces up in garrisons. After the siege of Hanoi, a relief column under Chinese commander Liu Sheng was defeated, partly by elephant attacks, losing 70,000 men, and the Hanoi garrison surrendered.

Lemnos, Battle of destruction in 924 of the forces of the Muslim pirate Leo, based in Tripoli, by the Byzantine navy.

Leo (VI) the Wise Byzantine emperor 886–912. He was the son of ◊Basil (I) the Macedonian, and proved to be an equally effective ruler. He campaigned against the Muslims in Italy and Bulgars in the Balkans, and is credited with writing a military treatise known as the *Tactica*.

Lepanto, Battle of sea battle fought on 7 October 1571 in the Mediterranean Gulf of Corinth off Lepanto (Italian name of the Greek port of Naupaktos), then in Turkish possession, between the Ottoman Empire under Ali Pasha and the 'Holy League' forces from Spain, Venice, Genoa, and the Papal States, jointly commanded by the Spanish soldier Don John of Austria. The combined western fleets broke Muslim sea power.

The battle was not decisive, but it marked a limit to Turkish expansion. It was the last major naval engagement to be fought by galleys.

Le Plessis-Bourré castle stronghold at Ecuillé, north of Angers, in the present-day *département* of Maine-et-Loire, France. It was built in the late 14th century for artillery defence, with an exterior low terrace for guns and a wide moat, and was modified as a château in the 15th century by Jean Bourré, the minister of Louis XI of France.

Now a rectangular platform with corner towers, the building is an important example of the architectural transition from castle to château. Jean Bourré acquired it in 1462.

Le Plessis-Grimoult castle early 11th-century Norman castle in Calvados, France, destroyed in 1047 when its lord Grimoult du Plessis lost all his possessions after rebelling against ◊William (I) the Conqueror. It is a ◊ringwork castle, with a simple ditch and bank enclosure. A stone wall topped the curtain. It had at least one wall tower and a stone gatehouse.

The site has been excavated, revealing a previous building, an unfortified 10th-century house.

Lê Thanh Ton (lived 15th century) Vietnamese king 1460–97. Vietnam was at war with its old enemy the kingdom of Champa (modern central Vietnam) from 1446. Lê Thanh Ton took the Cham capital Vijaya in 1471, killing 60,000 people and deporting 30,000, including the royal family. Most of Champa was annexed to Vietnam. A remnant Cham state existed in the far south until 1720, but it was virtually powerless.

lettre de retenue medieval French term comparable to the English ◊indenture, designed to raise troops for long-term service.

Leuctra, Battle of battle fought in Boeotia, Greece, in 371 BC in which the Boeotians, using revolutionary tactics, ended Sparta's dominance in pitched battle.

The Boeotian commander ◊Epaminondas massed his left 50 deep, refused his right, and led his line obliquely towards the left, aiming to smash the Spartan right. The Spartan cavalry, unusually placed in front of their phalanx, were driven back into their own infantry, who were still deploying, and the Theban infantry took advantage of the confusion to attack. The Spartans, though only 12 deep, held long enough to recover the body of their king Cleombrotus, killed in the opening exchanges. The remnants retreated to their camp and were later allowed to depart under truce.

leudes regional leaders of the Carolingian Franks.

Lewes, Battle of battle fought on 14 May 1264 at Lewes, Sussex, England, between the English barons led by Simon de ◊Montfort (the Younger), Earl of Leicester, and the royalist forces of Henry III (1207–72). The king was defeated and captured.

The royal army advanced in two parts, one under Henry and Richard of Cornwall, the other under Prince Edward. Edward broke the Londoners but his father was defeated before he returned to the field.

The battle resulted in a baronial regime for

one year, broken by de Montfort's death at Evesham in 1265 (see ◊Evesham, Battle of).

Lewes castle castle in Sussex, England, 13 km/8 mi northeast of Brighton. A ◊motte-and-bailey castle distinguished by having a motte at each end of the bailey, Lewes was built by William de Warenne, one of William the Conqueror's law lords, in about 1070.

The castle was given ramparts and a ditch, and one mound was carefully built from quarried chalk blocks. A shell keep was placed on one motte in the 12th century, and in the following century this was strengthened by the addition of wall towers. Later work saw the addition of a curtain wall, various domestic buildings, and finally a gatehouse and barbican.

Liang Wudi (died 549) (or *Liang Wu-ti*) southern Chinese emperor 502–49, founder of the Liang dynasty. Born Xiao Yan (or Hsiao Yen), he served as a garrison commander under the southern Qi and seized power in 501. He made two attempts to conquer the north, but was defeated by his treacherous general Hou Jing who captured the Liang capital and starved Wudi to death.

In 529 his general Chen Chingzhi invaded northern China with a small army, exploiting the confusion of ◊Erzhu Rong's coup, but Wudi sent him no support and Chen was overwhelmed. In 547 Hou Jing, a general of the eastern Wei dynasty, defected to Liang and Wudi gave him southern troops in another attempt to conquer the north. When he was defeated, Hou Jing instead tried to seize power in the south.

Liegnitz, Battle of battle fought on 9 April 1241 between the Mongols under Baidar, attacking Europe, and Duke Henry II of Silesia's German and Polish forces. The latter were trapped and crushed by the Mongols.

Leading the northern column of a two-pronged attack on Europe, Kaidu bypassed the fortress of Breslau and ravaged the territory to bring the Christians to battle. Duke Henry's force of 20,000 included picked Silesian and Polish knights. His Teutonic Knights and Silesian foot soldiers were drawn into a trap by the feigned flight of horse-archers, then counterattacked by heavier Mongol cavalry.

Li Guang (died 119 BC) (or *Kuang*) Chinese general of the emperor ◊Han Wudi. In 129 BC he was defeated by the ◊Xiongnu and sentenced to death in China. Subsequently reinstated, he was sent against the Xiongnu again in 121 and 119. In 119, under the general Wei Qing in a joint expedition with ◊Huo Qubing,

Li's force missed a rendezvous and he committed suicide rather than stand trial.

Li Guangli (died 89 BC) (or *Li Kuang-li*) Chinese general under the emperor ◊Han Wudi. He commanded two expeditions against the far western kingdom of Dayuan (present-day Ferghana, eastern Uzbekistan), and returned from the second with many 'heavenly horses'. He then fought against the ◊Xiongnu, who defeated him in 90 BC and put him to death.

The first expedition against Dayuan was in 104 BC, after its king had rejected demands for his 'heavenly horses' and killed Chinese envoys. Li lost many men on the long march and returned unsuccessful. He petitioned for more men and set off again in 102 with enough troops to overawe the local kings into providing supplies, and besieged the Dayuan capital, cutting off its water supply and forcing the defenders to surrender.

In 99 Li killed 10,000 Xiongnu enemy but was surrounded and barely escaped, and in 90 he was defeated and surrendered; the Xiongnu initially treated him well but then executed him.

Li Keyong (died 908) (or *Li K'o-yung*) Turkish general in China. He assisted the Tang Chinese court against the rebel leader ◊Huang Chao in 883, recovering the capital Changan. In the power struggles between the late Tang governors, Li's arch enemy was ◊Zhu Wen, who was unable to unseat Li north of the Yellow River. Li's descendants replaced Zhu's and ruled northern China for 35 years.

Li was a chieftain of the Shato Turks, a small nation on the Chinese frontier allied to the Tang court. He rebelled in 878, supported by 10,000 Tatars, but was legitimized as ◊*jiedu shi* (governor) of Bingzhou when the court needed his help against Huang in 883. His cavalry were highly effective against Huang's rebels, and he integrated them with Bingzhou's ◊*yabing* regulars and militia into combined ◊*fanhan* armies.

Zhu tried to murder Li as early as 884, and attacked Bingzhou twice but could not take it. Ultimately Zhu established a new imperial dynasty, but failed to oust Li.

Li Ling (lived 2nd–1st century BC) Chinese general under the emperor ◊Han Wudi, grandson of ◊Li Guang and, like him, a noted commander against the ◊Xiongnu.

In 99 BC he attacked the Xiongnu with 5,000 infantry to distract attention from a simultaneous assault under ◊Li Guangli. Ling's troops were surrounded by 80,000 Xiongnu. He formed up behind his wagons and held them off on an eight-day fighting retreat before running out of arrows and being forced to surrender.

Limerick castle (or *King John's castle*) castle in what is now Co. Limerick, Ireland. A Norman earthwork castle was built on this site around 1175, but this was soon replaced by a stone castle begun in about 1200. The plan was roughly rectangular, with round towers at each corner and a powerful two-towered gatehouse on the northwest wall. The southeast wall followed the river Shannon, and on the inner side of this wall a great hall was built during the reign of Edward I (1272–1307). It was captured by Edward ◊Bruce in 1316.

limes (plural *limites*) (Latin 'path' or 'boundary') Roman frontier zone. *Limites* could consist of a number of defensive features such as walls, ditches, forts, and watchtowers, for example ◊Hadrian's Wall in Britain, or in an area of low threat they could be just a road. The Roman Empire's first physical frontiers date to the late 1st century AD.

Limoges, Siege of siege of the French town of Limoges in 1370. After the bishop of Limoges, a supposed ally of England, surrendered his town to the French Duke of Berry, ◊Edward the Black Prince angrily stormed Limoges on 19 September. He fell ill, and was carried in on a litter. Some 3,000 citizens were killed, though the bishop and the French commanders were spared.

Linan, Siege of (*Hangzhou* or *Hangchow*) fall of the Song dynasty's capital Linan (modern Hangzhou in Zhejiang) in 1276 to ◊Khubilai Khan's general Bayan in the Mongol campaigns in China (see ◊China, Mongol campaigns in). Song troops in outlying towns mostly surrendered without a fight, and there was little fighting at Linan. After failing to negotiate terms which would allow the Song empire to continue as a tributary state, the Empress Dowager Xie surrendered the city.

Lincoln, Battle of (1141) battle fought on 2 February 1141 outside Lincoln, England, in which King Stephen (c. 1097–1154) was defeated and captured by supporters of Matilda, claimant to the English throne, and taken to Bristol. Matilda's supporters were led by her half-brother Robert, Earl of Gloucester.

Lincoln castle had fallen into rebel hands and Stephen came to relieve it. Gloucester arrived to help the rebels, and the battle was fought outside the city. Gloucester's victory and Stephen's capture temporarily put Matilda ahead in the battle for the crown, but she was defeated at Winchester in 1141 (see ◊Winchester, Battle of).

Lincoln, Battle of (1217) battle fought on 20 May 1217 at Lincoln, England, during the ◊Barons' War of 1215–17, between the supporters of Prince Louis of France (the future ◊Louis VIII) and William ◊Marshal, Earl of Pembroke, who gained the victory.

At the invitation of the English barons, Louis had invaded England and captured Lincoln in 1216, but the castle held out and the army under Marshal came to its relief. The English victory led to Louis abandoning his invasion.

Lincoln castle castle in east central England. It was one of the first Norman castles to be built after the Conquest and was unusual in having two mottes (castle mounds), one with a polygonal shell keep, the other with a square tower. Though extended and reworked in the 13th and 14th centuries, there are still ample traces of Norman stonework in the curtain wall and towers. The castle featured prominently in the 12th-century war between Stephen and Matilda.

Lindisfarne, raid on one of the earliest and most infamous Viking raids, which took place in 793 and resulted in the plundering of the church and monastery on the island of Lindisfarne off the Northumbrian coast. A raid on a holy place such as this was the most horrific crime possible in the eyes of the Christian inhabitants of England.

Lingzhou, Siege of (or *Ling-chou*, 1081) battle in 1081 in which the Tangut kingdom of Xixia defeated the Song Chinese in northwest China. Three hundred thousand Chinese troops invaded Xixia and besieged Lingzhou, but in mid-winter the defenders broke the Yellow River dykes and flooded the Song army, forcing them to retreat.

Lingzhou, Siege of (or *Ling-chou*, 1226) fall in 1226 of the major Tangut city to ◊Genghis Khan in his last campaign. He besieged Lingzhou in September. In December a Tangut relief force of 100,000 was defeated in a battle fought on the frozen flood plain of the Yellow River, and the city surrendered.

Lisbon, Siege of siege from 28 June to 24 October 1147 of the Muslim-held city of Lisbon, Portugal, by a fleet of Christians of the Second Crusade from northwest Europe who joined the Portuguese and reconquered the city.

Inspired by St Bernard of Clairvaux, a fleet of common troops from England, Normandy, the Low Countries, and the Rhineland set out in 116 ships. When they reached Portugal, King Alfonso I asked them to join his siege of Lisbon. On 1 July the allies captured the suburbs and the crusaders set about constructing siege equipment, including a flying bridge from the masts of their ships. An attack on 3 August was driven back by contrary winds, and the landward engines were set on fire by the defenders. By 8 September a new great siege tower was ready and on 29 September a mine was fired, bringing down 60 m / 200 ft of wall. Eventually the huge tower was edged up to the wall and the Muslims surrendered.

Li Tan (died 1262) Chinese warlord in Mongol service. Under the Mongol Great Khan Mangu he raided Song-held territory but remained aloof from the main Mongol war effort. He rebelled against Mangu's successor ◊Khubilai Khan in 1262. The Song failed to support him and he was defeated in five months by a large Mongol-Chinese army, and executed.

lithsman person employed for the fleet. The term, which is rarely used with a clear meaning, appears in the 11th century, suggesting a Scandinavian introduction in England by ◊Cnut the Great and his successors. Lithsmen may have been men of standing or hired men, possibly raised through a system of obligation comparable to ◊fyrd service.

The lithsmen of London helped choose Harold I as regent in 1036. Lithsmen are also mentioned in connection with Hastings and southeastern ports.

Liu Cong (died 318) (or *Liu Ts'ung*) ◊Xiongnu leader of the ◊Sixteen Kingdoms period in China, who ruled 310–18. He captured two Jin emperors, burning the capital Loyang in 311, and overran most of north China. He tried to maintain a Chinese-style state, but this antagonized the Xiongnu, and by his death Cong was confined to the northwest.

His father Liu Yuan, a descendant of Maodun, had ruled the southern Xiongnu on the Chinese border during the rebellions of the Eight Princes (see ◊Eight Princes, rebellions of the) against the Jin dynasty. In 304 Yuan rebelled with 50,000 troops to set up his own dynasty, Former Zhao. When Cong succeeded him, he captured and burned Loyang, capturing the emperor along with it; in 316 he captured a second emperor at the new capital Changan. Many of the Xiongnu defected to one of his father's generals, ◊Shi Le, who preferred the old nomad ways.

Liu Fang (died 605) Chinese general of the emperor ◊Sui Wendi. He reconquered the Chinese province in northern Vietnam in 602 and attacked Champa (now central Vietnam) in 605, sacking the capital.

Liu was sent out in 602 on ◊Yang Su's recommendation. He marched through Sichuan and Yunnan to approach Vietnam unexpectedly from the west, and the local leadership surrendered without a fight. In 605 he attacked Champa with an army and a fleet. Chinese archers defeated King Sambhuvarman's elephants, and Liu captured and sacked his capital. On the way home Liu and most of his army died of disease.

livery provision of food and drink, lodgings, clothing, and other maintenance to retainers or servants, mainly in medieval Europe. Also, the provisions themselves, especially the distinctive clothing, hood, or badge worn to indicate the retainer's service or loyalty to a particular lord or group. In the collective singular, retainers or servants in livery.

Llewellyn the Great (died 1240) (Llewellyn ap Iorwerth) ruler of Gwynedd (North Wales) 1201–40. He conquered Powys and Ceredigion in 1208, survived King John of England's invasion of 1211–12, benefited from the ◊Barons' War of 1215–17 to seize Swansea, and dominated Wales until his death.

Llewellyn flourished by a combination of military and diplomatic means. He married Joan, King John's illegitimate daughter, in 1205 and also allied himself with Ranulf, Earl of Chester, on his northeastern flank. The grandfather of ◊Llewellyn the Last, he assured the power of Gwynedd for two generations.

Llewellyn the Last (1240–82) (Llewellyn ap Gruffydd) Welsh prince who united Wales in the 1250s. He was an ally of Simon de ◊Montfort (the Younger) in 1264–65. War against ◊Edward I 1277–82 ended in his death at Radnor.

Llewellyn was able to exploit the weak rule of Henry III, supporting the rebel barons led by Simon de Montfort, and later Gloucester's revolt in 1267. In 1270 he invaded Glamorgan, but ◊Edward I was determined to crush him. Driven out of Shropshire in 1276, he was pinned back into Snowdonia. Pursuing the traditional Welsh harassing tactics worked at first, but Edward's forces were too large, and his policy of fortification narrowed Llewellyn's options. A breakout into South Wales was partially successful, but he was forced into battle at Radnor and outmanoeuvred.

lochagos (plural *lochagoi*) (Greek) commander of a *lochos*.

Loches castle stronghold on a rocky plateau southeast of Tours in present-day Indre-et-Loire *département*, France. The 9th-century fortress held by Fulk Nerra, Count of Anjou, was rebuilt as a castle in the 12th century. It has a forebuilding but no crosswall, and semicircular external buttresses.

Fulk Nerra built the keep. Loches has *en bec* (strengthening stone spur) towers built by ◊Philip (II) Augustus of France. The Martelet tower was added in the 15th century. The tomb of Agnès Sorel (d. 1450), mistress of ◊Charles VII, is here. The Italian patron of the arts and ruler of Milan, Ludovico Sforza, was imprisoned at Loches and spent time painting frescoes.

lochos (plural *lochoi*) (Greek 'men in ambush') military unit, varying in size but usually several hundred strong. In the Spartan army of ◊Xenophon's time it was a subunit of a ◊*mora* consisting of 160, 320, or 640 men. Prior to that, it was the largest unit in the Spartan army.

London, Roman (Roman *Londinium*) Roman provincial capital of Britain. Its city walls, constructed relatively late, were among the longest in the Roman Empire. London's earliest defence was provided by the Cripplegate fort, built in the late 1st century AD to house the governor's bodyguard and military staff. The city land wall, built in stone, was begun in the late 2nd century and ran for 3.2 km/2 mi. Between AD 250 and 270 a wall was built along the riverside to complete the circuit. The defences were improved in the late 4th century with the addition of bastions on the land wall.

London, Tower of English fortress; see ◊Tower of London.

longship Viking warship, probably developed in the 8th century. Longships were manoeuvrable and fast, well designed for raiding. They were long and slim, with a single sail attached to a mast fixed in a block, and powered also by a single bank of oars along each side.

They were of wooden construction, with overlapping planks riveted together. The rudder was on the starboard side. The rowers sometimes fixed their shields along the bulwark. The sail had either a striped or diagonal pattern.

Longwan, Battle of (or *Lung-wan*) battle on 23 June 1360 in which Ming commander ◊Zhu Yuanzhang defeated Chen Yuliang's Han state in the Chinese civil wars. Chen and most of his men escaped by ship, but 20,000 died and 7,000 were taken prisoner. The Ming also captured 100 large ships, giving them a powerful fleet for the first time. Han was neutralized until the Poyang campaign (see ◊Poyang, Battle of).

Chen sailed down the Yangtze to surprise the city of Nanjing with 100,000 men, equal to Ming numbers but with far more ships. After a failed attack by river, Chen landed at Longwan. Zhu had concealed 30,000 men in ambush to the north, others to the south, and hid his own reserve behind hills. Once Chen was disembarked, Zhu's reserve came down from the hills, and Chen advanced across the plain against this apparently isolated detachment. Zhu's ambushes then attacked the Han rear, and the surrounded Han were quickly defeated.

lorica Latin word for body armour. During the early republic the Romans used small rectangular or round metal breastplates, which remained in use until the 2nd century BC, or a linen cuirass sometimes reinforced with scales or overlapping rectangular plates, which was replaced by the ◊mail shirt. Mail was used in various forms during the empire. Articulated plate armour was introduced in the 1st century AD.

The mail shirt (*lorica hamata*) was cut to the same pattern as the original linen cuirass. Scale armour (*lorica squamata*) was also widely used during the empire. The articulated plate armour (known by the modern term *lorica segmentata*) was the main innovation of Roman body armour.

loricati (from Latin *lorica* meaning 'hauberk' or 'mail tunic') medieval European armed soldiers wearing a ◊hauberk. Soldiers in armour were well equipped and had social status. ◊William of Poitiers describes the better-armed Norman infantry at the Battle of Hastings in 1066 as 'loricatos'. The word was later equated with the meaning of 'knight'.

Loudoun Hill, Battle of battle fought in 1307 between the English and the Scots which signalled the turn of the tide against the English under ◊Edward I. An English force under Aymer de Valence, Earl of Pembroke, was blocked and defeated by ◊Robert (I) the Bruce at Loudoun Hill in Strathclyde, Scotland.

Three days later another English force under Gloucester was defeated. Together these clashes marked the rise of Scottish fortunes and of Robert the Bruce. Edward died marching north to recover the situation.

Louis VII (c. 1120–80) king of France from 1137, who in 1147 led the Second Crusade with Conrad III of Germany (1093–1152), a military disaster. He annulled his marriage to Eleanor of Aquitaine in 1152, whereupon Eleanor married Henry of Anjou, later ◊Henry II of England. Louis was involved in a bitter struggle with Henry 1152–74; he prevented Henry from gaining Toulouse.

Louis VIII (1187–1226) king of France from 1223. As prince he helped to defeat King John of England (1167–1216) and his allies in France at La Roche-au-Moine in 1214. He was invited to become king of England in place of John by the English barons, and unsuccessfully invaded England 1215–17. He participated in the ◊Albigensian Crusades, capturing Avignon, and brought Poitou under French control.

Louvain, Battle of victory in 891 by the Germans under King Arnulf over the Vikings, which effectively ended Viking raids into Germany.

Loyang, Battle of battle in 328 between two of the ◊Sixteen Kingdoms in northern China in which ◊Shi Le's northeastern army eventually defeated Liu Yao, ◊Xiongnu ruler of the northwest. The victory enabled Shi Le to destroy Liu power entirely.

Liu Yao defeated an attack by Shi Le's northeastern army. Liu followed up with 100,000 men and captured the key city of Loyang. Shi Le led 60,000 infantry and 27,000 cavalry to recapture the city. Liu's retreat was cut off, and he was defeated and captured in a battle fought at the gates of Loyang.

Lu classical Chinese walled city, capital of the state of Lu from the 11th century BC to the ◊Warring States period. The home of Confucius, it is now Qufuxian, Shandong. The circuit of the walls was an irregular variation on the standard rectangle, following features of the terrain, and with distinctive rounded corners. Rivers and a marsh were used to form the moat.

The pounded-earth walls were 11.7 km in circuit and had eleven gates. The gate-towers had foundations that projected outside the walls, so attackers would have to pass through a long corridor. Near the centre of the city was a fortified palace area, the *cheng* or inner city.

lu the standing army of the Chinese Shang dynasty, supplemented by ◊*zu* levies. The *lu* probably existed only in the later part of Shang history, around 1300–1027 BC. Ten thousand *lu* troops took part in one of the campaigns of ◊Fu Hao.

Lucullus, Lucius Licinius (110–56 BC) Roman general and consul. As commander against ◊Mithridates (VI) Eupator of Pontus 74–66 he proved to be one of Rome's ablest generals and administrators. His troops mutinied in 68, refusing to advance, and Lucullus was replaced by ◊Pompey the Great.

Ludlow castle castle in England, 40 km/25 mi south of Shrewsbury. First built by Roger de Lacy in 1085 on a rocky spur above the river Teme, with a great keep, a short curtain wall, and some lesser towers enclosing a bailey. This was extended in the 12th century by adding a longer curtain wall to enclose an outer bailey, and more towers and buildings were erected as this castle became a vital border fortress.

Lugdunum, Battle of battle fought in AD 197 near the present-day city of Lyon, France, between the Roman emperor Lucius ◊Septimius Severus and his rival Decimus Clodius ◊Albinus. The conflict was a hard fight between evenly matched armies; it was only decided when Severus' cavalry commander Laetus finally made a successful charge. Albinus committed suicide.

The battle was, according to the Roman historian Dio Cassius, one of the largest of its time, involving armies of 150,000 soldiers on each side.

Lukka tribal people who lived on the edge of the Hittite kingdom during the late Bronze Age, occupying the Lukka lands in southwest Anatolia (classical Lykia). Sometimes allied to the Hittites, they fought on the Hittite side at the Battle of Kadesh (see ◊Kadesh, Battle of) in 1275 BC, but they were also troublesome raiders by sea and land.

They attacked Alashiya (Cyprus) during the reign of Tudhaliyas II (c.1450 BC) and were a part of the coalition defeated by Pharaoh ◊Merenptah in 1213 BC, along with other ◊Peoples of the Sea. They conspired with Piyamaradus during the reigns of the Hittite Great Kings Muwatallis and Hattusilis III (13th century BC). They were defeated by the Hittite Great King Suppiluliumas II at sea and on land in the battles at Alashiya in about 1190 BC (see ◊Alashiya, battles of).

Luojian, Battle of (or *Lo creek*) battle in November 383 in which ◊Fu Jian's vanguard was defeated in his invasion of south China. This battle was a prelude to the great battle on the river Fei (see ◊Fei River, Battle of the).

Fu Jian's general Liang Cheng crossed the river Huai with 20,000 men and fortified a position near the Luojian stream, an arm of the river Fei. The southern commander Liu Laozhi, with 5,000 picked troops, crossed the Luojian to cut off the northerners' line of retreat and attacked at night from two sides. When Liang Cheng was killed, his army fled, losing 15,000 men.

Luscivus, Gaius Fabricus Roman general who conducted campaigns in southern Italy and against the invasion of ◊Pyrrhus, King of Epirus, in 280 BC, gaining a popular reputation as a military commander and ideal Roman citizen. As consul in 282 BC, Luscivus waged war in southern Italy against the Lucanians and Brutti, winning numerous successes and collecting an enormous amount of booty.

In 278 BC he was consul again and led the embassy that negotiated a peace with Pyrrhus, allowing him to resume the war in southern Italy where he gained further victories over the Lucanians and Brutti. As censor in 275 BC he was the first to strike a senator off the list for immoral behaviour; this, coupled with his refusal to have Pyrrhus assassinated, gained him a reputation as an ideal example of ancient Roman moral purity.

Ly Bi (c. 490–546) (or *Li Bon*) Vietnamese independence leader. A military official under the Chinese Liang dynasty, he led a rebel army called 'Troops of the Just Cause' to expel the Chinese in 541. Although he was initially successful, proclaiming himself Emperor of Nam Viet in 544, he was eventually defeated and killed by his Lao allies, who were bribed to kill him.

He defeated a counterattack and an invasion by ◊Rudravarman I in 544. The following year, however, another Chinese expedition under Chen Baxian (later Emperor) defeated Ly at Chu-dien in the Hong river plain and captured his capital. Ly raised an army including Lao mountain tribesmen, but Chen beat him again in a battle of boats on Dientriet Lake.

Lycus, Battle of battle fought in 66 BC between ◊Pompey the Great and the smaller army of ◊Mithridates (VI) Eupator of Pontus. It is sometimes known as the Battle of Nicopolis, after the city founded to commemorate Pompey's triumph.

Pompey had been pursuing Mithridates in an effort to finally defeat him. He attacked Mithridates at night, despite the risk of confusion, to ensure that the king did not escape. The night battle was successful for Pompey, the Pontic troops being routed with heavy losses, but Mithridates evaded capture.

Lympne castle castle in Kent, England, 11 km/7 mi west of Folkestone. A tower is said to have been built here on top of the cliffs by Lanfranc in around 1080. This appears to have been demolished, and in the 14th century a hall with two towers was built in its place. This may have had some defensive role, but then was abandoned. It later became a residence for the Archdeacon of Canterbury before being abandoned again.

Lysander (died 395 BC) Spartan admiral. In 407 BC he won the minor victory off Notium which resulted in ◊Alcibiades' dismissal. He destroyed the Athenian fleet at Aegospotami (see ◊Aegospotami, Battle of) in 405 BC, effectively ending the ◊Peloponnesian War. His influence waned when his policy of installing narrow oligarchies in Athens and elsewhere was repudiated by the Spartan authorities, and he supported ◊Agesilaus II's claim to the throne.

He accompanied Agesilaus to Asia Minor in 396, but quarrelled with his protégé and returned to Greece. He was killed at the beginning of the Corinthian War.

Lysimachus (c. 355–281 BC) Macedonian general and one of the 'successors' of ◊Alexander (III) the Great (see ◊*Diadochi*). At Alexander's death in 323 BC, he received Thrace as his province, assuming the title 'king' in 306/5. In 302 he invaded Asia Minor and, with Seleucus (I) Nicator, defeated and killed ◊Antigonus (I) Monophthalmus at Ipsus in 301 (see ◊Ipsus, Battle of). In 287 he joined Pyrrhus of Epirus to expel ◊Demetrius (I) Poliorcetes from Macedonia, and in 285 reached the zenith of his power when he took over the kingdom.

Domestic intrigues led to the intervention of Seleucus in Asia Minor, and Lysimachus was defeated and killed at Corupedium in 281.

MACEDONIAN WARS

Series of conflicts fought between Macedon and Rome which led to the destruction of the Macedonian Kingdom. The *First Macedonian War* 214–205 BC, began when Philip V of Macedon, concerned at Rome's growing influence in Illyria, on the eastern shore of the Adriatic Sea, made an alliance with ◊Hannibal the Great to fight Rome. In turn, the Romans made an alliance with Greece's Aetolian League. When the Aetolians withdrew their support in 206, Rome was forced to make peace. The *Second Macedonian War* 200–197 BC, resulted in Philip V giving up his fleet and his influence in Greece, and Macedon becoming a subordinate ally of Rome. After their victory over Carthage in the Punic Wars, the Romans declared war on Philip, carrying out a series of raids and surprise attacks on Macedonian strongholds, often with naval support. In 198 BC Titus Quinctius ◊Flamininus gained command of the Roman army and drove Philip out of the valley of the river Aoüs (possibly the modern river Vijosê in Albania). Afraid of losing his command for political reasons, he negotiated with Philip in an effort to gain credit for ending the war, but when his command was extended for another year he broke off the negotiations and smashed the Macedonian army at Cynoscephalae (see ◊Cynoscephalae, Battle of). The *Third Macedonian War* 172–167 BC, brought the dissolution of the Macedonian kingdom and its annexation as a Roman province. Rome declared war on Macedon in 172, using the pretext that it had attacked Roman allies. Though the Macedon of Philip's son and successor Perseus probably posed no real threat to Rome, Macedonian influence had gradually increased in Illyria and Thrace, and Rome may have considered the kingdom too strong and independent for a former enemy. There were several years of raids and sieges but no full-scale battles until Aemilius ◊Paullus defeated Perseus and destroyed his army at Pydna in 168 BC (see ◊Pydna, Battle of). The *Fourth Macedonian War* 149–148 BC, marked Macedon's final, and failed, attempt to reclaim its kingdom from Roman rule. Andriscus, who claimed to be an illegitimate son of Perseus, raised an army in Thrace and invaded Macedon in the hopes that the Macedonians would rally to his cause, but he failed to gain much support. The local authorities raised a militia to fight him, and in the battle that ensued Andriscus inflicted the only major disaster suffered by Rome in the course of the Macedonian Wars. He defeated the local militia and a Roman force and killed its commander, the praetor Publius Iuventius Thalna. He was soon defeated near Pydna by another praetor, Quintus Caecilius Metellus. After his defeat, Macedon became a province ruled directly by a Roman governor and containing a Roman garrison.

machaira sword found in southern Europe from the 7th century BC; see ◊*kopis*.

Machanidas (died c. 207 BC) regent of Sparta from about 210 BC. During the first of the ◊Macedonian Wars, Machanidas recovered territory lost to the Achaean League. He then allied with Philip V of Macedon to fight against Rome. Around 208, in the long-disputed area north of Sparta, he captured Tegea and threatened Elis and Argos. He was defeated and killed at the third battle of Mantinea (see ◊Mantinea, Battle of 207 BC).

machicolation projecting stone gallery on the wall or tower of a medieval fortification. It replaced the earlier wooden ◊brattices or hoardings. Its main purpose was to protect defenders who used the slots below for dropping objects onto attackers at the foot of the wall.

The word originally referred to the openings in the floor, but later came to mean the whole structure. Machicolation developed in the late 12th century; it was found at the castle in Niort, France, soon after 1175. The structure was supported by a row of corbels projecting from the wall.

machimoi hereditary soldiers of late pharaonic and Persian-ruled Egypt, composed of two castes: the Hermotybies and Kalasirieis. Each year 1,000 members of each caste provided the pharaoh's bodyguard. They were granted land tax-free for their maintenance as well as rations of bread, beef, and wine, and were forbidden to follow a trade.

About the time of King ◊Cambyses II's Persian conquest of Egypt (525 BC), the Greek historian Herodotus records 160,000 Hermotybies and 250,000 Kalasirieis. The independent Egyptian ruler Nekht-har-hebi fielded 60,000 *machimoi* in 351 BC.

maedate frontal crest or decorative motif on a Japanese helmet, which originated in the Muromachi period (1333–1568). The motifs could take the form of the family crest (*mon*), a religious symbol, or an animal or insect form; during the Momoyama period (1568–1600) the designs took almost any conceivable form.

Maes Maydog, Battle of battle fought in 1295 between the Welsh and the English under ◊Edward I. Madog ap Llewellyn led a Welsh rising, but an English army commanded by the Earl of Warwick defeated them.

Warwick 'placed one crossbowman between two cavalrymen'. The Welsh made a frontal attack, but were broken by the archers. The English lost only one squire and six footmen. Madog escaped, but was later captured and put in the Tower of London.

Magadha first Indian empire, c. 642–28 BC, in the lower Ganges valley, roughly corresponding to the middle and southern parts of modern Bihar. It was the seat of the Mauryan dynasty founded in the 3rd century BC. Its capital Paliputra (modern Patna) was a great cultural and political centre.

Its earliest dynasty was founded in about 540 BC by Bimbisara, the first Indian king known to history, with its capital at Rajagriha (modern Rajgir). A second dynasty, that of the Nandas, with its capital at Paliputra, came to power in about 413 BC. This in turn was overthrown by ◊Chandragupta Maurya in 325 BC. The last Mauryan king, Brahadratha, was overthrown by one of his generals, Pushyamitra Shunga, in about 183 BC. His grandson Vasumitra fought against a ◊Yavana invader, Menander (Milinda), but by the beginning of the Christian era the Magadhan empire had broken up into a series of successor states.

Magadha revived under the dynasty of ◊Chandragupta I and his successors (320–467) and again under ◊Harshavardhana (590–647), remaining the cultural centre of northern India until the mid-8th century.

magister equitum second in command to a Roman dictator under the Roman Republic. The *magister equitum* commanded an army's cavalry because, unlike the dictator, he was legally allowed to ride a horse. The term also refers to a subordinate commander in the late Roman army listed in the *Notitia Dignitatum*, a late 4th-century document containing Roman administrative information.

magister militum most senior military commander in the late Roman army (4th–6th centuries), literally 'master of soldiers'. In the Eastern Roman Empire the post was also known as *magister utriusque militiae* or 'master of all military services'.

magister peditum senior military commander in the late Roman army (4th–6th centuries), literally 'master of foot'. He was subordinate to the ◊*magister militum*, and despite his title could command both cavalry and infantry units.

Magnesia, Battle of decisive battle fought in 190 BC at Magnesia (present-day Manisa, western Turkey), in the war between the Syrian king ◊Antiochus (III) the Great and the Roman commander Lucius Cornelius Scipio. The smaller Roman force defeated a numerically larger Seleucid army.

Scipio had crossed into Asia Minor with an army of about 30,000. Antiochus met him at Magnesia with 60,000 infantry, 12,000 cavalry,

54 elephants, and a force of scythed chariots. The battle occurred after 11 days of manoeuvring and skirmishing. A charge by the scythed chariots failed to make an impression on the Roman line. Antiochus led a cavalry charge that punched through the Roman right, but this was halted by the force guarding the Roman camp and then defeated by reserve troops. Meanwhile the Roman advance was relentless, driving back the main ◊phalanx despite the elephants placed in close support. The Romans lost 350 men against alleged Seleucid losses of 53,000 killed and 1,400 men and 15 elephants captured.

Mago Barca (died 203 BC) Carthaginian general during the Second Punic War (see ◊Punic War, Second), brother of ◊Hannibal the Great.

He commanded forces at Trebia in 218 BC (see ◊Trebia, Battle of) and Cannae in 216 BC (see ◊Cannae, Battle of) before being sent to Spain in 215 BC to command an army of his own. In 205 BC he was sent to Liguria to try and open a second front in northern Italy that would prevent Publius Cornelius ◊Scipio from launching his invasion of Africa, but his army was ambushed and he was mortally wounded.

Magyars according to legend, the nomadic Magyars, the invaders and creators of Hungary, were made up of nine tribes, but were heterogeneous like many Eurasian nomadic groups. They were mobile horse-archers and devastated Europe on deep raids from their base on the Hungarian steppe between 898 and 955. They were defeated by the Holy Roman emperor Otto I in 955 (see ◊Lechfeld, Battle of). After 1000 they converted to Christianity and became valuable allies to the crusaders.

Mahdia, Siege of late crusading venture against the Muslim states in North Africa led by Louis II, Count of Clermont, in 1390. Mahdia, 320 km/200 mi southeast of Tunis, was an important base for Muslim raids on Christian merchant ships from Italian cities. The siege lasted ten weeks, but the city was not taken and an agreement was made.

Mahendravarman I king of the Tamil Pallava dynasty, ruling c. 600–25 from Kanchi. In accordance with the Hindu doctrine of ◊mandala, he began a series of wars against the Chalukya dynasty of the western Deccan, which continued for the next two centuries.

Mahmud of Ghazni (971–1031) (also known as *Mahmud the Iconoclast;* real name *Abu'l Qasim Mahmud ibn Sebuk-Tegin*) Amir and first sultan of Ghazni (central Afghanistan)

998–1031. He consolidated and extended the central Asian territories inherited from his father ◊Sebuk-Tegin before beginning a series of 17 expeditions into northwest India, defeating the armies of the ◊Rajput kings, plundering their cities, and destroying their temples.

He launched his first major raid into India in 1001, defeating ◊Jaipal I at the Battle of Peshawar (see ◊Peshawar, Battle of 1001). His most daring attack was on ◊Somnath in 1025, where 50,000 Hindu defenders were killed and treasure worth 2 million dinars was taken. He refused ransom for the sacred symbol of Shiva, ordering that it be smashed and the fragments built into the threshhold of his new mosque, 'the Bride of Heaven', at Ghazni, to be trodden underfoot by the faithful.

Mahmud Shah I (1400–69) sultan of Malwa (in the western part of present-day Madhar Pradesh, India) 1436–69. He campaigned against both his Hindu and Muslim neighbours. His attempts to conquer Delhi, Gujarat, Chitor, and the Deccan all ended in failure, but his successes against the Rajput states on his immediate borders enlarged and secured his own dominions.

Mahmud Shah Bigarha (1459–1511) (or *Begara*) Muslim king of Gujarat (in northwestern India) 1472–1511. The third ruler of the Ahmad-Shahi dynasty, he came to the throne at the age of 13. After establishing authority at home, he occupied the neighbouring provinces of Kathiawar and Kutch and the Rajput kingdom of Champaner (1484).

Mahmud the Iconoclast another name for ◊Mahmud of Ghazni, Sultan of Ghazni.

Mahoba city in Uttar Pradesh, northern India, deriving its name from the Sanskrit *Mahotsava* ('great sacrifice') performed there by Chandra Varman, founder of the ◊Rajput Chandela dynasty in the 10th century. Its main defences consisted of a series of artificial lakes.

Mahoba was captured by ◊Prithviraja Chauhana III in 1182, but regained independence after Tarain (see ◊Tarain, Battle of 1192). It fell to ◊Qutb al-Din Aibak in 1202, and thereafter its rulers paid tribute to the sultans of Delhi. Mahoba was established as a separate Muslim state about 1400.

Maiden castle the largest and most elaborate Iron Age hillfort in Britain, sited near Dorchester, England. Its fortifications represent both social prestige and the use of the sling as a defensive weapon in Celtic warfare.

A small stronghold with one ditch and rampart was established in the 6th century BC, but a massive redevelopment in the 2nd or 1st century BC almost tripled its size. Four steep earthen ramparts separated by deep ditches rose in successive levels, forcing attackers to always fight uphill under slingfire from the defenders above. Maiden castle fell to a Roman assault during the conquest of Britain in the early 1st century AD.

mail armour formed of circular (usually iron) links arranged so that each link passes through two others in the row above and two in the row below (except in the case of Japanese mail, where links of two different sizes are used to form a lattice structure).

The links are of four different kinds: riveted (each made of a length of wire with its ends overlapped, flattened, and joined by a rivet, the usual form of link); welded (the ends forge-welded together to form a solid link, used for alternating rows with riveted links in medieval Europe until about 1400 and in Indian mail until the 18th century); solid (punched from sheet metal, usually characteristic of alternate rows of some Turkish mail); or butted (in which the ends are merely butted together, producing a garment of little defensive capability, usually found in Indian and Persian mail of the 18th and 19th centuries).

Most mail is formed of iron links, but some European and Islamic garments have borders of brass links, and late Indian mail is often patterned with iron, brass, and copper links. The term 'mail' should be used for all forms of mail armour; 'chain mail' is a pleonasm, while other apparent types of mail such as 'mascled', 'rustred', and 'trelliced' describe different artistic representations of mail in the 19th century, not different types of mail.

mail, Roman armour made of interlocking rings, often erroneously called chain mail, which first appears in Celtic graves at the beginning of the 3rd century BC, and which may therefore have been a Celtic invention. It was the commonest form of body armour used by the Romans from the 1st century BC and had been generally adopted by the time of the Greek politician and historian ◊Polybius (150 BC).

Most Roman mail is made of iron rings about 6 mm/0.2 in in diameter, with alternate rings riveted. It was sometimes used in conjunction with scales.

maisnie medieval French medieval fighting unit; see ◊household, military.

Makri Plagi, Battle of battle fought in 1263 in the northeast of present-day Greece between the Achaian Franks under William II Villehardouin of Achaea (Greece), who had launched attacks on southern Morea (Pelopónnisos, Greece), and an imperial Byzantine force under Sevastokrator Constantine. The Byzantines were routed.

Following his release from captivity after the Battle of Pelagonia in 1259 (see ◊Pelagonia, Battle of), William began his attacks into southern Morea. Sevastokrator Constantine led a force of about 15,000 men to attack the Frankish capital at Adravida, but his Turkish mercenaries, unpaid for six months, deserted to William, who took the offensive and routed the Byzantines at Makri Plagi.

Malatesta, Carlo (lived 14th–15th centuries) ◊*condottiere* commander who served the Visconti of Milan, Venice, and Florence in the 1390s. As lord of Rimini he was not typical of the ◊*condottieri*, as he was assured a large following by his position and wealth. A cautious general, he fought without notable success. A Florentine commentator referred to him as 'very accustomed to losing'. He was defeated and captured at San Egidio in 1416.

Maldon, Battle of Danish victory in 991 over the Essex ◊fyrd, in which the ◊ealdorman Byrhtnoth was killed. An heroic Anglo-Saxon poem recounts how three warriors managed to prevent the Vikings from crossing a causeway until the Saxon commander, Byrhtnorth, allowed them across to engage in battle. Byrhtnoth was killed in the fighting and the Saxons were driven off.

Malesov, Battle of battle fought in 1424 between the Hussite religious dissidents of central Europe under their talented military leader Jan ◊Zizka and imperialist forces from Prague, at Malesov in the modern Czech Republic.

Zizka positioned his ◊*Wagenburg* on top of a hill, only approachable through the forest and across a marshy stream. As the Praguers approached, Zizka waited until half their forces were across the stream, then sent his cavalry to attack their flanks. The Hussites then rolled wagons laden with stones into their midst, smashing their formations. The Praguers broke, losing 1,200 men including the city's standard bearer, and the rear of the column fled without coming into action.

Malik Kafur (personal name *Hasan Bahri*) favourite general and deputy of Sultan ◊Ala al-Din Khilji of Delhi. His greatest feat was the invasion of southern India 1310–11. On the death of Ala al-Din in 1316, he imprisoned the sultan's widow and blinded his two eldest sons. The third son, Mubarak, had Malik Kafur killed and ascended the throne.

Malik Kafur established mosques and garrisons in a number of places in the south following his invasion, and took tribute and promises of subjection to Delhi from others (although the south was not completely conquered for Delhi until 1327).

Malik Shah, Jalal al-Daula Mu'izz al-Din Abu'l-Fath (1035–92) third of the great ◊Seljuk sultans 1072–92. His armies were victorious in campaigns in Transoxania and Kashgar (western China) to the southern Caucasus, Syria, Palestine, and the Arabian peninsula down to the Yemen.

Malik Shah inherited the throne from his father ◊Alp-Arslan, fighting off a challenge from his uncle Qavert, who was captured and strangled with a bowstring.

Maling, Battle of battle in 341 BC between the two Chinese ◊Warring States of Qi and Wei. Qi was victorious, and by weakening Wei, it contributed to Qin Shi Huangdi's eventual unification of China. The battle also marked the first decisive use of massed crossbows, which dominated Chinese warfare for centuries.

Attacking Wei's capital in an indirect relief of the state of Han, Qi commanders Tian Ji and ◊Sun Bin fell back when Wei forces were mobilized, lighting fewer fires each night to suggest their army was dispersing. Wei commander Pang Juan led mobile troops in a hasty pursuit, leaving his heavy infantry to follow. Sun set an ambush in a valley near Mount Maling. He concealed infantry in gullies, behind caltrops and a barricade of shields, with halberdiers in front and crossbows in the rear. He stripped bark from a tree and wrote on the trunk 'Pang Juan dies beneath this tree'. Arriving at dusk, Pang saw the message and struck a light to read it. At this signal 10,000 Qi crossbowmen opened up. The Qi attack destroyed the Wei army, and Pang Juan committed suicide.

Mameluke (or *Mamluk*) medieval Arabic term denoting troops recruited as slaves, trained, and then freed, serving the Ayyubid caliph. The Mamelukes were horse-archer lancers who trained to a very high standard by following the ◊*furusiya* manuals. During Louis IX of France's invasion of Egypt in 1248–50, the Mamelukes rebelled and one of their number, ◊Qutuz, seized power. Victors over the previously undefeated Mongols at Ain Jalut (see ◊Ain Jalut, Battle of) in 1260, the Mamelukes ruled Egypt and built a Levantine empire until they were conquered by the Ottomans 1488–1517.

Mamertine inhabitant of the city of Messana (now Messina) in Sicily. The Mamertines allied themselves with Rome in 264 BC, provoking the First Punic War (see ◊Punic War, First).

The Mamertines were originally mercenaries employed by Syracuse. In the 280s BC they seized the city of Messana and settled there under the name of their war god Mamers. They extended their territory but were defeated in battle by Syracuse (see ◊Hiero II) in 265 BC. To defend Messana they accepted an offer of Carthaginian protection in 262 BC (see ◊Hannibal Gisco), but later ejected the garrison and entered an alliance with Rome. When Syracuse and Carthage tried to regain Messana the Romans came to their defence.

Mammes, Battle of part of a pacification campaign in the wake of the Roman reconquest of Africa, in which the Romans, commanded by Solomon, defeated a large army of Moors, allegedly 50,000 strong, in 534.

The Moors set up a defensive position inside a ring of camels. This tactic had worked previously against the Vandals, because untrained horses will not close on camels. Initially the Romans had the same problem, but their general, Solomon, ordered his men to dismount and he personally led 500 soldiers in a charge on foot, which broke through the circle. Once the perimeter had been penetrated the remaining Romans were able to pour through and destroy the Moorish force.

mandala (Sanskrit 'circle', 'ring') classical Hindu doctrine, observed in India from about 500 BC until the Muslim conquests of the late 12th–early 13th century, that a king's neighbour must be regarded as a natural enemy and his neighbour's neighbour as a natural ally. It envisages a series of concentric circles spreading out from the territory of the king who desires to be a conqueror.

The king of the first circle is *vijigisu*, 'the desirer of conquest'; his neighbour is *ari*, 'the opponent'. Beyond him is *mitra*, 'the friend', then 'the enemy's friend', 'the friend's friend', and so on.

The *mandala* theory led to constant warfare, as when one king was conquered all the friendships and enmities beyond him went into reverse. It allowed Hindu kings to regard war as a royal sport, and acted against the rise of single empires, but had the disadvantage of leaving India at the mercy of invaders who would be welcomed by one king as an ally against another.

Mandalgarh city in Rajasthan, India, defended by a low rampart running for about 0.8 km/0.5 mi round a central hill, strengthened with bastions. It was built in the mid-12th century by the ◊Rajput chief of the Balnot clan and taken by the Muslims under Muzaffar Shah I of Gujarat at the end of the 14th century.

In 1446 it was besieged by Mahmud Khilji, Sultan of Malwa, who raised the siege in return for the promise of tribute. In 1457 he stormed the city walls, sparing the lives of the garrison in exchange for ransom.

Mandu fortress in central India on the summit of a flat-topped hill in the Vindhayan mountain range, defended by a wall some 37 km/23 mi long, with battlements, buttresses, and numerous gates. It was probably a stronghold from ancient times.

It was taken from the ◊Rajputs by a Muslim army under Ain al-Mulk in 1304, and a century later became the capital of the sultanate of Malwa under Hoshang Shah (ruled 1405–34). It was the scene of numerous battles and sieges.

mangonel stone-throwing engine. The term was often used indiscriminately by medieval chroniclers to refer to any type of stone-thrower. Specifically, a mangonel was an engine with a wooden arm ending in a spoon-shape on which the stone projectile was placed. It was operated by torsion through twisted ropes, the arm pulled back and released to impact against a crossbeam, throwing the stone forward on a low trajectory.

Maniakes, George (died 1043) Byzantine general and vigorous campaigner who won several victories over the Muslims and Normans in Syria, Sicily, and Italy between 1031 and 1042. He rose against the emperor Constantine IX in 1043, but died before he could reach Constantinople.

maniple tactical unit in the Roman republican ◊legion. The maniple, containing 60 or 120 men, was made up of two centuries (see ◊century) of infantry and commanded by the senior of the two centurions. A number of ◊*velites* (light-armed troops) were assigned to the maniples, giving them considerable versatility in battle.

By the late 2nd century BC the maniple was being replaced by the ◊cohort as the principal tactical unit within the legion.

Manlius, Lucius Roman general during the First Punic War (see ◊Punic War, First). As consul in 256 BC, he commanded the Roman fleet at Ecnomus (see ◊Ecnomus, Battle of) in which the Carthaginian fleet was destroyed.

As consul in 250 BC he was given command of the Roman fleet again and laid siege to Lilybaeum (Marsala), the Carthaginian headquarters on Sicily. He surrounded the city with strong siegeworks by land, but was unable to blockade the city by sea. His term of office

ended before the siege was complete and he returned to the Senate.

Manlius Vulso, Gnaeus Roman commander who conquered the Galatian tribes of Asia Minor in 189 BC. His army was attacked by Thracian tribesmen on the return to Italy and much of the booty taken in Asia was lost. He was criticized by the Roman Senate for his unprovoked invasion of Galatia and incompetence in Thrace.

He had also hoped to campaign against ◊Antiochus (III) the Great, but the latter proved unwilling to break the peace established after Magnesia in 190 BC (see ◊Magnesia, Battle of). Manlius' political connections enabled him to escape condemnation by the Senate and celebrate a lavish triumph in Rome.

Mannheim helmet alternative name for the ◊Coolus helmet.

Manorbier castle castle in Wales, 8 km/5 mi southeast of Pembroke. This was first built as an earthwork (fortification made of earth) some time in the 11th century, and was improved in the 12th century, firstly by the erection of a three-storied stone hall, then by the addition of a curtain wall with towers and a square, towered gatehouse. It the birthplace of Giraldus Cambrensis (c. 1150–22), a Welsh scholar and historian.

Mansurah, Battle of decisive battle between Mameluke Egyptian forces under the sultan Turan Shah and the crusader army of St Louis (Louis IX of France) during the Seventh Crusade, on 8 February 1250 at Mansurah in the Nile Delta, Egypt.

St Louis' crusaders were advancing upon Cairo, but were blocked at the town of Mansurah, 32 km/20 mi to the north. Seeking to outflank the position, Louis pushed crossbowmen across a Nile tributary, and they defended a bridgehead for the knights. The initial success was wasted when Robert of Artois led a rash charge into the town, where he was ambushed. The Templars suffered heavily, fighting as a rearguard to cover the crusader retreat.

Mantinea, Battle of (207 BC) defeat of the Spartan ◊Machanidas by ◊Philopoemen and the forces of the Achaean League, and one of the rare occasions in ancient warfare when artillery was employed on the battlefield.

To avoid missiles from the catapults along the Spartan front, Philopoemen launched his light cavalry on the left. Machanidas countered with a similar charge on his right, which drew in the mercenaries from both armies. At first the Spartans proved superior, but Machanidas pursued too far and Philopoemen was able to extend his citizen phalanx to the left and separate Machanidas from the rest of his army. The Spartans tried to advance but a dike impeded their progress and they were routed by Philopoemen's troops. Deserted by his mercenaries, Machanidas was killed by Philopoemen as he tried to cross the dike.

Mantinea, Battle of (362 BC) inconclusive battle that failed to restore Theban influence in the Peloponnese and, because of the Boeotian commander ◊Epaminondas' death, led to the beginning of Thebes' decline. Epaminondas used his cavalry as a strike force in this battle, marking the transition in the history of Greek warfare to this tactic which was later adopted by the Macedonians.

Having formed line as though for battle, Epaminondas led his phalanx off to the left and ordered it to lower its weapons as though about to make camp. As the enemy relaxed, he moved units from his right centre to behind his left, forming a deep left wing as at Leuctra (see ◊Leuctra, Battle of). Using Boeotian cavalry mixed with specially trained light infantry, he struck first on his left against the enemy right wing cavalry. The rout of their cavalry shook the enemy infantry next in line and it, too, gave way before the massed Boeotian left wing. In the moment of victory, Epaminondas was mortally wounded, and his men broke off the pursuit.

Mantinea, Battle of (418 BC) battle fought between Sparta and a mainly Argive, Mantinean and Athenian army, during the ◊Peloponnesian War, which ended Athens' hopes of creating an anti-Spartan coalition in the Peloponnese. Although the battle shows that Spartans could disobey orders, it also illustrates their tactical control.

Worried that his left was being overlapped, the Spartan king, ◊Agis II, ordered it to shift outwards while two units from the right plugged the gap. He hoped to overlap the enemy left because his line was longer, but his orders were disobeyed and the Spartan left was routed. However, most of the enemy centre fled and the Athenians on the left retreated. Agis ordered his right to wheel left

MANZIKERT, BATTLE OF

Decisive battle at Manzikert in eastern Turkey, on 19 August 1071, between the Seljuk Turks under Sultan ◊Alp-Arslan and the Byzantines led by Emperor Romanus IV (1067–71). It resulted in the destruction of the Byzantine regular army and the loss of most of Anatolia to the Turks.

Romanus gathered a large army in early 1071 to take the offensive against the Seljuk Turks. He advanced to the vicinity of Lake Van in eastern Anatolia, then divided his army in two, sending a force of Normans and Turks to forage while he besieged and captured Manzikert and began siege operations against Akhlat. Alp-Arslan sent an advance force under Soundaq to intercept the Byzantines while he gathered the remainder of his army. Soundaq successfully engaged the Byzantine covering forces in typical Turkish style, striking swiftly with mounted archers then vanishing when his opponents tried to engage decisively.

Romanus was surprised by the arrival of the main Seljuk army, but as he had superior numbers he rejected a peace offer and prepared for battle.

The Byzantines formed a typical two line formation, Romanus commanding the first line and the second led by Andronicus Ducas, nephew of the previous emperor and Romanus' political enemy. The Byzantines advanced towards the Seljuk camp but failed to pin down their opponents who retired in the face of their approach. At dusk, Romanus ceased trying to catch his elusive enemy and began to withdraw towards his own camp. The order caused confusion in the Byzantine ranks and the Turks seized the opportunity to attack. The Byzantine front line panicked while Ducas ordered the second line to continue the withdrawal, abandoning Romanus to his fate. Every man in the Byzantine front line was killed or captured, including the emperor who was taken prisoner.

past the Athenians and catch the victorious allied right in its unprotected flank as it streamed back across the battlefield.

Mantinea, Siege of attack on Mantinea in 385 BC, which illustrates the way Sparta disciplined its allies after the ◊Corinthian War.

After ravaging had failed to force the Mantineans to surrender, the Spartan king Agesipolis, who feared a long siege, dammed the river flowing through the brick walls surrounding the city. When the rising water began to undermine the walls, the Mantineans were forced to capitulate. They agreed to demolish the walls and to separate into the five villages which had constituted their original state.

mantlet (or *mantelet*) in medieval warfare, a covering used as a mobile shelter behind which defensive walls could be approached. Mantlets were light enough to be carried overhead and gave protection from above. They were also built around weapons and siege engines, like a wooden skirt, to give protection. A mantlet wall was a secondary defensive wall around a tower.

Manuel (I) Comnenus (1118–80) Byzantine emperor 1143–80. Faced with the loss of ◊Edessa in 1144, he supported the Second Crusade (see ◊Crusades) 1146–48. His invasion of Italy 1155–57 failed, leading to a neglect of his Anatolian frontiers, and Latin attacks on Egypt 1168–69 suffered disastrous defeat by Turks at Myriocephalon in 1176 (see ◊Myriocephalon, Battle of).

Manuel's policies included adopting western military practices, such as jousting, at his court. His attempts to recover territories in Italy were over-ambitious, and the result was that his attack on the ◊Seljuks 1146–47 was halted by a Sicilian invasion. Manuel recognized the need for cooperation with the Latins, but this proved difficult to organize.

Maranga, Battle of inconclusive victory in June 363 for the Romans commanded by the emperor Julian the Apostate over the Persians led by King Shapur. Although they won a tactical victory the Romans were far from home, cut off from supplies, and constantly harassed by the Persians. Strategically they had lost the campaign and were forced to withdraw. A few days later Julian was killed in a skirmish and his successor Jovian was forced to agree to unfavourable peace terms.

The Persian army consisted of heavily armoured ◊cataphracts, supported by archers, elephants, and spearmen. The Romans, whose strength lay in their infantry, advanced at the double to lessen the effects of the Persian

archery. The Persians, not willing to engage in close combat, withdrew in good order, and kept the Romans at bay through continual archery fire.

Marathon, Battle of battle fought in 490 BC on the Plain of Marathon, northeast of Athens, Greece, between the Athenians and their Plataean allies and the Persian invasion force of ◊Darius (I) the Great, which was resoundingly defeated. It is one of the most famous battles of antiquity.

The Persians had perhaps 25,000 men in all, including cavalry, while the Athenians and their Plataean allies had perhaps 10,000 ◊hoplites. Thinning their centre to cover the longer enemy line, the Greeks advanced, probably doubling the last few hundred yards to nullify enemy archery fire. The enemy wings almost immediately gave way and fled northeastwards to their ships; when their centre broke through, the Greek wings turned inwards to take it in both flanks as it tried to retreat. The Greeks then pursued the Persians to their ships, and although they captured only 7, their victory was complete, 6,400 Persians allegedly being killed for the loss of only 192 Athenians.

Marcellus, Claudius (died 208 BC) Roman general during the Second Punic War (see ◊Punic War, Second). He was Rome's most distinguished and popular commander of the war.

His fame was established during his first consulship in 222 BC when he killed the Gallic chieftain Viridomarus in single combat (see ◊Clastidium, Battle of). In 216 BC he was placed in command of the Roman army and pursued Quintus ◊Fabius Maximus' policy of containment against ◊Hannibal the Great. As consul in 214 BC he campaigned in Sicily, capturing Syracuse, and as consul again in 212 BC and 208 BC he campaigned in Italy. In this last command he was attacked and killed while reconnoitring near the Carthaginian camp.

March(er) medieval English term referring to the Welsh border lands, in which petty warfare was endemic. Always a militarized zone, it was highly castellated from the Norman Conquest onwards and an area for recruiting experienced troops.

The barons of the region were known as the Marcher Lords. They became especially important during periods of civil war, such as King Stephen's reign (1136–53), and played a part in English politics throughout the medieval period.

Marcomannic Wars series of wars 166–80 fought by the Roman emperor ◊Marcus

Aurelius against the Germanic tribes on the Roman Empire's Danubian frontier, involving in particular the Germanic tribal confederations of the Marcomanni and Quadi, but also the Sarmatian Iazyges.

In 167 the Germanic tribes mounted a series of massive raids across the frontier, at one point reaching as far as Aquileia in northern Italy. In a series of hard-fought campaigns involving large numbers of Roman troops fighting under the emperor's personal supervision, these tribes were forced into submission. Just before his death in 180, Marcus Aurelius was poised to annex a large area east of the Danube, a move that might have provided the empire with a more secure frontier.

Marcus Aurelius (AD 121–180) Roman emperor 161–180 and Stoic philosopher. He fought a series of campaigns on the Rhine–Danube frontier, known collectively as the ◊Marcomannic Wars. He had a column constructed in Rome bearing reliefs of campaign scenes, but these are considered less realistic than those on the more famous Trajan's Column.

Mardia, Battle of battle between the Roman emperor ◊Constantine (I) the Great and his eastern rival and co-ruler Valerius Licinianus Licinius in 315. A marginal victory for Constantine, Mardia was as hard-fought as the earlier battle of Cibalae (see ◊Cibalae, Battle of).

Constantine had concealed 5,000 men on high ground behind the enemy line, but their sudden attack was not enough to prevent Licinius' organized retreat.

Mardonius (died 479 BC) Persian general, nephew and son-in-law of ◊Darius (I) the Great. He commanded a campaign in Thrace in 492 BC, being defeated and wounded by the Brygi tribe before eventually subduing them. In 480 he accompanied Xerxes I's invasion of Greece and stayed with the army after its defeat by the Greeks at Salamis (see ◊Salamis, Battle of 480 BC). He was killed at Plataea (see ◊Plataea, Battle of).

After the defeat at Salamis he wintered in Thessaly, trying to break up the Greek alliance diplomatically. In 479 he advanced south, captured Athens, but fell back again to Boeotia in the face of the Spartan advance.

Margat castle castle in Syria, 160 km / 100 mi north-northwest of Tripoli. It was built by the Frankish Mazoir family in around 1110, and sold to the Knights Hospitaller (see ◊Military Order) in 1186. The largest of the crusader castles, it was concentric in form and always stocked for a five-year siege. It was abandoned around 1209 as the crusaders withdrew from Palestine.

The castle was besieged in 1285 by Sultan Kalaoun who mined the great tower, but he was reluctant to destroy such a work of architecture and invited the Crusaders to inspect the mine, whereupon they capitulated.

MARIUS, GAIUS (C. 157–C. 87 BC)

Roman consul and military commander, sometimes regarded as the great reformer of the Roman army, reputedly changing it from a citizen militia into a professional force by recruiting men who lacked the minimum property qualification for military service.

Born into an obscure family, Marius made his reputation as a cavalryman and junior officer, and in 133 BC attracted the attention of ◊Scipio Aemilianus (Scipio Africanus Minor) at ◊Numantia. In 109 BC he served in Numidia in North Africa as legate to Metellus, a commander in the ◊Jugurthine War. He returned to Rome in 108 to seek election to the consulship. Having gained this in 107 BC, he was given Metellus' command by popular demand, and, despite his claim to superior martial ability, won the war by following much the same strategy as his predecessor. By popular demand he also received a consulship from 104 to 100 BC to fight the Cimbri and Teutones, Germanic tribes whose migration threatened Italy, and his carefully trained army defeated the invaders. In 88 BC he provoked a civil war by attempting to steal the Asian command from ◊Sulla. When Sulla turned his troops on Rome, Marius fled to Africa where he raised an army from his veterans settled in the area. He returned to retake the city in 87 BC, but died just days later.

Margus, Battle of decisive confrontation between Roman emperor ◊Diocletian and Carinus, the brother of the deceased emperor Numerianus, in 285. The battle was fought between the armies of the eastern and western provinces at the town of Margus on the Danube. Carinus' army seemed to be gaining advantage when he was murdered by one of his own tribunes.

Marienburg castle (Polish *Malbork*) castle in Poland, 40 km/25 mi southeast of Gdansk. Headquarters of the Teutonic Knights (see ◊Military Order), it was built in the latter part of the 13th century in two main sections: the *Hochschloss* of the religious element and the *Mittelschloss* of the military element of the Order. In 1335–41 more construction led to the *Unterschloss*, containing services such as a brickworks.

Further improvements were made 1352–83, but in 1410 the Order was defeated by the Poles at Tannenberg (see ◊Tannenberg, Battle of). The castle was placed under siege for several months but did not fall. The power of the Order, however, was broken, and after various incidents the castle was formally ceded to Poland in 1466.

mariyanna (or *mariyanni*) elite class of people of the Late Bronze Age, particularly throughout Mitanni and Hurrian lands, mentioned in documents from Alalakh, Ugarit, and other north Levantine city-states, and associated with chariots.

Depictions of *mariyanna* show them wearing scale armour and helmets, sometimes with a gorget (neck guard). Kikkulis, a Hurrian *mariyanna*, wrote a treatise on training horses for chariot teams, which was discovered alongside other horse-training manuals at ◊Hattusas, the Hittite capital.

Marj 'Ayyun, Battle of battle between the Muslim forces of ◊Saladin, the Ayyubid sultan of Egypt, and the army of King Baldwin IV of the Christian Kingdom of Jerusalem on 10 June 1179, at Marj 'Ayyun in Galilee. Saladin defeated Baldwin's forces as they made an ill-disciplined pursuit of the Muslims.

Baldwin had marched to intercept Saladin who was attacking Sidon in Lebanon and ravaging the Syrian coastal plain. After an initial success against Muslim skirmishers, the Christians advanced too rapidly, their horse and foot soldiers becoming separated. When Saladin counterattacked with his main body, Baldwin's forces were defeated piecemeal.

Mark Antony (82–30 BC) (*Marcus Antonius*) Roman politician and soldier who was the last serious rival to Octavian's (later ◊Augustus) domination of the Roman world. He served in Palestine and Egypt 57–55 BC, and then with Julius ◊Caesar in Gaul and during the civil war, commanding the left wing at Pharsalus (see ◊Pharsalus, Battle of). After Caesar's assassination, he formed the Second Triumvirate with Octavian and Lepidus.

In 42 he defeated Brutus and Cassius at Philippi (see ◊Philippi, battles of). He took Egypt as his share of the empire and formed a liaison with the Egyptian queen Cleopatra, but returned to Rome in 40 to marry Octavia, the sister of Octavian. In 32 the Senate declared war on Cleopatra, and Antony, who had combined forces with Cleopatra, was defeated by Octavian at Actium (see ◊Actium, Battle of) in 31. He returned to Egypt and committed suicide.

Maroboduus king of the Germanic Marcomanni tribe who headed a confederation of Suebic tribes and massed a large semi-permanent army. In AD 6 he was saved from the attack of a large Roman army commanded by Tiberius when the Roman emperor was called away to suppress the Pannonian Revolt. In 17 Moroboduus was defeated by the German chieftain ◊Arminius and sought sanctuary within the Roman Empire.

Marsala wreck Carthaginian warship discovered off the coast of Sicily near Marsala and dated to the 3rd century BC. The ship was equipped with a ram with a single rowing bench, probably with 2 rowers to an oar and about 70 oarsmen. Excavation has revealed a sophisticated hull construction and the use of prefabricated components allowing speedy and efficient construction to a high combat potential.

marshal (or *maréchal*) medieval term for the military commander of a ruler or magnate. The marshal was responsible for the supply and maintenance of equipment, horses, and general logistical support. He also led the troops into battle.

Marshal, William (c. 1147–1219) First earl of Pembroke and regent of England 1217–19. He was a model chivalric warrior, jouster, and crusader. William's greatest military triumph was in defeating the French invasion 1216–18, including personally leading the charge at Lincoln in 1217 (see ◊Lincoln, Battle of) at the age of 70.

William is mostly known through a celebratory poem written in around 1225, which makes him out to be the perfect chivalrous knight and tells his story in the form of a romance. He was a successful jouster at tournaments in the 1170s, and made a living following Henry the Young King (the eldest son of ◊Henry II) until his death in 1184. William defended Henry II against the ambitions of his son ◊Richard (I) the Lionheart, actually unhorsing him in 1189. Richard bore no grudge, for he gave William the heiress to the earldom of Pembroke, with extensive lands in Wales and Ireland. William did not accompany Richard on crusade, but served him loyally. Often in dispute with King John, he nevertheless supported him at the end and was awarded the regency for the child Henry III.

Marwar Prakrit *Maru-war* 'the death region' desert area in Rajasthan, India, containing numerous ◊Rajput strongholds, including ◊Ajmer, Bikaner, ◊Jaisalmer, ◊Jodhpur, Umarkot, and others.

At the time of the early Muslim invasions the region was governed by Rajputs of the Pratihara clan. Their successors were ousted by the rival Rathor clan early in the 12th century. The area was captured by ◊Ala al-Din Khilji in 1307 and extensively raided by ◊Ahmad Shah, Bahmani ruler of the Deccan, in 1433.

marzban military governor of a Sassanian Persian frontier. In the Parthian period it is an officer superior to the satrap (provincial governor), perhaps in charge of several provinces.

The four ◊*spahbads*, one for each direction, set up by the Sassanian Persian king Chosroes (I) ◊Anushirvan were probably powerful *marzbans* under another name, though one source believes that the eastern frontier was governed by a *spahbad* with four *marzbans* under him. On the eastern frontier the title *kanarang* was a local synonym of *marzban*.

Masada Jewish hilltop stronghold which was occupied by Zealots in AD 66 and resisted a determined Roman siege. Sited on a plateau 400 m / 1,312 ft high and with only two treacherous approaches, the hill was developed into a fortress from the 2nd century BC. It became Herod the Great of Judaea's choice of refuge for his family during a Parthian invasion in 40 BC.

Herod strengthened the fortifications with 37 towers and added arsenals, cisterns, and huge storerooms, making Masada both impregnable and self-sustaining. In AD 66 a group of Zealots seized the fortress and were besieged by Roman forces for six months in 73. By building circumvallations and a massive ramp on the west side to bring siege engines up to the height of the wall, the Romans made slow progress until the defenders committed mass suicide.

Masada, Siege of Roman siege and capture of the Jewish-held fortress of Masada in the Roman province of Judaea (present-day Israel) in AD 73–74. Masada had been captured by the Zealots at the start of the Jewish rebellion against Roman rule in AD 66. It was the last stronghold to be taken by the Roman forces suppressing the rebellion. Rather than surrender to the Romans, the 960 defenders committed suicide.

Situated on a precipitous height near the west bank of the Dead Sea, the fortress seemed impregnable to direct assault, and could not be starved into submission because huge cisterns and large store rooms provided the garrison with plentiful supplies of food and water. The governor of Judaea, Flavius Silva, led the 10th Legion (*Legio X Fretensis*) to Masada. Surrounding the fortress with a wall, the Romans built a massive assault ramp against the cliffs of the western side of the mountain. A siege tower and ram ascended the ramp and breached the wall.

Masat Höyük site in present-day Turkey of the Hittite military outpost of Tapigga on the ◊Gasgan border, near the river Cekerek. Military reports dating from the Middle Kingdom period (1420–1340 BC) have been found here. As well as giving details of the military hierarchy, they record incursions of the Gasgans, deployment of troops and reconnaissance, and day-to-day administration.

Tapigga and Anziliya (Zile), 35 km/21 mi to the north, were used as bases by ◊Mursilis II in his early campaigns against the Gasgans, and refortified by Muwatallis and handed over to his brother Hattusilis III.

Masinissa (c. 50–148 BC) king of the Massylii of North Africa from 206/205 BC and king of Numidia from 202 BC, as prince regent. Masinissa was raised in Carthage and served the Carthaginians as an ally at the start of the Second Punic War (see ◊Punic War, Second). Following the Battle of Ilipa in 206 BC he joined the Roman cause and fought with the Romans at Zama in 202 BC.

He received Numidia as a reward from Rome for his assistance at Zama. He spent his last years expanding his kingdom at Carthage's expense, provoking it to war in 152 BC.

Masui, Battle of battle in 578 BC in which a coalition led by commander Marquis Li of Jin attacked and heavily defeated Duke Huan of the Chinese state of Qin. The victory brought Jin to the peak of its power, dominating all the Chinese states.

mata 'hundred' Aramaic term for a subdivision of the Achaemenid Persian ◊*degel*. The name confirms the decimal organization of Achaemenid troops known from other sources. Unlike his senior officer, the commander of a *mata* was generally of the same nationality as his men.

Mathos (lived 3rd century BC) Libyan mercenary leader in the ◊Mercenary War. He was elected general by his mutinous mercenaries and, along with ◊Spendius and ◊Autaritus, led the challenge to Carthaginian power in Libya. He was finally brought to battle by ◊Hamilcar Barca in 237 BC and was captured, suffering many tortures before death.

Maurice (*Mauricius*) East Roman (Byzantine) emperor 582–602 who successfully campaigned against the Persians and ◊Avars. He reformed the East Roman army, creating a more centralized, regular organization and reducing the number of semiprivate armies of ◊*bucellarii*. He also began to introduce new equipment and tactics, derived from the nomadic Avars.

Mauron, Battle of battle fought on 14 August 1352 during the ◊Hundred Years' War in which Walter Bentley's Anglo-Breton forces defeated the French under Guy de Nesle at Mauron, Brittany.

Bentley's 3,000 men, archers and dismounted men-at-arms, took up a defensive position on a slope behind a river. The French force, twice as large, was also dismounted except for 700 cavalry on the left flank. Pinning the English with his main force, de Nesle used his cavalry to outflank the English right. The English archers fled, but a counterattack in the centre threw the French back with heavy losses: about 2,000 men-at-arms were killed, including 89 knights of the newly formed Order of the Star.

Maxentius, Marcus Aurelius Valerius (279–312) Roman emperor from 306, son of ◊Maximian. He was appointed *princeps* in Italy and Africa following a popular rising in 306. With his father's assistance he drove Severus from Italy and was proclaimed *augustus* (emperor), then allied himself with ◊Constantine (I) the Great who married his sister. He defeated an attempt by the eastern emperor of Rome, Valerius Maximianus Galerius, to invade Italy and an attempt by his father to depose him, however, his position was not recognised by the Conference at Carnuntum. He was finally defeated by Constantine at the Milvian Bridge in 312 (see ◊Milvian Bridge, Battle of the). Maxentius

drowned during the retreat from this battle and his corpse was decapitated.

Maximian (c. 240–c. 310) (*Marcus Aurelius Valerius Maximianus*) Roman emperor from 286 to 305. He rose through the ranks of the army by conspicuous service under the emperors Aurelian and Probus before being named *caesar* (heir to the throne) in 285. After crushing the revolt of the Bagaudae in Gaul in 305, he was promoted to be *augustus* (emperor) of the western Roman provinces, equal in power to ◊Diocletian in the east. In 296–98 he fought a hard campaign against the Alamanni, but was unable to defeat ◊Carausius. He later campaigned against the Carpi on the Danube and the Mauretanians in Africa, but in 305 both he and Diocletian retired from public life. In 307 he reclaimed the position of *augustus* in an effort to help his son, Maximentius, defeat Severus and Galerius, but he later turned against his son and unsuccessfully attempted to depose him as *caesar*. He was persuaded to abdicate by Diocletian and returned to retirement in 308, living at the court of Constantine. In about 310 he committed suicide (or was executed) at Massilia (Marseille) after the failure of a revolt against Constantine that he had led.

Maximilian I (1459–1519) German king from 1486, Holy Roman emperor from 1493. He was the son of the emperor Frederick III (1415–93). He had acquired the Low Countries through his marriage to Mary of Burgundy in 1477. He married his son Philip I 'the Handsome' (1478–1506) to the heiress to the Spanish throne, and undertook long wars with Italy and Hungary in attempts to extend Habsburg power.

In Italy Maximilian lost Milan to Louis XII of France (1462–1515). In Germany he agreed the Perpetual Edict, forbidding private war and private armies, but this proved difficult to enforce. The Treaty of Basel (1499) granted independence to the Swiss.

Maximus, Marcus Valerius Corvus (c. 371–c. 271 BC) Roman general during the first Samnite War (see ◊Samnite Wars) whose strategic gains and military successes were to aid Roman supremacy in Italy.

At the age of 23 he served as an officer in campaigns against the Gauls, and gained his cognomen Corvus ('Raven') for killing an enemy chieftain in single combat. As consul in 346 BC he campaigned against the Volsci and destroyed their city of Satricum (modern Conca), an important commercial rival to Rome. As consul again in 343 BC he achieved two decisive victories over the Samnites in the first Samnite War. In 335 BC he was elected consul for a forth time and captured Cales (modern Calvi), which would become an important Roman base during the Samnite and Punic Wars. He died aged 100.

Maxstoke castle castle in England, 13 km/8 mi northwest of Coventry. Built under a licence to crenellate (build battlements) issued to the Duke of Huntingdon in 1346, this began as a fortified manor house. It was extended in the 15th century by the Duke of Buckingham to form a rectangular enclosure with six-sided towers at the corners and a well-protected gatehouse on one of the longer sides.

Mayor of the Palace high-ranking Merovingian Frankish noble who exercised power on behalf of the figurehead king of Gaul (France) and western Germany from 439 to 751.

Mazar Tagh 8th–9th century Tibetan fort controlling routes through the vassal-kingdom of Khotan in western Xinjiang. It was situated 150 km/93 mi northeast of Khotan on a sandstone cliff, the last spur of a range of hills, on the bank of the river Khotan. A small, squarish brick fort with a single watchtower, it was probably taken and burned during the 9th-century Uighur conquest of the area. Caches of Tibetan military documents have been found there.

Medway, Battle of the battle between the Romans and the Britons in AD 43, thought to have taken place on the river Medway in present-day Kent, England. It was the first encounter between the Britons and the Roman invasion force under Aulus ◊Plautius and was a major victory for the latter.

In a two-day engagement, Batavian auxiliaries crossed the river, taking the Britons by surprise. The future emperor Vespasian also distinguished himself in the battle.

Megat Iskander Shah (c. 1340–1424) (*Sri Paramesvara*) founder and first king of

MEGIDDO, BATTLE OF (1458 BC)

The first major battle of the first campaign of Pharaoh Tuthmosis III in 1458 BC. His victory over a Canaanite alliance ensured Egyptian control over the Levant south of the Lebanon, and influence as far north as Ugarit, on the north Syrian coast opposite Cyprus, and the great bend of the river Euphrates, near Carchemish.

When the female pharaoh Hatshepsut died in 1458 BC, her co-ruler Tuthmosis was determined to emulate the successes of his grandfather Tuthmosis I and restore Egyptian domination over the Levant. He marched north as far as Yaham, where intelligence reports informed him that the prince of Kadesh had amassed an army under 330 leaders from as far afield as Mitanni (northern Mesopotamia) and Qode (classical Cilicia). The ruler of Kadesh was based at Megiddo and controlled the routes north over the Carmel Range (Egyptian Mount User). One route headed north towards Jokneam and another along the Dothan Valley. A third route was a narrow defile that led direct to Megiddo along the Aruna Valley. After consultation with his staff, Tuthmosis chose this route.

The Canaanites had positioned their forces north and south of Megiddo, and the Egyptian army advanced unnoticed through the defile over the next two days. The armies faced each other in open battle on the third day, the Canaanites in two divisions, the Egyptians in three. The Egyptian army won the field but not the battle, which turned into a seven-month siege of Megiddo. The siege was successful, Tuthmosis capturing 924 chariots and over 200 coats of scale armour, including those of the prince of Megiddo.

In 1453 BC Tuthmosis struck north beyond the Lebanon Mountains and in 1452 BC he took Kadesh, the city of the leader of the forces at Megiddo, and then marched to the coast, cutting through ◊Amurru and capturing Sumur (Simyra). In these and subsequent campaigns, Tuthmosis razed the orchards of the towns after looting grain, fruit, and wine.

Malacca in the Malay peninsula. A prince of Palembang in Sumatra married to a Javanese princess of Majapahit, he fled Majapahit civil wars in about 1390 and usurped the throne of Tumasik (Singapore), killing the king, who was a vassal of the Thai king of Ayutthaya. He was expelled by the Thais or their Malay vassals, and settled about 1402 at Malacca, which he built into a major city.

Malacca was an insignificant fishing-village which with the help of Malay pirates he built up first into a pirate base and then into a great naval and commercial city that controlled the Straits of Malacca. He submitted to Ming China, which confirmed him as King of Malacca in 1405, and relied heavily on Chinese support against pressure from the Thai king ◊Intharaja I. Zheng He's fleet visited him in 1409. He took the name Megat Iskander Shah after converting to Islam at the age of 72.

Megiddo Bronze and Iron Age fortified site guarding the Esdraelon Valley (biblical Jezreel, modern Qishon) in northern Israel; it is famous for the victory of the Egyptian king Tuthmosis III over the Canaanites in 1458 BC (see ◊Megiddo, Battle of 1458 BC), and as the site of the final battle (Armageddon) of the Bible.

In the time of Pharaoh Merenptah (1213–1203 BC) Megiddo was taken over by the ◊Peoples of the Sea, perhaps as an Egyptian garrison force. Under Deborah and Barak, the Israelites conquered the Vale of Jezreel and Megiddo became a Hebrew town. It was refortified under Solomon (961–922 BC) only to be destroyed by Pharaoh Shishak in 924 BC. It was rebuilt and expanded under Ahab of Israel (860–842 BC).

Megiddo became the capital of the Assyrian province of Galilee after the Battle of Qarqar in 854 BC (see ◊Qarqar, Battle of), when the anti-Assyrian coalition of Levantine armies was defeated. It was here that Josiah, King of Judah, was defeated and killed by Pharaoh Necho II in 609 BC. This event marked, for all intents and purposes, the independence of Judah, thus symbolizing the last battle: Armageddon (Hebrew *Hâr-Megiddo*, 'Mountain of Megiddo') in Revelation 16.16.

Megiddo, Battle of (609 BC) battle fought in 609 BC between Judah and Egypt. It marked the end of Judah's bid for independence and resulted in the death of its king, Josiah (639–609 BC), and the country being placed again in the Egyptian sphere. Within a generation Jerusalem was sacked and the Hebrew people were deported to Babylonia – thus this battle became the Armageddon, the last battle between Good and Evil (Hebrew *Hâr-Megiddo*, 'Mountain of Megiddo') in Revelation 16.16.

Josiah was killed as he attempted to stop the advance of the Egyptian pharaoh Necho II, marching north towards ◊Carchemish to aid the Assyrians in their fight against the Chaldeans under Nebuchadnezzar. On returning south, Necho replaced Jehoahaz II with his brother Jehoiachin (608–598 BC) and Judah once again came under Egyptian influence, until the sack of Jerusalem by Nebuchadnezzar.

Mehmet (II) the Conqueror (1432–81) Ottoman sultan 1451–81, who finally achieved the long-held Ottoman objective of capturing Constantinople, in 1453. He also conquered the Greek cities of Mistra in 1460 and Trebizond in 1461, and invaded Italy 1479–80. His forces pressed east to take the Crimea in 1475 and westward into Italy, until his death.

In preparation for his attack on Constantinople, he built a fortress called Rumeli Hisar in 1452 to seal off the Bosporus. In the spring of 1453 he gathered a large army and fleet, together with heavy artillery to batter the city's huge walls. Freed to move westwards after the fall of the city, Mehmet subdued Serbia in 1454 and conquered it in 1459, but was defied by the Hungarian leader Janos Hunyadi at Belgrade in 1456 and by the Transylvanian ruler Vlad Tepes until 1462. Mehmet attacked Greece 1456–58 and took the last Greek outpost at Trebizond in Asia Minor in 1461.

Melanthius, Battle of Roman victory in 559 over the Bulgars in which ◊Belisarius led a small force of 300 veterans, together with locally raised levies, to drive the Bulgars from the walls of Constantinople. This was the last time Belisarius commanded a force in battle.

Melitene, Battle of victory in 576 for the East Romans over the Persians in a long and intermittent war between the two empires, which lasted for most of the 6th century. The Roman victory opened the way for a successful invasion of Persian Armenia and led to the Persians seeking a temporary truce the following year.

Memnon of Rhodes (died 334 BC) Greek commander in Persian service. He fought at the river Granicus (see ◊Granicus, Battle of the) in 334 BC against the invasion force of ◊Alexander (III) the Great, held Halicarnassus against the Macedonians although he had to evacuate the city, and led a naval counterattack in Alexander's rear, capturing Chios and Lesbos, where he fell ill and died.

From 366 BC he and his brother Mentor served under the satrap (provincial governor) Artabazos, their sister's husband. Artabazos rebelled, but the brothers fled into exile with ◊Philip (II) of Macedon, and in 344 Mentor secured Memnon's pardon. Later, Memnon opposed the army Philip sent to invade Asia, defeating it after its general Parmenio was recalled in 336. When ◊Alexander (III) the Great invaded the Persian Empire, Memnon proposed a scorched-earth withdrawal but was overruled by Darius III's satraps.

mengan mouke (or *meng-an mou-k'o*) military and socio-economic organization of the Jurchen Jin dynasty (1114–1234) under ◊Wanyen Aguda in Manchuria and north China. *Mengan mouke* is translated literally as 'units of 1,000 and 100'. Three hundred Jurchen families, each three providing one cavalryman, were grouped into a *mouke*, and ten of these formed a *mengan*. The cavalry thus raised provided the ◊*guaizi ma* formations.

Menggu jun (or *Meng-ku chün*) 'Mongol army', the ethnically Mongolian part of the army of the Mongol Yuan dynasty in China (1260–1368) that was under central government control, as opposed to the ◊*tammachi* troops and the Chinese ◊*Han jun* and ◊*xinfu jun*. Mongol troops were garrisoned in north China as well as in Mongolia itself, but were less widely used in the south where neither terrain nor climate was ideal for them.

Meng Tian (died 210 BC) (or *Meng T'ien*) Chinese general under the emperor ◊Qin Shi Huangdi. He campaigned on the northern border from about 220 BC, defeating the ◊Xiongnu in the ◊Ordos campaign and clearing them from the Ordos loop of the Yellow River and areas in Gansu and Inner Mongolia. He fortified the frontier with the first ◊Great Wall of China. He was ordered to commit suicide after the emperor's death.

menpo Japanese iron face mask worn with full armour, dating from the Muromachi period (1333–1568). It had an attached neck guard and was secured to the face by the helmet ties. The features were often exaggerated and the interior was usually lacquered red.

Menua king of Urartu (biblical Ararat; in present-day Armenia) 810–786 BC, the grandson of Sarduri I (c. 839–811 BC) who had first united the kingdom. Menua challenged the power of Assyria and expanded Urartu to its greatest extent.

He pushed north towards Qulhu (classical Colchis), west to the river Euphrates, and south towards Assyria itself. His successors, including his son Argishti I and grandson Sarduri II, succeeded in reaching the Black Sea at Qulhu and penetrating further east towards the Caspian Sea.

Mercadier (lived 12th century) English ◊routier leader who became the chief commander of ◊Richard (I) the Lionheart. He participated in Richard's successes in France at Vernon, and Fréteval (see ◊Fréteval, Battle of) in 1194. He was awarded the lordship of Périgord, in southwestern France. When Richard was wounded at Châlus-Chabrol (see ◊Châlus-Chabrol, Siege of) in 1199, Mercadier's surgeon, seeking to aid the king, hastened his death. Mercadier ignored the dying king's wish that the man who killed him should be well treated as an acknowledgement of his marksmanship, and the crossbowman was flayed alive.

Merceneries, medieval In the European medieval period, any soldier hired to fight. The commonest type of mercenary belonged to a company of experienced soldiers hired as a group under its captain. Famous captains included Mercadier for ◊Richard (I) the Lionheart of England and Cadoc for ◊Philip (II) Augustus of France.

Many mercenaries were recruited in France and the Low Countries, and were commonly foreigners in the lands where they functioned. They were usually unpopular, blamed for the policies of their masters: destroying crops, burning towns, and plundering. They were condemned by the Catholic Church.

Mercenary War (or *Truceless War*) war fought 241–237 BC between Carthage and its unpaid mercenaries and native Libyan population after the end of the First Punic War. The various rebel armies were finally defeated and their cities reduced by the Carthaginians.

Having been defeated by Rome, the Carthaginian government was unable to pay its extensive mercenary forces their arrears. Assembled at Sicca, the various nationalities – Iberians, Ligurians, Celts, Balearic Islanders, Greeks, Italians, and Libyans – united when negotiations broke down, and appointed ◊Mathos, ◊Spendius, and ◊Autaritus as their generals. They seized Tunis and promoted a major revolt of Libyan subject peoples and Phoenician cities.

The war was mismanaged by the Carthaginian general ◊Hanno the Great, who was defeated at Utica in 241 BC, and Carthage itself was later besieged. The Carthaginians showed great resilience and appointed ◊Hamilcar Barca who won a victory over Spendius' army at the river Bagradas in 240 BC and later was able to break the siege of Carthage.

The war was notable for the atrocities committed by both sides and the dangerous rivalry between Hamilcar and his political opponent Hanno. Eventually they were forced to make a reconciliation, in about 238 BC, and were able to annihilate the various armies of the rebels and reduce their cities.

Merenptah son and successor 1213–1203 BC of the Egyptian pharaoh Ramses II. Merenptah faced different enemies from his father: the Hittites were now allies, but south of the Lebanon Mountains he had to subdue rebellious tribes, including the people of Israel in 1210 BC. The main danger came from the sea and the western desert, with an attack by Libu (Libyan) tribesmen, whose allies included Shardana, ◊Lukka, and other ◊Peoples of the Sea, in 1208 BC.

Meretun, Battle of battle fought in the West Saxon kingdom of Wessex, England, in 871 in which the Danes under ◊Halfdan gained a victory over the Saxons commanded by King Aethelred and his brother Alfred (see ◊Alfred the Great).

The Saxons initially succeeded in driving back both divisions of Halfdan's army, but the Danes rallied and at the end of the day 'had possession of the place of slaughter'.

Mérida, Battle of victory in 428 for the Vandals over the Suevi, who were trying to break away from Vandal control in Spain.

Merv, Siege of (or *Marv*) seven-day siege in 1221 of the town of Merv (or Marv) in Khurasan (northeastern Iran) by a Mongol army under ◊Genghis Khan's youngest son Tolui. Surrendering on a promise that their lives would be spared, the population of over a million were all massacred except for 400 artisans and children taken as slaves.

The siege was part of Genghis Khan's invasion of the empire of ◊Ala al-Din Khwarazm Shah.

Mesad Boqeq fort (Roman *Castell Dimmidi*) Roman fort in Libya, the southernmost outpost on the Numidian frontier, 300 km/186 mi from the nearest legionary fortress at Lambaesis. It was constructed by the emperor Septimius Severus in AD 198. The defences followed the edge of the hilltop that it occupied, giving an irregular plan and area of 0.5 ha/1.2 acres.

The walls were built 2 m/6.5 ft thick and although no interval or corner towers have been uncovered, the finds of artillery ammunition within the fort suggests that such towers

existed. As the fort was abandoned in 238, it provides a snapshot of fortifications of the time, with less emphasis on defensive features. It lacks the thicker walls and reaching projecting towers found in later Roman forts, such as Xanten and Burg.

Metaurus, Battle of the battle fought in 207 BC, during the Second Punic War (see ◊Punic War, Second), in which the Roman army of Gaius Claudius ◊Nero defeated the Carthaginian army of ◊Hasdrubal Barca on the banks of the river Metaurus, Italy.

Hasdrubal had recently entered Italy with an army to reinforce his brother ◊Hannibal the Great when he was confronted by a large Roman army. He attempted to retreat, but was pursued and forced to make a stand beside the river. His elephants turned back on his own lines and, despite a desperate defence, the Romans stormed his position. Between 10,000 (according to the Greek historian Polybius) and 50,000 (according to the Roman historian Livy) Carthaginians were killed, including Hasdrubal; 2,000 Romans were lost.

mete zashi alternative name for the ◊*yoroi doshi*, a short, heavy Japanese dagger used in close combat to pierce armour. The name has connotations regarding the ritual hour appropriate for the weapon's use.

Methven, Battle of battle fought in 1306 in which English forces under the Earl of Pembroke attacked ◊Robert (I) the Bruce in his camp at Methven to the west of Perth, Scotland. Bruce had killed his rival John Comyn and been crowned king of Scotland. Pembroke attacked unexpectedly and Bruce was captured, but he escaped and sought refuge in Ireland.

Meuse, Battle of the battle fought in 55 BC on the banks of the river Meuse, eastern France, between the Roman army of Julius ◊Caesar and a German tribal army, during the ◊Gallic Wars, in which the Romans inflicted a massive defeat upon the Germans.

The migrating Germans had crossed the Rhine in the winter of 56 BC and by early 55 BC Caesar had led a Roman force to intercept them. Advance negotiations had concluded a truce, but when the advance guard of Roman cavalry arrived at the Meuse it was attacked by a force of German cavalry. Despite being only 800 to the Roman's 5,000 men, by a ferocious assault the Germans killed 74 and routed the rest. When the Germans sent an embassy of their senior chiefs to apologize for the incident, Caesar seized them and attacked their camp the following day. Those who escaped attempted to flee east across the Rhine but they were pursued by the Roman forces. Taken by surprise and leaderless, the Germans were almost annihilated.

meutrière (French 'murder-hole') small loophole in a defensive wall through which men with handguns could shoot at the enemy. They sometimes opened onto an area shut off by a ◊portcullis in which attackers could be trapped. They also proved useful for pouring water onto fires started by the attackers.

Michael (VIII) Palaeologus (1225–82)

Byzantine emperor 1258–82 and founder of the longest lasting Byzantine imperial dynasty. He restored the Greek Byzantine Empire after the interval of Latin control from 1204 by recovering ◊Constantinople in 1261.

He had acted as regent for John Laskaris, son of Emperor Theodore II Laskaris, whom he deposed and blinded. He won the at Pelagonia in 1259 (see ◊Pelagonia, Battle of), securing power for himself. He fought with King Charles I of the Two Sicilies to divert Latin efforts against Constantinople; the resulting Sicilian Vespers occurred in the year of his death.

Middleham castle

castle in England, 16 km / 10 mi south of Richmond, Yorkshire. Begun in 1287, it had one of the largest keeps ever built in England, 30 m / 100 ft by 24 m / 80 ft and three stories high. This was surrounded by a rectangular curtain wall with towers, and with walls dividing the interior into two wards. It was the favourite resort of Richard III, whose son was born here in the Prince's Tower in the 15th century.

Middleton, Sir John

English mercenary captain, employed by Charles the Bold, duke of Burgundy. Middleton commanded an ordinance company composed largely of English longbowmen; the use of longbowmen was part of Charles's reforms of the Burgundian army. Middleton was at the siege of Neuss in 1474–75 with 100 lances and 1,600 English archers (see ◊Neuss, Siege of). He also fought at Nancy in 1477 (see ◊Nancy, Battle of), where Charles was killed.

migdol ('tower') Egyptian fort, one of a line of 14 named garrisoned towers with wells protecting the Ways of Horus, the coastal road to from Tjaru to Gaza, and providing for the movement of troops. The third fort, near modern Tell el-Her, was called 'Migdol', and was avoided by the Israelites during the Exodus.

migfer Turkish term for a helmet of the type often called a 'turban helmet' in Western scholarship, an onion-shaped helmet fitted with a ◊nasal at the front and a mail ◊aventail

suspended from its lower edge.. This type was used throughout the Turkish dynasties until the 16th century, when it was gradually superseded by the *çiçak*, which was fitted with a neck defence and cheekpieces of plate.

Mihirakula (or *Mihirigula*)

'Sun-flower' last great king c. 502–30 of the ◊White Huns. He was a bloodthirsty tyrant and destroyer of temples. At the end of his reign he was defeated in western India by a confederation of Hindu princes and fell back to his base in Kashmir.

Mikata ga Hara, Battle of

indecisive battle fought in 1572 to the northwest of Hamamatsu, in present-day Shizuoka prefecture, between the forces of the Japanese warrior leader ◊Tokugawa Ieyasu, fighting on behalf of the military warlord ◊Oda Nobunaga, and the ◊*daimyo* Takeda Shingen.

Ieyasu was garrisoned at Hamamatsu castle and rather than risk defeat by defending Hamamatsu against the vastly superior forces of Shingen, he took the battle to Shingen on the nearby moorland of Mikata ga Hara. Shingen withdrew to consolidate his forces rather than sustain a long siege on the castle.

Milan, Siege of

unsuccessful attempt 402–03 by ◊Alaric's Visigoths to capture the city of Milan in northern Italy, at that time the West Roman capital. The city held out over the winter and the siege was broken when the West Roman general ◊Stilicho crossed the Alps from Gaul and launched a surprise attack against Alaric's army.

miles Latin 'soldier' originally a Roman soldier; from the 10th century the word began to be translated as 'knight'. The meaning changed gradually, coming to denote social status as well as military occupation. Its later meaning became common in the 11th century, but was used inconsistently.

A *miles* could still be described as 'ordinary', 'plebeian', and 'rustic', but in general was a man of rank who fought as a cavalryman.

miles gregarius ordinary soldier of the Roman army, who did not have special duties or higher pay. The term *caligati* ('booted one' or 'footslogger') was a frequently used synonym.

Miletus

ancient city founded on the coast of Asia Minor (modern Turkey) by the Ionian Greeks, which became an important Hellenistic centre. It was in Persian hands from 546 BC to about 479 and then again from 494 BC until its capture by Alexander the Great.

In 129 BC it was incorporated into the Roman province of Asia.

The city was built on a spur of land which was almost completely encircled by the city walls. These also incorporated an acropolis hill about 500 m/1,640 ft southwest of the city districts. It is uncertain when the walls were constructed, but most favour a Persian date. They

MILITARY ORDER

European orders of warrior monks who fought to defend and expand Christendom in the context of the ◊Crusades. Their heyday was from the mid-12th century to 1291 in the Holy Land, but they survived and flourished in Spain and on the German frontiers until the end of the Middle Ages. The Knights Hospitaller became the rulers of Rhodes (until 1480) and Malta (until 1798) and maintained religious warfare against the Ottoman Turks.

A product of crusading ideology which legitimized violence by Christians against non-Christian enemies, the first military order was that of the Temple of Jerusalem. The first *Knights Templar* took it upon themselves to protect pilgrims who wished to bathe in the river Jordan. In 1128 they were given a Rule by St Bernard and authorized by the papacy. By about 1150 the Knights of St John of the Hospital or *Hospitallers* (originally an order founded to tend to sick pilgrims) were also militarized. Entrants had to be mature and of knightly rank, and had to take vows of poverty, chastity, and obedience like ordinary monks.

These two orders became immensely popular as the recipients of grants of land and money and soon had bases (commanderies) all over Christian Europe. Their great wealth enabled them to construct (or take over from secular lords) large numbers of castles in the crusader states of the Holy Land. They also grew powerful in Spain. Although never great in number (both orders had probably no more than 300 knight brothers each in the East), their military contribution to the Crusades was incalculable. These international orders spawned many 'national' orders in imitation, especially in the border regions of Iberia and Germany. In Spain the *Order of Calatrava* was the first founded (1153), to be followed by many more. On the Baltic Coast eastwards to Prussia and Lithuania several orders grew up which in 1212 were combined as the *Teutonic Knights* (who also contributed to the defence of the Holy Land). They dominated this region until they were defeated by the Poles at Tannenberg in 1410 (see ◊Tannenberg, Battle of) and were effectively neutralized by 1466, after a 13-year war.

After the loss of Acre (see ◊Acre, Siege of 1291), the last Christian possession in the Holy Land, the international orders lost much of their credibility. They retreated to Cyprus, but in 1307 the Templars (who had become international bankers) were destroyed at the instigation of King Philip IV of France, who seized their assets. The last Grand Master was burned for heresy in 1314, and the Hospitallers inherited Templar property. In 1306–09 the Hospitallers established themselves on the island of Rhodes, constructing a magnificent fortified town and a fleet with which to raid Ottoman territories. After a long siege they were finally expelled by the Turks in 1480, and retreated to Malta. This island they also fortified and in 1565 defeated the fleet and army of the Ottoman sultan Suleiman I 'the Magnificent'. They retained their independence until succumbing to Napoleon on his way to Egypt in 1798, but by then they had lost most of their military significance.

MILITARY TEXTS, GREEK AND ROMAN

Military theory compiled in a series of textbooks from the Greek and Roman worlds of antiquity, many still surviving. The works can be divided into three main categories: general treatises on campaigning, such as *Epitome of Military Science* by ◊Vegetius; detailed technical works on topics such as artillery, the organization and drill of the Macedonian phalanx (see ◊Asclepiodotus) or encamping an army; and examples of military stratagems (see ◊Frontinus). Textbooks such as these provided information for military leaders who received no formal training in military science but were nonetheless expected to command troops and armies in battle as part of a political career.

The number of known treatises indicates the popularity of this type of work. Many were written by people with little or no experience of warfare, but it is clear that the advice generally reflects actual military practice, and some authors, including ◊Aeneas the Tactician, use examples to illustrate their advice. It is rare to find one of these books advocating particularly new or radical practices; even the more technical works on artillery include specifications of machines that were obsolete at the time of writing (although the details are such that it is possible to build a replica from the original instructions).

The more general textbooks cover military operations from recruitment to unit organization to campaigning techniques. Vegetius tends to give rather inflexible advice, listing seven different formations for the line of battle depending on the nature of the terrain and the enemy. On the other hand, ◊Onasander admits that war is an imprecise science and that it is impossible to predict all possible circumstances. He is less prescriptive in his advice and therefore more practical.

were strengthened about 200 BC and a new landward wall was constructed that abandoned the acropolis hill, requiring a much shorter distance to be guarded. This new wall across the neck of the spur was fortified with seven projecting towers.

Miletus, Siege of capture of the Greek city of Miletus, on the western coast of modern Turkey, by the Persians in 494 BC, effectively ending the Asiatic Greek revolt against Persian rule.

Few details are known, but ◊Herodotus says that the Persians 'dug under the walls and brought up all kinds of siege-engines', and that the surviving rebels were deported to Mesopotamia.

milites second-rate garrison troops of the late Roman period. In the early Middle Ages in western Europe the term was applied to military vassals who formed the bulk of mounted troops in early feudal armies.

Miltiades (550s?–489 BC) Athenian general. He joined ◊Darius (I) the Great of Persia against the Scythians, but returned to Greece to join the Greek revolt against the Persians early in the 5th century. He is credited with being responsible for the decision to confront the Persian invaders at Marathon in 490 BC (see ◊Marathon, Battle of), for persuading the polemarch Callimachus, to fight, and for the tactics used.

However, Callimachus was technically in command, and since he was killed in the battle, Miltiades' reputation as the architect of victory probably owes as much to the later influence of his son ◊Cimon as to reality. After the battle, he was wounded in an attack on the island of Paros, and died of gangrene.

Milvian Bridge, Battle of battle fought in 312 near Rome between the Roman emperor ◊Constantine (I) the Great and one of his main rivals, Marcus Aurelius Valerius ◊Maxentius. Constantine's forces won a notable victory against a numerically superior enemy.

Maxentius had prepared for a siege of Rome, but decided instead to fight Constantine's 40,000 men with his 100,000 troops when the latter approached, their shields displaying the newly painted Chi-Rho symbol, proclaiming Constantine's conversion to Christianity. Maxentius crossed the river Tiber over a bridge of boats constructed on the site of the demolished Milvian Bridge. Maxentius' inexperienced troops were outflanked by Constantine's cavalry and swiftly routed, but their flight proved difficult when the bridge collapsed under their weight. Maxentius was drowned and many of his troops suffered a similar fate or were slaughtered by their pursuers.

Minamoto family (also known as the *Genji*) ancient Japanese clan, members of which became the first ruling shoguns 1185–1219. Their government was based in Kamakura, near present-day Tokyo. After the death of the first shogun, ◊Minamoto Yoritomo, in 1199, real power was exercised by the regent for the shogun; throughout the ◊Kamakura shogunate the regents were of the ◊Hōjō family.

The Minamoto were an offshoot of the Japanese imperial family and one of four great families who dominated the court during the Heian period (794–1185). Minamoto Yoritomo, who established the first ◊Warrior Government of Japan in 1185, was a member of the Seiwa Genji branch of the family, which established itself as one of the most powerful provincial warrior families in eastern Japan.

Minamoto Sanetomo (1192–1219) third Japanese shogun of the Kamakura period, the second son of ◊Minamoto Yoritomo. He lacked the military vigour of his father and was more interested in court life than in consolidating his warrior heritage. He was assassinated by his nephew and the Seiwa Genji line of the Minamoto ended with him.

Minamoto Tametomo (1139–77) Japanese warrior and military leader. He was sent to Kyushu island in 1152, where he established himself as an influential warlord and defied the authority of the imperial court. He was forced to commit suicide following a failed attempt to seize power in Izu province (present-day Shizuoka prefecture), on O-shima island.

Minamoto Yorimasa (1104–80) Japanese aristocrat, poet, and warrior who was influential in the various uprisings against the ◊Taira family which resulted in the ◊Taira–Minamoto Wars (1180–85).

Having fought in the Hōgen and Heiji disturbances (1156 and 1160), when the Minamoto had been resoundingly crushed by the Taira, Yorimasa sided with the rebellious Prince Mochihito, son of the emperor Go-Shirakawa, against the Taira in 1180. The rebels sought help from militant monks and Yorimasa issued an edict calling for all Minamoto to join in the uprising. At the Battle of the Uji River

(see ◊Uji River, Battle of the) Yorimasa was wounded and committed *seppuku* (suicide by disembowelment) while composing his death poem.

Minamoto Yoritomo (1147–99) Japanese military leader and founder of the first warrior government of Japan, the ◊Kamakura shogunate, in 1185. He subdued most of his opponents of the Taira family and was declared shogun by the emperor Gotoba in Kyoto in 1192. His strength of character briefly unified Japan and his visionary form of government endured in various forms for nearly 700 years.

The third son of ◊Minamoto Yoshitomo, Yoritomo first saw military action with his father in 1160 in the ◊Heiji Disturbance. Following ◊Minamoto Yorimasa's call for support against the powerful Taira family in 1180, Yoritomo survived several battles with Taira forces and, having received pledges of support from other military leaders, established his new base at Kamakura. He consolidated his position through the creation of an impressive economic and political system of administration through family and vassalage ties. The ◊*samurai-dokoro* was created in 1180 for this purpose.

After several years of fighting, Yoritomo sent his half-brother ◊Minamoto Yoshitsune against the Taira forces in 1184 and forced them to retreat to the west of Japan; Yoshitsune finally defeated the Taira at the Battle of Dan no Ura in 1185.

Minamoto Yoshinaka (1154–84) Japanese warrior of the late Heian period who participated in the ◊Taira–Minamoto Wars. He welcomed the Minamoto call to rebellion against the Taira family in 1180, and in 1183 seized the imperial capital Kyoto where his troops caused havoc and created a third factional aspect to the wars. He was defeated and killed by the Minamoto.

Firstly the Taira sent forces against him, but they were forced to retreat together with the child emperor, Antoku. ◊Minamoto Yoritomo then sent his brother ◊Minamoto Yoshitsune to deal with this problematic clansman.

Minamoto Yoshitomo (1123–60) Japanese warrior of the late Heian period who saw action during the battles of the Hōgen and Heiji disturbances (1156 and 1160). In the latter series of conflicts, his father and brother fought against him and were killed. ◊Minamoto Yoritomo and ◊Minamoto Yoshitsune were his sons.

Minamoto Yoshitsune (1159–89) Japanese warrior of the late Heian period and one of the principal participants in the ◊Taira–Minamoto Wars. He was the half-brother and deputy of ◊Minamoto Yoritomo. His military skills and brilliant tactics secured the Minamoto victories over the Taira at the battles of Ichi no Tani and Dan no Ura (see ◊Ichi no Tani, Battle of and ◊Dan no Ura, Battle of). He was suspected of treason by Yoritomo and committed suicide.

His manipulation by the emperor in Kyoto gave rise to Yoritomo's suspicions and he sent an army against Yoshitune in 1185. Yoshitsune fled from Kyoto and hid himself and his family for several years, but was eventually forced to kill them all before killing himself.

Minatogawa, Battle of conclusive battle in July 1336 between Ashikaga Takauji and ◊Nitta Yoshisada and ◊Kusunoki Masashige, supporters of the Japanese emperor Go-Daigo, which effectively ended the ◊Kemmu Restoration and led to the establishment in 1338 of the Muromachi shogunate under Takauji.

The forces of Takauji were heading for Kyoto to attack the emperor when they were faced with the armies of Nitta Yoshisada and Kusunoki Masashige on the banks of the river Minato. Takauji's numerically superior troops destroyed the imperial forces and Takauji entered Kyoto, forcing the emperor to flee.

Minerve, Siege of siege of the Cathar fortress of Minerve, near Carcassonne, southern France, in June–July 1210 by northern French forces under Simon de ◊Montfort (the Elder), during the series of campaigns known as the ◊Albigensian Crusades.

The location of Minerve on a mountainous peak made it difficult to take, but it lacked a good water supply, the well lying in a vulnerable spot. After a failed sortie to obtain water, the defenders surrendered. The Cathars were promised their lives, but 140 were burned in a clearing outside the village.

Mingtiao, Battle of legendary battle in around 1763 BC in which ◊Tang of the Shang overthrew Jie, the corrupt last king of the Xia, China's first ruling dynasty. Tang led a surprise attack on the Xia, defeating their Kunwu allies and then crushing the Xia army during a thunderstorm at Mingtiao. Jie fled, but was captured and exiled.

Minturnae Roman colony (Italian Minturno) founded in 295 BC on the via Appia at the crossing of the river Liri in southwest Italy; a fine example of an early fortified Roman town.

Minturnae was founded in the aftermath of the ◊Samnite Wars, as Rome sought to increase its control over the region. The town was enclosed by a stone wall with square towers at the corners and flanking the gates on the west and east sides. The walls were built in the Roman 'polygonal masonry' style, using irregularly shaped stones fitted together without coursing or masonry, and were in use with only minor repairs until the sack of the town by the Lombards in 590 AD.

Miran 8th–9th century Tibetan fort in what is now eastern Xinjiang, on an open plain near the older city of Miran. It was an irregular rectangle, about 75 m/82 yds on the long sides, with massive oblong towers at the corners and another tower near the centre of each wall. It was built of sun-dried brick on foundations of pounded earth. Caches of Tibetan military documents and pieces of leather ◊lamellar armour have been found in the buildings inside the fort.

misericorde dagger used to strike a final blow and mercifully kill a seriously wounded opponent; also considered to be a last resort weapon. It was widely used from the 14th century, and was normally held with the point projecting downwards from the hand.

The misericorde was usually a straight dagger without a guard; the blade had a triangular section and only one cutting edge. From effigies it seems to have commonly been carried on a chain from the belt on the right side. Misericordes were often decorated with such scenes as the 'Dance of Death'.

Mita king of the Mushki (biblical Mesech) c. 738–c. 696 BC, identified with Midas, the Phrygian king from Greek sources. In 716 BC Mita supported Pisiris, the Neo-Hittite king of Carchemish, against the Assyrian king ◊Sargon II. Two years later he attacked the province of Hilakku (classical Cilicia) with the support of the Gasgans. Sargon ousted the Mushki and Gasgans from Hilakku and also from the Neo-Hittite dependent state of Tabal (biblical Tubal), in the Konya Plain. Mita eventually submitted to Sargon and in 706 BC betrayed Ambaris of Tabal to the Assyrians.

Mithradates I (died 138 BC) king of Parthia 171 BC–138 BC, who established Parthia as a major power. He conquered Media (present-day northwestern Iran) in 155 BC and captured Babylon, evading and countering the attacks of the Seleucid king Demetrios II.

Mithradates' conquests began in the border districts of the Greek kingdom of Bactria then, in a war from 161 BC to 155 BC, he conquered Media. In 141 BC Demetrios II launched an attack on Media, but rather than meet him directly, Mithradates invaded Babylonia, defeated another Seleucid army, and captured

Babylon. While he was fighting in Hyrkania, probably against nomadic invaders, Demetrios attacked Media again, this time in alliance with the kings of Persia, Elymais, and Bactria. After initial success, Demetrios was defeated and captured by Mithradates' generals. Mithradates then avenged himself on Elymais and probably also Persia about 139 BC.

Mithradates II king of Parthia 123–87 BC, who restored Parthian fortunes. He reconquered Babylonia, regained control of the eastern Parthian empire, made Armenia a Parthian vassal, and defeated Antiochos X, the Seleucid king of Syria, but lost Babylon to the rebel Gotarzes in 91 BC.

On Mithradates' accession Media (northwestern Iran) was overrun by nomad Saka invaders and Babylonia was lost to rebels, but he reconquered the latter within three years. In the east of the Parthian empire he probably established a loose overlordship over the Saka in Sakastan (parts of modern Iran and Afghanistan). He defeated Artavasdes of Armenia, making that country a Parthian vassal for the first time, and later put Artavasdes' son ◊Tigranes (I) the Great on the Armenian throne in exchange for frontier territory. About 92 BC Mithradates defeated and killed Antiochos X, prompting the Roman general ◊Sulla to send a mission that fixed the Roman-Parthian frontier on the river Euphrates.

Mithridates (VI) Eupator (120–60 BC) king of Pontus (on the Black Sea coast of modern Turkey), who became the greatest obstacle to Roman expansion in the east. He massacred 80,000 Romans in overrunning the rest of Asia Minor and went on to invade Greece. He was defeated by ◊Sulla in the first Mithridatic War 88–84 BC, by ◊Lucullus in the second 83–81, and by ◊Pompey the Great in the third 74–64.

Attempts to copy Roman tactics and equipment failed to improve his army's success rate. He was finally destroyed by a rebellion headed by his son Pharnaces, committing suicide in the fortress of Panticapaeum where he was preparing to renew the struggle with Rome.

Mizuki Japanese 'water fort' early Japanese fortification (c. 664) consisting of a substantial earthwork and moat built across a valley to protect the imperial government headquarters for administration of trade with China and Korea at Dazaifu, on Kyushu island, Japan. Large sections still exist today.

The original structure was approximately 1 km/0.6 mi wide, 14 m/46 ft high, and 35 m/115 ft thick at the base. The term *mizuki* has come to refer to other fortifications of this type found mainly on Kyushu and which effectively dam a stream or river.

Mohi, Battle of battle of 11 April 1241 in which invading Mongol forces under the princes Batu and Sübedei attacked and destroyed the army of the Kingdom of Hungary under King Béla IV at Mohi, Hungary.

Béla's army was riven by conflicts and undermined by the expulsion of valuable Cuman auxiliaries on the grounds that they were Mongol spies. While Batu attacked at a bridge, Sübedei crossed the river Sayo upstream at night. Surprised and surrounded, the Hungarians were overwhelmed by the Mongol cavalry.

Mohists philosophical school in ◊Warring States China. Mo Zi (Mo Tzu) taught universal love and denounced war and aggression, and some of his pupils put his philosophy into effect by specializing in the defence of Chinese fortified towns (see ◊fortified towns, Chinese) against sieges. The book that survives under his name, the *Mo Zi*, contains recommendations on moats, walls, signal-flags, defence against various kinds of assault, and what may be the first ever description of a simple man-powered ◊trebuchet.

mon Japanese crest or badge of a ruling ◊samurai family, frequently used from the Heian period (794–1185) as a decoration on arms and armour and used as an identifier on the ◊sashimono, a flag inserted at the back of a suit of armour.

Möngke (1209–59) fourth Mongol Great Khan 1251–59, and consolidator and expander of the Mongol empire. He used his brothers ◊Hülegü to conquer the west and ◊Khubilai Khan to conquer China. Although Möngke took command himself 1257–59 in the Chinese conquest and achieved a great deal, he contracted dysentery and died. The conquest took until 1279 to complete.

Monmouth castle castle 27 km/17 mi south of Hereford in Gwent, Wales. William FitzOsbern, Earl of Hereford, built an earthen enclosure and timber castle here in around 1068, on a triangular site at the confluence of the rivers Wye and Monnow. Henry of Monmouth, who became Henry V, was born in the castle gatehouse.

In about 1125 it was converted into a regular ◊motte-and-bailey castle with a two-story tower on the motte. A curtain wall and great hall were later added. Monmouth is also noteworthy for its unique fortified bridge across the river Monnow that also dates from the 13th century.

Mons-en-Pévèle, Battle of indecisive battle between Flemish foot soldiers under William of Jülich and a French army commanded by King Philip IV at Mons-en-Pévèle in modern Belgium on 18 August 1304.

After their successes at Courtrai in 1302 (see ◊Courtrai, Battle of) and Arques in 1303, the Flemings with 12,000–15,000 foot soldiers were prepared to take the offensive against the royal French army of 3,000 knights and 10,000 foot soldiers. But, lacking cavalry, they took up a defensive position with their rear protected by a barricade of wagons. An impasse followed: the French knights were unable to break the Flemish foot soldiers, while the Flemings were unwilling to risk an advance against their mounted opponents. Finally the Flemings charged, breaking into the French camp and almost killing Philip, but a French counterattack took a heavy toll, and William of Jülich was killed.

Mons Graupius, Battle of battle fought between the Roman general ◊Agricola and the British chieftain Calgacus in Scotland (perhaps near Inverness) in AD 84. It was the culmination of Agricola's series of campaigns in Scotland, and his victory pushed the Roman frontier northwards as far as the Firth of Forth.

Facing the Britons who had deployed on rising ground, Agricola made adroit use of his auxiliary infantry and cavalry to defeat the British army without having to engage his legions. The British casualties outnumbered the Roman by 28 to 1.

Mons Lactarius, Battle of (Italian *Monte Lacteria*) final Roman victory in 553 over the Goths, under Teias, their new king, in the long Italian War (534–54). A truce was arranged and the survivors agreed to leave Italy and never bear arms again against the Empire.

After their defeat at Taginae (see ◊Taginae, Battle of), the Goths continued to fight under Teias, a survivor of Taginae. For two months the Gothic and Roman armies faced each other in Campania, near Cumae (central Italy), without either side making a significant move, until the Romans managed to bribe the fleet which had been supplying the Goths.

The Goths then fell back to a strong position on Mons Lactarius (Milk Mountain) where they were besieged by the Romans. Impending starvation forced the Goths to attempt a breakthrough which they tried on foot, led from the front by Teias. The Gothic King fought heroically, taking twelve spears in his shield,

but he was eventually killed. The Goths fought on but were unable to break through and after two days of fighting they sued for peace.

Montefortino helmet Celtic helmet found in the 4th-century BC Gallic cemetery at Montefortino, near Ancona, Italy. In its widest sense, the term is used as a general name for all helmets with a back peak and integral topknot. Hundreds of examples have been found all over central and western Europe.

The Montefortino helmet was adopted by the Italic peoples and became the first truly Roman helmet. Most examples are made of bronze and many Celtic examples are partly lined with iron. Some, mainly from the Alpine area, are made totally of iron. The helmet type survived until superseded by the ◊Coolus helmet and ◊Imperial Gallic helmet around the end of the pre-Christian era (early 1st century BC).

Montfort, Simon de (1160–18) (the Elder) leader of the ◊Crusades against the Cathars in southern France. He won at Muret (see ◊Muret, Battle of) in 1213, in which ◊Pedro II of Aragon, an ally of the Cathars, was killed. He became Count of Toulouse 1213–18. In 1218 he besieged Toulouse (which had reaffirmed its loyalty to the former count) and was killed when a trebuchet, operated in part by women, threw a stone that hit him on the head.

Montfort, Simon de (c. 1208–65) (the Younger) English politician and soldier. From 1258 he led the baronial opposition to Henry III's misrule during the ◊Barons' War of 1264–67 and in 1264 defeated and captured the king at Lewes, Sussex. He was killed at Evesham (see ◊Evesham, Battle of).

Montlhéry, Battle of indecisive battle fought in 1465 to the south of Paris, France, during a rebellion of nobles in alliance with ◊Charles the Bold of Burgundy, then Count of Charolais, against the French king Louis XI. Charles held the field after the battle, but only because Louis went on to Paris. The monarch gained the advantage in the following years.

Montreal castle crusader castle on a hill in Shaubak, southern Jordan. ◊Baldwin I of the Christian Kingdom of Jerusalem supported the construction of the castle in 1115 on the communication route between Syria and Egypt. It fell to the Muslims following the Ayyubid sultan Saladin's victory at Hattin in 1187 (see ◊Hattin, Battle of), and underwent extensive rebuilding by the Muslims.

Montreuil-Bellay castle stronghold on the river Thouet south of Saumur, in Maine-et-Loire *département*, France. A natural chasm forms a defence around much of the castle. Fulk Nerra, Count of Anjou, built Montreuil-Bellay about 1000. He passed it to the Berlai family. Gerard Berlai's rebellion against ◊Geoffrey V, Count of Anjou, led to the castle being besieged 1148–51.

During the siege Geoffrey used ◊Greek fire for the first time in the West. The castle was destroyed by Geoffrey and rebuilt in the later Middle Ages in white stone. It contains an ancient kitchen.

Montségur castle early 13th-century fortress situated to the east of Foix, Ariège *département*, France, on a 152-m/500-ft peak, approximately pentagonal with a rectangular keep and thick curtain. It is the site of the massacre of the Albigenses in 1244 as the infamous climax to the ◊Albigensian Crusades.

After being besieged from 1243 for ten months by Hugh d'Arcis for Louis IX of France (1214–70), 255 heretics were burned to death on a pyre at the foot of the mountain.

mora (plural *morai*) (Greek) the largest unit in the ancient Spartan army. In the 4th and 3rd centuries BC, a *mora* had either 640 or 1280 men.

Morlaix, Battle of battle fought on 30 September 1342 during the ◊Hundred Years' War in which the English under the Earl of Northampton defeated the French under Charles of Blois with heavy losses at Morlaix, Brittany.

The 3,000-strong English force took up a defensive position behind a stream with woods to the rear, and also dug a concealed ditch. The French force outnumbered them four to one and advanced in three lines: first local foot soldiers, then mounted knights, then dismounted men-at-arms. The first two attacks were easily held off, the cavalry charge falling into the ditch, but as they were outnumbered and short of arrows the English were forced to withdraw into the woods. They escaped at nightfall, but Charles had already withdrawn.

Mortgarten, Battle of battle between Leopold, Duke of Austria, and the Swiss cantons near Lake Egeri in 1315. The Swiss had declared for Lewis of Bavaria against Frederick of Habsburg for the succession to the Holy Roman Empire, and Frederick's brother Leopold of Austria was seeking revenge. The Swiss victory was an important step in the progress towards independence.

Leopold advanced through the defile of Mortgarten, where the Swiss blocked the road. The Swiss infantry attacked, but Leopold escaped.

Mortimer's Cross, Battle of battle fought on 2 February 1461, during the English Wars of the Roses (see ◊Roses, Wars of the), between Edward, Earl of March, in a defensive position and Owen Tudor's Lancastrians.

Edward had hoped to join his father Richard, Duke of York, in Yorkshire, but Richard's death at the Battle of Wakefield in 1460 forced him back to the Marches. He drew up his men with their backs to a river. Tudor's men included good mercenaries on his left flank, but also poorly equipped Irish and Welsh troops. He drove back the Yorkist right, but his lines broke elsewhere as Edward led by example, fighting in the front rank.

motte-and-bailey medieval castle with a tower on a natural or artificial mound (motte) and a courtyard (bailey) on a lower level, with the motte serving as the main defence. There was much variety within the basic design: some castles had two mottes or two baileys, some had a keep, others did not. Motte-and-bailey castles seem to have first appeared as Frankish defences against the Vikings.

They were quick and cheap to build and useful in emergencies. Many were raised during the Norman Conquest and the 12th-century English invasion of Ireland. Excavation of the motte at ◊Abinger castle in England revealed evidence of a timber palisade and keep, similar to castles depicted on the ◊Bayeux Tapestry.

Motya, Siege of successful siege of the Carthaginian port of Motya by the army of Syracuse in 397 BC, part of a campaign to drive the Carthaginians out of Sicily. Motya was situated on an island off the coast of Sicily, connected to Sicily by a causeway. The defenders cut the causeway, but the Syracusans repaired and widened it to carry their siege engines.

The Syracusan tyrant ◊Dionysius I had invested heavily in siege machines and equipped his army with the most sophisticated engines yet devised. Advanced catapults kept the defenders at bay, while battering rams breached the walls. Mobile siege towers six storeys high were then pushed through the breaches and gave the Syracusans direct access onto the rooftops of the city houses. They sacked and destroyed the city.

Mount Gilboa, Battle of battle fought in 1004 BC between the Philistines and the Israelites, in which the Israelite army was defeated and King Saul and his son Jonathan were killed. After the battle the Philistines allowed ◊David to become king over the southern tribes of Judah.

Achish of Gath led the infantry and chariotry of the Philistine Pentapolis (the five cities of Ascalon, Ashdod, Ekron, Gaza, and Gath), plus mercenary forces such as those belonging to David. On reaching Aphek, the scene of the first victory of the Philistines over the Israelites around 1050 BC, Achish ordered David to return to his base at Ziklag. Saul brought his forces down from the mountain to attack the Philistines, who then used their superior mobility in chariotry to completely rout the Israelites. Up to this point Saul had successfully won back territory from the Philistines, who had occupied the whole territory after the Battle of Aphek.

Mu (died 621 BC) (Duke of Qin) ruler 659–621 BC of the westernmost Chinese state of Qin, who was involved in a long struggle with its neighbour Jin. He won more lasting success by conquering 12 Rong mountain tribes around the upper Wei River in 623, becoming known as 'Chief of the Western Rong'.

Mu helped Huai, Duke of Jin, gain his throne in 650, and when the territory promised as a reward was not forthcoming he defeated Jin at the Han Plain in 645 (see ◊Han Plain, Battle of). When the Jin succession was disputed again in 636, Mu put ◊Wen on the Jin throne. On Wen's death he began a war against Jin; defeated at the Xiao Gorge in 627, he renewed the attack but was defeated again at Pengya in 624 (see ◊Pengya, Battle of).

mubariz Arabic term for a warrior (from *baraza*, to meet in combat).

Mu, Battle of decisive battle in around 1122 or 1027 BC in which King ◊Wu of Zhou, advised by the ◊Taigong, defeated ◊Di Xin of Shang. The victory established a Zhou empire in northern China which lasted until the fall of ◊Hao.

Wu led 300 chariots, 3,000 ◊Tiger Warriors, and allied troops from eight states providing another 50 chariots and numerous infantry. The Shang army was larger, though claims of 700,000 Shang troops are exaggerated. The Shang deployed at Mu, a flat area of grazing land not far from the Shang capital, Yin (Anyang). At dawn the Zhou opened the battle with a charge of 350 chariots. Their forces gradually but steadily forced the Shang back, until they broke amid great bloodshed. By dusk the Zhou had taken Yin, where Di Xing was shot and beheaded and the royal palaces burned.

muffler modern term for the extension of the sleeve of a ◊mail shirt over the hands. This appeared in European mail shirts towards the end of the 12th century, and remained usual until the mid-14th century.

Mugello, Battle of fluid cavalry skirmish between Gothic and Roman forces in Italy, which took place in a wide valley in northern Italy in 542. The Romans showed a lack of resolve and were easily beaten off by the Goths, with few casualties on either side. The engagement the left the Goths in control of the Italian countryside, with the remaining Roman forces confined to garrisons.

Muhammad (c. 570–632) founder of Islam, who brought a monotheistic religion to the pagan Arab tribes. In 622 he fled persecution in his home town of Mecca on the Arabian peninsula to seek sanctuary in Yathrib (later Medina). From this point on (the 'Hegira' or flight which became year 1 in the Muslim calendar) he gained more converts and his power increased.

In 629, after establishing authority over many of the Arab clans, Muhammad launched an attack on the Byzantine frontier which, although defeated, marked the beginning of Arab expansion at the expense of the Byzantine Empire. He died on 7 June 632 while preparing another expedition against the Byzantines.

Muhammad (III) Bahmani (1454–82) (known as *Lashkari* 'the Soldier') sultan of the Deccan 1463–82. Under his rule the Bahmani Muslim kingdom expanded to its greatest extent, including the acquisition of Goa from ◊Vijayanagar in 1475. He owed much of his success to his able chief minister and commander in chief Mahmud Gawan (1404–82).

When Mahmud's enemies at court forged a letter in which he appeared to invite an invasion by the raja of Orissa (defeated in 1478), Muhammad, in a drunken rage, ordered his execution. Discovering his error too late, he drank himself to death.

Muhammad ibn Tughluq sultan of Delhi 1325–47. A megalomaniac tyrant, he brought ruin on himself and his kingdom by his capricious behaviour and grandiose schemes, suppressing the many revolts which these provoked with sadistic cruelty.

In 1337 he determined to conquer China, and sent a large army to invade by way of the Himalayas, where the whole force was annihilated by local tribesmen. A combination of natural disasters and the sultan's eccentric policies weakened his power and prestige, allowing provincial governors in the Deccan and Bengal to set up independent Muslim kingdoms there. He died in Sind, attempting to put down rebellion.

Muhammad of Ghur, Mu'izz al-Din Muhammad Shihab al-Din bin Sam

(died 1206) sultan of Ghazni (central Afghanistan) 1202–06. He conquered northern India in a series of expeditions between 1175 and 1193, invading previously unconquered Rajput lands, and defeating ◊Prithviraja Chauhana III in 1192 and ◊Jaichand Gaharwar in 1193. He was assassinated by Muslim extremists.

The nephew of ◊Ala al-Din Husain, 'the World-Burner', he became governor of Ghazni in 1173, captured Multan in 1175, imprisoned the last Ghaznavid sultan Chosroes Malik in 1186, invaded Rajput lands, and was defeated by Prithviraja at Tarain in 1191 (see ◊Tarain, Battle of 1191). In 1192 he again reached Tarain, where Prithviraja was defeated and killed. Muhammad's last victory in India was over ◊Jaichand Gaharwar the following year, after which he returned to Ghazni, leaving his lieutenant ◊Qutb al-Din Aibak to complete the conquest.

Muhammad succeeded his brother Ghiyath al-Din as sultan in 1202 and drove Ala al-Din Khwarazm Shah from Herat but was in turn defeated by the Khwarazm Shah and his Qara-Khitai allies at Andkui on the river Oxus (modern Amu Darya) in 1204. He returned to India to suppress a rebellion in the Punjab in 1205. On his way back to renew the war in Khurasan, he was assassinated.

Mukhali (1169–1223) (or *Muqali*) Mongol

warlord, one of ◊Genghis Khan's early commanders and a key figure in the Mongol campaigns in China (see ◊China, Mongol campaigns in). He brought all the territory north of the Yellow River under Mongol control.

Mukhali led the charge at Huanerzui in 1211 (see ◊Huanerzui, Battle of) and commanded a detached force in 1213. From 1214 he campaigned in Liaoning and captured the Jin northern capital. He also fought against Zhang Zhi, a Chinese who had submitted to the Mongols and then rebelled. Mukhali defeated Zhang's field forces at Yongde, and took his headquarters in 1216.

From 1219 he commanded the entire Chinese front while Genghis fought in the west. He had 50,000–70,000 troops: 15,000 Mongols, the rest other tribal cavalry and Chinese, including Chinese artillery which enabled him to besiege and take large towns. He conquered most of modern Shanxi in 1219, capturing the cities of Taiyuan and Pingyang. In 1220 he conquered part of Shandong, and in

1222 advanced up the river Wei and took Xian. In 1223 he began a campaign south of the Yellow River, but fell ill and died.

Munda, Battle of battle fought in 45 BC

between the forces of Julius ◊Caesar and ◊Pompey the Great. It was Caesar's final victory over the Pompeian forces in Spain, in probably the hardest fought battle of the Roman civil war. Pompey's numerous troops were commanded by Gnaeus Pompeius, Pompey's eldest son, but the quality of Caesar's veteran legionaries secured his victory.

Gnaeus offered battle, forming his army of 13 ◊legions on high ground outside his camp. Cavalry supported by 6,000 light infantry and a similar number of Spanish auxiliaries protected his flanks. Caesar commanded about eight legions supported by cavalry, including a contingent of Mauretanian light cavalry. His best legions were stationed on the flanks of his line. Caesar personally led his infantry uphill against the enemy to inspire his troops. After a long struggle Caesar's 10th Legion made a breakthrough on the right, and the left-wing cavalry simultaneously began to make ground. The Pompeians had no uncommitted reserves left and soon the whole line was in retreat. Caesar lost 1,000 men, Pompey allegedly 30,000.

Muntaner, Ramun (lived 14th century)

Catalan chronicler of the Aragonese conquest of Greece by the Catalan Company, 1304–06. Muntaner had a good eye for military and naval detail and gave a lively account of the extraordinary success of his compatriots, as well as a good analysis of contemporary warfare.

Murabitin medieval Arabic name for ascetic

warriors of northern Africa (also Almoravides) who conquered southern Spain 1086–1145. The name is believed to be derived from 'men of the 'ribat'' (a kind of fortified monastery).

Muret, Battle of battle fought on 12

September 1213 in which Simon de Montfort the Elder's Albigensian crusaders (see ◊Albigensian Crusades) defeated the allied forces of ◊Pedro II of Aragon and the citizens of Toulouse, France.

Besieged in Muret with 800 knights and a few foot soldiers, de Montfort faced Pedro with some 1,500 veteran knights to the north of the town, and a large force of Toulousain militia to the south. He launched a surprise dawn cavalry attack on the Aragonese and routed them; Pedro died in the conflict. De Montfort then recalled his knights to drive the unsuspecting Toulousains into the river Garonne with heavy losses.

Muromachi shogunate the second of Japan's ◊Warrior Governments, which ruled approximately 1333–1568 under the Ashikaga shoguns. They failed to create a strong centralized power base, and a series of successional disputes plunged the country into a century of civil war. Towards the end of the Muromachi period much of Japan was controlled by the emergent warlords of the ◊Sengoku period.

The military governors (◊*shugo*) of the Ashikaga greatly increased their personal powers during the period through the acquisition of land and vassals at the expense of the centralized shogunal interests. This decrease in centralized authority, brought about by successional disputes among the Ashikaga and the failure to administer efficiently and maintain a balance of power, led to the wars of the Sengoku period, commencing with the Ōnin Wars.

The last Ashikaga shogun, Yoshiaki, was deposed by ◊Oda Nobunaga in 1573, but he continued to act as though retaining full shogunal powers until his official resignation in 1588.

Mursa, Battle of victory in 351 for the East Roman army under Constantius II over the West Roman army commanded by the usurper Magnentius.

Prior to the battle, Constantius' troops discovered and destroyed an ambush in a ruined stadium. They then formed up in the classic order of battle for Eastern troops: infantry in the centre with heavily armoured ◊cataphract cavalry on their immediate flanks, and light horse-archers on the outer wings. Additional cavalry were kept in reserve behind the wings. Magnentius' dispositions are not known but his Western army probably contained more infantry and less cavalry, and it was outflanked by its opponents. The battle was hard fought, lasting until after dusk until Magnentius' flank crumbled, exposing his centre to a series of cavalry charges supported by archery. There were heavy losses on both sides.

Mursilis I Hittite king 1620–1590 BC. He conquered Halba (classical Aleppo) and raided the city of Babylon (see ◊Babylon, Hittite raid on) in about 1595 BC, which brought about the collapse of the Amorite kingdom and the beginning of Kassite rule over southern Mesopotamia.

Mursilis succeeded his uncle ◊Hattusilis I in an atmosphere of palace intrigues. Nevertheless he consolidated his authority and power sufficiently to organize the raid on Babylon, although the exploit cost him the throne. He was murdered, possibly because of the sacrilege of attacking Babylon, and succeeded by Hantilis.

Mursilis II (died 1295 BC) Hittite king 1321–1295 BC, who succeeded to the throne after the sudden deaths of his father Suppiluliumas I in 1322 BC and his brother, the crown prince, in 1321 BC. Mursilis re-established Hittite overlordship throughout his father's empire and extended it by conquering the western Anatolian kingdom of Arzawa 1319–1318 BC, regaining the lost province of Pala (classical Paphlagonia) in 1316 BC, and penetrating further into the ◊Gasgan lands across the river Kummesmaha (classical Iris) than other Hittite king before, in 1305 BC.

He also stopped Assyrian expansion across the river Euphrates by bolstering the forces of his brother, the king of Carchemish, and suppressed pro-Egyptian uprisings in the Levant 1314–1312 BC. He was succeeded by his son Muwatallis, who confronted a renewed attack from Egypt under the pharaohs Seti I and Ramses II.

Mürten, Battle of battle of 9–21 June 1476 in which Swiss forces defeated the army of Charles the Bold, Duke of Burgundy, at Mürten in Switzerland. Charles planned to extend Burgundian influence over the Swiss but was unable to overcome their military resistance.

The Bernese garrison of 500 mounted some 400 artillery pieces taken at Grandson (see ◊Grandson, Battle of) and inflicted heavy casualties until Charles's heavy bombards created breaches on 17 June. Aware of a Swiss relieving force, he revised his ready troops into earthworks and palisades facing the expected line of attack. Despite this precaution, when the Swiss attacked on 21 June, the defences were not properly manned. The 12,000 Burgundians were swept away by the charge of over 20,000 Swiss pike blocks, supported by René of Anjou's 1,800 cavalry, with heavy losses.

Muthul, Battle of battle of 108 BC during the Jugurthine War in which King ◊Jugurtha of Numidia (corresponding roughly to present-day Algeria) attempted to ambush the Roman army led by the consul Metellus which had invaded his kingdom. After heavy fighting, the Numidians were defeated.

Jugurtha had stationed his army in concealed positions on a hill running parallel to the Roman line of march. The Romans marched with their infantry in three columns which, as soon as the enemy were spotted, formed the ◊*triplex acies* battle formation; this caused Jugurtha to hesitate before launching his attack. As the Roman army was nearing exhaustion, Metellus massed four legionary cohorts that led an uphill charge and broke the Numidians. Roman losses were heavy, but those of the Numidians comparatively light due to the speed of their flight.

Mycale, Battle of battle fought in 479 BC, during the ◊Persian Wars, which marked the end of Persia's attempts to conquer Greece and the beginning of the Greek counterattack.

The remnants of the Persian navy, their morale shattered by Salamis (see ◊Salamis, Battle of 480 BC), had been drawn ashore at Mycale, on the western coast of modern Turkey opposite Samos. They and the army left to control Ionia took refuge in a stockade there, but were attacked by a Greek fleet of 110 ships commanded by the Spartan king Leotychidas, who landed his forces and advanced along the shore. The Persians sallied from their stockade but were driven back, and the Greeks managed to burst in with the fugitives. They then burned the enemy ships and stockade.

Mycenae prominent Greek citadel and town in the eastern Peloponnese, which gave its name to the Mycenaean (Late Bronze Age) civilization of Greece. Mycenae was centrally situated, some 16 km/10 mi north from its port of Tiryns, and dominated the Peloponnese and beyond. It grew in importance from about 1650 BC, when it became extremely wealthy. Before its final destruction about 1100 BC, it was burned at least twice and the fortifications were enlarged to enclose a grave circle and a postern gate.

Mycenae was small in comparison with the contemporary cities of ◊Knossos or ◊Hattusas, its citadel covering an area just under 4 ha/6.5 acres and surrounded by 900 m/985 yds of wall. The palace was centred on a megaron, or hall, with a central hearth with four posts supporting a skylight/smokehole. The cyclopean construction of the walls is reminiscent of Hittite architecture. The main entrance to the acropolis, the Lion Gate, is named after its early heraldic device: two lions supporting a column.

Mylae, Battle of sea battle fought in 260 BC off Mylae (modern Milazzo), on the northwestern coast of Sicily, between the Roman fleet under the consul Gaius Duillius and the Carthaginian fleet, during the First Punic War (see ◊Punic War, First). The Romans won their first naval victory of the war.

Despite being slower and less skilfully crewed, the newly built Roman fleet benefited from the invention of the ◊*corvus,* a device for grappling enemy ships for boarding. This negated the Carthaginian advantage of manoeuvrability and exploited the Roman superiority in the quality of their marines. The Punic fleet of 130 suffered 50 ships captured and for the next 10 years of the war were unable to match the Romans in naval engagements.

Myonnessus, Battle of naval battle off the coast of Asia Minor in September 190 BC in which the Romans defeated King ◊Antiochus (III) the Great of Syria. The battle was fought in the context of the ◊Syrian War.

Having repulsed Antiochus' invasion of Greece, the Roman army continued its pursuit by crossing to Asia Minor. Carried by the navy, which had received extra ships from the island of Rhodes, Roman naval supremacy was reinforced by a series of small engagements. Antiochus made a last desperate attempt to trap the Roman army by destroying the fleet, but was heavily outnumbered and defeated.

Myriocephalon, Battle of battle fought on 17 September 1176 near present-day Denizli, Turkey, between an invading Byzantine army under the emperor ◊Manuel (I) Comnenus and the Seljuk sultan Kilij Arslan II. As at Manzikert in 1071 (see ◊Manzikert, Battle of), the battle destroyed the Byzantine army and terminally weakened Byzantium.

The death of ◊Nur al-Din, Sultan of Egypt and Syria, in 1173 freed Kilij Arslan to confront Manuel. In 1176 Manuel decided to invade Seljuk territory with a large army and a substantial siege train. This made it a cumbersome force and when he approached Tzibritze Pass, the Turks launched an attack on his marching troops. Manuel's Frankish ally Baldwin of Antioch countercharged with his knights but was surrounded and killed. The Byzantine forces were unable to deploy and were massacred.

Nabis (died 192 BC) ruler of Sparta from 207 BC when he seized power following the death of his young ward, King Pelops. Rome initially recognized Nabis as king of Sparta, but his refusal to relinguish control of the Greek city of Argos led to war with Rome and its Greek allies. Nabis was forced to accept terms which ended Spartan control of even the coastal towns of Laconia. He tried unsuccessfully to recover these in 193, and was assassinated the following year.

As king, Nabis revived ◊Cleomenes III's radical reforms and aggressive foreign policy. In 198 he acquired Argos from Philip V of Macedon, and this was to lead to his downfall because his desire for Spartan control of Argos was in conflict with Rome's proclamation that the Greeks should be free.

naccara large Mongol drum used to direct troop movements. Drums were commonly used in battle in the Muslim world, but the Mongols took the use of drums to a higher level, controlling their squadrons of pony-mounted and camel-mounted cavalry to such a degree that almost no army could oppose them.

Nachhut medieval Swiss term for 'rearguard': see ◊*Vorhut*.

Nadol town in Rajasthan, India, defended by a fort of primitive design with square towers, set on a ridge. It was founded by Lachman Rao, a prince of the ◊Rajput Chauhana clan, at the end of the 10th century.

His family ruled over the surrounding area until defeated and dispossessed by ◊Qutb al-Din Aibak around the end of the 12th century. Nadol subsequently became a tributary of the Hindu ranas (local variant of 'rajas') of Udaipur.

naffatin medieval Arabic term for soldiers who threw incendiary bombs. The word is believed to derive from naptha, a naturally occurring petroleum mixture related to ◊Greek fire.

nagamaki Japanese polearm with a long, single-edged blade and handle of almost equal length, wielded in the manner of a sword. The use of the *nagamaki* was confined almost solely to the middle (1400–1500) of the Muromachi period.

Nagashino, Battle of major battle of 1575 in Japan's struggle for unification in the 16th century. The Japanese *Sengoku daimyo* ◊Oda Nobunaga and his ally ◊Tokugawa Ieyasu decimated the armies of the *daimyo* ◊Takeda Katsuyori near Nagashino castle in Mikawa province (now Honai Cho in Aichi prefecture) with some 3,000 troops armed with matchlock guns, forever changing the face of warfare in Japan.

Katsuyori had been besieging Ieyasu's castle at Nagashino when he was attacked. Nobunaga's major tactical ploy was the use of troops armed with matchlock guns who were arranged in ranks with orders to fire only when the enemy were in range, and then only to fire in volleys. Following fierce traditional hand-to-hand fighting, Katsuyori's cavalry came into range of the matchlocks. With 1,000 matchlocks in three ranks firing a round approximately every 20 seconds, Katsuyori's forces were wiped out. The besieged forces in Nagashino castle then attacked Katsuyori in the rear and the army was routed, although Katsuyori survived.

Nagaur city and fort in Rajasthan, India, deriving its name from the ◊Rajput Naga clan, and probably founded in the 9th or 10th century. The city wall was 6 km/4 mi long. The fort, rising above the city, had an outer wall 7.5 m/25 ft high and an inner wall 15 m/50 ft high.

Nagaur was taken from the Rajputs in the early 12th century by Muhammad Bahlim, Ghaznavid governor of the Punjab. It was subsequently governed by ◊Prithviraja Chauhana III, but again fell to the Muslims after his death in 1192. Nagaur was seized by Raja Chonda of Mandor about 1400. It was later recovered by the Muslims, and by the mid-15th century had become a dependency of Gujarat.

naginata Japanese polearm with a curving, single-edged blade, dating from the Heian period (794–1185). Its use increased following the Mongol invasions of Japan (1274 and 1281) in the Kamakura period, and it was a popular weapon of the various militant Buddhist sects during the Muromachi period (1333–1568).

Naissus, Battle of battle between the Roman emperor Claudius II and a Gothic army at Naissus (modern Nis, Serbia) in 269. Claudius achieved a great victory over the Goths, for which he earned the title 'Gothicus'.

He encountered the Gothic forces as they were returning overland after a series of seaborne raids on the European and Asian coasts. The battle began badly for the Romans, but the surprise attack of a small force positioned behind the Gothic army put them to flight with the loss of 50,000 men.

Najac castle castle in France on the River Aveyron, 80 km/50 mi northeast of Toulouse. Originally built in the 12th century, this castle was damaged in local insurrections in around 1250, and the present work was built on the ruins by Alphonse of Poitiers in around 1260. In 1356 the castle was ceded to the English, but they left the area in 1370 and the castle was thereafter abandoned.

The castle is a rectangular building with round towers on three corners, and a square keep-tower from the earlier 12th-century castle on the fourth. One of the round towers, larger than the others, became the keep of the newer castle. An outer polygonal wall with a gatehouse and two towers surrounded this.

Najéra, Battle of battle fought on 3 April 1367 in which ◊Edward the Black Prince of England defeated a Franco-Castilian force in Spain in an operation that was an extension of the ◊Hundred Years' War in France.

Edward invaded Spain from his duchy of Aquitaine in support of King Peter the Cruel of Castile. Peter's rival and half-brother Henry of Trastamara recruited French support including Bertrand du ◊Guesclin, with some 6,000 men. Edward's forces included 2,000 Navarrese cavalry on his right and his own dismounted men-at-arms and archers in the centre. The French attacked them but were repulsed with the loss of about 500 men. Henry's forces were routed, and about 2,000 nobles were captured including the masters of the Spanish ◊Military Orders.

Naka castle (Japanese *Naka Gusuku*) castle constructed in the centre of Okinawa island, Japan, around 1440. It overlooked the Pacific Ocean on the east and the China Sea on the west, and consisted of a series of terraced compounds which rose to the top of the flattened

hill. The compounds were surrounded by dry-stone walls over 10 m/33 ft high; remains of the walls survive.

It was built for defensive purposes by the Okinawan warrior Gozamaru, who had assisted Shō Hashi with his unification of the kingdoms of Ryukyu.

naker small drum carried by foot soldiers, Arabic in origin but widely used throughout the medieval world.

Nakijin castle (Japanese *Nakijin Gusuku*) late 13th-/early 14th-century hilltop castle at Hokuzan, Okinawa island, Japan, at that time ruled by one of the kingdoms of Ryukyu. It consisted of a series of fortifications surrounded by a stone wall. It was destroyed in 1429 in the battles which resulted in the unification of the three Ryukyu island kingdoms under Shō Hashi.

Nambokuchō period alternative name for the period of the ◊Northern and Southern Courts in Japanese history (1336–92).

Namri Songtsen (died 620) (or *gNam-ri slon-mtshan*) first *bTsan-po* ('emperor') of Tibet c. 570–620. Originally a chieftain of the Yar-lung Valley in south central Tibet, he defeated his overlord, the Zinporje of Naspo, and subdued neighbouring princes to create a sizeable kingdom. He was murdered and succeeded by his son ◊Songtsen Gampo.

Nancy, Battle of battle of 5 January 1477 between ◊René (II) of Anjou, Duke of Lorraine, and his Swiss allies and the smaller forces of ◊Charles the Bold, Duke of Burgundy. Charles, suffering from previous defeats by the Swiss, was besieging Nancy, René's capital. He was defeated and killed in the battle.

Charles had some 1,000 men-at-arms, 2,000 archers, and 2,500 infantry. The allied army was three times larger, including 6,000 veteran Swiss. Charles constructed field fortifications, including artillery, but, marching in appalling icy and snowy conditions, the allies managed to outflank and break the Burgundians.

Nanjing, fall of climax, in July 1402, of the rebellion of the Prince of Yan against his nephew, the second Ming emperor of China. After a successful offensive against the imperial capital, Nanjing, the Prince took the throne as Ming Chengzu, the Yongle Emperor, and moved the capital to Beijing.

In 1399 the Prince began strengthening his position around modern Beijing, defeating several imperial armies. In January 1402 he launched his final offensive against the imperial capital, Nanjing. He defeated an imperial cavalry army at Suzhou in April. In May, still pushing south, he was defeated by imperial commander Xu Huizu at Mount Qimen. Five days later, however, he surprised Xu at Lingbi and captured him. He crossed the Huai River in June but was stopped by the imperial fleet at the Yangtze on 1 July. The fleet, however, deserted to him, and he crossed the Yangtze and reached Nanjing unopposed. New armies had been recruited to defend Nanjing, but the prince's men were admitted by a turncoat commanding one of the city gates. In the street-fighting that followed the imperial palace was burned down and the Emperor declared dead – though his body was never found.

Nanjing, Siege of capture of the city of Nanjing on 10 April 1356 by ◊Zhu Yuanzhang in the Chinese civil wars at the end of the Yuan dynasty. Nanjing became Zhu's base for the unification of China and the first imperial capital of his Ming dynasty.

After the victory at Caishi in 1356 (see ◊Caishi, Battle of 1356), Zhu mopped up other Yuan forces to isolate Nanjing. The local Yuan field commander, the Mongol Chen Zhaoxian, surrendered, leaving the city inadequately garrisoned. Zhu's forces assaulted in three columns both by land and from the river, and the defenders surrendered once the wall was breached.

Narasinghavarman (or *Narasimhavarman*) king of the Tamil Pallava dynasty 625–45. He continued the war with the rival Chalukya dynasty for the possession of Vengi province, on the east coast of the Deccan, and assumed the title of Mambala (or Mahabala), 'Great Champion', to mark his defeat of the Chalukya king ◊Pulakeshin II in 642.

Narathihapate (1238–1287) Burmese king of Pagan from 1254, when he was 16. He suppressed rebellions in Arakan and elsewhere, but his reign was dominated by war with Mongol-ruled Yuan China under ◊Khubilai Khan. After suffering more than 10 years of defeats and a final surrender to the Mongols, his reputation was so undermined that his own son had him poisoned. He was subsequently known as Tarukphyi, 'the king who fled from the Mongols'.

After rejecting Mongol embassies, Narathihapate attacked the border state of Kaungai, which had submitted to Khubilai, in 1277. He was defeated at Vochan (see ◊Vochan, Battle of) by local Yuan forces. In December 1277 another Yuan army under the Muslim general Nasir al-Din took the Burmese fort at Kaungsin and secured Yuan control of the Yunnan-Burma border regions. In 1283 another

expedition defeated the Burmese at Ngasaungkyam (see ◊Ngasaungkyam, Battle of) and Narathihapate fled. In 1287 a third Mongol expedition under Khubilai's grandson Esen Timür finally took Pagan, and Narathihapate sent a mission of surrender to Khubilai.

Narbata, Siege of Roman siege and capture in AD 66–67 of the Judaean hilltop village of Narbata (in present-day Israel) during the early stages of the Jewish rebellion (66–73) against Roman rule, either during or after the Roman march on Jerusalem.

Archaeologists have uncovered Roman siege lines, camps, and an assault ramp very similar, but on a much smaller scale, to those at Masada (see ◊Masada, Siege of).

Narbonne, Battle of battle of 436 in which the West Roman general ◊Aetius gained a victory over the Visigoths who had settled in southern France, helping to bring temporary stability to France and leading to a cession of hostilities between the Visigoths and West Romans. This victory played a crucial part in the defeat of ◊Attila in 451.

Narses (478–573) East Roman general who defeated the Ostrogoths and Merovingians, completing the Roman reconquest of Italy. He successfully used infantry, archers, and cavalry in well coordinated combinations that maximized their strengths. His victories at Taginae in 552 (see ◊Taginae, Battle of) and Casilinium in 553 (see ◊Casilinum, Battle of) were models of effective combined arms tactics.

Because he was a eunuch, Narses posed no threat to the emperor ◊Justinian (a eunuch was not eligible to become emperor). Therefore, unlike ◊Belisarius, he was trusted with full control of a large army.

nasal modern term for the nosepiece of a helmet, either forged as part of the helmet (as in the Norman Spangenhelm or the Corinthian helmet), or attached by a bracket and adjustable (as in the Turkish çiçak and *migfer* and the Indian *kolah khud*).

Naulochus, Battle of naval battle fought in 36 BC near the Straits of Messana off Sicily where Octavian (the future Roman emperor Augustus) defeated the fleet of Sextus Pompeius, the son of Pompey the Great. The victory was mainly due to the skills of Octavian's admiral Marcus Vipsanius ◊Agrippa.

Octavian's land forces had been making advances against the Pompeian bases in Sicily, leading Sextus to risk a full-scale naval battle. Each fleet mustered about 300 ships, but

Agrippa had invented a new type of grapnel (grasping device) and planned boarding actions rather than manoeuvring. As soon as the battle started, his ships attempted to close as swiftly as possible. In the confused combat that resulted, Octavian's forces gradually gained the advantage, grappling and boarding ship after ship. Only three of his ships were sunk, compared to 28 of the Pompeian ships. Only 17 of Sextus's ships escaped; the others were captured or ran aground.

Naupactus, Battle of sea battle in 429 BC, the second of two victories won by the Athenian ◊Phormio in the Corinthian Gulf during the ◊Peloponnesian War. It provides a good example of the skill of Athenian galleys at this time.

Phormio, who had 20 triremes, was keeping watch on 77 Peloponnesian triremes when they suddenly turned towards him. He escaped with his leading 11 ships, but the others were driven ashore where some were captured and others were rescued by friendly troops. Meanwhile, the fastest 20 Peloponnesians pursued the Athenians to their base at Naupactus (modern Nafpaktos). Ten Athenian vessels made it safely into harbour but the eleventh, seeing that the leading pursuer had separated from the rest, rowed around a merchant ship anchored offshore. This concealed the Athenian warship until it emerged to ram its pursuer amidships. Taking advantage of the confusion, the other Athenians attacked, and the Peloponnesians fled, losing six of their ships and the Athenian vessels they had previously captured.

navarch from the Greek *nauarchos* 'ship leader' (Greek) admiral. In Sparta the position was an annual appointment.

nawak arrow guide used by Sassanian Persian archers to shoot short, light darts. It was a grooved length of wood held projecting backwards from the grip of the bow to enable archers to use darts too short to reach from bow to string when the bow was drawn.

The *nawak* may have been similar to the Byzantine ◊*solenarion*.

Naworth castle castle in Cumbria, England, 18 km/11 mi east of Carlisle. It was built by Ralph, Lord Dacre in 1335 as a fairly simple walled rectangle, with a great tower at one end and a gatehouse at the other, surrounded by a deep ditch on three sides.

Nearchus (lived 4th century BC) Cretan admiral of ◊Alexander (III) the Great 325–324 BC. He governed Lycia and Pamphylia for Alexander from their conquest in 334 until 329 BC. He took part in the Indian campaigns, com-

manding the fleet on the Hydaspes (modern Jhelum) and Indus rivers, and thence to the Tigris. He served ◊Antigonus (I) Monophthalmus 317–312.

Nebuchadnezzar (c. 630–c. 562 BC) or *Nebuchadrezzar II* king of Babylonia from 604 BC. Shortly before his accession he defeated the Egyptians at Carchemish and brought Palestine and Syria into his empire. Judah revolted, with Egyptian assistance, 596 and 587–586 BC; on both occasions he captured Jerusalem and took many Hebrews into captivity. He largely rebuilt Babylon and constructed the hanging gardens.

Nedao, Battle of crushing defeat of the Huns in 454 by a combined force of Germanic and Iranian subject peoples, which resulted in the destruction of the Hunnic empire.

Immediately after the death of ◊Attila, a power struggle broke out between his sons for control of his empire. Ellak, the eldest, fought off challenges by his two younger brothers, only to face a rebellion led by the Gepid King, Ardaric. Ardaric's forces decisively defeated the Huns by the Nedao River in Pannonia. Ellak was killed in the fighting and the power of the Huns broken.

nef (or *navis*) medieval round ship, used mainly for trade in the Mediterranean. It was broad in the beam and had a deep draught, with a relatively large space for cargo. It was used to transport bulky items such as wheat, salt, or timber. Twelfth-century carvings show two masts and a fairly prominent castle at the rear with steering oars, but *nefs* could vary in size and in the number of masts and decks.

Nemea, Battle of the battle fought in 394 BC, early in the ◊Corinthian War, near the River Nemea west of Corinth, between 18–19,000 Spartan hoplites and 24,000 Boeotian, Corinthian, Argive, Euboean and Athenian hoplites. In all, 2800 of the allies fell for only 1100 on the Spartan side. It was possibly the greatest hoplite battle ever fought and shows a development of the tactics employed at Mantinea (see ◊Mantinea, Battle of 207 BC)).

During the battle, both sides advanced diagonally to the right in a deliberate attempt to outflank the enemy left. Then, instead of simply pursuing the retreating enemy left, the Spartans wheeled their overlapping wing to form a right angle to the rest of their phalanx. Now, although defeated on their own left, they were in a position to take the victorious enemy in their unprotected flank.

Nepheris, battles of two battles, 149 and 147 BC, fought at Nepheris (Henchir bou Beker) during the Third Punic War between the Romans and Carthaginians (see ◊Punic War, Third).

Nepheris was the base of operations for the Carthaginian field army and the source of supplies for the city of Carthage. It was attacked twice in 149 BC by the Roman consul Manius Manilius. However, its defensive strength was such that this nearly led to disaster on the first occasion, when the Romans were counterattacked by ◊Hasdrubal Barca as they withdrew; on the second occasion the Romans were forced to disengage through lack of supplies.

In both expeditions the young military tribune ◊Scipio Aemilianus distinguished himself, and this contributed to his election to the consulship in 147 BC. With Scipio in command, the Romans attacked and destroyed the Carthaginian army in its camp and then captured the city of Nepheris itself in 147 BC. This victory enabled Scipio to choke off supplies to Carthage and concentrate on reducing the city by siege.

Nero, Gaius Claudius (lived 3rd century BC) Roman general during the Second Punic War (see ◊Punic War, Second). His greatest success was the defeat of the army of ◊Hasdrubal Barca on the banks of the river Metaurus in 207 BC (see ◊Metaurus, Battle of the).

As pro-praetor he commanded forces at the successful second siege of Capua in 212–211 BC (see ◊Capua, Siege of), and as praetor in 211 he commanded the Roman army in Spain against Hasdrubal Barca. Elected consul in 207 BC, he was leading the army shadowing ◊Hannibal the Great in Lucania when he learned of Hasdrubal's intention to rendezvous with his brother. By a rapid march over 475 km/295 mi he was able to join up with the Roman army shadowing Hasdrubal and destroy Hasdrubal's force before the union of the Carthaginian armies could take place.

Nerva (AD c. 30–98) (*Marcus Cocceius Nerva*) Roman emperor. He was proclaimed emperor on Domitian's death AD 96, and introduced state loans for farmers, family allowances, and allotments of land to poor citizens in his sixteen-month reign.

Neuss, Siege of siege of the town of Neuss, near modern Düsseldorf, Germany, by ◊Charles the Bold, Duke of Burgundy, with a huge army from 20 July 1474 to 13 June 1475. The defenders held out and Charles withdrew.

Charles's Burgundians mustered some 30,000 troops supported by the most modern artillery. The besieged numbered 3,000. Dividing their forces into three, they slept, ate, and fought in relays. Although supplies were

almost exhausted by 1475, they resisted grimly. The Holy Roman emperor Frederick II attempted a relief in May, but withdrew. Charles felt honour was satisfied and soon left to attack the Swiss.

Neva River, Battle of the battle fought on 15 July 1240 in which the Russian military leader ◊Alexander Nevsky defeated an invasion force of Swedes and Norwegians. It was little more than a skirmish in terms of numbers involved, but Alexander's victory demonstrated his determination to resist western attacks (see also ◊Lake Peipus, Battle of).

Neville's Cross, Battle of battle fought on 17 October 1346 between English forces under Ralph Neville and a Scottish invasion force under David II, King of Scotland, on difficult ground to the west of Durham, England. David was captured and held prisoner until 1357.

David was invading England in support of his ally Philip VI of France, who had been defeated at Crécy (see ◊Crécy, Battle of). He led some 20,000 men against the 15,000 northern English levies. The English adopted their usual three battle formation, with dismounted men-at-arms supporting archers. David's three battles also fought on foot, but found their advance cramped by a ravine to their right. After enduring a heavy barrage of arrows, they experienced an initial success before being hurled back by English countercharges, thrown into confusion, and routed.

Newark castle castle in Nottinghamshire, in central England. Originally a timber castle built by the Bishop of Lincoln early in the 12th century, it was replaced by a stone ◊motte-and-bailey work at the end of the century. The river undermined the gateway, and rebuilding was carried out in the 13th and 14th centuries, incorporating new towers and a water gate.

King John died here in 1216, and in 1218 it was besieged and severely damaged by Simon de ◊Montfort (the Younger) during the ◊Barons' War of 1264–67. It remained the Bishop's residence until the 15th century.

New Carthage, Siege of Roman siege and capture in 209 BC of the main Carthaginian base in Spain, New Carthage (present-day Cartagena), during the Second Punic War (see ◊Punic War, Second).

The army of the Roman commander Publius Cornelius ◊Scipio (later Scipio 'Africanus'), comprising 25,000 infantry and 2,500 cavalry, made a rapid and unexpected march into Punic-held territory and swiftly assaulted the city, which was situated at the end of an isthmus. Taking advantage of a low tide in the adjacent lagoon, 500 Romans crossed and seized an unguarded point of the wall while the defenders were occupied resisting a major assault on the city's landward side. Scipio sacked the town, enslaving the 'artisans' but letting citizens go free.

Newcastle upon Tyne castle castle in Northumberland, England, built in around 1080 by Robert Curthose to defend the northern border against the Scots and to cover a strategic ford across the River Tyne. Sited close to ◊Hadrian's Wall, it used much Roman material in its construction. The castle was the scene of fighting in various Scottish incursions in the 14th century.

Henry II had the keep built 1172–78, and the same architect who built Dover Castle keep planned it. The Scots attacked it in 1174, even before it was finished, but failed to make any impression on the 5.5 m/18 ft thick walls. After the keep was completed, new curtain walls were built, and other construction took place.

Ngasaungkyam, Battle of battle on 3 December 1283 in which the army of the Mongol-Chinese Yuan dynasty of ◊Khubilai Khan, commanded by the Mongol general Sangqudar, defeated the Burmese army of ◊Narathihapate. The battle was fought near the Bhamo River in Burma.

The Burmese were defeated and fell back on a fortified hill-top position, but Sangqudar marched southwest and retook the Burmese fort at Kaungsin on 9 December. Narathihapate evacuated the Burmese capital Pagan and fled to Bassein in the Irrawaddy delta. Sangqudar pursued, but did not catch the king or take Pagan.

Ngo Quyen (898–944) Vietnamese warlord, a son-in-law and general of Duong Dinh Nghe who ejected the Southern Han Chinese from Vietnam in 931. When Duong was assassinated by a pro-Chinese officer in 937, Ngo led the southern frontier army to avenge him. He defeated a Chinese expedition at the Bach-dang river (see ◊Bach-dang River, Battle of). In 939 he proclaimed himself king, setting up a Chinese-style court at the ancient city of ◊Co-Loa.

Nicaea Roman city (modern Iznik, Turkey) in the Roman province of Bithynia protected by a circuit of walls about the time of the reign of the emperor ◊Probus (ruled 276–82). The defences were supplemented by two types of tower that incorporated large amounts of material taken from demolished public buildings.

The D-shaped towers were made of concrete reinforced with timber lacing and lay upon a foundation raft of column drums. The square towers were constructed in high-quality ashlar blocks, clearly the fabric of a public theatre or temple.

Nicaea, Battle of (194) battle fought in 194 between the Roman emperor Lucius ◊Septimus Severus and the Roman governor of Syria, Percennius Niger, in the narrow mountain passes between Nicaea (now Iznik, Turkey) and Ascania. Severus' victory owed much to the skill, leadership, and personal courage of his general Candidus.

Nicaea, Battle of (1097) siege of the Seljuk capital of Nicaea (now Iznik, Turkey) by Christians of the First Crusade, lasting from 6 May to 19 June 1097, during which a major Seljuk relief attempt was beaten off. The city was taken by the crusaders' Byzantine allies using a fleet of boats on nearby Ascanian Lake.

The first main obstacle of the main crusading force, Nicaea was fiercely defended. Assaults launched by ◊Godfrey de Bouillon's Germans on the southern walls, and Raymond of Toulouse's Provencals on the east were both driven back. They then fought off an attack by the Seljuk sultan Kilij Arslan on 16 May. On 14 June, the northern French contingent under ◊Bohemond arrived to attack the north walls, and soon after a Byzantine fleet was launched on the lake to the east. Surrounded, the Turkish garrison surrendered to the Greeks, so denying the angry crusaders valuable booty.

Nicephorus (II) Phocas (died 969) Byzantine general and emperor 963–69, who presided over a revival of Byzantine power. In a series of victories from 956 to 969 he drove the Muslims from Eastern Anatolia, Syria, Crete, and Cyprus, and forced the Fatamid Caliphate to sue for peace. He was overthrown and assassinated by his nephew John ◊Zimisces in 969.

Nicias (c. 470–413 BC) Athenian general. During the ◊Peloponnesian War he negotiated the short-lived Peace of Nicias between Sparta and Athens in 421 BC. He opposed ◊Alcibiades' plan for the Sicilian expedition in 415, but was appointed one of its commanders. After Alcibiades' recall he remained in command with Lamachus and laid siege to Syracuse. He was captured by the Syracusans and executed.

Nicopolis, Battle of battle of 12 September 1396 fought on the banks of the Danube in Bulgaria in which the Ottoman sultan Bayezid I drew crusaders into a trap baited by horse-archers, surrounded, and captured them all.

Six thousand French and Burgundian crusaders were intending to rescue

Constantinople from Ottoman siege, in alliance with King ◊Sigismund of Hungary's 20,000 troops. They were opposed at Nicopolis by Bayezid with a well-balanced force of Janissary (standing Ottoman Turkish army) archers, horse-archers, and ◊spahi heavy cavalry. Sigismund advised caution and withdrew from the fight, but the crusaders charged head-long into a screen of horse-archers. They parted to reveal the Janissaries in a field of stakes. Losing horses to arrows and the stakes, the crusaders dismounted and dispersed the Janissaries, but were then counterattacked and captured by reserve *spahi* cavalry.

Nijmegen fortress (Roman *Batavodrum*) Roman legionary fortress established by the emperor Augustus in 20 BC on the Rhine River at present-day Nijmegen in the Netherlands as a base for the conquest of Germany. Covering at least 60 ha / 148 acres, it was intended to hold a campaign force of two legions.

Following the Roman withdrawal from Germany in AD 9 the garrisons were deployed elsewhere and Nijmegen was abandoned. It was re-established for a single legion by the emperor Vespasian I (reigned 69–79) to watch over the capital of the Batavi tribe following their recent revolt. With the acceptance of the Rhine frontier as permanent, a stone wall 1 m / 3.3 ft wide was built around the fortress under the emperor Trajan (reigned 98–117). The fortress was permanently abandoned about 117.

Nineveh, Battle of battle fought on 9 December 627 at Nineveh (now Al Mawsil, Iraq) between the forces of the Sassanid Persian Empire and the Byzantine Empire. It was the last major engagement between the two empires. The outcome was a decisive Byzantine victory.

Following the successful defence of Constantinople in 626 (see ◊Constantinople, Siege of 626), the Byzantines resumed their offensive against the Persians. The emperor ◊Heraclius led 70,000 troops through Syria, Mesopotamia, and Armenia into Assyria. Shahrbaraz, Heraclius' main opponent for the last few years, surrendered, but King Chosroes II of Persia ordered an army commanded by Rahzadh to make a stand near Nineveh,.

The battle opened with Rahzadh challenging Heraclius to personal combat. Heraclius accepted and, although wounded, succeeded in killing the opposing general. Despite low Persian morale, the battle was hard fought and it took the Byzantines all day to break their opponents. The Persians suffered heavy losses (said to be 50,000 men and 28 standards) but

withdrew in good order. Heraclius, despite his wounds and high losses in his own army, launched a vigorous pursuit driving on to the Persian capital of Ctesiphon.

The following spring King Chosroes II was murdered by his war-weary subjects and his son Kavadh II sued for peace.

Niort castle medieval stronghold between Poitiers and La Rochelle in the *département* of Deux-Sèvres, France. It was built by ◊Henry II of England in the late 12th century and has twin keeps separated by a courtyard. The curtain wall had 16 round towers and early ◊machicolation on the southern keep. A building linked the two keeps in the 15th century.

Niort was captured from King John of England by ◊Philip (II) Augustus of France and then recaptured. France finally won Niort in 1436. It was damaged by the Huguenots in 1588. The northern keep was repaired in the 18th century.

Nishapur Ghaznavid administrative capital of Khurasan (northeastern Iran) 1002–40. It was taken by the ◊Seljuk Turkomen in 1038, recovered by the Ghaznavid sultan Mas'ud in 1039, but abandoned, with all Khurasan, to the Seljuks after their victory at Dandanqan (see ◊Dandanqan, Battle of) in 1040.

Nisibis strategically important fortress on the borders between the Roman and Persian empires, and the site of battles in the 3rd and 4th centuries.

Third-century battle In 217 the Roman emperor Marcus Opelius Macrinus and the Parthian king Artabanus V fought at Nisibis. Macrinus, who had seized power after murdering the emperor Caracalla in 216, attempted to continue the latter's Parthian expedition, but was driven out of Mesopotamia and forced to pay the Parthians a heavy indemnity.

4th-century battles Nisibis was besieged three times, in 337, 344, and 349, by the Persian ruler Sharpur II. The Roman garrison, commanded by Lucilianus and actively supported by the citizens, repelled the Persian assaults each time.

Nisibis, Sieges of series of sieges by the Sassanid Persian king, Shapur II, in AD 337, 344, and 349 of the Roman fortress Nisibis, strategically sited on the border between the Roman and Persian empires. Each of the sieges was successfully repelled by the Roman garrison under Lucilianus with active support from the local citizens.

Nitta Yoshisada (1301–38) Japanese warrior. In the ◊Kemmu Restoration he sided with the emperor Go-Daigo and together with Ashikaga Takauji assisted in the brief restoration of imperial power. When Takauji revolted against the emperor in 1335 Yoshisada led imperial forces against him but was defeated in battle at Hakone.

Yoshisada was a member of the Japanese warrior family who in the late 12th century took their name from their lands in the Nitta district of what is now Gumma prefecture, Japan. The Nitta family sided with ◊Minamoto Yoritomo (founder of the Kamakura shogunate) in the Taira–Minamoto Wars and were subsequently powerful during the Kamakura period.

Yoshisada was killed by an ally of Takauji in a minor engagement in 1338.

nodachi (or *ō-dachi*) Japanese 'moor sword' extremely long Japanese sword which came into vogue during the Nambokuchō period (1336–92). Many of these swords had a cutting edge of over 1 m/3 ft and were very efficient when fighting cavalry on foot. Because the *nodachi* was too long to draw from the side, it was usually carried on the back and wrapped in a disposable scabbard.

Nogent-le-Rotrou castle early 11th-century comital castle of St-Jean, on a hill overlooking the River Huîsne, Eure-et-Loire *département*, France. It has a rectangular keep. Additions were made throughout the medieval period. Henry IV of France's minister the Duc de Sully owned Nogent-Le-Rotrou in the 17th century.

Nola, battles of series of unsuccessful battles and sieges of the strategic Italian town of Nola conducted by the Carthaginian general ◊Hannibal the Great in 216, 215, and 214 BC, during the Second Punic War (see ◊Punic War, Second).

In 216 BC, after the victory at Cannae (see ◊Cannae, Battle of), Hannibal was unable to dislodge the Roman commander Marcus Claudius Marcellus, despite pro-Carthaginian sympathizers within the city. Marcellus again saved it after a pitched battle in 215 BC and, following a further failure in 214, Hannibal abandoned any hope of gaining the town.

Norham castle castle in Northumberland, England, 13 km/8 mi southwest of Berwick-on-Tweed. It was sited on the banks of the Tweed to guard an important ford. The castle featured prominently in the various Scottish and Border wars of the 13th and 14th centuries and in the Wars of the Roses (1455–85).

A ditch that fed from the river surrounded two sides of the castle, the river covering the other two. Within this lay the outer ward, from which entrance to the inner ward was gained by a barbican and gate. The great keep, which is 27 m/90 ft high, with walls 4 m/12 ft thick, is in the corner of the inner ward.

Northallerton, Battle of battle fought in 1138 in Yorkshire, England, between Scottish invaders under David I and an army raised by Thurstan, Archbishop of York, including various northern nobles and royal household knights under Bernard de Balliol. The Scots were defeated, and the Scottish threat was diminished during the remainder of Stephen's reign in England.

The English formed around a ◊*carroccio* (standard). The armies met in the fog north of Northallerton and the Scottish infantry charge was opposed by English archers and annihilated.

Northampton, Battle of battle fought on 10 July 1460, during the Wars of the Roses (see ◊Roses, Wars of the), between the Yorkists under the Earl of Warwick and Henry VI (1421–1471), in which the Yorkists defeated Henry VI.

Warwick invaded England from Calais in June, and raised about 20,000 troops on his march north. The Lancastrians, 10–15,000 strong, had constructed an artillery camp backed onto the River Nene at Northampton. Their strong position was completely undermined by the defection of Earl Grey on the right flank, allowing the Yorkists in to massacre the surprised defenders.

Northern and Southern Courts (or *Nambokuchō period*) period of Japanese history from 1336 to 1392 when, due to conflicting political aspirations between Ashikaga Takauji and the Japanese emperor ◊Go-Daigo, there were effectively two imperial courts, one at Yoshino to the south with the exiled emperor Go-Daigo, the other at Kyoto in the north with the emperor Kōmyō who was placed there by Takauji. The two courts were reconciled by ◊Ashikaga Yoshimitsu in 1392.

The period was one of terrible civil war and Kyoto and the surrounding areas were repeatedly ravaged. The northern dynasty eventually emerged victorious.

Northern Army (*bei jun* or *pei chün*) central standing army in Eastern Han (AD 25–220) China, so named because it was garrisoned north of the capital. It was also called the 'Troops of the Five Colonels', these being the commanders of: Garrison Cavalry, Picked Cavalry, Infantry, the Chang River Encampment (◊Xiongnu and other nomad cavalry), and the Archers Who Shoot By Sound. They totalled about 4,000 men.

Norwich castle castle in Norfolk, England. Built in the 11th century as a ◊motte-and-bailey castle with two baileys, it was extensively rebuilt in 1160 with a large and ornate keep on the extended mound.

Notitia Dignitatum list of offices of the late Roman administration from the end of the 4th century, which includes a fairly complete listing of army organization and unit shield designs.

numerus vague term meaning unit. By the 2nd century it was most often applied to Roman units of irregulars raised from a specific ethnic group which were increasingly used as a cheap means of patrolling the empire's frontiers. The term was also applied to some cavalry units in the late Roman army.

Numistro, Battle of indecisive battle fought in 210 BC between the Roman commander Marcus Claudius ◊Marcellus and the Carthaginian general ◊Hannibal the Great, during the Second Punic War (see ◊Punic War, Second).

Nunney castle castle in Somerset, England, 5 km/3 mi west of Frome. John de la Mare, who had recently returned from the wars in France and had obviously been impressed by some French castles, built it in 1371. It is unique in Britain, being no more than a small rectangle with four huge towers at the corners, so close as to be almost touching at the ends of the work. The whole is crowned by ◊machicolation and enclosed in a wide moat.

Nur al-Din (born 1119) ruler of Aleppo 1146–74. He was the son of ◊Zengi, who had taken Edessa in 1146. Nur-al Din had the responsibility of holding these gains and defeating the Second Crusade. He was the victor at Inab in 1149 and captured Damascus in 1154, but he was defeated at Homs in 1163. Later he used his father's general, ◊Shirkuh, and his nephew, ◊Saladin, to good effect in protecting Egypt from Frankish incursions 1165–69 (see ◊Almaric).

After an illness in 1149 he was less active and was more of a strategist than a field commander. Saladin became his rival from 1170, but it was Nur al-Din's military achievements the formed the basis of Saladin's subsequent conquests.

Nutari no ki system of stockades (◊*saku*) constructed in about 647 in the northwest of Japan, near the modern city of Niigata, as a political and military administrative centre for

NUMANTIA, BATTLE OF

Hill town in Spain besieged by the Romans in 134–133 BC. It was situated on the river Douro in northern Spain, occupying a plateau surrounded by rivers and ravines. As the tribal capital of the Celtiberians it was naturally very well defended and had become the centre of stubborn resistance to the Romans. Attempts by various Roman generals to capture the town during the 2nd century BC had failed, and it was eventually blockaded in 134 BC by ◊Scipio Aemilianus, the man who had destroyed Carthage. The best account of the siege is given by Appian whose work was probably based on the eye-witness record of the Greek historian Polybius.

Scipio preferred to avoid battle with the experienced and eager Spanish warriors and had a 9 km/5.5 mi circumvallation wall and ditch thrown round the town. Towers were added every 30 m/98 ft and seven forts were built. He also blocked the river with revolving wooden beams studded with sharp blades, and devised a signalling system in case of trouble. These defences enabled the Romans to repel counterattacks by the Numantines and prevent supplies from reaching them. After an eight-month blockade the Numantines were starving (some sources claim they resorted to cannibalism) and they were forced to surrender. The occupants were sold into slavery and the town was razed to the ground.

Excavations at Numantia in the early 20th century revealed the Roman siegeworks and forts, as well as several other forts from the earlier, unsuccessful, actions.

the subjugation and control of the Ezo tribes.

The success of the campaigns against the Ezo tribes meant that by the early 8th century most parts of the system that had evolved from the original single stockade had been mostly abandoned as military bases.

Octavian (63 BC–AD 14) original name of ◊Augustus, the first Roman emperor.

Oda Nobunaga (1534–82) Japanese military warlord, one of the three great unifiers of Japan (with Toyotomi Hideyoshi and Tokugawa Ieyasu). In 1568 he occupied Kyoto in the name of the emperor and installed Ashikaga Yoshiaki as shogun, but in reality exercised full control himself. He suppressed all opposition to his authority, but was eventually assassinated.

The son of a warlord (◊*Sengoku daimyo*) of Owari province, Nobunaga inherited his father's estates at the age of 17. He quickly established a reputation for ruthlessness by seizing nearby territories and having his own brother killed on suspicion of plotting against him. His first major victory was at the Battle of Okehazama in 1560. His aspirations at this time are reflected in the wording of his personal seal, ' ◊*tenka fubu*', 'the realm under the military'.

In 1574 he ruthlessly put down a major uprising by the ikkō-ikki (militant Buddhist sect) of Nagashima, slaughtering some 20,000 people. Various military factions continued to cause him problems and the shogun Yoshiaki exploited this by involving other *daimyo* in conspiracies against Nobunaga. The powerful Takeda family was finally persuaded to fight against Nobunaga, but was all but destroyed at the Battle of Nagashino in 1575.

By 1582 Nobunaga was being invited by the emperor to take the title of shogun. He was assassinated by his vassal Akechi Mitsuhide at Honnōji temple, Kyoto, in June that year. Despite the turmoil left by his sudden death, he had paved the way to the final unification of the warring provinces of Japan.

Odawara, Battle of battle fought in 1590 in which the Japanese warlord Toyotomi Hideyoshi defeated the Hōjō family at the castle of Odawara (reputedly impregnable) in the Kantō region of Japan. The outcome of the battle, fought over a period of 100 days, removed the last military obstacle to the unification of Japan.

Odenwald *limes* stretch of the Upper German ◊*limes* (frontier) that formed part of Rome's German frontier from the reign of the emperor Domitian (AD 81–96) to the reign of Antoninus Pius (138–61). It was about 80 km/50 mi long and consisted of a cleared track running through the forests between the Main and Neckar rivers.

Watchtowers were positioned along the track to observe any movement, and under the emperor Hadrian (reigned 117–38) a timber palisade was added along the far side. Small irregular auxiliary units (*numeri*) provided the garrisons, with the regular forces stationed further to the west in reserve. By AD 161 the Odenwald *limes* was abandoned and the frontier advanced further east.

Odiham castle castle in Hampshire, England, 11 km/7 mi southeast of Basingstoke, built in around 1210 on an irregular moated site on the bend of a river and guarding a ford. The principal feature is the unusual octagonal tower keep faced with Caen stone, built by King John. A curtain wall followed this, and some further building was carried out in the 14th century.

Odoacer, Flavius (c. 433–93) (or *Odovacar*) Roman officer of German descent who deposed Romulus Augustulus, the last West Roman emperor, and became king of Italy in 476. He annexed Dalmatia in 481 and after a successful campaign against the Rugians added Noricum to his realm in 488. His kingdom was destroyed by ◊Theodoric the Great's Ostrogoths in 493 after a six-year campaign which culminated in the siege of Ravenna 490–93 (see ◊Ravenna, Siege of).

Odovacar, Flavius alternative, more correct spelling of Flavius ◊Odoacer, King of Italy 476–493.

Ōei Rebellion military insurrection in Japan from November 1399 to January 1400. The minor warlord Ōuchi Yoshihiro had established himself as military governor of a substantial area of western Japan, presenting a threat to the Muromachi shogunate. He was defeated after a two-month siege by the Muromachi at Sakai, near Osaka, Honshu island.

After this, the shogunate was briefly able to extend greater influence over the potentially rebellious provincial military lords (◊shugo daimyo).

Offa (died 797) king of the Anglo-Saxon kingdom of Mercia (west-central England) 757–97. He conquered Essex, Kent, Sussex, and Surrey; defeated the Welsh and the West Saxons; and established Mercian supremacy over all England south of the River Humber. He built the earthwork known as Offa's Dyke along the Welsh border to defend his frontier in the west.

Ogedei (died 1241) second Mongol Great Khan 1229–41, third son and successor to Genghis Khan. Not a great campaigner, Ogedei's role was as director of campaigns from his new capital rather than as field commander. He fortified Qaraqorum in 1235, launched the attack on Russia at a kuriltai and encouraged its expansion into eastern Europe 1240–41. His death in 1241 may have saved western Europe from Mongol assualt.

Oka castle (Japanese *Oka-jō*) Japanese castle built in the 12th century on a steep cliff overlooking two rivers. The natural site was additionally fortified by walls of rock and earth. The surviving walls are mostly of much later date, having being strengthened and rebuilt in the Edo period (1600–1868).

Okehampton castle castle in Devon, England, 40 km/25 mi west of Exeter. A ◊motte-and-bailey castle was built here in around 1070 in a commanding position on a ridge. A rectangular stone keep was then built on the motte and was later extended into a double building, and various domestic buildings were erected in the small at the foot of the motte.

In the 14th century the bailey was considerably extended along the ridge line, with a curtain wall ending in a gatehouse, to which a covered way led to a second gateway, the whole acting as a form of extended barbican. The result was one of the largest castles in the west of England.

Okehazama, Battle of battle fought in 1560 in which the young Japanese military warlord ◊Oda Nobunaga, with only about 3,000 troops, defeated the 25,000-strong force of Imagawa Yoshimoto, *daimyo* of Mikawa province (now Honai Cho in Aichi prefecture). It was Nobunaga's first major victory.

During a terrific thunderstorm, Imagawa was resting in the gorge of Dengaku Hazama, about 0.6 km/1 mi north of Okehazama, between Nagoma and Toyoako, following an earlier attack on one of Nobunaga's outposts. Knowing the area well, Nobunaga surprised his enemy with an attack as the storm abated. The battle was over quickly and Yoshimoto was killed.

Old Sarum castle castle near Salisbury, England. Often called the largest ◊motte-and-bailey castle in Europe, Old Sarum probably had Roman defensive works at an early stage, then became an Anglo-Saxon township.

After the Conquest it was the site for the new bishopric and cathedral, together with a curtain wall, gatehouse, and tower-keep. More domestic and commercial building took place, but in the early 13th century, after much friction between church and state, a new cathedral was begun some distance southwards. This became the nucleus of present-day Salisbury.

Olpae, Battle of small-scale battle fought in 426 BC at Olpae (somewhere near the modern Amfilochia), between the Athenian ◊Demosthenes and the Peloponnesians and local Abraciots. It illustrates a variation on the head-on clash of hoplites developed in the ◊Peloponnesian War, and Demosthenes' use of an ambush anticipates the tactics of Hannibal at Trebia (see ◊Trebia, Battle of).

Fearing that the more numerous enemy would outflank his army, Demosthenes placed 400 hoplites and light troops in position to ambush their left. He deployed the rest of his force in conventional formation, and the enemy hoplites formed a phalanx in the usual way. When the battle began, the Athenian ambush routed the enemy left. Panic spread and the enemy right, which had defeated Demosthenes' left, lost heavily while making its way back to Olpae.

onager stone-throwing catapult used in the Roman army, so named because it had a kick like the wild ass of that name. Developed by the 4th century AD, the *onager* was a powerful war machine and an important part of a Roman army's siege train.

Onasander Greek philosopher who wrote a treatise on generalship dedicated to Veranius, governor of Britain, in around 57 AD. His treatise emphasizes the importance of a general's character and offers practical advice on the use of psychology along with more mundane matters such as the deployment of troops and stratagems.

Ōnin Wars wars fought between 1467 and 1477 arising from a shogunal succession dispute within the Ashikaga family of the Muromachi shogunate in Japan. They were the beginning of what was to become almost a century of continuous civil war in Japan, known as the ◊Sengoku period, or the Warring States period.

The opening clashes of the war were between the provincial military governors (◊shugo daimyo) Hosokawa Katsumoto and Yamana Sōzen who found themselves on opposing sides over the complicated question of shogunal succession. This dispute highlighted the shugo daimyo's own factional problems. The shogunal question was resolved in 1473 with the appointment of Ashikaga Yoshihisa, but by that time the warring factions seemed interested only in mutual destruction. When the fighting in Kyoto eventually stopped in 1477, the Muromachi shogunate was in tatters and they were a government in little more than name.

Onomarchus (died 353 BC) Phocian commander in the Third Sacred War fought for control of Delphi, 356–346 BC, between Phocis and neighbouring states including Boeotia and Thessaly. Onomarchus cowed Phocis' smaller neighbours 354–353, twice invading its principal enemy Boeotia and re-establishing Orchomenus as a countercheck to Thebes. When ◊Philip (II) of Macedon threatened Phocian interests in the east central plain of Thessaly, Onomarchus drove him out, possibly with the help of stone-throwing catapults. He met Philip again at the Crocus Field (see ◊Crocus Field, Battle of the) in 353, but this time he was defeated and killed.

optio junior officer in a Roman ◊legion. The *optio* was second in command of a ◊century. According to the Greek politician and historian Polybius, he was distinguished by his helmet plumage and was responsible for ensuring that the rear ranks of his century did not waver in battle.

Orchomenus, Battle of battle fought in Greece in 86 BC between the Roman emperor Lucius Cornelius ◊Sulla and ◊Mithridates (VI) Eupator which ended the Pontic invasion of Greece and led to the conclusion of the First Mithridatic War. As at Chaeronea (see ◊Chaeronea, Battle of 86 BC), a small Roman force defeated a large but ineffective Pontic army.

The Pontic commander Archelaus positioned about 80,000 men on the flat plain outside the city of Orchomenus, seeking to make use of his numerically superior cavalry. On the first day, Archelaus sent a force against a party of Romans building a line of fortifications to restrict the enemy's movement. After an initial rout, the Romans were rallied by Sulla himself, who led them to defeat the enemy. The Romans advanced quickly, closing with the enemy archers before they could fire many arrows. Sulla decisively defeated the rest of the Pontic army the following day.

Order of the Garter royal order of chivalry founded by Edward III of England in 1348, designed to bind the military aristocracy more closely to a warlike king.

The order originally comprised two thirteen-man jousting teams, led by King Edward and his son Edward the Black Prince. Its name came from an incident at a royal ball when Edward III stooped to recover a lady's garter which had fallen off during an energetic dance. Turning to his scandalized courtiers, he said 'Honi soit qui mal y pense' (normally translated as 'Evil be to him who thinks evil', but more accurately 'Shame on anyone who thinks evil of this'). The Garter remains the highest knightly award of the British monarch to this day.

ordo elite armies of the Khitan Liao dynasty (907–1125). ◊Yelü Abaoji formed the first *ordo* in 922 as an expansion of his personal guard. They were political as well as military groups, and subject Chinese or tribal households were attached to the *ordo* to support the soldiers. Most *ordo* troops were Khitan or similar tribal cavalry, but others were Chinese infantry.

Each heavily-armoured cavalryman also supplied an armed forager and a groom, an arrangement reminiscent of the European ◊lance. The troops fought in three lines, with light cavalry (perhaps the armed grooms or tribal ◊jiu jun troops) in the first line, part-armoured cavalry (probably the foragers) in the second, and the heavily-armoured *ordo* regulars in the third.

Ordos campaign military camgaign in 215 BC in which ◊Qin Shi Huangdi's general ◊Meng Tian expelled the ◊Xiongnu nomads in China. A Chinese army of 300,000 cleared the Xiongnu from the Ordos, the semi-desert region inside the great loop of the Yellow River, and fortified the area.

Ordos Loop Wall wall that was built across the Ordos loop of the Yellow River after Wang Yue's victory at Hongyanchi (see ◊Hongyanchi, Battle of) expelled the Mongols, who had been using the area as a base for raids. Wang Yue and Yu Zijun used 40,000 men to build 1,100 kilometres of wall, including 800 forts and signal-towers. The wall proved its worth in 1482 when a Mongol raiding force was trapped against the walls and defeated.

Orford castle castle in England, 32 km/20 mi east of Ipswich, Suffolk. It was built 1165–73 by order of Henry II to act as a defence against possible invasion from the coast, and also to assert his rule in the face of the local barons. By the mid-14th century it had ceased to have military importance and was given by Edward III to the earls of Suffolk.

Originally surrounded by a rectangular curtain wall with towers, the keep, which still remains, is one of the most remarkable structures in Europe. Polygonal, with 20 sides, it is 9 m/30 ft in diameter and 27 m/90 ft high, with three large buttress-towers of about 2 sq m/20 sq ft. One of these contains a stone spiral staircase reaching from basement to roof; the other two contain the royal apartments, the chapel, constable's quarters, kitchens, and even a water cistern.

oriflamme scarlet banner given to French kings by the abbot of St Denis, Paris, and used as a rallying call to arms throughout France in the Middle Ages. It became the symbol of the French nation at war and was also displayed during battle.

In 1124 Louis VI took up the oriflamme when faced with a threat from Holy Roman emperor Henry V. Philip (II) Augustus also took up the oriflamme in 1190 as a symbol of the French effort in the Third Crusade.

Orléans, Siege of siege by English forces during the ◊Hundred Years' War of the well-fortified and strategically important city of Orlèans, in central France, from 12 October 1428 until 8 May 1429, when ◊Joan of Arc inspired French forces to liberate the city. Control of Orlèans would have given England access to France south of the Loire.

The English army suffered an initial setback when the earl of Salisbury was killed by a stray cannon ball on 3 November 1428. He was soon replaced by the energetic Lord Talbot who constructed a *bastille* (siege fort) at St Laurent, the first of ten designed to encircle Orlèans. In February an English supply column routed its attackers at nearby Rouvray, which further depressed French morale. Then Joan arrived on 29 April 1429. Her presence inspired the French to storm the *bastille* of St Loup, on the north bank of the river Loire, on 4 May. The next day the French crossed to the south bank to capture a fortified monastery. The English were still confident of holding the fortress complex of Les Tourelles, which included the bridge tower in midstream, but the French succeeded in gaining a foothold. The tower's garrison surrendered on 7 May and the siege was over.

Osaka castle castle in central Honshu island, Japan, built 1583–86 by the Japanese warlord ◊Toyotomi Hideyoshi as a centre for his military operations in subduing the area. Occupying a site of over 6 sq km/2.3 sq mi, situated on a hilltop, and bounded on two sides by rivers, the castle was deemed to be impregnable. It was destroyed in 1615; there is a replica on the site.

ost medieval French term for troops who were expected to serve outside their immediate region. Found in English as the biblical word 'host', the term is used to describe the conglomerations of medieval warriors serving in the retinues of their lord, or fighting for their city or country.

Ostia Roman fortification founded in the 4th century BC at the mouth of the river Tiber, Italy. It had the strategically important role of guarding the river and defending Rome's supply route to the sea.

The citadel (*castrum*) was constructed in the area that later became the city forum. It was rectangular in shape (194 × 126 m/637 × 413 ft) with walls made of large tufa blocks and gates in the centre of each side, and was divided by the intersecting streets into four equal parts. By the 2nd century BC Rome no longer needed to defend the Tiber mouth and the citadel walls were demolished. The civil settlement that had first begun as a village outside the citadel soon grew into a thriving city, fortified by land walls in 87 BC.

Oswestry, Battle of (or *Maserfeld*) defeat in 641of Oswald of Northumbria by Penda of Mercia, which temporarily established Mercia as the pre-eminent Anglo-Saxon kingdom in England.

othismos Greek 'shoving' crucial stage in a hoplite battle where the hoplites, individually or as a formation, forced their opponents back. Whether this was a literal or only metaphorical push is disputed.

Ōtomo family powerful military family at the Yamato court of Japan in the 8th century. Ōtomo Tabito (665–731) led a military force to Kyushu island to suppress a rebellion by the Hayato tribe in 720 and was later appointed to a government position in Kyushu.

Otterburn, Battle of (or *Chevy Chase*) battle fought on 15 August 1388 near Newcastle, England, in which a smaller Scottish army heavily defeated an English army under Henry 'Hotspur' ◊Percy, who was himself taken prisoner.

The battle followed a Scottish attack on

Otterburn castle, which failed. The Scottish commander, the 3rd Earl of Douglas, was killed in the battle.

Otto I (912–973) Holy Roman emperor from 962. He restored the power of the empire and asserted his authority over the pope and the nobles.

His son Liudolf led a German rebellion allied with the ◊Magyars, but Otto drew them from the siege of Augsburg (Bavaria) and ended the Magyar menace by his victory at Lechfeld (see ◊Lechfeld, Battle of) in 955. He refounded the East Mark, or Austria, as a barrier against them. As a result of Lechfeld the pope granted Otto the title of Holy Roman emperor. Otto made gains to the east, subjecting the Bohemians and defeating the Wends.

Otto IV (c. 1174–1218) Holy Roman emperor, elected in 1198. He was the son of ◊Henry the Lion, and was made Count of Poitou by his uncle ◊Richard (I) the Lionheart. He clashed with Philip, Duke of Swabia, in rivalry for the empire. He engaged in controversy with Pope Innocent III (c. 1160–1216), and was defeated by the pope's ally Philip (II) Augustus of France at Bouvines in 1214 (see ◊Bouvines, Battle of). Otto lost the throne to ◊Frederick II, and retired to Brunswick (Germany).

ouragos (plural *ouragoi*) Greek 'tail leader' in Greek warfare, the file closer (last man) in each file of a phalanx or cavalry formation.

Outremer medieval French 'overseas' term used to describe campaigning regions in the Holy Land or, more generally, outside Latin Christendom.

owi (Korean 'five commands') the central organization of the Korean army under the Yi dynasty in the 15th century, as finalized in 1457. The garrisons of the capital were organized into five divisions: Centre, East, West, South, and North. The Five Divisions each had nominal responsibility for the corresponding part of the whole country, but in practice the provinces were guarded by local *chinsugun* garrisons.

Each division was organized into five *pu* brigades, and each of those into four *tong* regiments. These were subdivided into *yo* battalions, *tae* companies, and *o* platoons. They were mostly recruited from a hereditary professional military class, though some *chongbyong* ◊conscripts were included.

ō-yoroi Japanese 'great harness' Japanese armour which developed during the Heian period (794–1185) from the earlier ◊*keikō* and continued to be worn well into the Kamakura period (1185–1333). Designed primarily as a defence against arrows, the *ō-yoroi* was a heavy yet flexible armour for the mounted warrior.

The cuirass (◊*dō*) was constructed from horizontal rows of lacquered plates of iron (◊*kozane*) laced vertically with an overall covering of leather (◊*tsurubashiri*) to prevent the bowstring from snagging. The armour covered all four sides of the body, joining on the right and covered at this point with an additional plate (*waidate*). The upper part of the chest was further protected by a solid iron plate (*munaita*). The fixings for the shoulder straps were protected on the left by a solid plate defence (*kyubi no ita*) and on the right by the *sendan no ita*, composed of lamellar strips. These two armour parts fell into place to protect the armpits when the arms were raised to fire the bow. Two large hanging shoulder pieces (*ō-sode*) additionally acted as shields to protect the arms when firing the bow. The back of the armour was adorned with a large decorative bow (*agemaki*) suspended from a substantial gilded metal ring to which cords securing the *ō-sode* and other smaller parts of the armour were attached to prevent them slipping out of position when fighting.

The left arm only was protected by a sleeve armour with integral gauntlets (*kote*) which was constructed of chain mail with solid iron plates on the upper arm and forearm. A skirtlike attachment (*kusazuri*) hung below the main armour to protect the hips and thighs of the mounted warrior. The body armour was completed with the addition of knee protectors (◊*hiza yoroi*) and shinguards (◊*suneate*).

The traditional helmet at this time was the ◊*hoshi kabuto*. The front of the helmet was decorated with two large, flat, gilded metal hornlike ornaments (◊*kuwagata*). The flexible neck guard (◊*shikoro*), together with its turned-back plates (◊*fukigaeshi*), *kyubi no ita* and *sendan no ita*, and *ō-sode* all fell into their appropriate positions and served to protect the warrior when firing his bow.

P

Pacorus (died 38 BC) Parthian general, son of King Orodes II. He invaded Roman Syria in 40 BC, and intervened in a civil war in the Roman province of Judaea and took Jerusalem. A Roman counterattack in 39 BC defeated Pacorus and he withdrew from Syria. He returned the following year but was defeated and killed.

In 51 BC Pacorus led an early successful raid on Roman Syria and Cilicia, but he was recalled in 50 BC under suspicion of plotting against his father. In 40 BC he was restored to a joint command with the Roman exile Quintus Labienus. They invaded Syria and defeated the Roman governor; while Labienus invaded Anatolia, Pacorus overran all Syria except Tyre. In Judaea he and his Jewish ally Antigonos defeated the high priest Hyrcanus and Herod the Idumaean (the future king), and took Jerusalem. The Roman counterattack was led by Publius Ventidius Bassus, who twice defeated Pacorus.

Paestum city (modern Pesto) founded by the Greeks as Poseidonia in about 700 BC, situated 60 km/37 mi southeast of Naples, Italy. In 273 it was taken by Rome and refounded as a Roman colony under the name Paestum. The defences almost certainly date to the 5th or 4th century BC, and are typical of Hellenistic fortifications of this time.

The defences incorporate the use of new artillery while also reducing the vulnerability of the defenders to enemy machines. Crenellations were rejected in favour of pitched roofs in the towers and screens along the mural wall. Artillery were placed in the upper storey of the towers and along the wall, firing through windows protected by shutters. Loopholes in the screen and tower lower storeys allowed archers to operate with a high degree of protection. The city gates had single narrow portals no more than 4 m/13 ft wide.

Paetus, L Caesennius Roman governor of Cappadocia (in present-day Turkey) who suffered a disaster at Rhandeia in AD 62 (see ◊Rhandeia, Battle of) at the hands of a Parthian army under Vologeses. After a disordered flight, Paetus' army surrendered and may have endured the humiliation of being forced to march under the yoke.

Palace Army Tang Chinese Imperial bodyguard, also known as Troops North of the Palace, Troops of the Northern Barracks, or the Army Defending the Emperor. The army was founded by ◊Tang Gaozu at the start of the dynasty, from 30,000 veterans of the civil war, and service became hereditary.

A professional standing force at the capital, the Palace Army supported and counter-balanced the ◊*wei* guard units recruited from ◊*fubing* troops, who were barracked to the south of the palace. Because of their duties guarding the Emperor and the imperial palace, the Palace forces were rarely used on campaign.

Palermo, Siege of siege of the important Muslim city of Palermo, Sicily, by the Norman knight Robert Guiscard, from the summer of 1071 to 10 January 1072. Guiscard captured the city and thereby secured Norman rule of Sicily.

Following his successful siege of the Byzantine stronghold of Bari in 1068–71 (see ◊Bari, Siege of 1068–71), Robert, again with his brother Roger of Sicily, led a fleet of 50 ships to besiege Palermo. Their previous attempt in 1064 had been driven off and there was a relief attempt by a North African fleet on the second occasion. The Norman fleet was stronger though, and in driving the Muslims back into the harbour, broke the chain and continued the siege on land. After a series of assaults the city fell to the Normans.

Palmyran Rebellion rebellion led by Queen ◊Zenobia of Palmyra, Syria, in 262–73, which led to a short-lived Palmyran dominance over the Roman east. It was brought to an end by the Roman emperor Lucius Domitius ◊Aurelian.

Zenobia's husband Odenathus campaigned successfully against the Persians in the aftermath of their success at Edessa (see ◊Edessa,

Battle of). Palmyra's independence ended when Aurelian defeated the kingdom in a campaign which included the battles of Antioch (see ◊Antioch, Battle of 272) and Emesa (see ◊Emesa, Battle of) and culminated in the destruction of Palmyra itself in 273.

palton Achaemenid Persian cavalry javelin, about 180 cm/71 in long, with a stout wooden shaft and an iron or bronze head. Two were normally carried; one was thrown, the second could also be thrown or kept as a thrusting weapon.

The Greek soldier and historian Xenophon recommended them for Greek cavalry because they were less likely to break than the slender Greek cavalry spear.

Panhala fortress in the Deccan, India, extensively strengthened by the Bahmani sultans during the early 15th century.

In 1490 its governor Khvaja Jahan joined Qasim Band the Mameluke, chief minister of the kingdom, in a revolt against ◊Muhammad (III) Bahmani. The rebels were defeated, but were allowed to retain their offices. A famous pirate, Bahadur Gilani, seized Panhala in 1493; when he escaped from the besieged city he was killed.

Panoramus, Battle of the last major land battle of the First Punic War (see ◊Punic War, First), fought in 251 BC between ◊Hasdrubal, son of Hanno, and the Roman consul L Caecilius Metellus, who held the Roman base at Panoramus (now Palermo), Sicily. The Carthaginians were heavily defeated.

As the Punic forces ravaged the territory near Panoramus, a skirmish close to the city walls developed into a general engagement. The Carthaginian war elephants were irritated into stampeding by the Roman missile troops and caused havoc in the Punic battle line. Metellus followed this up with his heavy troops and inflicted a bloody defeat on the Carthaginians, killing 130 of the 140 elephants and capturing the remainder.

Panormus, Siege of victory in 535 for the East Romans, led by the Byzantine general ◊Belisarius, over the Gothic garrison of Panormus, which gave the East Roman Empire control of Sicily.

Belisarius landed in Sicily with a force of only 7,500 men and was greeted as a liberator. Only the Gothic garrison at Panormus gave any resistance, but quickly surrendered when Belisarius brought ships into the harbour with archers in the mastheads who could overshoot the city walls.

Paraetacene, Battle of indecisive encounter between ◊Antigonus (I) Monophthalmus and ◊Eumenes of Cardia in 317 BC at Paraetacene (near modern Isfahan, Iran). Antigonus claimed victory because he was able to camp on the battlefield when Eumenes' army insisted on withdrawing to the baggage train.

This battle is a good example of the different ways troops were integrated at the time. Antigonus apparently had the larger phalanx and more cavalry, but fewer elephants and, perhaps, skirmishers. Eumenes was able to cover his weaker cavalry, on both wings, with elephants interspersed with skirmishers armed with missile weapons. The outer squadrons on his right, which he personally commanded, were angled back. Antigonus opened with a flanking cavalry attack on Eumene's right wing, but Eumenes countered by drawing light cavalry from his left. Meanwhile his phalanx drove back its counterpart, but it pursued too far and Antigonus was able to counterattack through the gap it left.

Parakrama Bahu king of Singhala (or Simhala, present-day Sri Lanka) 1153–86, during the Golden Age of Singhalese culture. He was famed as a soldier, statesman, and builder of temples, palaces, and other public works, especially irrigation systems, through which he controlled the economy of the island and united it under his rule.

He took advantage of the wars between the Chola and Pandya dynasties to invade the mainland and captured Madura (the present-day city of Madurai in Tamil Nadu).

Parantaka I third king (907–49) of the revived Tamil Chola dynasty ruling southeastern India, who re-established Chola power after centuries of subjection to the Pallavas. He was defeated and killed in battle by Krishna III, King of the Rashtrakuta dynasty ruling in the Deccan.

parapleuridia (or *side-protector*) large pieces of armour attached to a horse's saddle to protect both the horses's flanks and the rider's legs. The Greek soldier and historian Xenophon describes their use by Achaemenid Persian heavy cavalry on partly armoured horses (proto-◊cataphracts), and recommends them for Greek cavalry.

There is no sign that they were ever popular in Greece, but evidence that they were used by Persian and Anatolian riders can be found in art of the period (4th century BC).

parataxis (Greek) deployment of a line of battle, or the front rank of a phalanx.

Parenda fortress in the Deccan, India, constructed in the 15th century by Mahmud Gawan, chief minister of ◊Muhammad (III)

Bahmani. It was smaller in area than most other contemporary forts and its defences consisted of a wide moat and two strong walls, each with only one gate.

Parenda was used in 1498 as a place of refuge by Khvaja Jahan, governor of the sister fortress ◊Panhala, in the civil war leading to the break-up of the Bahmani sultanate.

Paris, Siege of unsuccessful 11-month siege of Paris in 885–6 by a large Viking army, under Sigfrid and Sinric. Their failure to take Paris is generally taken as the high-water mark of Viking incursions into western Europe.

A fleet of 300 Viking ships sailed up the Seine from Rouen. At that time Paris was a walled city on an island, linked to the mainland by fortified bridges, and the city blocked the route further up-river. Count Eudes and Bishop Joscelin conducted an energetic defence of the city, which succeeded in repelling all assaults. The Vikings beat off relief armies led by the Frankish King Charles the Fat and the Duke of Saxony, but were unable to completely cut off Paris from re-supply. The situation was in a stalemate until King Charles offered a ransom and gave the Vikings free passage to plunder Burgundy, which was not part of King Charles' kingdom.

Pasargadae Achaemenid Persian capital in the highlands of Fars, 43 km / 27 mi north of Persepolis; possibly the site of ◊Cyrus (II) the Great's victory over the Medes. Later kings moved the centres of government to Susa and Babylon, but Pasargadae remained a ritual centre – the kings were crowned there. It was unwalled but dominated by a fortified citadel, the Tall-i-Takht.

Patay, Battle of battle fought on 18 June 1429 at the village of Patay, 21 km / 13 mi northwest of Orléans, France, during the ◊Hundred Years' War, in which the French under the Duke of Alençon and ◊Joan of Arc surprised the English, captured John ◊Talbot, and inflicted heavy casualties.

PARTHIAN ARMY

Organized military forces of Parthia, c. 250 BC–AD 224. Parthian armies were famous for their cavalry and often entirely devoid of infantry in later stages. Early armies may have been more heterogeneous before being standardized under ◊Mithradates II. Accounts of the Seleucid king Antiochus VII's campaign against the Parthians in 129 BC suggest that the Seleucids had cavalry superior to the Parthians' at that stage, since the Parthians were noted as seeking the hills as protection from the Seleucid horsemen.

The developed army was divided into two specialized types: ◊cataphracts (fully-armoured cavalry) and unarmoured horse-archers armed only with composite bows. At Carrhae in 53 BC (see ◊Carrhae, Battle of), ◊Surena fielded 1,000 cataphracts and 9,000–10,000 horse-archers, but sometimes the proportion of cataphracts was higher. Horse-archers were used to harass the less mobile enemy, and if the enemy charged they would deliver the famous 'Parthian shot', shooting backwards while feigning retreat. After the enemy were sufficiently weakened, the cataphracts would charge and ride them down. If the cataphracts were committed prematurely, the army might well be defeated. The Greek philosopher Lucian recorded that Parthian cavalry were organized into units of 1,000 called dragons, perhaps an indication that they used draco standards. They were recruited from retainers or tribal followers of the Parthian nobles and vassal kings. Sometimes mercenaries were recruited, mostly from the nomadic Saka tribes. Although infantry were much less important than cavalry, they were available from various sources including the militias of Hellenistic cities in the Parthian Empire. One Syriac source notes that 20,000 infantry were recruited from its capital, Ctesiphon, about 100 km/60 mi above Babylon, in the 2nd century AD. One late attempt to use armoured camels was not successful, and unlike later ◊Sassanian armies the Parthians made virtually no use of war elephants.

In the wake of their failure to take Orléans, Lord Talbot and John Fastolf mustered 3,500 men in a good defensive position at Patay. They were surprised by the French, who charged into the vanguard of archers unprotected by stakes. Talbot was wounded and captured, with the loss of 2,000 men; Fastolf escaped with the remnant.

patrician originally an upper-class Roman citizen; in the late Roman Empire it became a title bestowed on very senior or influential commanders.

Pau castle stronghold on the Franco-Spanish border, overlooking the River Gave, in Pyrénées-Atlantiques *département*, southwest France. It was held by the Vicomtes of Béarn, including Gaston Phoebus who made additions in the later 14th century, including the Tour Montauzer. It later became a Renaissance château, and was used as a barracks during the French Revolution (1789–99).

Henry IV of France was born here. Restoration was done in the 19th century.

pauldron piece of plate shoulder armour with extensions to cover parts of the chest and back. Pauldrons appeared at the very end of the 14th century and became the usual form of shoulder defence on complete suits of plate armour thereafter, particularly in Italian armour.

Paulinus, Gaius Suetonius (lived 1st century AD) Roman governor of Britain about AD 58–61. He subdued the rebellious Iceni (native Britons) and defeated Boudicca, their queen, in AD 61. He was consul in AD 66, and during the civil wars of AD 69 sided with the emperor Otho's generals in the unsuccessful campaign against Vitellius (who had been proclaimed emperor by his troops). He later made his peace with Vitellius.

Paulinus campaigned in North Africa and became the first Roman to cross the Atlas Mountains in modern-day Morocco. In Britain he campaigned in Wales and conquered Anglesey, successfully crossing the Menai Straits, probably with units of Batavian auxiliaries. It was during his absence on campaign that the ◊Boudiccan Revolt erupted. Paulinus hurried south but was unable to prevent the destruction of London. Retreating before the advancing Boudicca, he succeeded in engaging the Britons on his own terms, using the topography of the battlefield to protect his small force from encirclement. Despite being vastly outnumbered (Tacitus claims by eight to one), Paulinus pulled off a spectacular victory; he was, however, unable to

settle the province down and was replaced shortly afterwards.

Paullus, Aemilius (died 216 BC) Roman general in the Second Punic War (see ◊Punic War, Second). As the consul of 216 BC, Paullus was commander of the Roman army at Cannae (see ◊Cannae, Battle of). Leading the right wing, he was injured by a slingstone at an early stage but stayed on the field to die in the fighting.

With both consuls present – the other being Gaius Terentius Varro – each took supreme command on alternate days. On the day of battle the evidence points to Paullus being in command.

Paullus, Lucius Aemilius (died 160 BC) (known as 'Macedonicus') Roman general. He concluded the Third Macedonian War (see ◊Macedonian Wars) by defeating Philip V of Macedon's son Perseus at Pydna in 168 BC (see ◊Pydna, Battle of).

As praetor in 191 BC he campaigned in Further Spain, and fought against the Ligurians of northwest Italy during his first consulship in 182. After Pydna he allowed his troops to sack Epirus, Greece, before returning to Rome to celebrate the most lavish triumph staged up to that date.

Pausanias (lived 5th century BC) regent of Sparta 479–c. 469 BC, and commander of the Greeks at Plataea in 479 BC, in which the Persians were routed (see ◊Plataea, Battle of). In 478 he overran Cyprus in command of a joint force, and captured Byzantium, but then began antagonizing his Greek allies and intriguing with the Persians. He is supposed to have been betrayed, and starved to death in a temple where he took sanctuary.

At Plataea he seems to have been out of his depth until he found himself isolated with his own Spartans and their Tegeate allies, but fighting the kind of hand-to-hand battle for which the Spartans trained all their lives, in the Greek historian Herodotus' words, he 'won the finest victory of all we know'.

Pavia, Siege of victory in 773–4 for ◊Charlemagne over the Lombard King Desiderius, in response to an appealed from the Pope help to stop the Lombard attacks on papal territory. Charlemagne forced Desiderius to abdicate and took the Lombard crown for himself, styling himself 'King of the Franks and Lombards and Patrician of the Romans.'

Pavia, Siege of successful attempt on 23 August 476 by the German soldiers of the West Roman army, led by ◊Odoacer, to capture the Italian city of Pavia where Orestes, who had refused land grants in Italy to the soldiers, was seeking refuge. Orestes was captured and executed, and on 4 September Odoacer forced Orestes' son Romulus Augustulus to abdicate and took control of Italy. This date is generally accepted as marking the end of the Western Roman Empire.

Orestes, former Roman secretary to ◊Attila, had deposed the emperor Julius Nepos and placed his son Romulus on the throne with the backing of the Italian army, which consisted almost entirely of German soldiers. When the soldiers demanded land grants in Italy, similar to those given to the Visigoths and Burgundians in France, Orestes refused. The army revolted and successfully stormed Pavia.

pavise large, rectangular shield used by medieval European infantry, often tapering slightly towards the top and sometimes fitted with a prop so that it could stand by itself. It appeared in the 14th century, for use by infantry archers and crossbowmen, and sometimes by spear-armed infantry called *pavisiers* in France, whose job was to protect missile troops. The pavise continued in use throughout Europe until the end of the 15th century.

Payns, Hugh de (died c. 1236) founder of the Knights Templar (see ◊Military Order) in 1120, whose original aim was to protect pilgrims en route to the Jordan. The order, however, became enormously wealthy, and was an important provider of troops and fortifications on every frontier of Christendom.

Hugh and a companion, Godfrey de St Omer, took monastic vows in 1118, intending to retain their military role as knights, a radical departure. King Baldwin II gave them quarters in the Temple of Jerusalem, after which their new organization was named. In 1126 Hugh wrote to St Bernard of Clairvaux, requesting a rule for his new order. It was provided, together with papal confirmation at the Council of Troyes in 1129.

Peace of God medieval term describing an attempt by the Western Church to restrict fighting. The 'Peace' was first preached by bishops in late 10th-century France, and was designed to protect ecclesiastics and civilians from the endemic warfare of the military classes.

Peasants' Revolt the rising of the English peasantry in June 1381, the result of economic, social, and political disillusionment. It was sparked off by the imposition of a new poll tax and led by Wat Tyler and John Ball. Rebels from southeast England marched on London and demanded reforms. The authorities put down the revolt by deceit and force.

Rebels burned John of Gaunt's palace at the Savoy and took the prisons at Newgate and Fleet. The young king Richard II attempted to appease the mob, who demanded an end to serfdom and feudalism. The rebels then took the Tower of London and murdered Archbishop Sudbury and Robert Hales. Again the king attempted to make peace at Smithfield, but Tyler was stabbed to death by William Walworth, the Lord Mayor of London. The king made concessions to the rebels, and they dispersed, but the concessions were revoked immediately.

pediform axe (*boot-shaped axe*) bronze battle-axe used by the Yue of southeastern China and the Vietnamese (about 600 BC–AD 100). A socketed head 8–10 cm/3–4 in long is fixed to the end of a curved haft. The rounded cutting edge of the axe rises to an upper point that could be used for thrusting. The curve of the blade enables it to be rolled to disengage it when stuck in a target.

pedites medieval Latin foot soldiers, distinct in terms of status from the *milites* (knights). ' ilites et pedites' was a standard phrase employed by medieval writers to describe military forces, and it was often stressed that these two components should operate together for best military effectiveness.

Pedro II (died 1213) king of Aragon 1196–1213. He played a major part in the Christian reconquest of Spain (see ◊*Reconquista*), commanding the left wing at Las Navas de Tolosa in 1212 (see Las Navas de Tolosa, Battle of). He formed an alliance with the Cathars in southern France, and fought against Simon de ◊Montfort (the Elder) at Muret (see ◊Muret, Battle of) in 1213, where Pedro was defeated and killed. His son was ◊James (I) the Conqueror.

Pei Ju (lived 5th–6th centuries) (or *P'ei Chü*) Chinese general and minister serving the emperor ◊Sui Wendi and his successor Sui Yangdi. After Wendi's conquest of southern China he ensured the submission of many indigenous tribes of the far south. He then masterminded Yangdi's expansionist strategy on the northern frontier. He advised Yangdi to attack Koguryo, leading to defeat in the resulting wars (see ◊Korea, Sui Chinese wars in).

At first successful on the northern frontier, he weakened the Eastern Turks by winning over border tribes and the city-kingdoms of the Tarim Basin silk-trade route. He also planned

PELOPONNESIAN WAR

War fought 431–404 BC between Athens and Sparta and their respective allies, involving most of the Greek world from Asia Minor to Sicily and from Byzantium (present-day Istanbul, Turkey) to Crete. It originated in Spartan fears of the growth of Athenian power, and was ended by the Spartan general Lysander's capture of the Athenian fleet in 405 at Aegospotami and his starving of the Athenians into surrender in 404. Sparta's victory meant the destruction of the political power of Athens.

The Peloponnesian War was a classic example of a war between a seapower and a landpower, with Athens controlling most of the Aegean and its coasts, and Sparta most of the Peloponnese and central Greece. This partly explains both its length and why so much of the early fighting was peripheral. The Spartans were unable to bring about the decisive battle they wanted by invading Attica, since the Athenians withdrew within the fortifications of Athens and the Piraeus, their supplies guaranteed by seapower. But, equally, Athenian raids on the Peloponnesian coast were ineffective even when extended by the occupation of permanent bases on and off enemy coasts 425–424, though the pressure this exerted brought about a spectacular Athenian success at Pylos in 425 (see ◊Pylos, Battle of). Following this, an Athenian attempt to win control of Megara failed, and an over-ambitious plan to knock Boeotia out of the war ended in disaster at Delium in 424 (see ◊Delium, Battle of).

Meanwhile, the Spartans at last devised a means of hitting Athens in a vital spot when they sent an expeditionary force over land to raise revolt amongst its allies in Thrace. However, the death of its charismatic leader Brasidas and that of Cleon, the Athenian principally opposed to negotiations, at Amphipolis (see ◊Amphipolis, Battle of), led to a temporary peace in 422/1.

During the early years of the peace Athens made use of the discontent of some of Sparta's allies to engineer an alliance in the Peloponnese and so match Sparta on land. The alliance disintegrated after Sparta's victory at Mantinea in 418 (see ◊Mantinea, Battle of 418 BC), and Athens fatally dissipated its strength by sending an expeditionary force to Sicily in 415. The annihilation of this force in 413 shattered Athenian seapower and encouraged Sparta and its allies to make a real effort at sea, Athens' allies to rebel, and Persia to throw its financial weight behind Sparta in the hope of recovering the Asiatic Greek cities lost to Athens in the years following the Persian king Xerxes I's defeat at Plataea in 479.

The great battles of the last ten years of the war were all fought at sea, in the northern Aegean, the Hellespont (present-day Dardanelles), or the Propontis (Sea of Marmara), as successive Spartan admirals strove to cut Athens' supply lines. Athens won a series of victories, notably off Cyzicus in 410 (see ◊Cyzicus, Battle of 410 BC) and the Arginusae Islands in 406 (see ◊Arginusae Islands, Battle of), but the end came with Lysander's destruction of the Athenian fleet at Aegospotami in 405 (see ◊Aegospotami, Battle of) and, after withstanding siege by both land and sea through the winter, Athens surrendered in 404.

the successful conquest of the Tuyuhun of modern Qinghai.

Pelagonia, Battle of battle between the Byzantine emperor ◊Michael (VIII) Palaeologus of Nicaea and Michael (II) Doukas of Epirus and his Frankish allies in October 1259. The Nicaean victory assured the subsequent restoration of Byzantine rule after the recapture of Constantinople in 1261 (see ◊Constantinople, capture of).

Michael II, allied with William II Villehardouin of Achaea and supported by 400 German knights, opposed Michael VIII's 600 Serbs, 300 Germans, 1,500 Hungarians, and 2,000 Cumans, with many Greek archers. Michael II's troops deserted under pressure from the Nicaean skirmishers, leaving the Franks to fight alone. Michael VIII's horse-archers outmanoeuvred, surrounded, and captured the Franks, including William and 30 of his barons.

Pelopidas (died 364 BC) Theban statesman and general. He helped expel the Spartan garrison from the citadel of Thebes in 379/8 BC. As commander of the elite 'Sacred Band' of Theban youth, he played a leading part at Leuctra (see ◊Leuctra, Battle of) in 371.

He furthered Theban interests in Thessaly by opposing Alexander of Pherae in 369–368, and serving as ambassador to Persia in 367. He

PEOPLES OF THE SEA

Egyptian *hau nebu* or *'imiu nebut-sen,* term used by the Egyptians to describe various enemy peoples from the islands and coastlands of the eastern Mediterranean, noted from the time of Pharaoh Amunhotep III until the time of ◊Ramses III (1183–1152 BC). Significant among them were the ◊Lukka, Shardana, Philistines, and Danuna.

The Shardana, or Sherden, were used as mercenaries in Ugarit and other Canaanite city-states from the 14th century BC and were formed into a bodyguard for ◊Ramses II at the Battle of Kadesh in 1275 BC. By the time of Ramses III they were again fighting against Egypt. They were linked with Sardinia, either taking their name from or giving their name to the island. However, Shardana may have become a general term for sea raider, like Viking.

The Philistines (Egyptian *Pelestu*) gave their name to Palestine, where they settled after their defeat in the land and sea battles against Ramses III in 1176 BC. They were used as garrison troops for the Egyptians in Megiddo, Taanach, and Bethshan. On the coast the five cities (Pentapolis) of Gaza, Gath, Ashkelon, Ekron, and Ashdod fought against the Israelites, successfully killing King Saul in 1004 BC at Mount Gilboa (see ◊Mount Gilboa, Battle of). They were conquered by King ◊David around 1000 BC, and eventually became subject to the Assyrians under ◊Sennacherib in 701 BC.

The Danuna, or Denyen (Hittite 'Adana folk'), are linked with Adaniya (near modern Adana, Turkey) in Kizzuwatna or Que (classical Cilicia) from the time of Ramses II. In the 8th-century BC Hittite–Phoenician bilingual inscription at ◊Azitawataya they are referred to as descendants of Muksas/Mpš – perhaps the Mopsus of Greek legend, which links them with Homer's Danaans (Danawoi). They also settled on Cyprus, known as Iadnana, the 'Island of Danuna', by the Assyrians. The Danuna were defeated by Ramses III in 1176 BC, and were probably allied with the Lukka against the Hittites in the battles off Alashiya (see ◊Alashiya, battles of).

Other Peoples of the Sea include the Teresh, or Tursha, the Ekwesh, and the Shekelesh who were defeated, alongside the Shardana and Lukka, by Pharaoh Merenptah in 1208 BC; and the Tjeker and Weshesh who were defeated, alongside the Shardana, Shekelesh (Hittite *Šikala*), Danuna, Teresh, and Philistines, by Ramses III in 1176 BC.

was killed defeating Alexander at Cynoscephalae.

peltast originally the Greek word for a particular type of Thracian light-armed soldier, so called from the shield – *pelta* – that they carried; the term came to be used of Greek light troops in general.

Pembroke castle castle in west Wales. Founded as a ditched encampment in 1090, construction of a permanent castle began under Gilbert de Clare, Earl of Pembroke, in around 1210. It was used by his son, Richard Strongbow, as the base for his conquest of Ireland. On his death it passed to the Marshall family who greatly enlarged and strengthened it between 1189 and 1245. During the Wars of the Roses (1455–85) it was occupied by both sides at various times.

Penafiel castle castle in Spain, 56 km/35 mi east of Valladolid, built in around 1450 by the Order of Calatrava (see ◊Military Order) on the site of an earlier work that had been built to protect a strategic crossing of the river Duero. It occupies the top of a large hill and consists of two curtain walls, the inner with numerous towers, as well as a central square keep with turrets on the corners and faces.

Pengcheng, Battle of (or *P'eng-ch'eng*) battle in 205 BC in which ◊Xiang Yu defeated Liu Bang (◊Han Gaozu) in China. Liu attacked Xiang's base at Pengcheng and took the city. As Liu's men were scattered looting Pengcheng, however, Xiang staged a dawn surprise attack and by noon had routed them. Liu Bang escaped under cover of a storm, but his whole army was lost.

Pengya, Battle of (or *P'eng-ya*) battle in 624 BC in which the Chinese state of Jin defeated Duke ◊Mu of Qin. Qin invaded Jin and captured several towns including Pengya. Jin leader Marquis Xiang sent military commander Xian Chuju to recover them. He defeated the Qin forces completely with a fierce chariot charge. Jin recovered most of the lost towns, including Pengya.

pennon triangular flag carried at the end of a knight's lance, frequently armorial and intended to identify his place in the battle-line above the dust of battle. When a knight was placed at the head of 25 other knights the pointed end of the pennon was ceremonially cut off, leaving a square flag known as a ◊banner, and he became known as a knight ◊banneret.

pentekonter (plural *pentekontor*) (Greek) galley rowed by 50 oarsmen, 25 a side.

pentekostys (plural *pentekostyes*) Greek 'fiftieth' in Sparta, a military unit consisting of four (or possibly two) *enomotiai* (see ◊enomotia).

Pepin the Short (c. 714–c. 768) king of the Franks from 751. The son of Charles Martel, he acted as Mayor of the Palace to the last Merovingian king, Childeric III, deposed him and assumed the royal title himself, founding the Carolingian dynasty. He was ◊Charlemagne's father.

Percy, Henry (1364–1403) (known as 'Hotspur') English soldier, son of the Earl of Northumberland. He commanded the English forces at their defeat by the Scots at Otterburn in 1388 (see ◊Otterburn, Battle of), but was victorious at Homildon Hill in 1402 (see ◊Homildon Hill, Battle of).

Hotspur was captured by the Scots at Otterburn, but later ransomed, and Homildon Hill resulted from his interception of a later Scottish border raid. He provided ◊Henry V's military education, and fought against Owen ◊Glyndwr. Percy was killed at Shrewsbury in 1403 while in revolt against Henry IV.

Perdiccas (died 321 BC) Macedonian general. Perdiccas was chiliarch (grand vizier) at Alexander's death, and received command of the main army as guardian of Alexander's half-brother, Philip Arrhidaeus, and his unborn son, later Alexander IV. His intrigues alarmed ◊Antipater and ◊Craterus in Europe, and when he invaded Egypt in 321 his troops mutinied and he was killed.

Pericles (c. 495–429 BC) Athenian politician under whom Athens reached the height of its power. He persuaded the Athenians to reject Sparta's ultimata in 432 BC, and was responsible for Athenian strategy in the opening years of the ◊Peloponnesian War.

His real influence began in the late 460s BC with the ostracism of ◊Cimon and the assassination of the democratic reformer Ephialtes, and he was probably behind much of Athens' imperialist foreign policy in the 450s and 440s.

Despite being repeatedly elected general, his military role was comparatively minor. He led a sweep into the eastern Mediterranean in the late 460s, won a victory near Sikyon and unsuccessfully attacked Oeniadae in 454, suppressed a revolt in Euboea in 446, helped to suppress one in Samos in 440/39, and led an undated expedition to the Black Sea.

periplous (Greek) a sailing round – for example, a military raid around the Peloponnese or the outflanking of a line of battle. It may also be an alternative term for *anastrophe*

Per-Ramses (or **Pi-Ramesse**) ('House of Ramses') Egyptian Delta capital of ◊Ramses II, significantly sited next to Avaris, the capital of the ◊Hyksos. Ramses wanted to create a new capital to rival Memphis, the administrative centre, and Thebes, the religious centre. It had temples, palaces, administrative offices, and barracks, but very little remains as it was plundered for building blocks for the new capital of the 21st and 22nd dynasties at Tanis (?1069–?715 BC).

The struggle with the Hittites for the control of the Levant had caused the Hittite Great King Muwatallis to move his capital from ◊Hattusas to the more southerly Tarhuntassas around 1285 BC. Ramses likewise created a new capital at Per-Ramses to be closer to the Levant.

Persepolis Achaemenid Persian capital in the highlands of Fars, built by ◊Darius (I) the Great. It was an occasional palace and ritual centre, housing one of the empire's treasuries, rather than administrative capital. It fell to Alexander the Great without a fight in 330 BC, and the royal palaces were burned. Surviving relief sculptures are an important source for the appearance of Persian troops.

Persepolis was constructed on an artificial terrace, walled in stone on the north side and with mud-brick walls 18 m/59 ft high reinforced by rubble-cored towers on the south and east; the precipitous west side was unwalled. The garrison troops were housed in mud-brick barracks against the eastern wall.

Persian Gates pass controlling the approaches to Persia from the west. In 330 BC the Achaemenid Persian general Ariobarzanes walled the pass to fortify it against ◊Alexander (III) the Great, thereby defeating his initial attack. However, Alexander outflanked the pass at night, attacked Ariobarzanes' rear at dawn, and went on to take the Persian capital ◊Persepolis.

Perugia, Siege of siege in 41 BC of the city of Perugia, central Italy, during the Roman civil wars. The city was held by ◊Mark Antony's wife and brother and, despite the alliance between Antony and Octavian (the future emperor ◊Augustus), the latter blockaded Perugia and starved the defenders into submission.

Peshawar, Battle of (1001) battle fought in 1001 at the foot of the Khyber Pass (in present-day Pakistan) in which the Ghaznavid sultan ◊Mahmud of Ghazni won a victory over the Rajput king ◊Jaipal I of Und. Mahmud returned to Ghazni with much plunder and

150 elephants for use in his central Asian campaigns.

Jaipal's Hindu army consisted of 12,000 cavalry, 300 elephants, and 30,000 infantry, pitted against the Muslims' 15,000 cavalry. Both sides began the battle by using their archers, but the Muslims shot to better effect, disabling many of Jaipal's elephants and opening the way to a decisive cavalry charge. This routed the Hindus, who fled with the loss of 15,000 soldiers.

Peshawar, Battle of (1008) battle fought in 1008 at the foot of the Khyber Pass (in present-day Pakistan) in which the Ghaznavid sultan ◊Mahmud of Ghazni, seeking to plunder and punish the Hindus, defeated the Hindu armies led by Anandapal, Raja of Und (or Waihind), the son and successor of ◊Jaipal I.

Anandapal, previously defeated by Mahmud in 1005, met the renewed invasion by forming a ◊Rajput alliance and assembling a huge army. Mahmud delayed battle for a month, after which Anandapal attacked. A charge by 30,000 tribesmen from Kashmir stormed Mahmud's flanking defences and he was considering a retreat, when Anandapal's elephant panicked and carried its rider from the field. The Hindu army then fled, losing 8,000 soldiers and 30 elephants.

Peter the Hermit (lived 11th century) prominent leader and legendary fomenter of the First Crusade (see ◊Crusades), 1096–99. An inspirational preacher, he led the first troops across to Asia Minor. They were poorly-equipped, unlike the retinues of the magnates who came later, and were severely defeated at Civetot. Peter escaped to join the other crusaders, but disgraced himself by running away from the siege of Antioch (see ◊Antioch, Battle of 1098).

Petra city in the Arabian desert (in present-day Jordan) founded by the Nabateans in the 4th century BC and serving as their capital from 312 BC to AD 106. It was captured by the Romans in 106 and destroyed by the Arabs in the 7th century. The natural geography of Petra offered good protection and walls were only built on the north and south sides, closing off approaches between the cliffs.

The north wall, about 1,400 m/1,530 yds long, was built 2 m/6.5 ft thick and stood just over 2 m/6.5 ft high. Rectangular bastions were built along the wall at strategic points, as well as independent free-standing towers fortifying other important positions. The largest of these strongpoints is the 'Conway Tower' at the northernmost point of the wall, 25 m/82 ft in diameter and surrounded by an outer ring wall

2 m/6.5 ft thick. The southern walls seem to have served as a territorial marker rather than for defence purposes, with the towers providing the security. Following the Roman occupation of the city the north walls were rebuilt partially on a new alignment behind the Nabatean wall, abandoning the Conway Tower.

petrary Latin *petra* 'stone' medieval stone-throwing engine, frequently mentioned in reference to the sieges of Jerusalem in the 11th century and Chinon, France, in the 12th century. The terms ◊mangonel and petrary were often used interchangeably.

Petra, Siege of Roman victory in 549–51 over the Persians. The East Roman Emperor ◊Justinian used the pretext of a persecuted Christian population to invade territory recently seized by the Persians. The Roman commander, Dagisteus, laid seige to Petra (in modern Jordan) with 8,000 troops, but was driven back by a Persian relief force. Reinforcements allowed the Romans to renew

PERSIAN WARS

Series of conflicts between Greece and Persia 499–479 BC. Greek involvement with Persia began with the conquest of the Greek cities of western Asia Minor by ◊Cyrus (II) the Great (reigned 559–530 BC) and ended with the conquest of Persia by ◊Alexander (III) the Great (reigned 336–323 BC), but the term 'Persian Wars' is usually applied particularly to the two Persian invasions of mainland Greece in 490 and 480/79. The Greek victory stemmed the tide of Persian conquest and ushered in the great days of classical Greece.

Probably in 499 many of the Greek cities of Asia Minor rebelled against Persian rule, briefly drawing support from Athens and Eretria in mainland Greece, and although the rebellion was crushed in 494, ◊Darius (I) the Great of Persia decided to avenge the part Athens and Eretria had played. Hence the seaborne expedition which came to grief at Marathon in 490 (see ◊Marathon, Battle of). Darius' death in 486 and a rebellion in Egypt delayed a renewal of the conflict, but in 480 Darius' son ◊Xerxes I invaded Greece by both land and sea.

Aware of Persian preparations for some time, the Greeks had formed an alliance under Spartan leadership in the autumn of 481, but their first attempt to halt the invasion, at the pass of Tempe between Mount Olympus and Mount Ossa, was abandoned even before Xerxes crossed the Hellespont (present-day Dardanelles), when it was realized that the pass could be turned. In August 480, despite the heroism of its defenders, the Greek position at Thermopylae was turned (see ◊Thermopylae, Battle of), while at sea an indecisive series of skirmishes was fought off Artemisium on the northeast coast of Euboea.

Eastern Greece as far south as Athens was now overrun, but the Athenians had already evacuated their city, and the Greek fleet managed to defeat the Persians in the narrow strait between the island of Salamis and Attica about 24 September (see ◊Salamis, Battle of 480 BC). The Persian fleet, its morale shattered, withdrew to Asia Minor and was followed by Xerxes himself and part of his land forces. However, Xerxes left the bulk of his army behind him under his general Mardonius, who wintered in Thessaly, and from there first tried to win Athens over by diplomacy, and then reoccupied the city in June 479. Eventually, when the Athenians threatened to make a separate peace, the Spartans and their allies mobilized and, joining the Athenians at Eleusis, advanced into Boeotia. Here, in the vicinity of Plataea, a complex three-week campaign ended in complete Greek victory in (?August) 479 (see ◊Plataea, Battle of).

the siege and the garrison fell after a spirited defence.

Pevensey castle castle in England, 24 km / 15 mi southwest of Hastings, Sussex, that was originally fortified by the Romans in around AD 280 as a coastal defence measure. After the Norman Conquest it was granted to William's half-brother Robert, but with the gradual recession of the seacoast, Pevensey's importance declined and the work fell into neglect.

Robert had divided off a part of the Roman ruins by digging a ditch and creating a mound. Utilizing part of the Roman walls he formed the castle bailey from the remaining area. In 1088 the castle was taken by William (II) Rufus after a siege, after which it changed ownership several times. It was again besieged during the wars of Stephen and Matilda in the 12th century. The curtain wall and towers were built by the Earl of Richmond in around 1250, and it withstood a siege by Simon de ◊Montfort (the Younger) 1264–65.

Pevensey fort (Roman *Anderidos*) late Roman fort (built about AD 330) on the south coast of England that formed part of the Saxon Shore defences. Notable for its irregular shape and the good preservation of its defences, it was one of the last Roman fortifications to be constructed in Britain.

Pevensey occupied a coastal peninsular whose shape dictated its oval plan. The 3.6-m/11.8-ft-thick walls enclosed an area of 4 hectares/9.9 acres and were supplemented by solid U-shaped external bastions. The only land approach was to the southwest and the main gate was located on this side. It consisted of a single portal, flanked by external bastions and internal guard chambers. A small undefended gate was located on the east side to give access to the harbour.

Peveril castle castle in England 16 km / 10 mi northwest of Buxton, in Derbyshire. Built in the late 11th century, this was simply a partly-walled enclosure on a natural defensive position on a precipitous ridge. The walling was extended in the 12th century, but the first (and only) major building was a square tower erected around 1180 by Henry II after he took the castle from its founders in 1155. It seems possible that he intended it as a minor residence, but it saw little use before falling into ruin.

peytral breast armour for a horse. The term is generally applied to all such armour in Europe, Asia, and Africa, and particularly to plate examples in Europe in the 15th and 16th centuries, when horse armour was relatively common.

The peytral was rare in the ancient world; some artistically decorated examples have been found from this period in southern Italy, but these were probably for ceremonial chariot horses. A lamellar example is shown on the Pergamon reliefs, and an archaeological specimen of the same type was found at the Hellenistic city of Ai Khanoun in Afghanistan. There is little evidence for such armour in the Classical period, but the whole body of the horse was often covered with scale armour during the later Empire (4th–5th century).

pezetairoi Greek 'foot companions' either all the soldiers in a Macedonian phalanx, or some elite units among them.

phalanx Greek 'rank' in ancient Greek warfare, term used to describe a massed formation, many ranks deep, of ◊hoplite and Macedonian-style armies.

Pharnabazus Achaemenid Persian general under ◊Artaxerxes (II) Memnon, King of Persia. He assisted the Spartan survivors after Cyzicus (see ◊Cyzicus, Battle of 410 BC) but in 394 BC defeated their fleet at Cnidus, sending the Spartans back to Greece. He led two failed attempts (385–383 BC and about 374 BC) to reconquer Egypt, which had been lost during Artaxerxes' reign.

Pharnabazus succeeded his father Pharnakes as satrap (provincial governor) of Daskylion, on the Hellespontine coast, about 413. At first he cooperated with the Spartans, leading cavalry into the sea to support their ships at Abydos and relieving their survivors after Cyzicus, but after 400 BC he obstructed their attempts to bring Asian Greeks into their orbit. In 395 his scythed chariots won a local victory against an isolated detachment of the Spartan king ◊Agesilaus II's forces before they captured his camp. A year later he and the Athenian ◊Conon defeated the Spartan fleet at Cnidus.

Pharsalus, Battle of battle fought on 9 August 48 BC between the forces of Julius ◊Caesar and those of his rival ◊Pompey the Great near Pharsalus (now Farsala) in Thessaly, Greece. After their comprehensive defeat by Caesar's veteran army, the remainder of Pompey's force surrendered, ending all organized resistance to Caesar's rule.

Pompey planned to exploit his cavalry advantage by massing his horsemen on the left flank to envelop the enemy right. Caesar formed his ◊legions in three lines with the flanks held by his best units. He then stripped a cohort from the third line of each legion and formed these as an oblique fourth line hidden behind his right flank. The Pompeian cavalry under Titus Labienus drove back Caesar's cavalry, but were then attacked and panicked by the sudden advance of Caesar's fourth line. Pompey's cavalry stampeded off the field exposing the left flank of their army. Caesar's main line advanced against the stationary Pompeian infantry. Caesar's veterans kept up a steady pressure and as the reserves were committed the inexperienced enemy infantry were driven back and began to flee. Caesar had 200 casualties, but claimed to have killed 15,000 and captured 24,000 men and 9 legionary eagles.

phidition (Spartan) military mess (*syssition*), probably consisting of about 15 members. Members were co-opted at age 20 and had to contribute dues in kind. Failure to do so meant expulsion and loss of their rights as citizens. Members up to age 30 were expected to both eat and sleep in the mess, and all members, even kings, were fined for not dining there.

Philip (II) Augustus (1165–1223) king of France from 1180. As part of his efforts to establish a strong monarchy and evict the English from their French possessions, he waged war in turn against the English kings ◊Henry II, Richard (I) the Lionheart (with whom he also went on the Third Crusade), and John (1167–1216).

Against Richard he suffered setbacks at Fréteval (see ◊Fréteval, Battle of) in 1194 and at Vernon, but against John he captured Château Gaillard in 1203–04 (see ◊Château Gaillard, Siege of) and destroyed the Angevin Empire. He defeated John's allies led by Emperor Otto IV at Bouvines in 1214 (see ◊Bouvines, Battle of).

Philip played a part in organizing the Fourth Crusade, and setting up the ◊Albigensian Crusades. He built many castles, a significant number with the new-style round towers.

Philip (II) of Macedon (382–336 BC) King of Macedon 359–336 BC. A master of both diplomacy and strategy, he not only saved and unified a state on the brink of disintegration, but made it the dominant power in the Balkans, and was poised to invade Anatolia when he died. His greatest achievement was the creation of the army, and particularly its ◊sarissa-armed infantry, with which his son and successor Alexander (III) the Great conquered the Persian Empire.

At Chaeronea (see ◊Chaeronea, Battle of 338 BC), Philip's pinning of the Illyrian centre with his infantry while his cavalry attacked their flanks and rear was novel, and the way in which he stretched the enemy line by withdrawing his right until a gap appeared for his cavalry to exploit, was more refined than his son's tactics at Gaugamela (see ◊Gaugamela, Battle of). He was also adept at the new techniques of siegecraft under development in the 4th century BC.

Philippi, battles of twin battles in 42 BC between the triumvirs ◊Mark Antony and Octavian (the future emperor ◊Augustus) and Julius Caesar's assassins, the Republicans Marcus ◊Brutus and Gaius ◊Cassius. The first battle was indecisive, but in the second the Republicans were destroyed.

The Republicans mustered 19 ◊legions and 20,000 cavalry plus light infantry, while the triumvirs fielded 19 rather stronger legions and 13,000 cavalry. In the first battle Antony, who was in overall charge, routed Cassius's legions on the left flank, capturing his camp. In despair Cassius committed suicide, unaware that the right wing under Brutus had enjoyed great success against Octavian's troops, inflicting heavy losses. After a three-week break, the triumvirs outmanoeuvred Brutus and forced him to offer battle. The clash between the main infantry lines was hard fought, but Octavian's infantry pushed back Brutus's troops. The second and third lines failed to stop the enemy advance and the whole army was put to flight. Brutus committed suicide soon afterwards.

Philippopolis, Siege of Gothic siege in AD 250 of the Roman city of Philippopolis (modern Plovdiv, Bulgaria) in Thrace. The Gothic army, led by King Cniva, took Philippopolis after a long resistance. An attempt by the Roman emperor Decius to relieve the city ended in disaster when his army was surprised and routed, losing its camp. Philippopolis is a rare example of a Germanic army mounting a successful siege.

Philomelion, Battle of battle fought in the autumn of 1116 when the Byzantine emperor ◊Alexius (I) Comnenus led a fighting march into Seljuk (Turkish) territory to rescue its Christian population and bring them back within the Byzantine Empire. Sultan Malik Shah's failure to defeat the Greeks led to his overthrow by his brother.

Marching southeast from Nicomedia, Turkey, towards Philomelion and Iconium, Alexius developed a march formation to counter Turkish harassment tactics. This slow-moving hollow rectangle, in which the infantry protected the cavalry, proved invulnerable to attack. On his return north, despite being hampered by refugees, Alexius used flying columns of cavalry to counter the Turks. This campaign strategy was enormously successful.

Philopoemen (c. 253–182 BC) Greek general of the Achaean League. He crushed the Spartans at Mantinea (see ◊Mantinea, Battle of 207 BC) and defeated ◊Nabis, tyrant of Sparta, in 192 BC. He was captured by the Messenians and poisoned.

Philopoemen first helped to defend Megalopolis against ◊Cleomenes III of Sparta in 223, and in the following year played a heroic part at Sellasia (see ◊Sellasia, Battle of). He was cavalry commander and vice-president of the League in 209, and president and general in 208/7 and 206/5. In alliance with Rome, he fought Nabis in 202–199 and again in 193/2.

ph'kak the most distinctive weapon of the Khmers. A long, straight shaft curves sharply backwards at the top, and to this curved portion is attached a narrow axe-blade. The weapon was used by both infantry and high-ranking elephant-riders on 12th–13th-century Khmer reliefs, and survived until the 20th century. It passed into Thai royal regalia as the 'hostage sword'.

Phocion (402–318 BC) Athenian general and politician. He served in Euboea in 348 and 341, at Megara (perhaps in 342), and against ◊Philip (II) of Macedon at Byzantium in 340/39, and defended Attica in the Lamian War of 322/1.

A conservative in politics, he often opposed those who favoured confrontation with Macedon, and used his influence to get better terms when such policies led to defeat. He was condemned to death during a brief democratic revival in Athens.

Phormio (?470s–420s BC) Athenian admiral in the early part of the ◊Peloponnesian War. In 430 BC he was sent in command of 20 ships to blockade the Corinthian Gulf, based on Naupactus, and in 429 twice defeated more numerous Peloponnesian squadrons, demonstrating how far Athenian skills in galley fighting had advanced.

Phraaspa, Siege of unsuccessful siege of Phraaspa, the capital of Media (now northeastern Iran), by ◊Mark Antony in 36 BC. It resulted in the failure of Antony's Parthian expedition.

Antony planned to take Phraaspa with a specially prepared siege train. Leaving this slow-moving column under the protection of two legions, he advanced the bulk of his army to blockade the city. A force of mobile Parthian cavalry slipped behind him and captured his siege train, destroying the guard. After attempting to take the city with improvised

siege engines, Antony's army began to run out of supplies and was forced to withdraw through Armenia. Harassed by the Parthians, the Romans won a series of unimportant rearguard skirmishes, but suffered a steady drain of casualties. During the whole campaign Antony lost 20,000 infantry and 4,000 cavalry, the majority to disease.

Piacenza, Battle of battle between the West Roman emperor Avitius and his German general ◊Ricimer at Piacenza, northern Italy, in October 456. Avitius was defeated and died shortly after the battle; for six months there was no western emperor.

Pickering castle castle in Yorkshire, England, 24 km/15 mi west of Scarborough. A ◊motte-and-bailey design dating from around 1200, this castle developed in an unusual manner.

Initially the motte, which had its own ditch, was crowned with a shell keep and a bailey to the north. A second bailey to the south later augmented this, and some time later a curtain wall was built from the keep, down the sides of the motte to link with the curtain wall of the north bailey. In the early 14th century the south bailey was also given a curtain wall, with towers, and a number of domestic buildings were erected in the two baileys. The overall effect was of a motte within the curtain walls, separating the two baileys.

pilos Greek 'felt' helmet, particularly the close-fitting conical helmet thought to have been worn in Sparta. The term's military meaning probably stemmed from the use of the word for anything made of felt, including shoes, mats and, especially, the linings of hats.

pilum javelin with a long, slim, iron shank between the wooden haft and the point, used by Roman legionaries primarily to break up the enemy charge. It was designed to penetrate a shield and wound the person behind it. If it failed to pierce the shield, or hit the ground, it usually bent and became unusable. Pila were in use until the 2nd century AD.

According to the Greek politician and historian ◊Polybius (150 BC), pila came in two types: a stout version attached to the haft with numerous rivets, and a slimmer version.

pilum muralis weapon used for fighting from walls or ramparts, mentioned in the 1st century BC by Julius Caesar in *De Bello Gallico* (V, 40). It may be the short, stocky type of ◊pilum.

Pingcheng, Battle of (or *P'ing-ch'eng*) battle in 200 BC in which Maodun of the ◊Xiongnu defeated Emperor ◊Han Gaozu of China near Pingcheng. Soon after the emperor made peace with the Xiongnu, appeasing them with regular payments.

Xin, a border governor, defected to the Xiongnu, and the Chinese emperor led a midwinter punitive expedition. Pursuing a feigned retreat, he and an infantry force were cut off and surrounded by Xiongnu cavalry on the White Peak near Pingcheng. The Xiongnu besieged him for seven days. The Xiongnu blockade lifted (it is said that Gaozu bribed Maodun's wife into allowing the Chinese to escape, but Maodun also feared treachery by his rebel Chinese allies) and under cover of fog, keeping the Xiongnu off with a cordon of crossbowmen, the emperor withdrew into the city of Pingcheng and joined up with the rest of the army.

Pingyin, Battle of battle in 555 BC in which a Chinese coalition led by commander Marquis Ping of Jin outsmarted and defeated the state of Qi.

The Qi army defended an earthwork and beat off allied attacks, though suffering heavy losses. The Jin commanders exaggerated the size of their army by setting up banners on hills and in marshes although there were no troops there, and by attaching carts to their chariots dragging branches to stir up dust clouds. Seeing this, the marquis of Qi believed himself outnumbered. He abandoned his position and fell back to the capital. The allies pursued, burned the suburbs, and devastated the countryside.

Placentia, Battle of battle between the Roman emperor Lucius Domitius ◊Aurelian and the Juthungi, an Alamannic (German) tribe, at Placentia, northern Italy, in 271. It was the first action in a campaign provoked by a large German raid on Italy.

Aurelian, marching in haste to intercept the Germans, was ambushed, and only his personal leadership allowed him to draw off a small part of his troops in some order, after suffering heavy losses.

plackart lower half of a two-part breastplate forming part of a medieval European suit of armour. Italian breastplates incorporating this feature were made from about 1420 to the end of the 15th century. The same term is used from the mid-16th century to the end of the 17th century to describe a reinforcing breastplate worn over the top of a complete breastplate.

Plataea, Siege of Sparta's successful siege of the southern Boeotian city Plataea from 429 to 427 BC. It provides proof that blockade was not the only technique used to take a walled city during the ◊Peloponnesian War.

There were only 480 defenders at Plataea during the siege, most of the city having been evacuated to Athens at the beginning of the war. The Spartans surrounded the city with a palisade then raised a siege mound and brought up battering rams. But the defenders raised Plataea's wall, built a second one behind it, undermined the siege mound, and either lassoed or broke the battering rams. Even a

PLATAEA, BATTLE OF

Decisive battle fought in 479 BC at Plataea, central Greece, between the Greeks under the Spartan commander ◊Pausanias and the invading Persian force of Xerxes I under ◊Mardonius. It was the final battle of the Persian Wars, and the Greek victory put an end to the Persian attempt to conquer Greece.

The Greeks first took up a position along the foothills of Mount Cithaeron, where they drove off the Persian cavalry and killed its commander. They then moved down to a position along the River Asopos, but although continuous reinforcements swelled their number to 38,700 ◊hoplites, they were subjected to constant harassment by Persian horse-archers and, deprived of their water supply, were compelled to risk a withdrawal at night. In the confusion, the centre retreated to Plataea, leaving the Athenians on the left separated from the Spartans and Tegeates on the right. The Persian commander Mardonius then allowed himself to be drawn into battle with the latter somewhere near modern Erythrae, while his Greek allies engaged the Athenians. Finding themselves unable to withstand hoplites in hand-to-hand combat, the Persians were routed and Mardonius was killed. The Athenians also defeated his Boeotian allies.

Spartan attempt to burn Plataea was frustrated by a thunderstorm. The besiegers finally settled down to starve the defenders out, but over two hundred of the garrison managed to escape to Athens before the rest were forced to surrender.

Plautius, Aulus first Roman governor of Britain 43–47. He commanded the Roman invasion force to Britain in 43, facing little resistance until the battles on the Medway (see ◊Medway, Battle of the) and Thames. He called the emperor Claudius to Britain for a triumphal entry into Colchester (Roman Camulodunum).

After further campaigns in the province, during which he conquered much of southern Britain, he was awarded the honour of an ovation in Rome.

plumbata late Roman missile weapon, described by the Roman military writer ◊Vegetius. It is also called a *martiobarbulus*. The names have generally been associated with a short javelin with a lead weight at the junction of the iron and wood, which is clearly derived from the *pilum*.

podestà medieval Italian term from the 12th century onwards for the military commander of a city-state, elected by the populace often in opposition to their feudal lord.

Poitiers, Battle of during the Hundred Years' War, victory for Edward the Black Prince 13 Sept 1356 over King John II of France. King John, his son Philip, and 2,000 knights were taken prisoner, and about 3,000 French were killed.

Poitiers, Battle of alternative name for the Battle of Tours between Charles Martel and the Muslims in 732; see ◊Tours, Battle of.

polemarch anglicized form of the Greek for 'war leader', originally used as the title of the commander in chief in many Greek states. Later, it was the title of a civilian official in Athens or a subordinate officer in Sparta.

poleyn piece of plate armour for the knee worn by medieval European men-at-arms.

It first appeared in artistic representations of armour about 1250, usually attached to gamboised cuisses (quilted thigh defences), and the term 'poleyn' first appeared in the inventory of Hues de Clermont of 1331. By about 1340 poleyns were represented with small side wings, and from 1370 onwards they were joined by articulating lames to solid plate cuisses.

Pollentia, Battle of battle fought in northern Italy on 6 April (Easter day) 402 between the West Roman army, commanded by ◊Stilicho, and the Visigoths led by their king ◊Alaric. Alaric was defeated and agreed to leave Italy, although he returned the following year.

After driving the Visigoths from Milan, Stilicho followed up with an army drawn from Britain and the Rhine frontier, together with Vandal and Alan allies. An initial cavalry charge by Stilicho's Alans was beaten back by the Visigoths, but the Roman infantry drove back the Goths and captured their baggage camp. Alaric's wife, who was in the camp, was also captured.

Polyaenus Macedonian writer who compiled a collection of stratagems dedicated to the Roman emperor Marcus Aurelius and his son, Lucius Verus. It includes stratagems practised by gods, mythological heroes, and women, as well as by historical Greek and Roman commanders.

Some of the anecdotes are valuable, but it is dangerous to rely on Polyaenus where better sources are available.

Polybius (c. 200–c. 118 BC) Greek historian. After Rome's defeat of Macedonia at Pydna (see ◊Pydna, Battle of) in 168, Polybius was deported to Italy as a political hostage. Here he became friendly with ◊Scipio Aemilianus and his circle, and gained access to the public records. He was with Scipio in the destruction of Carthage in 146 and of Numantia in Spain in 134. His history of Rome, in 40 books, covers the years 220–146 BC. The first five books remain intact and of the rest fragments and abstracts have survived.

Polyperchon Macedonian general who was appointed regent by ◊Antipater in 319 BC. This appointment annoyed Antipater's son, ◊Cassander, who declared war on Polyperchon and eventually drove him out of Macedonia in 316. Returning to the Peloponnese, Polyperchon surrendered the regency to ◊Antigonus (I) Monophthalmus.

In 309 he tried to recover Macedonia, ostensibly on behalf of Heracles, an illegitimate son of Alexander, but murdered him in return for recognition by Cassander as general in the Peloponnese. Thereafter he disappeared from history, apart from a brief mention in 303.

Pompeius, Sextus (c. 66–36 BC) Roman general, younger son of ◊Pompey the Great. He opposed Octavian (later the emperor ◊Augustus) and built up considerable power in Sicily and Sardinia, maintaining a large and effective fleet which he used to threaten the grain supplies to Rome. Although his navy was

POMPEY THE GREAT (106–48 BC)

(Gnaeus Pompeius Magnus)

Roman soldier and politician. Considered one of Rome's greatest generals, he had already commanded several armies before being admitted to the Senate as consul in 70 BC. After the death of his father, Pompeius Strabo, he raised an army from his father's veterans and clients which fought for ◊Sulla in the Social War. For this, Sulla gave Pompey the perhaps mocking title Magnus ('The Great'). He suppressed a rebellion in Italy in 77, then fought Sertorius in Spain the following year. He enjoyed some success with Sertorius' subordinates before being checked by Sertorius himself near the river Sucro (probably the modern Ebro). The conflict ended when Sertorius was murdered, and Pompey returned to Rome where he helped defeat the ◊Spartacus Revolt before entering the Senate. In 67 BC, Pompey received the extraordinary command to clear the Mediterranean of pirates, which he completed in three months. Sent to conclude the war with ◊Mithridates (VI) Eupator of Pontus, Pompey defeated him at Lycus (see ◊Lycus, Battle of) in 66 BC then received the surrender of ◊Tigranes (I) the Great of Armenia. In 63 he intervened in a civil war in Judaea, storming Jerusalem where he entered the Holy of Holies of the Jewish temple but left its treasures undisturbed. He later consolidated and organized Rome's eastern provinces, shaping their administrative structure for centuries to come. Political failures led to his alliance with ◊Caesar and Marcus Licinius Crassus (the Elder), the so-called First Triumvirate. After Crassus' death, Pompey refused to treat Caesar as an equal and supported his opponents in the Senate, culminating in the civil war of 49 BC. He abandoned Italy and built up a large army in Macedon which he planned to lead back to Rome. However, he was greatly hindered by the many prominent senators who fled to his camp and questioned his orders, perhaps causing his rather lacklustre generalship in the final campaign. Though far less experienced and confident than Caesar's legions, Pompey's army nearly defeated them at Dyrrachium (see ◊Dyrrachium, Battle of 49–8 BC) but was soundly beaten at Pharsalus (see ◊Pharsalus, Battle of). Pompey fled to Egypt where he was murdered.

---

successful for a long time, he was finally defeated at Naupactus. He escaped, but was caught and executed by ◊Mark Antony.

-pore suffix in south Asian place names; see -◊pur.

porpax (Greek) central armband of a hoplite shield, through which the left arm was thrust to the elbow.

Portchester castle castle in England at Portsmouth harbour, Hampshire. A Roman coastal defence fort dating from around 280, it is the only Roman fortress in Europe with completely intact walls. Abandoned by the Romans, it lay empty until the early 12th century, when the Austin friars built a priory in one corner. Shortly after, Henry I built a castle in the opposite corner, using the existing Roman wall for two sides and building two further sides inside the Roman work.

The castle was ditched, and a keep and wall towers were built to make it compact and strong. In the late 14th century Richard II built a palace within the ward. Later Henry V used it as a staging camp en route to the battle of Agincourt in 1415.

portcullis Old French *porte coleïce* 'sliding door' gate or grating that could be raised and lowered rapidly, forming part of the defensive gate of a castle or other fortification. The portcullis was probably introduced about 1100. It was strongly built of wood or iron to resist attack. Often the lower edge had points for striking attackers as it fell.

Portcullises were often built at the entrance and exit of a gatehouse, as at Hever castle in

Kent, England, so that attackers could be trapped between the two and shot at from ◊*meutrières*. The portcullis moved in slots built in the doorway, and was usually worked by pulleys in a chamber above the doorway. In some castles the operating machinery still exists or even works, as at the Bloody Tower in the Tower of London, England.

Potidaea, Siege of siege of the rebel city of Potidaea, on the western coast of modern Khalkidhiki, by Athenian forces in 432–429 BC, one of the incidents that led to the ◊Peloponnesian War. The Athenians walled Potidaea in from the north and south and at one time briefly used some sort of siege engines, but eventually the city was starved into surrender.

The battle outside its walls provides a rare example of the use of signals in ancient Greek warfare. The Corinthian Aristeus, who had come to the aid of Potidaea, arranged for some kind of signals to be hoisted when he engaged the Athenians. This would notify Potidaea's local allies, assembled at nearby Olynthus, to fall on the Athenian rear. But the Athenians secured a victory before this could be done. Aristeus routed the Athenian right but had considerable difficulty getting back to Potidaea when his own right was defeated.

pourpoint European medieval term for a fabric doublet worn under armour, synonymous with 'arming doublet'.

Poyang, Battle of naval battle August–October 1363 in which a Ming army under ◊Zhu Yuanzhang defeated Chen Yuliang's Han army in the Chinese civil wars. Zhu led a fleet from the Yangtze River into Lake Poyang to relieve the city of Nanchang, besieged by Chen. The Ming were eventually able to cut off the Han from their base. Zhu took over the Han fleet after it surrendered and overran Han territory, making him the strongest power in China.

Zhu's fleet of 100,000 was met by Chen's fleet of 200,000, built to replace that lost at Longwan, with exceptionally large three-decker towered ships. In fighting 30 August–2 September, the Ming destroyed much of the Han fleet with fireships, killing 60,000 men, but suffered heavy losses themselves. On the night of 2 September the Ming withdrew to the narrows at the mouth of the lake. This cut the Han off from their base, and in the following weeks of negotiations several Han officers defected. Eventually the Han fleet attempted a breakout. As they entered the Yangtze on 3 October the Ming again attacked with fireships. With less room to manoeuvre than in the lake, fighting

was heavy at close quarters. Chen was killed by an arrow and his son captured, and the next day the Han fleet surrendered.

praefectus castrorum Latin 'prefect of the camp' senior officer responsible for the day-to-day running of a Roman legionary fortress or campaign camp, including supply of food and equipment and logistics. He might be placed in command of the legion in the absence of the ◊legate and was of equestrian status.

During the empire the position was regularly held by a former ◊*primus pilus*.

praetor second highest annual magistracy in the Roman Republic. The praetors were often given command of a province and its army if the consuls were engaged elsewhere. They often commanded one ◊legion plus allied troops, but there was no set complement for a praetorian army.

praetorium headquarters of the commander of a Roman army on campaign. It was situated at the centre of the camp for maximum security and guarded by specially chosen soldiers (called the Praetorian Guard in the Republic). The large tent provided the commander's living space as well as his centre of operations.

prefect Roman title for various grades of officers. Prefects were most commonly found commanding the ◊*socii* during the republic and the ◊*alae* and cohorts of ◊*auxilia* under the principate. Prefects were usually equestrians rather than senators.

prick spur spur with a single point, attached to a horse rider's heels and used to drive his horse forwards. It is the earliest form of spur, first attested around the middle of the 1st millennium BC, and in continuous use thereafter.

Priene city founded by the Ionians about 350 BC beside the Maender River in southwestern Asia Minor. It occupied the lower slopes of Mount Micale, with the acropolis occupying the area of the summit to the north.

The circuit of city walls was not continuous, as the steep rise of Mount Micale made it both impractical and unnecessary to continue the western wall up to the acropolis. The acropolis itself had no defences on this side, relying on the terrain to provide security. The main gate was on the east side and was protected by square flanking towers. Elsewhere access through the defences was through three narrow posterns, one of which was protected by a square tower. Square towers, both external and internal, strengthened the defences at weak points.

primus pilus most senior centurion of a Roman legion, commanding the first ◊century of the first ◊cohort. The *primus pilus* was a man of great status. He held the office for one year, after which he became an equestrian and often went on to govern small provinces or receive the command of praetorian or urban cohorts.

principes (singular *princeps*) type of infantry of the Roman republican army. The *principes* held the second rank of the ◊legion's heavy infantry battle formation (see also ◊*hastati* and ◊*triarii*). Recruited from men in the prime of life, they were equipped with two javelins and a sword, fighting in the same manner as the ◊*hastati*.

In the 4th and 2nd centuries BC each legion had 1,200 *principes*, organized in the same manner as the *hastati*. By the 1st century BC the distinction between ranks had disappeared.

Prithviraja Chauhana III

Hindu ruler of Delhi in the latter part of the 12th century and king of the Chauhan ◊Rajputs, who controlled the Delhi–Ajmer region of north-central India. He commanded a coalition of Rajput forces which sought to halt the Muslim invasion of ◊Muhammad of Ghur at Tarain. Victorious in the first conflict in 1191, he died heroically in the second battle in 1192 (see ◊Tarain, Battle of 1191 and 1192).

He alone of the Rajput princes refused to acknowledge the overlordship of his eastern neighbour and rival ◊Jaichand Gaharwar, and carried off his daughter Padmavati after she selected Prithviraja as her husband by the ceremony of ◊*swayamvara*.

Probus, Marcus Aurelius (AD 232–282)

Roman emperor 275–82. One of ◊Aurelian's commanders who succeeded to the throne, he defeated the Alamanni and Franks, restoring the frontier on the Rhine and Danube. He also campaigned against the Vandals, and in the east concluded a treaty with the Persians. Despite his successes he was murdered when his own troops mutinied.

Procopius (c. 500–c. 560)

East Roman lawyer and rhetorician from Caesarea (Palestine). He was private secretary to the emperor Justinian's general ◊Belisarius, whom he accompanied on his campaigns in Persia, Africa, and Italy. He wrote a detailed *History of the Wars*, describing first-hand many of the key events of the Roman reconquest of the West and the Roman–Persian conflict.

His other works that survive include *The Secret History*, which is an attack on the emperor Justinian and his wife Theodora, and *The Buildings of Justinian*, which describes the major roads, bridges, and public buildings of the Roman Empire up to 558.

prodromoi Greek 'forerunners' the advance guard of a large army. In ancient Macedon it was a body of mounted scouts.

Prokop, Holy (lived 15th century)

Hussite priest-general, active 1426–33. Successor to Jan ◊Zizka, Prokop showed some of the same qualities as a commander, deploying his master's system to good effect. He twice defeated Emperor Sigismund's 'crusades', in 1427 at Tachov and 1431 at Domazlice, and took the war into Germany 1429–30 on his pludering raids into Saxony and Franconia. He could not maintain Zizka's iron discipline, however, and was imprisoned by his troops for a while shortly before his final defeat, at Lipany in 1433.

pronoia Byzantine term referring to the support of troops from the revenues of estates. It was close in form to the Ottoman *timar*, and has also been likened to the Western fief. It became hereditary from 1230, but it was more of a fiscal and administrative institution granted only by the emperor, and was not part of the social or judicial structure.

protectores veteran soldiers of the late Roman Empire who were selected for more senior command appointments. The system functioned somewhat like a staff college with the *protectores* being sent to join the staffs of commanders to gain experience before themselves being given a more senior command post.

Prudhoe castle

castle in Durham, England, 13 km/8 mi north of Consett. An early (around 1080) Norman ◊motte-and-bailey work, this was built on a promontory on the River Tyne, protected by a natural ravine on two sides and ditched on the other two.

A second bailey was added early in the 12th century, so that the motte was centrally located between the two, and a square tower-keep was built in the western bailey. Curtain walls and a gatehouse were added, and by 1173 it was strong enough to resist a siege by William the Lion of Scotland, which was repeated in 1174 and again resisted. A barbican was added in the 13th century, with a drawbridge leading to an inner barbican and the main gatehouse.

pseudocomitatenses former border troops (*limitanei*) who had been transferred to the mobile field army of the late Roman Empire.

psyloi Greek 'bare ones' in Greek warfare, light troops such as archers and slingers.

Pteria, Battle of

battle between the Persian king ◊Cyrus (II) the Great and ◊Croesus of Lydia at Pteria, eastern Anatolia, in 547 BC, when Cyrus won his first victory over Croesus.

After Cyrus had conquered Media (now northwestern Iran), Croesus invaded Persian territory and the armies met at Pteria in eastern Anatolia. Despite having equipped his infantry as Greek ◊hoplites, Croesus had the worst of a day-long indecisive battle. When Cyrus did not attack the next day, Croesus fell back to Lydia. He expected no more fighting until spring, but was surprised by Cyrus' march on the Lydian capital Sardis (see ◊Sardis, Battle of) which resulted in the Lydians' defeat.

pteriges rectangular strips of cloth or leather covering the shoulders and thighs shown on many Greek and Roman statues.

Ptolemy (I) Soter (367/6–282 BC) Ruler of Egypt from 323 BC, king from 305 BC, and founder of the Ptolemaic dynasty. He was one of the most successful of ◊Alexander (III) the Great's 'successors' (see ◊*Diadochi*).

On Alexander's death in 323 he made off with his body to Egypt and seized control of the country, taking Cyrene in 322 and repulsing ◊Perdiccas in 321. He does not appear to have shared some of the wider ambitions of the other successors, and worked instead for a balance of power. In 315 he allied himself with ◊Cassander and ◊Lysimachus against ◊Antigonus (I) Monophthalmus, and in 312 supported ◊Seleucus (I) Nicator's recovery of his kingdom. In 306 he repulsed Antigonus' invasion of Egypt, but lost Cyprus to ◊Demetrius (I) Poliorcetes. In 295 he recovered Cyprus, and from 291 became increasingly powerful in the Aegean, taking the title 'king' in 305.

pugio Roman military dagger, worn as part of military dress during the 1st century AD.

Of Spanish origin, it first appears on Roman sites in Spain in the second half of the 2nd century BC. Archaeological evidence of its existence disappears at the end of the 1st century AD, but it reappears in an evolved form, with a broader handle, in the 3rd century AD.

PUNIC WAR, FIRST

War fought between Rome and Carthage 264–241 BC. It was an inevitable result of contact between the Mediterranean's two greatest and most ambitious powers. The majority of the decisive engagements of the 23-year war took place at sea. Rome emerged victorious, gaining Sicily and command of the sea.

The war began in 264 BC over the ◊Mamertine city of Messina on Sicily. Rome sent an army to the island and raised the siege, defeating Hiero II of Sicily and winning his allegiance, but unable to break the Carthaginian army. In 256 BC Marcus Atilius Regulus launched a Roman invasion of Africa to break the deadlock, but his army was destroyed in battle and the fleet was destroyed in a storm, costing 100,000 lives in all. Without a fleet, the Romans concentrated on capturing the three Carthaginian ports on the island by land. Panoramus (Palermo) fell, but Lilybaeum (Marsala) and Drepana (Trapani) required lengthy sieges.

In 247 BC ◊Hamilcar Barca became the new Carthaginian commander and in 244 BC he concentrated on relieving Drepana, but became stuck in a strategic stalemate there for the next two years. This allowed the Romans time to build a new fleet at a critical moment. Carthage had been slow in organizing the supply lines to Sicily and as a result the garrisons were desperately short of food. Carthage had only two ports left and as the Roman navy was now rebuilt there was no guarantee that the grain fleet would be able to reach them.

This situation proved decisive in 241 BC when the Carthaginian supply fleet was intercepted off the Aegates Islands and destroyed. The garrisons on Sicily were left to face starvation and the Carthaginian council sent orders to Hamilcar that it was up to him to decide what to do next. He chose to surrender, negotiating the terms for the Treaty of Catulus that would end the war. Carthage conceded Sicily to Rome and agreed to pay heavy reparations.

Pulakeshin II (died 642) (or *Pulikesi II*) King 608–42 of the early Chalukya dynasty of the Deccan. He repulsed ◊Harshavardhana's attempted invasion of about 621, defeated the neighbouring kings of the Kadamba and Ganga dynasties, and exchanged ambassadors with the Sassanian shahanshah ◊Chosroes II Aparviz in 625. He was defeated and killed by ◊Narasinghavarman of the Pallava dynasty.

Pulcher, Publius Claudius (lived 3rd century BC) Roman general in the First Punic War (see ◊Punic War, First). He was consul in 249 BC and, as commander of the Roman army in Sicily, led a Roman naval attack on the Carthaginian port of Drepana (see ◊Drepana, Battle of). His fleet outnumbered the Carthaginian fleet, but it was newly trained and inexperienced. Losing the element of surprise, his fleet was broken and suffered heavy losses.

Purana Qila Persian 'the Red Fort' riverside fortress in Delhi, India, with numerous small towers and battlements, built in red sandstone. It was founded in the mid-11th century by Anang Pala, a king of the ◊Rajput Tonar clan. In 1193 it was captured by ◊Qutb al-Din Aibak for ◊Muhammad of Ghur. It became the symbolic centre of Muslim rule in India under the sultans of Delhi and their successors, the Mogul emperors, turning gradually from a military fortress into a palace and administrative centre.

Anang Pala's dynasty was supplanted in 1151 by Vigraharaja III, an early king of the Rajput Chauhana clan, whose grandson ◊Prithviraja Chauhana III led the Rajputs in their resistance to the Muslim invasions of the late 12th century. In 1206 Delhi became the capital of the new sultanate and dynasty of 'slave kings' established by Qutb al-Din Aibak.

Purandhar fort fortress in Maharashtra, India, on a hill rising 518 m/1,700 ft above the surrounding plain, defended mostly by cliffs of perpendicular rock, and surrounded by low

PUNIC WAR, SECOND

War fought between Rome and Carthage and their allies 218–201 BC. It is regarded as one of the most significant conflicts in world history. It featured two of the greatest commanders of the ancient world, ◊Hannibal the Great and Publius Cornelius ◊Scipio (Scipio 'Africanus'); was fought in Italy, Spain, and Africa; claimed hundreds of thousands of lives; and left Rome the undisputed master of the Mediterranean.

The war began with a deliberate act of aggression by Carthage in 219–218 BC in the form of an attack on Saguntum, a Spanish city that was under Rome's guarantee of protection. The attack was part of the Carthaginian preparations for an invasion of Italy and Roman diplomatic appeals over Saguntum were ignored, leading Rome to declare war. The architect of the invasion, Hannibal, immediately launched the campaign and crossed the Alps into Italy before the end of 218 BC.

Hannibal heavily defeated Roman armies at Trebia in 218 BC, Lake Trasimene in 217 BC, and Cannae in 216 BC, and in numerous other smaller engagements, winning the allegiance of several of Rome's allies as a result. Rome itself remained impregnable behind its city walls, and the strategies of Quintus ◊Fabius Maximus and Claudius ◊Marcellus prevented Hannibal from gaining more allies or the chance of a decisive victory. Hannibal had to rely on reinforcements sent from Carthage or Spain, which, due to Roman command of the sea, were frequently intercepted en route or on arrival. By 208 BC Carthage had lost Spain to Rome.

In 204 BC Scipio 'Africanus' invaded Carthage and defeated its home army at the Battle of the Great Plains the following year. Hannibal, whose hold on Italy had been steadily worn down, was recalled to come to his capital's defence. In 202 BC he was defeated by Scipio at Zama and Carthage sued for peace, signing the Treaty of Scipio.

PUNIC WAR, THIRD

War fought between Rome and Carthage 149–146 BC. It was the last of the three wars that had gripped the Mediterranean since 264 BC as the two great empires battled for supremacy. By the Third Punic War, Carthage had been reduced to its capital city and was fighting to avoid final obliteration. Carthage could not win, but fell to Rome with honour.

The Romans were unsure what to do with Carthage. It had surrendered and signed a truce, but resentment festered among many Romans who felt that the humiliation and devastation inflicted by ◊Hannibal the Great had not been truly avenged. Carthage still existed and its state continued as if the two previous wars had never happened. Vocal politicians also reminded the Senate that Carthage had not long abided by the Treaty of Catalus (ending the First Punic War). Thus when King ◊Masinissa of Numidia repeatedly encroached on Carthage's remaining territory, Rome refused to condemn its ally in the hope

that Carthage would strike back in self defence. In 150 BC it did so, breaching the Treaty of Scipio (ending the Second Punic War) and giving Rome reason to declare war.

Carthage soon realized the hopelessness of its position and surrendered. The Romans accepted and ordered the population to evacuate the city so it could be destroyed. Unable to accept such a prospect, Carthaginian nationalism and pride was stirred and the population resumed hostilities to fight to the end for their city. The Romans besieged them for three years (see ◊Carthage, Siege of) before the fortifications were finally breached, under the command of ◊Scipio Aemilianus, grandson of the victor of the Second Punic War. Desperate street fighting failed to stop the Roman advance, and the Byrsa citadel was the site of the last stand. The population was sold into slavery and the city was razed to the ground and ceremoniously cursed.

---

masonry curtain walls, bastions, and gateways flanked by towers. It was fortified about 1350 by Ala al-Din Hasan Gangu, founder of the Bahmani sultanate of the Deccan.

-pur (or *-pore*) Sanskrit *purum* 'fort' suffix in south Asian place names, originally meaning a stronghold or defended settlement, later a township or city.

Pydna, Battle of battle of 168 BC which ended the Third Macedonian War (see ◊Macedonian Wars). The Roman general Lucius Aemilius ◊Paullus defeated the army of Perseus of Macedon (c. 212–c.166 BC).

The battle began accidentally when skirmishing between the two armies' outposts escalated as supporting troops were drawn in. After some confused fighting, each side managed to form a main battle line. During its hurried advance from camp the Macedonian ◊phalanx fell into disorder. The more flexible Roman manipular formation took advantage of this, and centurions (see ◊century) led small parties of men into the gaps in the Macedonian line. Attacked from

the flank and unable to use their unwieldy pikes, the Macedonians were massacred by the Roman swordsmen, 20,000 being killed and 11,000 captured against a Roman loss of only 100. The battle lasted just over an hour.

pyknosis Greek 'close order' Greek military formation in which a distance of 1 m/3 ft separated the right shoulder of each man from the right shoulder of his neighbour – a close order, but not as close as ◊*synaspismos*.

Pylos (present-day *Ano Englianos*) late Bronze-Age palace site in Messenia, Greece, traditionally associated with Nestor, the ancient warrior in *The Iliad*. The palace complex is conventionally centred upon the megaron, a hall with a central hearth surrounded by four pillars supporting a light well/smoke vents. Although labelled Mycenaean, all the evidence points to Pylos being a totally independent state from Mycenae, but sharing a similar culture.

The fortification walls were dismantled in the 13th century BC, leaving only a gateway. By

PYRRHUS (319–272 BC)

King of Epirus (an area of northwestern Greece and southern Albania) from 307 BC. In the early years of his reign he struggled to maintain his throne and retain independence from Macedonian control. In 280 BC he invaded Italy as an ally of the Tarentines against Rome. He twice defeated the Romans, but with such heavy losses that a 'Pyrrhic victory' has come to mean a victory not worth winning. He returned to Epirus in 275 after his defeat at Beneventum, and was killed in street fighting at Argos.

In the turbulent wars and intrigues of the 'Successors' (see ◊Diadochi) to ◊Alexander (III) the Great, Pyrrhus' military career underwent rapid changes of fortune. Having been expelled from his kingdom in about 303/302 BC, where he had ruled as a minor, he served with ◊Demetrius (I) Poliorcetes at Ipsus in 301 BC (see ◊Ipsus, Battle of). Soon afterwards, ◊Ptolemy (I) Soter helped restore him to the throne of Epirus.

He then intervened in Macedonia, gaining territorial concessions, and when Demetrius made himself king there Pyrrhus allied himself with the other *Diadochi* to remove him. He divided Macedon and Thessaly with ◊Lysimachus but by 284 BC had been driven back to Epirus.

When Tarentum appealed to Pyrrhus for help against Rome, he crossed to Italy with 25,000 infantry, 3,000 cavalry, and 20 elephants. Despite bloody ('Pyrrhic') victories at Heraclea in 280 BC (see ◊Heraclea, Battle of, and Ausculum in 279 BC (see ◊Ausculum, Battle of) that won him allies in Samnium, Lucania, Bruttium, and the southern Greek cities of Italy, he failed to conclude peace with Rome. He nevertheless intervened in Sicily and campaigned in person against the Carthaginians on the island between 278 and 276 BC. However, a lack of decisive success drew him back to Italy and defeat at Beneventum against the Romans (see ◊Beneventum, Battle of 275 BC).

He returned to Epirus with about 8,000 of his original force, but was soon involved in Macedonia again, becoming king in 274 BC. This gain was squandered in an unsuccessful war in the Peloponnese and a failed attack on the city of Sparta in 273 BC. He attempted to seize Argos, but was killed by a roof tile thrown by a woman during street fighting.

the end of the 12th century BC the buildings were burned and deserted.

Clay tablets in Linear B from the site record ten detachments (*o-ka*) of watchers based around the coast under named officers and manned rowing stations (see ◊Defence of Pylos).

Pylos, Battle of action at Pylos in southwest Greece in 425 BC, during the ◊Peloponnesian War, that illustrates how the skilful Athenian use of sea power and light troops could defeat Spartan hoplites.

The rocky headland of Pylos had been seized by Athenian forces under ◊Demosthenes. He resisted all attempts by Spartan forces to dislodge him, and when the Athenian fleet arrived in force it trapped 420 Spartan hoplites on Sphakteria, the island south of Pylos. They held out for some time, but when the Athenian ◊Cleon arrived with reinforcements, Demosthenes was able to bring his hoplites and other troops ashore. Though greatly outnumbered, the Spartans confidently engaged the enemy hoplites, but under missile attack they retreated to the north end of the island where 292 survivors eventually surrendered. The Athenian threat to kill their prisoners prevented further Peloponnesian invasions of Attica.

pyolmuban Korean 'extraordinary army' created by King Sukchong (reigned 1095–1105) of the Koryo dynasty to supplement the regular ◊Two Guards and Six Divisions, whose effectiveness had declined. It consisted of a cavalry force (*sin'gigun*) recruited from aristocrats, an infantry force (*sinbogun*) recruited from free peasants, and a 'demon-subduing force' (*hangmagun*) of Buddhist monks.

The *pyolmuban* were used in 1107 for a massive offensive against the Jurchen of Manchuria, occupying part of Jurchen territory and garrisoning it with the Nine Forts (see ◊Koryo frontier fortifications).

Qadesh alternative spelling of ◊Kadesh.

Qadesh, Battle of Battle fought between the Egyptians and Hittites in 1275 BC; see ◊Kadesh, Battle of.

Qarqar, Battle of battle fought in 854 BC between the Neo-Assyrian Great King Shalmaneser III and a coalition of Levantine allies, near the city of Qarqar on the River Arantu (classical Orontes, modern 'Asi). Shalmaneser boasted that he killed 14,000 of his opponents (20,500 in a later account) and used their bodies as a bridge across the river, but it appears that, although they were defeated, the coalition forces were successful in stopping the advance of the Assyrians at the Arantu for over a decade.

Among the 12 coalition allies were King Ahab of Israel, bringing 2,000 chariots and 10,000 infantry, and King Hadad-ezer of Aram (Syria), with 1,200 chariots, 1,200 cavalry, and 20,000 infantry. Other contingents came from Egypt, Que (Cilicia), the Ammonites, the Arabs, and city-states like Hamath and Arvad, collectively forming a force of over 60,000 men.

Qash Bshier small Diocletianic Roman construction at Qash Bshier (Latin *castra praetorii Mobeni*, 'the fort of the governor of Mobeni') in Jordan, which may represent either a frontier fort or a fortified governor's residence. It is noted for the good state of preservation of its defences. It was rectangular in shape and had four massive towers in each corner and a single gateway.

qi Chinese term for a ◊halberd with a blade formed of a hook and an integral point, used from the late Zhou period to the end of the Han (5th century BC to 2nd century AD). It was a development of the *ge*, the halberd with a hooked blade and a separate spearhead or no point at all, used from the Shang to the Han period.

Qi is also a Chinese term (with a different Chinese character) for the head defence of a horse, the shaffron. Chinese shaffrons are found in chariot burials of the Warring States period, about the 5th century BC, and reappear with the arrival of armoured cavalry in China in the 3rd century AD. Chinese horse armour continues in use from then until the 19th century.

qil'a Arabic 'a fort' term variously transliterated in English works on south and central Asia as *killa, kalat, khelat, qalat*, and so on. Derived from it are 'killadar' (*qil'adar* 'fort holder') for commandant and 'killaband' (*qil'a-band*, literally 'fort shut') for besieged. It is also the name of a city and state, Kalat, in Baluchistan.

Qin Shi Huangdi (259–210 BC) (or *Ch'in Shih Huang-ti*) first emperor of China from 221 BC. He succeeded as King Zheng of Qin, the westernmost and strongest of the ◊Warring States, in 246. From 246 to 221 Qin armies, under Wang Jian, conquered the other six states, and in 221 Zheng declared himself Qin Shi Huangdi, 'First Qin Emperor'. His armies conquered the Yue of the south and under Meng Tian defeated the ◊Xiongnu in the ◊Ordos campaign and built the ◊Great Wall of China.

After his death, the revolts of ◊Chen She and ◊Xiang Yu brought down the Qin dynasty.

Qizilbash Persian 'red tops' heretical and eclectic Islamic sect, associated with Sufi mysticism, originating in northwestern Iran in the 15th century. The Qizilbash became a military brotherhood and defeated the rulers of Iran to found the Iranian Safavid dynasty under Ismail I in 1501. They were suppressed by Shah Abbas I in the 16th century.

In the mid-15th century Junaid, leader of the Safaviyya order and shaykh of Ardabil, realized the military potential of his followers and led them in holy wars against the Circassians. His son Shaykh Haidar introduced the wearing of a uniform headdress, the *taj-i-haidari*, which had 12 red stripes and gained the Qizilbash their name. Haidar continued the war against the Circassians, and attracted many Turkoman adventurers to join him. He was succeeded by his son Ismail, who gained the support of five major Turkoman tribes. They defeated the White Sheep Turkomen, the rulers of Iran, and Ismail became shah and founder of the Iranian Safavid dynasty. Under the early Safavids, the Qizilbash formed the military elite of the state.

quadrireme galley with four files of oarsmen on each side, Anglicized from the Latin words for 'four-oared' (see ◊bireme). There were probably two banks of oars, each oar rowed by two men.

quaestor junior Roman magistrate whose primary role was to oversee the finances of individual provinces under the Republic. Quaestors often commanded units in the army when the governor of the province fought a campaign.

quinquereme galley with five files of oarsmen on each side, Anglicized from the Latin words for 'five-oared' (see ◊bireme. There were probably three banks of oars, the oars in one rowed by single oarsmen and in the other two by two oarsmen each.

quintain from Latin *quintanus* 'street in a Roman camp' in medieval Europe, a post with an object attached as a target for tilting practice with a couched ◊lance. It was sometimes able to swivel on impact. The quintain occasionally consisted of a dummy dressed in a ◊hauberk and shield fixed to the post. Quintain use, reported in the 12th century, seems to have swiftly followed the development of the charge with couched lances in warfare.

Qutang Gorge, Battle of (or *Ch'ü-t'ang*) battle in July 1371 in which Ming forces under commanders Liao Yongzhong and Tang He defeated the Xia state in the Sichuan province of China.

◊Zhu Yuanzhang's Ming dynasty had unified most of China, and now Ming forces moved against the Xia state. While another column invaded Sichuan from the north, a riverfleet sailed up the Yangtze until it was halted at the narrow Qutang Gorge. The Xia defenders had blocked the gorge with suspension bridges from which catapults fired on enemy ships. Liao eventually destroyed the bridges with cannon-fire and broke through. The Xia capital soon fell, and the state surrendered.

Qutb al-Din Aibak (died 1210) ('Pole Star of the Faith') Turkish ◊ghulam of Muhammad of Ghur, and the most trusty of his lieutenants. In 1192 he was appointed viceroy of the Indian territories captured by Muhammad, and captured Delhi in 1193 and Benares (modern Varanasi) in 1194. He became sultan of Delhi 1206–10.

He established the line of Slave Kings who ruled until the accession of ◊Jalal al-Din Firuz Shah in 1290.

Qutuz (died 1260) first Mameluke sultan 1259–60, victor over the Mongols at Ain Jalut (see ◊Ain Jalut, Battle of), and conqueror of Damascus in 1260. Qutuz's time in command was brief, but his considered strategy and inspirational leadership inflicted the first major defeat on a Mongol force. He was assassinated soon after his conquest of Damascus.

R

rab haila Aramaic term for an Achaemenid Persian garrison commander, notably in 6th–5th-century BC Egypt. Generally Iranian, a *rab haila* would command several ◊*degels*.

Raby castle castle in County Durham, England, 10 km/6 mi northeast of Barnard Castle. Originally the residence of the Neville family, who received a licence to crenellate (build battlements) in 1379, the castle is generally held to represent the best of 14th century defensive ideas.

The castle was surrounded by a curtain wall, with towers, a strong gatehouse, and a moat. A barbican. Although considerably rebuilt over the years, the outward appearance still retains the original lines.

Radagaisus Germanic leader, probably a Goth, who led a large invasion of various tribes into Roman territory in 405. He was defeated by the West Roman general ◊Stilicho at Faestulae (see ◊Faestulae, Battle of), captured, and taken to Rome where he was executed.

The numbers of his followers have been grossly exaggerated, some accounts saying that there were as many as 500,000. Even taking into account women, children, and noncombatants, a tenth of that number is more likely, given the ease with which they were defeated by Stilicho's 20,000 men.

Radcot Bridge, Battle of battle fought in 1387 on the River Thames, England, between Richard II's supporters under Robert de Vere, Earl of Oxford, and rebel lords under the earls of Gloucester, Arundel and Warwick – the Lords Appellant. A rebel victory empowered them and led to the Merciless Parliament.

Oxford raised his force in Cheshire and headed to support the king in London. He attempted to evade the rebels by crossing the Thames at Radcot Bridge near Eynsham. The earls of Derby and Nottingham joined the Appellants. One force faced Oxford and another approached from the rear. The royal force was defeated, but Oxford escaped across the river and fled to France.

Raesana, Battle of poorly documented battle in 243 between the Persians and Romans under the emperor Gordian III. Both sides claimed Raesana as a victory. Given that the Roman army retreated afterwards, during which Gordian was murdered, it seems probable that the Persians had the advantage.

Raglan castle castle in Wales, between Newport and Monmouth, Gwent. The ornate castle-residence was built in the 15th century by Sir William ap Thomas on the site of a former Norman ◊motte-and-bailey work.

The motte was occupied by a massive six-sided keep, the 'yellow tower of Gwent' surrounded by its own ditch. The lines of the original bailey were occupied by the body of the castle: a towered curtain wall surrounding a great hall, domestic offices, apartments, and storerooms. The whole castle was fitted out in a very ornate manner with fountains, gardens, and a bowling green.

Ragnar Lothbrok Danish Viking leader who led a fleet up the River Seine in France to capture Paris in 845. His sons (especially ◊Halfdan) went on to lead the Danes in England.

Raichur fortress in southern India, dominating the military and commercial routes between the Kistna and Tungabhadra rivers, protected on one side by a steep hill and on the other three by a deep ditch and stone wall, each 3.5 m/12 ft long and 0.9 m/3 ft wide. Raichur was founded in 1294 by the Tamil prince Gore Gangaya Ruddivara.

It belonged to the Hindu rulers of ◊Warangal until seized by ◊Malik Kafur in the early 14th century and added to the sultanate of Delhi. Raichur was later held by Ala al-Din Hasan Gangu (ruled 1347–58), founder of the Bahmani sultanate of the Deccan. It withstood sieges by the Hindu armies of ◊Vijayanagar in 1378, 1398, and 1443 before being captured by the Hindus in 1490.

Raisen Sanskrit *Rajavasini* 'the king's dwelling place' hill fortress of Hindu rulers in

Bhopal, central India, on a northern spur of the Vindhayan mountain range, defended by a wall of massive sandstone blocks with nine gates.

It remained an independent ◊Rajput stronghold until the end of the 15th century, after which its chiefs paid tribute to the Rajput kings of Malwa, ruling from ◊Chitor.

Rajaraja I king 985–1018 of the later Tamil Chola dynasty. He conquered Kalinga, Vengi, and other Tamil lands and by 1005 was master of the entire south. He built a navy with which he protected his maritime commerce and launched expeditions to seize northern Lanka (Sri Lanka) and the Maldives.

Rajendra Deva I king 1012–42 of the later Tamil Chola dynasty, son of ◊Rajaraja I. He secured his existing borders by victories over the Chalukyas, expanded the navy, and launched a maritime expedition, unique in Indian history, against the pirate-infested coasts of Burma (modern Myanmar), Malaysia, and Sumatra.

He also used the navy to support an overland expedition which defeated Mahipala I, the Pala ruler of Bengal.

Rajput (Sanskrit *Rajyaputra* 'the sons of kings') military and ruling class of Hindu society from the 6th century to modern times. Probably descended from invaders such as the ◊White Huns, and other groups, Rajput chieftains ruled northern and central India and parts of Afghanistan until the coming of the Muslim invaders in the 12th century.

They developed a heroic culture in which honour was regarded of supreme importance and courage, skill-at-arms, and other martial attributes were held in the highest esteem. The Rajput kings encouraged commerce, patronized scholars, and erected great public buildings to mark their wealth and prestige. However, clinging to outdated military theories and rarely able to patch up their ancestral quarrels, the Rajputs were rapidly defeated by their Muslim invaders. Many were occupied; those that were not paid tribute, rebelling whenever Muslim power grew weak.

Rama Tibodi I (1312–) (or *Ramadhipati*) Thai founder of the Ayutthaya kingdom. He was originally a son-in-law and general of the king of Utong, a Mon state in modern southern Thailand. When the king died in 1350 the general seized the throne, taking the title Rama Tibodi (his personal name is unknown). He moved his capital to Ayutthaya, a commercial centre on an island in the Menam River, which remained the Thai capital for over 400 years.

Before seizing power, Rama Tibodi made Utong a significant regional power by conquering territory from Sukhothai, the first Thai kingdom (founded in 1238). As king he defeated Cambodia in 1352, making the Khmer king his vassal. He codified Thai law and became a Buddhist monk in 1361. His son Ramesuen, mistrusted because of the lack of military ability he had displayed in the Khmer war, was deposed by Rama Tibodi's brother-in-law, who reigned from 1370 as Boromoraja I.

Ramlah, Battle of (1101) battle of 6 September 1101 between ◊Baldwin I of the Christian Kingdom of Jerusalem and a Fatimid (Muslim) army in the Holy Land. Alarmed at the loss of the Syrian ports of Arsuf and Caesarea, the Fatimid vizier ◊al-Afdal sent troops to attack Jerusalem. They were surprised and defeated in a dawn attack at Ramlah by Baldwin's much smaller force.

Allegedly numbering 11,000 cavalry and 21,000 foot soldiers, the Fatimid Egyptian force was surprised by Baldwin's 260 knights and 900 foot soldiers. The Christian forces charged in five lines, but it was not until Baldwin led in the reserve that the inexperienced Egyptians broke, with heavy losses.

Ramlah, Battle of (1102) battle of 17 May 1102 in which ◊Baldwin I of the Christian Kingdom of Jerusalem was overwhelmed by a large Fatimid (Muslim) army from Egypt under Sharaf, son of the vizier al-Afdal, in the Holy Land, but escaped to return and defeat them.

Sharaf led about 20,000 troops against Ramlah. Baldwin's main army was at Jaffa (now Tel Aviv, Israel), and the 500 horsemen he was leading on a reconaissance encountered the Fatimid force by chance. He led a charge into the enemy, from which only he and a few knights escaped to take refuge in the tower at Ramlah. The Egyptians soon stormed it, taking 100 knightly prisoners and killing many. Baldwin again escaped, by boat. On 27 May, reinforced by crusaders, he led a force out of Jaffa and routed the Fatimid army.

Ramses II or *Rameses II*; known as *Ramses the Great* king (pharaoh) of ancient Egypt about 1279–1213 BC, the son of Seti I. He campaigned successfully against the Hittites, and built two rock temples at Abu Simbel in southern Egypt.

Ramses III or *Rameses III* king (pharaoh) of ancient Egypt about 1187–1156 BC. He won victories over the Libyans and the ◊Peoples of the Sea and asserted his control over Palestine.

ransom in the medieval period, money paid to recover a person captured in war, probably originating in the value placed on a man payable as fine for killing him, such as the wergild in Anglo-Saxon England. In the later medieval period it was a lucrative practice, notably for English captains in the ◊Hundred Years' War. Failure to pay could mean execution or imprisonment of the captive.

Ranthambhor Sanskrit *Ranastambhapura* 'the place of the pillar of war' city and fortress in Rajasthan, India, located at the top of an isolated crag, surrounded by a massive wall strengthened with towers and bastions. It was founded by the Jadon clan of ◊Rajputs, probably in the 10th century.

In the late 12th century it was taken by ◊Prithviraja Chauhana III, whose son Govindaraj founded a separate state there about 1200. ◊Qutb al-Din Aibak, Sultan of Delhi, seized the fortress in 1226, but it was reoccupied by the Chauhanas after his death until recovered by the Muslims under Sultan ◊Ala al-Din Khilji in 1301. It became part of the Bahmani kingdom of the Deccan in the mid-14th century and in 1446 passed to Malwa, one of its successor states.

Raphia, Battle of encounter between Ptolemy IV of Egypt and the King of Syria, ◊Antiochus (III) the Great, in 217 BC. It illustrates the superiority of Indian war elephants to African, and is interesting for Ptolemy's use of native Egyptian troops for the first time.

Ptolemy had 73 African elephants, 5000 cavalry and either 50,000 or 70,000 infantry, matched by Antiochus' force of 62,000 infantry, 6000 cavalry and 102 Indian elephants. Both sides used their elephants on the wings, with cavalry either behind or alongside them. But Ptolemy's smaller African elephants were mostly unwilling to face Antiochus' Indian elephants and their flight carried away much of his left wing, which Antiochus pursued off the field. Ptolemy took refuge behind his phalanx, and his presence encouraged it to advance and defeat Antiochus. The Syrian galloped back to retrieve the situation but, finding his whole line in retreat, could do nothing.

rath medieval Irish term for a native fortification, usually a stone ringwork, in existence before the introduction of castles to Ireland by the Normans.

Ravenna, Battle of (257) encounter in AD 257 between a large group of Alamannic raiders who had penetrated as far as Ravenna, Italy, and an army hastily raised by the Roman Senate around the nucleus of the Praetorian Guard. The raiders were forced to withdraw by the advancing Roman army.

After this, the Roman emperor Publius Licinius Egnatius Gallienus banned senators from military commands.

Ravenna, Battle of (432) battle of 432 at Ravenna, Italy, between ◊Aetius, the West Roman ◊*magister militum*, and Boniface, Count of Africa. Boniface defeated Aetius on the battlefield, but was mortally wounded. Aetius thus emerged as the unchallenged power in the West.

Ravenna, Siege of (490–93) final victory of ◊Theodoric the Great's Ostrogoths over King ◊Odoacer of Italy, besieged in Ravenna, Italy, from 490 to 493. Following his defeat of 11 August 490 on the Adda (see ◊Adda, Battle of), Odoacer sought refuge in Ravenna with the remnants of his mercenary army, where he held out for $2\frac{1}{2}$ years before suing for peace on 27 February 493.

Ravenna's situation amongst marshes and lagoons made it nearly impregnable. As it also had an excellent harbour, it could only be properly besieged in a combined land and sea operation. As a result Odoacer easily held out until a naval blockade combined with Theodoric's promise to share power induced him to sue for peace.

Ravenna, Siege of (538–39) victory by the Romans, led by ◊Belisarius, over the Goths under King ◊Witiges in 538–39. With the fall of the city of Ravenna and capture of the Gothic king, the Romans controlled all of Italy except for some regions of the north. Before Belisarius could complete the destruction of the Gothic kingdom he was recalled to Constantinople by ◊Justinian who feared Belisarius might set himself up as the Western emperor.

After failing to capture Rome in 538 (see ◊Rome, Siege of) the Goths fell back on Ravenna where they were besieged by Belisarius. Meanwhile, the Roman general had to contend with a new threat posed by a force of Burgundians sent by the Frankish king Theodebert to assist the Goths. Although they helped another Gothic army capture Milan from the Romans, they were prevented from linking up with Witiges by new Roman reinforcements. Witiges surrendered when fire destroyed his food supplies.

Razdarit (lived 14th–15th centuries) King of the Mons of Pegu in Lower Burma, 1385–1423. He fought a long and complex war against the Burmese kingdom of Ava, upholding Mon independence against Avan attempts to reunify Burma.

On Razdarit's accession his uncle rebelled, offering Pegu as a vassal state to

Myinkyiswasawke, King of Ava 1368–1401, in return for Burmese support. The Burmese and their Shan allies took the city of Prome and used it as a base for further attacks but failed to take Pegu. In 1404 Razdarit opened a second front by intervening against a Burmese puppet-king in the coastal kingdom of Arakan. In 1406 he sailed up the Irrawaddy River and almost reached Ava. He besieged Prome, but it was relieved by the Burmese king Minhkaung. Another riverborne raid behind Burmese lines forced Minhkaung to make peace in 1408. Fighting resumed soon afterwards. In 1410 the Burmese ejected Razdarit's ally from Arakan, but he defeated them in the Irrawaddy delta. In 1415 the Burmese prince Minrekyawswa overran most of the Mon kingdom, but was forced to withdraw by a Shan attack on Ava. Minrekyawswa was killed campaigning in the delta in 1417 and there were no further Avan attacks.

Reading, Battle of conflict between the Danes and the Saxons near Reading, England, in 871, in which the Danes defeated the Saxons. The main Saxon army of Wessex, under the command of King Ethelred and his brother Alfred, was reinforced by Ethelwulf's shire levies who scored an initial victory over the invading Danes at Englefield (see ◊Englefield, Battle of) four days before the Battle of Reading. This time the Danes had the upper hand, driving back the combined Saxon army and killing their ◊ealdorman, Ethelwulf.

Reconquista Spanish 'reconquest' Christian defeat and expulsion of the Moors from Spain during the 9th to 15th centuries. The Muslims conquered Spain between 711 and 728. Tradition commences the reconquest with the activities of the Visigothic nobleman Pelayo about 718. In the 10th century the Christian kingdom of León was established, and ◊El Cid became king of Valencia in the 11th century. Las Navas de Tolosa in 1212 (see ◊Las Navas de Tolosa, Battle of) was a key victory by Alfonso VIII of Castile. ◊James (I) the Conqueror of Aragón won the Balearic Islands in the early 13th century. Granada (see ◊Granada, Siege of) fell to the Catholic monarchs Ferdinand V (1452–1516) and Isabella I (1451–1504) to complete the reconquest in the 15th century.

Red Cliff, Battle of the battle in 208 in which an alliance master-minded by ◊Zhuge Liang defeated ◊Cao Cao, who invaded south China with a huge but dispirited northern army. This battle allowed Zhuge Liang's master Liu Bei to establish himself in the southwest, defining the frontiers of the ◊Three Kingdoms of China period.

The smaller southern army under Zhuge Liang held the Yangtze River at the Red Cliff. Cao's first attack from the river failed, and he regrouped on the north bank. One southern officer sailed across with fireships, claiming to be a defector until he got close enough to burn the northern fleet. Simultaneously a hidden southern force attacked Cao's camp by land. Cao's army fled.

Red Eyebrows, rebellion of the peasant rebellion AD 18–27 in China. This was the most serious revolt provoked by natural disasters following the usurpation of ◊Wang Mang in China.

The Red Eyebrows were founded by Fan Chong in Shandong and took their name from the red paint they applied to their foreheads for recognition. They were a disorderly movement with no military organization. Nevertheless they defeated local troops in AD 18 and a large imperial army at Chengchang in the winter of 22. Thereafter they spread out from Shandong, and in 25 took the capital Changan from the short-lived Green Woodsmen-backed regime of Liu Xuan (see ◊Green Woodsmen, rebellion of the). They used up all the supplies in Changan, however, and with no administrative base, had to go out raiding again. Finally trying to return to the eastern plains they were confronted by ◊Han Guangwudi's superior army and surrendered on 27 March.

Red Fort fortress in Delhi, India; see ◊Purana Qila.

Red Jackets, rebellion of the peasant rising 1211–25 in the Chinese province of Shandong against foreign Jurchen rule, begun for economic reasons but aggravated after 1215 when the Jurchen resettled in Shandong refugees from the Mongol campaigns in China (see ◊China, Mongol campaigns in). The rebels, led by Yang Aner, drove Jurchen forces out of most of Shandong, but a Jurchen counterattack regained much territory, and Yang died on campaign.

One rebel group, under Li Quan, went over to the Song of southern China when they invaded Shandong in 1218. Red Jacket troops were the basis of Quan's and his son ◊Li Tan's power. Other Red Jacket groups resisted all invaders until defeated by the Mongols in 1225.

Red Turbans, rebellion of the revolts 1351–63 against the Mongol Yuan dynasty in China, inspired by messianic Buddhist ideals that originated in the 1330s. The revolts originated from a rebellion among workers on a great Yellow River flood-control project in

1351. The rebels proclaimed their leader as emperor of a restored Song dynasty and expanded widely in northern China. They broke up into factions, however, and in 1359 were overwhelmed by the Mongol warlord Chaghan Temür. The Song court was finally destroyed in 1363.

A southern branch of the Red Turbans proclaimed the Tienwan ('Heaven Consummated') kingdom in Hubei in 1351 and expanded rapidly in the Yangtze valley. They attacked Nanjing in 1352, winning a battle at Yifeng Bridge (see ◊Yifeng Bridge, Battle of) but failing to hold the city. In 1357 Chen Yuliang seized control of the movement and proclaimed the Han kingdom. He fought against ◊Zhu Yuanzhang's Ming state – also a Red Turban offshoot – until beaten at Longwan (see ◊Longwan, Battle of) and Poyang (see ◊Poyang, Battle of).

Regensburg fortress (Roman *Castra Regina*) Roman legionary fortress on the Danube frontier notable for having the best-preserved gatehouse in the Roman Empire, the Porta Praetoria. Regensburg was founded during the reign of Marcus Aurelius (AD 161–80) to protect the frontier of the province of Raetia, and was the base for the 3rd Legion *Italica* for most of its occupation.

The fortress defences followed the 'playing card' shape (rectangular with rounded corners) with the short axis facing the River Danube. The gates were built to project completely beyond the curtain wall. Narrow, round-fronted towers flanked large guard chambers and only a single portal allowed passage. The first and second floors of the towers had wide window openings to serve as artillery embrasures.

Regulus, Marcus Atilius (died c. 250 BC) Roman general during the First Punic War (see ◊Punic War, First) who, despite early successes, was heavily defeated in an invasion of Africa in 256 BC.

As consul in 267 BC, Regulus had defeated the Sallentini of southern Italy and for his second consulship in 256 BC he was given command of the Roman fleet in Sicily, winning a decisive naval victory at Ecnomus (see ◊Ecnomus, Battle of). He landed with an army in Africa in an attempt to pressurize Carthage into withdrawing its forces from Sicily and though defeating the Carthaginians at Adys, his army was annihilated near Tunis and he was captured.

Reims campaign inconclusive initial campaign by the Roman governor Julian (later the emperor Julian the Apostate) in 356 against the Alamanni who had overrun much of eastern Gaul. Although the Romans had a number of small successes, they were prevented from concentrating their forces at Reims when an Alamannic ambush nearly destroyed two legions forming the army's rearguard.

The Romans did succeed in recovering Cologne and they repulsed an assault on the town of Sens.

Reise medieval German 'journey' crusades undertaken by the Teutonic Knights (see ◊Military Order) in the 14th century. They were keen to attract knights to take part in crusade against the pagan Lithuanians, and the *Reise* offered this opportunity. Many significant 14th-century figures, including Henry Bolingbroke (later ◊Henry IV of England), took part.

In order to glamorize campaigning in a desolate region, the Knights set up a Table of Honour to celebrate the chivalry of its visitors.

René (II) of Anjou (lived 15th century) duke of Lorraine and military ally of the Swiss Confederation who fought against ◊Charles the Bold 1475–77. In 1475 René joined the League of Constance, the opponents of Charles the Bold, who took the opportunity to seize his duchy. So exiled, the young duke was determined to recover his inheritance. He led the cavalry which supported the Swiss foot ◊phalanxes, playing a notable role in the crushing victories of Mürten in 1476 (see ◊Mürten, Battle of) and Nancy in 1477 (see ◊Nancy, Battle of).

Rennes castle castle of the counts of Rennes and dukes of Brittany by the River Vilaine, Ille-et-Vilaine *département*, Brittany, France. The ◊motte-and-bailey castle stood where the Square de la Motte is now. The ◊Bayeux Tapestry shows a timber palisade and roofed keep, a gateway and stairway up the motte, and a ditch and outer bank.

It was besieged by ◊William (I) the Conqueror in 1064, disputed by Charles de Blois and Jean de Montfort in the 1340s, and besieged by Henry of Lancaster in 1356. Old Rennes was destroyed by fire in 1720, and the castle was neglected in the newly designed city.

restor medieval French in the medieval period, the replacement of horses lost in battle or campaign by a knight's lord. This was a very important aspect of the financial relationship between lord and vassal or military employee.

Restormel castle castle in England, just north of Lostwithiel, Cornwall. Originally a wooden ◊motte-and-bailey castle, in the 12th century it was replaced by a shell keep. A stone wall was built around the mound, the ground levelled down within, and two-storied buildings erected in the courtyard. A ditch was then excavated around the mound. It later became a royal castle, occupied by the Black Prince in 1354 and 1365. It fell into disuse in the following century.

rgod conscript soldiers of the Tibetan empire. Rgod served for a fixed term in the regiment raised from their ◊stonsde. In 654 the Tibetan population was formally divided into rgod soldiers and gyung workers. A similar division may have been applied as early as the reign of ◊Namri Songtsen, since the stonsde system was already in operation.

Rhandeia, Battle of battle fought in AD 62 between the Parthians and a Roman army invading Armenia led by the Roman governor Lucius Caesennius ◊Paetus. The Parthians under Vologeses surprised Paetus's scattered forces, routing them and besieging the main camp. Paetus surrendered, pledging that Rome would abandon Armenia.

Although Gnaeus Domitius ◊Corbulo was on his way with a relief column, Paetus led his army in a disordered flight, giving up his baggage and abandoning his wounded.

Rhodes castle stronghold in the Old Town of Rhodes, Greece, with an excellent harbour. It was built by the Knights Hospitaller in the 14th century as an outpost of Christianity near the coast of Asia Minor that could threaten Muslim sea routes. It withstood sieges in 1480–81 (see ◊Rhodes, Siege of 1480–81) and 1522, but surrendered to the Ottoman sultan Suleiman the Magnificent in 1522.

Eight Langues (tongues) or 'nationalities' of knights each defended their own tower and section of wall.

Rhodes, Siege of (305–304 BC) siege of the town of Rhodes, on the island of the same name in the Aegean, in 305–304 BC, during the conflict between ◊Antigonus (I) Monophthalmus of Macedon and ◊Ptolemy (I) Soter of Egypt. It earned Antigonus' son, ◊Demetrius (I) Poliorcetes, his nickname (Poliorcetes means 'the Besieger') because of the sophisticated siege techniques he employed. But the Rhodians defeated all his efforts and he eventually made peace.

In his attacks on Rhodes' harbours, for example, Demetrius built sheds to protect his catapults. These were mounted on merchantmen surrounded by a floating barrier of logs joined with spikes to prevent ramming. On the landward side he constructed a huge ◊helepolis

equipped with artillery to protect his forces while they were filling the moat and manning the rams.

Rhodes, Siege of (1480–81) attack of 1480–81 against the stronghold of the Knights Hospitaller in Rhodes, on the island of the same name in the Aegean, by the Ottoman Turks under ◊Mehmet (II) the Conqueror during their period of expansion. The Ottomans abandoned the siege on the death of the sultan, but Rhodes fell to their forces after a second siege in 1522.

Peter d'Aubusson led the Knights, and was wounded in the head. The gunner Master George deserted the Turks for the Christians, in the course of the siege, but was hanged as a spy.

Rhuddlan castle castle in Wales, 39 km/24 mi northwest of Chester. Built by Edward I in 1277 as part of his Welsh strategy, it appears to be an early essay into the concentric form, later perfected in ◊Beaumaris castle.

A rectangular wall with twin gatehouse towers at opposite corners and residential towers at the other corners sat inside a somewhat irregularly shaped curtain wall with towers. A ditch fed from the nearby River Clwyd surrounded this, and an earth rampart with a palisade surrounded the ditch.

Riade, Battle of battle of 933 in which the German king ◊Henry (I) the Fowler inflicted the first significant defeat on the ◊Magyars who had terrorized Europe for half a century.

Henry led a cavalry army to intercept and destroy a Magyar raiding force. Because he feared that the Magyars would take flight once they saw his heavy cavalry, Henry masked them with Thuringian light horse. Having encouraged the enemy horse-archers to close, Henry charged with his knights and shattered the Magyar force.

ribaudequin (or **ribauds**) early light guns, most commonly used as massed small-scale artillery. The term, frequently mentioned in 14th century, could also be used to refer to guns in general.

Edward III of England had several guns clamped together with touchholes so that they could all be fired at once. At Verona, Italy, in 1387, 144 guns were placed together in 3 tiers in 4 sections of 12 tubes each. Four horses pulled the cart in which they were placed with a gunner on each tier, with the whole tower reaching a height of 60 m/20 ft.

ricasso European medieval term for a blunt section of a sword blade, next to the hilt, which could be gripped by the forefinger to increase control over the blade. This feature first appeared on 15th-century swords, and was usual by the evolution of the rapier in the 16th century.

Richard (I) the Lionheart (1157–1199)
king of England 1189–99. He defeated ◊Philip (II) Augustus at Fréteval in 1194 and Gisors in 1198, and ◊Saladin at Arsuf (see ◊Arsuf, Battle of) in 1191. Despite a careful fortress strategy designed to recover Jerusalem in 1192, he was thwarted and returned to Europe, first spending a year in German captivity. He was killed by a crossbow bolt while besieging Châlus-Chabrol in 1199, and left no heir.

Richard's experience in warfare came from controlling his rebellious vassals in Poitou in the 1170s and against his father, ◊Henry II, in 1183. He took up Henry's plans to recover Jerusalem on his accession in 1189 and set out to establish bases for crusades in Sicily in 1190 and Cyprus, which he took in 1191. Engaging in the siege of Acre, which he brought to a swift conclusion, he set off down the coast to Jaffa, conducting a fighting march against Saladin.

Once ransomed from the Germans, Richard recovered lands in France taken by Philip. In the Vexin, where he built◊ Chateau Gaillard, the great castle on the Seine, and in the Touraine and Poitou, he thwarted the French king's every manoeuvre.

Richard III (1452–1485)
king of England from 1483. The son of Richard, Duke of York, he was created Duke of Gloucester by his brother Edward IV, and distinguished himself in the Wars of the Roses (see ◊Roses, Wars of the). In 1485 Henry, Earl of Richmond, raised a rebellion, and Richard III was defeated and killed at Bosworth (see ◊Bosworth, Battle of).

Richborough fort
(Roman *Rutupis*) Roman fort on the east coast of Kent, England, that formed part of the defences of the Saxon Shore in Britain. It was built about AD 275 to guard a natural harbour in the Wantsum Channel (which no longer exists). Its construction introduced into Britain some of the latest innovations in military architecture, notably external bastions and an emphasis on defence.

The fort was rectangular in shape with free-standing walls 3.5 m/11.5 ft thick, enhanced by externally projecting towers that were round at the corners and square on the sides. It was surrounded by two deep ditches. The only gate was in the west; small posterns were built into the north and south sides. Occupation continued into the 4th century.

Richmond castle
castle in England, 19 km/12 mi southwest of Darlington, Yorkshire.

The castle was begun in 1071 and completed in the following century, and although much of it is now ruinous, it has the greatest collection of early Norman masonry outside the ◊Tower of London.

Located above the River Swale, the plan is triangular, and the great keep (30 m/100 ft high) dates from 1150, but is built upon a much earlier gatehouse. Scollard's Hall, overlooking the river, is one of the oldest stone buildings in the country.

Ricimer (456–472)
Roman officer of Germanic origin who rose to become the most powerful man in the Western Roman Empire. During most of his career he was the power behind the throne, playing a greater role in internal politics than in the defence of the Empire.

Ricimer's father was a Suevi, from the region in southern Germany later called Swabia (now part of Baden-Württemberg). His mother was the daughter of the Visigoth king, Wallia. Little is known of his career before 456 when he was made the most senior military commander in the Roman army (◊*magister militum*) by the emperor, Marcus Maecilius Avitius, and he met with immediate success in a campaign against the Vandals in Sicily and Corsica.

When Avitius fell from favour with the army, Ricimer deposed him in October 456. After virtually ruling the Western Roman Empire alone for six months, he backed Majorian as the next emperor. Ricimer turned against him, however, when he proved to be an active and successful military commander. He staged a mutiny, which was followed by Majorian's abdication in 461 and murder.

Because of his Germanic origin, Ricimer was unable to become emperor himself, so he ruled Italy through a series of puppet emperors who were deposed whenever they became troublesome. One of these was Anthemius (r. 467–72) who turned against Ricimer with the support of a band of Visigoths. Ricimer responded by marching on Rome, taking the city by assault and executing Anthemius. Shortly afterwards Ricimer died, leaving Italy in a state of anarchy.

Ridefort, Gerard de (died 1189)
Seneschal (commander) of the Knights Templar (see ◊Military Order) in 1183 and Grand Master 1185–89. He was defeated at Cresson and blamed for the Christian defeat at Hattin (see ◊Hattin, Battle of) in 1187. He died at the siege of Acre in 1189 (see ◊Acre, Siege of 1189–91).

He was a knight of Flemish origin who arrived in the Holy Land in the 1170s and by 1179 was Marshal of the Kingdom of Jerusalem. Failing to aquire an heiress, he turned to the Temple for preferment, and supported ◊Guy de Lusignan against Raymond of Tripoli in the power politics which made Guy king. When Raymond gave free passage to a Muslim scouting force in 1187, Gerard launched an attack on it. Unfortunately, he led 140 knights against several thousand Muslims, against the advice of the Master of the Hospitallers, who was killed in the ensuing massacre on 1 May. Gerard was also blamed for the advance toward Tiberias which led to the disastrous defeat at Hattin on 4 July.

ringwork simple, approximately circular bank-and-ditch fortification, usually employed for small, compact enclosures. The ringwork was an early form of castle, found throughout northwestern Europe.

◊Le Plessis-Grimoult castle in Normandy, France, possessed a 4-m-/13-ft-high rampart with a curtain wall of stone. Early post-Conquest British examples are Penmaen in Glamorgan, Wales, and Sulgrave in Northamptonshire, England.

Rio Salado, Battle of the battle fought on 30 October 1340 between Alfonso XI of Castile, with other Spanish and Portuguese allies, and Granadan and Moroccan Muslim troops besieging Tarifa, at the southernmost tip of Spain. The Christian victory enabled them to take ports along the Strait of Gibraltar and marked an end to North African intervention in the Iberian peninsula.

The Marinid Sultan Abu al-Hasan invaded Spain with a large army and besieged Tarifa in September. The Christians offered battle, the Castilians attacking the Moroccan troops while Alfonso IV of Portugal engaged the Granadans, but it was a sortie into the Muslim rear by the garrison which won the battle.

Robert (I) the Frisian (lived 11th century) count of Flanders 1071–93. Robert usurped the countship from his nephew Arnulf III, the latter being killed at the battle of Cassel (west central Germany) in 1071. Rebellions against Robert followed but were put down. He planned an invasion of England with the Danes in 1085, but it was abandoned on the death of his ally Cnut IV of Denmark. He maintained the tradition of Flemish interest in Asia Minor, fighting for the Byzantine Emperor ◊Alexius (I) Comnenus against the Turks in 1090.

Robert (II) Curthose (1052–1136) duke of Normandy 1087–1106. He was the son of William the Conqueror, and a noted crusader 1096–1100. When the English throne passed to his younger brother William II in 1087, Robert was unable to recover it by war. In 1106 Robert again attempted to recover England from ◊Henry I, but was defeated at Tinchebrai (see ◊Tinchebrai, Battle of) and imprisoned until his death.

Robert won undying fame for his role on the First Crusade, especially for his charge at Ascalon in 1099 (see ◊Ascalon, Battle of) when he captured the Egyptian banner. He turned down the offer to rule in Jerusalem, preferring to return home.

Robert Guiscard (born c. 1025) (actual name *Robert de Hauteville*) duke of Apulia 1059–85, Norman adventurer, conqueror of southern Italy, and invader of the Byzantine Empire. Arriving in Italy in around 1046, Robert, nicknamed 'Guiscard' (wily), began with one castle and rose to dominate all of southern Italy. He helped defeat Pope Leo IX at Civitate in 1053 (see ◊Civitate, Battle of), took Dyrrachium (modern Durres, Albania) in 1082, and defeated Corfu in 1084.

After his defeat of Pope Leo IX, Robert became a papal vassal in 1059, when he was made duke of Apulia. In a series of campaigns he conquered the last Byzantine territories, fortresses, and ports, taking Bari in 1071 (see ◊Bari, Siege of 1068–71). This enabled him to support his brother Roger's invasion of Sicily 1060–71. Guiscard besieged Dyrrachium 1081–82, and eventually took it despite a naval defeat by the Venetians. He defeated ◊Alexius (I) Comnenus decisively outside the city walls.

Robert (I) the Bruce (1275–1329) king of Scots from 1306, successful guerrilla fighter, victor at Bannockburn (see ◊Bannockburn, Battle of) over the English, and restorer of Scotland's independence.

Bruce murdered his main rival in 1306, enhancing his own claim to the Scottish throne. Prior to this he had been loyal to Edward I in the war against William ◊Wallace. Initially his resources were insufficient for anything more than harassment, but victory at Loudun Hill (see ◊Loudoun Hill, Battle of) displayed his tactical skill.

Defeat of the earl of Argyll at Loch Etive in 1309 freed him to take all the major castles and press upon Stirling. This threat eventually brought King Edward II of England north to confront him. Robert's victory against superior forces at Bannockburn enabled him to take the offensive, including an invasion of Ireland by his brother Edward. Taking Berwick, the Scots defeated the English again in 1319 and harried northern England. Large English expeditions of 1322 and 1327 were beaten by Robert's 'scorched earth' policy, apparently his deathbed advice on how best to conduct warfare.

Roche-Derrien, Battle of battle fought on 20 June 1347 between Thomas Dagworth and Charles of Blois, who was besieging the town of Roche-Derrien near the north coast of Brittany, France. Dagworth's small English force routed the much larger French force.

Dagworth had only 300 men-at-arms and 400 archers with which to attempt the relief of Roche-Derrien. Charles is attributed 1,800 men-at-arms, 2,000 crossbows, and 600 archers, plus many local militia. The odds seemed impossible, but by marching at night across difficult country and arriving from an unexpected direction, Dagworth's tiny force took the enemy completely by surprise. After initial success, the French began to recover, cutting the cords of their tents to obstruct their attackers. In the confusion Dagworth was wounded and captured, but a dawn sortie from the garrison routed the French, capturing Charles and assuring the English victory.

Rochester castle castle in England on the River Medway, 40 km/25 mi southeast of London. Begun in 1089 by Bishop Gundulf to replace a wooden castle built by William the Conqueror shortly after his arrival, it was subsequently modified and extended by various rulers. The keep is the tallest in England with a height of 38 m/125 ft.

In 1215 the keep was besieged by King John, who undermined the southeast corner and caused it to collapse. It was subsequently rebuilt but as a rounded corner. It withstood siege by Simon de ◊Montfort (the Younger) in 1264, but fell in the Peasants' Revolt of 1382.

Rochester, Siege of siege and capture of ◊Rochester castle in Kent, England, in 1215 by King John of England from rebel barons, after the signing of the Magna Carta. John's success was neutralized by his death the following year.

John's forces occupied the town and besieged the castle at the same time. Provisions for the rebels were short; Robert FitzWalter attempted to relieve the castle, but failed. The southeastern tower was destroyed (subsequently replaced by a round tower in contrast to the other rectangular towers) and the garrison surrendered when the keep was taken.

Rockingham castle castle in England, 13 km/8 mi north of Kettering, built around 1170 as a timber motte-and-two-bailey work and later expanded into a masonry keep. It was taken by Henry II in about 1155 and much rebuilt in the ensuing two centuries, a major feature being the twin-towered gatehouse built by Edward I towards the end of the 13th century.

Roger de Hautville (c. 1040–1101) known as the 'Great Count', Norman conqueror of Sicily 1060–91, victor of Palermo in 1072 and Syracuse in 1085, and conqueror of the Maltese islands 1090–91.

Roger intitially relied upon the support of his elder brother, ◊Robert Guiscard, to cross the Straits of Messina from Italy to attack Muslim Sicily. A raid in 1060 was followed by a more determined attack in 1061, when several hundred knights were shipped across with their horses and defeated the Muslims in battle. Roger's first attack on Palermo, in 1064, was thwarted by the arrival of a North African fleet, but returning in 1071, reinforced by vessels from newly-conquered Bari (see ◊Bari, Siege of 1068–71), he was able to capture the city and make it his capital. Catania had already fallen in 1071, followed by other crucial ports of Taormina in 1078 and Syracuse in 1086 (following a decisive victory at sea in 1085). Sicily was not fully-secured until 1091, by which time Roger had also seized Malta.

Rohtasgarh Prakrit 'Rohitaswa's hill' fortress in Bengal, India, commanding the confluence of the Koel and Son rivers. It was named after its founder, a son of the ◊Rajput king Hari Chandra, and may date back to the 8th or 9th century. It fell to the invading Muslims about 1100. In later centuries its walls were greatly strengthened and enlarged to give a circumference of 45 km/28 mi.

Roland (died c. 778) French hero. His real and legendary deeds of valour and chivalry inspired many medieval and later romances, including the 11th-century *Chanson de Roland* and Ariosto's *Orlando furioso*. A knight of ◊Charlemagne, Roland was killed 778 with his friend Oliver and the 12 peers of France at Roncesvalles (in the Pyrenees) by Basques. He headed the rearguard during Charlemagne's retreat from his invasion of Spain.

Rollo of Normandy (c. 860–c. 924) (or *Hrolfr*) first Viking ruler and duke of Normandy (although he never used the title). He founded the duchy of Normandy and established the dynasty of ◊William (I) the Conqueror. The city of Rouen is named after him.

Rollo left Norway about 875 and marauded, sailing up the River Seine to Rouen. By the Treaty of St-Clair-sur-Epte (912), Charles III 'the Simple' (879–929) of West Francia granted Rollo the eastern part of Normandy as a buffer against other Scandinavians and recognized him as duke. By 924 Rollo had extended his control into central Normandy.

Rome capital of the Roman Empire, on the river Tiber, Italy, enclosed by defensive walls befitting the status of the city in scale and grandeur. The walls of the early republic proved impregnable, while those of the late empire were to protect the city for over a thousand years.

The first wall, known as the Servian Wall following the Roman belief that it was begun by the king Servius Tullius (578–535 BC), was constructed about 386 BC and enclosed the Seven Hills in a circuit 10 km/6 mi in length. In 211 BC it prevented the Carthaginian general ◊Hannibal the Great from taking the city, but later Roman military successes made it redundant.

In about AD 271 a new circuit was begun, ordered by the emperor ◊Aurelian. The new walls of Rome were 18 km/11 mi long and 4 m/13 ft thick, and had 18 fortified gates and 381 towers – an astonishing feat of organization and engineering. Only through treachery were the defences ultimately penetrated in AD 410 and the city captured.

Rome, sack of (390/386 BC) sack of Rome in 390 or 386 BC by the Gallic Senones tribe, a direct result of the loss of the Roman army at the river Allia 18 km/11 mi north of Rome, where it had opposed the advancing Senones but been routed (see ◊Allia, Battle of the). Only the citadel on the Capitoline Hill managed to hold out as the Gauls were unable to organize a siege. They eventually wandered off or were bought off after about six months.

The fall of Rome to a barbarian enemy was a major psychological blow to the Romans. It had long-lasting effects on Roman morale and instilled an almost genocidal hatred among the Romans for the 'barbarians'.

Rome, sack of (410) capture and sack of Rome on 24 August 410 by the Visigoths under ◊Alaric.

Alaric had been waging an intermittent campaign against the Western Roman Empire for several years. After the death of his main opponent, ◊Stilicho, in 408, he marched on Rome but was bought off with a large bribe. In 409 he began negotiations with the emperor, Honorius, whose capital was at Ravenna. When Roman forces attacked his camp, Alaric broke off negotiations and again marched on Rome. The gates were opened by a traitor and Alaric's troops became the first foreign army to enter the city in nearly 800 years. Although Rome had long ceased to be the capital of the

Empire and the Goths remained in the city for only a few days, the psychological impact of the fall of the 'Eternal City' was tremendous.

Rome, sack of (455) capture and sack of Rome by the Vandals in 455. Their occupation and sacking of the city for two weeks from 2 to 16 June led to the word 'vandal' becoming synonymous with wanton destruction of property.

Following the murder of the Roman emperor Valentinian III, Petronius Maximus (who had arranged the murder) was elevated to the throne. He forced Eudoxia, Valentinian's widow, to marry him. She appealed to the Vandal king ◊Gaiseric for help and Gaiseric responded by sailing from Africa. Maximus attempted to flee but was killed by a mob and the Vandals entered Rome unopposed.

Rome, Siege of (472) successful siege of the city of Rome in 472 by the forces of ◊Ricimer, commander of the army of Italy, after which he deposed the reigning Roman emperor Anthemius and replaced him with Olybrius.

Although Ricimer had installed Anthemius as emperor in 467, relations between the two had deteriorated to such a degree that Italy had become divided between Anthemius in Rome and Ricimer in Milan. In 472 Ricimer marched on Rome, supported by Burgundians and Suevi, while Anthemius enlisted the support of Bilimer who commanded a force of Visigoths. Ricimer besieged Rome for three months, then launched a violent assault. Although Bilimer's troops conducted an active defence, Ricimer's men succeeded in breaking through into the city, which they then plundered. Anthemius was captured and beheaded.

Rome, Sieges of series of sieges of Rome during the long Roman-Gothic war in Italy. It was recaptured from the Goths in 536, who unsuccessfully besieged the city under King ◊Witiges 537–38, and again in 545 under King Totila. His forces took the city that year, but the Romans recaptured it in 546. The Goths again took Rome in 549, but the city was finally regained by the Romans in 553 (see ◊Mons Lactarius, Battle of).

Following their reconquest of Africa and Sicily, an East Roman army landed at Rhegium in Italy in 536. Gothic garrisons in southern Italy fell rapidly, including Rome which was betrayed by the population. The Roman general ◊Belisarius prepared the city's defences and was ready the following year when King Witiges led a large Gothic army against him. The Goths laid siege to Rome, assaulted the walls and gates, attempted blockade, and engaged the Romans in several battles and skirmishes outside the walls but failed all attempts to retake the city. The siege was lifted in 538.

Three years later, under the new energetic king Totila, the Goths took advantage of Belisarius' absence in Persia to try again. By 545 the Goths were again laying siege to Rome. Belisarius, recalled from Persia, attempted a relief but failed. On 17 December the disaffected garrison of Isaurian troops surrendered the city. The Romans, however, reoccupied it the following year.

The Goths regained the city in 549 when once again the garrison (which had not been paid) betrayed it. Rome finally ended up back in Roman hands after Narses' victory at Mons Lactarius in 553.

Romzug medieval German term for the Roman campaigns undertaken by the kings of Germany in order to be crowned emperor by the pope (see ◊Frederick (I) Barbarossa).

Roncesvalles, Battle of successful ambush of a Frankish army by the Basques, which took place in the Pyrenees in 778. The Frankish rearguard suffered heavy losses and several prominent commanders were killed, including the legendary Roland, Count of the Breton Marches. The destruction of the Frankish rearguard is celebrated in the epic poem *The Song of Roland*.

A successful Frankish expedition against the Muslims in Spain was returning home when they were ambushed by the Basques, whose light equipment and local knowledge allowed them to make hit and run attacks.

Roosebeeke, Battle of battle fought on 27 November 1382 in Flanders in which Charles VI of France defeated the Flemish troops of Philip van Artevalde by a double encirclement of flanking cavalry. Van Artevalde was besieging the nearby French-held town of Oudenarde, which Charles came to relieve.

Most of the French men-at-arms were dismounted in the centre, in front of the common foot soldiers, leaving two mounted wings. The Flemings attacked in a huge ◊phalanx, at first driving back their opponents, but allowing the French cavalry to swing in from both flanks. The Flemings found themselves crushed together, literally having the breath squeezed out of them. Van Artevalde was one of the many Flemings found dead without a wound.

Roscommon castle castle 32 km/20 mi northeast of Athlone in what is now Co Roscommon, Ireland. The design was based on the standard rectangular form, with towers at each corner and a powerful double-towered gatehouse in the centre of one long side.

It bears some resemblance to ◊Harlech castle, but was built some ten or fifteen years earlier. Built by the Lord Justice of Ireland, it was intended to subjugate the local chieftains, but they had their own ideas on the subject and in consequence it changed hands frequently throughout its history.

Roscrea castle castle in the modern Co Tipperary, Ireland, 64 km/40 mi northwest of Limerick. Begun by King John as a timber ◊motte-and-bailey castle in around 1213, this was later replaced by a masonry work erected around 1280 alongside it. Of irregular shape, its principal feature was a large gatehouse, which was later converted into residential use, and a fresh gate cut in the curtain wall.

Roses, Wars of the civil wars in England 1455–85 between the houses of Lancaster (badge, red rose) and York (badge, white rose), both of whom claimed the throne through descent from the sons of Edward III. As a result of ◊Henry VI's lapse into insanity in 1453, Richard, Duke of York, was installed as protector of the realm. Upon his recovery, Henry forced York to take up arms in self-defence.

Rouen castle former ducal castle near the River Seine, Seine-Maritime *département*, France, known as 'the Tower'; there are no remains. ◊Henry I of England built a turreted wall and improved the castle in the 11th century. Rouen was the key to Normandy and was besieged in every medieval invasion.

The ◊Bayeux Tapestry possibly shows William the Conqueror at Rouen castle. King John of England's murder of Arthur of Brittany probably took place here. In ◊Geoffrey V of Anjou's siege, one side of the castle collapsed and had to be rebuilt. ◊Henry V of England entered on a black horse in 1419; ◊Joan of Arc was burned here in 1431. The French recaptured Rouen castle in 1449.

Rouen, Siege of (1418–19) siege of Rouen, the capital of Normandy, France, by ◊Henry V of England from 30 July 1418 to 19 January 1419. There were no assaults, but the slow strangulation of blockade; Henry received the city's surrender when the defenders were reduced to starvation.

Henry crossed the River Seine at Pont de l'Arche on a bridge of boats and was able to besiege the large and well-fortified city, held for the Burgundians since January. He had the river blocked upstream, towards Paris, by piles driven into its bed and linked by a chain. Downstream, the French garrison of Caudebec promised not to send relief. On land a circumvallation of trenches spiked with stakes prevented a way out. Eventually, despairing of relief from Duke John the Fearless, the defenders surrendered.

Rouen, Siege of (1449) siege and capture of the city of Rouen, Normandy, by the French under ◊Charles VII in 1449. This was near the end of the ◊Hundred Years' War, when the French conquered Normandy from King Henry VI of England.

The Duke of Somerset had come to Rouen in 1448 as head of the English government for Henry in Normandy. Charles VII directed his attack from Pont de l'Arche. Rouen surrendered on 29 October, and Somerset and his entourage were given a safe-conduct. Charles entered Rouen, receiving the keys.

Rougemont castle castle in England, at Exeter in Devon, that began as a Roman walled enclosure. When William the Conqueror appeared in the area to crush rebellions, the locals were unable to defend it. William then built a ◊motte-and-bailey timber castle and a single-tower gatehouse within an angle of the walls.

In subsequent years it was periodically refurbished, eventually having a curtain wall with towers and a ditch, all surrounding numerous domestic buildings The castle fell into disuse in the 15th century, and very little now remains.

roundship medieval vessel. Originally an Arab type, the roundship was found throughout the Mediterranean from about 1050 to 1300. At its most developed form, in the 13th century, it weighed 800 tons and was a three-decked vessel, 35 m / 115 ft long, with two huge lateen sails. Roundships had crews of 80 men and could carry up to 200 fighting men and 100 horses.

routier term for a medieval mercenary, interchangeable with ◊cottereau and other similar terms. The Great Companies of the 1360s were grouped in routes according to nationality, the origin of the term. It was used especially of companies who hired themselves to princes, and who, acting on their own account, caused havoc. They sometimes had their own administrative system and uniforms.

Rouvray, Battle of battle fought in France on 12 February 1429 in which the Englishman John ◊Fastolf, commanding a wagon train of supplies (herrings) for the siege of Orléans (see ◊Orléans, Siege of), held off an ambush by Franco-Scottish forces. The English celebrated the victory as the 'Battle of the Herrings'.

Fastolf led 600 English troops and 1,000 Parisian militia as convoy guards for 300 wagons of herrings. The French mustered 4,000 under Charles de Bourbon and the constable of Scotland, John Stuart of Darnley. Informed of their approach, Fastolf formed his convoy into a rudimentary *Wagenburg*, but the French deployed guns which commenced a bombardment. Stuart dismounted his men-at-arms to storm the enclosure, but was killed, along with 600 Scots, by English archers. Fastolf then mounted up his own men-at-arms and charged out to rout the French.

ru Tibetan 'horn' military-administrative region of Tibet in the imperial period of the 7th–9th centuries. Each *ru* was divided into halves, and these into ◊stonsde, regiment-districts which were the basic units of recruitment.

In the 7th century the Central Tibetan heart of the Empire was divided into three *ru*: dbUs-ru in the centre (including Lhasa), gYo-ru in the 'left' or east (including Yarlung, the home of ◊Namri Songtsen's dynasty), and gYas-ru in the 'right' or west. A fourth, Ru-lag in the south, was later added.

Rudradaman great satrap (one of the Western Satraps, independent princes) who ruled over a successor state to the Kusana empire in western India, including Ujjain and parts of Maharashtra. He conquered Rajasthan, conducted punitive expeditions against hill tribes on his northern borders, and waged successful campaigns against the Andhra kingdom.

Rudravarman I (lived 6th century) king of Champa (modern central Vietnam), active during the period 529–43, and founder of a new dynasty shortly before 530. He attacked Vietnam in the summer of 543 but was defeated by a general of ◊Ly Bi. How much longer he reigned is unknown.

Rufus, Marcus Minucius (died 216 BC) Roman consul in 221 BC, dictator in 218, and ◊*magister equitum* in 217. He campaigned in Istria during his consulship, but is most famous for his dispute with the Roman dictator Quintus Fabius Maximus in 217/216 during the Second Punic War.

After the Battle of Lake Trasimene (see ◊Lake Trasimene, Battle of) in 217 BC, he was named as Fabius' master of horse (*magister equitum*), but disobeyed the command to refrain from battle against ◊Hannibal the Great. He won a minor victory at Gerunium and was subsequently given equal *imperium* with Fabius. Soon afterwards, however, Minucius' army was drawn by Hannibal into a trap but he was rescued by the arrival of Fabius' legions. According to the Roman historian Livy, he greeted Fabius as 'Father' and resumed a subordinate position for the rest of his term of office. He was killed at the Battle of Cannae in 216 BC.

Ruspina, Battle of hard-fought action in 47 BC in which Julius ◊Caesar barely managed to avoid defeat at the hands of a force led by Titus Labienus.

Caesar had led 30 cohorts, about 1,000 cavalry, and 150 archers out on a foraging mission when he was attacked by Labienus with 1,600 German and Gallic cavalry, 8,000 Numidian light horse, and a large body of supporting infantry. Avoiding a pitched battle, Labienus attempted to surround Caesar and cut him off from his camp. Harassed by missiles, but unable to reach their skirmishing opponents, Caesar's single line of cohorts were slowly worn down. Moving around the line Caesar managed to form half his units into a line facing to the rear, before sending them in desperate charges to both front and rear. Labienus was driven back and Caesar gained time to reorganize. He managed to gradually withdraw to his camp.

sabaton European medieval term for a piece of plate foot armour. Sabatons appeared throughout Europe in the early 14th century, and remained an essential part of a complete set of plate armour until the 17th century.

Sabi, Siege of siege in July 660 of Sabi, the capital of Paekche, one of the ◊Three Kingdoms of Korea, by the Chinese general Su Dingfang and his Silla Korean ally Kim Yusin, during the Tang invasions (see ◊Korea, Tang Chinese wars in). The city surrendered on 18 July.

Su Dingfang attacked Paekche by sea, landing at the mouth of the Kum River, defeating local forces and marching on the city with 130,000 men. Meanwhile a Silla Korean force of 50,000 under Kim Yusin attacked over land and defeated the outnumbered Paekche general Kyebaek at Hwangsan. The Paekche king fled Sabi, and the allies besieged it, forcing the abandoned defenders to surrender.

Sacred War war fought 356–346 BC in central Greece between the Boeotians and Phocians, so called because it involved the control of Delphi. The war weakened Boeotia and led to the intervention of ◊Philip (II) of Macedon.

It started as a result of Boeotia's attempt to damage Sparta and Phocis by getting the council that controlled Delphi to punish them for sacrilege. Encouraged covertly by both Sparta and Athens, the Phocians, under Philomelus, retaliated by seizing Delphi and using its accumulated treasures to hire mercenaries.

Philomelus was soon killed, but his successor Onomarchus forced the western Locrians into alliance, captured Orchomenos and Coronea in western Boeotia, and, when the war spread to Thessaly, twice defeated Philip. Onomarchus was killed at the Crocus Field in 352 (see ◊Crocus Field, Battle of the) and Thessaly passed under Philip's control, but when Philip marched south he found his path blocked by the Athenians at Thermopylae. Thereafter little changed for four years, though the Phocians, now led by Onomarchus' brother Phayllos, won some ground in eastern Locris.

In 347, however, the Boeotians invited Philip to intervene again, and when the Phocian commander at Thermopylae surrendered the pass to save himself and his men, Philip marched unopposed into Phocis and compelled its submission in 346.

saddle, Roman four-horned saddles are shown on many Roman cavalry tombstones, particularly in the Rhineland. They were first mentioned by Julius Caesar during the Gallic Wars (58–51 BC), when he noted that the Germans did not use them (by implication, his Celtic cavalry did). Statuettes of Parthians show a similar saddle, indicating that the four-horned saddle was also used in the Middle East during the same period.

The evidence of leather saddle covering from many sites, showing creases, signs of wear, and stretch lines, suggests that the leather was stretched over a rigid saddletree. Experiments with reconstructed Roman saddles prove that such a saddle gave the rider a secure seat, and that even before the advent of stirrups (around the 7th century AD), shock tactics were possible for Western horsemen.

Safed castle crusader castle strategically sited north of the Sea of Galilee in Israel. It was constructed in 1102–03 and enlarged by King Fulk of Jerusalem in the 1140s. The Knights Templar bought the site in 1168, but surrendered it to the Muslims in 1188 after a year's siege following the Christian defeat at Hattin in 1187 (see ◊Hattin, Battle of). A treaty of 1240 restored it to the Templars.

The castle was razed by the Abbuyid sultan al-Mu'azzam in 1219 to prevent it being used by members of the Fifth Crusade. After regaining the site, the Templars undertook an extensive rebuilding programme 1240–43. The new circumference was almost 914 m/1,000 yds in length, with 30-m/100-ft ramparts and a 15-m/50-ft moat surrounding them. Its wartime garrison exceeded 2,000 men. In 1266 Baibars besieged Safed for six weeks, but despite his large siege train could only take the castle through treachery.

sagaris picklike battle-axe used by Achaemenid Persian troops in the 6th to 4th centuries BC, and by the Saka tribes of Central Asia and the early Sarmatians. Apparently optimized for piercing helmets, it had an iron or bronze head comprised of a long, flattened spike in front and a hammer head or smaller spike at the back.

sageo flat braided silk cord used to tie the Japanese ◊*katana* (long sword of the Muromachi period) to the sash.

sagittarius archer in a Roman imperial army. The Romans recruited specialist units of archers from the Eastern provinces who used the composite bow (see ◊bow, composite). These units, some of which were mounted, were stationed throughout the empire.

Sagrajas, Battle of battle fought on 23 October 1086 in Spain between ◊Yusuf ibn Tashufin's Almoravid forces and Alfonso VI of Castile's forces. The Castilians were decisively defeated, temporarily reversing the Christian ◊*Reconquista* of Spain from the Moors.

Following his conquest of Toledo in 1085 (see ◊Toledo, capture of), Alfonso VI attacked southwest towards Badajoz but met the North African forces of the Almoravids. The Castilians charged the larger numbers of the well-disciplined Muslims and were defeated. Yusuf soon returned to Morocco, leaving only 3,000 cavalry behind.

Saguntum, Siege of siege and capture of the city of Saguntum (now Sagunto), Spain, by the Carthaginian general ◊Hannibal the Great in 219–218 BC, the cause for the Second Punic War with Rome (see ◊Punic War, Second).

Saguntum was a Roman protectorate, but its position on a hilltop dominating the eastern coastal route was of vital strategic importance in Hannibal's plans for the invasion of Italy. He assaulted the town in 219 BC and took it after an eight-month siege. The Romans demanded its release and when this was rejected war was declared in 218 BC.

saihai device used both for signalling on the Japanese battlefield and as a symbol of rank. It consisted of strips of paper, leather, or animal hair mounted onto the end of a baton, and was used from the Kamakura period (1185–1333) onwards.

St Albans, Battle of (1455) battle fought on 22 May 1455, during the English Wars of the Roses (see ◊Roses, Wars of the), in which Richard, Duke of York, defeated Lancastrian royalists in a skirmish at St Albans, Hertfordshire, England. Henry VI (1421–71) was captured, his chief advisors were killed, and Richard claimed the throne.

Henry VI's supporters were defending St Albans, protected by its town ditch and strong gates. The Yorkist rebels were restricted to attacking along the lanes leading to these gates without success. The earl of Warwick ordered Robert Ogle's border veterans to break in through the walls of houses, which they did, shouting his war cry, and the royalists were out-flanked and overwhelmed.

St Albans, Battle of (1461) battle fought on 17 February 1461 during the English Wars of the Roses (see ◊Roses, Wars of the), in which the Lancastrian forces of Queen Margaret, wife of Henry VI, defeated the Earl of Warwick in a scrambling encounter at St Albans, Hertfordshire, England.

After the Battle of Wakefield in 1460, when Richard, Duke of York, was killed, Warwick raised some 10,000 men in London and marched north to fortify St Albans with extensive field defences, but they were outnumbered and facing the wrong way. As in the first battle of St Albans, enterprising Lancastrians managed to spring the position, infiltrating the town and trapping its defenders. While the Yorkists tried to reorganize, the Lancastrian impetus drove them back northwards, eventually inducing a rout.

St Andrews castle castle 18 km / 11 mi south-east of Dundee in Fife, Scotland. Built in the late 12th century with a small stone tower and probably a timber palisade, on a rocky promontory overlooking the sea, this structure was demolished in around 1337. Toward the end of the century, the original tower was rebuilt, and two major new towers and a stone curtain wall were added.

Saintes, Battle of battle fought in western France in 1242 between Henry III of England and Louis IX of France. Henry, who was making an attempt to recover lands of the old Angevin Empire in France, retreated before the forces of Louis and renewed England's truce with France.

Henry had joined a rebellion by the Count of La Marche (married to his father King John of England's widow) and the Count of Toulouse. The French took Taillebourg, then faced Henry over the River Charente, but following a brief skirmish Henry retreated to Saintes. There was further skirmishing in and around the town, in which Simon de ◊Montfort (the Younger) was active. Henry retreated offering very little resistance and Saintes surrendered to Louis.

St Hilarion castle castle of three wards on a precipitous site 5 km/3 mi south of Girne (modern Kyrenia), northern Cyprus. It was first fortified by the Byzantines. The Lusignan kings made it their summer palace and built in the Gothic style around the peak. The Venetians reduced the site in the 16th century.

St Jakob-en-Birs, Battle of battle fought on 26 August 1444 in which Armagnac mercenaries (fighting for the French House of Orléans) invading Swiss territory overwhelmed a much smaller Swiss force using missile power.

About 40,000 Armagnac mercenary troops, unemployed from the Hundred Years' War in France, attacked Basel and Bern. Some 1,500 Swiss opposed them and drove in their vanguard, only to find themselves confronting the main body. Forming three close squares, they withdrew to the defended enclosure of St Jakob's Hospital. Here they were showered with arrows and bombarded to death by Armagnac artillery, but not before inflicting about 4,000 casualties on their enemies.

Saitobara tomb cluster group of late 5th-and 6th-century Japanese tombs in Miyazaki prefecture, Japan, which have yielded important finds of early weapons, armour, and horse trappings.

saku (or *ki*) early Japanese palisade or stockade. They first appeared as imperial defensive and administrative frontier forts in the northeast of Japan during the 7th-century campaigns against the Ezo tribespeople. Excavations have shown that as well as earth walls and fortifications, they contained substantial wooden structures.

Saladin (c. 1138–93) (*Salah al-Din Yusuf ibn Ayyub*) Kurdish conqueror of the Kingdom of Jerusalem, and nephew of ◊Nur al-Din's general ◊Shirkuh, who was his military tutor. Saladin became ruler of Egypt in 1169 and Aleppo in 1183. He defeated the forces of the Latin kingdom of Jerusalem at Hattin (see ◊Hattin, Battle of) in 1187, but was defeated at Arsuf by ◊Richard (I) the Lionheart in 1191.

Saladin won fame in Egypt at al-Babein (see ◊al-Babein, Battle of) and under siege in Alexandria in 1167, and in 1171, when the last Fatimid caliph was deposed, he was made governor. This position enabled him to seize Damascus in 1174 and Aleppo in 1183, so providing him with the resources of a hinterland stretching from the Nile to the Euphrates to turn against the crusader states. In 1187 he trapped King Guy at Hattin, taking him prisoner along with virtually the entire military forces of the Latin Kingdom. As a result Saladin was able to capture practically all the castles of the Christian Kingdom by 1189.

The Christian siege of Acre (see ◊Acre, Siege of 1189–91), successful after the arrival of Richard the Lionheart and other crusaders, and his defeat by Richard at Arsuf in 1191 did put Saladin on the defensive. He lived long enough, however, to see his greatest opponent leave for Europe without having recaptured Jerusalem, and proved himself the superior strategist.

Salamis, Battle of (480 BC) sea battle fought in the Strait of Salamis west of Athens, Greece, in 480 BC between the Greeks and the invading Persians. The Greek victory led to the withdrawal of the Persian fleet and paved the way for the defeat of ◊Xerxes I's invasion.

The Greeks had either 310 or 368 ships, commanded by the Spartan Eurybiadas. The Persians had possibly twice as many, but lost the advantage of their numbers and superior manoeuvrability by entering the Salamis Strait; tradition says that they were lured in by a message from the Athenian commander ◊Themistocles. The Greeks deployed at dawn, and the Persians possibly never recovered from the shock of finding them ready and waiting.

What happened is uncertain, but the Greeks may have succeeded in cutting off the Persian right wing and driving it ashore, before turning on the rest and driving them down the strait. The Persian morale had suffered a blow and the fleet withdrew to Asia Minor.

Salamis, Battle of (308 BC) sea battle off Salamis in Cyprus during the conflict between ◊Antigonus (I) Monophthalmus of Macedon and ◊Ptolemy (I) Soter of Egypt, notable as one of the few ancient sea battles in which artillery was used.

Ptolemy had 140–150 warships, all either quinqueremes or quadriremes. Antigonus' son and fleet commander, ◊Demetrius (I) Poliorcetes, had possibly 180 warships in all – mostly triremes, though some were even larger than Ptolemy's ships and carried both stone-throwing and spear-shooting catapults. With his heaviest ships on the left in a double line, Demetrius routed the enemy right and some of the ships next to them causing Ptolemy, who had won on his left with his heavier ships, to withdraw to Citium (modern Larnaka).

Demetrius possibly experimented with ship-borne artillery because of his familiarity with siege techniques (see ◊Rhodes, Siege of 305–304 BC). There is no record of any ship being sunk or disabled by catapults so it is likely their target was men rather than ships.

salgamum practice of Roman soldiers of the late empire of demanding more of their hosts than was required when they were billeted on the local population.

Salinator, Marcus Livius (born 254 BC) Roman general in the Second Punic War (see ◊Punic War, Second), one of the victors of Metaurus in 207 BC (see ◊Metaurus, Battle of the).

As consul in 219 BC he campaigned in Illryium, but was accused of stealing booty and withdrew to his country estate in protest. When ordered to perform his public duties in 210 BC, he protested by refusing to shave his hair, trim his beard, or mend his clothes. He was elected consul in 208 BC as colleague to Gaius Claudius ◊Nero. The two hated each other, but cooperated to defeat ◊Hasdrubal Barca at the river Metaurus.

sallet characteristic German helmet of the mid- and late 15th century. It had a typical 'sou'wester' form with a broad brim at the back, and was sometimes made in one piece covering the entire head, with a sight cut in the front or with a movable visor. Many sallets were made in Italy for export to the German lands, and they were also popular in western Europe.

Sallust (86–34 BC) (*Gaius Sallustus Crispus*) Roman historian. He served under Julius ◊Caesar in Gaul (France) and during the civil war, but retired from public life after a scandal involving his governorship of Africa. He wrote histories of the Catiline conspiracy and the Jugurthine War, as well as a Roman history of which only fragments survive.

Salsu River, Battle of the battle fought on 26 August 612 in which Koguryo, one of the ◊Three Kingdoms of Korea, defeated a Chinese invasion (see ◊Korea, Sui Chinese wars in).

While his main army besieged Liaodong fortress, the emperor Sui Wendi's son Sui Yangdi sent 300,000 men to strike directly at Pyongyang, the Koguryo capital. The Chinese besieged the city but could not take it. Running out of supplies and under constant attack from the Koguryo general Ulchi Mundok, they retreated towards Liaodong. Ulchi Mundok harried their retreat and then ambushed them as they tried to cross the Salsu River, killing or capturing all but 2,700.

Salzburg castle stronghold on a spur overlooking the Saale River above the town of Salzburg, Austria, built for the bishops of Würzburg in 1162. It was shared between families through the system known as *Ganerbenburgen*. It is approached from the east where there is a ditch, a wall with square towers, and a gatehouse. It encloses six sections, including the 13th-century Munze palace.

It was for a time a refuge for all the clergy in Bavaria opposing Paschal III as pope in the mid-12th-century schism. In 1418 the archbishop of Salzburg made a decree here demanding greater freedom for chaplains in castles.

Sambre, Battle of the battle fought in 57 BC in which the Roman army of Julius Caesar defeated an attack by the army of the Nerveii, Atrebates, and the Viromandui tribes, during the ◊Gallic Wars.

The Gauls had prepared an ambush beside the river Sambre, but the Roman army had arrived in greater numbers than expected. Waiting for the Romans to begin constructing their camp, the Gauls launched their attack, but Roman discipline carried them through the initial onslaught and they were able to repel the attack. Some 55,500 Gauls are claimed to have been killed or wounded.

sambuca name given to a type of ancient siege engine said to resemble the Roman *sambuca* harp. The Greek historian ◊Polybius, writing in the mid-2nd century BC, uses the term to describe an armoured ladder, raised by ropes and pulleys, used in the siege of Syracuse (see ◊Syracuse, Siege of).

The *sambuca* was mounted on two galleys that were lashed together in Syracuse harbour and the ladder was raised from the horizontal to the level of the battlements by pulleys attached to the masts. Wicker screens protected the ladder and also a platform at the top large enough to hold four men. The platform screens could be lowered to allow the men to mount the wall.

sambyolch'o (Korean 'three elite patrols') private troops of the Korean military dictators of the Ch'oe family, which held real power under the Koryo dynasty in 1196–1258. In the 13th century these troops were the core of anti-Mongol resistance, openly rebelling when the royal court made peace with the Mongols in 1270. By 1273 they were wiped out by combined Mongol-Korean forces.

In addition to a *tobang* personal bodyguard and a ceremonial cavalry troop, the *sambyolch'o* consisted of the Left and Right Night Patrols, originally military police, and the *sinuigun* or 'Army of Transcendent Righteousness'. The *sinuigun*, a later foundation than the Night Patrols, consisted of prisoners of war who had escaped from the Mongols.

Samnite member of an ancient Italian tribe occupying the region of Samnium in the central highlands. In the 4th century BC offshoots of the tribe had spread into

SAMNITE WARS

Three separate conflicts between 343 and 290 BC fought between the neighbouring tribes of the Romans and the ◊Samnites, as a result of which Rome won supremacy over Campania and its most powerful neighbours. The wars were also a test of tribal alliances, the Romans being supported by the Latin League and the Samnites by the members of the Samnite Federation.

The first war, 343–341 BC, consisted only of small skirmishes in Campania as both sides vied to gain control of the region. In 328 BC the Romans established a colony at Fregellae within recognized Samnite territory and the Samnites responded by instigating a coup in Naples which resulted in its withdrawal from the Latin League. War was declared, but seven years of indecisive fighting followed until the Romans launched a determined invasion of Samnium. This was blocked at the Caudine Forks in about 321 BC (see ◊Caudine Forks, Battle of the), though the Samnites gained nothing from the battle apart from a favourable truce.

The Romans broke the truce in 316 BC, but their three-pronged attack on Samnium was defeated and the Samnites advanced to within 30 km/19 mi of Rome itself. Despite having beaten all the available Roman forces and sparked revolts by many of Rome's allies, the Samnites halted their advance. An army from Sparta had landed in Italy en route to Syracuse and the Samnites seem to have thought that this was going to enter the war. The pause gave Rome critical time to regroup and counterattack, breaking the Samnite army. In 304 BC a peace agreement was signed.

In 298 BC hostilities began again and the Samnites combined with the Etruscans, Umbrians, and Gauls to attack Rome. At Sentium (see ◊Sentium, Battle of) in 295 BC the Romans defeated the coalition, largely because the Etruscans and Umbrians failed to show up. The Samnites were no longer able to stop the Roman tide and they sued for peace in 290 BC.

Campania and established independent subtribes. In the mid-4th century BC the Samnites established the Samnite Federation in response to the Latin League and tried to make their relatives join. Many of the Campanian tribes refused and when pressure was applied Rome attempted to intervene to ensure they remained independent. This lead to war with Rome (see ◊Samnite Wars), which would result in the subjugation of Samnium.

Samudragupta king of ◊Magadha 330–80, the son and successor of ◊Chandragupta I. He waged a series of campaigns which established his authority from Assam to the eastern Punjab, and as far south as Kanchi. His expansion to the west was blocked by the Shakas (Scyths), who still controlled much of Rajasthan.

He celebrated the ◊ashvamedha (the conqueror's horse-sacrifice) and took the title Sarva-rajachchheta, 'Destroyer of all other Kings'. Although a soldier and administrator, he was also a patron of the arts, a musician, and a man of letters, known to his subjects as Kavi-raja, 'the Poet-King'.

Samuel (976–1014) tsar of Bulgaria from 981. There was a brief resurgence of Bulgarian power early in his reign 981–96, but this was short-lived. The Byzantines decisively defeated the Bulgars at Balathista in 1014 (see ◊Balathista, Battle of), and Samuel is said to have died of shock when the victorious Emperor ◊Basil II blinded his 15,000 Bulgar captives.

samurai (or *bushi*) (Japanese 'one who serves') Japanese term for the warrior class which emerged from provincial obscurity to become the ruling military elite for almost 700 years.

The term originally referred to those with clan allegiances who formed the military groupings known as bushidan which evolved around the 10th century to protect and expand their provincial domains. From these early clan groupings developed an intricate system of loyalties which were later to become more feudal than family orientated.

samurai-dokoro office established in 1180 by the Japanese shogun ◊Minamoto Yoritomo to control the activities of both his family and vassals (*gokenin*). It was the main administrative office of his warrior government in Kamakura.

The *samurai-dokoro* also controlled provincial estates appointed by the shogun and provided guards for Kyoto, home of the emperor, and its surrounding area. It was abolished in the late 15th century.

Sandal castle castle in Sandal Magna, a suburb of Wakefield, in Yorkshire, England. This was a ◊motte-and-bailey castle built in around 1150 and subsequently expanded into a quite unusual design.

Construction in stone began early in the 13th century, and eventually there was a complex design comprising a turreted great tower on the motte linked to a curtain wall, which extended around the bailey. At the foot of the motte, in a widened section of the ditch, was a semicircular barbican approached from both motte and bailey by drawbridges. The remainder of the bailey was occupied by domestic buildings built against the curtain wall.

The castle was the scene of the Battle of Wakefield in 1460 (see ◊Wakefield, Battle of) in which the Duke of York was defeated by Queen Margaret, but soon after this it appears to have been abandoned.

San Egideo, Battle of battle of 1416 in which the ◊condottiere (professional mercenary commander) Braccio da Montone defeated Carlo ◊Malatesta and made himself ruler of Perugia, Italy.

Braccio divided his forces into smaller units and committed them gradually to the fray, in contrast to Malatesta's men who were constantly engaged in clumsy divisions. Braccio also ensured a ready supply of water to his troops over a long, hot summer's day. Malatesta lost 300 men and his army broke; he was captured in the rout.

Sanjar, Abu'l Harith Ahmad (1097–1157) last great ◊Seljuk sultan 1119–53. From 1130 he was engaged in warfare against Khwarazm, and abandoned Transoxania after being defeated by the Qara-Khitai near Samarkand in 1141. He put down a rebellion by ◊Ala al-Din Husain ('the World-Burner') in 1152, but was himself defeated and captured by the Ghuzz Turkomen near Merv in 1153.

His early victories included Nauslajan (1100), which helped his brother Muhammad take the Seljuk throne, and Ghazni (1117), in support of ◊Bahram Shah. In 1119 he defeated his nephew Mahmud, occupied Baghdad, and took the title sultan for himself.

His fall at the hands of the Ghuzz Turkomen, who had moved into Khurasan under pressure from the Qara-Khitai, was met with general astonishment and heralded the collapse of the Seljuk Empire.

San Romano, Battle of battle fought on 1 June 1432 in which the ◊condottiere (professional mercenary commander) Niccolo da Tolentino, leading Florentine forces, surprised and routed Sienese troops who were besieging the town of Montopoli.

In a lightning campaign, Tolentino left his infantry behind and attacked with his few cavalry troops. The Sienese were completely routed, with 150 men captured along with 600 horses. The battle is immortalized in a series of three paintings by the Renaissance artist Paolo Uccello, *The Rout of San Romano* (c. 1455).

San Servando castle castle in Toledo, Spain. The site was originally occupied by a Roman *castrum* (castle) and was fortified centuries later by the Moors in order to defend Toledo. The present castle was built on the Templar ruins in the 15th century and has a strong curtain wall with typical Moorish pointed *merlons* (◊crenellations) and round towers. The interior buildings formed the palace of the Archbishop of Toledo.

When Toledo was taken by the Christians in 1085 it became a Benedictine monastery, which was burned down by the Moors in 1099. Alfonso VI (1065–1109) rebuilt it as a fortification, but the monks abandoned it in the 12th century because it had become a focal point of the Moorish wars. It then became the property of the Knights Templar until the order was dissolved in the 14th century (see ◊Military Order).

sanshu (Chinese 'three corps') palace guards in Western Han (206 BC–AD 9) China, recruited from candidates for office serving a probationary period in the capital. Members were called *lang* ('gentlemen'), and the three units were the Gentlemen of the Palace, and the Left and Right Gentlemen of the Palace.

The *sanshu* commander, the Imperial Household Superintendent (*guangluzun*), also commanded two cavalry units, the Palace Gentlemen Rapid as Tigers and the Palace Gentlemen of the Feathered Forest.

Saone castle crusader castle, northeast of the port of Latakia, in northwest Syria. Originally the site of a Byzantine castle that was taken by Frankish crusaders in around 1106, major construction began in around 1120. Besieged and taken by ◊Saladin in 1188, it never thereafter left Arab hands and is thus a rare example of early fortification features, such as the deep channel hewn in solid rock to isolate the castle from the promontory upon which it was built.

Saphrax leader of the Alans. He joined with the Goths in 377 and played a major role in the ◊Adrianople campaign of 378, where he was one of the leaders of the cavalry charge which broke the Roman right wing.

Sardis, Battle of battle between the Persian king ◊Cyrus (II) the Great and ◊Croesus of Lydia fought to the east of the Lydian capital Sardis in 547 BC, in which Cyrus won a decisive victory over the Lydians.

After the Battle of Pteria (see ◊Pteria, Battle of), Cyrus pursued Croesus back to Lydia. On a plain just east of Sardis, Cyrus deployed with a camel corps in his front line, infantry behind them, and cavalry in the rear. The Lydians were reliant on their cavalry whose horses would not close with the unfamiliar camels. The riders dismounted and fought well, but were eventually defeated. The Persians then besieged and captured Sardis.

Sargon II (died 705) king of Assyria from 722 BC, who assumed the name of his predecessor. To keep conquered peoples from rising against him, he had whole populations moved from their homelands, including the Israelites from Samaria.

sarissa (or *sarisa*) pike used from the 4th to 2nd centuries BC by the Macedonians and their imitators. It varied in length from about 4 m/14 ft to 7 m/24 ft.

Sarus River, Battle of victory in 625 for the Byzantines, commanded in person by the Emperor ◊Heraclius, over a Persian army under Shahrbaraz which was defending the River Sarus in Cilicia (Asia Minor). The Byzantines forced their way across the river, broke the Persian army and pursued them north out of Cappadocia and Pontus (central Anatolia, now Turkey).

sashimono Japanese flag, usually decorated with the family crest, or ◊*mon*, inserted into a special tube at the back of a suit of armour to project above the head of the wearer. The *sashimono* developed during the massed infantry battles of the Muromachi period (1333–1568) as a means of identifying friend or foe on the battlefield.

satrap provincial governor in the Achaemenid Persian, Hellenistic, and Parthian empires. Persian satraps had both civil and military authority over a large area, often containing several peoples. They were in charge of local garrisons and conducted small-scale wars in their provinces although they were often superseded by commanders sent from court for major campaigns.

Under the Seleucids and Parthians the status of the title gradually declined as satraps came to rule smaller provinces.

Saumur castle stronghold between the Thouet and Loire rivers in Maine-et-Loire *département*, France, possibly dating from the 10th century. It was captured by Fulk Nerra, Count of Anjou. The Duc de Berry turned it into a 'fairy-tale' castle of Gothic tracery and flying turrets, with corner turrets, ◊machicolation, and a turreted barbican.

Saumur castle is illustrated in the *Très Riches Heures du Duc de Berry*. It has been used as a prison and a barracks, and now houses an equestrian museum.

saunion (or *soliferreum*) ancient Spanish javelin, similar to a ◊*pilum* but made totally of iron. It had a barbed head and a pointed butt and varied in length from 1.6 m/5.25 ft to 2 m/6.5 ft.

sax (or *seax*) large, single-edged knife commonly used by Germanic warriors in the 5th–7th centuries, both as a weapon and a tool.

Saxon Shore, forts of the defensive chain of Roman forts along the south and east coasts of England, from Hampshire to Norfolk. Identification is not entirely secure, but they are generally accepted as modern Bradwell, Dover, Lympne, Brancaster, Burgh Castle, Reculver, Richborough, Pevensey, and Walton Castle. The forts were sited to guard harbours suitable for use by Roman naval forces as anchorages and by enemy raiding parties as landing sites. They were not constructed as a single system, but were built at various times, with almost a hundred years separating the construction of Reculver and Pevensey.

Shortly after AD 293 the Roman emperor Diocletian appointed a *comes litoris saxonici* ('Count of the Saxon Shore') to command these defences, from which the name arises.

saya Japanese scabbard, generally made from magnolia wood (*mokuren*), decorated with lacquer and highly ornate soft metal fittings. When the sword was not in use it was kept in a plain wooden scabbard called a *shirasaya*.

SASSANIAN ARMY

Military force of the Sassanid empire in Persia, AD 224–651. Like the Parthian army from which it developed (see ◊Parthian army), it relied on the ◊asavaran (cavalry), but it was more varied and sophisticated than its predecessor. The men were generally brave but cautious in battle and very able in siege warfare, using captured Roman ◊ballistae and, probably, man-powered, Chinese-style ◊trebuchets. Although the armies fortified their camps, they were vulnerable to night attacks because of their poor camp discipline.

The cavalry were recruited from nobles and their retainers. Attempts to turn them into a standardized central force had limited success although the various guards units, including ◊Immortals, *pushtigbansalar* (Imperial bodyguard) and *janavaspar* ('self-sacrificers'), may have been under central control. Most cavalry were archers, using the ◊*nawak* (used to shoot short, light darts) as well as conventional composite bows. At first both cavalry and horses were heavily armoured, some even fully-armoured ◊*clibanarii*. ◊Chosroes (I) Anushirvan 531–79 attempted to standardize the cavalry armament to lance, bow, shield, and horse armour, but cavalry equipment appears to have become lighter by 600.

According to the Byzantine Emperor ◊Maurice, the typical Persian cavalryman at that time had bow, sword, and body armour but no lance, shield, or horse armour. The sculpture of Chosroes II at Taq-i-Bustan, however, shows that some troops still used heavy equipment albeit in new styles that included frontal ◊lamellar armour for horses. The heavy cavalry were supported by lighter horsemen, including Arab and Central Asian auxiliaries, and by infantry and elephants. Most Sassanian infantry were spearmen, carrying cane and leather shields like the old ◊*spara*. They were despised by their Roman opponents, and completely absent from some armies. Sources are ambiguous about whether or not there were more competent infantry, but if so they must have been few in number since they made very little impact. Sassanian armies in battle usually formed three divisions, sometimes of equal size but often with the centre much larger than the wings and including the army's reserve. The centre would contain the ◊Kaviani banner, if present, and often the elephants. Elephants carried towers containing archers but were not themselves armoured, and were sometimes closely escorted by infantry. Infantry typically formed a second line of the centre.

scale armour armour made of small, usually D-shaped plates sewn either individually or in rows (with the individual scales wired together) to a fabric lining, characteristically overlapping downwards. Scale is probably the earliest form of armour, appearing among the Hurri-Mitanni around the 17th century BC, with Egyptian examples and representations dating from the beginning of the New Kingdom in the 16th century BC. Scale armour continued to be manufactured through the Roman period into the early medieval period in Europe, and right through to the 19th century in Asia. The Romans used both bronze and iron scales.

They vary enormously in size, some tiny examples being no more than 15 × 19 mm / 0.6 × 0.75 in, others being as much as 80 × 54 mm / 3.1 × 2.1 in.

Scapula, Ostorius (died AD 52) Roman governor of Britain AD 47–52. He succeeded Aulus ◊Plautius as governor and carried the Roman conquest through to Wales and the Midlands, putting down a minor revolt of the Iceni in Norfolk and defeating the British king ◊Caratacus.

He may have founded the Roman colony of Camulodunum at Colchester. He had ambitions for further conquests in the province but died before he could embark on these, exhausted by the campaigns in Wales.

scara elite Carolingian Frankish unit of full-time soldiers.

Scarborough castle castle in Yorkshire, England, built in around 1130 at the top of cliffs overlooking the sea. It was taken by Henry II in around 1155, who then continued building, completing the great tower and curtain wall begun by the founder. The triangular barbican with its twin-towered gatehouse was added in the 13th century.

SCIPIO, PUBLIUS CORNELIUS (236–190 BC)

(called Scipio 'Africanus')

Roman general whose tactical and strategic abilities turned the tide of the Second Punic War (see ◊Punic War, Second) and established his reputation as one of Rome's greatest commanders. He learned from observing the Carthaginian general ◊Hannibal the Great that the only way to gain victory was to emulate his enemy's audacity and mobility, and use whatever means were necessary to gain the advantage. His military operations won control of Spain from Carthage and at Zama in 202 BC (see ◊Zama, Battle of) he achieved the final victory that won the war for Rome.

At the age of 18 he served with his father (also called Publius) and saved his life at the River Ticinus in 218 BC (see ◊Ticinus, Battle of the). He probably also fought at the Battle of Trebia in 218 BC and was certainly at Cannae in 216 BC (see ◊Cannae, Battle of), which gave him the opportunity to observe Hannibal's tactics and attempt to work out a solution. He recognized that the Roman army was too rigid, relying too heavily on infantry and fatally neglecting cavalry, a situation that made it unable to cope with the mobility and flanking manoeuvres used by Hannibal. He also advanced the use of scouts and reconnaissance patrols to gather as much military intelligence as possible, a practice that Hannibal had used to good advantage in Italy.

In 211 BC he offered himself as a candidate in the election to find a new general in Spain, following the death of his father and uncle. He was elected unanimously, despite being too young to hold the office, and arrived in Spain with his first independent command. His campaign began with an audacious act. Learning that the Carthaginian armies were widely dispersed and not within ten days' march of their Spanish capital at Carthago Nova (New Carthage, present-day Cartagena), he attacked and captured the city, achieving an immense propaganda victory. With the city came over 300 hostages that Carthage had taken from the Iberian nobility, and by restoring these to their tribes Scipio won over a large number of Carthage's old allies.

He won control of Spain for Rome in two decisive battles, destroying the army of ◊Hasdrubal Barca at Baecula in 208 BC (see ◊Baecula, Battle of, and Ilipa in 206 BC (see ◊Ilipa, Battle of). As a result Scipio was elected consul in 205 BC and used his influence to press for an invasion of Africa. Landing with an army near Utica, he defeated the Carthaginian and Numidian armies at an ambush near the Tower of Agathocles and in a night attack on their camps on the Bagradas River in 204 BC (see ◊Bagradas, Battle of the). At the Battle of the Great Plains in 203 he defeated the army of Hasdrubal Barca in a pitched battle. At Zama in 202 he defeated the army of Hannibal, thus securing Roman victory in the war and leading to the peace treaty that bore his name. He adopted the name 'Africanus' in recognition of the place of his greatest victory, but he felt that his achievements had not been sufficiently rewarded and retired to his villa embittered.

schiltron medieval Scottish term for a body of pikemen or long spearmen who adopted a very close formation as a defence against English knights, sometimes making a circular 'hedgehog' with their weapons. The formation was efficient in repelling cavalry, but its weakness was its immobility.

At Falkirk in 1298 (see ◊Falkirk, Battle of) English archers decimated schiltrons pinned by the threat of knightly charges.

schola unit of the Roman emperor's bodyguard in the late imperial period, probably created by ◊Constantine (I) the Great in the 4th century. There were originally five cavalry units each with about 500 soldiers. By the end of the 4th century there were five units in the Western Empire and seven in the East, possibly each with strengths of around 300 men.

The *scholae* survived into Byzantine times where they became part of the ◊tagmata.

Scipio, Gnaeus Cornelius (died 211 BC) Roman general in the Second Punic War (see ◊Punic War, Second). He commanded a Roman army in Spain from 218 BC until his death there in 211 BC.

Scipio was sent to Spain in 218 BC and established his base at Tarraco (now Tarragona). He defeated ◊Hasdrubal Barca's navy at the mouth of the river Ebro in 217 BC and his army at Ibera in 215, but at Ilorci (now Lorqui) in 211 his army was destroyed and he was killed in the fighting.

Scipio Aemilianus, Publius Cornelius (185–129 BC) (known as 'Scipio Africanus Minor') Roman general. He was the son of Lucius Aemilius ◊Paullus, but was adopted into the Scipionic family. He served with distinction under his father at Pydna (see ◊Pydna, Battle of), and then in Spain in 155 BC. The only officer to win renown in the early campaigns of the Third Punic War (see ◊Punic War, Third), he was elected to the consulship by a landslide and was sent to take command in Africa. His careful assault concluded the siege of Carthage in 146, when he razed the city to the ground.

In 134 BC he was elected consul again and sent to Spain to quell the rising centred on the city of Numantia. Refusing to face the Numantines in battle, despite his numerical superiority, he blockaded the city and starved the defenders into submission.

scorpio name given to a small, rapid-fire ◊ballista (stone-shooting machine), used, mainly by the Romans, in the 1st and 2nd centuries BC.

scutage in medieval Europe, a feudal tax imposed on knights as a substitute for military service. It developed from fines for non-attendance at musters under the Carolingians, but in England by the 12th century it had become a purely fiscal measure designed to raise money to finance mercenary armies, reflecting the decline in the military significance of feudalism.

scutum curved shield used by Roman legionaries from the mid-Republic until the 2nd century AD. Its was semicylindrical in shape, giving better protection than a flat shield, and enabled the Romans to fight in a loose formation. During the Republic (509–27 BC) the shield was generally oval in shape, but it became rectangular in the 1st century AD.

Sebastopolis, Battle of Muslim victory in 692 over the Byzantines, which resulted in the conquest of Armenia, and cleared the Byzantines from any territory east of the Taurus mountains. The Byzantines were forced to agree to joint control over Cyprus.

Sebuk-Tegin, Abu Mansur Samanid amir (governor) of Khurasan (northeastern Iran) 974–97 and Ghazni (central Afghanistan) 977–97, founder of the Ghaznavid empire of eastern Iran and northwestern India.

A Qarakhan Turk, captured in a tribal war and sold as a slave to the Samanids, he became a member of the royal ◊ghulam guard and rose rapidly through the ranks. He joined the household of ◊Alp-Tegin and later succeeded him as Samanid governor of Ghazni. In 974 he assisted the Samanids to put down a rebellion in Khurasan, and was rewarded with the governorship.

Sekigahara, Battle of the decisive battle in the unification of warring 16th-century Japan, fought in 1600. The eastern forces of the warrior leader ◊Tokugawa Ieyasu defeated the opposing forces of the powerful western *daimyo* Ishida Mitsunari, after which Ieyasu seized the balance of power in Japan and founded the Tokugawa dynasty of shoguns.

Following the death of the warlord ◊Toyotomi Hideyoshi in 1598, Japan had once more been plunged into civil strife. By 1600 the many factions had broadly divided into eastern and western divisions. The opposing armies faced each other at the small village of Sekigahara in thick fog following heavy rain. The early fighting was indecisive but with the defection on the battlefield of five *daimyo* previously loyal to Mitsunari, the armies of Ieyasu crushed the opposing western forces.

Seleucus (I) Nicator (c. 358–281 BC) founder of the Seleucid dynasty of Syria and, with Ptolemy (I) Soter, one of the most successful of ◊Alexander (III) the Great's 'successors' (see ◊*Diadochi*).

Becoming governor of Babylonia on Alexander's death, he was ousted by ◊Antigonus (I) Monophthalmus in 316 BC, and took refuge in Egypt. He returned in 312 and by 307 had recovered Babylonia and much of the neighbouring area as far as Bactria. In 306 he invaded India, but ceded the old Persian territories there to Chandragupta in return for the elephants which helped him win at Ipsus in 301 (see ◊Ipsus, Battle of).

This gave him access to the Mediterranean via Syria, where he founded Antioch. Further campaigns consolidated Seleucid control over the eastern Persian Empire, and victory over ◊Lysimachus at Corupedium in 281 gave him Asia Minor. Perhaps now aiming to take over Lysimachus' possessions in Thrace and Macedonia, he crossed the Hellespont (modern Dardanelles), but was murdered soon after landing at Lysimacheia.

Seljuk member of a dynasty of ◊Turkoman origin, ruling over Iran, Iraq, and most of the lands of the Eastern Caliphate from the mid-11th to mid-13th centuries AD. They were succeeded in the east by the Khwarazm-shahs in the later 13th century and in the west by the Ottomans in the 14th century.

The founder of the dynasty was Duqaq Temur-Yaligh 'Iron Bow', who with his son Seljuk (or Saljuk) led one of the nine tribes of the Toquz Oghuz Turks. In about 900 Seljuk lost favour with the military leader of the Oghuz and fled with his followers to Jand (to the east of the Aral Sea), where he embraced Islam. During the following century, they took part as mercenaries in wars in and around central Asia, and pressed into eastern Iran, where their lawless Turkoman ways had disastrous effects on the economy of the country. A major expedition against them, led by the Ghaznavid sultan Mas'ud in person, was defeated at Dandanqan in 1040 (see ◊Dandanqan, Battle of) by Seljuk's grandson Toghril Beg.

The Seljuks then advanced through Iran and reached Baghdad in 1055. Under Sultan ◊Alp-Arslan they took Herat and the holy cities of Arabia, and defeated and captured the Byzantine emperor in Anatolia. Under Malik Shah, towards the end of the 11th century, they conquered Egypt, Syria, Bukhara, and Samarkand. The last of the great Seljuk sultans, ◊Sanjar, was unexpectedly defeated by the Ghuzz Turkomen in 1153, leading to the collapse of the Empire and its partition among a number of successor states.

Sellasia, Battle of conflict in 222 BC between ◊Cleomenes III and the Macedonian ◊Antigonus (III) Doson, which ended Cleomenes' attempts to reassert Spartan dominance over the Peloponnese.

Antigonus fought at Sellasia, about 5.5 km/9 mi north of Sparta, at the request of the Achaean League. He had 28,000 infantry and 1200 cavalry while Cleomenes had 20,000 men in all. The battle developed into three separate engagements, two on the hills Cleomenes had occupied and one in the valley between them, along which ran the road to Sparta. The decisive engagement was fought on one of the hills between the two phalanxes, each commanded by its king. After his defeat, Cleomenes fled to Egypt where he later committed suicide.

Sempach, Battle of battle fought on 9 July 1386 in Lucerne, central Switzerland, between Swiss Confederates and Leopold of Austria, in which the Swiss gained a victory over the Habsburgs.

Leopold led 4,000 knights against 6,000–8,000 Swiss. He ordered his men to dismount and fight on foot with their lances to counter the Swiss ◊halberds. Initially this was successful, and the front ranks of the Lucerne troops suffered heavily. However, the Swiss formations were able to manoeuvre and attack the Austrian left rear, precipitating a rout. The Austrians lost 1,500 men, the Swiss 200.

Sengoku daimyo Japanese warlord of the ◊Sengoku period (1467–1568) who displaced the officially appointed provincial military governors. As the *Sengoku daimyo* fought for military control, they established their own centres of administration and built castles and castle towns.

The military warlord ◊Oda Nobunaga emerged from among these minor *daimyo*, and they pledged allegiance to him in the first steps towards a unified Japan.

Sengoku period (or *Warring States period*) period of Japanese history 1467–1568 which began with the ◊Onin Wars and ended with the assumption of power by the *Sengoku daimyo* ◊Oda Nobunaga, and later by the military defeat of all opposing *daimyo* by the warrior leader ◊Tokugawa Ieyasu at Sekigahara in 1600 (see ◊Sekigahara, Battle of).

The leadership of the Ashikaga shoguns of this period was particularly weak and minor provincial military leaders exploited the opportunity to increase personal control of their own domains. These leaders fought amongst themselves for military and political domination and it was not until the emergence of Nobunaga that potential unification was possible. Despite the constant fighting, the age was also one of great artistic and cultural developments.

Sennacherib (died 681 BC) king of Assyria from 705 BC. Son of ◊Sargon II, he rebuilt the city of Nineveh on a grand scale, sacked Babylon 689, and defeated Hezekiah, King of Judah, but failed to take Jerusalem. He was assassinated by his sons, and one of them, Esarhaddon, succeeded him.

Sens, Siege of unsuccessful six-month siege of the city of Sens in France (886–87) by the Vikings, who had just recently failed to capture Paris (see ◊Paris, Siege of).

Sentium, Battle of battle fought in 295 BC in present-day Umbria, Italy, between the Romans and a coalition of ◊Samnites and Gauls that finally ended the ◊Samnite Wars and gave Rome dominance over its neighbours.

Hostilities had begun in 298 BC with a combined assault on Roman territory by an alliance of Samnite, Gallic, Etruscan, and Umbrian tribes. The alliance armies were rendezvousing at Sentium, near present-day Sassoferrato, when the Roman army attacked. The Etruscans and Umbrians had not yet arrived and the Romans were able to overcome the Samnite and Gallic armies after a bitter fight.

Sepeia, Battle of battle in 494 BC between Sparta and Argos in which 6,000 Argives are said to have died. Because they were afraid the Spartans would play some kind of trick on them, the Argives decided to imitate the Spartan manoeuvres. When the Spartan king, ◊Cleomenes I, realized this he instructed his men to attack next time the herald ordered them to fall out for breakfast. When the Argives heard the Spartan herald give the order to fall out, they did so but the Spartans kept their ranks and attacked. The result was a rout of the Argives, made even worse by Cleomenes' treacherous massacre of fugitives who took refuge in a nearby sacred grove.

seppuku (or 'hara-kiri', belly slitting) Japanese form of ritual disembowelment as a means of atonement or to avoid dishonour (such as being captured alive by one's enemies). The earliest recorded instances of this custom were the suicides of ◊Minamoto Tametomo in 1177 and ◊Minamoto Yorimasa in 1180, after the Battle of the Uji River.

Septimus Severus, Lucius (AD 145–211) Roman emperor 193–211. Following the murders of the emperors Publius Helvius Pertinax

and Didius Severus Julianus, Severus was proclaimed emperor with the support of the legions on the Rhine and Danube frontiers. Concluding a truce with the Roman general Decimus Clodius Albinus by recognizing him as Caesar, Severus defeated his other rival Percennius Niger, Roman governor of Syria, at Issus, Asia Minor, in 194, and then returned to shatter Albinus' army at Lugdunum (Lyon) in 197 (see ◊Lugdunum, Battle of).

He then led a highly successful expedition against the Parthians, sacking Ctesiphon, and turning Mesopotamia into a province. In 208 he went to Britain to campaign against the Caledonians who had overrun the north of the Roman province. He died of an illness there, at Eboracum (York).

Serdica, Battle of battle fought at Serdica (modern Sofia, Bulgaria) in 550 in which the East Romans led by Germanius, nephew of the emperor Justinian, gained a victory over the Slavs who were starting to make inroads into imperial territory.

sergeant (from Latin *servus* 'slave'), through Old French *serjant* in the medieval period, term for an ordinary soldier, commonly a cavalryman who was not a knight, but also used for infantry. A sergeant was also a tenant owing military service to a lord, but sergeanty tenure, not always military, was an inferior form of tenure. A sergeant might also be an officer with police duties.

servitium debitum ('service owed') knight service or military service during the medieval period.

Its introduction into England was gradual, by individual bargain rather than by mass imposition. There had been military obligations in Anglo-Saxon England, often the basis of service after the Norman Conquest. Tenants in chief later provided a number of knights (the quota) for annual military service to the king for a set period in return for lands, the knight's fee being the basis of assessment. Later this was often commuted.

Seven Military Classics the canonical works of Chinese military theory, which include: *Bing Fa* (Art of War), *Six Secret Teachings, Three Strategies of Huang Shigong, Methods of the Sima, Wuzi, Wei Liaozi,* and *The Questions and Replies between Tang Taizong and Li Jing.*

Bing Fa (Art of War) by ◊Sunzi, was the most famous military work of the period. *Six Secret Teachings* was attributed to the ◊Taigong, but was really a much later work, perhaps of the 3rd century BC, ranging widely from government to tactics. *Three Strategies of Huang Shigong* was also traditionally attributed to the Taigong, but perhaps came from the 1st century BC. It is a Daoist work more about government than warfare. *Methods of the Sima* was a 4th century BC compilation of older material on military administration. *Wuzi* was written by ◊Wu Qi in the 4th century BC. *Wei Liaozi* probably came from the 4th–3rd century BC, and emphasized military discipline and morale. *The Questions and Replies between Tang Taizong and Li Jing*, ostensibly a dialogue between ◊Tang Taizong and one of his generals, was in fact probably a 9th–10th-century work that discusses classical principles in the light of medieval conditions and techniques. The recently rediscovered *Bing Fa* of ◊Sun Bin might be added as an eighth classic.

shamshir scimitar-style sword characteristic of southern and central Asia and the Middle East, used from about 1500 BC to the present day. It has a curved blade with a single edge tapering to a point, and a hilt in the shape of an inverted L, with a crossguard strengthened by langets.

It is designed for use as a light cavalry sword, and features as part of the parade uniform of senior officers in several modern Western armies.

Shang Yang (lived 4th century BC)
Chinese reformer of Qin, one of the ◊Warring States. He redirected Qin's government and economy with the sole aim of increasing its military power, encouraging agriculture and warfare at the expense of trade and making social status dependent on military achievement. His reforms paved the way for the emperor ◊Qin Shi Huangdi.

Shang Yang was originally an official in Wei, but he defected to Wei's enemy Qin in 361 and became chancellor. He was executed in 338 when a prince whom he had offended came to the throne.

Shaoxing, Siege of
(or *Shao-hsing*) siege of Shaoxing (in modern Zhejiang) February–June 1359, by ◊Zhu Yuanzhang's Ming forces, commanded by Hu Dahai, in the Chinese civil wars. The city was held by Lü Zhen, a general of Zhang Shicheng's Wu state, semi-independent but nominally loyal to the Mongol Yuan dynasty. The Ming never had a firm command of the siege, and abandoned it after plague broke out in May.

Shaoxing was entirely surrounded by broad waterways, and the Ming forces were never able to encircle it completely. They could not therefore cut off supplies, and the siege was disorganized, with skirmishes and frequent sorties. Lü's defenders set up ◊trebuchets over each gate, and both sides used ◊bombards.

Shapur I Sassanian Persian king from about 242 to 273, the son of ◊Ardashir I. He conducted three campaigns against Rome 243–60 and conquered ◊Dura Europus and Antioch from the Romans about 255. He also conquered the Kushan kingdom at the eastern border of the Persian Empire, stretching his influence as far as Peshawar, Sogdia, and Tashkent.

In the first of his campaigns against Rome (243–44), he defeated and killed the Roman emperor Gordian III. During the second campaign (about 255), he defeated a large Roman army and conquered Dura Europus and Antioch. In 259–60 he defeated and captured the Roman emperor ◊Valerian, but his attempts to conquer Syria were defeated by Odenathus of Palmyra.

Shayuan, Battle of battle in northern China in 537 in which western Wei warlord ◊Yuwen Tai defeated eastern Wei's Gao Huan.

Yuwen's 10,000 men fell back through the Tongguan pass in front of Gao's huge army, reported at 200,000 men. Yuwen then deployed with his back to the Wei River, much of his army concealed in long reeds. Gao hastily attacked Yuwen's left flank, hoping to catch the outnumbered westerners against the river, but cavalry hidden on Yuwen's right charged into Gao's flank and cut through his army. The easterners were defeated, and 6,000 were killed.

She jun (or *She chün*) auxiliary force from the She, a tribe of the Yao ethnic minority from Fujian, used by the Song dynasty of China against the Mongols. They surrendered to ◊Khubilai Khan in 1277 and were demobilized in 1285.

shence jun (or *shen-ts'e chün*) (Chinese 'Divine Strategy Army') main imperial field army of late Tang China. A northwestern frontier army founded in 754, it was sent east against the rebellion under ◊An Lushan and protected the Emperor's flight from the Tibetan occupation of ◊Changan in 763. It was finally disbanded when Chu Wen seized power in 903.

After the occupation of Changan, the *shence jun* was incorporated into the ◊Palace Army and commanded by palace eunuchs, as a counterbalance to the provincial armies of the ◊*jiedu shi*. Its quality and numbers declined, but when Emperor Xizong fled the capture of Changan by ◊Huang Chao, he recruited a new *shence jun* of 54,000-man regiments. The court, however, could no longer pay such a force.

Shenzhou, Siege of (or *Shen-chou*) battle in 1004 between the Khitan and Song China. After defeating Song attacks at Gaolianghe (see ◊Gaolianghe, Battle of) and again in 986, the Khitan invaded China. A cavalry army led by Khitan emperor Shengzong penetrated to the Yellow River opposite the Song capital Kaifeng. Attacking Shenzhou on the northern bank, the Khitan were ambushed by its Song commander Li Geilong. When the Song emperor Zhenzong personally reinforced Shenzhou, the Khitan invasion stalled. The two empires reached a peace that lasted, with occasional interruptions, for a century.

Shibao, Siege of (or *Shih-pao*) siege in 749 of Shibao, a Tibetan fort near Koko Nor which dominated routes from China into northeast Tibet and Central Asia, by Turkish general Qoshu Khan. After previous Chinese attacks had failed, Qoshu Khan led 63,000 men against Shibao. After several days of unsuccessful fighting, Qoshu threatened to execute his subordinates unless they took the fortress. They did so, capturing the Tibetan commander and 400 of his men, but several tens of thousands of Chinese troops died in the assault.

shieldwall poetic description of a battle formation used by the English and those fighting in the Scandinavian style from the first Viking era to the Norman Conquest of 1066. The word suggests a very tight formation, difficult for an enemy to penetrate, such as was adopted by the English at the Battle of Hastings in 1066 (see ◊Hastings, Battle of).

shikoro flexible hanging neck guard of a Japanese helmet (◊*kabuto*), usually made of linked rows of lacquered iron or leather lamellae (◊*kozane*) laced vertically. It was used from the Heian period (794–1185).

Shi Le (lived 4th century) leader of the Jie, a fair-haired ◊Xiongnu tribe of western origin, in the Chinese ◊Sixteen Kingdoms period. He became a general of the Xiongnu ruler Liu Yuan, but attracted his own following and established a principality in present-day Hebei. He gained control of the east, and proclaimed his own Later Zhao dynasty in 319.

While Yuan and his son ◊Liu Cong tried to preserve – and tax – the conquered Chinese, Shi preferred traditional nomadic looting and massacre, turning Chinese farmland into nomads' horse pastures. In a great raid in 310 he killed 100,000 Chinese. Such opportunities for plunder led many tribesmen to desert Liu Cong for him. When establishing his own principality, he defeated ◊Xianbei attacks and adopted ◊*tiema* cavalry using horse armour

captured from them. Although he never openly fought Liu Cong, by the latter's death Shi controlled the east. He attacked Liu Cong's successors, defeating them at Loyang in 328 (see ◊Loyang, Battle of) and annexing their state.

Shirburn castle castle in England, 23 km/14 mi southeast of Oxford. It was built in around 1377 under a licence to crenellate (build battlements) issued to Warine de Lisle, who thereby converted the family mansion into a castle. Of the usual style for the period, it was rectangular with half-round corner towers and a gatehouse in front of the curtain, and is a very early example of the use of brick in its construction.

Shirkuh (lived 12th century) Kurdish general under ◊Nur al-Din from 1146. His energy and strategic and tactical skills made him a good model for his nephew ◊Saladin, who first fought with him aged 26. Shirkuh seized Cairo for Nur al-Din, drove out the Franks, and was made vizier in 1169. He died soon afterwards, of something he ate, although whether this was due to poison or excess is unclear.

Facing an alliance between the Fatamid vizier Shawar and Almaric, King of Jerusalem, Shirkuh did well with limited resources. His victory at al-Babein in 1167 (see ◊al-Babein, Battle of) enabled him to seize Cairo for Nur al-Din. Reinforced to some 7,000 cavalry (500 his own Mamelukes) in 1169, he was able to drive the Franks out and secure the country.

Shivner hill fortress in Maharashtra, India, built on a triangular rock rising 305 m/1,000 ft above its surrounding area. The hillside was fortified halfway up by bastioned walls and outworks. The citadel, defended by a massive wall with five gates and supplied with natural springs, was a Buddhist centre in the 1st and 2nd centuries.

Shivner commanded an important route from the west coast to the interior of the Deccan. It fell to the Delhi sultanate under ◊Ala al-Din Khilji about 1300, and later fell to the Bahmani sultans, the Sultan of Ahmadnagar, and eventually to the Mogul Empire.

Shizugatake, Battle of major battle fought in 1583 in present-day Shiga prefecture, Japan, during the struggle for the unification of the country between the forces of the warlords ◊Toyotomi Hideyoshi and Shibata Katsuie, who had allied himself with Nobutaka, the son of the military warlord ◊Oda Nobunaga. Hideyoshi personally reinforced his troops and gained the victory.

Following Nobunaga's assassination in 1572, Hideyoshi had employed various military strategies and political moves to establish and consolidate his position of authority. By 1583 forces opposed to him felt strong enough to pose a serious military threat. After a significant defeat by these rival forces, Hideyoshi joined his army at the mountain of Shizugatake and his smaller forces gained the advantage over Shibata's army.

shogun Japanese term for military dictator and abbreviation for *'seii tai shogun'* – 'great barbarian-conquering general'. The title was first given in the Nara period (710–94) to generals who had achieved great success in the struggles to suppress the Ezo tribespeople of northern Japan. It is normally associated with the military leaders of the Kamakura and Muromachi periods (1185–1568).

shogunate (Japanese *bakufu* 'tent (or camp) government') military government of a Japanese ◊shogun. The term alludes to the military origins of the ◊samurai and the simple aspirations and values of the battlefield. The two great shogunates of pre-modern Japan were those of the Kamakura and Muromachi shoguns.

Sholapur fortified city in Maharashtra, India, founded about 90 BC by a king of the Andhra dynasty. The fortifications attributed to Ala al-Din Hasan Gangu Bahman consisted of a double line of high battlemented walls protected by a moat on three sides and a lake on the fourth.

Sholapur was ruled by the Chalukyas from 550, by the Rashtrakutas from 750, by the Western Chalukyas from 973, by the Yadavas of Deogir (later Daulatabad) from 1156, by the sultans of Delhi from 1318, and by the Bahmani kings of the Deccan from about 1350 until 1489, after which it changed hands several times between the sultanates of Bijapur and Ahmadnagar.

Shōsōin the Japanese imperial repository in Nara, Japan, founded in 756. Among the many treasures are early examples of arms and armour.

Records indicate that there were originally 90 ◊keikō and 10 ◊tanko in the collection, but these were never returned after being requisitioned for use by imperial troops in the suppression of an early revolt against the emperor and in the campaigns against the northern tribes of Japan in the 8th century.

Shrewsbury castle castle in Shropshire, England. Built in timber by Roger de Montgomery in around 1068 as a ◊motte-and-bailey work in a bend of the River Severn, it was converted to masonry shortly afterwards. It eventually had a curtain wall, barbican, and

gatehouse, and was continuously refurbished during the 13th and 14th centuries when it served as a garrison against the Welsh. By the late 14th century it had fallen into disuse.

shugo Japanese military governor originally appointed by the ◊Kamakura shogunate (1185–1333). A *shugo* was appointed from among those favoured by the new ruling military elite in Kamakura and exercised local authority on behalf of the shogun over his vassals (◊gokenin).

Many *shugo* preferred to discharge their authority through deputies, *shugodai*, rather than take up a position which seemed to offer few material rewards.

shugo daimyo Japanese provincial military lord of the Muromachi period (1333–1568). In contrast to their Kamakura predecessors (see ◊shugo), many *shugo* of the Muromachi period took up residence in their appointed provinces and expanded their own power base until they attained the position of a minor *daimyo*.

By the end of the Onin Wars, most *shugo daimyo* had been defeated by their own conflicts and had been replaced by the superior forces of the ◊Sengoku daimyo.

Shuri castle (Japanese *Shuri-jō*) Japanese castle of the early 15th century, situated in the hills outside the modern city of Naha, on the island of Okinawa, Japan. It is believed to have been built by Shō Hashi, the unifier of the Ryukyu islands, as his new capital.

The perimeter walls, which were over 1 km/1.6 mi long and 6 m/20 ft high by 3 m/10 ft wide, were punctuated by various gateways which had wooden towers constructed above.

shuriken Japanese throwing knife, usually of one piece, made of steel, and triangular in section. It was used in close combat, mostly by non-samurai.

Sicilian Vespers popular revolt against French rule by the Sicilians in 1282, named after the church bells for vespers that were ringing at the start of the revolt. It sparked a 20-year war that brought the end of the Angevin French domination of the island (dating back to Norman colonization in the 11th century) and the beginning of the Aragonese (Spanish) domination that lasted into the 18th century.

On Easter Monday 1282 in the Sicilian capital of Palermo a French sergeant insulted a Sicilian woman before vespers. Her husband knifed the sergeant, which led to a French attack in which 2,000 people were killed. In response, the Messinese rose against the French garrison, which retreated to Mategriffon castle. Charles I of Anjou, the king of Naples and Sicily, attempted to restore French power at Messina, but his siege in 1293 failed. The arrival of Pedro III of Aragon, in alliance with the Sicilians, turned the revolt into a war, and Pedro entered and saved Messina.

Sigismund (1368–1437) Holy Roman emperor from 1411, king of Hungary 1387–1437, and king of Bohemia 1419–37. He convened and presided over the Council of Constance 1414–18, where he promised protection to the religious reformer John Huss (c. 1372–1415), but imprisoned him after his condemnation for heresy and acquiesced in his burning. He led the military campaign against the ◊Hussites, agreeing peace in 1436.

Sigismund took part in the defeated Crusade of Nicopolis in 1396 (see ◊Nicopolis, Battle of), and recovered Bosnia, Herzegovina, and Serbia from the Turks.

signifer standard-bearer in the Roman army. Each ◊century or ◊*turma* in the imperial army had its own standard (◊*signum*), carried by the *signifer* who received higher pay for the honour and responsibility. Like the ◊*aquilifer* (see ◊*aquila*), he was expected to show courage in battle.

signum standard of a Roman ◊century from the mid-Republic, shown on many military tombstones and imperial monuments. It consisted of a series of discs and other emblems attached to a pole, often surmounted by a hand.

Silchester (Roman *Calleva Atrebatum*) fortified city in southern England. It was first fortified in the Celtic period when it was a tribal capital of the Atrebates and was protected by rings of massive earthworks. The first defences of the Roman city were raised at the end of the 2nd century AD and consisted of a clay and gravel rampart with a double line of ditches in front. Around AD 260–80 the front of the rampart was cut away and a stone wall was inserted into the space.

This new defence consisted of a 3-m-/10-ft-thick wall built of flint and faced in stone, with a single 14-m-/46-ft-wide ditch in front. The circuit, which was 2.5 km/1.5 mi long in both phases, is still complete, though robbed of most reuseable materials. The town gates were built in stone from the start.

Silfke castle oval castle of a single circuit in southern Turkey reflecting crusader and Armenian influences. Already a Byzantine fortress in 1111, Silfke displays many features associated with Greek and Armenian fortification. The Knights Hospitallers (see ◊Military

Order) added a ◊donjon, hall, and improved water cisterns during their ownership 1210–25.

The castle walls are studded with equally spaced horseshoe towers rising from a talus (sloping wall on a bank) above a dry moat. The Holy Roman emperor ◊Frederick (I) Barbarossa drowned in the river below the walls during the Third Crusade in 1190.

Silistra, Battle of battle fought in 1086 at Silistra in present-day Bulgaria, in which the nomadic Pechenegs, who had allied themselves with the heretic Manichaeans, were victorious over a Byzantine force under Pakourianus and Branas. Both Byzantine commanders were killed, and it took the Byzantines until 1091 to finally push the Pechenegs back across the River Danube.

Singara, Battle of battle fought in 344 or 348 between the Persian ruler Sharpur II and the Roman emperor Constantius II. The battle was initially favourable to the Romans, but they exploited an early breakthrough too impetuously and were defeated by fresh Persian troops.

siphon weapon used on medieval Byzantine ships to shoot inflammable ◊Greek fire against enemy vessels. No examples survive, but it was apparently a brass tube into which the fuel was sucked and then expelled by a pair of bellows.

Siphons were used to destroy the fleet engaged in the first Arab siege of Constantinople in 674–78.

Sirmium, Battle of victory in 488 for the Ostrogoths, led by ◊Theodoric the Great, over the Gepids. The Ostrogoths had been induced to move from Thrace (modern Bulgaria) to invade Italy on behalf of the East Roman Empire. Their passage was blocked by the Gepids near Sirmium (west of modern Belgrade in Serbia), but they were defeated, and the Ostrogoths moved on to invade, and later conquer, Italy.

Sis castle asymmetrical Armenian castle built along the top of a long ridge 40 km/25 mi north of Adana, southern Turkey. In typical Armenian style, the castle walls straggle along the broken ridge, at times substituted by sheer rock faces. The circuit is 0.8 km/0.5 mi in length and originally stood above an Armenian royal town.

The two gateways of the lower eastern ward are particularly heavily defended. To the south stands a strong ◊donjon overlooking a sheer drop. The place proved invulnerable to attack until the kingdom finally fell to the ◊Mamelukes in 1375.

Six Armies the six ◊*jun* that formed the most prestigious part of the Western Zhou (about 1100–770 BC) Chinese royal army. These were not the only forces directly under royal control, since inscriptions also mention the Eight Yin Armies (originally ex-Shang troops). However, the Six Armies became a standard term for imperial military power in later periods, regardless of the actual military organization of the time, while the Eight Armies were forgotten.

Six Garrisons, rebellion of the revolt of Toba soldiers 524–28 in northern China. Various tribal factions joined them and united under the leadership of commander Ge Rong to become one of two main military forces in the area. In 528 they were defeated by the other main force, loyalists under ◊Erzhu Rong, but the Toba government never fully recovered.

As the Toba elite ruling north China grew in wealth and Chinese culture, they downgraded the mobile tribal armies responsible for the successful ◊Toba campaigns against the Ruanruan. Instead they fortified the frontier and settled the Toba soldiers in poverty in six garrisons. The frontier leaders were neglected and their soldiers under-supplied. A successful Ruanruan attack by ◊Anagui in 523 showed the failure of the new static defence.

In 524 one garrison commander refused to issue grain to his starving troops. They mutinied, and the other garrisons followed. As various tribes joined the rising, the government lost control of vast areas and even called in Anagui's Ruanruan to attack the mutineers. Many surrendered, but rose again in 526 when they were transferred to the south. After combining under the leadership of Ge Rong, they overran all the country north of the Yellow River. In 528 Ge marched on the capital and met Erzhu Rong and his heavily tribal but nominally loyal army at Ye (see ◊Ye, Battle of). Erzhu Rong's victory put an end to the rebellion.

Skanderbeg (1405–68) (adopted name of *George Kastrioti*) Serb leader of Albania who led a national movement against the Turks from 1443. As a boy he was captured by Turks and brought up as a Muslim soldier, becoming a commander for Sultan Murad II 1404–51,

---

SIXTEEN KINGDOMS

Foreign-ruled states of northern China in the 4th and 5th centuries.

The united rule of the Western Jin dynasty was weakened by the rebellions of the Eight Princes 291–306 (see ◊Eight Princes, rebellions of the), and 'barbarian' tribes settled within the empire sought independence. The proto-Tibetan Di seized modern Sichuan in 304 and proclaimed the Cheng Han kingdom. More important was the revolt of the ◊Xiongnu under Liu Yuan and ◊Liu Cong, who captured the Jin capital and emperor, forcing Jin loyalists to flee south and establish a new Eastern Jin dynasty. The Xiongnu-ruled Former Zhao state held most of the north until in 319 ◊Shi Le, a Jie tribesman and general of Liu Yuan, rebelled. His Later Zhao dynasty defeated the Liu at Loyang in 328. He in turn was challenged by the Murong tribe of the ◊Xianbei; Murong Hui built up a state and army even before the Jin fell, and in 337 his successor Murong Huang proclaimed the Former Yan dynasty in the northeast. Meanwhile Eastern Jin, the Chinese regime in the south, tried to reconquer the north; Huan Wen had some success before being beaten at Xiangyi (see ◊Xiangyi, Battle of). The greatest figure of the period was ◊Fu Jian, a Di tribesman whose Former Qin state conquered Later Zhao and Former Yan to unite the north. He invaded the south but was crushed at Luojian (see ◊Luojian, Battle of) and the Fei river (see ◊Fei River, Battle of the). His generals rebelled, Murong Chui re-establishing Xianbei independence as Later Yan after a victory at Zheng in 384 (see ◊Zheng, Battle of); between 383 and 409, a total of ten states emerged. The victor in this confusion was the Toba clan of the Xianbei, previously unimportant until ◊Toba Gui led them to the conquest of all of northern China by 439 as the Northern Wei.

who named him Alexander with the title *bey* (governor), hence Skanderbeg. He joined the ◊Hunyadi crusade and was defeated by the Turks at Kosovo, Serbia. After further defeat at Berat in Albania, he won at the battle of Albulena in 1457. Albania retained its independence while he lived.

Skenfrith castle castle in east Wales, 10 km/6 mi north of Monmouth, and one of the 'three castles of Gwent'. Sited so as to command a crossing of the River Monnow, it was set in the valley so as to allow the building of a wet ditch. An early ◊motte-and-bailey work was rebuilt in stone by Hubert de Burgh in around 1203, with a rectangular curtain wall with four drum towers and a stone keep within. Owned by the house of Lancaster, it appears to have fallen into disuse by the 15th century.

Skipton castle castle in England, 32 km/20 mi west of Harrogate in Yorkshire. Built as an earthwork (fortification made of earth) in the late 11th century, this was then rebuilt in stone and provided with a powerful quadrilateral keep and a twin-towered gatehouse in the 14th century.

Skylitzes, John (lived 11th century) Byzantine historian active in the second half of the 11th century. He wrote a chronicle covering the years 811–1057. He was not a great military historian, but the Madrid manuscript of his work contains almost 600 miniature illustrations, providing a unique visual record of mid-11th-century Byzantine arms, armour, troop types, and transport by land and sea.

Sluys, Battle of battle of 24 June 1340 in which ◊Edward III of England, invading France through the Low Countries, engaged the Franco-Genoese fleet at anchor off the coast of Flanders, sinking or capturing almost all the vessels.

Edward commanded over 120 vessels crewed by about 1,000 men-at-arms and several thousand archers. They were arranged in groups so that they were mutually supporting, just as on land. The French had over 200 ships, most them chained together in three lines, but lacked fighting men (they had only 150 men-at-arms and 500 crossbowmen, the rest being sailors). The English fleet was able to manoeuvre and attack at will, using an arrow storm followed by boarding. They took 190 ships, and some 16,000 Frenchmen died.

Social War see ◊Italian Social War, 91–89 BC.

socii (Latin 'associates') autonomous tribes and states allied to Rome that provided the Roman army with light infantry and cavalry or,

as *socii navales,* ships for the navy. The *navales* later also supplied sailors and crews for the ships.

At times the *socii* made up over half the Roman army. They formed units similar in size and organization to the Roman citizen forces and were usually deployed on the wings. In 91 BC the allies gained Roman citizenship as a result of the Social War (see ◊Italian Social War)

sodang (Korean 'banner') elite troops of the Silla kingdom in the ◊Three Kingdoms of Korea period. They may originally have been oath-bound retainers of their commanders, but later swore an oath directly to the king. Each unit had collars in a distinctive regimental colour.

After unification in the 7th century, there were nine *sodang* units at the capital while ◊chong garrisons held the province; six of the nine *sodang* were recruited from areas outside the original Silla kingdom, to promote national unity.

sode-garami Japanese polearm, over 2 m/6.5 ft in length, with barbed hooks and spikes on the upper part which were used to entangle the long sleeves of the kimono and thereby apprehend a miscreant without inflicting personal injury. It was used from the 16th century by non-samurai.

sōhei Japanese Buddhist warrior monk. The favoured weapon of the *sōhei* was the ◊naginata (a polearm with a curving blade). Their aggression and seizure of territory caused local and national problems from the late Heian period (12th century) through to the end of the Muromachi period (16th century).

Soissons, Battle of (486) defeat in 486 of the Gallo-Roman warlord Syagrius by the Salian Franks, under ◊Clovis which gave Clovis control of most of northern France.

Soissons, Battle of (719) decisive victory in 719, and culmination of a campaign by the Austrasian ◊Mayor of the Palace Charles Martel (he acquired the name Martel – 'the Hammer' later) over the Neustrians and Aquitainians. Austrasia was a kingdom in France which consisted of most of northern France, Belgium, and part of Germany. From this point on Charles exercised royal power over all of France, even if he did not actually have the title of 'king'.

Solcinium, Battle of battle fought in 367 between the Roman emperor *Valentinian I* and the Alamanni (a German tribe), who had crossed the Rhine into Gaul. The Roman victory was the culmination of Valentinian's campaign against the tribe.

After inflicting three defeats on the Alamanni, Valentinian took to the field in person and led a successful expedition down the River Neckar. He remained inside Alamannic territory for seven years, stabilizing the Rhine frontier by building a series of fortifications and by enlisting the help of the Burgundians who were enemies of the Alamanni.

soldeier medieval French mercenary, the word being the etymological origin of the modern soldier. The term is generally suggestive of a warrior below knightly rank.

soldurii (singular *soldurius*) infantrymen who made up the bulk of ◊Celtic armies. The rewards gained by displays of personal courage and skill in battle made the Celtic *soldurii* ferocious and aggressive soldiers.

While nobles wore helmets and, from about 300 BC, mail armour, the *soldurii* fought naked or stripped to the waist, carrying only a shield. Effects such as war paint and lime-washed hair were used to intimidate their opponents. By engaging in battle cries, taunts, boasts, and acts of intimidation the *soldurii* worked themselves into a frenzy before they engaged the enemy in a mass charge.

The battle lines were open-order to allow each man room to use his slashing sword or thrusting spear in single combat. The head of the vanquished was taken as proof of valour, while booty from the enemy camp was also motivation for determined fighting. These trophies enhanced the status of individuals within their society.

solenarion early form of crossbow used by the Byzantines.

soliferreum Roman name for a type of javelin called a ◊saunion in Spain before the Roman conquest in 218 BC.

Solygeia, Battle of battle between the Athenians and Corinthians in 425 BC, one of very few in the ◊Peloponnesian War in which cavalry appears to have been important.

An Athenian force, including 200 cavalry, landed at dawn south of the Isthmus of Corinth on the shore overlooked by the hill of Solygeia. Warned in advance, the Corinthians had mustered their forces at the Isthmus, but they were surprised by the dawn landing. When beacons alerted them of the danger, they left half their army to guard a nearby harbour, detached one unit to occupy Solygeia, and engaged with the rest. Thucydides says the presence of Athenian cavalry proved decisive in the end, though he fails to explain why, and

the Corinthians retreated in good order. When the rest of the Corinthian army came up in support, the Athenians retired to their ships.

somatophylax (Greek 'bodyguard') in Alexander the Great's army, some of the young nobles in the king's entourage. Later the term meant a guards unit.

Somnath city flourishing from the 8th century on the south coast of Kathiawar, Gujarat, India, protected on three sides by a deep trench cut through solid rock and on the fourth by a square fort extending to the shoreline. Somnath is traditionally the site of the earthly death of the divine hero Krishna, and it is one of the greatest shrines of Shiva.

Its fame and wealth attracted the notice of ◊Mahmud of Ghazni, who captured the city in 1025, destroyed its idols, and plundered its treasuries. Somnath was later recovered by Rajputs of the Rathor clan, but finally fell to a Muslim army led by Ulugh Khan (later Sultan ◊Muhammad ibn Tughluq) in 1298.

Song Taizu (died 976) (or *Sung T'ai-tsu*; originally *Zhao Kuangyin* or *Chao K'uang-yin*) emperor of China 960–76. He commanded the Palace Corps of the Later Zhou dynasty in north China, and was forced by his officers to seize power in 960. He brought the army under civil control, and conquered five of the other seven Chinese states.

He started with the weakest – Chu and Jingnan in the Yangtze River valley – in 963–65. Next he attacked Shu (Sichuan), with one army coming from the north and another up the Yangtze. In 970 he overran Southern Han, based at Guangzhou (Canton). In 975 he attacked the largest state, Jiangnan, crossing the Yangtze River on ◊Fan Ruoshui's bridge. The coastal state of Wuyue short-sightedly helped his campaign. The victories owed much to the failure of the victims to unite, and to the superior quality of the Song army, though these ◊yangbing troops were later to deteriorate.

Songtsen Gampo (died 650) (or *Srong-brt-san-sgam-po*) bTsan-po ('emperor') of Tibet c. 620–50, the real founder of the Tibetan empire which his father ◊Namri Songtsen had created. He conquered the Sumpa in the north, defeated the Tuyuhun in Qinghai, restored King Narendradeva of Nepal to his usurped throne and made Nepal a vassal state, and opened diplomatic relations with the emperor ◊Tang Taizong of China.

He demanded a Chinese princess in marriage to match the Nepalese princess he had already wed; when China refused, he attacked the border town of Songzhou in 638. A Chinese force surprised and defeated the Tibetans, but Taizong agreed to the marriage. In 648 Songtsen Gampo lent troops to Taizong's ambassador ◊Wang Xuance for use in India.

Sons of Heaven medieval Vietnamese standing forces established by ◊Dinh Bo Linh along with the ◊Ten Circuit Army militia. Their equivalents under later dynasties were the 'Permanent Troops' of the Ly (1009–1225) and the 'Troops Under Arms' of the Trân (1225–1413).

Sontius, Battle of (modern *Isonzo*) inconclusive Ostrogothic victory on 28 August 489 in the first battle for control of Italy between the invading Ostrogoths, led by ◊Theodoric the Great, and Italian ◊foederati, under ◊Odoacer. Although the Ostrogoths succeeded in driving Odoacer's men back towards Verona (see ◊Verona, Battle of 489), they were unable to destroy the army.

At the urging of the Eastern Roman Emperor Zeno, Theodoric led the Ostrogoths from Thrace (modern Bulgaria) over the Alps into northeastern Italy. They were met by Odoacer's force of Germanic veterans of the Roman army, who had seized power in Italy for themselves in 476. The strengths of the opposing armies are unknown but the numbers were probably quite small as all of the Ostrogothic people were later able to be lodged in the fairly small town of Pavia.

spahbad Sassanian Persian general. The commander in chief of the Empire's armies was the *Iran-spahbad*. Below this rank, the term was loosely applied to generals of all types.

The Sassanian Persian King Chosroes I established *spahbads* for the north, south, east, and west who may have been powerful ◊marzbans under another name.

spahi Ottoman word for a heavily armoured cavalryman, either raised from the provinces supported by a ◊timar estate or supported in the sultan's bodyguard.

Spangenhelm German word applied to any helmet made in segments riveted to a metal frame. This type of helmet became standard in the late Roman Empire and continued in use into the medieval period.

spara large Achaemenid Persian shield used by infantry in the 6th and 5th centuries BC. It was made of canes or thin wooden rods woven decoratively through a sheet of thick leather, and was rectangular in shape, about 160 cm/63 in tall.

The Greek historian Herodotus describes defensive barricades made of *sparas* at the battles of Plataea and Mykale (both 479 BC). Smaller shields were later used by Sassanian Persian infantry. Two examples from Dura Europus, dated about 255 AD, are approximately 1 m/39 in tall and a third measures 155 cm/61 in. All come to a point at one end, presumably the bottom, and there is a single wooden handle.

sparabara Achaemenid Persian infantry army in the 6th and 5th centuries BC. *Sparabaras* fought several ranks deep, probably ten. The front rank was armed with spears and large ◊sparas (shields); succeeding ranks were primarily archers. Persian, Median, and other Iranian units, including the ◊Immortals, were equipped this way.

They proved effective against Near Eastern opponents, including Scythian horse-archers, but could not stand against Greek ◊hoplites after the front rank's barricade of shields was breached.

Spartacus Revolt revolt against the Romans by gladiators and runaway slaves under the Thracian gladiator Spartacus that spread through southern Italy and Cisalpine Gaul from 73 to 71 BC. Spartacus inflicted numerous defeats on the hastily raised Roman armies sent against him before being defeated by the Roman general Marcus Licinius ◊Crassus (the Elder) in 71 BC.

When the Roman Senate finally gave the command to Crassus, he was placed at the head of eight ◊legions. He restored discipline to the demoralized troops and was able to defeat the slave army when internal disputes caused them to divide. Spartacus was killed and 6,000 captured slaves were crucified along the length of the Via Appia from Rome to Capua as a dreadful warning against servile revolt.

Spartolus, Battle of battle at Spartolus, in the Chalcidice (modern Khalkidiki) fought in 429 BC, during the ◊Peloponnesian War, that illustrates how well-handled light troops and cavalry could defeat Athenian hoplites.

The Athenians initially drove the Chalkidian hoplites, cavalry, and light troops back inside the city walls. When fresh light troops reached Spartolus, the defenders made a sortie. Each time the Athenians charged their opponents gave way, but a barrage of javelins held the Athenian hoplites at bay. The Chalkidian cavalry also made repeated charges, and eventually the disheartened Athenians fled to nearby Potidaea, losing all three of their commanders and 430 men.

spatha slashing sword used by the Roman cavalry during the early empire (1st century AD), evolved from the Celtic long sword. It became more generally used in the 2nd century. By the 3rd century *spatha* had become the general word for a sword, although many of the later Roman weapons hardly fit the original meaning of the word.

Blade lengths varied greatly, some being no longer than the Pompeian and Mainz type ◊*gladius*, while others were 80 cm/31 in or more. Some blades had parallel sides while others were tapered. The most noticeable change was that the sword was later suspended on the left side.

spaudler modern term for a medieval European piece of plate armour for the shoulder formed of narrow articulating lames, as opposed to the ◊pauldron in which the main plates were extended to cover parts of the chest and back. Spaudlers appeared before pauldrons, in the early to mid-14th century. They were usually permanently attached to the upper cannons of the ◊vambraces (or rerebraces).

spear-bearer (also called *apple-bearer, doruphoroi,* or *arötibara*) Achaemenid Persian household infantry, one or two regiments of 1,000 men recruited from the nobility. They were the infantry equivalent of the ◊Kinsmen. They were probably equipped as ◊*sparabara* in battle.

The Greek historian Herodotus describes two such regiments in the Persian king Xerxes' invasion of Greece in 480 BC, but might have confused one of them with the ◊Immortals. They may have later been re-equipped as ◊hoplites.

Spendius (lived 3rd century BC) escaped Italian slave who, together with ◊Mathos and ◊Autaritus, was one of the principal instigators of the ◊Mercenary War against Carthage.

Despite a major defeat at the River Bagradas in 240 BC at the hands of ◊Hamilcar Barca, his forces continued to harry the Carthaginian field army by avoiding the plains where the Punic war elephants and Numidian cavalry had the advantage. In 238 BC his force were trapped in a defile and starved. After their men had resorted to cannibalism, Spendius and Autaritus surrendered to save their troops. However, the weakened mercenaries (apparently numbering 40,000) were massacred and Spendius was crucified before the rebel base at Tunis.

Sphrantzes, George (1401–78) Byzantine historian and diplomat, and governor of Patras from 1430 and Mistra from 1442. He was taken prisoner at the fall of Constantinople in 1453 (see ◊Constantinople, Siege of 1453). His history covers 1413–77. He also wrote a section of another work dealing with the siege of the city.

spiculum late version of the ◊*pilum* described by the Roman military writer ◊Vegetius in the 5th century, with a head 22 cm/8.7 in long and a wooden shaft 147 cm/4.8 in long.

Spitamenes (died 328 BC) Sogdian leader who resisted ◊Alexander (III) the Great. He led a rebellion against Alexander in Bactria and Sogdia, besieging the Macedonian garrison of Marakanda (now Samarkand, Uzbekistan). Alexander's relief force was ambushed by Spitamenes and Alexander had to relieve Marakanda himself. In 328 BC Coenus defeated Spitamenes and sent his head to Alexander as a peace offering.

Spitamenes was allied with ◊Bessus in 329 BC but betrayed him to Alexander's general ◊Ptolemy (I) Soter, shortly before leading the general rebellion in Bactria and Sogdia.

Split palace (Roman *Salona*) palatial residence constructed by the Roman emperor Diocletian on the coast of Dalmatia (modern Croatia) at the beginning of the 4th century AD. Aware of the external and internal threats to the empire, Diocletian combined imperial luxury with strong security. When he abdicated in 305 and retired to Split it was to a palace that was designed as a fortress.

The rectangular complex (2.9 ha/7 acres) was enclosed by a circuit of walls 2.1 m/7 ft thick and 17 m/56 ft high. Gates at the centre of the east, west, and north sides were protected by octagonal flanking towers and had inner and outer gateways to create an open courtyard killing zone. External square towers stood at each of the four corners and in the intervals between these and the gates. Interval towers and gates were absent on the south side which was built against the Adriatic Sea and contained the imperial residence.

Sri Vidyanandana (lived 12th century) (or *Suryavarman*) king of Champa (modern central Vietnam), active during the period 1182–1203. As an exile in Cambodia, he was given command of a Khmer army. He defeated Cham forces, seized a kingdom for himself in Champa, then broke from the Khmers. He subsequently defeated several Khmer attacks until 1203, when he was driven out by a Khmer army commanded by his own uncle, Ong Dhanapatigrama. He fled by sea to Vietnam, but was refused help and disappeared. Champa was a Khmer province until 1220.

As a young exiled prince Vidyanandana took refuge with ◊Jayavarman VII of Cambodia in 1182, and distinguished himself fighting rebels. In 1190 Cambodia was again attacked by the Cham King ◊Jaya Indravarman IV. Jayavarman gave command of the Khmer army to Vidyanandana, who defeated and captured Jaya Indravarman, taking the Cham capital, Vijaya. Vidyanandana set up Jayavarman's Cham brother-in-law as a puppet king and seized a kingdom for himself at Panduranga in the south, where he reigned as King Suryavarman. When rebels deposed the puppet the next year, Vidyanandana defeated them. The Khmers also sent the captive Jaya Indravarman IV against the rebels, but Vidyanandana turned on him and defeated and killed him in turn in 1192. He thus became king of a reunited Champa free of Khmer rule.

Stafford castle castle in England, 24 km/15 mi north of Wolverhampton. A timber ◊motte-and-bailey castle was erected here in around 1070, but it was destroyed by 1086 according to the *Domesday Book*. A fresh work was in existence early in the 12th century, but nothing is known of its form. In 1348 the Earl of Stafford commissioned a new work and had a rectangular three-storied, turreted tower built on the mound. It survived the Wars of the Roses (1455–85).

Stainmore, Battle of ambush by Anglo-Saxon forces in 954 of the exiled King of Norway, ◊Erik Bloodaxe, in the Northumbrian Moors, in northern England. Erik, who had tried to seize northern England, was killed in the battle. The ambush was set by Oswulf Ealdulfing, the High Reeve of Bamburgh, who supported the Saxon king of England, ◊Eadred. As a result of Erik's death, the independent Norse kingdom of Northumbria was brought under English control.

stakes mobile field defence system used by medieval English archers, consisting of sharpened stakes driven into the ground, which enabled them to hold the line against cavalry attack. They were first used at Agincourt (see ◊Agincourt, Battle of) in 1415, when ◊Henry V of England ordered his archers to cut 2-m/6-ft stakes, sharpened at both ends, and drive them into the ground.

Even the famed English bowmen could not stand unprotected against cavalry charges. They usually took cover behind fixed defences such as hedges, ditches, or potholes, which restricted their tactical movement. Portable stakes, the sharpened ends of which formed a barrier to prevent enemy cavalry charging into the archers' positions, gave them a new mobility on the battlefield.

Stamford Bridge, Battle of surprise attack at Stamford Bridge, in northern England, on 25 September 1066 by ◊Harold (II) Godwinson, King of England, who defeated and killed his rebel brother Tostig and his ally Harald Sigurdsson (◊Harald Hardrada), King of Norway.

The exiled Tostig had brought Harald and his army to England in a bid for the throne. After their victory over the northern English at Fulford Gate on 20 September, the Norse troops were resting outside York. Harold marched with exceptional speed from the south coast, where he had been waiting for William, Duke of Normandy, and caught the enemy army unprepared. Many had no armour and the English, delayed for a while by a solitary defender of a bridge, slaughtered most of them. Both Tostig and Harald were killed, and only about 1,000 Norsemen escaped alive.

standard (derived from French) large battle flag. The term first appeared in the 12th century. The Battle of Northallerton in 1138 (see ◊Northallerton, Battle of) is also known as the Battle of the Standard because the English army mounted a large standard on a ◊carroccio as its command centre.

Stefan Urosh (IV) Dushan (died 1355) king of Serbia from 1331 and Rumania from 1345. After the conquest of Serres in 1345, Dushan was proclaimed tsar (emperor). He built the empire of Serbia, although it did not survive long after his death.

Following his father's victory at Velbuzd in 1330 which established Serbian authority over Macedonia, Dushan imprisoned him and seized power. He was particularly astute at exploiting Byzantine weaknesses during the civil war of 1341–47, and as a result was able to annex Epiros, Albania, and Thessaly. This extended his power from the Danube to the Gulf of Corinth and from the Adriatic to the Aegean.

Stilicho, Flavius (AD 365–408) Roman general, notable for his defence of the Western Roman Empire against a series of invasions by Germanic tribes. He campaigned successfully against ◊Alaric's Visigoths and broke the power of a large Germanic invasion led by ◊Radagaisus. He was, however, unable to prevent the crossing of the Rhine in the winter of 406–07 by the Vandals, Suevi, Burgundians, and Alans. He was blamed for mishandling the political and military situation in the West and was executed at Ravenna.

Stilicho was the son of a Vandal who had fought on the Roman side at Adrianople in 378 (see ◊Adrianople campaign), although his mother was Roman. He enjoyed the patronage of the emperor ◊Theodosius and was given a series of high-level appointments. By 394 he held a military command at Frigidius (see ◊Frigidius, Battle of) and after Theodosius' victory he was appointed ◊*magister militum* in the West and made the guardian of the young Western emperor Honorius. He married the adopted daughter of Theodosius and married his own daughter to Honorius.

Although a very able military commander, Stilicho was less adept at political manoeuvring and he made powerful enemies at court, due in large part to his hostility towards the Eastern Empire. In 408 his troops were encouraged to mutiny and he was captured and executed.

stimuli equestrian spurs, widely used in the ancient world; also the term used by the Roman general and political leader Julius Caesar for antipersonnel devices, such as partially buried spikes.

Stirling castle castle in Scotland, 32 km/20 mi northwest of Glasgow. Built as a timber and earth castle probably late in the 11th century, it is sited on a rock so as to command the road to the Highlands.

During much of the 12th and 13th centuries it was attacked, razed, rebuilt, burned, or besieged until it was finally taken by Edward I in 1304. Ten years later, after the Battle of Bannockburn in 1314 (see ◊Bannockburn, Battle of) it was regained by the Scots and was then demolished. The site remained empty until work began in the 15th century under the Stewarts.

stirrup, impact of although stirrups certainly made riding a horse more comfortable and provided a firmer base from which the rider could use his weapons, their military impact has often been overstated by modern historians. An Asiatic invention, stirrups were probably introduced into western Europe in the early 7th century by the ◊Avars. Effective cavalry operated long before this and many European armies had already become predominantly cavalry forces. Prior to the introduction of stirrups, Celtic, Roman, and Middle Eastern saddles were built up with horns, arches, or pommels to provide the rider with a secure seat, enabling him to use his weapons effectively.

Stoke, Battle of battle fought on 16 June 1487 during the English Wars of the Roses (see ◊Roses, Wars of the), in which Henry VII (1457–1509) defeated rebels including many foreign mercenaries led by the English impostor Lambert Simnel (c. 1475–c. 1535). The battle, fought outside Newark, Nottinghamshire, marked the end of wars going back three decades to the Battle of St Albans in 1455.

Henry led some 15,000 men, with 6,000 in the vanguard under the skilful Earl of Oxford. The rebels mustered 8,000, including 2,000 mercenary German and Swiss pikemen, but with substantial numbers of poorly equipped Irish troops and too few archers. Their tight formation drove back Oxford's men initially, but Oxford began to pour arrows into the rebels' packed ranks. A massacre followed, many dying in a ravine (the Red Gutter), with possibly 50% casualties.

Stokesay castle castle in England, 32 km/20 mi south of Shrewsbury, in Shropshire. It is among the best-preserved fortified manor houses in existence.

Stokesay began in around 1202 as a simple two-story rubble masonry tower with a wall turret. Later in the century the building was extended by the addition of a long hall structure to the south side of the tower. Finally, in around 1290, a second tower was built at the southern end of the hall, three stories high and with a crenellated (indented square) parapet. From the two towers a curtain wall ran to enclose a bailey to the east.

stonsde the regimental districts into which the ◊*ru* of the Tibetan Empire were divided. There were ideally eight large and one small *stonsde* for each *ru*. Like the *ru* they were territorial as well as military units, and hence the basis of local government.

Small tribes formed one *stonsde*, while larger tribes were divided. The name means 'districts of a thousand', so they may originally have provided 1,000 troops each, but by the imperial period they provided more than that, and commanders of a thousand were a lower rank than the overall *stonsde* commander. The system was extended to conquered territories including the former Tuyuhun kingdom (now in Qinghai) and even to occupied Chinese territory.

stradiot medieval Italian light cavalryman, similar to the later Hungarian hussar, used for skirmishing and hanging on the flanks of an enemy force, employed by the Venetians and others during the medieval period.

strategos, Byzantine (plural *strategoi*) Greek term for a general or commander of an army; a senior military appointment in the Byzantine Empire.

strategos, Greek (plural *strategoi*) Greek general in the Classical period. In Athens, ten were elected each year. The Arcadian and Achaean Leagues, as well as other parts of Greece, had one *strategos* who served as both president and commander in chief.

Strongbow (lived 12th century) (nickname of *Richard FitzGilbert* of Clare) earl of Pembroke 1148–76 who conquered Dublin and Leinster 1170–71. 'Strongbow's' reputation probably owes much to his name, but he was typical of the English military adventurers of his time: French in language and military culture but operating in a British context. He was so successful (partly by marrying the daughter of Dermot, King of Leinster) that Henry II brought over a large expedition, 1171–72, to bring him under control.

Strongbow brought heavily-armoured men and archers into territories largely lacking both, which gave the invaders the upper hand. His victory at Castleknock in 1171 over the High King Rory O'Connor was achieved by combining mounted knights, archers, and Irish foot soldiers. Like all invaders of Ireland he also adopted the native techniques of raiding and burning to achieve his domination.

Subeibe castle castle on a ridge in the Golan Heights region of Israel/Syria, built by the crusaders after 1129 and enlarged later by Muslim rulers. It was besieged by Muslims in 1157 but was rescued by a relief force. The Knights Hospitallers (see ◊Military Order) took over the upkeep of Subeibe in return for half the town of Banyas just below it, but it fell in 1164 and never returned to Christian hands.

The castle is over 411 m/450 yds long and 59 m/65 yds wide, and runs along a sharp ridge. The northern wall stands above a sheer drop and has no towers. The citadel at the eastern end is particularly strong. Thirteenth-century Ayyubid caliphs reconstructed the site, as did the Baibars in 1260.

Su Dingfang (lived 7th century) (or *Su Ting-fang*) Tang Chinese general. In 657 he defeated a Western Turk rebellion, completing the destruction of their power begun under the Emperor ◊Tang Taizong. Su then served in the Korean wars (see ◊Korea, Tang Chinese wars in), capturing the Paekche capital Sabi in 660 (see ◊Sabi, Siege of) in alliance with ◊Kim Yusin. In 662 he besieged Pyongyang, capital of Koguryo, but had to withdraw because the siege could not be supplied through the winter.

Sui Wendi (541–604) (or *Sui Wen-ti*) emperor of China 581–604. During his reign his general ◊Yang Su conquered the Chen dynasty of south China in 589, thus reuniting China after 270 years of division. The general and minister ◊Pei Ju pacified the southern tribes and the general ◊Liu Fang reconquered Vietnam and raided Champa. Less successful foreign campaigns included the first of the invasions of Korea (see ◊Korea, Sui Chinese wars in).

Yang Jian, as the future emperor was originally called, enlisted at the age of 14 under the tribal general ◊Yuwen Tai and became a general under Tai's heirs in northwest China, the northern Zhou. He participated in the Zhou conquest of northern Qi in 577 which reunited the north. He seized power after defeating local opponents at Ye, proclaiming himself Emperor Wendi of the Sui dynasty in 581.

suji kabuto Japanese helmet whose bowl is formed of separate iron plates joined together with the edges turned outwards to form vertical ridges, introduced in the early Muromachi period (1333–1568) and used continuously by the samurai. There could be over 100 plates in a single bowl of a *suji kabuto*.

With the exception of minor modifications to the neck guard (◊*shikoro*), which in some types became more vertical, the turned-back side plates (◊*fukigaeshi*), which generally became smaller and more rudimentary, and the bowl itself, which changed shape to accommodate different hairstyles, the parts of the *suji* ◊*kabuto* were similar in most respects to those found on the earlier kabuto.

Sun Bin (lived 4th century BC) (or *Sun Pin*) Chinese military theorist and general of the Chinese ◊Warring States state of Qi, whose lost *Bing Fa/Art of War or Military Methods* was rediscovered in 1972. He was a descendant of the theorist ◊Sunzi. He masterminded two great victories over the state of Wei, at Guiling in 354 BC (see ◊Guiling, Battle of) and Maling in 341 BC (see ◊Maling, Battle of). His victory at Maling is the first recorded use of massed crossbows.

Like Sunzi, Sun Bin stressed identification and manipulation of the enemy's weaknesses, assessing the balance of strength, and the classification of terrain. Changes in warfare since Sunzi's time were reflected by the importance assigned to crossbows and field fortifications.

surcoat long, flowing fabric tunic worn over armour, which carried the personal arms or

SULLA, PUBLIUS CORNELIUS (138–78 BC)

Roman general and dictator. He was elected consul in 88 BC after defeating the Samnites several times during the Social War (see ◊Italian Social War). When, in the same year, ◊Marius tried to deprive him of the command against ◊Mithridates (VI) Eupator of Pontus, Sulla took the unprecedented step of marching on Rome, executing or putting to flight his rivals. His campaign against Mithridates ended successfully in 85 BC, and Sulla returned to Italy in 83 where his opponents had raised armies against him. Sulla defeated them in 82 and massacred all his opponents. After holding supreme power as dictator and carrying out a series of political reforms, he retired to private life in 80 BC.

Sulla came from an old but impoverished family and entered politics late in life. He made a reputation for himself in 107 BC when, as Marius' quaestor, he arranged the capture of the African king ◊Jugurtha. His reputation was further enhanced by his command at Campania during the Social War in 90 BC, and his defeats of the Samnites eased his election to the consulship. After defeating Marius in 88 BC, Sulla left Italy for the war against Pontus, in northeast Asia Minor. He stormed Athens after a long siege and subjected it to a brutal sack, then defeated the forces of the Pontic king Mithridates at Chaeronea (see ◊Chaeronea, Battle of 86 BC) and Orchomenus (see ◊Orchomenus, Battle of). Before the second battle, he built strong fieldworks to defend his army's flanks against the numerically superior enemy. When enemy attacks dispersed the Romans working on these fortifications, Sulla rallied his troops by seizing a standard and proclaiming that they must fight or abandon him. Sulla's enemies seized power during his absence from Rome, but on his return in 83 he defeated one army near Capua, a town in southern Italy, then persuaded another to defect to him. He blockaded Marius' son until the main Marian army, including a large contingent of Samnites, advanced on Rome and forced him to abandon his siege in some haste. In 82 he confronted them in a fierce battle outside Rome's Colline Gate, where both sides suffered heavily before the enemy withdrew. Sulla's victory was accompanied by mass executions of his opponents. Like Caesar and Pompey, Sulla was always keen to portray himself as a lucky general, a virtue the Romans admired.

device of a medieval European knight for the purpose of identification.

Surena (c. 80–c. 52 BC) Parthian general and member of the Suren family, one of the great royal families of Parthian Iran. He defeated the Roman commander Publius Licinius ◊Crassus at Carrhae (see ◊Carrhae, Battle of) in 53 BC. The Parthian king had Surena killed not long afterwards because he was jealous of his reputation.

Surena was left to defend Mesopotamia with 10,000 cavalry in 53 BC while the main Parthian army awaited Crassus' Romans in Armenia. When Crassus made a surprise attack across the open plains instead, Surena met and defeated him at Carrhae. Crassus was killed during surrender talks, perhaps after Roman treachery.

suriage Japanese custom of cutting down the long cavalry swords of the Heian and Kamakura periods (794–1333) to a more suitable length for the style of warfare on foot that evolved during the Muromachi period (1333–1568).

Suryavarman I (lived 11th century) king of Cambodia 1002–50, the son of a Malay king of Tambralinga and a Khmer princess. He landed in eastern Cambodia in 1001 to assert his rather weak claim to the throne against Udayadityavarman, who came to the throne in that year. He defeated Udayadityavarman in 1002, and then fought his successor

SUNZI (OR *SUN TZU* OR *SUN WU*)

Chinese military theorist whose book, *Sunzi Bing Fa/Master Sun's Art of War*, is the most famous of the ◊Seven Military Classics and still influential today. While some of his work is cryptic, partly because it is expressed briefly and in abstract terms, and some critics suggest that his principles are obvious generalities, the work's brevity, comprehensiveness and level-headed realism have influenced many later commanders. Sunzi's disciples include ◊Cao Cao, ◊Takeda Shingen, whose flag bore a quote from Sunzi, and Mao Zedong.

Sunzi (literally 'Master Sun') was probably the same as the historical Sun Wu, an officer of ◊Holu of Wu. Some scholars argue that the *Sunzi Bing Fa* is a later Warring States work since it is too sophisticated for Sun Wu's time. But it is becoming clear that early Chinese warfare was more advanced than sometimes supposed and the *Bing Fa* probably is based on Sun Wu's ideas, though heavily edited later. A copy from a tomb dated 134 BC is in essentially its modern form. In contrast to the mystical streak present in some later Chinese military writing, Sunzi emphasized rational calculation. He argued that warfare should be thoroughly analysed and that the balance of forces on opposing sides be assessed and compared. Aware of the heavy financial cost of warfare, he warned against protracted campaigns and sieges and recommended getting provisions from enemy territory. Best of all, he said, avoid battle: 'To defeat the enemy without fighting is the peak of excellence'. Sunzi stressed intelligence, secret agents, speed, deception and exploiting the enemy's weaknesses. The general must be inscrutable and self-controlled, never revealing his plans even to his own officers. He must be neither reckless, cowardly, nor easily provoked. He must assess the enemy's dispositions without revealing his own and attack only when he has created suitable conditions for victory: 'Know the enemy and know yourself; in a hundred battles you will not be in danger'. Like many Chinese philosophers, Sunzi stressed that government must be devoted to the welfare of the people, rewarding the deserving and punishing the unruly, in order to unite the nation behind the ruler and the army. Similarly, the troops must be fiercely disciplined but their welfare cannot be neglected. Sunzi used the philosophical distinction between orthodox or direct (*zheng*) methods and those that are unorthodox, indirect, or extraordinary (*qi*). The exact implications depend on context, but to engage an enemy frontally with heavy troops would be *zheng* and then to turn a flank from an ambush would be *qi*, for example. Neither is necessarily superior to the other. There is no single secret to victory: 'None of the five elements is constantly dominant'. This image from Chinese philosophy suggests that change is continual and that the general must adapt to it using the right tactics to fit the circumstances.

Jayaviravarman and took the capital, Angkor, in 1010. Suryavarman expanded the Khmer frontier to the northwest, conquering the Mon states of Haripunjaya and Lavo in the lower Menam valley.

Suryavarman II (died 1150) king of Cambodia from 1130, usurping the throne from Dharanindravarman I by leaping onto the head of the king's elephant to kill him in single combat. Suryavarman led Khmer armies further than ever before, especially in raids on Dai Viet (Vietnam), but with limited success. He died of fever, probably on the way to meet Vietnamese enemy troops.

In 1128 he led 20,000 men against Dai Viet, but was defeated. In 1129 he raided the Vietnamese coast with 700 ships. He forced Jaya Indravarman III, King of Champa, to join another attack on Dai Viet in 1131. When this failed, Jaya Indravarman made peace with Dai Viet and did not support Suryavarman's unsuccessful attack in 1138. In revenge, Suryavarman attacked Champa in 1145, took the capital, Vijaya, and captured or killed Jaya Indravarman. He occupied northern Champa and attacked the south with an army of Khmers and Chams, but was defeated by Jaya Harivarman I at Rajapura and Virapura in 1148. Suryavarman set up a puppet Cham king to win local support, but in 1149 Jaya Harivarman defeated the puppet at Mahisa and expelled the Khmers. In the west Suryavarman extended Khmer rule among the Mon kingdoms.

Sviatoslav (died 971) prince of Kiev 964–72 who campaigned successfully against the Khazaks, Pechenegs, and Bulgars. He helped the Byzantines conquer Bulgaria 967–69, but went to war with his former allies over the division of the spoils of the campaign. He was decisively defeated by the Byzantines in 971 (see ◊Silistra, Battle of), and on his way home to Kiev was ambushed and killed by the Pechenegs.

Svoldr, Battle of victory in 1000 for a combined Swedish-Danish fleet over the Norwegians, in which the Norwegian King Olaf Tryggvasson was killed. As a result of the battle, the Danish King ◊Swein Forkbeard became overlord of Norway.

The Norwegian king, betrayed by the ◊Jomsvikings and some of his own followers, was ambushed off the Island of Svoldr (probably off the Baltic coast of Germany). He lashed his eleven ships together with his flagship *Long Serpent* in the centre. The Danes and Swedes suffered heavy losses attacking King Olaf's line, but their Norwegian allies under Jarl Eric attacked Olaf's flanks, destroying ship after ship, until only the *Long Serpent* was left. Eric's men boarded Olaf's ship, and after hard fighting cleared its decks. Olaf jumped overboard and was drowned.

swayamvara (Sanskrit 'maiden's choice') Rajput custom that allowed a princess to choose her own husband from noble suitors assembled at her father's court.

The event was marked by displays of martial prowess, archery contests, and skill-at-arms competitions, accompanied by feasting and other entertainments, at the conclusion of which the princess threw her garland over the favoured suitor. Attendance at the ceremony implied that the suitor accepted the overlordship of the princess's father.

Swein Forkbeard Danish king from about 987 who took the kingdom by force from his father Harald Bluetooth (r. 958–87) and went on to conquer Norway and England.

Sybota, Battle of sea battle in 433 BC at the Sybota islands (probably the modern Sivota and Ayios Nikolaos), one of the greatest ever fought between Greeks and an immediate cause of the ◊Peloponnesian War.

The battle involved 10 triremes from Athens plus 110 triremes from Kerkyra (modern Corfu) against 150 from Corinth and its allies. The Athenians, who had come to Kerkyra's aid, were ordered not to interfere except to prevent a landing on the island itself, but they joined in when their outnumbered allies began to give way. Even Athenian skills were not enough to save the Kerkyraians, however, and they were driven back to land with the loss of 70 ships. After towing away the captured vessels, the Corinthians prepared to renew the fight, but they were frightened off by the approach of 20 Athenian ships which they mistakenly thought heralded a larger fleet.

Syene (Syrian name *Sin*) fortress in Upper Egypt, on the River Nile at Syene (modern Aswan), opposite Elephantine. Under the Persians in the 6th and 5th centuries BC it had a Syrian garrison, the Aramaeans of Sin the Fortress, organized much like the Jewish garrison at Elephantine. The Syene garrison left records written in Aramaic on papyrus.

Symeon tsar of Bulgaria 893–927. He campaigned successfully against the Byzantines for most of his reign, inflicting several defeats and repeatedly threatening Constantinople.

synaspismos ('joined shields') in Greek warfare, the closest-order military formation. Only 46 cm/18 in separated the right shoulder of each man from the right shoulder of his neighbour – the formation was thus literally shoulder-to-shoulder.

syntagma in Greek warfare, any body of troops drawn up in order. In the ideal army of ◊Asclepiodotus, a unit of 256 men.

Syphax (died 201 BC) king of the Numidian tribe of the Masaesyles (in north Africa) who united his nomadic subjects into a strong state and established a formidable army. He was an ally of Carthage during the Second Punic War (see ◊Punic War, Second), apart from a brief period of support for Rome.

His loyalty to Carthage was secured by marriage, and he fought against Publius Cornelius ◊Scipio's invasion of Africa with the Carthaginian army. Exhausted by the conflict, his army was defeated in 203 BC in his own kingdom near Cirta. He was captured and his kingdom was given to ◊Masinissa by the Romans. Syphax was sent to Italy as a prisoner and died there within the year.

Syracuse, Battle of battle between Athens and the city of Syracuse in southeast Sicily in 415 BC, during the ◊Peloponnesian War, that provides a rare example of the use of reserves in a hoplite battle.

After luring the Syracusan army away with false information, the Athenians landed unopposed in the Grand Harbour southwest of the port of Syracuse. When the Syracusans returned the next day, the battle began. The Athenians drew up half their army eight deep, with their allies to right and left. The other half was kept in reserve to protect their camp and the non-combatants. Unusually, the Syracusans and their allies drew up 16 deep with all their cavalry on the right. The decisive moment seems to have come when a thunderstorm frightened the inexperienced Syracusans. Shortly afterwards the Argives on the Athenian right forced the Syracusan left wing back. The Athenians broke through in the centre, cutting the Syracusan forces in half and forcing them to flee.

Syracuse, Siege of Athens' failed siege of the Sicilian city of Syracuse from 414 to 413 BC which, with the annihilation of the besieging Athenian forces, became a turning point in the ◊Peloponnesian War.

The siege began when Athenian forces captured the Epipolai heights, a plateau to the north and northwest of the city of Syracuse. There they established a heavily defended spot known as The Circle. To counter, Syracuse's Spartan ally Gylippus built defensive fortifications north of The Circle.

With reinforcements under ◊Demosthenes, the Athenians attempted to take these fortifications in a daring night attack in 413, but the attack failed and Demosthenes advised the general ◊Nicias to withdraw. Nicias delayed because of an eclipse of the moon on 27 August 413, and when, after two failures to break out by sea, the Athenians tried to escape by land,

they were hunted down and forced to surrender.

Syr-Darya campaign campaign 1389–92 by ◊Timur Leng (Tamerlane) of Samarkand in the basin of the river Syr-Darya in Central Asia, against local rulers who had taken advantage of his absence in the west to invade Transoxiana. By securing his northern and eastern flanks, the campaign allowed Timur to concentrate his forces for further offensives, against first Iran, and then Delhi.

Timur rapidly dispersed his opponents and followed up his success by plundering and enslaving the population of Khwarazm and by defeating his former protégé Tokhtamish, Mongol Khan of the Golden Horde.

Syria and Egypt, Persian conquest of series of conquests by the Persian king, ◊Chosroes II, over the Byzantines between 603–20 which resulted in Sassanid Persian occupation of most of Armenia, Anatolia, Syria, and Egypt.

Chosroes launched the attacks to take advantage of civil war and anarchy in the Byzantine Empire. In 614 the Persians conquered Damascus and Jerusalem, capturing the Christian relic the True Cross. In 616 a Persian army commanded by Shahin took Chalcedon (modern Kadiköy), an ancient Greek city in Bithynia on the Bosporus, after a long siege. In the same year, an army under Shahrbaraz invaded Egypt and cut off the vital corn supplies to Constantinople. Although these conquests were the greatest military achievements of the Sassanians against the Romans or Byzantines, they were not sustainable and fell to a counterattack led by the Emperor ◊Heraclius a few years later.

Syrian War war fought 195–190 BC between Rome and King ◊Antiochus (III) the Great of Syria. It was concluded by a treaty which involved Rome in Eastern affairs.

Following the Roman destruction of the state of Macedonia, Antiochus invaded Greece to try and take advantage of the power vacuum created there. A Roman army intercepted him and he was pushed back to Asia Minor and defeated at Magnesia (see ◊Magnesia, Battle of) and Myonnessus (see ◊Myonnessus, Battle of) in 190 BC.

syssition alternative name for the Spartan ◊phidition.

tabar (plural **tabarzin**) Persian term for a 'saddle axe', a short axe used by cavalry throughout the Islamic world.

tabard form of ◊surcoat worn in late medieval Europe. In the 14th century the tabard was a sleeveless overgarment worn by the lower classes, and by 1400 the term was applied to the surcoat, decorated with (in fact called) a herald's coat of arms. From the 1430s the term was applied to a knight's short-sleeved surcoat, open at the sides and decorated with his coat of arms.

Tacfarinas (died AD 24) deserter from a Roman auxiliary unit who built up a following amongst the Numidian and Mauretanian tribes and from AD 17 to 24 raided the Roman province of Africa. He was finally killed when the Romans mounted a surprise attack on his camp.

tachi Japanese slung sword, originating in the Heian period (794–1185) and used continuously for cavalry use and carried with the cutting edge facing down. Different styles of *tachi* were also worn at court and on ceremonial occasions.

T'aejo king of the Koryo kingdom in northern Korea 636–43; see ◊Wang Kon.

Taga castle (Japanese *Taga-jō*; originally known as *Taga no ki*) Japanese fortification built in the 8th century in the north of Honshu island, Japan, as imperial military and administrative headquarters in the wars to subjugate the Ezo tribespeople. The original stockade was destroyed in 737 and rebuilt as a castle in 780, eventually falling into disuse after the successful military operations in Honshu.

Taginae, Battle of decisive battle in the Byzantine–Gothic war in Italy that gave the Byzantine forces control of Rome. It was fought in 522 at Taginae, a narrow mountain valley near modern Gualdo Tadino, and is a classic example of the effective use of properly coordinated infantry, archers, and cavalry.

For the first time in this war, the Byzantine army was large and well funded. It was commanded by the eunuch ◊Narses and comprised nearly 30,000 men, including contingents of Lombards, Gepids, Heruls, Huns, and Persians in addition to Roman troops. The Goths, commanded by King ◊Totila, were significantly outnumbered, with probably no more than 15,000–18,000 troops. The two armies met face to face in the Apennines and encamped close to each other on a plain surrounded by hills.

Totila first tried to compensate for his weakness in numbers by attempting to seize a hill from which he could outflank the enemy position, but he was stopped by a unit of 50 Roman infantry. Having held the hill, Narses deployed his army in a strong defensive position: his infantry in the centre, bolstered by dismounted Lombards and Heruls, with cavalry and archers on the wings curving out from the centre in a crescent. He also deployed a unit of 1,000 Roman cavalry on the right wing to act as a flanking force.

Totila delayed while waiting for an additional 2,000 cavalry to join him, then, after attempts to draw out the Romans had failed, he launched an attack after the midday meal. His troops attempted to break through the Roman centre with a cavalry charge. Relying solely on close combat weapons, they took heavy casualties from the Roman archers and were forced back. Repeated charges made no impression on the Roman line, and when the Goths were sufficiently weakened Narses launched his flanking force which broke the enemy. The Gothic infantry, who were deployed in a second line, played no part in the battle and were swept up in the rout. More than 6,000 Goths, including Totila, were killed, with minimal Roman losses.

Tagliacozzo, Battle of battle fought in central Italy on 23 August 1268 in which Charles of Anjou, King of Sicily, defeated his Hohenstaufen rival Conradin of Germany and secured his Sicilian crown.

Charles defended a dried-up river line with 4,000 men, keeping 1,000 as a hidden reserve. Conradin attacked with 6,000. His vanguard tried to force a bridge but was checked; half its force crossed further upstream and fell on the left flank of the Angevin main body, which lost its commander and standard-bearer. Victory seemed assured for Conradin. While his men went in pursuit and search of plunder he remained on the battlefield with his small bodyguard. Suddenly, Charles emerged from ambush and attacked and scattered the Germans. Conradin escaped but his army dispersed. He was later captured and executed by Charles on 29 October.

tagma Byzantine tactical unit of approximately 300 men; the same as a ◊*bandon*.

tagmata central regular Byzantine army based at Constantinople (modern Istanbul, Turkey), consisting of three cavalry regiments: the *Scholae, Excubiti,* and *Viglae* with a fourth regiment (the *Ikanatoi*) added in the 9th century.

Tahir the Ambidextrous (real name *Tahir bin al-Husain Dhu'l Yaminain*) general of the Abbasid caliph al-Mamun, and founder of the Tahirid dynasty, the first line of Iranian rulers of Khurasan (northeastern Iran) after the Muslim conquest.

In the war of succession between the two sons of Harun al-Rashid, Tahir supported al-Mamun against al-Amin, and led his army to victory at the battle of Ray in 810, where he gained his nickname by cutting a soldier in half with his left hand. After a campaign in which the Arab west was defeated by the Iranian east, Tahir's soldiers captured Baghdad and killed al-Amin.

In 821 Tahir intrigued with al-Mamun's vizier Ahmed ibn Abi Khalid to obtain the governorship of Khurasan, but once there declared his independence of the caliphate. He died in 822, poisoned by the vizier's agents.

taifa term for the small Muslim kingdoms that appeared in Spain in the 11th century during the Christian ◊*Reconquista,* following the disintegration of the caliphate of Córdoba. There were 7 major *taifas* and about 16 lesser ones.

They were mostly based on alliances formed by existing ethnic communities (mainly Berbers or Arabs), with Christian or Muslim principalities, often involving payment of *parias* (tributes). Many fell to the Almoravids (a Berber dynasty) in the 11th century. They disappeared as Spain was reconquered by the Christians.

Taigong (lived 12th–11th centuries BC) (or *T'ai Kung*) Chinese general who served

King ◊Wu of Zhou. His name was Jiang Shang or Lu Shang; the exact meaning of his title Taigong is unclear. He commanded the Zhou army at the victory of Mu (see ◊Mu, Battle of), and was rewarded with the duchy of Qi in the east.

After Wu's death he helped the regency authorities put down a rebellion by ◊Di Xin of Shang's son and disaffected Zhou princes.

He is traditionally credited with writing the *Six Secret Teachings* and the *Three Strategies of Huang Shigong,* two of the ◊Seven Military Classics.

Taiheiki (Japanese 'the chronicle of great peace') one of Japan's war tales (◊*Gunki monogatari*) written in the late 14th century, consisting of some 40 volumes and dealing with the events which surrounded the creation of the ◊Northern and Southern Courts.

The tale is divided into three parts. The first deals with the ◊Kemmu Restoration, the second with the rebellion of Ashikaga Takauji and the creation of the two courts, and the third with the creation of the ◊Muromachi shogunate and the victory and establishment of the Northern Court.

The tales are Confucian in their approach to the social disorder of the time and deal particularly with the phenomenon known in Japanese as ◊*gekokujō* (the overthrow of the ruling military or political classes by the lower classes).

Taila II (or *Taipala II*) king c. 973–95 of the western Chalukya dynasty. He overthrew his Rashtrakuta overlords in 973 and replaced them as the major power in the Deccan. He was a rival of ◊Rajaraja I, his southern neighbour.

Taira Atsumori (1168–84) member of the Japanese ◊Taira family remembered for the probably apocryphal story of his death at the Battle of Ichi no Tani, the decisive battle of the ◊Taira–Minamoto Wars.

Caught fleeing by the Minamoto warrior Kumagai Naozane, he was spared on account of his youthful beauty and resemblance to Kumagai's own son. Seeing other Minamoto arriving and knowing that they would kill Atsumori, Kumagai slew him and then abandoned his life as a warrior and entered the priesthood. The story has become one of Japan's most enduring and poignant themes of literature and drama.

Taira family (or *Heike*) one of the four great Japanese families of the Heian period (710–94). As the emperor was polygamous, a process known as dynastic shedding evolved, whereby offspring far removed from the direct line were given noble surnames and appointments in the provinces. It is from this distinguished lineage that the Taira evolved as a military and political power.

Taira Kiyomori (1118–81) Japanese warrior. After the ◊Hōgen Disturbance of 1156, he was rewarded more generously than ◊Minamoto Yoshitomo for defending the emperor. Yoshitomo's disaffection led to the ◊Heiji Disturbance of 1160 in which Kiyomori crushed the Minamoto and gained military control of Kyoto and the court, thereby setting the scene for future intrigues which would result in the ◊Taira–Minamoto Wars.

Kiyomori is the central figure of the war chronicle ◊*Heike monogatari*.

Taira Masakado (died 940) Japanese warrior of the Heian period who was the first of the military class to attempt to take power by force from the court. He attacked the Kantō headquarters of the government in 940 and assumed the title of 'New Emperor', but was quickly defeated by imperial forces.

Taira–Minamoto Wars (or *Gempei Wars*) major conflict of 1180–85 between the ◊Taira family and the ◊Minamoto family of Japan, which resulted in the crushing defeat of the Taira and the establishment of a ◊Warrior Government by ◊Minamoto Yoritomo, which was to last in various forms for almost 700 years.

In the aftermath of the Hōgen and Heiji disturbances (see ◊Hōgen Disturbance and ◊Heiji Disturbance), the Minamoto had been all but crushed by the Taira who were heavily influential at the imperial court. In 1180 ◊Minamoto Yorimasa and the second son of the retired emperor called for an uprising and Yorimasa sent edicts to all Minamoto asking that they join them. This uprising was crushed at the Battle of the Uji River (see ◊Uji River, Battle of the). Minamoto Yoritomo gathered forces to attack the Taira but he in turn was defeated and retreated to Kamakura. Having established a strong military base, he once again attacked the Taira at Fujigawa (see ◊Fujigawa, Battle of the), this time securing a significant victory.

Between late 1180 and 1183 the wars consisted of little more than minor skirmishes while both sides consolidated their power bases. In late 1183 ◊Minamoto Yoshinaka took control of Kyoto, but his provincial warriors proved to be almost as unacceptable to the population of Kyoto as the Taira had been. The Taira forces which counterattacked were defeated. Yoritomo sent ◊Minamoto Yoshitsune to Kyoto and Yoshinaka was defeated in February 1184. Yoritomo followed up this victory with a series of crushing defeats against the Taira, notably at Ichi no Tani, Yashima, and finally at Dan no Ura (see ◊Ichi no Tani, Battle of, ◊Yashima, Battle of, and ◊Dan no Ura, Battle of).

Taiyuan, Battle of (or *T'ai-yüan*) battle in 541 BC in which the Chinese state of Jin defeated a coalition of barbarian tribes. Jin invaded the area to its north and was confronted in a narrow ravine by a large army of Di and Wuzhong infantry. The Jin commander dismounted his chariot-crews to fight as infantry, deploying in five bodies. One officer who refused to dismount was beheaded. The Jin infantry then attacked and defeated the barbarians before they could deploy properly.

taka light shield, probably crescent-shaped, carried by Persian ◊*peltasts*, or possibly ◊*takabara*, in the later 5th and 4th centuries BC. They were similar to the Greek *pelte*, but sometimes larger.

The term may also have been used for the leather violin-shaped shields carried by Persian guards on the Persepolis reliefs.

takabara Persian term for bearers of ◊*taka* (light shields). It may have been the name for the new ◊*peltast* units in Persian armies of the later 5th and 4th centuries BC.

These unarmoured infantry who carried crescent-shaped or round shields, short spears, and swords or light axes sometimes fought in conjunction with archers. They wore Persian dress but most, except the peltast units kept at the royal court, may have been mercenaries rather than ethnic Persians.

Takamatsu, Battle of battle fought in Japan in 1582 between the warlord ◊Toyotomi Hideyoshi and the Mōri family, old rivals of the *Sengoku daimyo* ◊Oda Nobunaga. Hideyoshi, commanding the siege of Takamatsu castle, called for reinforcements from Nobunaga, but after Nobunaga was assassinated in the ◊Honnōi Incident he made a private deal with the Mōri and the castle was surrendered.

Takeda Katsuyori (1546–82) Japanese *daimyo* of the late Muromachi period, the son of ◊Takeda Shingen. He attempted to invade Mikawa, the homeland of the warrior leader ◊Tokugawa Ieyasu, but was defeated at the Battle of Nagashino (see ◊Nagashino, Battle of). Nobunaga launched a massive invasion of the Takeda domains and Katsuyori was forced to commit suicide.

Takeda Shingen (1521–73) Japanese *daimyo* of the late Muromachi period, member of a family of ◊*shugo* (military governors) established in the Kamakura period (1185–1333). Shingen fought almost constantly with his neighbour Uesugi Kenshin; they fought no less than five battles at Kawanakajima (see ◊Kawanakajima, battles of).

Around 1565 there began a series of temporary alliances, none of which gained more than a short-term shift in the balance of power. In 1572 Shingen headed for Kyoto with his army to attack ◊Oda Nobunaga, gaining minor victories en route. In 1573 he was wounded in an attack on Noda castle, held by one of the warrior leader ◊Tokugawa Ieyasu's generals, and died several weeks later.

Talbot, John (c. 1387–1453) earl of Shrewsbury from 1442. He spent a life in arms, fighting at Shrewsbury in 1403 and at Harlech in 1409. In Ireland 1414–19, he proved himself a ruthless raider, and imposed English rule and peace for ◊Henry V. He was at Henry's last siege; but he is chiefly known for his part in the long, losing war against the French recovery in the ◊Hundred Years' War.

Captured by ◊Joan of Arc's forces at Patay in 1429, he fought stalwartly after his release in defence of Normandy 1435–45 and 1448–49. When the duchy was finally lost he was chosen for the expedition to relieve the English possessions in Gascony. This was going successfully until his rash attack on a French artillery camp at Castillon, south of Bordeaux, led to his own death in battle.

talwar curved sword used by all types of soldier in south Asian armies from medieval times onwards. It is distinguished from the ◊shamshir by the pattern of its hilt, which ends in a disc-shaped pommel, and by the generally uniform width of its blade.

The curve of the *talwar* blade may vary from almost straight to a crescent shape.

tama-ire Japanese bullet pouch, in use following the introduction of firearms to Japan by the Portuguese in 1543.

Tamerlane (1335–1405) Turco-Mongol ruler of Samarqand, Uzbekistan, from 1369: see ◊Timur Leng.

tammachi (or *tanmachi jun* or *t'an-ma-ch'ih chün*) private Mongol armies of hereditary leaders who enjoyed a privileged status under the Mongol Yuan rulers of China (in contrast to the ◊Menggu jun). Their semi-independence went back to the granting of appanages to their leaders by ◊Genghis Khan, and lasted at least until 1369.

Tanagra, Battle of great battle in 457 BC, during what is sometimes called the First Peloponnesian War, in which 11,500 Peloponnesians, perhaps with some Boeotian help, defeated 14,000 Athenian, Argive, and other allied troops at the city of Tanagra in Boeotia. The historian Thucydides says that the Thessalian cavalry deserted the Athenians during the battle and that, after much slaughter on both sides, the Spartans won.

Tancred (1077–1112) prince of Antioch, nephew of ◊Bohemond, and leader on the First Crusade (see ◊Crusades). After the capture of Antioch (see ◊Antioch, Battle of 1098), he took part in the siege of Jerusalem (see ◊Jerusalem, Siege of 1099) and then fought at Ascalon (see ◊Ascalon, Battle of), before returning to Antioch in 1101 to act as regent when Bohemond was taken captive.

An energetic crusader, Tancred broke away from the main army in 1097 to seize Tarsus. At Antioch he fortified a siege castle at the south side of the city. After its capture he served Raymond of Toulouse, who could afford to pay his troops. When Jerusalem fell, he seized the Tower of David and the booty of the al-Aqsa mosque. He fought as fiercely against Christians as Muslims, imprisoning his old master Raymond for a while, and took Lattakiah from the Greeks in 1103 after a two-year siege.

Tang (lived 18th century BC) legendary founder and ruler 1766–1753 BC of the Shang, the first definite historical Chinese dynasty.

Tang was originally the ruler of a very small principality under the overlordship of the shadowy Xia dynasty. After conquering several neighbouring statelets, he overthrew the Xia at Mingtiao (see ◊Mingtiao, Battle of), traditionally dated to 1763 BC. (The real date for the founding of the Shang may be closer to 1600 BC.)

Tang Gaozu (566–635) (or *T'ang Kao-tsu*) emperor of China 618–26, the founder of the Tang dynasty. He defeated the Sui, declared himself emperor in 618, and spent six years suppressing rival claimants. His son Li Shimin (the future ◊Tang Taizong) conquered the northwest and took Loyang and the eastern plain. Finally Tang forces invaded the south, and by 624 had pacified the whole country.

Gaozu's heir was his eldest son Li Jiancheng. In circumstances that are still unclear, Shimin staged a coup in 626, had Jiancheng murdered, and persuaded his father to abdicate in his favour. Gaozu lived as a neglected 'Retired Emperor' until his death.

Tang Xuanzong (683–761) (or *T'ang Hsüan-tsung*) emperor of China 721–56. In a

TAN TAIZONG (601–649)

(or *T'ang T'ai-tsung* or *Li Shimin*)

Emperor of China from 626, son of the first Tang emperor, ◊Tang Gaozu. As a young man he fought in Gaozu's revolt against Sui Yangdi, the son and successor of ◊Sui Wendi, who was commanding troops at Huoyi and Yinma Spring, but he did not mastermind the revolt as later propaganda implied. After the Tang took Changan (modern Xi An) in December 617, he subdued northwestern China. In 621 he besieged the Sui general Wang Shichong at Luoyang, in North Henan province on the Luo River, then lured a relief force into ambush at Sishui, 50 km/19 mi east of Luoyang, which resulted in Wang's surrender. In 626 Shimin had his elder brother, Jiancheng, murdered on the pretext that his own life was in danger, persuaded Tang Gaozu to abdicate, and succeeded as Tang Taizong. His only major defeat as emperor was in Korea (see ◊Korea, Tang Chinese wars in).

While emperor, Taizong extended Chinese rule into Central Asia. In 629 his armies captured the Eastern Turks, who were resettled in Chinese territory, while further campaigns brought the Western Turks under Chinese overlordship. As a result, he was able to employ Turkish troops in conquering the oasis cities of the silk route, such as Kucha (modern Kuzhe Kuerluo in Xinjiang). In the latter part of his reign, Taizon's influence extended into northern India, due partly to his alliance with ◊Songtsen Gampo of Tibet.

long war of attrition against Tibet's eastern frontier combined with diplomatic efforts and long-distance expeditions to win over the petty states of the west, Xuanzong's generals won victories at Koko Nor in 726–27 (see ◊Koko Nor, Battle of), Wakhan and Balur in 747 (see ◊Wakhan and Balur, conquest of), and Shibao in 749 (see ◊Shibao, Siege of). In 751 China was defeated on several fronts, and Xuanzong was forced by his courtiers to abdicate in 756.

When Chinese fortunes changed in 751, the Arabs defeated the general Gao Xianzhi at Atlakh (see ◊Atlakh, Battle of), King ◊Geluofeng of Nanzhao rebelled in the southwest, and the Khitan beat ◊An Lushan in the northeast. An, his position threatened by court intrigue, rebelled in 755 and overran vast areas. The general Guo Ziyi and others were pushing back the rebels when Xuanzong mistakenly ordered an attack which led to disaster at Tongguan (see ◊Tongguan, Battle of). He fled to Sichuan as An approached the capital and was forced to abdicate, dying in retirement.

Tanjore fort fortress in southern India, with a massive inner citadel built by the Chola monarch ◊Rajaraja I about 1000.

It was captured and burned by Maravarman Sundara I of the rival Pandya dynasty in 1220, and taken by a third Tamil dynasty, the Hoysalas, later in the 13th century, but soon recovered by the Pandyas who held it until the Muslim conquest of southern India in the early 14th century. Control of Tanjore passed to the Bahmani rulers of the Deccan in the mid-14th century.

tanko Japanese armour of the Kofun period (c. 300–645), introduced from mainland Asia. It consisted of a solid construction of broad iron plates which were tied or riveted together, opened by a long hinge at one side and closing at the front.

Tannenberg, Battle of victory of a combined Polish and Lithuanian army over the Knights of the Teutonic Order (see ◊Military Order) in 1410, at Tannenberg, a village in northern Poland (now Grunwald). The battle broke the Knights' hold over Old Prussia (approximately modern Poland); their defeat led to the Treaty of Thorn and to an independent Polish state.

The rule of the Knights in Poland was oppressive and in 1410 the population, led by King Władysław Jagiello, Grand Duke of Lithuania and king of Poland, rose against them. Władysław led an army of 20,000 to meet some 15,000 Knights near Tannenberg and completely defeated them, slaughtering several thousand Knights.

Tanshihuai (c. 133–180) (or *T'an-shih-huai*) unifier of the ◊Xianbei, elected their paramount chief in 156. He led regular successful raids on Han China, and subdued neighbouring nomad tribes from Manchuria to Kazakhstan and southern Siberia. He organized his empire into groups of tribes whose leaders owed personal allegiance to him; without any formal structure, the system collapsed on his death.

Tantallon castle castle in Scotland, 40 km/25 mi northeast of Edinburgh. Built in the 14th century, it was the stronghold of the earls of Douglas.

tantō form of Japanese dagger with a small guard, which would have been carried by a ◊samurai at all times.

Tarain (or Taraori), Battle of (1191) battle fought in 1191 near Karnal in the Punjab in which the Hindu army under ◊Prithviraja Chauhana III defeated the invading Muslim forces led by ◊Muhammad of Ghur. The Muslims were forced to return to Afghanistan, giving India a brief respite before the invasion was renewed the following year.

The Hindu success was achieved by weight of numbers, which overwhelmed the Muslims on both flanks. In a desperate counterattack on the Hindu centre, Muhammad engaged in personal combat with Prithviraja's brother Govind Rai, and wounded him in the face with a lance thrust. Govind wounded Muhammad in the arm with a javelin, causing him to turn and follow his army from the field, fainting from loss of blood.

Tarain (or Taraori), Battle of (1192) battle fought in 1192 near Karnal in the Punjab in which ◊Muhammad of Ghur finally defeated the ◊Rajput alliance led by ◊Prithviraja Chauhana III, opening the way to the Muslim conquest of northern India.

The numerically superior but less manoeuvrable Hindu army was attacked on both flanks and in the rear by four divisions of Muhammad's army, consisting of mounted archers. After the Hindu ranks had become disordered under the impact of Muslim arrows, Muhammad charged the centre with his fifth division, a force of 12,000 heavy cavalry. The Hindus were routed, with Prithviraja himself being taken and killed.

Tarain (or Taraori), Battle of (1216) battle fought in 1216 near Karnal in the Punjab in which the sultan of Delhi, Shams al-Din Iltutmish (or Altamsh), successor and son-in-law of ◊Qutb al-Din Aibak, defeated Taj al-Din Yildiz, governor of Kirman and pretender to the Ghurid throne, who had marched into India to take the Punjab.

Yildiz, driven out of Kabul by ◊Ala al-Din Khwarazm Shah in 1214, was challenged by Iltutmish in his invasion of India, but reached Tarain before being defeated, captured, and subsequently put to death.

Iltutmish extended his own rule over the former Ghurid territories in the Punjab in 1217, reuniting them with the Delhi sultanate.

Tarascon castle castle in France, on the Rhone, 96 km/60 mi north of Marseille. Begun in around 1400 by Louis d'Anjou, King of Naples, and completed by King René, it became the seat of the rulers of Provence, then independent of France.

The castle is important architecturally as an early and well-developed example of the 'bastille' system of building towers and curtain wall to the same height, so as to provide a wide wall-top round which troops could be quickly moved to any threatened point.

target (or *targe*) round shield held with ◊enarmes rather than with a boss for carrying, used throughout medieval Europe. The term was first recorded about 1400.

tarida medieval ship, a galley-type form of horse transport. The *tarida*, originally an Arab vessel, was distinctive in that it had a square stern with two or three stem-posts, providing space for one or two doors. This meant that it could be backed onto a shelving beach and could deliver its mounted cargo similar to a modern ferry.

It may even have been possible for cavalry to ride out fully armed and ready for battle, as described by Robert de Clari at the Frankish siege of Constantinople 1203–04 (see ◊Constantinople, Siege of 1203–04).

tatami Japanese type of folding armour in use from the late Muromachi period (1333–1568): body armour (◊*dō*), helmet (◊*kabuto*), or a full suit of armour (◊*ō-yoroi*). *Tatami* armour was constructed of small plates (◊*kozane*) linked together with mail so that the entire protective covering could be folded up for transportation.

Tattershall castle castle in England, 24 km/15 mi southeast of Lincoln. The existing keep, an impressive brick-built structure, was built by Ralph, 4th Baron Cromwell, in the 15th century on the site of earlier work. The outer works comprised three wards, a wall, and double ditch.

Taunton castle castle in Somerset, England. A timber and earthwork Norman castle was built here in the 12th century, to which a large masonry hall was later added. The great hall was the scene of the Bloody Assizes and today houses the county museum.

Additions in the 12th century included a rectangular tower with turrets and various domestic buildings. In the 13th century the great hall was rebuilt and a constable's tower added.

taxis (Greek 'drawing up' or 'deployment') a rank or body of soldiers in Greek warfare. In Athens, the division of hoplites from each of the ten citizens' *phylai* (tribes). In the ideal army written about by tacticians, *taxis* is a body of 128 men.

tehen no ana opening in the top of a Japanese helmet bowl which provided ventilation for the wearer.

Telamon, Battle of battle fought in 225 BC between the Romans and a large force of invading Gauls. A major incursion of northern Italian Gallic tribes into central Italy was halted at Telamon where two consular armies, approaching from different directions, surrounded and destroyed a Celtic army of 50,000 infantry and 20,000 cavalry and chariots.

The military objectives of the Gallic campaign appear to have been the acquisition of large amounts of plunder, although the Greek historian Polybius suggests the Boii and Insubres also feared Roman expansionism. They gathered allies and mercenary ◊Gaesati from the Alpine tribes and proceeded to march through Etruria, causing panic and mauling a Roman force at Faesulae. They were harassed by consul Lucius Aemilius as they began to withdraw northwards, but encountered the southbound legions of Gaius Atilius who had recently returned from Sardinia. The Gauls deployed with the Boii and Tauriscan allies facing Atilius, while the Insubres and Gaesati faced in the opposite direction to meet Aemilius. A long cavalry fight for control of a commanding hill gave the Romans the advantage despite the death of Atilius. After the Gaesati had been driven back by ◊velites, a stubborn infantry melee raged. This turned into a massacre when the Gallic cavalry fled, and the victorious Roman horse fell on the Gallic flank. About 40,000 were killed and 10,000 captured. Aemilius conducted a counter-raid in the territory of the Boii and then held a triumph (victory procession) in Rome.

Ten Circuit Army medieval Vietnamese peasant militia founded by ◊Dinh Bo Linh in 974. They were originally 100,000 strong, organized into squads of 10, companies of 100, brigades of 1,000, and finally 10 armies of 10,000. The troops wore distinctive leather-covered square hats, the four sides of the brim meeting in a point at the top. They were mobilized only in wartime, and were supplemented by a standing army initially called the ◊Sons of Heaven.

teppō general Japanese term for a firearm. Firearms were first introduced to Japan by the Portuguese survivors of a shipwreck on the island of Tanegashima in 1543. The Japanese quickly learned how to copy and improve on the basic European design, and by about 1570 the gun had become their most important offensive weapon.

The introduction of the gun brought about radical changes in the way that battles were fought. Not only did the forms of armour have to change to meet this new threat, but traditional fortifications underwent a major transformation and large stone castles began to be built.

Although seen as an effective battlefield weapon, the gun was never regarded as an 'honourable' weapon.

Tertry, Battle of decisive victory in 687 by Pepin II, the Austrasian ◊Mayor of the Palace, over the Neustrian mayor Berthar. This left Pepin II as the sole mayor, exercising power over the entire Frankish kingdom, with the exception of Aquitaine, which remained independent. Following his victory the Austrasian Franks re-established their control over the Alamanni and Bavarians east of the Rhine.

testudo (Latin 'tortoise') Roman infantry formation in which the soldiers completely covered themselves on all sides and overhead with their shields, usually while approaching an enemy wall during a siege.

In the late Roman/Byzantine period the formation became known as the ◊*fulcum*. The term *testudo* may also occasionally have used to refer to a piece of siege equipment with a similar function – that is, a moveable shed or covering for soldiers approaching an enemy wall.

tetrarch ruler of one-fourth of the Roman Empire, an administrative position created by the emperor ◊Diocletian when he divised the tetrachic system of government in the 3rd century. He divided imperial rule between two Augusti (himself in the East and Maximian in the West), and appointed two assistant Caesars: Constantius Chlorus, ruling over Britain, Gaul, and Spain, and Galerius, ruling Illyricum and the Danube valley.

Teutoberger Forest, Battle of the battle fought in AD 9 between a Roman army commanded by Publius Quinctilius ◊Varus and German forces under the chieftain ◊Arminius, in the Teutoburger Forest in northern Germany. A shattering Roman defeat led to abandonment by the Romans of the recently conquered German province stretching from the Rhine to the Elbe rivers.

Varus had been warned of possible Germanic unrest, so he hastily gathered the greater part of three legions, six auxiliary cohorts, and three *alae* (see ◊*ala*), and marched to confront the Germans. As the Roman column passed through the difficult terrain of the Teutoberger Forest, it was mercilessly harried in a series of ambushes over several days. Finally trapped in a hopeless position, Varus committed suicide, and his army was massacred.

Teutonic Knights order of Crusading knights: see ◊Military Order.

Tewkesbury, Battle of battle fought on 4 May 1471, during the English Wars of the Roses (see ◊Roses, Wars of the), in which ◊Edward IV defeated the Lancastrian forces of Queen Margaret, wife of Henry VI, at Tewkesbury, Gloucestershire. Henry's only son, Prince Edward (1453–71), was killed. Edward IV's throne was never seriously challenged again.

After his victory at Barnet in April, Edward moved swiftly west to deal with the Lancastrians who had landed at Weymouth. He forced them to fight at Tewkesbury, where they took up a strong position on a slope behind a stream. Edward led some 5,000–6,000 men, including 2,000 good archers. The Lancastrians had 6,000–7,000 men, and planned a right flank manoeuvre led by the Duke of Somerset through broken ground. Edward sent a covering force of 200 lances, which hid in some woods. Somerset's attack almost worked, but was driven back and then caught in the rear by the ambush party, and was defeated in Bloody Meadow.

thalamian (or *thalamite*) oarsman at the lowest level in a ◊trireme.

Thapsus, Battle of battle fought between Julius ◊Caesar and the Pompeian forces in the Roman province of Africa in 46 BC. The larger Pompeian army under Scipio proved unable to defeat Caesar's veterans. Caesar's victory ended the second Roman civil war and led to the capture or suicide of many prominent Republicans.

Caesar's army was besieging the city of Thapsus, but he decided to march out and face Scipio when he attempted to relieve the city. Caesar had nine ◊legions, 4,000 cavalry, and 2,000 light infantry. Scipio had about 10 larger but inexperienced legions, 1,600 cavalry, as well as King Juba I of Numidia's 64 elephants, 18,000 light cavalry, and a body of infantry including 4 legions of men equipped and trained in the Roman manner.

Caesar formed his army into three lines, but took ◊cohorts from the rear line and formed two smaller fourth lines of five cohorts each in the areas threatened by the elephants. Missiles from Caesar's skirmishers panicked the elephants, whose flight disrupted the Pompeian line. The advance of Caesar's infantry quickly put Scipio's troops to flight. Caesar's army suffered light casualties, allegedly 50 dead, compared to a Pompeian loss of 5,000.

theme military district of the Byzantine Empire which was settled by men with hereditary military obligations who could be called up to serve in regional armies.

Themistocles (c. 524–c. 460 BC) Athenian admiral and politician. In 480 BC he commanded the Athenian contingent at Artemisium (see ◊Artemisium, Battle of) and Salamis (see ◊Salamis, Battle of 480 BC), where he is alleged to have lured the Persians to defeat by sending ◊Xerxes I false information.

Although generally regarded as responsible for the victory at Salamis, he disappears from the scene at the end of the year. After the war against the Persians, he pursued an anti-Spartan line which got him ostracized, possibly in 471, and some years later he fled to Asia Minor, where he died.

Theodoric the Great (c. 455–526) king of the Ostrogoths 471–526. He led the Ostrogoths from the Danube frontier regions of the Roman Empire to conquer Italy, where he established a peaceful and prosperous kingdom. Although remembered for his benevolent rule in later years, Theodoric was ruthless in his efforts to attain power.

He succeeded his father Theodemir at a time when the Ostrogoths were divided between rival factions which were being played off against each other by the Eastern Roman Empire. Theodoric ended the conflict by murdering his rival in 481. He was given the rank of patrician and induced to invade Italy by the emperor Zeno, who wished to rid the Eastern Empire of the Ostrogoths.

Theodoric led his entire people over the Alps into Italy where they fought against ◊Odoacer's army of Germanic ◊*foederati* who had been ruling Italy since 476. Although initially successful at the battles of Sontius and Verona in 489, Theodoric was defeated at Faenza in 490. He managed to finally destroy Odoacer's army at Adda in 490 (see ◊Adda, Battle of), with help from the Visigoths and Burgundians. Odoacer held out in Ravenna for another $2\frac{1}{2}$ years (see ◊Ravenna, Siege of 490–93) until a naval blockade combined with Theodoric's promise to share power induced him to sue for peace in 493. Theodoric broke his promise, murdered Odoacer, and massacred his troops, thus becoming sole ruler of Italy.

He then established himself at Ravenna as king of the Ostrogoths and the emperor's representative in Italy. During his reign Theodoric successfully extended his borders, becoming master of all of Italy, Sicily, and much of Noricum, Dalmatia, and Pannonia (roughly southern Bavaria, western Austria, Slovenia, and Croatia). After the defeat of the Visigoths by the Franks and death of their king Alaric II (Theodoric's son-in-law) at Vouillé in 507, Theodoric's grandson Amalaric became king of the Visigoths, giving Theodoric virtual control over Spain and Provence.

Theodosius, Flavius (c. AD 346–95) East Roman emperor 379–95, who has gone down in history as 'Theodosius the Great' because of his devout but intolerant Christianity. He brought stability to the East in the wake of the disaster at Adrianople in 378 (see ◊Adrianople campaign). Unable to expel the Goths from the Empire, he allowed them to settle in Thrace, under their own laws, in return for military service. Following his victory at the Frigidius in 394 (see ◊Frigidius, Battle of), he became emperor of a briefly reunited Roman Empire.

Thermopylae, Battle of (191 BC) battle fought in 191 BC between the Syrian king ◊Antiochus (III) the Great and the Roman leader Marcus Acilius Glabrio. Antiochus' invasion of Greece was halted at Thermopylae by Glabrio's Roman force.

Antiochus, failing to rally much support within Greece, had stationed his 10,000 infantry and 500 cavalry in a strongly entrenched position in the narrow pass of Thermopylae in central Greece. Glabrio detached two forces of 2,000 men from his army of 20,000 and sent them under the command of his legates Marcus Porcius ◊Cato and Lucius Valerius Flaccus to outflank the enemy position. Cato's column drove off the Aetolian troops guarding the route around the enemy flank and appeared behind Antiochus' army. Only about 500 of his troops escaped.

Thermopylae, Battle of (480 BC) battle fought in 480 BC between the Greeks, under the Spartan king Leonidas, and the invading Persians, under Xerxes I, at the narrow mountain pass of Thermopylae, leading from Thessaly to Locris in central Greece. Although the Greeks were defeated, the heroism of those who fought to the last against the Persians boosted Greek morale.

After being held in the pass for two days by their opponents, the Persians, guided by a local Greek, found a way through the mountains, brushing aside a force set to guard it. Warned in time, most of the Greeks in the pass withdrew,

but the Spartans and some of the others remained, including those from Thespiae, to fight to the death. The last stand was made on the hillock opposite the modern monument.

thiufadus Visigothic general, commander of a *thiufa* (1,000 men).

Thracian helmet type of helmet adopted by the Greeks during the 5th century BC and which became the elite helmet during the Hellenistic period (300–30 BC). It was ideally suited to front rankers in the ◊phalanx, giving much the same protection as the ◊Corinthian helmet, but with better vision and hearing.

thranite oarsman at the top level in a ◊trireme; his oar passed through the vessel's outrigger.

Thrasybulus (died 388 BC) Athenian statesman and soldier. As a ship's captain in 411 BC he became one of the leaders of the opposition to the oligarchs who had seized power in Athens, and was elected general. He served at Cynossema, Abydos, Cyzicus, Phocaea, and Arginusae (all in modern Turkey), but when Athens surrendered in 404 he was exiled by the Thirty Tyrants, the puppet government installed by Sparta, and fled to Thebes. Returning to Athens in 403, as the head of other exiles, he helped pull down the Thirty Tyrants and restore democracy under an amnesty brokered by Sparta.

He commanded a fleet 390–389 in the northern Aegean and Propontis, during the war between Athens and Sparta. He was killed near Aspendos (modern Bal-kiz in southern Turkey) the following year.

Thrasylus (died 406 BC) Athenian democratic politician and soldier in the latter part of the ◊Peloponnesian War. In 406 he was one of the eight commanders at Arginusae (see ◊Arginusae Isles, Battle of the), and was executed with five others for failing to pick up survivors.

He commanded the left at Cynossema (see ◊Cynossema, Battle of) in 411 BC and off Abydos before returning to Athens from Samos as a leader of the opposition to the oligarchs who had seized power in Athens. After outfacing King Agis of Sparta as he approached Athens, Thrasylus was sent to Asia Minor in 410, where he won a battle near Ephesus, won over Colophon, but was defeated outside Ephesus. He then sailed north and in 409 helped ◊Alcibiades defeat a sortie from Chalcedon.

Threave castle castle on a small island in the River Dee, 1.6 km/1 mi west of Castle Douglas, in Galloway, Scotland. The main structure, built in around 1370, is a massive rectangular tower, some 21 m/70 ft high with walls 3 m/10 ft thick, which acted both as a defence and a residence.

In about 1454 the tower was surrounded by a wall with four towers and a gatehouse, enclosing various domestic buildings. The provision of gun-loops was made in this wall, making it the earliest example of artillery defence in Britain.

Three Kingdoms of China period of division (220–65) after the fall of the Han dynasty. Han power disappeared before 200, and the battle of the Red Cliff established a division between the Wei in the north under Cao Cao, the Wu in the southeast under Sun Quan, and the Shu Han in the southwest under Liu Bei and ◊Zhuge Liang.

After Cao Cao's death his son Cao Pi proclaimed himself emperor, and the others followed suit. Endemic warfare continued (see ◊Xianmi, Battle of and ◊Chencang, Siege of) until ◊Deng Ai led the campaign that destroyed Shu Han in 263. In 265 the Wei dynasty was overthrown by one of its generals, and his Western Jin regime conquered Wu in 280, reuniting China. This unity was short-lived, however, shaken by the Eight Princes' rebellions (see ◊Eight Princes, rebellions of the) and ended by the turmoil of the ◊Sixteen Kingdoms.

Three Kingdoms of Korea the period about 300–668 when Korea was divided between Koguryo (the north, including much of Manchuria), Paekche (the southwest), and Silla (the southeast). The Three Kingdoms fought against each other, the ◊Xianbei to the northwest, Japanese raiders, and the Chinese during their invasions (see ◊Korea, Sui Chinese wars in). Silla finally allied itself with China (see ◊Korea, Tang Chinese wars in) to destroy the other two states and unify Korea.

The kingdoms developed from tribal leagues, and at first there were other states, notably Kaya (between Silla and Paekche) and Chinese colonies in the northwest (since the Han Chinese conquest: see ◊Korea, Han Chinese conquest of). Koguryo, the largest of the Three Kingdoms, was powerful under ◊Kwanggaeto and for much of the period, but Silla grew in power, with a well-organized army of ◊chong and ◊sodang led by ◊hwarang knights, and under King ◊Chinhung it became dominant.

Thucydides (460s?–390s? BC) Athenian historian. He was briefly general in 424, when he failed to save Amphipolis from the Spartan general ◊Brasidas, and, as a result, spent the rest of the war in exile. His *History of the Peloponnesian War* gives a detailed account of the conflict down to 411.

The work is remarkable not only for the detail and lucidity of the narrative, but the insight into motives and the reasons why things happened as they did

thumb ring term used in archery for a ring worn on the right thumb (if shooting a bow right-handed) in order to protect the thumb from the bow string during release. There are two basic types: the Chinese, formed of a cylinder, often of jade; and the Islamic, which has a triangular projection worn on the inside of the thumb, the part worn on the outside being quite narrow.

Tian Dan (lived 3rd century BC) (or *T'ien Tan*) general of the Chinese ◊Warring State of Qi. He became governor of Jimo, one of the few cities that held out against the Yan occupation of Qi in 284 BC, following Qi's defeat by an alliance of neighbours. In 279 he defeated the Yan besiegers (see ◊Jimo, Siege of), drove Yan forces out of the rest of the country, and restored the crown prince to his father's throne.

The weakened state of Qi remained a minor power after the Yan occupation, allying with Qin until the conquests of ◊Qin Shi Huangdi.

Tiaoyushan, Battle of battle in 1265 in which forces under ◊Khubilai Khan defeated Song Chinese mountain fortresses in Sichuan, during the Mongol campaigns in China (see ◊China, Mongol campaigns in). The Mongols also captured 146 ships, which became the nucleus of a Mongol river fleet.

tiara Achaemenid Persian military headgear, a hoodlike cap with a broad neck flap and two narrower flaps that covered the cheeks and were often tied over the chin. The top of the cap flopped over to the front or the side; to wear the *tiara* stiffened so that the top stood up was a mark of royalty. The cap was usually yellow, sometimes white.

Ticinus, Battle of the battle fought on the banks of the river Ticinus in 218 BC between the Carthaginian and Roman armies, during the Second Punic War (see ◊Punic War, Second). It was ◊Hannibal the Great's first action in Italy and showed that he was willing to use whatever means gave him the advantage.

Ticinus was a significant skirmish rather than a full-scale battle. A Roman force of cavalry and light infantry was ambushed while scouting for the Carthaginian camp across the river. Though wounded, Publius Cornelius ◊Scipio escaped and lead most of his force through the river to safety.

tiema (or *t'ieh-ma*) (Chinese 'iron horses') one of several Chinese terms for ◊cataphract cavalry who dominated 4th–6th century warfare. Introduced in around AD 300 by the ◊Xianbei armies of the ◊Sixteen Kingdoms, they spread to other tribes, the native Chinese, and the Koreans. Riders and horses used ◊lamellar armour, sometimes red or black-lacquered leather rather than iron.

Some commanders emphasized formation-keeping, one Xianbei general even chaining his cavalrymen together, but descriptions of individual heroics and head-taking suggest formations often broke up in confused melees. Cataphracts were overshadowed in the 7th century by mobile Turkic-style cavalry tactics, but smaller numbers were used throughout the medieval period.

Tieqiao, Battle of (or *T'ieh-ch'iao*) revolt in 784 of the Yunnanese kingdom of Nanzhao against the Tibetan Empire. When Tibet demanded 10,000 Nanzhao troops for a war against the Uighur Turks, King Yimouxian feigned agreement, but planned a revolt instead. The troops he sent were a vanguard of a larger Nanzhao force who joined them in treacherously attacking the Tibetans from two directions. They seized the Tibetan fortress of Tieqiao on the upper Yangtze River and destroyed the iron chain suspension bridge that was the main Tibetan route into Yunnan.

Tiger Warriors a common term for Chinese elite troops. The Zhou King ◊Wu had 3,000 Tiger Warriors at Mu, possibly making up his entire Zhou army. ◊Cao Cao's bodyguard were also called Tiger Warriors or Tiger Cavalry, and 8th–9th-century Tibetan documents call some troops 'tigers'.

Tigranes (I) the Great (139–55 BC) king of Armenia from 95 BC, who briefly turned Armenia into a great power. He conquered Media and northern Mesopotamia, took the Parthian title 'King of Kings', and in 83 BC annexed Seleucid Syria. He supported Mithradates VI Eupator of Pontus against Rome in 72 BC and was defeated by the Roman general ◊Lucullus at Tigranocerta in 69 BC (see ◊Tigranocerta, Battle of) and again at Artaxata in 68 BC (see ◊Artaxata, Battle of).

After the Parthian king ◊Mithradates II defeated his father Artavasdes, Tigranes was held hostage until 95 BC when he was enthroned by the Parthians in exchange for 70 frontier valleys. The new king allied himself with Mithradates VI of Pontus and assisted his conquest of Cappadocia in 93. When Mithradates II of Parthia died in 87, he attacked the usurper Gotarzes and regained the 70 Armenian valleys.

In 66 BC his son Tigranes the Younger rebelled and, when defeated, called in Phraates of Parthia. Phraates went home when his siege of Artaxata dragged on, and Tigranes defeated his son's remaining forces. Tigranes the Younger took refuge with the Roman general Pompey, obliging his father to buy Pompey off. When Phraates occupied Gordyene the following year, Pompey recovered it for Tigranes.

Tigranocerta, Battle of battle fought at Tigranocerto (modern Siirt, Turkey) in 69 BC between a Roman force led by Lucius Licinius ◊Lucullus and the Armenian army of ◊Tigranes (I) the Great, allied to ◊Mithridates (VI) Eupator of Pontus. The Armenian army was defeated.

Lucullus' 12,000 infantry and 3,000 cavalry advanced against the much larger enemy, surprising them by the boldness of their attack. His main effort concentrated on Tigranes' heavily armoured ◊cataphracts. Pinning them with his infantry, Lucullus also outflanked them with his cavalry, putting them to flight before the Romans made contact. Under the ferocity of the Roman advance the Armenian army collapsed and routed.

timar Ottoman term for an estate whose revenues supported a ◊spahi cavalryman, perhaps based on the Byzantine ◊pronoia. Ottoman provincial troops from Asia Minor could be described as *timariot* cavalry.

Timur Leng (1335–1405) (or *Tamerlane*) Turco-Mongol ruler of Samarqand, Uzbekistan, from 1369 who conquered Persia, Azerbaijan, Armenia, and Georgia. He defeated the Golden Horde (Mongol–Tatar army that terrorized Europe) in 1395, sacked Delhi in 1398 (see ◊Delhi, Battle of), invaded Syria and Anatolia, and captured the Ottoman sultan Bayezid I (c. 1360–1403) in Ankara in 1402 (see ◊Ankara, Battle of); he died invading China.

Timur Leng claimed to be a descendant of the Mongol leader ◊Genghis Khan, and was the great-grandfather of Babur (1483–1530), founder of the Mogul Empire of India. His descendants ruled Persia.

Tinchebrai, Battle of battle fought in 1106 between Henry I of England and his brother Robert Curthose, Duke of Normandy. Henry invaded Normandy in 1105 and besieged the castle of Tinchebrai, held by a vassal of Curthose. Robert came to its relief and fought Henry outside its walls, but Henry gained control of Normandy.

This was the first Anglo-Norman battle in which the tactic of dismounting knights to fight on foot occurred. Curthose's cavalry failed to break through them, and a reserve for Henry under Helias of Maine made a flank charge which settled the battle. Curthose was captured and imprisoned until his death in 1134.

Tissaphernes (died 395 BC) Achaemenid Persian satrap (provincial governor) who featured in Persian relations with the Greeks. In 401 BC he warned the Persian king Artaxerxes II of Cyrus the Younger's revolt using Greek mercenaries, and his cavalry trampled the Greek *peltasts* at Cunaxa (see ◊Cunaxa, Battle of). A year later he opposed the Spartan king ◊Agesilaus II attempts to bring the Asian Greeks into the Spartan orbit, and was defeated by him in 395 BC. Discredited at court, he was murdered at the instigation of Cyrus' mother.

Tissaphernes became satrap of Lydia about 416 BC after arresting his disloyal predecessor Pissouthnes. In 414 Pissouthnes' son Amorges rebelled with support from Athens. Tissaphernes allied himself with the Spartans who captured Amorges for him, but his intrigues with the Athenian general ◊Alcibiades alienated the Spartans who transferred their support to his colleague and rival ◊Pharnabazus. In 401 Tissaphernes fled with 500 cavalry to warn Artaxerxes of Cyrus the Younger's revolt.

Titus (AD 41–81) (Titus Flavius Sabinus Vespasianus) Roman general and emperor, 79–81. In 67 he served under his father ◊Vespasian as legate of *Legio XV Apollonaris*, playing a distinguished role in the storming of Jotopata (see ◊Jotopata, Siege of) and Gamala (see ◊Gamala, Siege of) and the capture of Tarichaeae. Left in charge of the Judaean army after Vespasian became embroiled in the civil war, Titus commanded the Roman army at the siege of Jerusalem (see ◊Jerusalem, Siege of AD 70).

The historian ◊Josephus provides a very flattering account of his leadership in this campaign against Jerusalem, emphasizing his personal heroism. After the fall of the city Titus returned to Rome to celebrate a joint triumph (victory procession) with his father, before becoming commander of the Praetorian Guard.

Tiverton castle castle in Devon, England, 19 km / 12 mi north of Exeter. Built in around 1106 to the orders of Henry I, this castle passed into the Courtenay family by marriage in the early 15th century, after which it was much rebuilt. It eventually formed a rectangular enclosure with towers at the corners, surrounded by double ditches.

Toba campaigns Toba campaigns 391–458 in north China to expel the Ruanruan (or Juanjuan or Jou-jan). The Toba won victories in 391 and throughout the 420s, but the Ruanruan were more successful in the 430s and 440s. The Toba finally succeeded in driving them out in 458, and they left China alone until the Wei began to neglect the frontier troops, provoking a renewal of Ruanruan attacks under ◊Anagui (see ◊Six Garrisons, rebellion of the).

The Ruanruan were a nomadic confederacy, possibly descendants of the ◊Xiongnu. They were founded in around 308 and dominated Mongolia 402–550. When they first raided north China, it was ruled by ◊Toba Gui. The Toba, of steppe nomad origin themselves, fielded large mobile cavalry armies that could cross the Gobi without heavy baggage to fight the Ruanruan on their own ground. They attacked in spring when nomads were most vulnerable because their horses were weak from winter. Their aim was to weaken the Ruanruan by capturing their herds and depopulating the steppe.

Toba Gui himself defeated the Ruanruan in 391, capturing half the nation. Toba Dao defeated a Ruanruan invasion in 423 and counterattacked across the Gobi in 425 and 429, both times surprising and defeating the Ruanruan. The Ruanruan were more successful in the 430s and 440s but were defeated again on the frontier in 449. Toba Dao attacked them in 458 with 100,000 troops and 150,000 supply carts, forcing them west and winning over many subject tribes.

Toba Gui (died 409) (or *T'o-pa Kuei*) founder and ruler 386–409 of the Northern Wei dynasty in China that replaced the ◊Sixteen Kingdoms. He established a well-organized tribal-Chinese state, with tribesmen settled as soldiers supported by Chinese taxpayers, used by his successors to conquer all of northern China.

Toba Gui was chieftain of the minor Toba clan of the ◊Xianbei, who had been subject to ◊Fu Jian until his death in 385. On Gui's accession the Toba were still nomads. He waged the first of the ◊Toba campaigns against the Ruanruan from 391, driving the Ruanruan away from the Yellow River. He then conquered eastern China from the Murong Xianbei and declared his new Wei dynasty in 396. He absorbed the Murong soldiers and their Chinese officials into his new state.

Tokugawa Ieyasu (1543–1616) Japanese warrior leader of the late Muromachi period. He was an ally of the military warlord ◊Oda Nobunaga but was forced to pledge allegiance to the warlord ◊Toyotomi Hideyoshi. After Hideyoshi's death in 1598 Ieyasu formed new alliances, won a major victory at Sekigahara in 1600 (see ◊Sekigahara, Battle of), and established the Tokugawa dynasty of shoguns.

Both he and Nobunaga gained much military benefit from the alliance established between them in 1561, which enabled them to accumulate and secure territories from rivals. Ieyasu's relationship with Hideyoshi was quite different, and there were several inconclusive conflicts between the two leaders before Ieyasu submitted. After Hideyoshi's death, Ieyasu broke his promises to maintain his master's lineage, and by his victory at Sekigahara set Japan on a settled course for the next 250 years.

Tolbiac, Battle of Zulpich (German) decisive victory in 496 for the Franks, under Clovis, over the Alamanni. This victory, which was the culmination of a ten-year campaign against the Alamanni, left Clovis as the most powerful man in the west, controlling all of northern France and the Rhine Valley. According to legend Clovis, a pagan, was inspired by his Burgundian Catholic wife, Clotilda, to convert to Christianity at a critical point in the battle.

Toledo, capture of capture of Muslim-ruled Toledo, Spain, by Alfonso VI of Castile and León in 1085. Alfonso was allied to the Kingdom of Toledo under the Muslim al-Mamun until the latter's death in 1075. The alliance continued under al-Qadir, but Alfonso decided to take control in 1085, with little need for violence.

The kingdom and city of some 28,000 inhabitants became the largest in Alfonso's realm.

Tonbridge castle castle in Kent, England. A Norman earthwork castle was noted here as early as 1088, covering a strategic ford across the River Medway. It was then rebuilt by Richard, Earl of Clare, in around 1105.

Richard placed a shell enclosure on the motte (castle mound), and from it a wall that went down to a gatehouse tower and then enclosed the rectangular bailey before rejoining the shell. Gilbert de Clare (the builder of ◊Caerphilly castle) added a large gatehouse-tower in around 1265.

Tongguan, Battle of (or *T'ong-kuan, Tong Pass*) battle in 756 in which ◊An Lushan's rebels defeated Tang Chinese imperial forces. The battle enabled An to take the capital, Changan, and forced Emperor ◊Tang Xuanzong to flee.

An's advance on Changan was stopped by imperial commander ◊Gao Xianzhi in a prepared position in the Tongguan (pass). Despite this success Emperor Tang Xuanzong had Gao executed for failing to defeat An, and put Tongguan under Qoshu Khan, victor of Shibao (see ◊Shibao, Siege of). As An's forces were weakened by counterattacks elsewhere, Xuanzong was urged by Qoshu's enemies at court to order an attack. Qoshu initially refused to leave his impregnable position, but he was given no choice. He advanced with 180,000 men and was ambushed in a defile between the Yellow River and the mountains, and his army was wiped out. He tried to organize a last stand, but he was forced by his officers to surrender.

tosei gusoku (Japanese 'equipment of the times') style of Japanese armour developed during the Momoyama period (1333–1568) to give protection from missiles, including firearms, as well as cutting weapons such as the sword or polearm.

The matching set of equipment would typically include a helmet (◊*kabuto*), iron face mask (◊*menpo*), cuirass (◊*dō*), armoured sleeves (◊*kote*), shoulder pieces (*ō-sode*), a split armoured apron (*haidate*), and shinguards (*suneate*). Some armour was made of solid plate in European style in order to withstand bullets. Many of the sets made at this time incorporated fantastic designs and decoration, particularly on the helmet.

tōsu small personal knife carried by members of the Japanese court during the Nara period (710–94). There are many examples in the Shōsōin, the imperial repository in Nara, Japan.

Totila (died 522) king of the Ostrogoths 541–52, who led a brief resurgence of the Ostrogoths against the East Roman forces in Italy. He defeated several imperial armies and captured Rome. He managed to keep the meagre forces of the Roman general ◊Belisarius at bay but was eventually defeated and killed by a large Roman army commanded by ◊Narses at Taginae in 552 (see ◊Taginae, Battle of).

Toulouse, Battle of victory in 721 by the Aquitanians, under Duke Eudo, over the Muslims who had moved north from Spain to occupy Septimania (the coastal strip of France between the Rhone and Pyrenees), and were pushing into Aquitaine. The Muslim governor of Spain was killed in the fighting and his forces were driven back.

Toulouse, sieges of unsuccessful attacks in 1211 and 1217 on the southern French city of Toulouse, seat of Raymond VI, Count of Toulouse, by Simon de ◊Montfort (the Elder) during the ◊Albigensian Crusades. De

Montfort was killed in 1217 by a block of masonry thrown by a trebuchet (stone-throwing machine) operated by defenders of the city.

De Montfort first besieged Toulouse in 1211, but abandoned the attempt after two weeks. In 1217 he renewed the attack, but again could not encircle the town. He was hit on the head and killed on 25 June.

tournament in medieval western Europe, sporting mock combat between two teams of knights on an open battlefield. It gradually came to apply to all forms of knightly combat for sport, en masse or individual, and the social occasion that accompanied these displays.

The tournament originated in 11th-century France where the technique of using a couched lance on horseback was first developed. It seems likely that tournaments emerged as a means of group training in this new skill. In its earliest form the tournament was fought over several miles of countryside with no formal boundaries. Bands of knights took part under the leadership of the lords they followed in battle. Often there were up to 200 combatants on each side. Sometimes the knights and lords were accompanied by foot soldiers drawn from their lesser tenants and townsmen. There were no rules to distinguish the tournament from real warfare other than the creation of certain designated 'safe havens' within the tournament area and the general understanding that the object was to capture and ransom the opposition rather than to kill, though fatalities were not uncommon.

From France the tournament quickly spread throughout western Europe. By 1130 tournaments had attracted the condemnation of the church, but despite this opposition they increased in popularity among the knightly classes. A new style of courtly and chivalric literature in the late 12th century also contributed to their popularity. This literature catered to the rich, powerful, and cultured men and women of France and the Low Countries, and it echoed and praised their interests in tournaments. A cult of tourneying developed, and young men recently knighted often spent months or years on the tournament circuit gaining experience, reputation and, for the more successful, income through ransoms and booty gained on the tournament field.

The popularity of the mêlée-style tournament began to dwindle by the end of the 13th century as it was gradually replaced by the smaller-scale joust. Gradually the spectacle of the tournament became more important than its role as training for war and by the 16th century the tournament operated ultimately as a means of princely display with no remaining competitive element.

Tours, Battle of (or *Battle of Poitiers*) battle fought near Poitiers, France, in 732 between the Franks under ◊Charles Martel and the Muslims. The outcome was a decisive victory for the Franks, ending Muslim expansion into western Europe. Although the Muslims again raided into southern France, the Battle of Tours (or more accurately the Battle of Poitiers) ended the possibility of further Muslim conquests in France.

After their defeat at Toulouse in 721 (see ◊Toulouse, Battle of), the Muslims of Spain, under their new governor Abd ar-Rahman, renewed raids into southern France. They captured Nîmes and consolidated their hold on the Frankish province of Septimania. In 732 a large army (70,000–80,000) led by Abd ar-Rahman defeated the Aquitainians under Duke Eudo at the Battle of Bordeaux and advanced towards the Loire River. Eudo appealed for help to Charles, the Frankish ◊Mayor of the Palace, and in return for Aquitainian allegiance, Charles led an army against the invaders.

The Muslims began to withdraw from the area of Tours and, after a series of skirmishes, engaged the Franks near Poitiers in October 732. The Franks dismounted their cavalry and formed in a solid shieldwall which successfully beat off successive Muslim cavalry charges. Realizing their primarily light cavalry army could make no headway against the Frankish phalanx, the Muslims began to withdraw, but the death of Abd ar-Rahman in the fighting turned the withdrawal into a rout. The Franks held their ground and did not pursue.

Tower of London fortress on the bank of the River Thames, London, England. William (I) the Conqueror established a palisaded camp here immediately after his coronation in 1066, and in 1078 Gundulf of Bec, Bishop of Rochester, began building the White Tower, the centrepiece of the fortress and probably the finest and best-preserved Norman keep in existence. The remaining works were added to at various times by different monarchs.

The inner ward is surrounded by a wall with 13 towers; the outer ward by another wall with 6 towers on the river face and 2 semicircular bastions. A ditch – formerly fed by the river but now dry – surrounds the whole complex. The Tower has served variously as a fortress, palace, prison, arsenal, and barracks.

Towton, Battle of battle fought on 29 March 1461 during the English Wars of the Roses (see ◊Roses, Wars of the) in which Edward of York, who had declared himself King Edward IV on 4 March, defeated his Lancastrian opponents at

Towton, Yorkshire, in the decisive battle of the first war.

Fighting in a snowstorm, the Yorkists gained an early advantage when Lord Fauconberg saw that their archers could outrange the Lancastrians, who had the wind in their faces. The Yorkist barrage forced the Lancastrians to attack, and a dour slog followed. The battle was decided by the arrival of Norfolk's forces on the Lancastrian left. There was no possibility of flight in the tightly packed mass, and when the Lancastrians broke they suffered great slaughter.

Toyotomi Hideyoshi (1537–98) Japanese warlord of the late Muromachi period who is credited with the military unification of the country which had been begun by his predecessor ◊Oda Nobunaga.

Of humble origins, he entered Nobunaga's service in 1558 and became one of his foremost generals. He proved himself an able strategist in battle and was particularly adept at siege craft. Following Nobunaga's assassination in 1582, Hideyoshi styled himself 'the great avenger' and persuaded many of the senior *daimyo* (major regional military landholders) of the time to follow him. There ensued a period of military conquests of the outlying provinces and, following the ◊Komaki Nagakute campaign, he and ◊Tokugawa Ieyasu came to a mutually acceptable military agreement.

TRAJAN (AD 52–117) (*MARCUS ULPIUS TRAJANUS*)

Roman emperor from AD 98. Born in Seville, Spain, he was adopted as heir by the Roman emperor ◊Nerva, and became the first non-Italian emperor. He acquired a reputation for military achievement but, more significantly, for his fair rule and good relations with the Senate, earning the title Optimus Princeps, the best of emperors. Trajan was a great campaigner, conquering the province of Dacia on the Danube and vast areas from the Parthians which extended the Roman Empire beyond the Euphrates.

Trajan established his military reputation as governor of Germany under Nerva, continuing the Flavian policy of consolidating the frontiers in this area with defences on high ground to the east of the Rhine. Despite his adoption and subsequent ascent to the throne, Trajan remained in the northern provinces for some months, firmly establishing his position with the armies of the area, before returning to Rome. He was not there long, however, before planning a campaign against the Dacians and their hostile king Decebalus. Two ◊Dacian Wars were fought and each time Trajan led his army in person. He wrote commentaries on the campaigns, which did not survive, and created another impressive record of the wars, Trajan's Column. The figure of the emperor features regularly on the Column, prominently displayed and indicating the good relationship he had developed with his soldiers.

In 106 the kingdom of Arabia was annexed, and in 114 relations with Parthia deteriorated after disagreement over control of Armenia. Rome and Parthia had experienced relatively peaceful relations since the treaty arranged by ◊Corbulo under Nero, but Trajan, possibly eager for further expansion, refused Parthian diplomacy. Between 115–16 he created the provinces of Armenia and Mesopotamia, captured the Parthian capital of Ctesiphon, about 100 km/60 mi above Babylon, and reached the Persian Gulf. His conquests were not properly consolidated, however, and he was forced to return to deal with Jewish revolts. Trajan planned to return to Italy but died at Antioch, in southern Turkey, in 117. Although his Dacian province survived until the late 3rd century, most of the eastern provinces he established were quickly abandoned by his successor, ◊Hadrian. Trajan had overstretched the resources of the Empire, but his memory remained popular with Senate and army alike.

By 1585 Hideyoshi had been appointed regent by the emperor and thereby held all military and civil power by imperial decree. There only remained pockets of resistance in Kyushu and parts of the Kantō and by 1591 these had been overcome by military and political means. He ensured the safety of his domains by redistributing control of the provinces to his own trusted followers, and introduced a new system of land survey which was to further effectively control the country. With Japan now under his control, Hideyoshi was free to embark on his grandiose plans for the invasion of China (see ◊Korea, Japanese invasions of).

He began to show apparent signs of mental instability from about 1593, and prior to his death in 1598 he created a council of Five Great Elders (*Gotair*) to ensure that his heirs would succeed him. The chief among these, Tokugawa Ieyasu, was to ensure that his own schemes would take preference over any promises made to Hideyoshi.

Trapani, Battle of see ◊Drepana, Battle of, sea battle fought in 249 BC between the Romans and Carthaginians.

Trebia, Battle of battle fought in 218 BC between the Roman and Carthaginian armies, during the Second Punic War (see ◊Punic War, Second). It was ◊Hannibal the Great's first major battle against the Romans in Italy, and he routed them.

By constantly raiding the Roman camps, Hannibal lured them into accepting his offer of battle, regardless of his strong position, the fact they had not eaten breakfast, and the fact that they had to wade through a freezing river. Using his cavalry and spearmen to strip the Roman wings, he called in the 2,000 cavalry and infantry he had hidden overnight under his brother ◊Mago Barca to attack the rear of the Roman centre. The Romans were thrown into confusion and routed, leaving 20,000 dead.

trebuchet missile-launching weapon resembling a catapult, with a beam pivoted on an axle and terminating in a sling. It was invented in China between the 5th and 3rd centuries BC, and reached Europe around AD 500. The most powerful trebuchets could launch missiles weighing a tonne or more.

tresantes literally 'tremblers', people considered guilty of cowardice in ancient Sparta. They suffered various penalties, including loss of their rights as citizens.

triarii (singular *triarius*) type of heavy infantry of the early Roman republican ◊legion.

The *triarii* held the third line in the battle order (see also ◊hastati and ◊principes). Recruited from citizens of an older age group and numbering 600 in each legion, they were experienced veterans placed at the back to give the lines strength. They were equipped with spears and carried swords for close combat.

They only entered the battle when the *hastati* and *principes* had been defeated.

tribune title given to a range of officers in the Roman army. Under the Republic, six tribunes were placed in charge of a ◊legion. Under the Principate, each legion possessed one senatorial tribune (*tribunus laticlavius*) who was second in command to the ◊legate, and five equestrian tribunes (*tribunes angusticlavii*).

Tricamarum, Battle of battle at Tricamarum, 29 km/18 mi from Carthage (modern Tunisia), in 533 that ended in a Roman victory over the Vandals, effectively ending organized resistance to the East Roman reconquest of the Vandal kingdom in North Africa.

Following his victory at AD Decimum (see ◊Ad Decimum, Battle of) and capture of the city of Carthage, the Roman general ◊Belisarius sought to destroy the Vandal army under King ◊Gelimer. He used skirmishing tactics in an attempt to draw the Vandals across a stream, but without much success. The Romans then crossed in force and engaged the Vandals in a fierce fight. The Vandals had been ordered to use only swords, probably to ensure that they would fight at close quarters where they might have an advantage over the skirmishing Romans. However, the best Vandal warriors fighting in the front line suffered heavy casualties and one of their princes was killed. The remaining Vandals fled, including Gelimer. Casualties are recorded as 50 Romans and 800 Vandals.

Trier (Roman *Augusta Treverorum*) Roman city in southwest Germany notable for the survival of its north gate, the Porta Nigra. One of the finest examples of monumental defensive architecture in the Roman Empire, it incorporates civic ostentation with heavily defensive features – a portcullis, killing grounds, and artillery embrasures.

Begun in about AD 170, the city's curtain wall incorporated the amphitheatre on the east side, which served as an east gate and citadel. The Porta Nigra, thought by some to be a 4th-century construction, follows plans first used in Augustan times (for example at ◊Aosta). An inner and outer set of passageways is flanked at the sides by deep towers, creating a central open courtyard. Wide embrasures in two storeys over the gates and a third storey in the towers allowed missiles to be directed down on all sides of an attacker who had entered the open courtyard. The outer gates were closed by a portcullis.

trimarcisia (Celtic 'three horses') Celtic combat system involving one cavalryman and two supporting mounted servants, developed after the introduction of the four-pommel saddle in the 3rd or 2nd century BC. The cavalryman engaged in the battle and the two servants, based at the rear, each in turn provided their master with a new mount or took his place in battle if he fell.

Celtic cavalry originally operated without a reliable means of holding the rider on his horse; the four-pommel saddle (one pair at the rear and one pair angled over the thighs at the front) gave the cavalryman the means to fight securely on horseback. Within a short time cavalry had completely replaced chariots as the mobile wing of Celtic armies on the European mainland. Celtic experience and skill with cavalry made them prized mercenaries and allies with foreign armies, notably for Carthage during the Second Punic War.

Trim castle castle 40 km / 25 mi northwest of Dublin in the modern County Meath, Ireland. This castle probably began as a timber ◊motte-and-bailey work when the first Anglo-Normans moved into Ireland. It was converted into a masonry work in around 1173 and subsequently became one of the major Norman Irish castles.

Commanding the River Boyne, it was roughly triangular in form, two sides being walled and the third being a sloping escarp above the river. There was a square, turreted great tower in the centre of the enclosure, a gatehouse, a barbican tower as a secondary entrance, and several mural towers.

trinoda necessitas 'threefold necessity' or obligations levied from those holding bookland (granted by royal charter) in Anglo-Saxon England. Evidence of the obligations date from 749 in the kingdom of Mercia. The obligations were ◊fyrd or army service, fortress work, and bridge work, probably from Frankish example.

King ◊Offa of Mercia demanded 'army service against the pagans, the building of bridges and the fortification of fortresses'. It was the basis of the burghal defence system.

triplex acies most common Roman battle formation from the 3rd century BC onwards, in which the heavy infantry ◊legions were deployed in three distinct lines. This tactic proved more flexible than the Hellenistic practice of deploying in a single line, since it

provided reserves of fresh troops to reinforce a success or oppose an enemy breakthrough.

The three lines were known as the *hastati, principes,* and *triarii*. Each line was divided into ◊maniples. After the adoption of the ◊cohort, the *triplex acies* remained the most common formation for Roman armies.

trireme ancient galley with three banks of oars, Anglicized from the Latin words for 'three-oared'. Of the most common types of galleys, the ◊bireme, trireme, ◊quadrireme, and ◊quinquereme, the trireme was probably the fastest.

Troy city in Asia Minor (modern Hisarlik in Turkey) that has a long and complex history from about 3000 BC to AD 1200, with 46 building phases. The site was identified as Troy in 1820, but its actual name is unknown.

Consisting of a citadel hill and lower town, the first fortifications appeared on the citadel in the Early Bronze Age. These were a stone wall with a mudbrick battlement and a gate protected by flanking towers. By the Middle Bronze Age the defences had been enlarged and required at least four gateways, two of which were protected by towers. The defences were breached about 1270 BC and the city was sacked. The city and its defences were rebuilt, but suffered a similar fate about 1050 BC. These two destructions, of Troy VI and VIII respectively, have been suggested as the sack of the city in the Trojan War related by the Greek poet Homer.

Truceless War alternative name for the ◊Mercenary War, 241–237 BC.

Trung Trac (died AD 43) Vietnamese chieftain's wife who led a rebellion, with her sister Trung Nhi, against China in AD 40. Chinese forces were ejected and Trung Trac crowned queen. The following year, however, imperial commander Ma Yuan defeated the rebels, and the Trung sisters were executed.

When Han China conquered Vietnam, Chinese rule was initially light, but higher taxes and the imposition of Chinese law eventually caused the Trung sisters to lead a revolt. In AD 41 Ma Yuan led 20,000 Chinese troops down the coast, supplied by sea. He defeated the rebels near ◊Co-Loa. The Trung sisters withdrew westwards but were caught. The last rebel remnants were mopped up by the spring of AD 44.

tsuba Japanese sword guard, found on blades of all periods, a primary vehicle for decoration. The blade passes through the central opening and there are separate holes for sliding out the bodkin (◊kōgai) and small knife (◊kozuka), if fitted in the scabbard.

tuan Chinese 'battalion' at several periods. Tang dynasty ◊*fubing* troops were organized into 200-man ◊*tuan* commanded by a *xiaowei*. The *tuan* was divided into 50-man *dui* companies under a *zheng* and 10-man *huo* squads under a *huozhang*.

tuanlian (or *t'uan-lien*) local militia in Tang China. They first appeared as an emergency measure in the northeast during a Khitan invasion in 697, but were particularly important in the south where fewer ◊*fubing* units or ◊*jianer* regulars were stationed. Later they were an important source of manpower in the late Tang and the following periods, used by the Huaixi governors and the Shatuo Turks under ◊Li Keyong, among others.

The effectiveness of the *tuanlian* varied considerably, depending on the local leadership at the time. In 876, facing ◊Huang Chao's rebellion, the government ordered 'archers, swordsmen, and drummers' to be recruited in every village in the empire. This was the first time that local militias were centrally authorized.

tümen Mongol term technically meaning a force of 10,000 men, based on the decimal system instituted by ◊Genghis Khan (with lesser units of 10, 100, and 1,000). This total number should not taken literally on all occasions, however, and it should be understood as a term parallel to 'division'.

Tumu Incident battle August–September 1449 in which the Mongols decisively defeated Ming China. Ming Emperor Yingzong, encouraged by the eunuch adviser Wang Zhen, led an ill-disciplined, poorly-supplied army of 500,000 to the frontier fortress of Datong to counter raids by Prince Esen's 70,000 Mongol cavalry. At Datong, opposition to endangering the Emperor finally prevailed, so the expedition started back for Beijing. They were attacked repeatedly by the Mongols, however, and Wang Zhen and half the Chinese army were killed.

On August 30, after the Ming army began their retreat, the Mongols ambushed and wiped out the rearguard. A new rearguard of 50,000 cavalry was led straight into another ambush, and destroyed in turn. On August 31 the Chinese camped at Tumu post station. There was no water, and Esen cut them off from the river. The Mongols attacked Chinese outposts throughout the night. On 1 September, as the imperial entourage moved off, the Mongols attacked again. Chinese soldiers trying to surrender were slaughtered. The Emperor was almost killed, but he was captured by a Mongol officer. Esen, however,

could not exploit his unexpectedly complete victory. He marched on Beijing, but the court refused to negotiate and appointed a new emperor. In November Esen withdrew to the steppes, having gained much loot but little else.

Tunis, Battle of battle fought in 255 BC between the Romans and Carthaginians, in which Marcus Atilius ◊Regulus' Roman army of 4 legions (about 16,000 men) was defeated by a Carthaginian army of 12,000 infantry, 4,000 cavalry, and 100 war elephants, led by the Spartan mercenary Xanthippus. Regulus was captured and this defeat ended Rome's attempt to resolve the First Punic War (see ◊Punic War, First) by campaigning in Africa.

The location of the battle is unknown, though it is likely to have taken place near Tunis, North Africa. Regulus' attempt to counter the Punic elephants by deploying his infantry in an unusually deep formation failed spectacularly and the Romans were disordered and suffered heavily. The Carthaginian superiority in cavalry also contributed to the victory by being able to outflank the Romans and fall on the rear of the army. The disciplined formation of the Carthaginian infantry made short work of the surviving Romans. Only 2,000 escaped to ◊Clypea.

Tunis Crusade Louis IX of France's second crusade to North Africa in 1270. He intended to head for Tunis and on to the East, probably hoping to encourage the Christian conversion of the emir of Tunis, but died from typhus in Africa.

Louis took up the crusading cause again in 1267 and recruited support throughout western Europe. The crusaders camped by the ancient city of Carthage, near Tunis, and captured the fort. After Louis's death his brother Charles I of Anjou made an agreement with the ruler of Tunis, who seemingly had no intention of converting, and the crusade was abandoned.

tuntian (or *t'un-t'ien*) Chinese military-agricultural colonies where the armies could grow their own food. In the Tang period (618–907) they were staffed by ◊*jianer* soldiers, their families, and convicts. They were also an important part of the Ming ◊*wei so* system.

turcopole initially an 11th-century Byzantine military unit formed from the descendants of Turkish mercenaries; later a term used by the west European crusaders for Turks who had converted to Christianity and served in their armies.

Turin, Breseia, and Verona notable phases in ◊Constantine (I) the Great's rapid campaign in Italy in 311, which culminated in his victory over Marcus Aurelius Valerius ◊Maxentius at Milvian Bridge, near Rome, in 312 (see ◊Milvian Bridge, Battle of).

Maxentius' general Ruricius Pompeianus managed to break Constantine's centre with his cavalry outside Turin, but his cavalry was then defeated by reserves, allowing Constantine to drive the enemy from the field and capture the city. Constantine then took Verona, defeating and killing Ruricius in a battle fought nearby.

Turkoman (or *Turkman*) nomadic pastoralist Turkish inhabitant of Central Asia, a member of an unruly and intractable group which continued to harass its neighbours by slave-raiding, sheep-rustling, caravan-looting, and the disruption of agriculture by the pasturing of flocks on arable land until conquered by the Russian Empire in the second half of the 19th century.

Turkic peoples migrated westwards through Siberia to reach regions around the Aral Sea, the Caspian, and the Volga during the 8th century AD. In the 9th century they provided auxiliaries, the 'Tourkopoulai', for the armies of Byzantium. During the 10th and 11th centuries Turkoman adventurers and mercenaries took part in most of the wars in and around their Central Asian homeland, while continuing the depredations on their neighbours whenever civilized governments were unable to control them.

During the 1030s several great cities of the Ghaznavid Empire, including Nishapur and Marv, voluntarily surrendered to the Turkoman ◊Seljuks. The defeat of a great Ghaznavid punitive expedition at Dandanqan in 1040 (see ◊Dandanqan, Battle of) by its more mobile Turkoman adversaries led to the fall of the Ghaznavids and the establishment of the Seljuk Empire. This empire lasted for a hundred years before its last great sultan, ◊Sanjar, was defeated by the Ghuzz Turkomen in 1153.

The various successor states of the Seljuk Empire fell to the Mongols in the 13th century, but when Mongol power declined in the 14th century that of the Turkoman revived. Rival Turkoman groups, the 'White Sheep' and the 'Black Sheep', controlled most of Iran until the establishment of the Safavid dynasty by Shah Ismail I, leader of the ◊Qizilbash, in 1501.

turma subunit of an ◊*ala* in a Roman army. Commanded by a decurion, the *turma* was a squad of cavalry men about 30 strong. Like the ◊century of an infantry unit, the men would live and presumably fight together.

Tuyuhun Raid attack on two towns in China in 621 by the Tuyuhun, a seminomadic tribe from what is now Qinghai, who often raided the Chinese borders in the 5th–7th centuries. In this raid they surrounded a relieving army under commander Chai Shao, shooting arrows from higher ground. Chai sent a musician and two dancing-girls towards the Tuyuhun to distract them. As they crowded round watching, he sent cavalry to attack the tribesmen from behind, dispersing them.

Two Guards and Six Divisions central army of the Koryo dynasty in Korea (981–1392), distinct from the provincial ◊*kwanggun*. They were descended from the personal units of the founder of the dynasty ◊Wang Kon, and organized about 995 into the following divisions: Division of the Left and Right (*Chwauwi*), Divine Tiger Division (*Sinhowi*), Elite Striking Division (*Hungwiwi*), Internal Security Division (*Kumowi*), Thousand Bull Division (*Ch'onuwi*), and the Capital Guards Division (*Kammunwi*). The Two Guards – the Soaring Falcon Guards and Dragon-Tiger Guards – were royal bodyguard units added later.

They totalled 45 *yong* regiments of 1,000 men, mostly infantry but including cavalry, ceremonial, and security units. By the 11th century they were declining and were supplemented by the ◊*pyolmuban*, and by the time the ◊*sambyolch'o* were founded after 1195 they had virtually disappeared.

Tyre, Siege of (332 BC) six- or seven-month siege of Tyre, a port in modern Lebanon, by Alexander the Great in 332 BC, part of his strategy to weaken Persia's superiority at sea by capturing its ports.

The siege was complicated by Tyre's position on an island, but Alexander built a breakwater with towers to protect his engineers from attack. When the towers were burned by Persian fire ships, the breakwater was widened and warships from Rhodes, Cyprus, and other towns blockaded the Tyrian harbours. Despite the ingenuity of the defenders, the city was doomed once Alexander won command of the sea, and it was eventually taken by assault from both land and sea.

Tyre, Siege of (1124) successful crusader siege of Tyre, the last Syrian port in Muslim hands, from 15 February to 7 July 1124. The Christian success was achieved with the support of the Venetian fleet.

Tyre was well fortified and effectively an island. An earlier Christian siege of 1111–12 had failed, but in 1124 the arrival of a crusading Venetian fleet made a blockade possible.

Relief attempts by land from Egypt and Damascus were half-hearted, and although the Venetians feared attack by the Fatimid (Muslim) fleet, this never materialized. Low on food and water, the defenders surrendered after six months of bombardment.

U

uchigatana early name for the ◊*katana*, a Japanese 'striking sword' used by foot soldiers in the Muromachi period (1333–1568).

Originally used only by lower ranking ◊samurai, the *uchigatana* subsequently became standard wear for all samurai.

uchi ne Japanese short javelin or throwing spear believed to have been carried by passengers when travelling in a palanquin. It was in use from the Muromachi period (1333–1568), and possibly earlier.

uchiwa Japanese nonfolding fan used as a symbol of rank by senior officers in battle as well as a means of signalling. When mounted in metal, the uchiwa could also be used as a weapon.

ujibumi o yomu Japanese ◊samurai custom of declaring one's ancestry prior to traditional one-to-one battle, to ensure that the opponent was worthy of killing or, more importantly, being killed by. It was regarded as a great dishonour to be killed by one of lesser birth or rank. The custom was practised from the Heian period (794–1185).

Uji River, Battle of the first major battle, fought in 1180, of the ◊Taira–Minamoto Wars in Japan. A huge Taira force defeated a small number of Minamoto rebels and warrior monks at the bridge over the Uji River, and their leader ◊Minamoto Yorimasa committed ritual suicide.

The bridge was of major strategic importance, lying on the main road from Kyoto to Nara. Yorimasa had already destroyed part of it before being overtaken, but the Taira force of cavalry was so huge that by sheer numbers they forged their way across the river. Yorimasa was forced back to the Byōdō-in, one of Japan's oldest and most beautiful temples, where he committed ◊*seppuku*.

Ujjain (Sanskrit *Avanti*) chief city of the Rajput kingdom of Malwa, central India, and holy city of the Hindus. It was ruled by ◊Ashoka as viceroy in about 260 BC, prior to his accession to the throne of ◊Magadha, and is the legendary seat of Raja Bikram (a folk memory of ◊Chandragupta II, who captured the city about AD 390).

It fell to the Paramara Rajputs in the mid-9th century, and thereafter changed hands repeatedly between rival Rajput princes. It was sacked in 1235 by Sultan Altamsh (Iltutmish) of Delhi.

Ulchi Mundok (lived 6th–7th centuries) Korean general from Koguryo in the ◊Three Kingdoms of Korea period, who fought with distinction in the Chinese invasions (see ◊Korea, Sui Chinese wars in). He planned to defeat the massive Sui invasion of 612 by holding the strong frontier fortresses along the river Liao. When part of the Sui army bypassed these defences he defeated them at the river Salsu (see ◊Salsu River, Battle of the).

umabari (Japanese 'horse needle') small, flattened, triangular double-edged bodkin carried in battle or on campaigns in place of the ◊*kōgai* in the Japanese sword.

Umar (c. 581–644) second Islamic caliph 634–44, successor to ◊Abu Bakr, who presided over the initial Muslim onslaught against the Byzantines. He laid the foundations of a regular, organized Muslim army while employing the brilliant ◊Khalid ibn al-Walid to lead his armies in battle. He was murdered by a Persian slave.

umbo Latin name for a metal shield boss protecting the handgrip of a Roman shield.

unnamed battle (Julius Caesar against Ariovistus) battle fought at an unknown site in 58 BC, in which the Roman army of Julius ◊Caesar defeated the German army of ◊Ariovistus during the ◊Gallic Wars.

Originally invited into Gaul as mercenaries, the German Suebi tribe had seized the lands of their hosts and begun to settle. Caesar determined to drive them out and succeeded in drawing them into battle. Breaking through on the right, the Roman left struggled against the superior German numbers, but the timely commitment of the reserves broke the tribes and they were routed. Ariovistus and the survivors withdrew across the Rhine.

Urban (lived 15th century) Hungarian gunsmith who played a major role in the Turkish siege of Constantinople in 1453 (see ◊Constantinople, Siege of 1453). Employed by the Byzantines, he was bribed by the Turks and defected. Urban was a trained engineer who specialized in making heavy cannons. One gun needed up to 50 yoke of oxen and 2,000 men to move it. He began a tradition of Turkish giant cannons, which were used in their sieges for a century.

Urbicas, Battle of battle in 456 between the Germanic Suevi in Spain and the Visigoths under Theodoric II, in which the Suevi, who had been expanding their power in northern Spain under King Rechila at the expense of the Romans since the 430s, were defeated by the Visigoths fighting on behalf of the Romans.

Lacking the military strength to act against the Suevi, the West Roman emperor Avitius encouraged the Visigoths of southern France to attack them on his behalf. Their success paved the way for the eventual move of Visigothic power from southern France to Spain.

Usamah ibn Munkhid (1095–1188) Arab-Syrian nobleman of Shaizar and author of memoirs which explore the conflicts and relationships between Muslims and crusaders in his time. From the age of 24 he had an active military career. He served ◊Nur al-Din 1130–38, and was then employed defending Damascus until 1144. After this he spent a decade in Egypt fighting the crusaders, returning to serve Nur al-Din and ◊Saladin.

Usamah's military lifestyle led to him being called a Muslim knight, for he shared the same interests in hunting and war as his Christian counterparts. He retired to write his memoirs, a lively exploration of warrior lifestyle, packed with interesting anecdotes.

Utus, Battle of inconclusive battle at Utus (modern Vid) in 447 in which the East Roman army, although bettered on the battlefield, managed to turn ◊Attila's Huns away from the Byzantine capital Constantinople (modern Istanbul, Turkey).

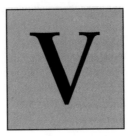

Valens, Flavius Julius (c. AD 328–78) East Roman emperor 364–78. He was elevated to the throne by his brother and co-emperor ◊Valentinian I and, after eliminating a number of usurpers, spent much of his reign directing campaigns against the Goths (367–69 and 377–78) and Persians (373–77). He was killed fighting the Goths at Adrianople (see ◊Adrianople campaign).

Unlike his brother, he seems to have been an incompetent military commander. His actions at Adrianople showed poor judgement, faulty reconnaissance, and a lack of control over his troops.

Valentinian I (Flavius Valentinianus) Roman emperor from 364 who permanently divided the Empire into two administrative halves: the West with Rome as the capital (later Milan, then Ravenna), and the East governed from Constantinople. He retained rule in the West and elevated his brother ◊Valens to the eastern throne.

Valentinian was an able and energetic military leader who personally directed campaigns against the Picts, Scots, and Saxons in Britain and against the Alamanni and Sarmatians on the Rhine and Danube frontiers. He campaigned deep inside German territory, and after defeating the Alamanni in battle built up a series of fortifications along the upper Rhine. He made efforts to strengthen the army and improve conditions of service for the soldiers. He died while planning a campaign against the Quadi, and the dynasty he founded lasted nearly a century.

Valerian (died AD 260) (Publius Licinius Valerianus) Roman emperor 253–60. Commander of the Rhine army in 253, he was proclaimed emperor by his troops following the murder of the emperor Trebonianus Gallus. In 259 he went east to confront the Persians under Sharpur I who had overrun most of the eastern empire, but his army was defeated at Edessa in 260 (see ◊Edessa, Battle of).

Valerian was publicly humiliated after this defeat. One account claims that he was stuffed and put on display in a Persian temple.

Val-ès-Dunes, Battle of battle in January 1047 fought by the young Duke of Normandy (◊William (I) the Conqueror) and his ally Henry I of France against rebels led by William's cousin, Guy of Burgundy. Guy had sought to claim the duchy with the support of a number of Norman magnates, but his defeat at Val-ès-Dunes firmly established William in Normandy.

According to the Anglo-Norman historian Wace, writing more than a century later, the French army advanced through Mézidon towards Caen where they were met at Laison by a smaller contingent of Normans loyal to Duke William. From there the army marched through Valmeraye to the plain of Val-ès-Dunes, bordered by the hamlets of Serqueville, Begrenville, Bill, and Airan. There they encountered and defeated the rebel forces who had crossed the river Orne. More contemporary accounts of the battle are brief, stating only that the strength of the enemy was considerable and that after many engagements between groups of cavalry the rebels were routed and many who tried to flee were drowned in the river Orne. Guy of Burgundy escaped the battlefield and held the castle of Brionne against William for three years before being forced to surrender.

valet (medieval French) knight's servant, in English 'varlet', who replaced the squire in the later Middle Ages. The title designated some military usefulness: varlets would ride the men-at-arm's horses as cavalry when their masters dismounted to fight (see ◊Agincourt, Battle of).

vambrace plate armour for the arm, used throughout medieval Europe. In the 14th century the term was applied to the armour for the forearm, the word 'rerebrace' being applied to the upper arm (and shoulder) armour. Modern terminology generally follows the 16th-century usage, in which the vambrace comprises the upper and lower arm armour (called the upper and lower canons of the vambrace), including the ◊couter but excluding the shoulder defence, which is normally a separate piece of armour.

varadiot elite military unit in the Byzantine army after the Battle of Manzikert of 1071 (see ◊Manzikert, Battle of), recruited from Turks who had converted to Christianity.

Varangian (Old Norse, *varan* 'to swear') member of the Byzantine imperial guard founded 988 by Vladimir of Kiev (955–1015), which lasted until the fall of Constantinople 1453. The name (meaning 'the sworn') came to be used for a widespread Swedish Viking people in eastern Europe and the Balkans.

From the late 11th century, the Byzantine guard included English and Norman mercenaries, as well as Scandinavians. It was feared and respected as an elite military force.

Varaville, Battle of battle on August 1057 at which the Duke of Normandy (◊William (I) the Conqueror) routed a contingent of the French forces that had invaded Normandy under the joint leadership of his overlord, Henry I of France, and his neighbour, Count Geoffrey of Anjou. The invaders had entered the duchy by way of the Hiémois and had marched towards Bayeux and Caen. William's army shadowed them until they attempted to cross the river Dives near Varaville. The incoming tide made it impossible for the entire force to cross together, and the Normans fell upon those who had been left behind. French losses were so heavy that the invaders had to retreat from Normandy.

Varna Crusade unsuccessful attempt in 1444 to halt the expansion of Turkish power into Europe. Responding to a call by Pope Eugene IV in 1443, an eastern European army of 20,000 advanced east to besiege Varna, Bulgaria, but the Christian fleet failed to arrive in time. Sultan Murad II (1404–51) came to relieve the city and an indecisive battle resulted.

King Wladyslaw III of Poland and Hungary (1424–44) was killed and the siege was abandoned. The fall of the Byzantine capital Constantinople (modern Istanbul, Turkey) was imminent.

Varro, Gaius Terentius Roman consul and commander of the army destroyed by ◊Hannibal the Great at Cannae in 216 BC (see ◊Cannae, Battle of). He survived the battle and, although condemned by historians for his demagogic politics and military incompetence, was granted a vote of thanks in the Roman Senate for refusing to negotiate with Hannibal after the defeat.

Although given some positions of authority in the remainder of the war, he never again commanded in a major battle.

Varus, Publius Quinctilius (died AD 9) Roman commander who led his army to disaster in the Teutoburger Forest (see ◊Teutoberger Forest, Battle of the) in northern Germany in AD 9.

In 4 BC, as governor of Syria, he had quelled disturbances following the death of Herod the Great by marching into Judaea with a hastily raised army to bluff potential rebels into submission by a show of force. He attempted to repeat this operation in Germany, to put down unrest led by ◊Arminius, but came up against concerted opposition and lost his entire army. He committed suicide as the battle drew to a close.

vassus (or *vassallus*) medieval European vassal, subject to a lord. The term was used in the context of the feudal relationship between a free man and his lord, voluntary subordination being offered in return for protection and maintenance. The vassal gave an oath of fidelity and commended himself to his lord, later doing homage. A vassal could later be of high rank.

vavassor in the medieval period, a lesser vassal under a tenant. It is generally an alternative to 'vassal', though of a lesser kind. In the 11th-century English Domesday Book vavassors are lesser free men.

In the 1133 Bayeux Inquest a vavassor was a free tenant with military obligations depending partly on land, expected to serve with arms, armour, and horse. Sometimes a vavassor held a fraction of a knight's fee.

Veii strongly fortified Etruscan city to the northwest of Rome, Italy. It was founded on the top of a plateau in the late 4th century BC when a wall 2 m/6.5 ft high and about 2 m/6.5 ft wide was constructed along the plateau rim. The steep cliffs and slopes were used to supplement the defences. A small detached hill at the southeast corner was fortified as a citadel. Ten gates gave access through the walls, but neither these nor any point of the wall seems to have had towers.

The fortifications protected the city from a Roman siege in 406 BC (see ◊Veii, Siege of), with only starvation forcing it to surrender in 396.

Veii, Siege of siege and capture of the Etruscan city of ◊Veii by the Roman army 406–396 BC. The city's defences were finally breached by the use of a tunnel, which may have been one of the drainage ditches that passed beneath the wall, closed off by the defenders. The capture of Veii removed a powerful rival of Rome.

velites (singular *veles*) Roman light infantry used for skirmishing who appeared in the Roman army about 211 BC and were last men-

VEGETIUS (*FLAVIUS VEGETIUS RENATUS*)

Roman military theorist. Very little is known about his life, but he seems to have held a senior position in the imperial bureaucracy of the late empire, late 4th–early 5th centuries. He wrote two works, one on equine and bovine veterinary practices and his *Epitome of Military Science*. The latter is the only general military treatise in Latin to have survived from antiquity and it became very influential in the medieval period.

Vegetius' treatise comprises four books: recruitment and training; the structure and battle order of the legion; field campaigns; and siege and naval warfare. It provides a vast amount of information about the Roman army but is not without problems. As an *epitome*, it is a compilation and precis of earlier treatises. Vegetius acknowledges a number of these works at times, two of his major sources are Cato and ◊Frontinus, but it is impossible to tell which sections are copied or summarized from earlier works and which, if any, describe the contemporary situation. Nor is Vegetius known to have had any military experience. Although *Epitome* is based on the works of earlier writers who commanded armies themselves, Vegetius does not describe how the Roman army operated but how he felt it ought to be organized and operated.

He has been accused of being reactionary and attempting to turn back the clock to a time when the Roman army was successful in all it did, but he does not ignore the political and military situation at the end of the 4th century AD when Rome suffered a disastrous defeat at Adrianople at the hands of their erstwhile allies (see ◊Adrianople campaign). He advises against using barbarians in the Roman army, concentrating instead on the organization and use of the citizen legion. He condemns the quality of soldiers and their lack of professionalism compared with their counterparts of the early empire, and he stresses the importance of proper equipment and training. The section on siege warfare shows most clearly the influence of the late empire's circumstances: Vegetius concentrates solely on the defence of fortified positions, covering a range of issues such as fortifications, supplies, and dealing with siege engines.

tioned in 109/108 BC, during the Jugurthine War. They consisted of the youngest and poorest 1,200 recruits who presented themselves at a muster. They were equipped with small javelins and a sword and had no armour apart from a helmet and a round shield.

Instead of having their own line, the *velites* were added to the maniples of the ◊*hastati*, ◊*principes*, and ◊*triarii*, with 60 men assigned to the first two and 40 to the third.

Vellore city in southern India, on the Palar River, founded in 1274 by the refugee Dravidian chieftain Bomni Reddi. It is defended by a fort considered to be among the finest examples of military architecture in the region.

The fort, surrounded by a wet ditch, could only be entered via a winding roadway, through massive gates protected by a drawbridge. It was annexed by the rising power of ◊Vijayanagar in the 15th century, though the surviving fortifications are mostly of a later date.

Vercellae, Battle of battle fought in 101 BC between the Roman army and the Cimbri tribe near Vercellae (near modern Rovigo) in northeast Italy. When the Cimbri entered Italy, intending to settle in Cisalpine Gaul, the Roman consul Gaius ◊Marius was sent to intercept them. He inflicted a heavy defeat on the Cimbri.

Using his superior cavalry and disciplined army, Marius manoeuvred the Cimbri into a tight column where they were too cramped to be able to use their slashing weapons. They were slaughtered with losses claimed as 140,000–120,000 dead and 60,000 taken prisoner. It was the last invasion Italy was to have for almost 500 years.

Vercingetorix (died 46 BC) chieftain of the Averni tribe, who joined the Gallic revolt (see ◊Gallic Wars) in 52 BC and became its commander in chief. Unable to stem the tide of Julius Caesar's counteroffensive, he was forced to make a stand at the stronghold of Alesia. With his surrender came the end of Gallic resistance to the Roman conquest of Gaul.

Vercingetorix's father, a member of the Avernian nobility, had ruled the tribe but had been executed for showing too much ambition. When the revolt against the Romans broke out in 53 BC Vercingetorix was expelled by the tribal leaders for agitating for the Averni to join it. He responded with a coup and took power, pledging the support of his tribe. The Averni dependants and allies joined him and in 52 BC the preparations were complete and his army entered the war. The chieftain of the Treveri tribe, ◊Indutiomarus, had been beaten and Vercingetorix soon took the mantle of leader for the resistance to Rome.

The superiority of the Romans in a pitched battle was shown at Noviodonum, and Vercingetorix accordingly switched to guerrilla tactics and scorched earth. At Avaricum a large part of his army was besieged and destroyed, but at his own capital of Gergovia the Roman assaults were repulsed. Realizing that the revolt was losing momentum and strength, he decided to risk everything on achieving a decisive victory, but was defeated. His army retreated to the hilltop fortress of Alesia and made a stand there. Allied Gallic armies tried to raise the Roman siege of Alesia, but even combined assaults were unable to breach the Roman double circumvallations. Faced with starvation, Vercingetorix was forced to surrender before the end of 52 BC. He was captured and taken to Rome where he was ritually executed during Caesar's triumphal celebrations of 46 BC.

Verneuil, Battle of battle fought on 17 August 1424 in France, during the ◊Hundred Years' War, in which John, Duke of Bedford, English regent of France for Henry VI, defeated a French force under the Count of Aumâle and his Scottish allies in a hard-fought encounter. Bedford's heralds recorded over 7,000 dead on the field, the Scots losing 50 noblemen.

Building on the victory at Cravant in 1423, Bedford mustered the Norman feudal levy and marched to oppose the Franco-Scots forces advancing from Tours. He led 8,000 men-at-arms and 1,000 archers which he dismounted in two battles, leaving some as baggage guards. Aumâle led 15,000, including 6,000 Scots under Alexander, Earl of Douglas, on the right wing, and 500 Italian cavalry wide on each flank. Bedford advanced to a position north of the town of Verneuil. The ground was so hard that the archers had difficulty driving in their stakes, and those on the left flank were driven off by the Italian cavalry, who dispersed after attacking the baggage train. The men-at-arms then fought a very bloody melee. Bedford's battle broke the French and then returned to surround and crush the Scots.

Verona, Battle of (403) battle fought in June 403 between the West Roman general ◊Stilicho and the Visigoths commanded by ◊Alaric. Stilicho's victory prevented Alaric from renewing his invasion of Italy.

After the battle Alaric accepted the authority of the Western emperor and was given Illyricum (former Yugoslavia) to hold in his name.

Verona, Battle of (489) decisive victory for the Ostrogoths, led by ◊Theodoric the Great, over the Italian *foederati*, led by ◊Odoacer in

VESPASIAN (9–79) AD

Roman general and emperor. As the legate of the 2nd Legion (*Legio II Augusta*), he took part in the invasion of Britain in AD 43 by Claudius, playing a distinguished role in the Roman victory at the Medway (see ◊Medway, Battle of the). He then led his legion in an independent command to conquer much of southwestern England. In 66–67 the emperor Nero sent him to suppress the Jewish rebellion (see ◊Jewish War). He reconquered Galilee through a series of hard-fought sieges, capturing the cities of Jotopata (see ◊Jotopata, Siege of), Gamala (see ◊Gamala, Siege of), and Gischala and accepting the defection of Sepphoris. During campaigns in 68–69, he suppressed Samaria and much of Judaea before the war to determine Nero's successor (see ◊Year of Four Emperors) demanded his attention. He left his son ◊Titus to complete the Jewish War, then consolidated his position in Egypt and sent an army to Italy. The civil war was decided in Vespasian's favour by the actions of his subordinate commanders, without his having to participate in a single battle.

this follow-up to Sontius (see ◊Sontius, Battle of) a month earlier, which took place on 30 September 489. Odoacer was driven back to his capital at Ravenna, leaving the Ostrogoths in control of northern Italy. They laid siege to Ravenna, but behind its protective marshes and with sea access, Odoacer was secure.

verutum Roman javelin with a head approximately 22 cm/8.7 in long and a wooden shaft approximately 105 cm/41 in long, described by the Roman military writer ◊Vegetius in the 5th century.

vervelle pierced brass or iron lug on a ◊basinet, used to secure the ◊aventail.

Vesuvius, Battle of battle fought in 339 BC between Rome and its Latin allies near Mount Vesuvius, southwest Italy, that established Roman suzerainty over the Latin tribes.

War had begun in 340 BC over Rome's refusal to appoint a Latin as one of its consuls, with the Latins, Volscians, and Campanians forming a coalition against Rome. Though outnumbered and facing opponents well trained in fighting methods, the Romans carried the battle. Rome was aware of how much it needed the allies and rather than subjecting them harshly, it dissolved the Latin League and awarded them privileged status.

vexillatio detachment from a larger unit in the 3rd-century Roman army. From the 4th century it was a cavalry unit of about 500–600 men.

vexillum square, flaglike standard used by Roman cavalry regiments (see ◊alae, ala). It was also used by detachments of legionaries.

Vietnam, Mongol invasion of invasion of Vietnam (Annam) in 1257 by the Mongol general Uriyangkhadai, continuing ◊Khubilai Khan's campaigns in southern China. He marched down the Red River and briefly occupied Hanoi, but his troops suffered from heat, disease, and guerilla activity, and he withdrew when Vietnamese Emperor Tran Thai-ton accepted Mongol overlordship. Peace lasted until the Mongol invasion of Champa in 1282–87 (see ◊Champa, Mongol invasion of).

Vijaya (lived 13th–14th centuries) (*Kritarajasa Jayavardhana*) founder of the Majapahit empire of Java, taking the name Kritarajasa Jayavardhana as king 1293–1309. After suppressing rebels in the northeast and forcing Chinese invaders to evacuate, he eventually secured control over all Java and its neighbouring island Madura.

Son-in-law of King Kritanagara of the Singhasari dynasty, Vijaya was campaigning in northern Java against rebels when Kritanagara was killed in 1292 by Jayakatwang, viceroy of Kadiri in eastern Java. Vijaya initially defeated Jayakatwang but was forced by Kadiri reinforcements to flee to King Viraraja of Madura. With Madurese help he established himself at Majapahit in northeastern Java.

In 1293 a Mongol-Chinese expedition sent by ◊Khubilai Khan and commanded by ◊Yikomusu arrived. Vijaya promptly offered his submission, and Yikomusu's troops helped him defeat Jayakatwang's attack on Majapahit. The allies marched on Kadiri, Vijaya forming the rearguard, defeated the Kadiri army, and captured Jayakatwang. Vijaya returned to Majapahit ostensibly to collect tribute for Khubilai; but he massacred his Chinese escort and began to attack detachments of Chinese troops, who had split up to pacify Java. He eventually made their position so difficult that Yikomusu evacuated Java.

Vijayanagar (Sanskrit/Prakrit 'Victory City') capital of the last great Hindu empire (also named Vijayanagar) in India between the 14th and 17th centuries, situated on the river Tungabhadra, southern India. The empire attained its peak under the warrior Krishna Deva Raya (reigned 1509–65), when the city had an estimated population of 500,000. Thereafter it came under repeated attack by the Deccani Muslim kingdoms of Ahmadnagar, Bijapur, and Golconda.

The empire was established by Harihara I (reigned 1336–57), a warrior chief from the Sangama dynasty. He and his brother Bukka founded and fortified the capital 1336–43 as a centre of resistance to the Muslim invasion of southern India. At its greatest extent the city covered an area of some 165 sq km/64 sq mi, in a series of seven citadels and concentric walls.

The empire was extended to the south and northeast by Bukka (reigned 1344–77) and by Devaraya II (reigned 1422–46). The Sangama dynasty was overthrown in 1485 by the provincial governor Saluva Narasimha (reigned 1486–91), and the Saluvas were replaced by the Tiluvas (c. 1505–65). The capital was destroyed after defeat by the Muslims at the Battle of Talikota in 1565.

Vikramaditya I king 652–80 of the Chalukya dynasty ruling in southern India, the son and successor of ◊Pulakeshin II. He ended a long-standing dynastic war on his southern borders by conquering the Cholas and Pandyas in 655 and avenged the death of his father at the hands of Narasinghavarman by defeating the Pallavas in 675.

He occupied the Pallava capital Kanchi, but spared it the pillage and slaughter which they had previously inflicted upon his own capital, Vatapi.

Vikramaditya II king 730–40 of the Chalukya dynasty ruling in southern India, the grandson of ◊Vikramaditya I. He continued the war with the Pallava dynasty, capturing the Pallava capital Kanchi on three occasions.

Villehardouin, Geoffrey de (c. 1150–c. 1218) marshal of Champagne in 1185 and historian of the Fourth Crusade 1202–04. Villehardouin was involved in the Venetian transport of Crusaders to the Holy Land. His *Conquest of Constantinople* represents the view of the crusade's leaders. It is a detailed account of military operations and provides valuable insights into such contemporary practices as the division of booty. He settled in the East and his descendants became rulers of mainland Greece.

Viminacium, Battle of battle between a Byzantine force and the ◊Avars led by ◊Bayan in 601. The decisive Byzantine victory checked Avar expansion into southern Europe.

Vincennes castle castle-fortress in Paris, begun on the site of an earlier work by Philip VI of France in the 14th century, and continued and completed by John and Charles V. The castle comprised a large rectangular curtain wall with nine towers, all but one of which were later cut down to wall height, and within this is the large, turreted keep, 51 m / 167 ft in height. A ditch surrounded the curtain wall, and an interior ditch isolated the keep from the bailey.

Vindolanda fort Roman fort (modern Chesterholm) that formed part of the northern frontier defences of Roman Britain from the 1st to the 5th centuries AD. Archaeological excavations have uncovered large quantities of wooden and leather objects, including the documents and letters known as the Vindolanda Tablets, that provide an insight into everyday army life.

A succession of forts were built between AD 85 and 105 to guard the Stanegate road that ran between Carlisle and Corbridge. The site was reoccupied a few years later and remained in use following the construction of ◊Hadrian's Wall, providing a reserve unit to strengthen the central sector. The emperor Hadrian stayed here while overseeing the construction of the Wall, accommodated in a palatial timber building constructed beside the fort. A large civil settlement grew up outside the west gate of the fort, which included an inn.

Viriathus (died 140 BC) leader of the Spanish Lusitanian people in a war against Rome. He won battles in 147 and 146 BC and trapped a Roman army at Erisane in the Roman province of Lusitania in 141 BC, forcing Rome to negotiate a peace treaty that recognized Lusitania as an independent ally. In 140 BC the treaty was repudiated and his ambassadors were bribed to assassinate Viriathus while sleeping in his tent.

Viriathus escaped a Roman attempt at genocide on his tribe in 151 BC, joined the war fought by the survivors, and emerged as their leader in 147 BC. He was able to employ guerrilla tactics and local knowledge to gain numerous successes against the Roman forces sent against him.

Visconti, Gian Galeazzo (1351–1402) (Duke of Milan) Milanese ruler. He succeeded his father Galeazzo II in 1378 as joint ruler of Milan with his uncle Bernabo, whom he put to death in 1385, when he assumed the title of duke. Under his rule Milan expanded its control southwards, over Lucca, Pisa, Siena, and Bologna, dominating northern Italy.

Vitkov, Battle of battle fought on 14 July 1420 between the ◊Hussites, defending the Bohemian capital Prague and Vitkov Hill (in the modern Czech Republic) outside the city, and a crusader army. The Hussites forced the crusaders into negotiations, proving in the battle that they were militarily effective.

A large force of crusaders besieged Prague at the end of June, and its citizens defended the fortified bridge over the river Vltava determinedly. The Hussite military leader Jan ◊Zizka fortified Vitkov Hill, which granted access to the countryside with field defences, but his troops were ill equipped. When the crusaders launched an attack on his positions his blockhouses (forts), which mounted guns, held out, forcing the besiegers into negotiations.

Vitruvius (lived late 1st century BC) (*Marcus Vitruvius Pollio*) Roman architect and military engineer. His ten-volume interpretation of Roman architecture *De architectura/On Architecture* includes several chapters on artillery and military machinery.

During the civil wars of the late Republic, Vitruvius supported Julius Caesar and then Octavian (later Augustus) and supervised the construction of artillery for the latter. *De architectura* is dedicated to the emperor Augustus and the final book includes detailed information on artillery and specifications for the construction of catapults. He also describes other pieces of siege machinery.

Vlad Tepes (c. 1430–76) ('the Impaler') ◊*voivode* of Wallachia in 1448, 1456–62, and 1476. The legendary Dracula, he had a reputation for cruelty, and spent as much time fighting rivals as he did fighting against the Turks. He fought at Kossovo in 1448, ambushed Mehmet II at Turnu in 1462, and was eventually killed by the Turks. Vlad was typical of many eastern European potentates trapped between Christendom and the Turks in the border warfare of the mid-15th century.

The fragmented dates of Vlad's reign show how insecure was his rule. His rebellion against Mehmet II was bold, and he forced the Sultan to retire from Wallachia in 1462. He was then imprisoned for political reasons by Matthias Corvinus, King of Hungary. On his release, Vlad took part in the capture of Bucharest before Mehmet took his revenge.

Vochan, Battle of battle in April 1277 in which ◊Narathihapate of Burma invaded the border-state of Kaungai in Yunnan, a vassal of the Mongol-Chinese Yuan dynasty under ◊Khubilai Khan. Twelve thousand Yuan troops from Yunnan under Hudu (Quduqu) met the Burmese at Vochan (Yongchang), in Kaungai. The Burmese were able to defeat the Mongols by shooting arrows at their elephants, scattering and confusing the army.

The Burmese army was 40,000–60,000 strong, relying on 800 elephants. The outnumbered Yuan troops deployed in front of a forest, but met the Burmese advance across the plain with a mounted counterattack. When the Mongol horses, unused to the elephants, refused to go near them Hudu fell back into the wood and ordered his men to dismount and shoot. Their archery wounded and panicked the elephants, which fled into bamboo thickets, throwing their riders. The Mongols remounted and charged the disordered Burmese, routing them in heavy close-quarters fighting.

voivode medieval name for a ruler and military commander in Serbia, Romania, and Moldavia, controlling 'voivodates' as military territories. ◊Vlad Tepes 'the Impaler' was *voivode* of Wallachia.

Vorhut medieval Swiss term for the vanguard of their pike and ◊halberd formations. The equivalent term for the main body was *Gewalthut*, and for the rearguard *Nachhut*.

voud Flemish term used in the 14th century for a military unit raised from the cities, usually associated with their guild forces; it could contain both infantry and cavalry.

Vouillé, Battle of decisive victory in 507 for the Franks, under ◊Clovis, over the Visigoths in southern France, in which Clovis is said to have personally defeated and killed the Visigothic king Alaric II. This battle completed the conquest of most of France by the Franks. Intervention by the Ostrogothic king, ◊Theodoric the Great, prevented the Franks from taking Septimania (the western Mediterranean coastal strip up to the Pyrenees).

Wagenburg (German 'wagon-fortress') medieval mobile fortification developed in the early 15th century. It consisted of a number of horsedrawn wagons loaded with weapons and fighting men which were moved into a strategic position on the battlefield to form a formidable mobile fortress. *Wagenburgs* were notably used by ◊Hussite armies.

The Hussites had scores of large wagons, many armoured, filled with crews of crossbowmen, handgunners, and ◊halberd and ◊flail-men, drawn by teams of horses. This provided them with strategic mobility. Tactically, when the wagons were drawn up in a circle and interspersed with gunpowder artillery they proved almost invincible.

Wakefield, Battle of battle fought on 30 December 1460 during the English Wars of the Roses (see ◊Roses, Wars of the) in which Richard, Duke of York, was ambushed and killed outside Sandal castle, Yorkshire, by Lancastrians.

Northern Lancastrian forces had been gathering in Yorkshire. York advanced to his base at Sandal, his forces gathering to the south of the castle, while the Lancastrians surrounded it to the north. For an unknown reason, York left the safety of the castle, but did not join up with his supporting forces. His small troop was surrounded and defeated.

Wakhan and Balur, conquest of conquest in August–September 747 in which the Tang Chinese captured the mountain kingdom of Wakhan from a Tibetan army of 9,000 and then captured the neighbouring kingdom of Balur unopposed. This victory blocked a major route from Tibet to the west.

The Tang general ◊Gao Xianzhi led 10,000 cavalry and mounted infantry from Kashgar over the almost impassable Pamir mountains to Wakhan. He surprised the Tibetans by fording a supposedly uncrossable river, enabling him to take high ground and defeat them. He then invaded Balur, whose king was influenced by his Tibetan queen, captured the capital, and executed pro-Tibetan officials. He

destroyed a cane suspension bridge just in time to prevent the arrival of Tibetan reinforcements.

waki-biki small protective devices of mail, or ◊kozane, sewn to a cloth backing and worn with Japanese armour, typically the ◊dōmaru, ◊haramaki, or ◊tosei gusoku, to protect the armpits. They were in use from the Muromachi period (1333–1568).

wakizashi Japanese 'companion sword', the shorter of the two swords which formed the ◊daishō (matching pair of swords worn by Japanese ◊samurai at all times).

It was introduced in the Muromachi period (1333–1568) as a side arm for use in close combat by the *ashigaru*, who would traditionally have been armed only with a spear (◊yari) or polearm (◊naginata).

Wallace, William (1272–1305) Scottish nationalist who led a revolt against English rule in 1297, won a victory at Stirling against Earl Warenne, and assumed the title 'governor of Scotland'. He was styled 'Knight' in a charter of 1298. Edward I defeated him at Falkirk in 1298 (see ◊Falkirk, Battle of). Wallace was defeated in a minor conflict in 1303, captured, and executed in 1305.

Wallingford castle castle 19 km/12 mi southeast of Oxford, in Berkshire, England. It originated as a timber ◊motte-and-bailey castle shortly after the Conquest, located to protect a useful ford across the river Thames.

The castle came into prominence during the 12th-century wars of Stephen and Matilda and was considerably strengthened by a great tower and curtain walls, which allowed it to survive three sieges. The Treaty of Wallingford, between Stephen and Matilda, was signed there in 1153.

Wang Anshi (1021–86) (or *Wang An-shih*) Song Chinese military reformer who was in power 1068–85 as part of the 'New Laws' movement aiming to reform government and finance. His reforms were only partially successful, and when his patron Emperor

Shenzong died Wang was dismissed in disgrace and most of his measures lapsed.

He tried to reduce reliance on the expensive ◊yangbing professional army by forming ◊baojia peasant militia. He tackled the chronic shortage of cavalry horses by making them available to peasants who were responsible for their upkeep and could use them in peacetime but supplied them to the army in war. He also established a new government office to oversee and standardize weapons manufacture.

Wang Jian (c. 290–220 BC) (or *Wang Chien*) Chinese general who led the emperor ◊Qin Shi Huangdi's conquest of the ◊Warring States. He conquered Zhao in 229–228 BC, and destroyed Yan in 227–226 after its crown prince had failed in a plot to assassinate Qin Shi Huangdi. Jian then retired, but was recalled in 223 to command against Chu.

Another general had rashly attacked Chu with 200,000 men and suffered defeat. Jian insisted on using a force of 600,000. He sat in a fortified camp until the Chu troops slackened their guard, then attacked and crushed them. In the next two years he campaigned south of the Yangtze River, conquering Chu completely.

Wang Kon (died 943) founder and ruler 918–43 of the Koryo kingdom in northern Korea, which he created out of the Silla kingdom when it collapsed in rebellion. He took power for himself in 918, becoming King T'aejo in 936 after the last Silla king's abdication.

The Silla kingdom that had united Korea at the end of the Tang Chinese Wars in Korea collapsed in rebellion about 900. Wang Kon was a general of one rebel regime, 'Later Koguryo', who carried out successful amphibious operations against its rebel rival 'Later Paekche'. He defeated 'Later Paekche' at the battles of Koch'ong (930) and Unju (934). The last Silla king surrendered peacefully in 935 and abdicated in Wang Kon's favour the following year.

Wang Mang (45 BC–AD 23) Chinese regent and usurper. He was appointed regent for an infant emperor in 1 BC. When the emperor died in AD 6 he appointed another infant, proclaiming himself emperor of the Xin 'New' dynasty in AD 9. He subdued several rebellions but was defeated by the Green Woodsmen in AD 23 (see ◊Green Woodsmen, rebellion of the) and beheaded.

In AD 11 Wang mobilized 300,000 men against the ◊Xiongnu, who were becoming more assertive, and briefly imposed a peacefully inclined ruler. Natural disasters – two shifts in the course of the Yellow River – provoked the revolts of the Green Woodsmen, aided by dissident Han princes, and the Red Eyebrows (see ◊Red Eyebrows, rebellion of the). The latter defeated imperial armies in 22. In 23 the Green Woodsmen defeated Wang's army at Kunyang (see ◊Kunyang, Battle of), and took Loyang and the capital Changan.

Wang Xuance (lived 7th century) (or *Wang Hsüan-ts'e*) Tang Chinese guards officer. In 648 he was sent by the emperor Tang Taizong to India, responding to an embassy sent by the Hindu emperor Harshavardhana. By the time he arrived Harsha had died, and a local king (Aluonashun in Chinese sources, possibly Arunāsva) seized the embassy's treasure. Wang escaped to Tibet, where ◊Songtsen Gampo supplied him with 1,200 troops and 7,000 cavalry. Returning to India, Wang defeated the Indian king, pillaged his country, and received tribute from neighbouring kingdoms.

Wanyen Aguda (1067–1123) (or *Wan-yen A-ku-ta*) Jurchen founder of the Jin (Chin, Kin) or 'Golden' dynasty of Manchuria and northern China. He was the chieftain of a Jurchen tribal alliance under the rule of the Khitan Liao dynasty, but rebelled against the Khitan in 1114 and defeated the Liao emperor at Huanglong in 1115 (see ◊Huanglong, Battle of). From 1122 he was allied to the Song Chinese, who tried to take the Liao capital at modern Beijing, but failed twice; the fate of the ex-Liao territories in China sparked war between the Song and Jin and led to the Jurchen conquest of all northern China.

Wanyen Liang (died 1161) (originally *Digunai;* also *Hailing Wang*) Jurchen emperor of the Jin dynasty in northern China 1149–61, grandson of ◊Wanyen Aguda. In 1161 he launched a massive attack on the Song dynasty in the south, defeating Song forces on the Huai River, though losing much of his fleet in the conflict. He attempted to cross the Yangtze River, but was assassinated during the Battle of Caishi (see ◊Caishi, Battle of 1161).

Liang came to power by murdering the previous emperor, his cousin. He strengthened imperial control to undermine the Jurchen nobles, alienating conservative Jurchen including the hereditary ◊mengan mouke soldiers. He began preparations for the offensive against the Song dynasty in 1158, recruiting 120,000 Jurchen and Khitan troops and 150,000 Chinese, including 30,000 sailors for a newly built fleet. The strain of this massive conscription led to Chinese and Khitan rebellions before the attack began.

Warangal city in the southeastern Deccan (in the present-day state of Andhra Pradesh), India, founded in the 12th century by Proda Raja, a prince of the Kakatiya dynasty. His successors fortified the city with a stone wall 7.25 km/4.5 mi in circumference and an outer wall of earth, enclosing a total area 3 km/2 mi in diameter.

In 1310 King Pratapa Rudra Devi II submitted to the sultan of Delhi and agreed to pay tribute. When this was later withheld, the sultan's eldest son, Ulugh Khan (later Sultan

WARRING STATES

Period of Chinese history, around 475–221 BC, marked by intensification of warfare. The decisive trend of the period was the rise of the western state of Qin, revitalized by the reforms of ◊Shang Yang after 359 BC. The period was also marked by an increase in the size of armies, from the low tens of thousands to hundreds of thousands, and by great strides in military theory. Several of the ◊Seven Military Classics were compiled during this period, as was the work of ◊Sun Bin.

The 15 states of the start of the period were reduced by 300 BC to seven – Han, Wei, Zhao, Yan, Qi, Chu, and Qin – plus the prestigious but powerless Zhou kings. Han, Wei, and Zhao were successors of the state of Jin, which fragmented after the siege of Jinyang in 453 (see ◊Jinyang, Siege of) – a partition formalized in 403. Qi was powerful in the mid-4th century thanks to the generalship of Sun Bin and his victories at Guiling (see ◊Guiling, Battle of) and Maling (see ◊Maling, Battle of). In 284, however, it was almost destroyed by its neighbours, and only rescued by ◊Tian Dan's victory at Jimo (see ◊Jimo, Siege of). Chu, in the Yangtze and Huai valleys, expanded by destroying the semi-barbarian coastal state of Yue in 333 and the ancient states of Song in 286 and Lu in 255. A Chu-led alliance failed to defeat Qin at the Hangu Pass in 318 (see ◊Hangu Pass, Battle of), and thereafter various attempts to assemble alliances against Qin met with failure. Qin outflanked Chu by conquering Shu (modern Sichuan) in 316 and was thus able to take Ying from Chu in 278 (see ◊Ying, fall of 278 BC). In 260 Qin crippled Zhao at Changping (see

◊Changping, Battle of). ◊Qin Shi Huangdi conquered all the remaining states 246–221.

The increase in the size of armies was made possible by agricultural improvements that increased the population and by improvements in iron technology that equipped large armies – though some of the most prestigious weapons were still of bronze alloys, as in Qin Shi Huangdi's terracotta army. Most of the soldiers were conscript infantrymen, divided into crossbowmen and close-combat troops with spears, swords, or halberds. Chariots (see ◊chariot, Chinese) declined in importance, and though ◊Wuling of Zhao introduced cavalry, they remained a minority, armed mostly with bows and crossbows for skirmishing.

Armies were led by professional generals rather than the hereditary nobles of earlier periods. They were thoroughly drilled and strictly controlled on the battlefield by flag and drum signals. Ferocious offensives were emphasized, especially in Qin where social advancement could be gained by taking enemy heads, but stubborn defences from behind elaborate field fortifications were well known. Tactics of manoeuvre, deception, and ambush were highly developed. The increasing sophistication of Chinese fortified towns (see ◊fortified towns, Chinese) and the defensive techniques developed by the ◊Mohists meant that sieges were long and difficult, but whereas ◊Sunzi in around 500 BC had advocated avoiding fortified cities, Warring States generals had the organization and resources to carry out sieges that lasted for months or years.

◊Muhammad ibn Tughluq) captured the city in 1323. It was renamed Sultanpur, and paid tribute to Delhi. In 1422 it was captured by the Bahmanis, and later passed to a successor state, Golconda.

Warkworth castle castle in Northumberland, England, 11 km/7 mi southeast of Alnwick, that was the seat of the Percy family. Begun as a simple ◊motte-and-bailey work in the 12th century, it was subsequently enlarged and built in stone to the same layout, the present towerhouse being sited on the motte.

The curtain wall dates from the 13th century and contains corner and flanking towers and a large double-tower gatehouse with a bridge across the surrounding ditch. The keep, or tower-house, is a complex rectangular, three-storey structure, with a tower protruding from each face.

Warring States period another name for the ◊Sengoku period of Japanese history (1467–1568).

Warrior Government (or *buke seiji*) form of government under the leadership of a ◊shogun appointed by the figurehead emperor, which dominated Japan for almost 700 years from the time of the ◊Kamakura shogunate (1185–1333) to 1872. It was established as a result of the ◊Taira–Minamoto Wars (1180–85).

The court of the preceding Heian period (794–1185) had relied on the control of its provinces by officials who had local, rather than courtly, allegiances. The influence of these provincial warrior chieftains, as they became, began to expand into court life to the extent that by the mid-12th century factional disputes over imperial succession were being decided by force of arms, with those on the winning side further increasing their influence at court.

The Taira–Minamoto Wars, fought between two families with significant influence at court and having their origins as provincial military rulers, saw the establishment of Japan's first true Warrior Government under a shogun.

Warwick castle castle in England 32 km/20 mi southeast of Birmingham. The first defences were constructed here in Saxon times. A wooden castle with a ditch was built in around 1065–67 by the Earl of Warwick, which was then appropriated by William the Conqueror and given to Henry de Newburgh.

This work appears to have lasted until 1263 when it was severely damaged in the ◊Barons' War of 1215–17 and that of 1264–67. It then passed into the Beauchamp family's hands (though still Crown property), and in 1345 the building of the present stone castle began.

Warwick the Kingmaker (1418–71) (actual name *Richard Neville*) earl of Warwick and captain of Calais. A prominent participant in the Wars of the Roses, Warwick first supported the Yorkists and was instrumental in their victory at St Albans in 1455. He was defeated at the second Battle of St Albans in 1461 and campaigned in the north 1461–64. He manoeuvred Edward IV off the throne in 1470, but when the king returned in 1471, Warwick was defeated and killed at Barnet (see ◊Barnet, Battle of).

A member of one of the most prominent families in medieval England, made the richest earl by marriage. A cautious commander, he became seemingly more so as he got older, but was politically ambitious. His support for Edward, earl of March, and later switch to the Lancastrians, led to his 'Kingmaker' nickname.

wei Chinese guards units. The Sui dynasty (581–617) established 12 *wei* at the capital, which survived under the early Tang after 618. They were recruited from ◊*fubing* territorial troops, and counterbalanced by the professional ◊Palace Army. They declined in numbers and were replaced by the ◊*changcong suwei*.

Wei River, Battle of battle in 203 BC in which general Han Xin under ◊Han Gaozu defeated general Long Chu under ◊Xiang Yu at the River Wei in China. By night, Han blocked the river above their position with sandbags. He then began a withdrawal, and as the Chu forces pursued he had the sandbag dam broken. The flood cut the Chu army in half. Those who had crossed were easily defeated, and those on the far side fled, to be pursued and captured later.

wei so military system of early Ming China, strongly linked to farming, established by ◊Zhu Yuanzhang in 1364. His forces were organized into 5,000-strong ◊*wei* divided into five ◊*qianhu so* (battalions), comprising ten *bohu so* (companies) of 100 men. There were about 500 *wei*, theoretically giving 2,500,000 troops, and membership was hereditary.

Some units had ◊*tuntian* farmlands to provision themselves, and after 1368 this became standard, every *wei so* unit receiving land. Only 30% of the soldiers performed military duties, while 70% worked on the land. Field armies would be formed from detachments of different units so farming could continue. The units fell below their establishment, and most men became more farmers than soldiers. In the 15th century the ◊*ying* were established to train them, and they were also supplemented by new volunteer mercenary units.

Wen (died 627 BC) (Marquis of Jin) second *ba* (hegemon) of the Chinese states 636–627 BC, after ◊Huan, Duke of Qi. Exiled for 19 years, he seized the throne with troops supplied by ◊Mu, Duke of Qin. He then restored the king of Zhou to his throne, killing the brother who had expelled him. When the half-barbarian southern state of Chu attacked Jin's ally Song, Wen defeated Chu at Chengpu in 632 (see ◊Chengpu, Battle of).

Wen reorganized Jin's army, expanding it from two ◊*jun* to three in 633 and in 632 raising three new armies – called 'columns' (*hang*), since only the Zhou king was allowed more than three *jun*. Two 'new armies' (*xinjun*) were created in 629.

Western Garden, Army of the army created by the Han Chinese court in 188 to counter the Yellow Turbans (see ◊Yellow Turbans, rebellion of the). It was commanded by a court eunuch, but prominent military leaders including ◊Cao Cao and ◊Yuan Shao were named 'Colonels of the Western Garden' in the hope of bringing their semiprivate forces under central control. It was never an effective force.

white armour (or *alwhite armour*) complete set of plate armour worn in late medieval Europe as uncovered, bright metal. The first sets of this type appeared in the 1420s and continued as the standard form of knightly armour during the remainder of the medieval period.

At this time the 'international' style of armour worn in the 14th century gave way to regional styles, centred on Italy and Germany.

White castle castle in Wales 27 km/17 mi southwest of Hereford and the third of the 'three castles of Gwent', guarding the road from Abergavenny to Ross-on-Wye. Originally a ditched palisade, it was converted to masonry in around 1235, formed as a hexagon with six towers, two of which formed the entrance. It was unusual for its period in being primarily a fortress rather than a residence. It featured in some minor local skirmishes but fell into disuse in the 14th century.

White Huns a people of Turkic stock, known to the Byzantines as Hephtalites and in India as *Hunas*. They entered northwestern India around the mid-5th century and then invaded Iran; by the early 6th century their empire stretched from Iran to Khotan (present-day Hotan, west China). It collapsed about 530 under attack from other Turkish peoples.

The White Huns moved southwards from Bactria into India during the reign of ◊Kumaragupta I, ruler of ◊Magadha, but were turned back by his son and successor Skandagupta (lived 455–67). They invaded Iran next, defeating and killing the Sassanian king Firuz, before returning to the Punjab where they overthrew the Kusanas and other local kings and took tribute from the Gupta kings. The Huna empire reached its peak in the 6th century under Toramana and his son ◊Mihirakula.

William (II) Rufus (c. 1056–1100) ('the Red') king of England from 1087, the third son of ◊William (I) the Conqueror. He spent most of his reign attempting to capture Normandy from his brother ◊Robert (II) Curthose, Duke of Normandy.

His extortion of money led his barons to revolt and caused confrontation with Archbishop Anselm. He was killed while hunting in the New Forest, Hampshire, and was succeeded by his brother Henry I.

William of Poitiers (lived 11th century) knight, priest, and historian, active 1020s–70s. He is the author of the *Deeds of Duke William (the Conqueror)*, containing detailed descriptions of warfare, including the Battle of Hastings in 1066.

William was a Norman knight who developed a religious vocation and received a high-quality classical education at the schools of Poitiers. His history is a eulogy of his subject. He describes 11th-century warfare, largely a matter of raids and ambushes, based around the control of fortresses and castles, set in the context of William the Conqueror's career. He also provides a rare and detailed set-piece description of the Battle of Hastings.

William of Ypres (died 1162) illegitimate son of Philip of Ypres who twice attempted and failed to become count of Flanders. In exile he became a mercenary captain and chief lieutenant for King Stephen of England in his civil war with Matilda.

William became earl of Kent in all but name. He led Stephen's cavalry on the left at Lincoln (see ◊Lincoln, Battle of 1141); they were defeated, but William escaped. He continued to act as military commander for Stephen's queen Matilda, recovering London, and capturing Robert of Gloucester at Winchester (see ◊Winchester, Battle of) in 1141. He fought on in the war until becoming ill and blind. Under Henry II he retired to Flanders.

William (I) the Lion (1143–1214) king of Scotland from 1165. He was captured by Henry II while invading England 1174, and forced to do homage, but Richard I aban-

WILLIAM (I) THE CONQUEROR (1028–87)

King of England from 25 December 1066, and duke of Normandy from 1035. He defeated his rival, King ◊Harold (II) Godwinson of England, at the Battle of Hastings (see ◊Hastings, Battle of) on 14 October 1066.

William's early years were marked by violence and disorder. In 1046 his cousin, Guy of Burgundy, led a revolt which forced the young duke to seek the aid of his overlord, Henry I of France. With Henry's help, William defeated Guy at Val-és-Dunes (see ◊Val-és-Dunes, Battle of), and firmly secured control over Normandy. In 1051–52 William and Henry besieged and captured ◊Domfront castle and Alençon (see ◊Alençon, Siege of) in Maine, France. Almost immediately afterwards, William, Count of Arques, rebelled against the duke with the support of Henry I, who was increasingly concerned about Normandy's growing power. William quickly besieged the rebel ◊Arques-la-Bataille castle and it was surrendered to him in 1053. In 1054 Henry I and Geoffrey of Anjou invaded Normandy, but the annihilation of part of their force at Mortimer forced them to withdraw. Their second invasion, in 1057, was defeated at Varaville (see ◊Varaville, Battle of).

In 1051 Edward the Confessor had nominated William as heir to the English throne, but when he died in January 1066 ◊Harold (II) Godwinson was crowned. William immediately began preparations for an invasion of England. On 28 September his forces landed unopposed at Pevensey, Sussex. Harold was in the north of England defeating an invasion led by Harald Hardrada, King of Norway, (see ◊Stamford Bridge, Battle of) but immediately marched south to meet William. Their armies clashed in the Battle of Hastings on 14 October 1066. Harold was slain and William achieved a decisive victory. On Christmas Day 1066 William was crowned King of England in Westminster Abbey.

In 1067 William forcibly brought southwest England under his control. In 1068 he marched north and east to establish a number of strategic fortifications. In the summer of 1069 Swein ◊Estrithson of Denmark landed with a considerable force in the Humber and was welcomed by the northern English earls who joined him in expelling the Norman garrison at York. William immediately marched north, destroying everything in his path, and reoccupied York. He undertook a systematic harrying of the north, setting his troops to kill and burn in order to leave nothing that could support future rebellion. The Danish fleet was bought off and departed.

In 1072 William led an invasion that forced King Malcolm of Scotland to surrender hostages and swear fealty. In 1073 he was back in France suppressing rebellion in Maine. His regents dealt with a rebellion by the English earls in 1075, and in the latter years of his reign, William twice faced rebellion in Normandy led by his eldest son, ◊Robert (II) Curthose. In 1087 William sacked the French-controlled town of Mantes in the Vexin. In the fighting he suffered a fatal internal injury after being thrown against the pommel of his saddle. He was taken to the priory of Saint-Gervais near Rouen where on 9 September he died.

doned the English claim to suzerainty for a money payment in 1189. In 1209 William was forced by King John to renounce his claim to Northumberland.

Wilton, Battle of (871) victory in 871 for the Danes, led by ◊Halfdan, over the Saxons of Wessex, under ◊Alfred the Great, in the last major engagement of the campaign of 870–01.

Alfred secured a fragile peace by buying off the Danes and inducing them to leave Wessex for Mercia and Northumbria.

There had been a brief pause in the fighting following the Danish victory over the Saxons at Meretun, during which time King Aethelred of Wessex had died (shortly after Easter) and Halfdan's Danes had been reinforced by newcomers from overseas. Alfred, who had succeeded his brother Aethelred, led a small Saxon force against the Danish army at Wilton. Although outnumbered, the Saxons initially succeeded in driving back the Danes, but in the end were defeated.

Wilton, Battle of (1142) battle fought between King Stephen of England and the late King Henry I's daughter Matilda in Wiltshire, England, in 1142. It formed part of a civil war between them over the English throne. Matilda's cause was defended by a force under Robert, Earl of Gloucester. The battle was a setback for the king, but he escaped and recovered.

Stephen's castle at Wilton was an outpost in enemy territory, where he assembled a new army. Gloucester's forces besieged him in the castle. Stephen made a sortie and the battle was fought in what are now the grounds of Wilton House. Gloucester charged and Stephen, rather than repeat the disaster of Lincoln (see ◊Lincoln, Battle of 1141), escaped.

Winchelsea, Battle of sea battle of 1350 off Winchelsea, East Sussex, England, between ◊Edward III of England and a Castilian fleet during the ◊Hundred Years' War. Edward's victory helped to win English domination in the war for a time.

The English fleet at Sandwich under Lord Morley was joined by Edward and his sons ◊Edward the Black Prince and John of Gaunt. The Castilian fleet under Don Carlos de la Cerda had the windward and was armed with throwing engines. The battle depended on grappling and boarding. Edward's ship was sunk but he boarded an enemy galley. Fourteen Castilian ships were captured and their crews were thrown into the water; the others fled.

Winchester, Battle of battle fought on 14 September 1141 at Winchester, England, between the forces of Matilda, claimant to the throne, and the royalist supporters of King Stephen (c. 1097–1154). Matilda's forces besieged Wolvesey castle, the episcopal residence of Stephen's younger brother Henry of Blois, but were defeated by the royalist relief force holding the castle. Her forces were themselves besieged by ◊William of Ypres and militia from London, and were defeated as they tried to break out.

Robert, Earl of ◊Gloucester, was captured, forcing Matilda to release Stephen, who had been held since his defeat at Lincoln in February (see ◊Lincoln, Battle of 1141) in exchange for him.

Winchester castle castle in Hampshire, England. Built as a timber earthwork castle by William the Conqueror in 1067, this work was later expanded as Winchester became the capital city of England. Various walls and towers were added, including a square tower built by Henry II and a round tower on the motte (castle mound) built by Henry III. The existing great hall was built under Henry II in 1222–35.

Windsor castle castle 35 km/22 mi west of London, in Berkshire, England. Although construction work went on for several centuries, it can still be discerned as a Norman ◊motte-and-bailey castle. It was founded by William (I) the Conqueror, who had a motte cut into the chalk of the river cliffs and embellished with two ditched baileys.

Henry I began converting the work into stone; Henry II improved this work, planted a vineyard, and built a great tower inside his father's shell keep; Edward III built the Chapel of St George; and after that almost every monarch up to George IV added or rebuilt some part of the castle.

Winkelried, Arnold (lived 14th century) Swiss hero of Sempach in 1386 (see ◊Sempach, Battle of). The Swiss halberdiers were outmatched by well-armoured Austrian men-at-arms who had dismounted and were using their lances in a kind of pike formation. Apparently Winkelried, a man of huge size and strength, grabbed hold of many of these weapons and took their impact on his body. This created a gap in the Austrian line, allowing the halberdiers to break into it, eventually leading to victory.

Winwaed, Battle of victory in 655 for the recently Christianized Northumbrians, under Oswy of Bernicia, over the pagan Mercians and East Angles. Although outnumbered, the Northumbrians destroyed the pagan army, killing King Penda of Mercia, and Aethelhere, crown prince of East Anglia. As a result, Oswy became the undisputed *Bretwalda* (ruler of Britain). Northumbria became the pre-eminent Anglo-Saxon kingdom and Christianity rapidly spread throughout all of Britain.

Witiges king of the Ostrogoths 536–40. He was defeated by the Roman general ◊Belisarius at Ravenna (see ◊Ravenna, Siege of 538–39). He surrendered and spent the remainder of his life in exile in the East Roman Empire.

Worringen, Battle of battle fought in Germany on 5 June 1288 between John I of Brabant and the Archbishop of Cologne. John was besieging Worringen in support of the citizens of Cologne, who had expelled their ruler, when he was attacked. He emerged the victor.

John had 2,000 knights and 3,000 foot soldiers, his opponents a few more. He deployed in three battles in very close order. The archbishop's line was thinner and extended, allowing his troops to overlap and attack John's camp. The cavalry encounter was drawn out and equal, but the arrival of the Cologne militia in the archbishop's rear compelled him to surrender.

Wu (lived 12th–11th centuries BC) king of Zhou in northern China about 1133–1115 or 1038–1021 BC. His father King Wen was a vassal of the last Shang king ◊Di Xin, but had built up powerful support among the Shang's western vassals. With the help of his general ◊Taigong, Wu rebelled against Di Xin, defeating and killing him at Mu about 1122 or 1027 BC (see ◊Mu, Battle of) and establishing Zhou rule over all northern China from a new capital at Hao.

Wu Ding (lived 14th–13th centuries BC) (or *Wu Ting*) king of the Shang dynasty in northern China about 1324–1265 BC (these dates are traditional and may have been closer to 1200 BC). He brought Shang power to its greatest extent, a success perhaps connected with the adoption of chariots about this time (see ◊chariot, Chinese).

He led several successful campaigns against tribes to the northwest of Shang territory, including a three-year war against the Guifang 'demon country' for which he levied 23,000 men. Other campaigns were led by his queen ◊Fu Hao. He also fought in the south, extending Shang influence to the Yangtze basin.

Wuling (died 298 BC) king of Zhao 325–298 BC in the Chinese ◊Warring States period. In 307 he recruited the first ever Chinese cavalry, copying the clothing and equipment of the neighbouring steppe nomad horse-archers. With this new force he defeated the nearest nomad tribes and established a Zhao protectorate over them, and attempted to outflank neighbouring Qin from the north.

Wu Qi (c. 440–361 BC) (or *Wu Ch'i*) Chinese general and theorist of the ◊Warring States period, whose *Wuzi/Master Wu's Book* is one of the ◊Seven Military Classics. He fought successively for the states of Lu, Wei, and Chu, and was never defeated, but made political enemies who forced his exile from Lu and Wei and his death in Chu.

The *Wuzi* probably embodies his ideas edited by his disciples. It stresses the need for military power to defend a just state, discusses control and discipline, and has an interesting comparison of the troops of the different Chinese states.

Wu rebellion rebellion by the king of Wu in 154 BC, after ◊Han Gaozu unified China, making some regions into kingdoms with limited autonomy, ruled by his generals or his relatives. The rebel defeat resulted in the reduction of the kingdoms' territories.

The king of Wu, joined by six other kings in the southeast, pushed west with a mainly-infantry army, vulnerable in the plains to the Han cavalry and chariots, which cut his supply lines. Forced by lack of food to attack an entrenched Han army at Xiayi, he was defeated and fled to the barbarian chief of Eastern Yue, who was bribed to kill him. The remaining rebels were crushed.

Xanten Roman city (Colonia Ulpia Traina), now within modern Birten, north Germany, founded by the emperor Trajan beside the Rhine River in about AD 100 for soldiers retired from the nearby legionary fortress of Vetera.

The city was defended by walls with corner and interval towers and main gates on the north, south, and west sides. These were destroyed in the Frankish attack of AD 275, and were replaced by a new construction under ◊Constantine (I) the Great between 306 and 311. This new fortress (390 × 390 m/426 × 426 yds) occupied the centre of the ruined city and consisted of a wall 4 m/13 ft thick reinforced by 44 semicircular projecting towers. It had gates only on the north and south sides. The fortress was rebuilt by the emperor Julian (reigned 361–63) following damage by further Frankish raids and served until its final capture by the Franks in the 5th century.

Xenophon (c. 430–c. 350 BC) Athenian soldier and writer. He joined the Persian prince ◊Cyrus the Younger against his brother Artaxerxes II in 401 BC, and after Cunaxa (see ◊Cunaxa, Battle of) emerged as one of the leaders of the Greek mercenaries in their long march home to Byzantium.

He then served various commanders until he returned to Greece with ◊Agesilaus II in 394. Exiled by Athens, he lived on an estate near Olympia granted him by the Spartans, until expelled after Leuctra (see ◊Leuctra, Battle of) in 371 BC. He died in Corinth.

His works include the *Anabasis*, an account of his mercenary service; the *Hellenika*, a history of Greece from 411 to 362; and two of the earliest theoretical military works, the *Cyropaedia*, a treatise on the ideal commander under the guise of a fictional biography of the founder of the Persian Empire, and the *Hipparchikos/Guide for a Cavalry Commander*.

Xerxes I (c. 519–465 BC) Achaemenid king of Persia 486–465 BC, the son and successor of ◊Darius (I) the Great. He suppressed Babylonian revolts in 484 and 482, then in 480, at the head of a great army supported by a fleet, he crossed the Hellespont (Dardanelles) on bridges of boats and marched through Thrace into Greece. He occupied Athens, but the Persian fleet was defeated at Salamis (see ◊Salamis, Battle of 480 BC) and Xerxes was forced to retreat. His general ◊Mardonius remained behind, but was defeated by the Greeks at Plataea in 479 BC (see ◊Plataea, Battle of).

As the Persian survivors evacuated Greece after their defeat at Plataea, the Greek allies followed up their success, defeating Persian forces in Ionia at Mykale, and liberating Thrace and Ionia. About 466 a new Persian fleet was defeated by the Greeks at Eurymedon. Xerxes had brought disaster to Persia, and was murdered soon afterwards by the hazarapatiš Artabanus.

Xianbei (or *Hsien-pi*) group of nomadic tribes from southern Manchuria, probably proto-Mongolian since the Khitan and Mongols were regarded as their descendants. They allied with Han China AD 87–90 to defeat the northern ◊Xiongnu and conquer Mongolia, absorbing many Xiongnu.

The tribes were disunited, briefly uniting under ◊Tanshihuai. Some provided auxiliary troops to Chinese factions in the 2nd–3rd century disorders. From 285, the Murong tribe under Murong Hui developed a stable government, absorbing many frontier Chinese and other tribes. In 337 Murong Huang proclaimed the Former Yan dynasty – one of the ◊Sixteen Kingdoms – and invaded north China. By now Xianbei armies supplemented their traditional light horse-archers with ◊*tiema* armoured cavalry and Chinese-officered infantry. Another Xianbei tribe, the Toba, unified northern China under ◊Toba Gui after 386 and dominated the north until the 6th century.

xiangbing (or *hsiang-ping*) Chinese troops raised by ◊Yuwen Tai of the Western Wei dynasty to supplement the ◊*jinwei jun* after a defeat in 543. They were raised from local defence forces that already existed under the command of local Chinese military families, and became part of the central government system. They were organized into 24 ◊*jun* armies, and divided into 48 ◊*tuan* battalions and 96 *yitong fu*, or territorial units.

Xiangyang and Fancheng, sieges of (or *Hsiang-yang* and *Fan-ch'eng*) sieges 1268–73 of twin cities on opposite banks of the Han River which obstructed Khubilai's advance on the Yangtze valley. These were part of the conquest of Song-ruled southern China by ◊Khubilai Khan, during the Mongol campaigns in China (see ◊China, Mongol campaigns in). The Mongol army under the Chinese defector Liu Cheng, with 50,000 ◊*Han jun* conscripts and many ◊*gantaolu* volunteers, eventually succeeded in taking both cities.

Xiangyang, under Lu Wenhuan, was particularly strongly fortified and equipped with ◊*zhen tian lei* bombs. Liu blockaded the cities, building forts on the river at Lumenshan and constructing a river fleet to interdict supplies. He defeated a sortie from Xiangyang in 1268, and defeated a relief force with 3,000 boats at Lumenshan in 1269. In 1270, 10,000 men and 100 boats breaking out of Xiangyang were again defeated at Lumenshan. In September 1272, 3,000 Song troops succeeded in breaking in with supplies, though their commander was killed and some supplies lost. Blockade was clearly not enough, so Khubilai's nephew Abakha sent for Muslim engineers from Persia. These men built the latest counterweight ◊trebuchets, which breached the walls of Fancheng within a few days in December 1272. They were then set up against Xiangyang, and their effectiveness finally persuaded Lu to surrender in March 1273.

Xiangyang, Siege of (or *Hsiang-yang*) siege of Xiangyang, south of the Han River in what is now Hubei, December 1206–March 1207 by an alleged 200,000 Jurchen men. This was a counterattack after an invasion by the Song empire of the south. After unsuccessful attempts to take the city, the Jurchen grew low on supplies and withdrew.

The Song commander Zhao Chun had 10,000 men whom he reinforced with militia, and originally 16 ◊trebuchets, building another 98 during the siege. The Jurchen tried to divert the course of the river to put the city on their side of its new course, but failed. They built earth assault-ramps, but the defenders burned their wooden substructures.

Xiangyi, Battle of (or *Hsiang-i*) battle in 369 in which Xianbei tribal cavalry defeated Chinese infantry. Retreating from his campaign in the north with 50,000 men, the Chinese commander Huan Wen was pursued by the Xianbei. The Xianbei commander Murong Chui harried the Chinese retreat with 8,000 cavalry, while his colleague Murong De took 4,000 cavalry past them and ambushed them at Xiangyi. Caught between the two forces, 30,000 of Huan's men were killed. This battle demonstrated the decisive superiority of 4th-century northern ◊*tiema* cavalry over Chinese infantry.

Xiang Yu (232–202 BC) (or *Hsiang Yü*) Chinese aristocrat from the former southern Chinese kingdom of Chu. He rebelled against Qin and organized an alliance of rebel leaders throughout China, including Liu Bang (later the emperor ◊Han Gaozu), who took the Qin capital but was deprived of it in the settlement that followed. Liu started the war again in 206, and in 203 Liu and Xiang agreed to divide China between them. In 202 Liu broke the agreement, attacked from several directions, and trapped Xiang at Gaixia (see ◊Gaixia, Battle of); Xiang committed suicide.

Xianmi, Battle of (or *Hsien-mei*) battle in December 221 in which the Wei Chinese defeated the ◊Xiongnu nomad rebels on the northern frontier. The Wei general Zhang Ji expected an attack on his camp and organized an ambush of 3,000 men and a cavalry of 1,000 to attack the Xiongnu cavalry and feign flight. The Xiongnu took the bait and pursued recklessly. They were surrounded by the ambushers and defeated.

Xianyun invasion (or *Hsien-yün*) offensive in 823 BC in which the obscure Xianyun barbarians invaded the Zhou empire in northern China from a base somewhere on the upper Yellow River. They sacked the Zhou capital, ◊Hao, but it was recovered by an army led by Zhou commander Yin Jifu. In a campaign lasting from spring to winter, the Xianyun were driven out.

Xinan, Battle of (or *Hsi-nan*) battle in 207 BC in which Chu rebels under ◊Xiang Yu defeated and massacred Qin Chinese troops. Xiang defeated Qin forces under commander Wang Li at Julu, and then negotiated for the surrender of Chang Han, whose army had been defending Wang's supply lines. For some time the Chu and Qin armies confronted each other during negotiations. Xiang Yu eventually treacherously attacked by night and massacred more than 200,000 Qin troops.

Xincheng, relief of (or *Hsin-ch'eng*) relief of the fortress of Xincheng on 12 March 1365 by a Ming force under commander Li Wenzhong. The fortress had been besieged by Wu general Li Bosheng with 200,000 men. The battle ended Wu's last offensive against Ming.

In the Chinese civil wars, ◊Zhu Yuanzhang's Ming forces built the fortress of Xincheng as a frontier defence against the coastal state of Wu. Li personally led a cavalry charge which broke the Wu army, and as they retreated past Xincheng a sally by the garrison completed their rout. Wu was defeated in a series of sieges in 1365–67. Decisive cavalry actions like that at Xincheng were rare in the wars in south China.

Xindian, Battle of (or *Hsin-tien*) battle on 30 November 757 in which the Tang Chinese defeated rebels under commander An Chingxu. Although the rebellion dragged on for several more years, it was no longer a real threat after this battle.

After the imperial victory at ◊Changan, the rebels fell back to the eastern capital Luoyang. A large rebel army under commander Yan Zhuang drew up on the lower slopes of a mountain at Xindian, west of the city. A Tang army under Guo Ziyi pushed the rebels back but became disorganized as they followed up, and were themselves forced back. Meanwhile the Tang's Uighur allied cavalry defeated a rebel ambush force. When they learned of the main army's plight, the Uighurs rode round behind the rebel army and charged downhill into their rear. The rebels broke, and lost 100,000 men to a savage Uighur pursuit. Most of the survivors surrendered, and An Chingxu fled.

xinfu jun (or *hsin-fu chün*) (Chinese 'newly-adhered army') south Chinese troops of the Mongolian Yuan dynasty (1260–1368), originally recruited after 1273 from troops of the defeated Song dynasty. They were thought to be unreliable, so were originally officered by Mongols or northern Chinese and were of lower status than the ◊*Menggu jun* or ◊*Han jun*.

The *xinfu jun* were alternatively known as 'hand-marked troops of the perished Song' from the Song practice of tattooing soldiers on the hand to identify deserters. Despite their reputation for unreliability, they were used in the Mongol attacks on Japan (see ◊Japan, Mongol invasions of), in expeditions to southeast Asia, and in garrisons in the Uighur territories in what is now Xinjiang.

xingjun (or *hsing-chün*) (Chinese 'mobile army') campaign army in Tang China (618–907). The forces were recruited in the early period from ◊*fubing* called up for campaign duty. A *jiangjun* of one of the ◊*wei* guards units with the title ◊*tianxia bingma yuanshui* ('Imperial Generalissimo of Foot and Horse') generally commanded them.

XIONGNU (OR *HSIUNG-NU*)

Nomadic confederacy, possibly of Turkic origin, that proved to be a powerful force against Chinese armies. Maodun founded their power in Mongolia in about 200 BC, and ◊Qin Shi Huangdi built the ◊Great Wall of China against them. They were eventually conquered and the survivors absorbed.

The Xiongnu defeated ◊Han Gaozu at Pingcheng (see ◊Pingcheng, Battle of). ◊Han Wudi launched a series of campaigns against them under ◊Huo Qubing, ◊Li Guang, ◊Li Ling, and ◊Li Guangli, but armies had difficulty coping with their horse-archers' hit-and-run tactics. China eventually broke their power by fomenting civil wars, one of which saw ◊Chichi flee to the west while another split the Xiongnu into northern and southern factions.

An alliance of Chinese, southern Xiongnu, and ◊Xianbei destroyed the northerners, who fled to the Ili valley (southern Kazakhstan) in AD 92. They resisted the Chinese reconquest of the Tarim cities, and thereafter disappeared, perhaps moving west to play a part in forming the Huns.

The southerners settled on the Chinese border, intervening in civil wars like the Eight Princes' rebellion (see ◊Eight Princes, rebellions of the , and in 304 rebelled under Liu Yuan and ◊Liu Cong to establish one of the ◊Sixteen Kingdoms. The Jie) a Xiongnu subject-tribe, rebelled in their turn under ◊Shi Le. The Xiongnu states were successively conquered by ◊Fu Jian and ◊Toba Gui and his successors, and the survivors were absorbed.

Xuge, Battle of (or *Hsü-ko*) battle in 707 BC in which the Zhou Chinese king was defeated by his nominal vassals at Xuge. This battle confirmed the loss of royal power evident at the fall of ◊Hao.

King Huan led a coalition of lords against the powerful Earl Zhuang of Zheng in an attempt to restore royal authority. The king deployed in the centre, with allied lords on both flanks. The Zheng army also drew up in three bodies, each in ◊fish-scale formation so that chariots and infantry could support each other. They attacked on both flanks, and the unreliable troops of the allied lords fled. All three Zheng bodies then converged on the centre. King Huan was wounded by an arrow but led a controlled retreat.

ya Japanese arrow. Arrows were used by warriors from the Nara period (710–94). The many types of arrowhead (*ya no ne*) include the armour-piercing square- or lozenge-sectioned variety, those of flatter and elongated section used for cutting through armour, barbed arrows for cutting and piercing flesh, those with large forked heads said to be for cutting through rope, and whistling arrows with wooden heads, used for signalling or terrifying the enemy.

yabing private armies of the ◊*jiedu shi* military governors in late Tang China (618–907) and the following period. The core was a *yajun* bodyguard, originally the guards of the governor's residence. A new governor taking over a province would bring his own *yajun*, but sometimes had trouble winning over his predecessor's *yabing*.

yabusame Japanese term for archery from horseback. From the Heian period (794–1185) to the Muromachi period (1333–1568), the bow was the traditional weapon of the mounted ◊samurai.

As well as demonstrating his skill with the bow in battle, the samurai on occasions would perform *yabusame* as a form of religious rite in the precincts of a Shinto shrine. While at full gallop, he was required to fire arrows at three targets in quick succession. The first recorded instance of this was in 1096 before the retired emperor Shirakawa.

Yamana Sōzen (1404–73) (adopted religious name of *Yamana Mochitoyo*) Japanese military commander of the early Muromachi period. He was a major participant in the disputes surrounding the Ashikaga shogunal successions of 1465 which were one of the main causes of the ◊Ōnin Wars.

During the wars Sōzen was commander of the troops loyal to Ashikaga Yoshihisa and opposed to ◊Hosokawa Katsumoto who supported Ashikaga Yoshimi.

Yamazaki, Battle of major battle fought in 1582 in which the Japanese warlord ◊Toyotomi Hideyoshi defeated Akechi Mitsuhide, the assassin of the military warlord ◊Oda Nobunaga, and paved the way for the military unification of Japan.

Following the assassination of Nobunaga, Hideyoshi rallied his own and other *daimyo*'s forces against Mitsuhide. Mitsuhide had failed to get the support he had hoped for from other *daimyo* and withdrew with his force of 16,000 to Shōryūji castle. The castle quickly fell to the experienced Hideyoshi and his 40,000-strong force, and Mitsuhide was killed by peasants as he fled.

yangbing (or **yang-ping**) regular troops of Song China (960–1279). They were recruited from the lower social classes and supplemented by amnestied convicts and conscripts, so although professionals, their status was low and they were often inefficient. Song armies were very large – 378,000 in 960 and 1,259,000 by 1041 – and well equipped with armour, crossbows, and gunpowder weapons including the ◊*huoqiang* and ◊*zhen tian lei*. The army was thus very expensive. ◊Wang Anshi tried to reduce costs by establishing the ◊*baojia* system.

Yang Su (died 606) Chinese general who served his distant relative the emperor ◊Sui Wendi. He commanded the Sui conquest of south China in 589, subdued southern rebellions, and commanded on the northern frontier.

In 589 Yang's force sailed down the Yangtze River with a fleet built in Sichuan. The largest ships were five-deckers carrying 800 men each and equipped with spiked booms for smashing enemy ships. When blocked by a superior Chen fleet at difficult rapids, Yang had his infantry and heavy cavalry storm the Chen stockaded camp, and their fleet fled. Further downstream the Chen made a final stand, but were defeated when ten ships were broken by the spiked booms of the Sui ships.

On the northern frontier Yang used aggressive cavalry tactics to defeat the Eastern Turk nomad cavalry. After the emperor

Wendi's death, Yang put down a rebellion by the new emperor's brother; shortly afterwards he fell ill, and his suspicious new sovereign made sure that he did not recover.

Yanling, Battle of (or *Yen-ling*) battle in 575 BC in which the northern Chinese state of Jin defeated the southern state of Chu, both powers having sent armies to support warring allies. The battle ended the peaceful hegemony that Jin had enjoyed since Masui (see ◊Masui, Battle of), but confirmed Jin's power.

King Gong of Chu deployed his army with the best troops in the centre, his less reliable wings including wild southern tribesmen. Jin commander Marquis Li drew up his centre behind a marsh to protect it from the Chu elite, and attacked with chariots on both flanks. After fierce fighting all day, both armies were still intact, though Chu had suffered heavier losses. While Jin prepared for a second day's battle, King Gong ordered a retreat.

yari general Japanese term for a spear which was used to cut and thrust, but was never intended for throwing. The blades were usually of triangular or diamond-shaped section and some were modified with additional transverse blades (◊*jūmonji-yari* and ◊*katakama yari*). Smaller *yari* were sometimes remounted as daggers.

The significance of the *yari* as a weapon became evident during the Mongol invasions of 1274 and 1281 when the Japanese first experienced the extensive and effective use of armies of foot soldiers equipped with polearms against traditionally armed cavalry. In the Muromachi period (1333–1568) the massed armies of *ashigaru* were principally armed with the yari. From 1600 the *yari* was mainly used ceremonially, but it was again prominent in the civil wars about 1870.

Yarmuk, Battle of decisive Arab victory over the Byzantines which took place 12–20 August 636, resulting in the conquest of Syria by the Muslims under ◊Khalid ibn al-Walid.

A large Byzantine army was formed to drive the Muslims from Syria. Outnumbered, Khalid's Muslims abandoned the recently captured cities of Damascus and Emesa and fell back to the Yarmuk River.

Although suffering from dissension and ill discipline, the Byzantines were confident of victory. When initial attempts at subversion failed, the Byzantines attacked. Six days of hard fighting followed. Initially the Byzantines had the upper hand, breaking through the Muslim lines only to be halted by a hastily organized defence of the Muslim encampments. On the fourth day the tide

began to turn: Muslim cavalry scored a number of successes, and a flanking movement by Khalid's men exploited a gap between the Byzantine cavalry and infantry, driving off the former. The Byzantines were finally routed two days later, their escape was cut off and thousands died falling off high cliffs while others were slaughtered by the pursuing Muslims.

Yashima, Battle of penultimate battle, fought in 1185, of Japan's ◊Taira–Minamoto Wars. The Minamoto forces under ◊Minamoto Yoshitsune launched a surprise attack on the Taira at the fortress of Yashima (present-day Takamatsu), on the island of Shikoku, and they were forced to flee with the child emperor Antoku.

Following their defeat at the Battle of Ichi no Tani (see ◊Ichi no Tani, Battle of) in 1184, the Taira forces had regrouped at the fortress of Yashima. The opposing Minamoto forces were at a disadvantage as they were lacking in boats and had little experience of warfare on water. Several months were spent organizing materials and establishing supply routes before Yoshitsune decided to launch an attack, not directly from the sea, but from inland. The Taira sustained light casualties.

Yavana (Sanskrit 'Ionian') term applied in classical India (c. 500 BC–c. AD 1000) to the Greeks or other Hellenized westerners, and hence to all other Europeans.

First contact was with the invading armies of ◊Alexander (III) the Great and his successors, who established Hellenistic kingdoms in Bactria and northwest India, one of the best known being that of Menander (or Milinda), invader of ◊Magadha in 175 BC. The last of the Yavana monarchs, Hermaeus, ruling in Kabul, was overthrown by the ◊Kusana dynasty in about AD 50.

Yazdagird III last Sassanian Persian king 632–51, the grandson of ◊Chosroes II. His empire was attacked relentlessly by Muslim Arabs, who captured his capital Ctesiphon (modern Iraq) and defeated him at Nihawand in 642. Yazdagird retreated, trying to organize resistance, but was murdered in Merv.

After the death of Chosroes in 628, civil wars raged in Persia until the young Yazdagird was enthroned by Persian nobility. His empire was immediately attacked by Muslim Arabs and they took the frontier city of Hira in 633. Yazdagird sent an army to retake Hira and it defeated the Arabs at the Battle of the Bridge in 634. The victory was short-lived; Caliph ◊Umar sent a fresh army that defeated the Persians at Buwaib and retook Hira. In 637 a full-scale

Arab invasion of Iraq destroyed a Persian army at Qadisiyya. Ctesiphon was soon captured and Yazdagird fled to gather a new army. In 642 the Arabs defeated him at Nihawand. Yazdagird retreated successively to Istakhr, Kirman, and Khurasan, and was eventually killed at Merv.

Ye, Battle of classic cavalry charge in which ◊Erzhu Rong defeated the mutineers of the Six Garrisons (see ◊Six Garrisons, rebellion of the) under commander Ge Rong at the northern Chinese city of Ye in 528.

The mutineers, near the city of Ye, threatened the north Chinese capital Loyang which Erzhu controlled. He marched to Ye with 7,000 armoured ◊*tiema* cavalry, against an enemy allegedly 1,000,000 strong, and certainly greatly outnumbering him. Erzhu's troops approached in open order, stirring up dust-clouds to conceal their small numbers. They were forbidden to use swords, so the charge would not be slowed by men stopping to behead fallen enemies, but instead used 'miraculous cudgel' maces. The mutineers were broken by one charge across the plains, Erzhu himself taking them in the rear to complete the victory. Ge Rong was captured and his survivors surrendered.

Ye, capture of battle in 580 in which Yang Jian, who dominated north China, defeated commander Weichi Qiong and captured Ye. While Yang's general Gao Jiong fought Weichi Qiong outside the city, many citizens came out to watch. Gao had his archers shoot these spectators, and as they fled into the city, stampeding the rebel army with them, Gao's men followed up and stormed the almost undefended walls. The victory helped Yang Jian establish himself as Emperor ◊Sui Wendi.

Yellow River campaign attack in 1049 by the Khitan Liao empire on the Tangut Xixia state in northwest China. The Khitan launched a two-pronged attack on Xixia, one column sailing up the Yellow River with large war junks and supply boats cooperating with an army on the bank, while Liao emperor Xingzong led the main column. The Tangut defeated them by scorched-earth tactics.

Yellow Turbans, rebellion of the massive peasant rising 184–92 against the Eastern Han regime in China. The main Yellow Turban armies were defeated by ◊Dong Zhuo and other Han generals 184–85, but roving bands still threatened the capital in 189. They were not really crushed until 300,000 of their fighters, over a million people including dependants, surrendered to ◊Cao Cao in 192.

YEAR OF FOUR EMPERORS

Roman civil war, AD 68–69, prompted by the death of Nero. It marked the end of the Julio-Claudian dynasty and culminated in the capture of Rome by the Flavians.

After a reign of just three months, Nero's successor Galba was murdered by the Praetorian Guard. Otho was proclaimed emperor in Rome, but the legions on the Rhine refused to accept him and nominated their own commander, Vitellius, who led an army into Italy and won a great victory at the First Battle of Cremona in northern Italy. At this, Otho committed suicide. Meanwhile, the legions in Egypt, Syria, and Judaea had proclaimed ◊Vespasian emperor, and he had dispatched an army into Europe. This was led by the Syrian governor, Mucianus, and headed by an advance column under Antoninus Primus. Primus was joined by legions from the Danubian provinces and the remnants of Otho's army before proceeding to Italy. The large Vitellian army waiting to meet it was without clear command, and Primus defeated it in the Second Battle of Cremona (see ◊Bedriacum, Battle of) then led his troops in sacking Cremona. The Flavians captured Rome soon afterwards.

Founded by Zhang Jiao, the Yellow Turbans took their name from the yellow headscarves they wore for identification. They were the most important of several movements believing that omens proclaimed the end of the Han. Yellow Turban forces were better organized than most, into 36 *fang* divisions of 6,000–10,000 men each.

Yelü Abaoji (lived 10th century) (or *Yeh-lü A-pao-chi*) first emperor of the Khitan in southern Manchuria 901–26. He campaigned in the steppes, defeating the Kirghiz and establishing control over Mongolia, and in 926 conquered the wealthy Korean-Manchurian kingdom of Bohai (Po-hai, or Parhae). He laid the foundations for a strong Khitan state that later – under the name Liao – briefly overran all northern China, and held part of it for 200 years.

Originally the chief of one of several Khitan tribes, Abaoji led successful attacks on divided China and on neighbouring Turkish and Jurchen tribes; he carried off many captives, especially Chinese, and settled them in his territories. This enabled him to combine Khitan tribal cavalry – establishing the first ◊ordo army – with a base of Chinese agricultural wealth. In 907 he declared himself Emperor of the Khitans, and in 913 and 918 put down rebellions by Khitan who objected to the new monarchy.

Yelü Liuge (died 1220) (or *Yeh-lü Liu-ko*) Khitan general, one of several members of the Yelü clan who rebelled against the Jurchen Jin dynasty (which had ruled the Khitan since ◊Wanyen Aguda) and joined the Mongol leader ◊Genghis Khan. With Genghis's support, he regained control of the ancestral Khitan homeland.

Liuge raised an army in 1212; Genghis sent Mongol troops under Jebe to assist him in the Liao River region (modern Liaoning). Jebe captured the city of Liaoyang by a feigned withdrawal, and Liuge made it the capital of a revived Liao kingdom. In 1215 he was expelled by a rebellion of his own supporters, but regained his territory with ◊Mukhali's assistance and chased the Khitan rebels into Korea where combined Khitan, Mongol, and Korean forces wiped them out in 1217.

Yeomen of the Guard (popularly known as *Beefeaters*) medieval English royal bodyguard established by Henry VII and still existing as a pensioner unit at the ◊Tower of London.

Yifeng Bridge, Battle of (or *I-feng*) battle in 1352 in which the Red Turbans (see ◊Red Turbans, rebellion of the) defeated the Miao army, southern tribal troops serving the Mongol Yuan dynasty of China. The Red Turbans attacked Hangzhou, one of the largest and most strongly garrisoned cities of southern China. At Yifeng Bridge the Miao fled ignominiously, and the Red Turbans occupied Hangzhou for about a fortnight before being ejected by local irregulars.

Yikomusu (lived 13th century) (or *I-k'o-mu-ssu* or *Yighmis*) central Asian Uighur who was an admiral in the service of the Mongol Great Khan ◊Khubilai Khan. With the Mongol Shibi and the Chinese Gao Xing, he commanded an expedition against Java in 1292 that was initially successful but was withdrawn as Javanese resistance stiffened.

The expedition sailed late in the year, with 20,000 troops in 1,000 ships. Its aim was to punish Kritanagara of Singhasari for mutilating an envoy sent to demand his submission, but when it arrived in early 1293 Kritanagara had been overthrown by Jayakatwang of Kadiri. Yikomusu captured the Javanese fleet at the mouth of the Surabaya strait. Kritanagara's son-in-law ◊Vijaya submitted to the expedition and joined a successful attack on Kadiri.

Yikomusu and his colleagues then allowed Vijaya to return home with an escort of 200 of their troops; he massacred these and began to attack the rest of the Sino-Mongol forces. Shibi was nearly killed, returning with difficulty to Yikomusu's ships, and the commanders decided to evacuate Java.

ying Chinese 'division'. Under the Eastern Han (AD 25–220), it was the command of a ◊*jiangjun* in wartime, divided into *bu* regiments. In 1415 the Ming government set up three *ying* as training camps in Beijing, one each for infantry, cavalry, and firearms, to counter the declining standards of ◊*wei so* troops.

Ying, fall of (506 BC) fall of the capital of the Chinese state of Chu to the coastal state of Wu in 506 BC. Ying was not permanently lost, however, because Wu's success provoked a rescue expedition from the state of Qin.

A Chu army held the Han River against Wu invaders. After indecisive fighting 5,000 picked Wu troops attacked the Chu camp at dawn, surprising and routing their army. The Wu forces pursued to Ying, where they defeated another hastily mustered Chu army, including stampeding wild elephants urged on by men carrying flaming torches.

Ying, fall of (278 BC) fall of the capital of the Chinese state of Chu to its neighbour Qin in 278 BC. From Sichuan the Qin general Bo Qi attacked down the Yangtze, probably taking advantage of the current to sail on barges. He took Ying, forcing the Chu army to retreat to the Huai valley, and permanently annexed the western parts of Chu.

Yinma Spring, Battle of battle on 12 October 617 in which the Tang rebels under ◊Tang Gaozu defeated the army of the Sui dynasty, commanded by Qutu Tong, in China.

After Huoyi (see ◊Huoyi, Battle of), Tang Gaozu's army had to cross the Yellow River to reach the capital, Changan. He left a force to cover the Sui army, and the Tang vanguard under Li Shimin (the future ◊Tang Taizong) successfully crossed the river. Qutu, however, sent his subordinate Sang Xianhe to surprise the main Tang body as it crossed. The Sui attack was successful until 500 Turkish cavalry allied to the Tang attacked Sang in the rear and defeated him.

Yongde, Battle of (or *Yung-te*) battle in July in which the Mongols defeated Zhang Zhi's rebels in the northeast during the Mongol campaigns in China (see ◊China, Mongol campaigns in). The rebel commander, Zhang Dongping, was killed, and 13,000 of his men were killed or taken. ◊Mukhali dismounted part of his Mongol force to shoot at the unarmoured Chinese infantry, showing that Mongol archers were as dangerous afoot as mounted.

Zhang sent his nephew Zhang Dongping with 8,000 cavalry and 30,000 infantry to relieve a fort besieged by the Mongols under Mukhali. Mukhali marched by night to intercept Dongping, surprising him near Yongde at dawn. The Zhang rebellion was not finished for another year, but could not put an army in the field again.

York (Roman *Eboracum*) site in northeast England of a Roman legionary fortress founded in AD 71 and a high-status city, separated by the navigable river Ouse. An important centre for imperial campaigns in the north, York was the permanent headquarters of the 6th Legion (*Legio VI Victrix*) for most of the Roman period. The independent civil settlement that developed on the opposite river bank gained the status of a colonia (implying civic dignity, imperial favour, high status, municipal autonomy, and citizen rights) and a provincial capital.

The fortress at York commanded the volatile northern tribe of the Brigantes and the main north–south road routes from the frontier. It was first occupied by the 9th Legion (*Legio IX Hispana*), then replaced by the 6th Legion from the early 2nd century. The combination of a strategic fortress and a successful city made York an ideal base for directing frontier campaigns, and the Roman emperors Septimius Severus and Constantine I made it their headquarters.

York, Battle of (867) battle between the Danes under ◊Halfdan and the Northumbrians at York, England, in 867. Following their decisive victory, the Danes established settlements in the region and York became the main Viking centre in England.

York, Battle of (1069) battle fought at York, England, in February 1069 in which ◊William (I) the Conqueror defeated English rebels. He subsequently ordered his troops to devastate

Yorkshire to prevent any revival of opposition to his rule.

A rebellion in Durham in January had resulted in the massacre of the Norman garrison. William quickly marched north and surprised the English rebels in the streets of York.

York castle castle in Yorkshire, England. William the Conqueror built two ◊motte-and-bailey castles at York 1068–69, both of which were destroyed by Viking raids. Both were rebuilt; one fell into disuse quite quickly, the other became York castle.

The motte was reinforced by layers of clay, stone, and timber, and a large wooden tower was built on it in around 1070 and burned down in around 1190. The motte was heightened and a second tower was built which blew down in a gale in 1228. Finally, under Henry II (1154–89), masonry work began and a curtain wall with towers and a gatehouse was built, followed by *Clifford's Tower* on the motte. This unusual great tower was quatrefoil (four-lobed), with a forebuilding between two of the quadrants.

yoroi doshi (Japanese 'armour piercer') short, thick, triangular-sectioned Japanese dagger used for penetrating upwards into armour in close combat, worn on the right side of the waist with the cutting edge uppermost. It is also referred to as a *mete zashi*.

youth (Latin *juvenis*, French *jeune*) term used in 12th-century western Europe for knights bachelor or for the period during which a knight had this status. Youths, who had not yet received honours and were unmarried, sought to display prowess to earn these rewards. Princes who had not come into their inheritance, such as the 'Young King' Henry, son of Henry II of England, formed courts of such followers and engaged in ◊tournaments.

The youth of the great jouster William ◊Marshal lasted 22 years after his knighting. Youths also featured on crusades, with the slightly different meaning of young, common warriors setting themselves in the front rank in order to win full military equipment.

Yrfon Bridge, Battle of battle fought in 1282 between the English and the Welsh at the River Yrfon, Powys, Wales, during ◊Edward I of England's Welsh wars. The English commander John Giffard learned of a ford across the river, captured the bridge, and attacked the Welsh, holding a height that defended the crossing.

Giffard used 'new and momentous tactics' in the battle, which involved combining archers and cavalry in attack.

Yuan Shao (died 202) Chinese general in the civil wars of the late Han dynasty. He was the most powerful warlord in China until he fell out with his former ally ◊Cao Cao, who defeated him at Guandu in 200 (see ◊Guandu, Battle of). After this he never regained the initiative.

He fought against the Yellow Turbans (see ◊Yellow Turbans, rebellion of the) and became a colonel in the Western Garden Army (see ◊Western Garden, Army of the) in 188. When the Han emperor Lingdi died in 189, Yuan Shao and his half-brother Yuan Shu massacred the court eunuchs who were trying to seize power, but were prevented from taking control themselves by the arrival of the warlord ◊Dong Zhuo's army. Shao led an alliance of generals against Dong from a northeastern power base.

Yuan Shu (died 199) Chinese general in the civil wars of the late Han dynasty, the half-brother of ◊Yuan Shao.

He assisted in Shao's massacre of the court eunuchs in 189, and joined the alliance against the warlord ◊Dong Zhuo. He built up a power base south of the capital Loyang, and when ◊Cao Cao took control of the Han emperor in 196, Shu proclaimed his own dynasty but gained little support. He was defeated at Xiapi in 197 by Cao's ally Lu Bu, and most of his followers deserted him.

Yubi, Siege of (or *Yü-pi*) unsuccessful siege in 546 of Yubi fortress in China in which the Eastern Wei warlord Gao Huan was defeated by Western Wei's ◊Yuwen Tai.

Yubi, a four-sided fortress on a commanding height, blocked the Fen river valley down which Gao advanced in a general offensive against Western Wei. Gao successively built an earthen ramp up against the south wall, tunnelled under it, attacked it with a ram, and sapped the east wall, but the defending commander Wei Xiaokuan countered him each time. Desperate, Gao massed against the precipitous north wall, but failed there too. Finally, having fallen sick during the siege, and possibly wounded by a defending crossbowman, he broke the siege and abandoned the campaign. He never recovered.

Yue Fei (1103–41) (or *Yo Fei*) Song Chinese general, revered as a patriotic hero. The Jurchen Jin invaded Song China in 1126 and he led counterattacks from 1130, recovering Loyang and winning a major battle at Yancheng, Henan, in 1140. He advocated a determined counteroffensive to push the Jurchen out of China, but was recalled. When the emperor accepted a peace ceding all the north to the Jin, Yue Fei was executed.

Yumbu Lagang castle (or *Yum-bu-bla-sgang*) the oldest dwelling in Tibet, possibly built in the 7th century. Traditionally used by Tibetan kings, it was a five-storey castle of wood and stone with a single tall tower overlooking the Tsangpo River in the Yarlung valley, where the dynasty of ◊Namri Songtsen originated.

yumi Japanese bow of composite construction, consisting of a length of hardwood sandwiched between two pieces of bamboo, generally bound with rattan and sometimes lacquered. The *yumi* was normally about 2 m / 6.5 ft long and had the grip approximately one-third up from the bottom of the bow. It was used from the Heian period (794–1185).

It was fired from horseback and this differential enabled the archer to pass the bow quickly over the horse's body as he stood up in the solid stirrups (*abumi*) to aim and fire.

yurt (or *ger*) Mongolian term for a circular tent made of felt bound onto a wicker frame, having a low conical roof with a central vent for smoke from the fire.

Yusuf ibn Tashufin (c. 1030–1106) Almoravid ruler, conqueror of North Africa from 1070. He defeated Alfonso VI at Sagrajas in 1086 (see ◊Sagrajas, Battle of) and gradually reconquered the Muslim south. On Yusuf's death he left forces of 17,000 cavalry and a reorganized and refortified Muslim Andalusia.

A cousin of the Almoravid movement's founder, Abu Bakr, Yusuf was given charge of its forces based in Marakesh, soon after the city's foundation in 1070. He successfully dominated North Africa 1074–79, and following the fall of Toledo (see ◊Toledo, capture of) to the Christians in 1085, he launched an invasion of Andalusia and the Muslim south. Only the Muslim buffer state of Zaragoza remained independent. Almoravid armies were defeated by ◊El Cid, whom Yusuf never confronted in person, but Valencia was recovered in 1102.

Yuwen Kai (lived 6th–7th centuries) chief engineer of the Chinese Sui dynasty. He carried out irrigation projects and supervised the building of the Grand Canal. In 612, during the invasions of Korea (see ◊Korea, Sui Chinese wars in), he bridged the river Liao with two specially designed pontoon bridges (after a first attempt produced three bridges that were too short).

Yuwen Tai (505–56) tribal general in north China, a member of the Yuwen tribe of the ◊Xianbei. He opposed ◊Erzhu Rong's Chinese general Gao Huan and decisively defeated him at Yubi in 546 (see ◊Yubi, Siege of). In 554 he invaded the Liang empire of southern China and besieged the capital, installing a puppet ruler after its fall in 555.

Tai became an officer of the Six Garrisons leader Ge Rong (see ◊Six Garrisons, rebellion of the). He was captured by Erzhu Rong at Ye in 528 (see ◊Ye, Battle of) and enlisted with his captor. By 532 Rong was dead and Gao Huan was in power. Tai led the western armies in opposition to him and took control of the emperor; Gao Huan appointed a rival emperor, dividing north China between Western and Eastern Wei. Fighting between them centred on border areas round Loyang and the Tongguan Pass. In 537 Tai defeated an eastern attack through the pass, pursued, had to retreat from Huan's main army, but defeated it at Shayuan (see ◊Shayuan, Battle of). This pattern of attack, pursuit, and retreat was repeated several times, notably when Tai was heavily defeated at Mangshan in 543.

After this he supplemented his ◊*jinwei jun* tribal cavalry with Chinese ◊*xiangbing,* and secured his victories over Gao Huan and the Liang empire.

Zab, Battle of battle of 591 in which a Roman army won a decisive victory, having intervened in a Persian civil war to restore ◊Chosroes II to the Persian throne after he had been overthrown by Bahram Chobin.

Zangdihe, Battle of (or *Tsang-ti-ho*) battle in 1115 in which Tangut cavalry defeated Song Chinese troops. While the Jurchen under ◊Wanyen Aguda were conquering the Khitan Liao state, the Tangut kingdom of Xixia attacked the Song, preventing them from giving aid to the Jurchen.

Zanhuang, Battle of (or *Tsan-huang*) battle in July 1225 in which the Mongols defeated the Song Chinese during the Mongol campaigns in China (see ◊China, Mongol campaigns in). A Song army under commander Peng Yibin invaded Mongol-held Hebei, and at Zanhuang, near the Wuma hills, fought Shi Tianze, a Chinese general in Mongol service. Afraid of

ZAMA, BATTLE OF

Battle fought in 202 BC between the Roman army of Publius Cornelius ◊Scipio 'Africanus' and the Carthaginian army of ◊Hannibal the Great, at Zama, near Carthage in North Africa. It decided the Second Punic War (see ◊Punic War, Second) and established Rome as the undisputed champion of the Mediterranean.

Hannibal arrived back in Carthage from Italy in 202 BC and advanced his army to Hadrumentum (present-day Sousse, Tunisia) and from there to a place called Zama (the exact site is unknown), about five days' march from Carthage. There he pitched camp about 5 km/3 mi away from Scipio and, after an attempt to arrange a meeting failed, the two commanders drew up their armies on the plain between the camps.

Hannibal placed his 80 elephants in the front line, then his mercenaries (Celts, Moors, Balearics, and Ligurians), and behind them the Liby-Phoenicans and the Carthaginians. At the rear he placed his veterans and on his wings the cavalry, the Carthaginians on the right and the Numidians on the left. Scipio drew up his forces in the standard three lines (see ◊hastati, ◊principes, and ◊triarii) but instead of the draughtboard formation he placed the maniples in rows with a gap between. On the left wing were the Italian cavalry and on the right the Numidian cavalry of the Roman ally ◊Masinissa.

The elephants charged, but Scipio was prepared. Roman trumpets scared many into flight, and the ◊velites lured the remainder down the gaps in the legions where they could be safely picked off. The Roman cavalry wings charged their Carthaginian and Numidian counterparts and routed them. The *hastati* and *principes* then charged the Carthaginian infantry and broke the first two ranks who fled the field. Regrouping, Scipio placed the *triarii* and *principes* on the wings of the *hastati* and advanced on the Carthaginian veterans. Outflanked, the veterans put up stubborn resistance until the Roman cavalry returned from their pursuit and attacked them from behind.

being outflanked by Shi's cavalry, Peng set fire to the slopes of the hills behind him. Nonetheless, some of Shi's archers got onto the slopes in the Song rear. Caught from both directions the Song were crushed. Peng was captured and executed.

zarad (or **dir'**) Arabic term for a mail shirt. The same word is transliterated as *zereh* in Persian and Urdu and *zirh* in Turkish.

Zela, Battle of battle fought in 47 BC between Julius ◊Caesar and the army of Pharnaces, King of Pontus and the Bosporus, who had overrun much of the Eastern Roman Empire during the confusion of the Roman civil war. The Romans captured the Pontic camp and destroyed their army.

Caesar had marched swiftly with his force of four legions to confront Pharnaces, and camped close to his army, with only a ravine separating them. At dawn on 2 August, Pharnaces surprised Caesar by crossing the ravine to attack him. A charge by scythed chariots threw the Romans into confusion, but the difficult ground delayed Pharnaces enough to allow them to put together a battle line. After heavy fighting, the veteran VIth Legion drove back Pharnaces' left. A general onslaught forced the Pontic infantry down the slope, which led to their collapse, enabling the Romans to gain the victory.

Zengi, Imad al-Din (c. 1100–46) atabeg (ruler) of Mosul from 1127. Although unable to capture Damascus in 1139, he controlled Mosul and most of northern Syria, giving him the resources to challenge the crusader states of Antioch and Edessa. He took Edessa after a four-week siege in 1144 and so precipitated the ◊Crusades. He threatened to take more Christian territory but was murdered by a disgruntled eunuch on his way to attack Damascus again.

Zenobia queen of Palmyra (now Tadmur, Syria) 267–72. She assumed the crown as regent for her son Vaballathus, after the assassination of her husband Odaenathus, and led the city to a spectacular but short-lived dominance over most of the Roman East before being defeated at Emesa (see ◊Emesa, Battle of) by the emperor Aurelian in 272 and taken captive to Rome.

She occupied Antioch, much of Egypt apart from Alexandria, as well as Cappadocia and Bithynia. Her forces were defeated both at Antioch and Emesa in 272 and she was captured at the fall of Palmyra. Led in Aurelian's triumph (victory procession) in Rome, she was spared execution and lived out her life in comfortable captivity.

Zhao Tuo (257–136 BC) (or **Chao T'o** or **Trieu Da**) Chinese general who founded the Nan Yue (Nam Viet) state in south China and northern Vietnam. When ◊Han Gaozu reunified China, Zhao acknowledged Han China's overlordship and was left alone. He expanded south into Vietnam, subduing the Au Lac kingdom of ◊Co-Loa. Zhao died aged 121. His successors rejected Chinese overlordship, provoking Han Chinese conquest in 111 BC.

◊Qin Shi Huangdi conquered several southern tribal states including Nan Yue, centred at Panyu (Guangzhou). When the Qin empire collapsed in revolt, Zhao Tuo, deputy governor of this southern province, declared the independent kingdom of Nan Yue in 207 BC. Zhao's original army was the Qin garrison, recruited from conscripted convicts, probably supplemented by local tribesmen. A Chinese ban on horse exports to Nan Yue suggests that he tried to raise Chinese-style chariots or cavalry.

Zhe, Battle of (or **Che**) battle in 717 BC between the Chinese states of southern Yan and Zheng. Yan invaded Zheng, and near the town of Zhe was met by the main Zheng army. While this delayed the invaders, the Earl of Zheng's sons led a small force behind the Yan army and entered Zhe. They then led its garrison against the Yan rear, surprising and defeating Yan.

Zheng, Battle of (or **Cheng**, 713 BC) battle in 713 BC in which the Chinese state of Zheng defeated invading Northern Rong barbarians. The Earl of Zheng was afraid that the swift though disorderly barbarian infantry would overwhelm the Chinese chariots, indicating the weakness of chariots if unprepared. On the advice of his son Du, the Earl sent out a small force which lured the Rong into pursuit, and then ambushed them with the rest of the army. The first Rong body was surrounded and annihilated, and the rest fled.

Zheng, Battle of (or **Cheng**, 384) battle in 384 in China in which the Xianbei chief Murong Chong defeated a Qin army of 50,000 under commander Fu Hui. Chong was one of several subordinates who rebelled, wishing to reconstitute Murong Hui's kingdom after ◊Fu Jian's defeat at the river Fei (see ◊Fei River, Battle of the).

Chong attacked the Qin defensive position at dawn with a decoy charge by women mounted on oxen, carrying poles to look like standards and holding bags of dust. At a signal they released the dust, which the wind blew into the faces of the Qin troops. Blinded, the troops were then attacked and routed by the rest of Chong's army.

Zheng He (1369–1434) (or Cheng Ho)

Chinese admiral, a Muslim eunuch from modern Yunnan. He commanded voyages of exploration in the South China Sea and the Indian Ocean between 1405 and 1433, setting up a fortified base at ◊Megat Iskander Shah's Malacca and sailing as far as East Africa.

Zheng's expeditionary fleets were large – 27,000 men on 317 ships in 1405 – and used impressively large ships, the biggest being nine-masted junks 135 m/440 ft long. The voyages were mostly peaceful, but Zheng defeated Chinese pirates in Sumatra in 1407, intervened in a war between two Javanese kings in 1408, defeated a Sri Lankan king who tried to plunder the fleet in 1411, and intervened in a Sumatran succession war in 1413.

zhen tian lei (or chen t'ien lei) (Chinese

'heaven-shaking thunder') medieval Chinese explosive bombs first used by the Jurchen Jin dynasty at the siege of the Song Chinese city of Qizhou in 1221. Bombs made from bamboo tubes filled with ◊gunpowder were used from the 11th century, but the zhen tian lei had a cast-iron casing to produce a genuine fragmentation bomb.

Zhen tian lei were used by the Jin in defence of Kaifeng (see ◊Kaifeng, Siege of), by the Song defenders of Xiangyang (see ◊Xiangyang, Siege of) and other cities, and in the Mongol invasions of Japan. They were launched from ◊trebuchets, or even lowered on chains into besiegers' approach trenches. The fragments pierced iron armour and the explosion could be heard 50 km/31 mi away.

Zhongdu, sieges of (or Chung-tu) two

attacks on the Jin capital (modern Beijing) 1214–15 during the Mongol campaigns in China (see ◊China, Mongol campaigns in). ◊Genghis Khan assaulted Zhongdu in March 1214, but withdrew soon after. In another attack in September 1214, forces under Mongol commander Samuqa successfully besieged the city until it surrendered in June 1215.

The first assault failed because the Mongols were short of supplies and suffering from disease. Negotiations led to them withdrawing with considerable tribute in May. When the Jin moved their capital south to Kaifeng, Genghis sent Samuqa with Mongol, Khitan, and Chinese troops to besiege Zhongdu again. He blockaded the city rather than storm its formidable defences. The starving defenders were reduced to cannibalism. When the Mongols defeated a Jin relieving force, the city's commander took poison.

zhongxiao jun (or chung-hsiao chün)

(Chinese 'loyal and filial troops') Chinese irregulars noted for their courage but also for their indiscipline. They were raised by the Jurchen Jin dynasty to fight the Mongols in the 13th century in response to the decline of the ◊mengan mouke system.

Zhuge Liang (181–234) (or Chu-ko Liang)

Chinese statesman and general, minister of Liu Bei at the end of the Han and the early ◊Three Kingdoms of China period, and one of the most famous strategists in Chinese history. He masterminded the Red Cliff victory in 208 (see ◊Red Cliff, Battle of the), and in 221 persuaded Liu Bei to assume the title 'Emperor of (Shu) Han'.

He was responsible for the first use of the wheelbarrow to transport military supplies, a method particularly effective in mountains too difficult for wagons. Chencang in 229 (see ◊Chencang, Siege of) was one of his rare defeats. Shu Han began its decline after his death, falling to the Wei general ◊Deng Ai in 263.

zhupin double-ended javelin used by the

Daylami infantry of northern Iran.

Zhu Wen (died 912) (or Chu Wen) Chinese

general and emperor 907–12. He took control of the court in 903, deposing the Tang and proclaiming the (Later) Liang dynasty in 907. Zhu only controlled part of the north, and his coup ushered in a period of division until ◊Song Taizu's reunification. He was murdered by his son.

He joined ◊Huang Chao's rebellion but deserted to the Tang government in 882, and after winning battles against his former allies was made jiedu shi (governor) of Bianzhou in Henan. He fought against rebels and rival governors, notably ◊Li Keyong whom he could never eliminate, for territory and for influence in the imperial court, until he was able to take control.

Zhu Yuanzhang (1328–98) (or Chu Yüan-

chang, Ming Taizu, Hungwu) first Ming Chinese emperor from 1368, victor over the Mongols. He took Nanjing from the Mongol Yuan dynasty and made it the capital of his Ming state. He defeated the state of Han and absorbed its territory to become the strongest power in China. Next he defeated the state of Wu, then moved north against the Mongols, capturing their capital (modern Beijing) and proclaiming the new Ming dynasty in 1368.

Zhu became a leader of the Red Turban rebels against the Yuan dynasty (see ◊Red Turbans, rebellion of the), gradually increasing his independence from the movement. In 1356 he defeated the Yuan at Caishi (see ◊Caishi, Battle of 1356) and took Nanjing (see ◊Nanjing, Siege of). Caught between the states of Han further up the Yangtze River and Wu on the coast, he fought unsuccessfully against Wu at Shaoxing (see ◊Shaoxing, Siege of), but defeated Han attacks at Longwan (see ◊Longwan, Battle of) and crushed them at Poyang (see ◊Poyang, Battle of). He reorganized his armies into the ◊*wei so* system in 1364, then defeated Wu at ◊Xincheng (see Xincheng, relief of) and took its capital Suzhou in a ten-month siege 1366–67. He conquered the remaining southern Chinese warlords without difficulty.

He then moved north against the Mongols, capturing their capital and proclaiming the Ming dynasty. Victory at Dingxi completed the pacification of the north. Isolated regimes in Sichuan and Yunnan were mopped up (see ◊Qutang Gorge, Battle of). War with the Mongols continued, with battles at Karakorum in 1372 (see ◊Karakorum, Battle of) and Buyur Nor in 1388 (see ◊Buyur Nor, Battle of).

Zimisces, John Byzantine emperor 969–79, who campaigned successfully against the Russians and Muslims.

Zizka, Jan (c. 1378–1424) blind Hussite general. He came to the fore during the Hussite revolution of 1419, and devised a system of warfare employing battle-wagons for mobility and as mobile fortresses against armies of knights (see ◊*Wagenburg*). He achieved victories at Sudomer and Vitkov in 1420, Kutna Hora in 1421, Hörice in 1422, and Malesov in 1424 (see separate entries for these actions), but failed in his invasion of Hungary in 1423. He died of plague the following year.

Zizka fought at Tannenburg in 1410, and later lost an eye fighting for Wenceslas IV of Bohemia. Sudomer proved the value of his wagon formation, repeated at Vitkov, which gave the Hussites control of Prague. Facing the new king (and emperor) Sigismund, who invaded Bohemia in 1421, Zizka was first driven back at Kutna Hora, then returned to storm Kasik Hill and establish a *Wagenburg* which repelled the imperialists. He was then involved in civil wars until his death. His invasion of Hungary failed because light cavalry harassed his line of march, prevented foraging. The Hussites barely escaped starvation.

Zosimus Greek philosopher and historian. He wrote *New History*, which covered the Roman Empire from Augustus to the sack of Rome in 410. He was a pagan.

zu (or *tsu*) the clan, or basic social and military unit of the Shang state in China (about 1763–1027 BC), based at least theoretically on kinship. Towns might be populated entirely by one *zu*. Its members formed a military unit in wartime. In one case, ◊Fu Hao's *zu* provided 3,000 troops; others may have been smaller. In the early part of the Shang period *zu* levies may have been the only source of manpower. Later they were supplemented by a ◊*lu* standing army.

Zulpich alternative (German) name for Tolbiac (see ◊Tolbiac, Battle of).

Zurzach fort (Roman *Tenedo*) late Roman fort in present-day Switzerland built to protect an important Rhine crossing on the Raetian frontier. Zurzach is unusual as it seems to consist of two independent forts only 40 m/130 ft apart. Both were constructed by the emperor Diocletian (reigned 284–305) and though physically separate, they performed the unified function of commanding the road to and from the bridge.

The fort on the left, 'Kirchlibuck', was almost oval in shape, with walls 3.5 m/11.5 ft thick. The landward south and east walls survive, with closely spaced round towers and a gate on the south side. The 'Sidelen' fort to the east was a smaller 48 × 50 m/158 × 164 ft diamond with a spur wall on the east side that stretched down to the river. Valentinian I added a bridgehead fort at Rheinheim on the opposite bank of the river.

Zvikov castle (or *Klingenberg*) castle in Bohemia (now the Czech Republic), about 25 km/15 mi northwest of Strakonitz, on a headland overlooking the confluence of the Vltava and Otava rivers. A residence and castle, it had an unusual type of mural tower, rounded on the inner face and pointed on the outer, thus giving a bastionlike defence. Bavor II built this and a similar tower at Strakonitz between 1265 and 1280.

zygian oarsman at the middle level of a ◊trireme.

Select Bibliography

Ancient and Classical warfare

Anderson, J K *Greek Military Theory and Practice in the Age of Xenophon* (1970)
authoritative study of classical Greek warfare at its height.

Bar-Kochva, B *The Seleucid Army* (1976)
one of the few modern studies of post-Alexander armies.

Best, J G P *Thracian Peltasts and their Influence on Greek Warfare* (1969)
study of an important and neglected side of Greek warfare.

Bosworth, A B *Conquest and Empire* (1988)
up-to-date and sensible account of Alexander's career.

Buckler, J *The Theban Hegemony 371–362 BC* (1980)
includes excellent accounts of the battles of Leuctra and 2nd Mantinea.

Burn, A R *Persia and the Greeks* (1962)
vivid and scholarly account of the Persian Wars.

Cawkwell, G *Philip of Macedon* (1978)
readable but scholarly account of Alexander the Great's father.

Cook, J M *The Persian Empire* (1983)
the best modern general history of the Achaemenid empire and its campaigns.

Connolly, P *Greece and Rome at War* (1981)
excellent on armour and weapons.

Ducrey, P *Warfare in Ancient Greece* (1986)
good, general account of Greek warfare.

Engels, D W *Alexander the Great and the Logistics of the Macedonian Army* (1978)
pioneering study of a neglected aspect of ancient warfare.

Hamilton, C D *Sparta's Bitter Victories* (1979)
comprehensive account of the Corinthian War.

Hanson, V D *The Western Way of War: Infantry Battle in Classical Greece* (1989)
one of the few groundbreaking books on ancient warfare.

Hanson, V D (ed) *Hoplites: the Classical Greek Battle Experience* (1991)
distinguished collection of essays by various experts.

Head, Duncan *The Achaemenid Persian Army* (1992)
illustrated account summarizing all the evidence for the Persian army.

Hignett, C *Xerxes' Invasion of Greece* (1963)
good corrective to some more cavalier approaches to the subject.

Kagan, D *The Archidamian War* (1974)
comprehensive account of the first ten years of the Peloponnesian War.

Kagan, D *The Peace of Nicias and the Sicilian Expedition* (1981)
covers the middle years of the Peloponnesian War.

Kagan, D *The Fall of the Athenian Empire* (1987)
completes the author's monumental account of the Peloponnesian War.

Lazenby, J F *The Defence of Greece, 490–479 BC* (1993)
account of the two Persian invasions of Greece, with full discussion of the
evidence.

Morrison, J S and Coates, J F *The Athenian Trireme* (1986)
excellent account of the reconstruction of an ancient trireme.

Sekunda, Nick *The Persian Army 560–330 BC* (1992)
good illustrated account of the Achaemenid army, especially good on later
military dress.

Spence, I G *The Cavalry of Classical Greece* (1993)
the best study of ancient Greek cavalry.

Turney-High, H *Primitive Warfare: Its Practice and Concepts* (1971)
perhaps the best general study available.

Yadin, Yigael *The Art of Warfare in Biblical Lands in the Light of Archaeological Study*
(2 vols, 1963)
the best guide to warfare in the Middle East in Biblical times.

Roman warfare

Breeze, David and Dobson, Brian *Hadrian's Wall* (1987)
a very useful introduction to the subject.

Connolly, Peter *Greece and Rome at War* (1981)
a very useful and copiously illustrated survey.

Debevoise, Neilson C *A Political History of Parthia* (1938)
old but still useful narrative of Parthia's wars.

Dixon, Karen and Southern, Pat *The Roman Cavalry* (1992)
a useful introduction to the subject.

Dodgson, Michael H and Lieu, Samuel N C (eds) *The Roman Eastern Frontier and
the Persian Wars AD 226–363* (1991)
invaluable collection of translated contemporary documents on
Roman–Sassanian wars.

Elton, Hugh *Warfare in Roman Europe, AD 350–425* (1996)
the best available study of the later Roman army.

Goldsworthy, Adrian *The Roman Army at War, 100 BC–AD 200* (1996)
a detailed study of the army on campaign and in battle.

Hubert, H *The Greatness & Decline of the Celts* (1934) trans M R Dobie
classic work on Celtic history.

James, S *Exploring the World of the Celts* (1993)
excellent introduction to Celtic society and history.

Keppie, Lawrence *The Making of the Roman Army* (1984)
a very good survey of the army's development.

Lancel, S *Carthage: A History* (1995)
good, up-to-date account of Carthaginian society and history.

Lazenby, J F *Hannibal's War* (1978)
excellent account of the Second Punic War.

Lazenby, J F *The First Punic War* (1996)
clearest account of the first war between Rome and Carthage.

Luttwak, E N *The Grand Strategy of the Roman Empire* (1976)
a valuable, if now largely rejected, study of imperial defence.

Nicolle, David *Sassanian Armies: The Iranian Empire early 3rd to mid-7th centuries AD* (1996)
illustrated overview of Sassanian military development, especially dress and equipment.

Peddie, John *Invasion: The Roman Conquest of Britain* (1987)
very interesting study of the logistics of a major Roman campaign.

Warmington, B H *Carthage* (1960)
classic account of Carthaginian history.

Webster, Graham *The Roman Imperial Army* (1985)
a dated, but still very good introduction to the subject.

Medieval warfare

Bradbury, J *The Medieval Archer* (1985)
a wider discussion of medieval warfare than its title suggests.

Bradbury, J *The Medieval Siege* (1996)
excellent survey of all spects of medieval siege warfare.

Contamine, P (trans Michael Jones) *War in the Middle Ages* (1984)
good thematic survey of the whole subject.

France, J *Victory in the East: a Military History of the First Crusade* (1994)
excellent, revisionist 'new military history' study.

Hewitt, H J *The Black Prince's Expedition of 1355–57* (1958)
excellent analysis of a Hundred Years' War campaign, including the Battle of Poitiers.

Hooper, N and Bennett, M *Cambridge Atlas of Warfare: the Middle Ages 778–1485* (1996)
valuable survey of western and crusading warfare with dozens of maps.

Keen, M *Chivalry* (1984)
a sophisticated analysis explaining the real impact of chivalric ideas.

Marshall, C *Warfare in the Latin East 1192–1291* (1992)
sole study of a neglected period of crusading warfare.

Morillo, S *Warfare under the Anglo-Norman Kings 1066–1135* (1994)
helpful synthesis on 12th-century warfare.

Morris, J E *The Welsh Wars of Edward I* (1901, reprinted 1997)
a model monograph for the study of a particular war.

Nicolle, D *Medieval Warfare Source Book* (2 vols, 1996 and 1997)
a useful guide to weaponry and much more; well illustrated.

Prestwich, M *Armies and Warfare in the Middle Ages: the English Experience* (1996)
detailed and perceptive study of all aspects of warfare.

Smail, R C *Crusading Warfare 1097–1193* (1958, numerous reprints)
a little dated, but still a valuable assessment.

Strickland, M *Anglo-Norman Warfare* (1992)
a wide-ranging collection of essays on military organization, battle tactics, and chivalry.

Vale, M *War and Chivalry* (1981)
a convincing proof that chivalry was a practical and flexible code of war even in times of changing military technology.

Verbruggen, J F *The Art of War in the Middle Ages* (1997)
provides great insights into troop types and tactics.

Chinese warfare

Backus, Charles *The Nan-chao Kingdom and T'ang China's Southwestern Frontier* (1981)
the only coherent account of Nanzhao and its wars with China and Tibet.

Barfield, Thomas J *The Perilous Frontier: Nomadic Empires and China* (1989)
modern history of the northern frontier, particularly good for the Xiongnu and the Sixteen Kingdoms.

Beckwith, Christopher I *The Tibetan Empire in Central Asia* (1987)
fascinating chronicle of Tibet's wars with China, the Arabs, and the Turkish
empires.

De Crespigny, Rafe *The Last of the Han* (1969)
annotated translation of sections of the medieval Chinese historian Sima Guang
(Ssu-ma Kuang) covering the turmoil of AD 181–220.

Fang, Achilles *The Chronicle of the Three Kingdoms* (1965)
annotated translation of sections of the medieval Chinese historian Sima Guang
(Ssu-ma Kuang) covering the Three Kingdoms wars of AD 220–265.

Legge, James *The Chinese Classics, Volume V: The Ch'un Ts'ew with the Tso Chuen,*
(1872, reprinted since)
the only translation of the *Zuo Commentary* on the *Spring and Autumn Annals*, the
main Chinese history of the 8th to 5th centuries BC.

Mackerras, Colin *The Uighur Empire according to the T'ang Dynastic Histories* (1972)
includes the original narratives of the battles of Changan and Xindian.

Martin, H Desmond *The Rise of Chingis Khan and his Conquest of North
China* (1950).
the best military account of the early Mongol campaigns in China.

Needham, Joseph and Yates, Robin D S *Science and Civilisation in China, Volume V
Part 6, Military Technology: Missiles and Sieges* (1994)
one volume of an immense and wonderful series, others of which have useful
military information too.

Pan Ku *The History of the Former Han Dynasty by Pan Ku* trans and notes by
Homer H Dubs (1938)
two-volume translation with some valuable military material.

Peers, C J *Ancient Chinese Armies 1500–200 BC* (1990)
accessible illustrated history of Chinese armies from the Shang to the Qin.

Peers, C J *Medieval Chinese Armies 1260-1520* (1992)
good illustrated history of Yuan and early Ming armies.

Peers, C J *Imperial Chinese Armies: (1) 200 BC–589 AD* (1995)
well-illustrated account of Chinese armies from the Han empire to the Sui
reunification.

Peers, C J *Imperial Chinese Armies: (2) 590–1260 AD* (1996)
covers the period from the Sui to the Mongol conquests, including the best
illustrations of the series.

Ranitzsch, Karl Heinz *The Army of Tang China* (1995)
very useful illustrated account, in greater depth than the 1996 Peers volume.

Sawyer, Ralph D (translation and commentary) *The Seven Military Classics of
Ancient China* (1993).
probably the only translated edition of all seven manuals; well annotated and
very readable.

Sawyer, Ralph D (translation and commentary) *Sun Pin: Military Methods* (1995)
a good edition of Sun Bin's *Bing Fa*, a companion to the same translator's 1993
volume.

Sunzi *The Art of War* trans Samuel B Griffith (1963)
influential translation of Sunzi (Sun Tzu), with the work of Wu Qi in an
appendix.

Waldron, Arthur, *The Great Wall of China* (1990)
excellent, myth-dispelling summary of the Wall's history.

Wright, Arthur *The Sui Dynasty* (1978)
good history of the Sui re-unification of China.

Japanese warfare

Harris, Victor and Ogasawara, Nobuo *Swords of the Samurai* (1990)
catalogue of Japanese arms and armour from the 8th century to the 19th, by
period.

Joly, Henri *The Armour Book in Honcho Gunkiko* (various reprints from 1913)
a classic translation of Arai Hakuseki's 18th-century treatise on Japanese armour.

Joly, Henri *The Sword Book in Honcho Gunkiko* (various reprints from 1913)
a classic translation of Arai Hakuseki's 18th-century treatise on the Japanese
sword.

Robinson, H Russell *Oriental Armour* (1967)
standard reference work covering Persia, Turkey, the Middle East, India, Ceylon,
Phillippines, China, Korea, Tibet, Bhutan, and Japan.

Sasama, Yoshihiko *Dictionary of Japanese Arms and Armour* (1981)
extensive work in Japanese with line drawings and photographs showing
Japanese arms and armour from the earliest periods.

Sato, Kazan *The Japanese Sword* trans Joe Earle (1983)
an excellent work on all aspects of the Japanese sword.

Turnbull, Steven R *The Samurai, A Military History* (1977 and 1996)
well illustrated and sound, if somewhat romanticized, history of the samurai.

Varley, Paul *Warriors of Japan as Portrayed in the War Tales* (1994)
well-researched work on the Taira and Minamoto Wars of the 12th century.

Central, South, and Southeast Asian warfare

Basham, A L *The Wonder that was India: a Survey of the Culture of the Indian Sub-continent before the coming of the Muslims* (1954)

Boyle, J A (ed) *The Cambridge History of Iran: (vol 5) The Saljuq and Muslim Periods* (1968)

Burn, R (ed) *The Cambridge History of India: (vol IV) the Mughal Period* (1937)

Coedes, G *The Indianized States of Southeast Asia* (1968)
classic account of ancient and medieval Southeast Asian history.

Frye, R N (ed) *The Cambridge History of Iran: (vol 4) from the Arab Invasion to the Saljuqs* (1975)

Haig, W (ed) *The Cambridge History of India: (vol III) Turks and Afghans* (1928)

Jackson, P (ed) *The Cambridge History of Iran: (vol 6) the Timurid and Safavid Periods* (1986)

Quaritch Wales, H G *Ancient South-east Asian Warfare* (1952)
now scarce but indispensable study.

Rawlinson, H G *India: A Short Cultural History* (1937)

Taylor, Keith Weller *The Birth of Vietnam* (1983)
excellent account of Vietnam to the 10th-century wars.